the book of **wisdom**

the book of **wisdom**

the heart of tibetan buddhism

commentaries on atisha's seven points
of mind training

This book is a transcript of a series of original talks by Osho given to a live audience.
Some parts have been edited to keep the work contemporary in accordance with Osho's request.
All of Osho's talks have been published in full as books, and are also available as original audio recordings.
Audio recordings and the complete text archive can be found via the online OSHO Library at www.osho.com

Osho comments in this work on excerpts from: *The Great Path of Awakening*, by Jamgun Kongtrul,
translated by Ken McLeod, © 1987, 2005 by Ken McLeod.
Reprinted by arrangement with Shambhala Publications Inc., Boston, MA. www.shambhala.com.

OSHO MEDIA INTERNATIONAL

New York • London • Mumbai
an imprint of
OSHO INTERNATIONAL
www.osho.com/oshointernational

Distributed by Publishers Group Worldwide
www.pgw.com

Library of Congress Cataloging-in-Publication Data is available

ISBN 13: 978-0-9818341-1-5
ISBN 10: 0-9818341-1-6

Printed in China

10 9 8 7 6 5 4 3 2 1

Design by Terry Jeavons
Copyright on Osho-image on jacket: © OSHO International Foundation

Table of contents

preface

Atisha, as Osho explains in The Book of Wisdom, was a 10th-century mystic who is credited with establishing the foundations of Buddhist teachings in Tibet. In the following introduction, taken from a discourse series Om Mani Padme Hum, Osho talks about the priceless contribution of Tibet to the international community, and gives his unequivocal support for Tibetan independence and autonomy.

The only country in the world that has devoted all its genius to the inner exploration is Tibet. But unfortunately, Tibet has fallen into darkness. Its monasteries have been closed, its seekers of truth have been forced to work in labor camps. The only country in the world that was working with a one-pointed genius, with all its intelligence put into the search for one's own interiority and its treasures, has been stopped by the communist invasion of Tibet.

And it is such an ugly world that nobody has objected to it. On the contrary, because China is big and powerful, even countries that are more powerful than China can ever be, like America, have accepted that Tibet belongs to China. That is sheer nonsense — just because China is powerful and everybody wants China to be on their side. Even India has not objected! It was such a beautiful experiment, and Tibet had no weapons to fight with, they had no army to fight; they had never thought about it. Their whole thing was an introverted pilgrimage.

Nowhere has such concentrated effort been made to discover man's being. Every family in Tibet used to give their eldest son to some monastery where he was to meditate and grow closer to awakening. It was a joy to every family that at least one of them was wholeheartedly, twenty-four hours a day, working on the inner being. They were also working in this way but they could not give all their time; they had to create food and clothes and shelter, and in Tibet it is a difficult matter. The climate is not very helpful; to live in Tibet is a tremendous struggle. But still, every family used to give their first born child to the monastery.

There were hundreds of monasteries...and these monasteries should not be compared with any Catholic monasteries; they had no comparison in the whole world. These monasteries were concerned with only one thing: to make you aware of yourself.

Thousands of devices have been created down the centuries so that you can blossom and you can find your ultimate treasure. But the destruction of Tibet should be known in history, particularly when man becomes a little more aware and humanity a little more humane.... This is the greatest calamity of the twentieth century, that Tibet has fallen into the hands of materialists who don't believe that you have anything inside you. They believe that you are only matter and your consciousness is only a by-product of matter. And all this is simply without any experience of the inner — just logical, rational philosophizing.

Not a single communist in the world has meditated, but it is strange — they all deny the inner. Nobody thinks about how the outer can exist if there is no inner. They exist together, they are inseparable. The outer is only a protection for the inner, because the inner is very delicate and soft. But the outer is accepted and the inner is denied. And even if sometimes the inner is accepted, the world is dominated by such dirty politicians that they use even inner experiences for ugly ends.

America is now training its soldiers in meditation so that they can fight without any nervous breakdown, without going mad, without feeling any fear — so they can lie down in their ditches silently, calm and cool and collected. No meditator may have ever thought that meditation can also be used for fighting wars, but in the hands of politicians everything becomes ugly — even meditation. Now the army camps in America are teaching meditation so that their soldiers can be more calm and quiet while killing people.

But I want to warn America: you are playing with fire. You don't understand exactly what meditation will do. Your soldiers will become so calm and quiet that they will throw away their weapons and they will simply refuse to kill. A meditator cannot kill; a meditator cannot be destructive. So they are going to be surprised one day that their soldiers are no longer interested in fighting. War, violence, murder, massacre of millions of people — this is not possible if a man knows something of meditation. Then he also knows not only himself, he knows the other whom he is killing. He is his brother, they all belong to the same oceanic existence.

In other countries also, they are interested in meditation. But the purpose is the same — not realization of yourself, but making you stronger so that you can kill and bomb and use nuclear weapons and missiles to kill whole nations.

But they are all going on a dangerous path, unknowingly — it is good, they should be helped! Once meditation spreads among their soldiers, those soldiers will become mystics! So I am immensely happy that their idea is different, and they don't know anything about meditation. They have only heard that it makes people calm and cool so they can fight without any fear, without looking back. Meditation gives them a feeling of immortality; hence their fear will disappear.

But meditation will not only give them the experience of their own immortality — it will also give them the experience that everybody is immortal. Death is a fiction. Why unnecessarily harass people? They will be living, you cannot kill them. Not even your nuclear weapons are going to kill them.

Krishna, in the Gita, has a beautiful statement: *Nainam chhindanti shastrani; naham dahati pavakahr.* "Neither can any weapon destroy me nor can any fire burn me." Yes the body will be burned, but I am not the body....

Meditation gives you the feel, for the first time, of your authentic reality.

If humanity were a little more aware, Tibet should be made free because it is the only country that has devoted almost two thousand years to doing nothing but going deeper into meditation. And it can teach the whole world something that is immensely needed.

But Communist China is trying to destroy everything that has been created in two thousand years. All their devices, all their methods of meditation — their whole spiritual climate is being polluted, poisoned. And they are simple people; they cannot defend themselves. They don't have anything to defend themselves with — no tanks, no bombs, no airplanes, no army. An innocent race, which has lived without any war for two thousand years... It disturbs nobody; it is so far away from everybody — even to reach there is a difficult task. They live on the very roof of the world. The highest mountains, eternal snows, are their home. Leave them alone! China will not lose anything, but the whole world will be benefited by their experience.

And the world will need their experience. The world is getting fed up with money, power, prestige, all that scientific technology has created — people are getting fed up. They are finished with it. People in the advanced countries are no longer interested in sex, are no longer interested in drugs. Things are falling away, and a strange despair like a dark cloud is descending on the advanced countries — of deep frustration, meaninglessness, and anguish. They will all need a different climate of meditation to dispel all these clouds and bring again a new day into their lives, a new dawn, a new experience of themselves, a discovery of their original being.

Tibet should be left as an experimental lab for man's inner search. But not a single nation in the world has raised its voice against this ugly attack on Tibet. And China has not only attacked it, they have amalgamated it into their map. Now, on the modern Chinese map, Tibet is their territory.

And we think the world is civilized, where innocent people who are not doing any harm to anybody are simply destroyed. And with them, something of great importance to all humanity is also destroyed. If there were something civilized in man, every nation would have stood against the invasion of Tibet by China. It is the invasion of matter against consciousness; it is the invasion of materialism against spiritual heights....

You may have all the pleasures and comforts and luxuries of the world, but unless you know yourself, unless your inner lotus opens, you will go on missing something. You may not be certain what you are missing but a feeling... that something is being missed, that "I am not complete," that "I am not whole," that "I am not what existence wanted me to be." This "missing" feeling goes on nagging everybody. Only the expansion of your consciousness will help you to get rid of this feeling, of this nagging, of this anguish, this angst.

Even people like Jaspers, Kierkegaard, Heidegger, Marcel, Jean-Paul Sartre, the highest geniuses of the West, are agreed on a few things. They all say that life is nothing but boredom, that life is nothing but anxiety, anguish, that life is accidental, it has no significance... that it is absolutely futile to search for any blissful space; there exists none. And when great philosophers like these agree on such points, the ordinary masses simply follow them.

Whatever they are saying is absolutely wrong, because none of them has ever meditated; none of them has entered into his own subjectivity. They are just in their heads. They have not even moved to their hearts, what to say about their beings? What to say about their disappearing into the universal?

Unless you disappear into the universal ocean just like a dewdrop, you will not find significance. You will not find your real dignity. You will not find that existence showers so much joy and so much celebration on you that you cannot contain it; you have to share it. You become a rain cloud, so much burdened with rain that it has to shower. A man of deep insight, a man of intuition, a man who has reached to his being becomes a rain cloud. He is not just a blessing to himself, he becomes a blessing to the whole world.

chapter 1
Atisha the Thrice Great

First, learn the preliminaries.
Think that all phenomena are like dreams.

Examine the nature of unborn awareness.
Let even the remedy itself go free on its own.

Settle in the nature of basic cognition, the essence.
Between sessions, consider phenomena as phantoms.

Train in joining, sending and taking together.
Do this by riding the breath.

Three objects, three poisons, three bases of virtue.
Train with phrases in every mode of behavior.

Religion is not a science.... Religion is not a science in the sense physics, mathematics and chemistry are sciences. But still it *is* a science because it is the ultimate knowing: the word *science* means knowing. And if religion is not a science, what else can be? It is the highest knowing, it is the purest knowing.

Ordinary science is knowledge, not knowing: religion is knowing itself. Ordinary science is object-oriented — it knows something, hence it is knowledge. Religion is not object-oriented; it has no object, it knows nothing. Knowing knows itself, as if the mirror is reflecting itself. It is utterly pure of all content. Hence religion is not knowledge but knowing.

Science is a lower kind of knowing, religion is a higher kind. Religion is *Philosophia Ultima*: the ultimate knowing. The difference between the two is not of the spirit — the spirit is the same — but the difference is certainly of purity.

Science is mixed with much mud. Religion is pure essence, pure fragrance. The mud has disappeared, the lotus has appeared. And at the ultimate stage even the lotus has disappeared, only the fragrance abides. These are the three stages of knowing: the mud, the lotus and the fragrance.

Religion cannot be grasped, because there is no object in it. But still it can be understood. It cannot be explained, but it can be experienced. There is no way of informing you about religion, because it cannot be reduced to information. But you can be shown the way, the path to it — fingers pointing to the moon. The fingers are not the moon, obviously, but the fingers can point to the moon.

These "Seven Points of Mind Training" of the great master Atisha, are fingers, seven fingers pointing to the moon. Don't be caught by the fingers, don't become too much obsessed with the fingers. That is not the point, that will be missing the point. Use the fingers and forget them, and look where the fingers are pointing. And when you see the moon, who bothers about the fingers? Who remembers them? They automatically become nonessential; they disappear.

That's why for those who have experienced religion, all the scriptures become utterly useless, all methods become nonessential. When the goal is achieved, the path is forgotten.

Atisha is one of the rare masters, rare in the sense that he was taught by three enlightened masters. It has never happened before, and never since. To be a disciple of three enlightened masters is simply unbelievable — because one enlightened master is enough. But this story, that he was taught by three enlightened masters, has a metaphorical significance also. And it is true, it is historical too.

The three masters that Atisha remained with for many years were: first, Dharmakirti, a great Buddhist mystic. He taught him no-mind, he taught him emptiness, he taught him how to be thoughtless, he taught him how to drop all content from the mind and be contentless. The second master was Dharmarakshita, another Buddhist mystic. He taught him love, compassion. And the third master was Yogin Maitreya, another Buddhist mystic. He taught him the art of taking the suffering of others and absorbing it into your own heart: love in action.

This could happen because all these three masters were great friends. They had started their search together; while they were on the way they had remained together, and when they attained they were still together.

Atisha became a disciple of Dharmakirti. Dharmakirti said to him, "I will teach you the first principle. And for the second you go to Dharmarakshita, and for the third to Yogin Maitreya. This way you will know all the three faces of the ultimate reality, the three faces of God — the trinity, the *trimurti*. And this way you will learn each face from the person who is the most perfect in it."

These are the three ways people reach to the ultimate. If you reach through emptiness you attain the other two also, but your path remains basically that of emptiness — you know more about emptiness, so emptiness will be emphasized in whatsoever you teach.

That's what happened in Buddha's case. He had attained through emptiness, hence his whole teaching became emptiness-oriented. There is no God in Buddha's teaching, because God is a thought, a content, an object — God is the other, and Buddha had attained by dropping the other. Buddha had attained by emptying his mind totally, hence there is no place for God, no place for anything at all. His path is the purest *via negativa*.

That was also the case with Dharmakirti. He was the perfect master of emptiness, a master par excellence of emptiness. And when Atisha had learned how to be empty, the master said, "It will be better for you to go to Dharmarakshita for the next step, because he has attained from a totally different path. Just as you can reach Everest from different sides, he has reached from a totally different path, the path of compassion. I can also teach you the path of compassion, but my knowing about that path is only known from the top.

"I have reached through the path of emptiness. Once you reach the top, you can look down at all the paths, they are all available to your vision. But to follow a path in its different dimensions, to follow a path in all its details, small details, is a totally different thing." And to look at it from a helicopter or from the mountain-top is certainly a different vision; it is a bird's-eye view.

And Dharmakirti said, "If there had been nobody available here, I would have taught you the other too. But when a man like Dharmarakshita is just here, my neighbor, living in another cave just nearby, it is better you go to him."

First one has to become empty, utterly empty. But you have not to cling to emptiness, otherwise your life will never know the positive expression of religion. Your life will miss the poetry, the joy of sharing; you will remain empty. You will have a kind of freedom, but your freedom will be only freedom *from*, it will not be freedom *for*. And unless a freedom is both – freedom from and freedom for – something is missing, something is lacking; your freedom will be poor. Just to be free from is a poor kind of freedom.

The real freedom starts only when you are free *for*. You can sing a song and you can dance a dance and you can celebrate and you can start overflowing. That's what compassion is.

Man lives in passion. When the mind disappears, passion is transformed into compassion. Passion means you are a beggar with a begging-bowl; you are asking and asking for more and more from everybody; you are exploiting others. Your relationships are nothing but exploitations — cunning devices to possess the other, very clever strategies to dominate. When you are living in the mind, in passion, your whole life is power politics. Even your love, even your social service, even your humanitarian works, are nothing but power politics. Deep down, there is a desire to be powerful over others.

The same energy, when the mind is dropped, becomes compassion. And it takes a totally new turn. It is no longer begging; you become an emperor, you start giving. Now you have something — you had it always, but because of the mind, you were not aware of it. The mind was functioning like darkness around you, and you were unaware of the light within. The mind was creating an illusion of being a beggar, while all the time you had been an emperor. The mind was creating a dream; in reality you never needed anything. All had already been given. All that you need, all that you can need, is already the case.

God is within you, but because of the mind – mind means dreaming, desiring — you never look within, you go on rushing outwards. You keep yourself in the background, your eyes are turned towards the outside, they have become focused there. That's what the mind is all about: focusing the eyes on the outside.

And one has to learn how to unfocus them from there — how to make them loose, less rigid, more liquid, so that they can turn inwards. Once you have seen who you are, the beggar disappears. In fact it had never existed; it was just a dream, an idea.

The mind is creating all your misery. With the mind gone, misery is gone, and suddenly you are full of energy. And the energy needs expression, sharing; it wants to become a song, a dance, a celebration. That is compassion: you start sharing.

Atisha learned compassion from Dharmarakshita. But compassion has two faces. One is inactive compassion: the meditator sits silently in his cave, showering his compassion over the whole existence. But it is a very inactive kind of compassion. You have to go to him to partake of it, he will not come to you. You will have to go to the mountains to his cave to share his joy; he will not come to you. He will not move in any way, he will not take any active step. He will not flow towards others, he will not seek and search for the people with whom he can share his dance. He will wait.

This is a feminine kind of compassion: just like a woman waits — she never takes the initiative, she never goes to the man. She may love the man, but she will never be the first to say "I love you." She will wait; she will hope that one day or other, sooner or later, the man will propose. Woman is inactive love, passive love. Man is active love, man takes the initiative.

And in the same way, compassion has two possibilities: the feminine and the masculine. From Dharmarakshita, Atisha learned the feminine art of being in love with existence. One more step was needed: Dharmarakshita told him, "Go to Yogin Maitreya" — these three masters were all living together in the same vicinity — "Go to Yogin Maitreya and learn how to transform the baser energy into active energy, so love becomes active."

And once love is active, compassion is active, you have passed through all the three dimensions of truth — you have known all. You have known utter emptiness, you have known compassion arising, you have known compassion showering. Life is fulfilled only when all these three have happened.

Because Atisha learned under three enlightened masters, he is called Atisha the Thrice Great. Nothing more is known about his ordinary life, when and where exactly he was born. He existed somewhere in the eleventh century. He was born in India, but the moment his love became active he started moving towards Tibet, as if a great magnet were pulling him there. In the Himalayas he attained; then he never came back to India.

He moved towards Tibet, his love showered on Tibet. He transformed the whole quality of Tibetan consciousness. He was a miracle-worker; whatsoever he touched was transformed into gold. He was one of the greatest alchemists the world has ever known.

These "Seven Points of Mind Training" are the fundamental teaching that he gave to Tibet — a gift from India to Tibet. India has given great gifts to the world. Atisha is one of those great gifts. Just as India gave Bodhidharma to China, India gave Atisha to Tibet. Tibet is infinitely indebted to this man.

These seven points, the smallest treatise you can find, are of immense value. You will have to meditate over each statement. They are the whole of religion condensed: you will have to unfold each statement. They are like seeds, they contain much. It may not be apparently so, but the moment you move into the statements deeply, when you contemplate and meditate and start experimenting with them, you will be surprised — you will be going into the greatest adventure of your life.

The first sutra:

First, learn the preliminaries.

What are the preliminaries? These are the preliminaries. First: truth is. Truth is not something to be created, truth is not something that is far away. Truth is herenow, truth surrounds you like the ocean surrounds the fish. The fish may not be aware — once the fish becomes aware of the ocean, the fish is enlightened. The fish is not aware, cannot be aware, because the fish is born in the ocean, has always lived in the ocean, is part of the ocean as any wave is part of the ocean. The fish is also a wave — a little more solid, but born out of the ocean, lives in the ocean and one day disappears in the ocean. The fish may never come to know about the ocean. To know something, a little distance is needed. To know something, perspective is needed. And the ocean is so close, that's why the fish may not be aware of it.

And so is the case with truth, or if you like you can use the word *God*. So is the case with

God. It is not that he is far away, and that's why we don't know about him; it is because he is not far away but very close by. Even to say that it is close by is not right, because you *are* it. He is within you and without: he is all and all.

This is the first thing that has to be allowed to sink deep in your heart: truth already is, we are in it. This is the most fundamental thing to begin with. You are not to discover it; it is not covered. All that is needed is a new kind of awareness which is missing in you. Truth is there, but you are not aware, you are not mindful, you are not alert. You don't know how to watch, you don't know how to observe, you don't know how to look and see. You have eyes but still you are blind, you have ears but you are deaf.

The first preliminary is: truth is.

The second preliminary is: mind is the barrier. Nothing else is hindering you from truth, just your own mind. Mind surrounds you like a film, like a movie that goes on and on, and you remain engrossed in it, fascinated by it. It is a fantasy that surrounds you, a continuous story that goes on and on. And because you are so fascinated by it, you go on missing that which is. And mind is not; it is only a fantasy, it is only a faculty for dreaming.

Mind is nothing but dreams and dreams — dreams of the past, dreams of the future, dreams of how things should be, dreams of great ambitions, achievements. Dreams and desires, that is the stuff mind is made of. But it surrounds you like a China Wall. And because of it the fish remains unaware of the ocean.

So the second preliminary is: mind is the only barrier.

And the third: no-mind is the door. Atisha calls no-mind *bodhichitta*: that is his word for no-mind. It can be translated as Buddha-mind, Buddha-consciousness, too. Or if you like you can call it Christ-consciousness, Krishna-consciousness. It doesn't make any difference what name is used, but the basic quality of *bodhichitta* is that it is no-mind. It looks paradoxical: the mind in the state of no-mind. But the meaning is very clear: mind without content, mind without thoughts, is what is meant, is what is indicated.

Remember the word *bodhichitta*, because Atisha says the whole effort of religion, the whole science of religion, is nothing but an endeavor to create *bodhichitta*, Buddha-consciousness: a mind which functions as a no-mind, a mind which dreams no more, thinks no more, a mind which is just awareness, pure awareness.

These are the preliminaries.

The second sutra:
Think that all phenomena are like dreams....

Now the work starts. Atisha is very condensed, seedlike. That is the meaning of a sutra: it is just a thread, just a hint, and then you have to decode it.

Think that all phenomena are like dreams.

"Phenomena" means all that you see, all that you experience. All that can ever be experienced is all phenomena. Remember, not only are the objects of the world phenomena and dreams, but also objects of consciousness. They may be objects of the world, they may be just objects of the mind. They may be great spiritual experiences. You may see kundalini rising in you: that too is a phenomenon – a beautiful dream, a very sweet dream, but it is a dream all the same. You may see great light flooding your being, but that light is also a phenomenon. You may see lotuses blooming inside you and a great fragrance arising within your being: those too are phenomena, because you are always the seer and never the seen, always the experiencer and never the experienced, always the witness and never the witnessed.

All that can be witnessed, seen, observed, is phenomena. Material phenomena, psychological phenomena, spiritual phenomena – they are all the same. There is no need to make any distinction. The basic thing to remember is: that which can be seen is a dream.

Think that all phenomena are dreams.

This is a tremendously powerful technique. Start contemplating in this way: if you are walking on the street, contemplate that people passing by are all dreams. The shops and the shopkeepers and the customers and the people coming and going, all are dreams. The houses, the buses, the train, the airplane, all are dreams.

You will be immediately surprised by something of tremendous import happening within you. The moment you think "All are dreams" suddenly, like a flash, one thing comes into your vision: "I am a dream too." Because if the seen is a dream, then who is this "I"? If the object is a dream, then the subject is also a dream. If the object is false, how can the subject be the truth? Impossible.

If you watch everything as a dream, suddenly you will find something slipping out of your being: the idea of the ego. This is the only way to drop the ego, and the simplest. Just try it — meditate this way. Meditating this way again and again, one day the miracle happens: you look in, and the ego is not found there.

The ego is a by-product, a by-product of the illusion that whatsoever you are seeing is true. If you think that objects are true, then the ego can exist; it is a by-product. If you think that objects are dreams, the ego disappears. And if you think continuously that all is a dream, then one day, in a dream in the night, you will be surprised: suddenly in the dream you will remember that this is a dream too! And immediately, as the remembrance happens, the dream will disappear. And for the first time you will experience yourself deep asleep, yet awake — a very paradoxical experience, but of great benefit.

Once you have seen your dream disappearing because you have become aware of the dream, your quality of consciousness will have a new flavor to it. The next morning you will wake up with a totally different quality you had never known before. You will wake up for the first time. Now you will know that all those other mornings were false; you were not really awake. The dreams continued — the only difference was that in the night you were dreaming with eyes closed, in the day you were dreaming with eyes open.

But if the dream has disappeared because awareness happened, suddenly you became aware in the dream.... And remember, awareness and dreaming cannot exist together. Here, awareness arises, and there, the dream disappears. When you become awake in your sleep, the next morning is going to be something so important that it is incomparable. Nothing like it has ever happened. Your eyes will be so clear, so transparent, and everything will look so psychedelic, so colorful, so alive. Even rocks will be felt to be breathing, pulsating; even rocks will have a heartbeat. When you are awake, the whole existence changes its quality.

We are living in a dream. We are asleep, even when we think we are awake.

Think that all phenomena are like dreams.

First, objects will lose their objectivity. And second, the subject will lose its subjectivity. And that brings you to a transcendence. The object is no longer important, the subject is no longer important, then what is left? A transcendental consciousness: *bodhichitta* — just a witnessing, with no idea of "I" and "thou"; just a pure mirror which reflects that which is.

And God is nothing but that which is.

The third sutra:
Examine the nature of unborn awareness.

Now you know what awareness is. You have known this transcendental awareness where objects and subjects are no more existential. You have known for the first time this purity, this crystal-clear mirror. Now examine the nature of this awareness.

Look into it, look deep into it. Shake yourself into as full alertness as possible. Wake up and see! And you will start laughing — because now you will see there has never been a birth, and there is never going to be a death.

This is unborn and undying consciousness. It has always been here. It is eternal, it is timeless. And how afraid you were of death, and how afraid you were of old age, and how afraid you were of a thousand and one things! And nothing has ever happened: all was a dream.

Seeing this, one smiles, one laughs. Your whole life up to now has been ridiculous, absurd. You were unnecessarily afraid, unnecessarily greedy, unnecessarily suffering. You were living in a nightmare and it was your own creation.

Examine the nature of unborn awareness.

And you are freed from all misery, all suffering, all hell.

Let even the remedy itself go free on its own.

And now don't start clinging to the remedy, to the method. That temptation arises. It is the last temptation, the very last effort of the mind to survive. The mind comes from a back door, it tries once more. Before it disappears forever, it makes one more effort, and that effort is to cling to the method — the method of thinking that all phenomena are dreams.

It has given you such joy, such a deep experience of reality, that naturally you would like to cling to it. And once you cling you are back in the same old rut again: the mind is back in disguise. Cling to anything and the mind is back, because clinging is mind. Hold on to anything, depend on anything, and the mind is back, because the mind is dependence, slavery. Possess anything – even a spiritual method, even a method of meditation — become a possessor, and you are possessed by it. Whether you possess money or you possess a tremendously significant method of meditation, it doesn't matter. Whatsoever you possess, you will be possessed by it and you will be afraid to lose it.

Once a sufi mystic was brought to me. For thirty years continuously he had used the Sufi method *zikr*, and he had attained to great experiences. One could see it; even ordinary people were aware that he was living in a totally different world. You could see it in his eyes, they were shining with joy. His very being had a vibe of the beyond.

His disciples brought him to me, and they said, "Our master is a realized soul. What do you say about him?"

I said, "Leave your master with me for three days, and then come back."

The master stayed with me for three days. On the third day he was very angry, and he said, "You have destroyed my thirty years' work!" Because I told him a simple thing — just this sutra of Atisha: *Let even the remedy itself go....*

I told him, "Now for thirty years you have been remembering one thing, that all is divine. The tree is God, the rock is God, the people are God, the dog is God, everything is God — for thirty years you have been remembering it continuously." And he had really made a sincere effort.

He said, "Yes."

I said, "Now stop remembering. How long are you going to remember? If it has happened, then stop remembering and let us see what happens. If it has really happened, then even after dropping remembering, it will remain."

It was so logical that he agreed. He said, "It *has* happened."

I said, "Then give it a try. For three days you forget remembering, stop remembering."

He said, "I cannot stop, it has become automatic."

I said, "You just wait and try."

It took him at least two days, forty-eight hours, to stop. It was hard to stop, it had become automatic. There was now no need to remember; for thirty years he had been remembering, it was simply there like an undercurrent. But within forty-eight hours it stopped.

And on the morning of the third day he was very angry. He said, "What have you done? All that joy has disappeared. I am feeling very ordinary, I am feeling the same as I was before I started on the journey thirty years ago." He started crying out of anger and out of sadness; tears started coming to his eyes. He said, "Give me back my method — please don't take it!"

I said, "Just look! If this is so dependent on the method, then nothing has happened. It is just an illusion that you are creating by continuous remembering. This is nothing but autohypnosis."

All the great masters say this, that one day you have to drop the method. And the sooner you drop it, the better. The moment you attain, the moment awareness is released in you, immediately drop the method.

Just look: this is only the fourth sutra. In the third sutra Atisha says:

Examine the nature of unborn awareness.

And in the fourth, immediately:
Let even the remedy itself go....

Now no more examination, no more mindfulness, no more remembering that all is a dream. Once the first taste of awareness has happened on your tongue, be quick! Because the mind is very cunning — the mind can start telling you, "Look, you are no longer ordinary, you are extraordinary. Look, you have attained. Look, you have become a buddha, you are enlightened. Look, this is the goal of all human beings, and very rarely, one in a million attains. You are that one in a million."

The mind will say all these beautiful sweet nothings, and of course the ego can come back. You can start feeling very good, holier than thou. You can start feeling special, spiritual, saintly. And all is lost. Through the remedy, the disease is back. Cling to the remedy, and the disease is back.

One has to be very alert about dropping the method. Once you attain something, immediately drop the method, otherwise your mind will start clinging to the method. It will talk very logically to you, saying, "It is the method that is important."

Buddha used to tell a story again and again. Five idiots passed through a village. Seeing them, people were surprised, because they were carrying a boat on their heads. The boat was really big; it was almost crushing those five idiots, they were almost dying under the weight of it. And people asked, "What are you doing?"

They said, "We cannot leave this boat. This is the boat that helped us to come from the other shore to this shore. How can we leave it? It is because of it that we have been able to come here. Without it we would have died on the other shore. The night was coming close, and there were wild animals on the other shore. It was as sure as anything that by the morning we would have been dead. We will never leave this boat, we are indebted forever. We will carry it on our heads in sheer gratitude.

This can happen, because all minds are idiots. Mind as such is idiotic.

The origin of the word *idiot* is beautiful to remember. Idiocy means something private, something special, something that is your own, something eccentric. That is the basic meaning of idiocy — to function in an eccentric way.

The mind always functions in an eccentric way, the mind is always an idiot. The really intelligent person has no mind. Intelligence arises out of no-mind, idiocy out of the mind. Mind is idiotic, no-mind is wise. No-mind is wisdom, intelligence.

Mind depends on knowledge, on methods, on money, on experience, on this and that. Mind always needs props, it needs supports, it cannot exist on its own. On its own, it flops.

So the ultimate effort of the mind to come back will be when you attain to some awareness. It will say, "Look, so we have arrived." The moment something inside you says, "We have arrived," beware! Be very, very cautious now, each step has to be of great caution.

Let even the remedy itself go free on its own.

Now please don't cling to the remedy, to the method. This is the emphasis of J. Krishnamurti — but this is his first sutra. It should be the fourth. That's where he is wrong; it cannot be the first sutra. How can you drop a method that you have never used? You can only drop a method that you have used.

Atisha is far more logical, far more scientific, than J. Krishnamurti. But I can understand why he emphasizes it, because he is afraid that if you go into the first three sutras the fourth may never arrive, you may be lost in the first three. Many are lost in the preliminaries, many are lost in the methods. So he has become too cautious, extremely cautious.

Those five idiots were carrying the boat, and J. Krishnamurti is on the other shore teaching people: "Don't enter the boat" — too cautious! — "because if you enter the boat, who knows, you may start carrying the boat on your head. So please don't enter it."

And there are many who have become afraid of entering the boat. But to be afraid of entering the boat is the same idiocy; there is no difference. One who is afraid of entering the boat is the same person who will carry the boat; otherwise why should you be afraid?

There are old friends of mine who have followed J. Krishnamurti for their whole life. They come to me and say, "We would like to come here, but we are afraid of all the methods that you teach. Methods are dangerous," they say.

Methods are dangerous only if you are unaware; otherwise they can be used beautifully. Do you think a boat is dangerous? It is dangerous if you are thinking to carry it on your head for your whole life out of sheer gratitude; otherwise it is just a raft to be used and discarded. All methods are rafts to be used and discarded, used and abandoned, used and never looked back at again — there is no need, no point!

These are two extremes. At one extreme are those five idiots, and at the other extreme are the followers of J. Krishnamurti. There is no need to be either. My approach is: Use the boat, use beautiful boats, use as many boats as possible; with this awareness, when the shore is reached the boat is abandoned with no clinging. While you are in the boat, enjoy it, be thankful to it. When you get out of the boat, say thank you and move on.

The fifth sutra:
Settle in the nature of basic cognition, the essence.

If you drop the remedy, automatically you will start settling in your being. The mind clings; it never allows you to settle in your being. It keeps you interested in something that you are not: the boats.

When you don't cling to anything, there is nowhere to go — all boats have been abandoned, you cannot go anywhere; all paths have been dropped, you cannot go anywhere; all dreams and desires have disappeared, there is no way to move. Relaxation happens of its own accord. Just think of the word *relax*. Be, settle, you have come home.

Settle in the nature of basic cognition, the essence.

And when you settle, there is pure awareness, with no effort, with no method. If awareness needs a method it is still not true awareness, not the essential awareness, not the natural spontaneous awareness. It is still a by-product of the method; it is cultivated, created. It is a by-product of the mind, it is not yet the truth.

Settle in the nature of basic cognition, the essence.

Now there is nothing to do. See, be, enjoy: only this moment exists. This now, this here, this cawing of the crows…and all is silence.

To know this serenity is to know who you are, what this existence is all about. This is *samadhi*, in the words of Patanjali. This is *sambodhi*, in the words of Gautam Buddha. This is *bodhichitta*, in the words of Atisha.

Between sessions, consider phenomena as phantoms.

Now Atisha is really very aware of the disciple. He knows that these experiences of settling into your being will be only momentary in the beginning. One moment you will find yourself relaxed into your being, another moment it will be gone. In the beginning it is bound to be so: one moment you are flooded with the unknown, with the mysterious, another moment it is no more there. One moment all is fragrance, and the next moment you are searching for it and you cannot find it, where it has gone.

Only glimpses will happen in the beginning. Slowly, slowly they become more and more solid, they abide more and more. Slowly, slowly, slowly, slowly, very slowly, they settle forever. Before that you cannot be allowed to take it for granted; that will be a mistake. Hence he says: Between sessions….

When you are sitting in meditation, a session of meditation, this will happen — but it will go. So what are you supposed to do between sessions?

Between sessions, consider phenomena as phantoms.

Between sessions, continue to use the method. Drop the method when you are deep in meditation. The moment comes, as awareness is getting purer and purer, when suddenly it is utterly pure: drop the method, abandon the method, forget all about the remedy, just settle and be.

But this will happen only for moments in the beginning. Sometimes it happens here listening to me. Just for a moment, like a breeze, you are transported into another world, the world of no-mind. Just for a moment, you know that you know – but only for a moment. And again the darkness gathers and the mind is back with all its dreams, with all its desires and all its stupidities.

For a moment the clouds had separated and you had seen the sun. Now the clouds are there again; it is all dark and the sun has disappeared. Now even to believe that the sun exists will be difficult. Now to believe that what you had experienced a moment before was true will be difficult. It may have been a fantasy; the mind may say it may have just been imagination.

It is so incredible, it looks so impossible, that it could have happened to *you*. With all this stupidity in the mind, with all these clouds and darknesses, it had happened to you: you saw the sun for a moment. It doesn't look probable — you must have imagined it; maybe you had fallen into a dream and seen it.

Between sessions start again, be in the boat, use the boat again.

... consider phenomena as phantoms.

Atisha is very considerate to the disciples. Otherwise the fourth sutra would have been the last – or, at the most, the fifth:

Settle in the nature of basic cognition, the essence.

If Atisha had been a man like Bodhidharma, the treatise would have finished at the fifth sutra, or even at the fourth:

Let even the remedy itself go free on its own.

Then the settling happens on its own. Bodhidharma was very miserly, he would not have used the fifth, but Atisha is very considerate to the disciple. He had been a disciple, so he knew the difficulties of a disciple. And he had been a disciple of three great masters, so he knew all the difficulties that a disciple has to face. He had been a pilgrim; he knew all the problems. And he had been a pilgrim on three paths, all the three possible paths, so he knew all the problems and all the difficulties and all the pitfalls and all the obstacles that are bound to arise on the path of a disciple. Hence his considerateness. He says: Between sessions....

Between these moments of meditativeness, between these moments of utter joy, emptiness and purity, between these moments of being, remember that all are dreams, that every phenomenon is a phantom. Go on using this method till the settling has happened forever.

Train in joining, sending and taking together.
Do this by riding the breath.

Now emptiness has been experienced – this is what he had learned. Up to this sutra he had been with the first master, Dharmakirti. With this sutra, the second master, Dharmarakshita.

Train in joining, sending and taking together.
Do this by riding the breath.

Now he says: Start being compassionate. And the method is, when you breathe in — listen carefully, it is one of the greatest methods – when you breathe in, think that you are breathing in all the miseries of all the people in the world. All the darkness, all the negativity, all the hell that exists anywhere, you are breathing it in. And let it be absorbed in your heart.

You may have read or heard about the so-called positive thinkers of the West. They say just the opposite — they don't know what they are saying. They say, "When you breathe out, throw out all your misery and negativity; and when you breathe in, breathe in joy, positivity, happiness, cheerfulness."

Atisha's method is just the opposite: when you breathe in, breathe in all the misery and suffering of all the beings of the world — past, present and future. And when you breathe out, breathe out all the joy that you have, all the blissfulness that you have, all the benediction that you have. Breathe out, pour yourself into existence. This is the method of compassion: drink in all the suffering and pour out all the blessings.

And you will be surprised if you do it. The moment you take all the sufferings of the world inside you, they are no longer sufferings. The heart immediately transforms the energy. The heart is a transforming force: drink in misery, and it is transformed into blissfulness…then pour it out.

Once you have learned that your heart can do this magic, this miracle, you would like to do it again and again. Try it. It is one of the most practical methods – simple, and it brings immediate results. Do it today, and see.

That is one of the approaches of Buddha and all his disciples. Atisha is one of his disciples, in the same tradition, in the same line. Buddha says again and again to his disciples, "*Ihi passiko*: come and see!" They are very scientific people. Buddhism is the most scientific religion on the earth; hence, Buddhism is gaining more and more ground in the world every day. As the world becomes more intelligent, Buddha will become more and more important. It is bound to be so. As more and more people come to know about science, Buddha will have great appeal, because he will convince the scientific mind — because he says, "Whatsoever I am saying can be practiced. And I don't say to you, Believe it, I say, experiment with it, experience it, and only then if you feel it yourself, trust it. Otherwise there is no need to believe."

Try this beautiful method of compassion: take in all the misery and pour out all the joy.

Train in joining, sending and taking together. Do this by riding the breath. Three objects, three poisons, three bases of virtue.

There are three objects which can either function as three poisons or can become three bases of infinite virtue. Atisha is talking of the inner alchemy. The poison can become the nectar, the baser metal can be transformed into gold.

What are these three objects? The first is aversion, the second is attachment, and the third is indifference. This is how the mind functions. You feel aversion to whatsoever you dislike, you feel attachment to whatsoever you like, and you feel indifferent to things which you neither dislike nor like. These are the three objects. Between these three, the mind exists. These are the three legs of the tripod called the mind: aversion, attachment and indifference. And if you live in these three as they are, you are living in poison.

This is how we have created a hell out of life. Aversion, dislike, hatred, repulsion — that creates one-third of your hell. Attachment, liking, clinging, possessiveness — that creates the second one-third of your hell. And indifference to all that you are neither attracted to nor repulsed by — that creates the third part, the third one-third of your hell.

Just watch your mind, this is how your mind functions. It is always saying, "I like this, I don't like that, and I am indifferent to the third." These are the three ways the mind goes on moving. This is the rut, the routine.

Atisha says: These are the three poisons, but they can become the three bases of virtue. How can they become three bases of great virtue? If you bring in the quality of compassion, if you learn the art of absorbing suffering, as if all the suffering of the world is coming riding on the breath, then how can you be repulsed? How can you dislike anything and how can you be indifferent to anything? And how can you be attached to anything? If you are unconditionally taking in all the suffering in the world, drinking it, absorbing it in your heart, and then instead of it pouring blessings onto the whole of existence *unconditionally* — not to somebody in particular, remember; not only to man but to all: to all beings, trees and rocks and birds and animals, to the whole existence, material, immaterial — when you are pouring out blessings unconditionally, how can you be attached?

Attachment, aversion, indifference: all disappear with this small technique. And with their disappearance the poison is transformed into nectar, and the bondage becomes freedom, and the hell is no more a hell, it is heaven.

In these moments you come to know: This very body the buddha, this very earth the lotus paradise.

And the last sutra:

Train with phrases in every mode of behavior.

Atisha is not an escapist. He does not teach escapism, he does not tell you to move from situations which are not to your liking. He says: You have to learn to function in *bodhichitta*, in Buddha-consciousness, in all kinds of situations — in the marketplace, in the monastery; with people in the crowd or alone in a cave; with friends or with enemies; with family, familiar people, and with strangers; with men and with animals. In all kinds of situations, in all kinds of challenges, you have to learn to function in compassion, in meditation – because all these experiences of different situations will make your *bodhichitta* more and more ripe.

Don't escape from any situation — if you escape, then something will remain missing in you. Then your *bodhichitta* will not be that ripe, will not be that rich. Live life in its multidimensionality.

And that's what I teach you too: Live life in its totality. And living in the world, don't be of it. Live in the world like a lotus flower in water: it lives in water, but the water touches it not. Only then will *bodhichitta* flower in you, bloom in you. Only then will you come to know the ultimate consciousness which is freedom, which is joy, eternal joy, which is benediction. Not to know it is to miss the whole point of life; to know it is the only goal. The *only* goal — remember it.

And remember, Atisha's sutras are not philosophical, not speculative, not abstract. They are experimental, they are scientific.

Let me repeat again: religion is a science in the sense that it is the purest knowing. Yet it is not a science in the sense of chemistry and physics. It is not the science of the outward, it is the science of the inward. It is not the science of the exterior, it is the science of the interior. It is the science that takes you beyond, it is the science that takes you into the unknown and the unknowable. It is the greatest adventure there is. It is a call and a challenge to all those who have any courage, any guts, any intelligence.

Religion is not for cowards, it is for people who want to live dangerously

Chapter 2
The Enlightenment of the Lily

> This sounds like a silly question. I am not sure that I want to become
> enlightened. I am surprised to see so many people around who seem to have
> that desire. I feel very much attached to my country and I love my work there.
> Still I want to take sannyas. Is that possible? Is it not a contradiction?

All questions are silly and so are all answers. Questions come out of the mind like leaves come out of the trees. Questions are part of the mind that has to be dropped; questions keep the mind nourished.

A question is really a search for food. The answer is the food. The question is a groping: the mind is feeling hungry, it wants to be strengthened, it wants to be fed, it searches for food. Wherever it can find something satisfying…any answer that makes the mind knowledgeable, that gives the mind the feeling "Now I know," functions as a food. And the mind can go on and on asking, collecting answers, becoming knowledgeable.

The more knowledgeable the mind is, the more difficult it is to drop it. And it has to be dropped, because unless questioning ceases in you, you will never be silent. Unless questioning disappears totally, you will not find that space, that serenity, that stillness, which can make you aware of who you are, and of what this reality is.

Remember, reality is never going to come to you in the form of an answer. It has never happened that way, it is not going to happen that way. It can't happen that way, it is not in the nature of things. Reality comes to you when there is no question left; reality comes to an unquestioning state of awareness.

So the first thing to be remembered is: all questions are silly, and all answers are too. Then you will be a little puzzled – why do I go on answering your questions? If you look deep down into my answers you will see that they are not answers. They don't nourish your mind, they destroy your mind, they shatter you. They are meant to be shocks. The purpose of my answering is to hammer your mind – it is hammering, it is not answering.

In the beginning, when you come here for the first time and you don't understand me and my purpose, you may think that I am answering you. The longer you are here, the deeper you become attuned with me, the more you know that my answering is not to give you answers. It is not to make you more knowledgeable – just the opposite. It is to take your knowledge away, to make you unknowledgeable, to make you ignorant – ignorant again, innocent again – so that questioning disappears.

And when there is no questioning, there is a totally new quality to your consciousness. That quality is called wonder. Wondering is not questioning, it is feeling mystified by existence. Questioning is an effort to demystify existence; it is an effort not to accept the mystery of life. Hence we reduce every mystery to a question. The question means the mystery is only a problem to be solved, and once solved, there will be no mystery.

My effort in answering you is not to demystify existence but to mystify it more. Hence my contradictions. I cannot be consistent, I am not answering you. I cannot be consistent, because I am not here to make you more knowledgeable. If I am consistent, you will have a body of knowledge — very satisfying to the mind, nourishing, strengthening, gratifying.

I am deliberately inconsistent, contradictory, so that you cannot make any body of knowledge out of me. So if one day you start gathering something, another day I take it away. I don't allow you to gather anything. Sooner or later, you are bound to be awakened to the fact that something totally different is transpiring here. It is not that I am giving you some dogma to be believed in, some philosophy to be lived by, no, not at all. I am utterly destructive, I am taking everything away from you.

Slowly, slowly your mind will stop questioning. What is the point? When no answer answers, then what is the point? And the day you stop questioning is a day of great rejoicing, because then wondering starts. You have moved into a totally new dimension; you are again a child.

Jesus says, "Unless you are like small children you will not enter into my kingdom of God." He means unless you are ignorant again, innocent again, unquestioning and wondering, certainly.

Hence there is a difference between the question of a child and a grown-up person. The difference is of quality. The child asks, not to be answered; he is simply being articulate about his wonder. So if you don't answer the child he forgets about his question and he starts asking another question. His purpose is not to be answered, his purpose is simply that he is talking to himself. He is being articulate about his wonder, he is trying to figure out what it is – the wonder, the mystery. He is not hankering for an answer, so no answer will satisfy him. If you give him an answer he will ask another question about the answer. His wondering continues.

When a grown-up person — educated, sophisticated, well-read, informed — asks a question, he asks it out of his knowledge, to gather more knowledge. The mind always hankers for more and more. If you have money, it hankers for more money; if you have prestige, it hankers for more prestige; if you have knowledge, it hankers for more knowledge. Mind lives in the "more."

And this is the way you go on and on avoiding reality. Reality is a mystery, it is not a question to be asked. It is a mystery to be lived, a mystery to be experienced, a mystery to be loved, a mystery to be dissolved in, to be drowned in.

I am answering you, not to answer but to simply destroy the question. I am not a teacher. The teacher teaches you; the master does not teach you, he helps you unlearn.

Goran Strandberg, you say: "This sounds like a silly question." Not only does it sound, it is. All questions are — what can I do? What can you do?

You say: "I am not sure that I want to become enlightened."

That shows how the mind functions, it is never sure of anything. Mind is always unsure; it lives in unsureness. Mind lives in confusion, it can never have any clarity. Clarity is not part of the mind at all; clarity is the absence of the mind, confusion is the presence of the mind. Confusion and mind are synonymous.

You can't have a clear mind. If you have clarity, you cannot have the mind; if you have the mind, you can't have clarity. The mind is always divided against itself, it lives in conflict. Divisibility is its nature. Hence those who live in the mind never become individuals, indivisibles. They remain divided: one part wants this, another part wants that.

Mind is a crowd of many desires; it is not a single desire. Mind is multi-psychic, and all the fragments are falling apart in different directions. It is a miracle how we go on keeping ourselves together; it is a hard struggle to keep oneself together. Somehow we manage, but that togetherness remains only on the surface. Deep down there is turmoil.

You fall in love with a woman: are you sure that you are in love? Really sure? I have never come across a lover who is really sure. You may even get married, but were you sure? You may have children, but were you sure that you really wanted to have children?

That's how you are living: nothing is sure. But one has to do something or other to keep oneself occupied, so you go on keeping yourself occupied. But surety is not of the mind, it cannot be. And the same problem will arise on every level. The same problem is facing you again.

You say: "I am not sure that I want to become enlightened."

But there must be a certain desire, otherwise why the question? A part of your mind must be saying, "Strandberg, become enlightened" — just a part. Another part must be saying, "Are you mad? Have you lost your senses? You have a wife at home, and children, and work, and you love your country — and you are trying to become enlightened? You must have become a victim of mass hypnosis: so many people in orange, it is dangerous to live with such mad people. So many mad people, enjoying and laughing and loving and looking so happy! Strandberg, keep on remembering: you have a wife, children, a job. Keep alert!"

But again and again the desire will come. When so many people are interested in enlightenment, there must be something in it. You can deceive one, you can deceive two, but how can you deceive so many? Thousands of people interested in enlightenment? It can't be all bullshit. So a desire arises: have a little taste of it. And fear is there too.

But this is the situation; always it is so, in everything it is so. You want to purchase a car, and it is the same: whether to purchase a Chevrolet or a Ford or a Benz? If your wife is not there to help you, you will never purchase any car! Women are more decisive; they are still less in the mind than men. They function out of the heart, their feeling side is still alive. Fortunately they are not yet so civilized; they are still primitive, a little wild, leaning towards the intuitive and not towards the intellect, still capable and courageous enough to act decisively, to act intuitively, to act illogically.

All decisions come from the heart. The mind is never decisive, it cannot be. If you want to decide through the mind, you never can. And I am not talking about great things like enlightenment and the existence of God or the existence of life after death. I am not talking about great things, just small things — whether to purchase this soap or that, or which toothpaste — and you will find the same difficulty. Mind is fragmentary, divided. Hence my consistent insistence that you get out of the mind and start living. The mind only thinks and never lives. It thinks beautiful thoughts, but they are thoughts all the same, just dreams.

Get out of the mind if you want to live. Get out of the mind if you want to live *this* moment. The mind cannot live in this moment, because first it has to decide, and the moment is lost in thinking. And by the time the mind has decided — if it ever decides — that moment is gone already. You are always lagging behind. Mind is always running after life, and lagging behind and missing it continuously.

Many of you must have dreamed something like this: Anand Maitreya continuously dreams that he is going to catch a train, and in the dream he always misses it. Many people, I think almost everybody, has dreams of that kind — that you are just going to make it, just going to make it...and you miss it. By the time you reach the platform, the train has left. You see it leaving, but it is too late; you cannot get on it.

Anand Maitreya's dream is a very significant dream and a very universal one. This is simply how the mind functions; this dream symbolizes the mind: it is always missing the train. It is bound to be so, because mind takes time to think, and time cannot stop for you; it goes on and on slipping out of your hands.

You never have two moments together in your hands, only one single moment. It is such a small moment that there is no space for thinking to move, no space for thoughts to exist. Either you can live it, or you can think. To live it is to be enlightened, to think is to miss.

Enlightenment is not a goal that you have to decide whether to accept it or not. It is not a goal. Enlightenment is the realization that we have only the present moment to live. The next moment is not certain — it may come, it may not come.

In fact, the tomorrow never comes. It is always arriving and arriving, but never arrives. And the mind lives in the tomorrows...and life is possible only in the present.

Jesus says to his disciples, "Look at the lilies in the field, how beautiful they are! Even the great Solomon was not so beautiful attired in all his grandeur as these poor lily flowers." And what is the secret? The secret is that they think not of the morrow. They live now, they live here.

To live now is to be enlightened, to live here is to be enlightened, to be a lily is to be enlightened this very moment! Don't think about what I am saying. Don't think about it, just be here. This is the taste of enlightenment. And once you have tasted it, you will want to taste it more and more.

Don't make a goal out of it; it is not a goal, it is the most ordinary state of consciousness. It is nothing extraordinary, it is nothing special. Trees are enlightened, and the birds are enlightened, and rocks are enlightened, and the sun and the moon are enlightened. Only man is not, because only man *thinks* and goes on missing.

The moment you realize that you are missing because you are brooding too much, then small glimpses start happening. Small gaps in the traffic of the mind, small gaps when there is no traffic: those are the moments of meditation. They can happen anywhere....

Yes in your country too! So, no need to be worried – you need not be in India. India has no copyright on enlightenment; it is not patented yet, it cannot be patented. You can be enlightened anywhere. You can be enlightened remaining a husband, a father, a mother, a wife. You can be enlightened as an engineer, as a doctor, as a carpenter, as a vagabond — even as a hippie. You can be enlightened *anywhere*.

Enlightenment is not something you have to work for, to strive for. It is something that you have to relax for — not strive, but relax. Relax, and this moment you are enlightened. Many times you will become enlightened, and many times you will become unenlightened again, just because of the old habit.

You say: "I am surprised to see so many people around who seem to have that desire."

If they have that desire, they will never become enlightened. Either you can have the desire, or you can have enlightenment; you can't have both. Either you can eat the cake, or you can have it; you can't do both. If you have a desire for enlightenment, then enlightenment is never going to happen to you — never, never. Because desiring is what prevents it, so enlightenment cannot be desired; that will be a contradiction in terms.

Either you are enlightened or you are not, it is as simple as that. And enlightenment is not caused by anything, it is your nature. So it is not a question of making a great endeavor. It is not an enterprise; you need not plan for it. It is already the case!

That is Atisha's first preliminary: Truth is.

Enlightenment is: it is as much as the sunlight showering all around. But you can remain with closed eyes, and you are in a dark night although the sun is showering everywhere. Open your eyes and the night disappears and there is no darkness. Even when you were thinking there was darkness, there was not. It was a very private affair, idiotic; it was something eccentric that you were doing.

To be unenlightened is something that you have earned; great effort has been invested in being unenlightened. And continuously you have to go on making an effort to remain unenlightened. Just drop making any more efforts to remain unenlightened, and you are enlightened. Enlightenment is your natural state; it is what you are.

So please don't misunderstand my people. Newcomers are certainly desirous; they have come out of desire, in search of something. But those who have been here with me a little longer are no more in any desire. They are living moment to moment, enjoying the extraordinary ordinariness of life. Small things — sipping hot tea in the morning: you can sip it in an enlightened way, and you can sip it in an unenlightened way. If, sipping hot tea early in the morning, you are not in the moment but thinking of something else – that you have to go to the morning discourse — you are unenlightened. You missed an enlightened cup of tea. And remember, if that is your habit, you will miss the discourse too — because this again is nothing but a cup of tea. Then in the discourse you will be thinking, "I have to do the Sufi meditation, I have to rush to do this and that and then come back."

It is not a question of one moment, it is a question of your pattern, your gestalt. If this is your gestalt, that you are always rushing ahead of time, thinking of the next moment, then you remain unenlightened. And this is your effort, this is something that you are doing.

For enlightenment nothing is needed to be done, only this understanding…"Why should I go on keeping myself unenlightened?"

That's what I decided one day: "Enough is enough. I have lived so many lives in an unenlightened way." And since then I have lived in an enlightened way. This is simply an understanding, it is not a desire.

You say: "I feel very much attached to my country and love my work there."

Perfectly good! Love your work, love your country, go back — but live there in such a simple moment-to-moment way that you remain enlightened. Don't lag behind, don't rush ahead. Just be herenow, wherever you are, whatsoever you are doing.

"Still," you say, "I want to take sannyas. Is that possible? Is it not a contradiction?"

It is a contradiction. But you are living in contradictions, and this is the last contradiction. Before you can come out of your contradictory life, your life of conflict, you have to close the doors of that life. Sannyas is nothing but closing the doors – the last thing. It is simply a declaration that "I have lived in the mind for so long, and nothing but misery has been my experience. Now I am taking a jump out of the mind into the unknown. I am going into a totally different kind of life."

Sannyas is just a gesture from your side that yes, understanding has dawned, and you would like to come closer to me to see what it actually is.

To be close to a master, to be related to a master, to be intimate with a master, is nothing but an approach towards your own ultimate understanding, your own enlightenment. Your mind will make you very much frightened of the unknown, it will drag you back. And it is always safer to live with the known; it is familiar, you are efficient in living with it. To move into the unknown, you will need a guide – a guide who has moved into the unknown, who lives in the unknown, who lives in innocence. Just to imbibe the spirit you need the guide – not for any guidance, but just to imbibe the spirit of the unknown, the joy of the unknown, the celebration of the unknown.

Once you start drinking something of the master, you will not go back to the old ways of the mind. That's what sannyas is all about.

Yes you can take sannyas. In the beginning it is bound to be the same conflict again: whether to take it or not, whether to go into it or not. It is natural, because that's how you have functioned for many lives. This has become your second nature.

I persuade you, I seduce you into sannyas. Great persuasion is needed, great seduction is needed. And that's why I have created sannyas. Otherwise there was no need; you could have come here, listened to me, and gone. You would have listened to me, but you would not have come close to me. This is a bridge. You would have heard me, but you would not have tasted of my silence. You would have known what I say about love, but you would not have known my love.

Sannyas makes it possible. It is an energy-field, it is a buddhafield. It is communion: nonverbal, heart-to-heart, and, one day, being-to-being.

> I have noticed that when I see a woman who is particularly lovely, and I am taken into that sweet silence, I forget all about philosophy or religion, but I am lost and found entering a moment. I think animals are wise because God doesn't trouble them with metaphysics. Still, I want to throw my books out... But still I like them.

A woman is metaphysics, philosophy, poetry. So is a man. Certainly one will forget metaphysics and philosophy when one comes across alive metaphysics, alive philosophy, alive poetry. That simply shows that you are still alive. To appreciate beauty, to be drowned and drunk with it, is something immensely valuable.

There would have been something wrong if, seeing a beautiful woman, you still remembered the Old Testament or the Bhagavadgita or the Koran. That would have shown that something is wrong with you. This simply shows you are natural, human.

Let this sensitivity grow, and slowly, slowly, as you become more and more sensitive, more and more sensuous, you will see more and more beauty around. The deeper your insight, the greater the beauty. And when you see this whole existence as a tremendous dance, a celebration, you are liberated by it.

It is celebration that liberates, it is love that liberates, it is beauty that liberates — it is not metaphysics or philosophy.

But I am not saying that you have to throw your books out — because there are beautiful books too; they are by-products of great experiences. Don't be lost in them, but to read something of Shakespeare or Kalidas or to read something from Buddha or Atisha is to move into the same world of beauty from a different door.

There are many doors to God's temple. Beauty is one, wisdom is another, love still another, and so on and so forth. Music can do it, poetry can do it, literature can do it. The flowers on the trees are beautiful – what do you think of great poems? They are flowers of consciousness.

You need not throw away your books. In fact, by throwing away your books, you will simply be saying that you are still attached to them. Hate is nothing but love standing on its head, love doing *sirshasana*, a headstand. Love and hate are not separate, they are one. In fact we should stop using these two words separately, we should make one word: lovehate. Not even a hyphen is needed between the two; they are simply one energy like hot and cold, summer and winter, life and death, darkness and light.

There is no need to throw away your books: enjoy them! And there is no need to stop enjoying the beautiful form of a woman, because that too is divine. Enjoy life in all its dimensions. Why this continuous obsession to become one-dimensional, either this or that? Why not both? Why live in either/or? Why not live in both/and? That's my approach: live in both/and, and drop living in either/or.

Soren Kierkegaard has written a book, Either/Or. He lived his whole life in either/or. He could not decide whether to marry the woman he loved – and loved tremendously; he could not decide. That either/or continued for so long that finally the woman decided to go with somebody else. For years he could not decide.

His book became so famous, he himself became so famous, that when he used to walk in Copenhagen, urchins and children and people would shout behind him, "Either/Or! Either/Or! Here goes Either/Or!" Even children had come to know that he used to stand at crossroads thinking, "Where to go? Either/Or – to move this way or that? Both roads lead to the same goal, both go to the station, but which one to follow?" And he would stand at the crossroads, thinking, for hours.

He lived only in thought; he was really a metaphysician. His father had left a heritage; he had enough money, so there was no need to work either. So the whole day, for twenty-four hours, he was thinking. And when he had drawn the last money from the bank, on the way home, he dropped dead. He did well – otherwise he would have been in difficulty.

My feeling is that he must have been thinking, "To be or not to be? Either/or." Because now there was no money left. He must have suffered a heart attack between that either/or. That had been his whole way of life.

There is no need to choose. Why not live choicelessly? Why not live all that life makes available to you? Don't be a spiritualist and don't be a materialist: be both. Don't be a Zorba and don't be a Buddha; be both: Zorba the Buddha. Enjoy all that God has showered on you.

That's my message to my sannyasins. You are not yet my sannyasin, but if you start living in totality, accepting all, giving each moment its due, respecting all, and when a beautiful woman passes suddenly you are thrilled, that shows you are *alive*, that you are not dead yet.

But this need not be just a sexual stirring in you – that is very poor. It has to be something more; it can be a spiritual stirring too. I am not against sex, but to live only a sexual life is to live life at the minimum. Why not live the whole spectrum of it, from sex to samadhi?

When a really beautiful woman passes by, if only your sexuality is stirred, then the animal is alive but you are not. But if your spirituality is also stirred, then you are alive in your totality. And to be alive in totality is the way to God.

Chapter 3
Sitnalta and the Seventeen Chakras

? Why don't I trust you?

Trust is possible only if first you trust in yourself. The most fundamental thing has to happen within you first. If you trust in yourself you can trust in me, you can trust in people, you can trust in existence. But if you don't trust in yourself then no other trust is ever possible.

And the society destroys trust at the very roots. It does not allow you to trust yourself. It teaches all other kinds of trust – trust in the parents, trust in the church, trust in the state, trust in God, ad infinitum. But the basic trust is completely destroyed. And then all other trusts are phony, are bound to be phony. Then all other trusts are just plastic flowers. You don't have real roots for real flowers to grow.

The society does it deliberately, on purpose, because a man who trusts in himself is dangerous for the society – a society that depends on slavery, a society that has invested too much in slavery.

A man trusting himself is an independent man. You cannot make predictions about him, he will move in his own way. Freedom will be his life. He will trust when he feels, when he loves, and then his trust will have a tremendous intensity and truth in it. Then his trust will be alive and authentic. And he will be ready to risk all for his trust, but only when he feels it, only when it is true, only when it stirs his heart, only when it stirs his intelligence and his love, otherwise not. You cannot force him into any kind of believing.

And this society depends on belief. Its whole structure is that of autohypnosis. Its whole structure is based in creating robots and machines, not men. It needs dependent people – so much so that they are constantly in need of being tyrannized, so much so that they are searching and seeking their own tyrants, their own Adolf Hitlers, their own Mussolinis, their own Josef Stalins and Mao Zedongs.

This earth, this beautiful earth, we have turned into a great prison. A few power-lusty people have reduced the whole of humanity into a mob. Man is allowed to exist only if he compromises with all kinds of nonsense.

Now, to tell a child to believe in God is nonsense, utter nonsense – not that God does not exist, but because the child has not yet felt the thirst, the desire, the longing. He is not yet ready to go in search of the truth, the ultimate truth of life. He is not yet mature enough to inquire into the reality of God. That love affair has to happen some day, but it can happen only if no belief is imposed upon him. If he is converted before the thirst has arisen to explore and to know, then his whole life he will live in a phony way, he will live in a pseudo way.

Yes, he will talk about God, because he has been told that God is. And he has been told authoritatively, and he has been told by people who were very powerful in his childhood – his parents, the priests, the teachers. He has been told by people and he had to accept it; it was a question of his survival. He could not say no to his parents, because without them he would not be able to live at all. It was too risky to say no, he *had* to say yes. But his yes can't be true.

How can it be true? He is saying yes only as a political device, to survive. You have not turned him into a religious person, you have made him a diplomat, you have created a politician. You have sabotaged his potential to grow into an authentic being. You have poisoned him. You have destroyed the very possibility of his intelligence, because intelligence arises only when the longing arises to know.

Now the longing will never arise, because before the question has taken possession of his soul, the answer has already been supplied. Before he was hungry, the food has been forced into his being. Now, without hunger, this forced food cannot be digested; there is no hunger to digest it. That's why people live like pipes through which life passes like undigested food.

One has to be very patient with children, very alert, very conscious not to say anything that may hinder their own intelligence from arriving, not to convert them into Christians, Hindus and Mohammedans. One needs infinite patience.

One day that miracle happens when the child himself starts inquiring. Then too, don't supply him with readymade answers. Readymade answers help nobody, readymade answers are dull and stupid. Help him to become more intelligent. Rather than giving him answers, give him situations and challenges so that his intelligence is sharpened and he asks more deeply – so that the question penetrates to his very core, so the question becomes a question of life and death.

But that is not allowed. Parents are very much afraid, the society is very much afraid: if children are allowed to remain free, who knows? They may never come to the fold the parents belonged to, they may never go to the church – Catholic, Protestant, this or that. Who knows what is going to happen when they become intelligent on their own? They will not be within your control. And this society goes into deeper and deeper politics to control everybody, to possess everybody's soul.

That's why the first thing they have to do is to destroy trust – the trust of the child in himself, the confidence of the child in himself. They have to make him shaky and afraid. Once he is trembling, he is controllable. If he is confident he is uncontrollable. If he is confident he will assert himself, he will try to do his own thing. He will never want to do anybody else's thing. He will go on his own journey, he will not fulfill somebody else's desires for some trip. He will never be an imitator, he will never be a dull and dead person. He will be so alive, so pulsating with life, that nobody will be able to control him.

Destroy his trust and you have castrated him. You have taken his power: now he will always be powerless and always in need of somebody to dominate, direct and command him. Now he will be a good soldier, a good citizen, a good nationalist, a good Christian, a good Mohammedan, a good Hindu. Yes, he will be all these things, but he will not be a real individual. He will not have any roots, he will be uprooted his whole life. He will live without roots – and to live without roots is to live in misery, is to live in hell. Just as trees need roots in the earth, man is also a tree and needs roots in existence or else he will live a very unintelligent life. He may succeed in the world, he may become very famous....

Just the other day, I was reading a story:
Three surgeons, old friends, met on holiday. On the beach, sitting under the sun, they started

boasting. The first said, "I came across a man who had lost both of his legs in the war. I gave him artificial legs, and it has been a miracle. Now he has become one of the greatest runners in the world! There is every possibility that in the next coming Olympics he is going to win."

The other said, "That's nothing. I came across a woman who fell from a thirty-story building: her face was completely crushed. I did a great job of plastic surgery. Now just the other day I came to know through the newspapers that she has become the world beauty queen."

The third was a humble man. They both looked at him and asked, "What have you done lately? What's new?"

The man said, "Nothing much – and moreover, I am not allowed to say anything about it."

Both his colleagues became more curious. They said, "But we are friends, we can keep your secret. You need not be worried, it will not leak out."

So he said, "Okay, if you say so, if you promise. A man was brought to me: he had lost his head in a car accident. I was at a loss to know what to do. I rushed into my garden just to think what to do, and suddenly I came across a cabbage. Finding nothing else, I transplanted the cabbage in place of the head. And do you know what? That man has become the prime minister of India."

You can destroy the child; still, he can become the prime minister of India. There is no inherent impossibility of becoming successful without intelligence. In fact it is more difficult to become successful *with* intelligence, because the intelligent person is inventive. He is always ahead of his time; it takes time to understand him.

The unintelligent person is easily understood. He fits with the gestalt of the society; the society has values and criteria by which to judge him. But it takes years for the society to evaluate a genius.

I am not saying that a person who has no intelligence cannot become successful, cannot become famous – but still he will remain phony. And that is the misery: you can become famous, but if you are phony you live in misery. You don't know what blessings life is showering on you, you will never know. You do not have enough intelligence to know. You will never see the beauty of existence, because you don't have the sensitivity to know it. You will never see the sheer miracle that surrounds you, that crosses your path in millions of ways every day. You will never see it, because to see it you need a tremendous capacity to understand, to feel, to be.

This society is a power-oriented society. This society is still utterly primitive, utterly barbarian. A few people – politicians, priests, professors – a few people are dominating millions. And this society is run in such a way that no child is allowed to have intelligence. It is a sheer accident that once in a while a Buddha arrives on the earth – a sheer accident.

Somehow, once in a while, a person escapes from the clutches of the society. Once in a while a person remains unpoisoned by the society. That must be because of some error, some mistake of the society. Otherwise the society succeeds in destroying your roots, in destroying your trust in yourself. And once that is done, you will never be able to trust anybody.

Once you are incapable of loving yourself, you will never be able to love anybody. That is an absolute truth, there are no exceptions to it. You can love others only if you are able to love yourself.

But the society condemns self-love. It says it is selfishness, it says it is narcissistic. Yes, self-love *can* become narcissistic but it is not necessarily so. It can become narcissistic if it never moves beyond itself, it can become a kind of selfishness if it becomes confined to yourself. Otherwise, self-love is the beginning of all other loves.

A person who loves himself sooner or later starts overflowing with love. A person who trusts himself cannot distrust anybody, even those who are going to deceive him, even those who have already deceived him. Yes, he cannot even distrust them, because now he knows trust is far more valuable than anything else.

You can cheat a person – but in what can you cheat him? You can take some money or something else from him. But the man who knows the beauty of trust will not be distracted by these small things. He will still love you, he will still trust you. And then a miracle happens: if a man really trusts you, it is impossible to cheat him, almost impossible.

It happens every day in your life, too. Whenever you trust somebody it becomes impossible for him to cheat you, to deceive you. Sitting on the platform in a railway station, you don't know the person who is sitting by your side – a stranger, a complete stranger – and you say to him, "Just watch my luggage, I have to go to purchase a ticket. Please, just take care of the luggage." And you go. You trust an absolute stranger. But it almost never happens that the stranger deceives you. He could have deceived you if you had not trusted him.

Trust has a magic in it. How can he deceive you now that you have trusted him? How can he fall so low? He will never be able to forgive himself if he deceives you.

There is an intrinsic quality in human consciousness to trust and to be trusted. Everybody enjoys being trusted, it is respect from the other person; and when you trust a stranger it is more so. There is no reason to trust him, and still you trust him. You raise the man to such a high pedestal, you value the man so much, it is almost impossible for him to fall from that height. And if he falls he will never be able to forgive himself, he will have to carry the weight of guilt his whole life.

A man who trusts himself comes to know the beauty of it – comes to know that the more you trust yourself, the more you bloom; the more you are in a state of let go and relaxation, the more you are settled and serene, the more you are calm, cool and quiet.

And it is so beautiful that you start trusting more and more people, because the more you trust, the more your calmness deepens, your coolness goes deeper and deeper to the very core of your being. And the more you trust, the more you soar high. A man who can trust will sooner or later know the logic of trust. And then one day he is bound to try to trust the unknown.

It is only when you can trust the unknown that you can trust a master, never before it, because the master represents nothing but the unknown. He represents the uncharted, he represents the infinite, the unbounded. He represents the oceanic, he represents the wild, he represents God.

You say: "Why don't I trust you?"

It is simple: you don't trust yourself. Start trusting yourself – that is the fundamental lesson, the first lesson. Start loving yourself. If you don't love yourself, who else is going to love you? But remember, if you *only* love yourself, your love will be very poor.

A great Jewish mystic, Hillel, has said, "If you are not for yourself, who is going to be for you?" And also, "If you are *only* for yourself, then what meaning can your life ever have?" – a tremendously significant statement. Remember it: love yourself, because if you don't love yourself nobody else will ever be able to love you. You cannot love a person who hates himself.

And on this unfortunate earth, almost everybody hates himself, everybody condemns himself. How can you love a person who is condemnatory towards himself? He will not believe you. He cannot love himself – how can you dare? He cannot love himself – how can you love him? He will suspect some game, some trick, some trip. He will suspect that you are trying to deceive him in the name of love. He will be very cautious, alert, and his suspicion will poison your being.

If you love a person who hates himself, you are trying to destroy his concept about himself. And nobody easily drops his concept about himself; that is his identity. He will fight with you, he will prove to you that he is right and you are wrong.

That's what is happening in every love relationship – let me call it every so-called love relationship. It is happening between every husband and wife, every lover and beloved, every man and every woman. How can you destroy the other's concept about himself? That is his identity, that is his ego, that's how he knows himself. If you take it away he will not know who he is. It is too risky; he cannot drop his concept so easily. He will prove to you that he is not worth loving, he is only worth hating.

And the same is the case with you. You also hate yourself; you cannot allow anybody else to love you. Whenever somebody comes with loving energy around you, you shrink, you want to escape, you are afraid. You know perfectly well that you are unworthy of love, you know that only on the surface do you look so good, so beautiful; deep down you are ugly. And if you allow this person to love you, sooner or later – and it is going to be sooner than later – he will come to know who you are in reality.

How long will you be able to pretend with a person with whom you have to live in love? You can pretend in the marketplace, you can pretend in the Lions' Club and the Rotary Club – smiles, all smiles. You can do beautiful acting and role-playing. But if you live with a woman or a man for twenty-four hours a day, then it is tiring to go on smiling and smiling and smiling. Then the smile tires you, because it is phony. It is just an exercise of the lips, and the lips become tired.

How can you go on being sweet? Your bitterness will surface. Hence by the time the honeymoon is over, everything is over. Both have known each other's reality, both have known each other's phoniness, both have known each other's falsity.

One is afraid to become intimate. To be intimate means you will have to put aside the role. And you know who you are: worthless, just dirt. That's what you have been told from the very beginning. Your parents, your teachers, your priests, your politicians, all have been telling you that you are dirt, worthless. Nobody has ever accepted you. Nobody has given you the feeling that you are loved and respected, that you are needed – that this existence will miss you, that without you this existence will not be the same, that without you there will be a hole. Without you this universe is going to lose some poetry, some beauty: a song will be missed, a note will be missed, there will be a gap – nobody has told you that.

And that's what my work here is: to destroy the distrust that has been created in you about yourself, to destroy all condemnation that has been imposed on you, to take it away from you and to give you a feeling that you are loved and respected, loved by existence. God has created you because he loved you. He loved you so much that he could not resist the temptation to create you.

When a painter paints, he paints because he loves. Vincent van Gogh continuously painted the sun his whole life, he loved the sun so much. In fact it was the sun that drove him mad. For one year continuously he was standing and painting under the hot sun. His whole life revolved around the sun. And the day he was content painting the painting that he had always wanted to paint – and to paint this painting he had painted many others, but he had not been contented with them – the day he was contented, the day he could say, "Yes, this is the thing that I wanted to paint," he committed suicide, because, he said, "My work is done. I have done the thing that I came for. My destiny is fulfilled, now it is pointless to live."

His whole life a devotion to a certain painting? He must have been madly in love with the sun. He looked at the sun so long that it destroyed his eyes, his vision, it drove him mad.

When a poet composes a song it is because he loves it. God has painted you, sung you, danced you. God loves you! If you don't see any meaning in the word *God* don't be worried; call it existence, call it the whole. The existence loves you, otherwise you would not be here.

Relax into your being, you are cherished by the whole. That's why the whole goes on breathing in you, pulsating in you. Once you start feeling this tremendous respect and love and trust of the whole in you, you will start growing roots into your being. You will trust yourself. And only then can you trust me. Only then can you trust your friends, your children, your husband, your wife. Only then can you trust the trees and the animals and the stars and the moon. Then one simply lives as trust. It is no more a question of trusting this or that; one simply trusts. And to trust is simply to be religious.

That's what sannyas is all about. Sannyas is going to undo all that the society has done. It is not just accidental that priests are against me, politicians are against me, parents are against me, the whole establishment is against me; it is not accidental. I can understand the absolutely clear logic of it. I am trying to undo what they have done. I am sabotaging the whole pattern of this slave society.

My effort is to create rebels, and the beginning of the rebel is to trust in oneself. If I can help you to trust in yourself, I have helped you. Nothing else is needed, everything else follows of its own accord.

**John Lilly has said, "What the mind believes is true or becomes true."
Would you please comment on this?**

That's what has been happening down the ages. That is the way of autohypnosis. John Lilly is absolutely wrong. "What the mind believes," he says, "is true…." It is not. It only appears true.

And he says "…or it becomes true." It never becomes true by being believed, but it starts *appearing* true. Yes, for the believer it becomes true, although it is not true, because belief begins in ignorance. Belief cannot create truth; truth is already the case.

Remember the first preliminary of Atisha: truth is. You need not believe in it for it to be. Your belief or your disbelief is not going to make any difference to the truth. Truth is truth, whether you believe or you disbelieve.

But if you believe in something it starts appearing as true to you at least. That's what the meaning of belief is: belief means to believe in something as true – you know that you don't know, you know that the truth is unknown to you, but in your ignorance you start believing, because belief is cheap.

To discover truth is arduous, it needs a long pilgrimage. It needs a great emptying of the mind, it needs a great cleansing of the heart. It needs a certain innocence, a rebirth: you have to become a child again.

Only very few people have ever dared to discover truth. And it is risky, because it may not console you; it has no obligation to console you. It is risky: it may shatter all that you have known before, and you will have to rearrange your whole life. It is dangerous: it may destroy all your illusions, it may shatter all your dreams. It is really going through fire; it is going to burn you as you are, it is going to kill you as you are. And who knows what will happen later on?

How can the seed know that by dying in the soil it will become a great tree? It will not be there to witness the happening. How can the seed know that one day, if it dies, there will be great foliage, green leaves, great branches, and flowers and fruits? How can the seed know? The seed will not be there. The seed has to disappear before it can happen. The seed has never met the tree. The seed has to disappear and die.

Only very few people have that much courage. It really needs guts to discover truth. You will die as yourself. You will certainly be born, but how can you be convinced of it? What guarantee is there? There is no guarantee.

Hence, unless you are with a master who has died and is reborn, who has crucified himself and is resurrected – unless you come across a man like Christ or Buddha or Atisha – you will not be able to gather enough courage.

Seeing Atisha, something may start stirring in your heart, a chord may be touched, something may be triggered, a synchronicity. The presence of somebody who has arrived may create a great longing in you, may become the birth of an intense passionate search for truth.

Belief cannot give you the truth, it only pretends. It is cheap, it is a plastic flower. You need not take all the trouble of growing a rosebush, you can simply go to the market and purchase plastic flowers – and they are more lasting too, in fact they are almost eternal. Once in a while you can wash them, and they are fresh again. They will not deceive you, but at least they can deceive the neighbors, and that is the point. You will know all along that they are plastic flowers. How can you forget it? You have purchased them! The neighbors may be deceived, but how can *you* be deceived?

And I don't think that even the neighbors are deceived, because they have also purchased plastic flowers. They know they are deceiving you, they know you are deceiving them. Everybody is perfectly aware that everybody else is deceiving. "But this is how life is," people say. Nobody is really deceived. People just pretend to be deceived. You pretend that you have real flowers, others pretend that they are deceived. Just watch, observe, and what I am saying will be experienced by you. It is a simple fact; I am not talking philosophy, just stating facts.

What John Lilly says is utter nonsense. He says, "What the mind believes is true." It is never true, because belief has nothing to do with truth. You can believe that this is night but just by your believing, this is not going to become night. But you can believe, and you can close your eyes and for you it is night – but only for you, remember, not in truth. You are living in a kind of hallucination.

There is this danger in belief: it makes you feel that you know the truth. And because it makes you feel that you know the truth, this becomes the greatest barrier in the search. Believe or disbelieve and you are blocked – because disbelief is also nothing but belief in a negative form.

The Catholic believes in God, the communist believes in no God: both are believers. Go to Kaaba or go to the Comintern, go to Kailash or to the Kremlin, it is all the same. The believer believes it is so, the nonbeliever believes it is not so. And because both have already settled without taking the trouble to go and discover it, the deeper is their belief, the stronger is their belief, the greater is the barrier. They will never go on a pilgrimage, there is no point. They will live surrounded by their own illusion, self-created, self-sustained; it may be consoling, but it is not liberating. Millions of people are wasting their lives in belief and disbelief.

The inquiry into truth begins only when you drop all believing. You say, "I would like to encounter the truth on my own. I will not believe in Christ and I will not believe in Buddha. I would like to become a christ or a buddha myself, I would like to be a light unto myself."

Why should one be a Christian? It is ugly. Be a christ if you can be, but don't be a Christian. Be a buddha if you have any respect for yourself, but don't be a Buddhist. The Buddhist believes. Buddha knows.

When you can know, when knowing is possible, why settle for believing? But again, the society would like you to believe, because believers are good people, obedient, law-abiding. They follow all formalities and etiquette, they are never trouble-makers. They simply follow the crowd, whichever crowd they happen to be in; they simply go with the crowd. They are not real men, they are sheep. Humanity has not yet arrived.

Somebody once said to George Bernard Shaw, "What do you think about civilization?"

He said, "It is a good idea. Somebody should try it."

It has not yet been tried. Humanity is still arriving; we are still groping between animality and humanity. We are in limbo: man has to be born, man has to be given birth to; we have to prepare the ground for man to appear.

And the most significant thing that will help that man to come will be if we can drop believing – if we can drop being Christians, Hindus, Mohammedans, Jainas, Buddhists, communists. If you can drop believing, immediately your energy will take a new turn: it will start inquiring. And to inquire is beautiful. Your life will become a pilgrimage to truth, and in that very pilgrimage you grow.

Growth is a by-product of the inquiry into truth. Believers never grow, they remain childish. And remember, to be childlike and to be childish are poles apart, they are not the same thing. It is beautiful to be childlike. The man of trust is childlike and the man of belief is childish. To be childlike is the ultimate in growth; that is the very culmination – consciousness has come to the ultimate peak. To be childlike means to be a sage, and to be childish means to be just un-grownup.

The average mental age of human beings on the earth today is not more than twelve years. When for the first time this was discovered, it was such a shock. Nobody had ever thought about it; it was just by accident that it became known. In the First World War, for the first time in human history, the people who were candidates, who wanted to enter the army, were examined. Their mental age was inquired into, their IQ was determined. This was a great revelation – that they were not more than twelve years; the average age was just twelve years.

This is childishness. The body goes on growing, and the mind has stopped at the age of twelve. What kind of humanity have we created on this earth? Why does the mind stop at twelve? Because by the time one is twelve, one has gathered all kinds of beliefs; one is already a believer, one already "knows" what truth is. One is a Christian, another is a communist; one believes in God, one does not believe in God; one believes in The Bible and the other believes in *Das Kapital*; one believes in the Bhagavadgita, another believes in the *Red Book* of Mao Zedong.

We have drilled concepts and ideologies into the innocent minds of poor children. They are already becoming knowers. Do you know – by the age of seven, a child already knows fifty percent of all that he will ever know. And by the time he is fourteen he has almost arrived; now there is nowhere to go, he has only to vegetate. Now he will exist as a cabbage. If he goes to college then, as they say, he may become a cauliflower. A cabbage with a college education is a cauliflower. But there is not much difference, just labels change. The cabbage becomes an MA, a PhD, this and that, and just to show respect we call it a cauliflower. But the mental age is twelve.

The real man grows to the very end. Even while he is dying, he is growing. Even the last moment of his life will still be an inquiry, a search, a learning. He will still be inquiring – now inquiring into death. He will be fascinated: death is such an unknown phenomenon, such a mystery, far more mysterious than life itself – how can an intelligent man be afraid? If in life he has not been afraid to go into the uncharted and the unknown, at the moment of death he will be thrilled, ecstatic. Now the last moment has come: he will be entering into the darkness, the dark tunnel of death. This is the greatest adventure one can ever go on; he will be learning.

A real man never believes; he learns. A real man never becomes knowledgeable; he always remains open, open to truth. And he always remembers that "It is not that truth has to adjust to me, but just vice versa: I have to adjust to truth." The believer tries to adjust truth to himself, the seeker adjusts himself to truth. Remember the difference; the difference is tremendous. One who believes, he says, "Truth should be like this, this is my belief."

Just think of a Christian…. If God appears not like Jesus Christ but like Krishna, not on the cross but with a flute and girlfriends dancing around him, the Christian will close his eyes; he will say, "This is not my cup of tea." Girlfriends? Can you think of Jesus with girlfriends? The cross and girlfriends can't go together. Jesus hanging on the cross and girlfriends dancing around? It won't fit, it will be very bizarre. He was waiting for Christ to appear, and instead of Christ this guy, Krishna, appears: he seems to be debauched. And the flute? The world is suffering and people are hungry and they need bread – and this man is playing on the flute? He seems to be utterly uncompassionate, he seems to be indulgent. The Christian cannot believe in Krishna: if God appears as Krishna, then the Christian will say, "This is not God."

And the same will be the case with the Hindu who was waiting for Krishna: if Christ appears, that will not be his idea of God – so sad, such a long face, so gloomy, with such suffering on his face.

Christians say Jesus never laughed. I don't think they are right, and I don't think they are representing the real Christ, but that's what they have managed to propagate. The Hindu cannot accept the revelation; he must think this is some kind of nightmare. Jesus will not appeal to him.

The believer cannot even trust his own experience. Even if truth is revealed, he will reject it, unless it fits with him. He is more important than truth itself: truth has an obligation to fit with him. He is the criterion, he is the decisive factor. This kind of man can never know truth; he is already prejudiced, poisoned.

The man who wants to know truth has to be capable of dropping all concepts about truth. Everything *about* truth has to be dropped. Only then can you know truth. Know well: to know about truth is not to know truth. Whatsoever you know may be utter nonsense; there is every possibility that it *is* utter nonsense. In fact people can be conditioned to believe any kind of nonsense; they can be convinced.

Once I went to address a conference of theosophists. Now, theosophists are people who will believe any bullshit – *any*! The more shitty it is, the more believable. So I just played a joke on them. I simply invented something; I invented a society called "Sitnalta." They were all dozing, they became alert. "Sitnalta?" I made the word by just reading *Atlantis* backwards. And then I told them, "This knowledge comes from Atlantis, the continent that disappeared in the Atlantic ocean."

And then I talked about it: "There are really not seven chakras but seventeen. That great ancient esoteric knowledge is lost, but a society of enlightened masters still exists, and it still works. It is a very, very esoteric society, very few people are allowed to have any contact with it; its knowledge is kept utterly secret."

And I talked all kinds of nonsense that I could manage. And then the president of the society said, "I have heard about this society." Now it was *my* turn to be surprised. And about whatsoever I had said, he said that it was the first time that the knowledge of this secret society had been revealed so exactly.

And then letters started coming to me. One man even wrote saying, "I thank you very much for introducing this inner esoteric circle to the theosophists, because I am a member of the society, and I can vouch that whatsoever you have said is absolutely true."

There are people like these who are just waiting to believe in anything, because the more nonsensical a belief is, the more important it appears to be. The more absurd it is, the more believable – because if something is logical, then there is no question of believing in it.

You don't believe in the sun, you don't believe in the moon. You don't believe in the theory of relativity: either you understand it or you don't understand it; there is no question of belief. You don't believe in gravitation; there is no need. Nobody believes in a scientific theory – it is logical. Belief is needed only when something illogical, something utterly absurd, is propounded.

Tertullian said, "I believe in God because it is absurd: *Credo quia absurdum*, my creed is the absurd."

All beliefs are absurd. If a belief is very logical, it will not create belief in you. So people go on inventing things.

Man is basically a coward, he does not want to inquire. And he does not want to say "I don't know," either.

Now, that president of the theosophical society who said, "I have heard about this society" – he cannot say that he does not know, he does not have even that much courage. To accept one's ignorance needs courage. To accept that you don't know is the beginning of real knowledge. You go on believing, because there are holes in your life which have to be filled, and belief is easily available.

There are three hundred religions on the earth. One truth, and three hundred religions? One God, and three hundred religions? One existence, and three hundred religions? And I am not talking about sects – because each religion has dozens of sects, and then there are sub-sects of sects, and it goes on and on. If you count all the sects and all the sub-sects, then there will be three thousand or even more.

How can so many beliefs, contradictory to each other, go on? People have a certain need – the need not to appear ignorant. How to fulfill this need? Gather a few beliefs. And the more absurd the belief is, the more knowledgeable you appear, because nobody else knows about it.

There are people who believe in a hollow earth, and that inside the earth there is a civilization. Now, if somebody says so you cannot deny it; you cannot accept it, but at least you have to listen attentively. And that serves a purpose: everybody wants to be listened to attentively. And one thing is certain, this man knows more than you. You don't know whether the earth is hollow or not; this man knows. And who knows? He may be right. He can gather a thousand and one proofs; he can argue for it, he can propound it in such a way that you at least have to be silent if you don't agree.

Believers and believers and believers – but where is truth? There are so many believers, but where is truth? If John Lilly is right, then the world would be full of truth, you would come across it everywhere. Everybody would have truth, because everybody is a believer. No, it is all nonsense.

He says, "What the mind believes is true or becomes true." No. What the mind believes is *never* true, because truth needs no belief. Belief is a barrier to truth. And what the mind believes never becomes true, because truth is not becoming, truth is being; it is already the case. You have to see it – or you can go on avoiding seeing it, but it is there. Nothing has to be added to it, it is eternally there.

And the best way to avoid truth is to believe. Then you need not look at it. Your eyes become full of belief; belief functions as dust on the eyes. You become closed into yourself, the belief becomes a prison around you. Belief closes you: then you are living within yourself in a windowless existence, and you can go on believing whatsoever you want to believe. But remember, it is belief, and belief is a lie.

Let me say that even when the truth is told to you, don't believe in it! Explore, inquire, search, experiment, experience: don't believe in it. Even when truth is conveyed to you, if you believe in it, you turn it into a lie. A truth believed is a lie, belief turns truth into a lie.

Believe in Buddha and you believe in a lie. Believe in Christ and you believe in a lie. Don't believe in Christ, don't believe in Buddha, don't believe in me. What I say, listen to it attentively, intelligently; experiment, experience. And when you have experienced, will you need to believe in it? There will be no doubt left, so what will be the point of belief? Belief is a way of repressing doubt: you doubt, hence you need belief. The rock of belief represses the spring of doubt.

When you know, you know! You know it is so; there is no doubt left. Your experience has expelled all darkness and all doubt. Truth is: you are full of it. Truth never creates belief.

How to attain to truth? By dropping all kinds of beliefs. And remember, I am saying *all* kinds – belief in me is included. Experience me, come along with me, let me share what I have seen, but don't believe, don't be in a hurry. Don't say, "Now what is the point? Now Osho has seen it, all that is left for me is to believe it."

What I have seen cannot become your experience unless *you* see it. And it is the experience of truth that delivers you from ignorance, from bondage, from misery. It is not the belief that delivers you, it is truth.

Jesus says, "Truth liberates." But how to attain to truth? It is not a question of belief, but a question of meditativeness. And what is meditation? Meditation is emptying your mind completely of all belief, ideology, concept, thought. Only in an empty mind, when there is no dust left on the mirror, truth reflects. That reflection is a benediction.

**? All the beautiful methods are no good anymore. 'I' will let the mind drop
     and the methods too. I fear that you will send me back to hell.**

Methods are never of any use. Methods have never been any good, but they still serve a purpose. The purpose is negative. If you have a thorn in your foot, you need another thorn to pull it out. Once the first thorn is pulled out by the second, don't put the second back in the wound just out of gratefulness. Throw away both! The second thorn is as much a thorn as the first; their qualities are not different.

Because your mind is so full of rubbish, you need something to pull it out. But whatsoever is going to pull it out is rubbish in its own way; it is the same. Poison is needed to kill poison. Don't cling to the second poison, thinking it is medicine; don't become addicted to the second poison.

It is good that you say: "All the beautiful methods are no good any more."

They never were. But they still serve a purpose, because man lives in such stupidity that he has to be pulled out of it. And remember, your lies, your beliefs, your ignorance, have to be dropped somehow; some ways and means have to be invented. Once your mind is dropped, you will see the whole ridiculousness of all the methods. Then you will understand that they were never needed at all.

But don't start talking about it to others, because there are many people who may drop them from the very beginning, seeing that if they are not needed then why bother? They are needed, although there comes a time when they have to be dropped. Use them, and drop them. All methods are like ladders: when you have climbed up the ladder and you have reached the upper floor, you need not bother about it, it can be thrown away.

In fact it *should* be thrown away. Keeping it may show some unconscious desire in you to go back; you want to keep the ladder there in case you decide to go back to your old rubbish. The ladder can help in that way too. A ladder is neutral – it can take you to the upper floor, it can bring you back down to the old situation. But the ladder cannot direct you.

In fact the moment you have climbed up the ladder, you have used it and reached a different plane of life, a different plane of understanding, throw the ladder away immediately, before you start clinging to it.

So it is good that you think methods are no good any more.

"…'I' will let the mind drop and the methods too."

If methods are no good any more, where is the mind? And if the mind is still there to be dropped, then please don't be in a hurry: the methods still have a little function to fulfill.

You will not be able to let the mind drop. Who are you except the mind? Who will drop the mind, who will let the mind drop? You are not yet; you will know yourself only when the mind is dropped. When the mind disappears, you will know who you are. Before that, you don't know. It is just the mind thinking about dropping the mind. Mind is very subtle, very cunning; it can go on playing new games. It can say, "Yes it is so beautiful to drop the mind." And it is still the mind! And the mind can say, "There is no need for any method. You can drop me easily – it is up to you."

The mind is playing a very subtle trick. It is helping you to drop the methods first, and then the mind thinks, "We will see – we will see if you can drop me!"

If it has really been understood – that methods are no longer useful – it is synonymous to that understanding that the mind is dropped. They mean the same thing: to know that methods are no longer needed, no longer useful, is to see that the mind is no more there. Mind is method, mind is technique. Mind cannot exist without methods, methods cannot exist without mind; they go together. They are two aspects of the same energy.

And you say: "I fear that you will send me back to hell."

If methods are really dropped, there is no way to go back to hell. Even if I want to send you, I cannot. Methods are needed to go to hell. Methods are needed to come out of hell, methods are needed to go into hell, but no method is needed to go to heaven. When you are out of hell, you are in heaven.

So the whole question is how to be out of hell? Out of hell is heaven. Heaven is not some place where you have to go, otherwise methods would be needed, paths and ways would be needed. No paths and no ways are needed. All paths, all ways, lead into hell. But if you are in hell, then you will have to use the same paths and the same ways to come back.

Let me tell you one of the most beautiful parables that has ever been invented by man, the parable of Adam and Eve eating the fruit of the Tree of Knowledge. The moment they have eaten the fruit of the Tree of Knowledge they fall – the original fall. They are no more in paradise, they are no more deathless, they are no more in eternity; they have lost contact. What has happened? Mind has been created.

That is the meaning of the parable. Eating from the Tree of Knowledge creates the mind; the moment they ate the fruit of the Tree of Knowledge, mind was created. Adam and Eve are still in the same place, in the same space, they have not gone anywhere. But the mind is created

– and once the mind is there, paradise is lost, forgotten. One falls asleep and starts dreaming of hells, death, etcetera, etcetera. Now you will have to vomit the fruit of knowledge.

You will have to vomit the mind out of your system. Once you have vomited knowledge out of your system, suddenly you will be awakened to the fact that you are in paradise. And you will start laughing at the whole ridiculousness of it, because you will know, you will become perfectly aware, that you had never been anywhere else. You have always been here, always and always: you had just fallen asleep and had a nightmare. Now that the poison is out of your system, the nightmare is finished.

We *are* in the garden of Eden, right now, this very moment. Nobody can send you to hell except knowledge, except methods, except the mind.

Try to understand. Rather than being in a hurry to drop anything, try to understand. Become more aware, become more alert, more watchful, more observant, and methods will disappear and mind will disappear in the same instant. And then there is no hell – in fact there never has been, you had only imagined it. It is all paradise and always paradise. We *are* in God, we are gods.

Chapter 4
The Last Chance to Rebel

Some time ago, while asleep in the night, I dreamed I was at a lecture. In the morning I could not remember anything you'd said except the phrase "Poetry is surrender." Since then I have been wondering what poetry has to do with surrender, and vice versa, and how poetry can be a path like love, prayer and meditation.

Poetry contains all: it contains love, it contains prayer, it contains meditation, and much more. All that is divine, all that is beautiful, all that can take you to the transcendental, is contained in poetry.

Poetry is not just poetry: poetry is essential religion. Poetry means a state of being where the mind is no longer interfering between you and existence; when there is communion between you and existence – direct, immediate; when you are suddenly possessed by the whole, where you disappear as a separate entity and the whole starts speaking through you, starts dancing through you; where you become a hollow bamboo and the whole transforms you into a flute.

Poetry is the whole descending into the part, the ocean disappearing into the dewdrop. Poetry is a miracle.

And when I use the word *poetry* my fingers are not pointing to the Shakespeares, the Kalidases; they are only partial poets. Yes, they knew certain moments of poetry, but they are not poets. They had a few glimpses when the doors of the unknown were open to them, they had some access to the deepest sources of life, but those moments were sheer gifts from the unknown. They knew nothing of how to reach them, they knew nothing about how the whole reached them. It was almost a state of unconsciousness. It happened in a dream, just as it has happened to you in a dream. They were dreamers.

All the so-called great poets of the world, great painters, musicians, sculptors, they were all dreamers. Yes, they had a few glimpses in their dreams: something infiltrated, here and there a ray of light was able to pass through the dream barrier, and even that single ray was enough to create a Shakespeare or a Kalidas. But that's not what I am pointing to.

When I say poetry, I mean that which flowed through the buddhas. That is true poetry. Buddha is not a dreamer, Atisha is not a dreamer; if they are anything they are awakened people. Dreams have disappeared, evaporated. Now it is not only a glimpse of truth that comes to them unawares, possesses them, and then leaves them empty, spent, exhausted….

The ordinary poet simply hops; for a moment he is off the ground, but only for a moment, and then he is back on the ground again.

A buddha has wings – he does not hop. He knows how to go to the farthest star. He knows the way to approach the unknown, he has the key to unlock the doors to the mysterious. He is a master. And then something starts flowing through him which is not his own. He is only a medium: he is possessed. Then whatsoever he says is poetry; or, even if he keeps silent, his silence is poetry. His silence has tremendous music in it; whether he speaks or not doesn't matter. Speaking, he speaks poetry; not speaking, he remains poetry. He is surrounded by poetry: he walks in poetry, he sleeps in poetry, poetry is his very soul, it is his essential being.

How does this poetry happen? It happens in surrender, it happens when the part gathers enough courage to surrender to the whole, when the dewdrop slips into the ocean and becomes the ocean.

Surrender is a very paradoxical state: on one hand you disappear, on the other hand you appear for the first time in your infinite glory, in your multidimensional splendor. Yes, the dewdrop is gone, and gone forever; there is no way to recapture it, to reclaim it. The dewdrop has died as a drop, but in fact the dewdrop has become the ocean, has become oceanic. It still exists, no more as a finite entity, but as something infinite, shoreless, boundless.

This is the meaning of the myth of the phoenix. He dies, he is utterly burned, reduced to ashes, and then suddenly he is reborn out of the ashes – resurrection. The phoenix represents Christ: crucifixion and resurrection. The phoenix represents Buddha: death as an ego, and a new birth as utter egolessness. It represents all those who have known; to know means to be a phoenix. Die as you are, so that you can be that which you really are! Die in all your inauthenticity, phoniness, separation from existence.

We go on believing that we are separate. We are not, not even for a single moment. In spite of your belief, you are one with the whole. But your belief can create nightmares for you; it is *bound* to create them. To believe that "I am separate" means to create fear.

If you are separate from the whole, you can never get rid of fear, because the whole is so vast and you are so small, so tiny, so atomic, and you constantly have to fight the whole so that it does not absorb you. You have to be constantly alert, on guard, so the ocean does not simply take you in. You have to protect yourself behind walls and walls and walls. All this effort is nothing but fear. And then you are constantly aware that death is reaching you and death is going to destroy your separation. That's what death is all about: death is the whole claiming the part back. And you are afraid that death will come and you will die. How to live long? How to attain a kind of deathlessness? Man tries it in many ways. To have children is one of the ways, hence the continuous urge to have children. The root of this desire to have children has nothing to do with children at all, it has something to do with death.

You know you will not be able to be here forever; howsoever you try, you are going to fail, you *know* it, because millions have failed and nobody has ever succeeded. You are hoping against hope. Then find some other ways. One of the simplest ways, the most ancient way, is to have children: you will not be here, but something of you, a particle of you, a cell of you, will go on living. That is a vicarious way of becoming immortal.

Now science is finding far more sophisticated ways – because your child may look a little bit like you, or may not look like you at all, and he will only be just a little bit like you; there is no intrinsic necessity for him to appear exactly like you. So now science has found ways to duplicate you. Some of your cells can be preserved, and when you die, a duplicate can be created out of those cells. And the duplicate will be exactly like you; not even twins are so alike. If you meet your duplicate you will be surprised: he will be exactly like you, absolutely like you.

Now they say that to be safer, a duplicate can be created while you are alive, and the duplicate can be kept in deep freeze, so if some accident happens, if you die in a car accident, you can be immediately replaced. Your wife will never be able to detect it, your children will never come to know that this daddy is just an imitation, because he will be exactly like you.

Men have tried in other ways also, far more sophisticated than this one. Write books, paint pictures, compose great symphonies: you will be gone but the music will remain; you will be gone, but your signature will be there on the book; you will be gone, but the sculpture that you created will be there. It will remind people of you, you will persist in their memories. You will not be able to walk on the earth, but you will be able to walk in people's memories. It is better than nothing. Become famous, leave some marks in the history books – of course they will be only footnotes, but still, something is better than nothing.

Man has been trying, down the ages, somehow to have some kind of immortality. The fear of death is so much, it haunts you your whole life.

The moment you drop the idea of separation, the fear of death disappears. Hence I call this state of surrender the most paradoxical. You die of your own accord and then you cannot die at all, because the whole never dies, only its parts are being replaced. But if you become one with the whole, you will live forever: you will go beyond birth and death.

That's the search for nirvana, enlightenment, *moksha*, the kingdom of God – the state of deathlessness. But the condition that has to be fulfilled is very frightening. The condition is: first you have to die as a separate entity. That's what surrender is all about: dying as a separate entity, dying as an ego. And in fact it is nothing to be worried about, because you are not separate, it is only a belief. So only the belief dies, not you. It is only a notion, an idea.

It is as if you have seen a rope in the darkness of the night, and you have got the notion that it is a snake, and you are escaping from the snake in tremendous fear, trembling, perspiring. And then somebody comes along and says, "Don't be worried. I have seen it in daylight, and I know perfectly well that it is only a rope. If you don't trust me, *ihi passiko*, come with me! I will show you that it is only a rope!"

And that's what the buddhas have been doing down the ages: "*Ihi passiko*, come with me! Come and see!" They take the rope in their hand and they show you that this is only a rope, the snake was never there in the first place. All fear disappears, you start laughing. You start laughing at yourself, at how foolish you have been. You have been escaping from something which never existed in the first place! But whether it existed or not, those drops of perspiration were real; the fear, the trembling, the heartbeat going faster, the blood pressure – all those things were real.

Unreal things can trigger real things, remember it. If you think they are real, they function for you as reality – only for you. It is a dream reality, but it can affect you, it can affect your whole life, your whole lifestyle.

The ego is not there. The moment you become a little alert, aware, conscious, you will not find the ego at all. It will be a rope that you had misconceived as a snake; you will not find the snake anywhere.

Death does not exist, death is unreal. But you create it: you create it by creating separation. Surrender means dropping the idea of separation: death disappears automatically, fear is found no more, and your whole flavor of life changes. Then each moment is such crystal purity, a purity of delight, joy, bliss. Then each moment is eternity. And to live that way is poetry, to live moment-to-moment without the ego is poetry. To live without the ego is grace, is music; to live without the ego is to live, to really live. That life I call poetry: the life of one who is surrendered to existence.

And remember, let me repeat it again: when you surrender to existence you are not surrendering anything real. You are simply surrendering a false notion, you are simply surrendering an illusion, you are surrendering maya. You are surrendering something that you never had with you in the first place. And by surrendering that which you don't have, you attain to that which you have.

And to know that "I am at home, I always have been and I always will be," is a great moment of relaxation. Knowing that "I am not an outsider, I am not alienated, I am not uprooted," that "I belong to existence and the existence belongs to me," all becomes calm and quiet and still. This stillness is surrender.

The word *surrender* gives you a very very wrong idea, as if you are surrendering something. You are not surrendering anything; you are simply dropping a dream, you are simply dropping something arbitrary that the society had created.

The ego *is* needed, it has certain functions to fulfill in the society. Even when one is surrendered to God, one goes on using the word *I* – but now it is only something utilitarian, nothing existential. He knows he is not; he uses the word because not using it will be unnecessarily creating trouble for others, it will make communication impossible. It is already impossible! It will be more difficult to communicate with people. So it is just an arbitrary device. If you know it is a device, arbitrary, utilitarian, useful, but nothing existential, then it never creates any problem for you.

Your dream has given you a glimpse, your dream has allowed you to see something, something you may not be allowing while you are awake. It sometimes happens. The conscious mind is more egoistic, obviously; the ego never penetrates into the unconscious. The society can only teach the conscious; the society cannot teach the unconscious, at least not yet – they are trying hard.

In Soviet Russia particularly, they are trying hard to teach the unconscious. And unfortunately they are succeeding. They are teaching people while they are asleep. When you are asleep your conscious is no longer functioning; your unconscious functions. Now, in Russia particularly, they are doing great experiments in teaching people while they are asleep. It can be done, it *is* being done.

This is one of the great dangers that the future generations will have to face. If the politicians have gadgets with them which can teach people while they are asleep, then there will never be any possibility of rebellion.

While he is asleep, you can make a person a communist, Catholic, Hindu, Buddhist, Christian, Mohammedan, and because it will be in his unconscious he will be absolutely unable to go beyond it. He will not be able to get rid of it, because the unconscious is nine times more powerful than the conscious. The conscious is only the tip of the iceberg: one tenth of your mind in conscious, nine tenths is unconscious. If the politician can reach the unconscious, then humanity is doomed. Then children will be taught while they are asleep. Even sleep will not be your own and private; even sleep will not be a personal thing, it will be owned by the state. You will not even be allowed to dream private dreams; the state will decide what dreams you can dream – because you may be dreaming some anti-state dreams, and the state cannot afford them. Your dreams can be manipulated, your unconscious can be manipulated, but fortunately it has not happened yet.

You may be the last generation which has the possibility to rebel. And if you don't rebel, there may be no more chances: humanity can be reduced to a robotlike existence. So rebel while there is still time! I don't think there is much time left, maybe just this last part of the century, these coming twenty or twenty-five years. If humanity can rebel in these next twenty-five years, this is the last opportunity; otherwise people will be utterly unable to, their unconscious will dominate them. Up to now, the society has only been able to pollute your conscious mind – through education, through the church, through propaganda – but only your conscious mind; your unconscious is still free.

It happens more often that you are closer to the truth, closer to reality, when you are deeply asleep. It is very strange, it should not be so; you should be closer to reality while you are awake. But your wakefulness is no longer yours; it is Hindu, it is Christian, it is Mohammedan, it is no longer yours; society has already impinged upon it, interfered with it, distorted it. But the unconscious is still yours.

Hence psychoanalysis became so interested in your dreams, because in your dreams you are truer. In your dreams you are less false, in your dreams all the censors of the society disappear. In your dreams you are saying things as they are, seeing things as they are, seeing yourself as you are. The moment you are awake, you start pretending. Your wakefulness is a long, long pretension.

Hence sleep is so relaxing, because to be continuously on guard and say the things which are supposed to be said, and do the things which the society requires to be done, is tiring, very tiring. One needs to fall into deep sleep every day for eight hours to get rid of all this, to be natural again, to forget the society and the nightmare and the hell that it has created.

The more alert you become, the more watchful you are, the more free from the bondage of the society and its clutches, then only your body will need sleep, and even in your sleep there will continue an undercurrent of awareness. Your mind will not need any sleep; there is no intrinsic necessity for it to go to sleep, it is a created necessity.

When your mind is clear, untethered, free, you will have less and less need for the mind to go to sleep. And then a miracle happens: if you can remain alert even while the body is asleep, you will know for the first time that you are separate from the body. The body is asleep and you are awake: how can you both be identical, how can you both be one? You will see the difference; the difference is so vast.

The body belongs to the earth, you belong to the sky. The body belongs to matter, you belong to God. The body is gross, you are not. The body has limits, is born and will die; you are never born and you will never die. This becomes your own experience, not a belief.

Belief is fear-oriented. You would like to believe that you are immortal, but belief is just a belief, something pseudo, painted from the outside. Experience is totally different: it wells up within you, it is your own. And the moment you know, nothing can ever shake your knowing, nothing can destroy your knowing. The whole world may be against it, but you will still know that you are separate. The whole world may say there is no soul, but you will know there is. The whole world may say there is no God, but you will smile – because the experience is self-validating, it is self-evident.

Your dream may be very significant. What you have not allowed in your waking consciousness has sprung up in your dreaming consciousness. A ray of light has entered you.

In the West, before Freud, waking consciousness was thought to be the only consciousness; not so in the East – even after Freud, although dreaming consciousness has been accepted as valuable, one thing has still not yet happened: dreamless sleep is still ignored. This is not so in the East. The East has always accepted waking consciousness as the most superficial, dreaming consciousness as far deeper and more significant, and sleeping consciousness as even deeper, even more significant than dreaming consciousness. The West needs yet another Freud to introduce sleep as the most significant part.

But the East knows something still more. There is a point, the fourth state of consciousness. It is called *turiya*, simply "the fourth"; it has no other name. Turiya means the fourth. When waking, dreaming and sleep all disappear, one is simply a witness. You cannot call it waking, because this witness never sleeps; you cannot call it dreaming, because for this witness no dream ever appears; you cannot call it sleep, because this witness *never* sleeps. It is eternal awareness. This is the *bodhichitta* of Atisha, this is Christ-consciousness, this is buddhahood, enlightenment.

So always be careful. Be more careful of your dreams than your waking, be more careful again of your dreamless sleep than of dreaming. And remember that you have to search for the fourth, because only the fourth is the ultimate. With the fourth you have arrived home. Now there is nowhere to go.

You say you have forgotten all about the dream, but only remembered one phrase, "Poetry is surrender." That is the very essence of my teaching. The most fundamental thing about my message to the world is, poetry is surrender – and vice versa, surrender is poetry.

I would like my sannyasins, all of my sannyasins, to be creative – poets, musicians, painters, sculptors, and so on and so forth. In the past, the sannyasins of all the religions have lived a very uncreative life. They were respected for their uncreativity, and because of this uncreativity they have not added any beauty to the world. They have been a burden; they have not brought something of paradise to the earth. In fact they have been destructive – because you can either be creative, or you are bound to be destructive. You cannot remain neutral; either you have to affirm life with all its joys, or you start condemning life.

The past has been a long, long drawn-out nightmare of destructive attitudes, life-negative approaches. I teach you life-affirmation! I teach you reverence for life. I teach you not renunciation but rejoicing. Become poets! And when I say become poets, I don't mean that you all have to become Shakespeares, Miltons and Tennysons. If I come across Shakespeare and Milton and Tennyson, then too I will say please become poets – because they are only *dreaming* about poetry.

Real poetry happens in the fourth state of consciousness. All the great so-called poets have only been dreamers; they were confined to the second state of consciousness. Prose remains confined to the first – waking consciousness, and your poetry is confined to the second.

The poetry I am talking about is possible only in the fourth. When you have become fully alert, clear, when there is no mind any more, then whatsoever you do will be poetry, whatsoever you do will be music. And even if you don't do a thing, poetry will surround you, it will be your fragrance, it will be your very presence.

You ask me: "Since then I have been wondering what poetry has to do with surrender, and vice versa, and how poetry can be a path like love, prayer and meditation."

Love is a path, prayer is a path, meditation is a path, because they are ways to poetry. Anything that leads you to God is bound to lead you to poetry. The man of God can be nothing but a poet. He will sing a song, not his own any more of course: he will sing God's song. He will give utterance to the silence of God, he will be a mouthpiece to the whole.

I teach you meditation, prayer, love, only because they all take you to the center. And the center is poetry. They are all ways to poetry. To dissolve yourself in poetry is to dissolve yourself in God – and certainly without surrender it is not possible. If you remain too much, God cannot happen. You have to be absent for him to become a presence in you.

Die, so that you can be.

Utter confusion is my part. Good and bad have ceased to exist. I am neither proud nor ashamed and yet I am both. Whatever I have achieved seems lost in a fog, resolved together with my failures. Like smoke I feel, but through the smoke a tremendous sadness arises like a sharp rock with a velvet covering. Osho, I can't perceive the end of it – or is there no end? Is it ecstasy carrying the weight of impurity? Please, Osho, give me sannyas.

Confusion is a great opportunity. The problem with people who are not confused is great – they think they know, and they know not. The people who believe that they have clarity are really in great trouble; their clarity is very superficial. In fact they know nothing of clarity; what they call clarity is just stupidity.

Idiots are very, very clear – clear in the sense that they do not have the intelligence to feel confusion. To feel confusion needs great intelligence. Only the intelligent ones feel confusion; otherwise the mediocres go on moving in life, smiling, laughing, accumulating money, struggling for more power and fame. If you see them you will feel a little jealous; they look so confident, they even look happy.

If they are succeeding, if their money is increasing and their power is increasing and their fame is growing, you will feel a little jealous. You are so confused and they are so clear about their life; they have a direction, they have a goal, they know how to attain it, and they are managing, they are already achieving, they are climbing the ladder. And you are just standing there, confused about what to do, what not to do, what is right and what is wrong. But this has always been so; the mediocre remains certain. It is only for the more intelligent to feel confusion, chaos.

Confusion is a great opportunity. It simply says that through the mind there is no way. If you are really confused – as you say, "I am utterly confused" – if you are *really* confused, you are blessed. Now something is possible, something immensely valuable; you are on the verge. If you are utterly confused, that means the mind has failed; now the mind can no longer supply any certainty to you. You are coming closer and closer to the death of the mind.

And that is the greatest thing that can happen to any man in life, the greatest blessing – because once you see that the mind is confusion and there is no way out through the mind, how long can you go on clinging to the mind? Sooner or later you will have to drop it; even if you don't drop it, it will drop of its own accord. Confusion will become so much, so heavy, that out of sheer heaviness it will drop. And when the mind drops, confusion disappears.

I cannot say that you attain to certainty, no, because that too is a word applicable only to the mind and the world of the mind. When there is confusion, there can be certainty; when confusion disappears, certainty also disappears. You simply are – clear, neither confused nor certain, just a clarity, a transparency. And that transparency has beauty, that transparency is grace, it is exquisite.

It is the most beautiful moment in one's life when there is neither confusion nor certainty. One simply is, a mirror reflecting that which is, with no direction, going nowhere, with no idea of doing something, with no future, just utterly in the moment, tremendously in the moment.

When there is no mind there can be no future, there can be no program for the future. Then this moment is all, all in all; this moment is your whole existence. The whole existence starts converging on this moment, and the moment becomes tremendously significant. It has depth, it has height, it has mystery, it has intensity, it has fire, it has immediacy, it grips you, it possesses you, it transforms you.

But I cannot give you certainty; certainty is given by ideology. Certainty is nothing but patching up your confusion. You are confused. Somebody says, "Don't be worried," and says it very authoritatively, convinces you with arguments, with scriptures, and patches up your confusion, covers it with a beautiful blanket – with The Bible, with the Koran, with the Gita. And you feel good; but it is temporary, because the confusion is boiling within. You have not got rid of it, it has only been repressed.

That's why people cling to beliefs, churches, scriptures, doctrines, systems of thought. Why do people invest so much in systems of thought? Why should somebody be a Christian or a Hindu? Why should somebody be a communist – for what? There is a reason, a great reason too. Everybody is confused, and so somebody is needed to supply you with certainty. He can be the pope or he can be Mao Zedong, he can be Karl Marx or he can be Manu or Moses – anybody will do. And whenever there are great times of crisis, any stupid person who has the stubbornness to shout, to argue, who can pretend certainty, will become your leader. That's how Adolf Hitlers, Josef Stalins and Mussolinis became important people.

People have always been wondering why Adolf Hitler was able to dominate a great intelligent race like the Germans. Why? It appears a paradox that a man like Martin Heidegger, one of the greatest thinkers of this age, was a supporter of Adolf Hitler. The great professors of the great German universities supported Adolf Hitler. Why? How was it possible?

And Adolf Hitler is just a stupid person, uneducated, unsophisticated. But he has something in him that the professors were lacking, that intelligent people were lacking, that the Martin Heideggers were lacking. He has something in him which no intelligent person can have: he has absolute certainty. He is idiotic – but he can say things with no ifs and no buts; he can make statements as if he knows. He is a madman, but his madness had great impact. It changed the whole course of human history.

It is not a surprise that the Germans became so interested and impressed by him. They were intelligent people, some of the most intelligent people on the earth, and intelligence always brings confusion. That is the secret of Adolf Hitler's success. Intelligence brings confusion and confusion brings trembling, fear; one knows not where to go, what to do, and one starts looking for a leader. One starts searching for somebody who can say things with absoluteness, who can assert categorically.

The same has happened in India; it has happened just now. This is one of the most ancient countries of the world, with the longest tradition of thinking and contemplation, the longest tradition of philosophizing. No other country has philosophized so much.

Whenever people are in confusion they fall prey to third-rate minds. The first-rate minds fall prey to third-rate minds because the third-rate mind has no confusion. The third-rate mind knows that just by drinking your own urine all diseases can be cured – even cancer is curable by drinking your own urine. It is only possible to assert this if you really are utterly unintelligent.

The intelligent person hesitates, ponders, wavers. The unintelligent never wavers, never hesitates. Where the wise will whisper, the fool simply declares from the housetops.

Lao Tzu says, "I may be the only muddle-headed man in the world. Everybody seems to be so certain, except me." He is right; he has such tremendous intelligence that he cannot be certain about anything.

I cannot promise you certainty if you drop the mind. I can promise you only one thing, that you will be clear. There will be clarity, transparency, you will be able to see things as they are. You will be neither confused nor certain. Certainty and confusion are two sides of the same coin.

But you are in a beautiful moment, and the world too is in a beautiful moment. Whenever there is a crisis of identity, whenever people don't know who they are, whenever the past loses its grip, whenever people are uprooted from the traditional, whenever the past no more seems relevant, this crisis arises, a great crisis of identity – who are we? what are we supposed to do?

This opportunity can turn into a curse too, if you fall victim to some Adolf Hitler; but this curse can become a great opening into the unknown if you are fortunate enough to be in the vicinity of a buddha. If you are fortunate enough to be in love with a buddha, your life can be transformed.

People who are still rooted in tradition, and who think they know what is right and what is wrong, will never come to a buddha. They will continue to live their life – the routine life, the dull, the dead life. They will go on fulfilling their duties as their forefathers used to do. For centuries they have been following a track and they will go on following that trodden track. Of course, when you follow a trodden track, you feel certain – so many people have walked on it. But when you come to a buddha and you start moving into the unknown, there is no highway, no trodden path. You will have to make your own path by walking; the path will not be found ready-made.

That's what I want each of my sannyasins to understand. You are not here to depend on me, you are not here to follow me, you are not here to simply accept me and believe in me. You are here to experiment; you have to move on your own. I can give you encouragement to move on your own, I can trigger a process of inquiry in you; but I will not give you a system of thought, I will not give you any certainty. I will only give you a pilgrimage – a pilgrimage which is hazardous, a pilgrimage which has millions and millions of pitfalls, a pilgrimage in which you will have to face more and more dangers every day, a pilgrimage that will take you to the top of human consciousness, to the fourth state. But the higher you go, the more is the danger of falling.

I can only promise you a great adventure, risky, dangerous, with no promise that you will attain it – because the unknown cannot be guaranteed.

So, if you have come to me to find some remedy for your confusion, then you have come to the wrong person, I am not the right person to be with. But if you have come to drop confusion *and* certainty, and be free of the mind that can either give you confusion or certainty, if you have come to me to go on the ultimate adventure in search of God, if you have come to me to dare, to accept the challenge of the uncharted sea, the roaring waves, with no possibility of seeing the other shore, then you have come to the right person. Then much is possible. I only say "possible" – I cannot say it is absolutely certain. It is always a possibility; you may be able to make it, you may not be able to make it, there is no guarantee. It is not a commodity which can be guaranteed; it is a gamble.

And if you are ready to gamble, enter into this buddhafield. No need to wait any longer – you have already waited enough, for many, many lives.

You ask me: "Please, Osho, give me sannyas." It is not a question of my giving you sannyas; it is a question of you *taking* it. Open your heart! I am always giving it. The question is of your receiving it, welcoming it.

You say: "Good and bad have ceased to exist." That is good, that's beautiful. Good and bad are all manmade, sinners and saints are all manmade. And they are not different at all; the difference is only superficial, very superficial, not even skin-deep. Scratch a little, and in your saint you will find the sinner.

This guy went to the pope and he said, "Hey pope, fuck you!"

The pope could not believe it. He said, "Me? The head of the Catholic Church? Me, the spiritual head of millions and millions? Me, the direct descendant of Jesus Christ? Me, the only representative of God on earth? Fuck me? Fuck *you!*"

There is not much difference. Just scratch a little, and you will find sinners in the saints and you will find saints in the sinners. All good, all bad, is just arbitrary, man-made.

It's a beautiful space you are entering. If good and bad have ceased to exist, so far, so *good*! Now enter another dimension, not man-made, where distinctions are of no relevance, where nothing is good and nothing is bad, where whatsoever is is, and whatever ain't ain't. There is no question of good and bad; either something is or something is not. Good and bad are nothing but alternatives to be chosen – either choose this, or choose that. They keep you in the division of either/or.

The moment you start seeing the hocus-pocusness of all good and bad, when you start seeing that they are socially manufactured things…. Of course they are utilitarian, and I am not saying to go into the marketplace and behave as if there is nothing good and nothing wrong. I am not saying to walk in the middle of the road, saying what does it matter whether one walks on the right or the left.

When you are with people, remember, for them good and bad still exist. Be respectful to them and their dreams. It is not for you to disturb anybody's dream. Who are you? It is not for you to interfere. Be polite to people and their stupidities, be polite to them and their games. But all the time remember, deep down nothing is good, nothing is bad.

Existence is simply there; there is nothing to choose between. And remember, when there is nothing to choose between, you will become undivided. When there is something to choose between, it divides you too. Division is a double-edged sword: it divides reality outside, it divides you inside. If you choose, you choose division, you choose to be split, you choose schizophrenia. If you don't choose, if you know there is nothing good, nothing bad, you choose sanity.

Not choosing anything is choosing sanity, not choosing is to be sane, because now there is no division outside, how can you be divided inside? The inside and the outside go together. You become indivisible, you become an individual. This is the process of individuation. Nothing is good, nothing is bad. When this dawns in your consciousness, suddenly you are together, all fragments have disappeared into one unity. You are crystallized, you are centered.

This is one of the greatest contributions of Eastern consciousness to the world. The Western religions still go on hanging around the idea of good and bad. That's why it is so difficult for the Christian to understand the Upanishads, Lao Tzu, Chuang Tzu; it is impossible for them to understand. They are always looking with the Christian mind, "Where are the commandments?" And there are none! The Upanishads never say what is good and what is wrong, they never say what to do and what not to do, they don't command. They are poetic assertions, they are poetry. They exult in existence, they are ecstatic, overflowing; they are just ecstatic ejaculations.

The Upanishads say, "God is, and you are that: *tat tvam asi.*" The Upanishads say, "God is, and I am God." These are assertions arising out of ecstasy. They have no ethics, no morality, no reference even. The Christian mind, the Mohammedan mind, the Jewish mind, cannot understand why these books are thought to be religious. They may be good literature, but why are they thought to be religious?

And if you ask one who has reached the same ecstasy as the Upanishadic seers, he will say The Bible, the Talmud, the Koran, they are ethical, moral, but what do they have to do with religion? They are good, because they make a society move smoothly, but they have nothing religious in them – or maybe only a few statements here and there. The major part is ethical; the religious part seems to be so small that it can be neglected, ignored. And it *has* been ignored.

To come to know that nothing is good, nothing is bad, is a turning point; it is a conversion. You start looking in; the outside reality loses meaning. The social reality is a fiction, a beautiful drama; you can participate in it, but then you don't take it seriously. It is just a role to be played; play it as beautifully, as efficiently, as possible. But don't take it seriously, it has nothing of the ultimate in it.

The ultimate is the inner; the indivisible soul knows it. And, to come to that soul, this is a good turning-point.

You say: "Good and bad have ceased to exist." This is the right moment to take sannyas, this is what sannyas is all about. Now there is no need to wait, now there is no need even to ask my permission. Sannyas is already happening. Enter into this buddhafield. Long you have waited – too long, really.

I have heard: An old couple reached the divorce court. They were really ancient, ninety-five years old, and they had been married for seventy-five years. The judge could not believe his eyes. He said, "So you are thinking of divorce now, after seventy-five years of married life? Why now?"

They looked at each other, and then the old man said, "Well, we waited till all the children were dead."

People go on waiting and waiting and waiting.... Now, what a hope! There is no need to wait any more. You are welcome, you are ready. Even people who are not ready, I welcome them – because those who are not ready today may be ready tomorrow. Those who are not ready when they take sannyas, may be ready *after* they have taken sannyas. And who am I to refuse you if God accepts you? I am nobody to refuse you.

That's why nobody is refused, no condition is made, nobody is thought to be unworthy. If God thinks you worthy of being alive, that's enough proof that you are also worthy of becoming a sannyasin.

You say: "I am neither proud nor ashamed and yet I am both." That's the state of confusion. You will find everything like that – neither this nor that, yet both.

"Whatever I have achieved seems lost in a fog" – you are really blessed – "resolved together with my failures."

Many should feel jealous of you. To know that all has failed is the beginning of a new journey. To know that "All that I have achieved is lost" is the beginning of a new search for something that cannot be lost. When one is utterly disillusioned with the world and all its successes, only then does one become spiritual.

"Like smoke I feel, but through the smoke a tremendous sadness arises like a sharp rock with a velvet covering." It is bound to be so. When life has been lived through illusions and one day one suddenly feels all has been meaningless, useless – "I was chasing shadows" – a great sadness arises.

But I can see your perceptiveness. Sadness is there, but "with a velvet covering." Yes, sadness is there because of the past, and the velvet covering is what is possible; it only becomes possible now. Out of all this confusion is sadness; but because of this confusion and its utterness, deep down a new stirring is happening. You may not yet be aware of it, but something is stirring, a new joy is arising behind the curtain of sadness – a joy of a new search, of a new adventure, of a new life, of a new way to be.

"Osho, I can't perceive the end of it – or is there no end?" There is a beginning of the mind and there is an end of the mind, there is a beginning of the ego and there is an end of the ego, but there is no beginning to you and no end to you. And there is no beginning to the mystery of existence and no end to you. It is an ongoing process. Mysteries upon mysteries are waiting for you, hence the thrill and the ecstasy.

Feel ecstatic that there is no end to life, that when you have reached one peak, suddenly another peak starts giving you challenges – a higher one, a more arduous climb, a more dangerous reach. And when you have reached the other peak, there will be another peak; peaks upon peaks. It is an eternal Himalayas of life.

Just think of a point where you arrive, and now there is nothing else left. You will be utterly bored then; boredom will be your only fate then! And life is not boredom, it is a dance. Life is not boredom, it is exultation, exuberance.

Many, many things are going to happen, and many, many things will always remain to happen. The mystery never ends, it cannot end. That's why it is called a mystery, it cannot even be known. It will never become knowledge, that's why it is called a mystery; something in it is eternally elusive. And that's the whole joy of life. The great splendor of life is that it keeps you eternally engaged, searching, exploring. Life is exploration, life is adventure.

You ask: "Osho, I can't perceive the end of it or is there no end?" There is an end to you, but there is no end to the real you.

"Is it ecstasy carrying the weight of impurity?" There is no impurity anywhere. All is pure. Impurity is just a shadow of the confusion that you are feeling right now. When the confusion and the confusing mind are dropped, the shadows will disappear of their own accord.

Your innermost core has always been pure; purity is intrinsic to you, it cannot be taken away. Your virginity is eternal; you cannot lose it, there is no way to lose it. You can only forget about it or remember it. If you forget about it, you live in confusion; if you remember it, all is clear. Again, I will not say "certain," but just "clear." All is transparent. That transparency is freedom, that transparency is wisdom. This transparency is your birthright; if you are not claiming it, nobody else is responsible except you. Claim it! It is yours. It is yours just for the asking.

Sannyas is an effort to reclaim that which is yours and to drop that which is not yours. Sannyas is an effort to drop that which you really don't have, and to claim that which you always had with you all along.

Ecstasy is our very nature; not to be ecstatic is simply unnecessary. To be ecstatic is natural, spontaneous. It needs no effort to be ecstatic, it needs great effort to be miserable. That's why you look so tired, because misery is really hard work; to maintain it is really difficult, because you are doing something against nature. You are going upstream – that's what misery is.

And what is bliss? Going with the river – so much so that the distinction between you and the river is simply lost. You are the river. How can it be difficult? To go with the river no swimming is needed; you simply float with the river and the river takes you to the ocean. The river is already going to the ocean.

Life is a river. Don't push it and you will not be miserable. The art of not pushing the river of life is sannyas.

You are ready. This moment of confusion, this moment of chaos in your life, can open a new door, can turn a new leaf. Don't wait any more.

Chapter 5
Sowing White Seeds

Begin the development of taking with yourself.
When evil fills the inanimate and animate universes
change bad conditions to the bodhi path.
Drive all blame into one.
Be grateful to everyone.
The insurpassable protection of emptiness
is to see the manifestations of bewilderment as the four kayas.
An excellent means is to have the four provisions.
In order to bring any situation to the path quickly as soon as it is met,
join it with meditation.
The concise epitome of heart instruction: work with "five forces."
The instructions for transference in the Mahayana are the "five forces."
Behavior is important.
The purpose of all dharma is contained in one point.

Meditation is the source, compassion is the overflow of that source. The non-meditative man has no energy for love, for compassion, for celebration. The non-meditative person is disconnected from his own source of energy; he is not in contact with the ocean. He has a little bit of energy that is created by food, by air, by matter – he lives on physical energy.

Physical energy has limitations. It is born at a certain moment in time, and it dies at another moment in time. Between birth and death it exists. It is like a lamp that burns because of the oil in it – once the oil is exhausted, the flame goes out.

The meditative person comes to know something of the infinite, becomes bridged with the inexhaustible source of energy. His flame goes on and on, his flame knows no cessation. It cannot disappear, because in the first place it never appears. It cannot die, because it is unborn.

How to bridge oneself with this inexhaustible source of life, abundance, richness? You can call that inexhaustible source God or you can call it truth or anything that you wish to call it. But one thing is absolutely certain; that man is a wave of something infinite.

If the wave looks inward it will find the infinite. If it goes on looking outwards it remains disconnected – disconnected from its own kingdom, disconnected from its own nature. Jesus calls this nature the kingdom of God. He again and again says, "The kingdom of God is within you. Go within."

Meditation is nothing but a bridge to go within. Once meditation has happened, the only thing that remains to happen is compassion.

Buddha, the original master in Atisha's line, said that unless compassion happens, don't remain contented with meditation itself. You have gone only halfway, you have yet to go a little further. Meditation, if it is true, is bound to overflow into compassion. Just as when a lamp is lit it immediately starts radiating light, it immediately starts dispersing darkness, once the inner light is lit, compassion is its radiation.

Compassion is the proof that meditation has happened. Love is the fragrance that proves that the one-thousand-petaled lotus in the innermost core of your being has bloomed, that the spring has come – that you are no more the same person you used to be, that that personality has ceased and individuality is born, that you are not living any more in darkness, that you are light.

These sutras are practical instructions, remember it. Atisha is not a philosopher, no wise man ever is. He is not a thinker; thinking is only for the mediocre, the foolish. The wise does not think, the wise knows. Thinking is an effort to know; it is guesswork, groping in the dark, shooting arrows in the dark.

Wisdom is knowing. And when you know, you need not guess. You are not guessing that this is morning and the birds are singing and the trees are bathed in sunlight. You are not guessing it, you are not thinking that it is so. If somebody is guessing it, then he must be blind or at least drunk. It is an experience, and every experience is self-validating.

Atisha is not a speculative thinker. What he is saying is not a philosophy or a system of thought. It is how he has attained; he is showing you the way. And the buddhas can only show the way – you will have to walk on it, nobody else can walk for you. Nobody else can do it for you; no proxy is possible in existence.

Yes, others can communicate how they attained, what pitfalls to avoid, how to go on judging whether you are moving in the right direction or not, what energies to use and what energies to discard, what is helpful and what is a hindrance. They can give you little hints about the path – and I say "little hints"; they cannot give you a complete map either, because each individual will have to follow a path that is a little bit different, and each individual will come across unique experiences that nobody has come across before and nobody may ever come across again.

Each individual is so unique that no absolute map can be given, only hints, vague hints, indications.

You are not to cling to these instructions. Just understand them, absorb them, and don't be a fanatic. Don't say, "This has to be like this. If it is not like this then I am not going to follow it, then something is wrong." It will be something like this, but in a very vague way. It will have a similar fragrance but it will not be exactly the same; similar, yes, but not the same. One has to be aware of it. If one is not aware, then one becomes a fanatic – and fanatics have never arrived, their very fanaticism prevents them.

These are small hints. These are not mathematical, these are not like two plus two is four. In the world of the mysterious, sometimes two plus two is three, sometimes two plus two is five. It is very rarely that two plus two is four, very rarely; it is the exception, not the rule. It is not mathematics, it is music. It is not logic, it is poetry.

When you read a logical treatise, you read with a different mind. If you read poetry you need a totally different approach. In logic there is a clear-cut process, the process of syllogism – you know that this is so, and this is so, therefore *this* is bound to be so. There is a "therefore."

In poetry there is no "therefore." Poetry takes quantum leaps. Poetry is a vision, not a logical process; a song, not a syllogism. Yes, even the song has some intrinsic logic in it, but it is not on the surface. And it is not for those who are on the path, it is only for those who have arrived.

Once you have arrived you will see the whole logicalness of each step that you had taken, but not before it. You will see why you had to jump, why you had to take a certain step. When you were taking that step, nothing was clear, nothing was absolutely certain or guaranteed. You were taking that step according to your feeling, not according to your thinking. But later on, recapitulating, looking back, thinking can be revived. Now you can search for the undercurrent of logic.

Those who have arrived are very logical. But those who are on the path, if they try to be logical, they will never survive. This is one of the paradoxes to be understood. Hence the statements of Buddha, Tilopa, Saraha and Atisha are really very logical, but only for those who have arrived. The logic can be felt only backwards. When you are progressing towards the goal, the ultimate, everything is vague, hidden behind a cloud. It is like the early morning mist. In the afternoon, in the full noontide, the mist will have disappeared. But that full noontide has yet to happen.

So think, meditate, feel these instructions, but don't take them in dead seriousness. There are bound to be a few differences. A few things are going to happen on your way which did not happen on Atisha's way. A few things are going to happen on your way which have not happened on my way. There are as many ways in the world as there are people. Nobody can stand in your place; even those who are standing very close to you are not standing in exactly the same place. Your angle of vision is bound to be a little bit different from the angle of vision of somebody who is standing just by your side holding your hand. No two persons can see the world in exactly the same way, it is impossible. And everybody has to move from his own place, his own space.

Now, Atisha existed one thousand years ago. He must have seen a totally different world, he must have walked through a totally different world, with a different kind of language – where a different kind of understanding was prevalent, where different attitudes and approaches were still valid. They are no more valid, they are no more relevant, that world has disappeared. Atisha's world exists no more.

Still, his instructions are of tremendous importance, taken nonfanatically. Taken fanatically, you miss the whole point. One has to be very, very loose and relaxed. While thinking about the past buddhas, one has to be available to them, open to them, but unclinging and detached, knowing perfectly well that centuries have passed, knowing perfectly well that "I am not Atisha, so how can I follow these instructions absolutely?"

But Atisha is not telling you to follow his instructions absolutely. He is simply giving a glimpse of his vision and the way he has arrived at it. He is simply sharing his poetry with you, his compassion with you.

Remember it – otherwise it is very easy for people to become fanatics. Why do millions of people in the world become fanatics? For a simple reason: by becoming a fanatic you avoid all experimenting, by becoming a fanatic you escape from thinking on your own, feeling on your own. By becoming a fanatic you throw all responsibility on somebody else's shoulders – Jesus, Buddha, Krishna, Atisha.

Remember, your responsibility is such, it cannot be given to anybody else, it cannot be thrown on somebody else. Your responsibility is absolutely yours. You will have to think, you will have to feel, you will have to meditate, you will have to walk, for yourself. And let me remind you again: you may come across scenes which Atisha has never come across.

If you go to the Himalayas and you want to climb Everest, there are many ways to climb it, many sides. From one side you may come across beautiful valleys and rivers and trees. From the other side you may not come across any river, you may not come across trees at all, you may come across only rocks and rocks. From the third side you may come across glaciers, virgin snow that has never melted. And you all will reach the top.

Those who have reached the top will always be considerate and liberal. They cannot be stubborn, they cannot say, "This is the only path," because from the top they can see that there are many paths. They can see many pilgrims arriving, reaching from different routes. And each route has its own world. Atisha followed a certain route. But he was very fortunate to have three enlightened masters; he reached Everest by at least three routes. His vision is very comprehensive, his vision is wide, it is not narrow.

Jesus says, "My path is narrow but straight." He followed only one master. Naturally his path is very narrow and straight. It is not the case with Atisha; his path is very zigzag and very wide. It contains many paths in it, it is a great synthesis.

The first sutra:

Begin the development of taking with yourself.

Let me remind you, in the last sutra Atisha was saying that when you take the breath in, let it become your meditation that all the suffering of all the beings in the world is riding on that incoming breath and reaching your heart. Absorb all that suffering, pain and misery in your heart, and see a miracle happen.

Whenever you absorb somebody else's misery, pain and suffering, the moment you absorb it, it is transformed. The natural tendency is to avoid it; the natural tendency is to protect yourself against suffering. The natural tendency is to keep aloof, not to sympathize, not to empathize. People, even when they sympathize, sympathize only formally. They pay lip-service; they don't mean it. If they really meant it, they could have helped the other person. They could have absorbed his suffering, they could have drunk his suffering.

And it happens a few times, and you know it: there are people, if you meet them you feel an unburdening. When they are gone, you feel light, you feel flowing, you feel more vibrant, more alive – as if they have taken a great burden off your head, off your chest, as if they have poured some nectar into your being. You feel a dance left within your heart when they leave. You wait again and again for them to come to you; you seek their company, you enjoy it, because you are nourished by their presence.

The opposite kind of people also exist. If they meet you they leave you more burdened than you ever were. They leave you in a kind of despair, disgust. You feel you have been sucked, your energy is lower. They have taken something from your energy and they have not given anything to you. This is an ordinary experience.

If people avoid you, remember, they are not responsible. Something in you makes them avoid you. If people don't want to meet you, if they find excuses to escape from you, remember, they are not responsible. You must be doing something negative to their energy.

If people seek you, if people become friendly immediately, if people feel a certain affinity – even strangers would like to come and sit close to you, would like to hold your hand, would just like to be with you – that means you must be knowingly or unknowingly helping them. Everybody is burdened with great misery, everybody is under great suffering, everybody's heart is hurting. There is much pain.

Atisha says before you can do this with the whole existence, you will have to start first with yourself. This is one of the fundamental secrets of inner growth. You cannot do anything with others that you have not done in the first place with yourself. You can hurt others if you hurt yourself, you will be a pain in the necks of others if you are a pain in the neck to yourself, you can be a blessing to others only if you are a blessing to yourself.

Whatsoever you can do with others, you must have done to yourself before, because that is the only thing that you can share. You can share only that which you have; you cannot share that which you don't have.

Atisha says:

Begin the development of taking with yourself.

Rather than starting by taking the whole misery of the world and absorbing it in the heart, start with your own misery. Don't go into the deep sea so fast; learn swimming in shallow water. And if you immediately start taking the misery of the whole existence, it will remain simply an experiment in speculation. It won't be real, it can't be real. It will be just verbal.

You can say to yourself, "Yes, I am taking the misery of the whole world" – but what do you know of the misery of the whole world? You have not even experienced your own misery.

We go on avoiding our own misery. If you feel miserable, you put on the radio or the TV and you become engaged. You start reading the newspaper so that you can forget your misery, or you go to the movies, or you go to your woman or your man. You go to the club, you go shopping in the market, just somehow to keep yourself away from yourself, so that you need not see the wound, so that you need not look at how much it hurts within.

People go on avoiding themselves. What do they know of misery? How can they think of the misery of the whole existence? First, you have to begin with yourself. If you are feeling miserable, let it become a meditation. Sit silently, close the doors. First feel the misery with as much intensity as possible. Feel the hurt. Somebody has insulted you. Now, the best way to avoid the hurt is to go and insult him, so that you become occupied with him. That is not meditation.

If somebody has insulted you, feel thankful to him that he has given you an opportunity to feel a deep wound. He has opened a wound in you. The wound may be created by many, many insults that you have suffered in your whole life; he may not be the cause of all the suffering, but he has triggered a process.

Just close your room, sit silently, with no anger for the person but with total awareness of the feeling that is arising in you – the hurt feeling that you have been rejected, that you have been insulted. And then you will be surprised that not only is this man there: all the men and all the women and all the people that have ever insulted you will start moving in your memory.

You will start not only remembering them, you will start reliving them. You will be going into a kind of primal. Feel the hurt, feel the pain, don't avoid it. That's why in many therapies the patient is told not to take any drugs before the therapy begins, for the simple reason that drugs are a way to escape from your inner misery. They don't allow you to see your wounds, they repress them. They don't allow you to go into your suffering and unless you go into your suffering, you cannot be released from the imprisonment of it.

It is perfectly scientific to drop all drugs before going into a group – if possible even drugs like coffee, tea, smoking, because these are all ways to escape.

Have you watched? Whenever you feel nervous you immediately start smoking. It is a way to avoid nervousness; you become occupied with smoking. Really it is a regression. Smoking makes you again feel like a child – unworried, nonresponsible – because smoking is nothing but a symbolic breast. The hot smoke going in simply takes you back to the days when you were feeding on the mother's breast and the warm milk was going in; the nipple has now become the cigarette. The cigarette is a symbolic nipple.

Through regression you avoid the responsibilities and the pains of being adult. And that's what goes on through many, many drugs. Modern man is drugged as never before, because modern man is living in great suffering. Without drugs it will be impossible to live in so much suffering. Those drugs create a barrier; they keep you drugged, they don't allow you enough sensitivity to know your pain.

The first thing to do is close your doors and stop any kind of occupation – looking at the TV, listening to the radio, reading a book. Stop all occupation, because that too is a subtle drug. Just be silent, utterly alone. Don't even pray, because that again is a drug, you are becoming occupied, you start talking to God, you start praying, you escape from yourself.

Atisha is saying: Just be yourself. Whatsoever the pain of it and whatsoever the suffering of it, let it be so. First experience it in its total intensity. It will be difficult, it will be heart-rending. You may start crying like a child, you may start rolling on the ground in deep pain, your body may go through contortions. You may suddenly become aware that the pain is not only in the heart, it is all over the body – that it is aching all over, that it is painful all over, that your whole body is nothing but pain.

If you can experience it – this is of tremendous importance – then start absorbing it. Don't throw it away. It is such a valuable energy, don't throw it away. Absorb it, drink it, accept it, welcome it, feel grateful to it. And say to yourself, "This time I'm not going to avoid it, this time I'm not going to reject it, this time I'm not going to throw it away. This time I will drink it and receive it like a guest. This time I will digest it."

It may take a few days for you to be able to digest it, but the day it happens, you have stumbled upon a door which will take you really far, far away. A new journey has started in your life, you are moving into a new kind of being – because immediately, the moment you accept the pain with no rejection anywhere, its energy and its quality changes. It is no longer pain. In fact one is simply surprised, one cannot believe it, it is so incredible. One cannot believe that suffering can be transformed into ecstasy, that pain can become joy.

But in ordinary life you are aware that opposites are always joined together, that they are not opposites but complementaries. You know perfectly well, your love can at any moment become hate, and your hate can at any moment become love. In fact if you hate too much, intensely and totally, it is bound to become love.

That's what happened to the person called Saul who later on became Paul and founded this ugly phenomenon, the Christian church. Jesus is not the founder of the Christian church, the founder of the Christian church is Saint Paul. And the story is worth remembering.

When he was born, his name was Saul. And he was so anti Christ that his whole life was devoted to destroying Christians and Christianity. His whole dedication was to persecute Christians, destroying any possibility of Christianity for the future, and effacing the name of Christ. He must have hated tremendously, his hate cannot be ordinary. When you devote your whole life to the object of your hatred, it is bound to be really total. Otherwise who cares? If you hate something you don't devote your whole life to it. But if you hate totally, then it becomes a life-and-death problem.

Persecuting Christians, destroying Christians, destroying their power-holds, arguing with Christians, convincing them that this was nonsense, that this man Jesus was mad, a neurotic, a pretender, a hypocrite, one day it happened, the miracle happened. He was going to persecute more Christians in another town. On the way he was alone, and suddenly he saw Jesus appearing out of nowhere and asking him, "Why do you persecute me?"

Out of shock, terror, he fell on the ground, apologizing, crying great tears of repentance. The vision disappeared, and with the disappearance of the vision the old Saul disappeared. To remember this point he changed his name to Paul; the old man was dead, a new man had arrived. And he became the founder of the Christian church. He became a great lover of Jesus – the greatest lover the world has ever known.

Hate can become love. Jesus did not appear; it was just the intensity of his hate that projected Jesus. It was not Jesus who asked him, "Why do you persecute me?" It was his own unconscious which was suffering so much because of this hatred for Jesus. It was his own unconscious that asked him, "Why do you persecute me?" It was his own unconscious that became personified in the vision of Jesus. The miracle happened because the hate was total.

Whenever anything is total it turns into its opposite. This is a great secret to be remembered. Whenever something is total it changes into its opposite, because there is no way to go any further; the cul-de-sac has arrived.

Watch an old clock with a pendulum. It goes on and on: the pendulum goes to the left, to the extreme left, and then there is a point beyond which it cannot go, then it starts moving towards the right.

Opposites are complementaries. If you can suffer your suffering in totality, in great intensity, you will be surprised: Saul becomes Paul. You will not be able to believe it when it happens for the first time, that your own suffering absorbed willingly, welcomingly, becomes a great blessing. The same energy that becomes hate becomes love, the same energy that becomes pain becomes pleasure, the same energy that becomes suffering becomes bliss.

But start with your own self.

Make a small experiment with your own pains, sufferings and miseries. And once you have found the key, then you can share it with the whole existence. Then you can take all the suffering of all the world, or all the worlds.

Ride on the incoming breath and your small heart is bigger than the whole universe, if you know what miracles it can do. And then pour out your blessings. It is the same energy passing through your heart that becomes bliss, that becomes a blessing. Then let blessings go riding on the outgoing breath to all the nooks and corners of existence.

Atisha says: This is compassion. Compassion is to become a transforming force in existence – transforming the ugly into the beautiful, kissing the frog and transforming it into a prince, transforming darkness into light. To become such a medium of transformation is compassion.

Begin the development of taking with yourself.
When evil fills the inanimate and animate universes
change bad conditions to the bodhi path.

This is the Buddhist alchemy: all evil can be transformed into the bodhi path, the path to become a buddha. Evil is not against you, you just don't know how to use it. Poison is not your enemy, you just don't know how to make medicine out of it. In wise hands poison becomes medicinal, in foolish hands medicine can become poison. It all depends on you, on your artfulness.

Have you ever looked at the word *evil*? Read backwards, it is live. Life can become evil, evil can become life; it all depends on how you read it.

There are three things to be understood about this sutra, to change bad conditions to the bodhi path so that you can attain to *bodhichitta*, the mind or no-mind of a buddha. The first is: do not resist evil. That is a saying of Jesus; there is every possibility that Jesus got it from Buddhist sources. He traveled in India; he had lived in India before he started his mission in Israel.

That's why in The Bible there is almost no account of his life. Only once is he mentioned as having gone with his parents to the great temple and that he argued with the rabbis there. He must have been nearabout twelve at that time. After that incident there is no life story in The Bible. For eighteen years he simply disappears from Israel, and then suddenly when he is thirty he appears again. His ministry lasted only for three years; by the age of thirty-three he was crucified.

Where had he been for eighteen years? It is a long period. And why does The Bible mention nothing about it?

In Tibet there are still books available which relate everything about those eighteen years. He had been in the East. In fact that was one of the reasons why he could not be accepted by the Jews, because he brought something very alien and strange. Although he was quoting the prophets from the Old Testament, he was giving to those old ancient statements new meanings that had never been heard before. He was bringing something foreign into the Jewish world.

For example, this statement: Do not resist evil. Now this is very un-Jewish. The Jewish God is very much against evil; he is so much against it that there are stories that he destroyed whole cities like Sodom and Gomorrah. He destroyed whole cities because those cities had fallen into evil. There were good people there too, but to destroy the evil people even the good people were destroyed.

The Jewish God says, "I am a very jealous God; if you don't obey me you will be destroyed." He is very dictatorial. And the Old Testament says evil has to be punished, an eye for an eye.

Jesus says again and again, "You have been told that if somebody throws a brick at you, throw a stone or a rock at him. But I say unto you, if somebody hits you on one cheek, give him the other also."

This is alien, strange, to Jewish thinking. But this is not alien to Buddhist thinking, this is pure Buddhism. Do not resist evil. That is the first thing if you want to absorb evil in your heart and transform it. If you resist it, how can you transform it? Accept it.

Jesus says, "Love your enemies." The Jewish God cannot love his enemies, so why should man? If God is incapable of loving his enemies, how can you expect poor man to? "And love your enemies," Jesus says, "as you love yourself." Again, he got it from some strange sources that the Jews were not aware of. This is a Buddhist approach, this is the contribution of Buddha to the world – one of the greatest contributions ever, because this is the inner alchemy. Accept evil. Don't resist it, don't fight with it, don't be angry with it; absorb it, because it can be transformed into good.

The art of transforming suffering, pain, evil, into something good is the art of seeing the necessity of the opposite. Light can exist only if darkness exists. Then why hate darkness? Without darkness there will be no light, so those who love light and hate darkness are in a dilemma; they don't know what they are doing.

Life cannot exist without death. Then why hate death? Because it is death that creates the space for life to exist. This is a great insight, that death is the contrast, the background, the blackboard on which life is written with white chalk. Death is the darkness of night on which life starts twinkling like stars. If you destroy the darkness of the night the stars will disappear. That's what happens in the day. The stars are still there – do you think they have disappeared? They are still there, but because there is too much light you cannot see them. They can be seen only in contrast.

The saint is possible only because of the sinner. Hence, Buddha says don't hate the sinner, he makes it possible for the saint to exist. They are two aspects of the same coin.

Seeing this, one is neither attached to good nor detached from bad. One accepts both as part and parcel of life. In that acceptance you can transform things. Only through that acceptance is transformation possible.

And before you can transform suffering you will have to become a witness; that is the third point. First: do not resist evil. Second: know that opposites are not opposites but complementaries, inevitably joined together, so there is no choice – remain choiceless. And the third is: be a witness, because if you are a witness to your suffering you will be able to absorb it. If you become identified with it you cannot absorb it.

The moment you become identified with your suffering you want to discard it, you want to get rid of it, it is so painful. But if you are a witness then suffering loses all thorns, all stings. Then there is suffering, and you are a witness to it. You are just a mirror; it has nothing to do with you. Happiness comes and goes, unhappiness comes and goes, it is a passing show; you are just there, a mirror reflecting it. Life comes and goes, death comes and goes; the mirror is not affected by either. The mirror reflects but remains unaffected; the mirror is not imprinted by either.

A great distance arises when you witness. And only in that witnessing can you become able to transform the baser metal into gold. Only in that witnessing do you become a scientist of the inner, a detached observer. Now you know the opposites are not opposites, so they can be changed into each other. Then it is not a question of destroying evil in the world, but of transforming evil into something beneficial; transforming poison into nectar.

Drive all blame into one.

The third sutra. The ordinary mind always throws the responsibility on somebody else. It is always the other who is making you suffer. Your wife is making you suffer, your husband is making you suffer, your parents are making you suffer, your children are making you suffer, or the financial system of the society, capitalism, communism, fascism, the prevalent political ideology, the social structure, or fate, karma, God…you name it.

People have millions of ways to shirk responsibility. But the moment you say somebody else – x, y, z – is making you suffer, then you cannot do anything to change it. What can you do? When the society changes and communism comes and there is a classless world, then everybody will be happy. Before it, it is not possible. How can you be happy in a society which is poor? And how can you be happy in a society which is dominated by the capitalists? How can you be happy with a society which is bureaucratic? How can you be happy with a society which does not allow you freedom?

Excuses and excuses and excuses – excuses just to avoid one single insight that "I am responsible for myself. Nobody else is responsible for me; it is absolutely and utterly my responsibility. Whatsoever I am, I am my own creation." This is the meaning of the third sutra:

Drive all blame into one.

And that one is you. Once this insight settles: "I am responsible for my life – for all my suffering, for my pain, for all that has happened to me and is happening to me – I have chosen it this way; these are the seeds that I sowed and now I am reaping the crop; I am responsible" – once this insight becomes a natural understanding in you, then everything else is simple. Then life starts taking a new turn, starts moving into a new dimension. That dimension is conversion, revolution, mutation – because once I know I am responsible, I also know that I can drop it any moment I decide to. Nobody can prevent me from dropping it.

Can anybody prevent you from dropping your misery, from transforming your misery into bliss? Nobody. Even if you are in a jail, chained, imprisoned, nobody can imprison you; your soul still remains free.

Of course you have a very limited situation, but even in that limited situation you can sing a song. You can either cry tears of helplessness or you can sing a song. Even with chains on your feet you can dance; then even the sound of the chains will have a melody to it.

The fourth sutra:

Be grateful to everyone.

Atisha is really very, very scientific. First he says: Take the whole responsibility on yourself. Secondly he says: Be grateful to everyone. Now that nobody is responsible for your misery except you, if it is all your own doing, then what is left?

Be grateful to everyone.

Because everybody is creating a space for you to be transformed – even those who think they are obstructing you, even those whom you think are enemies. Your friends, your enemies, good people and bad people, favorable circumstances, unfavorable circumstances – all together they are creating the context in which you can be transformed and become a buddha. Be grateful to all.

A man once came and spat on Buddha, on his face. Of course his disciples were enraged. His closest disciple, Ananda, said to him, "This is too much!" He was red-hot with anger. He said to Buddha, "Just give me permission so that I can show this man what he has done."

Buddha wiped his face and said to the man, "Thank you, sir. You created a context in which I could see whether I can still be angry or not. And I am not, and I am tremendously happy. And also you created a context for Ananda: now he can see that he can still be angry. Many thanks, we are so grateful! Once in a while, please, you are invited to come. Whenever you have the urge to spit on somebody, you can come to us."

It was such a shock to the man, he could not believe his ears, what was happening. He had come expecting that he would anger Buddha. He had failed. The whole night he could not sleep, he tossed and turned and could not sleep. Continuously the idea haunted him – his spitting on the Buddha, one of the most insulting things, and Buddha remaining as calm and quiet as he had been before, as if nothing had happened, wiping his face and saying to him, "Thank you, sir. And whenever you have this desire to spit on somebody, please come to us."

He remembered it again and again. That face, that calm and quiet face, those compassionate eyes. And when he had said thank you, it had not been just a formality, he was really grateful. His whole being was saying that he was grateful, his whole atmosphere was grateful. Just as he could see that Ananda was red-hot with anger, Buddha was so cool, so loving, so compassionate. He could not forgive himself now, what had he done? Spitting on that man – a man like Buddha!

Early the next morning he rushed back, fell down at the feet of Buddha, and said, "Forgive me, sir. I could not sleep the whole night."

Buddha said, "Forget all about it. There is no need to ask forgiveness for something which has already passed. So much water has gone down the Ganges." Buddha was sitting on the bank of the Ganges under a tree. He showed the man, "Look, each moment so much water is flowing down! Twenty-four hours have passed – why are you carrying it, something which is no longer existential? Forget all about it.

"And I cannot forgive you, because in the first place I was not angry with you. If I had been angry, I could have forgiven you. If you really need forgiveness, ask Ananda. Fall at *his* feet – he will enjoy it!"

Be grateful to everyone.

To those who have helped, to those who have hindered, to those who have been indifferent. Be grateful to all, because all together they are creating the context in which buddhas are born, in which you can become a buddha.

The insurpassable protection of emptiness is to see the manifestations of bewilderment as the four kayas.

Atisha talks about the four bodies. These four bodies are significant to be understood. The first is called *dharmakaya*: the body of the ultimate law. And what is the ultimate law? Emptiness is the ultimate law: all is empty.

If you really want to grow, you will have to let this insight soak into you: all is empty. Life is empty, death is empty, all phenomena are empty – because nothing abides, everything passes by, all is dream stuff. If this is understood, this will protect you. How can you be insulted if all is empty? How can you be miserable if all is empty? How can there be pain if all is empty? You are empty, the other is empty, so you must have seen a dream that the other was insulting you, that the other spat on you.

If you really want to protect your understanding, this is the first body to grow around yourself, the body of emptiness, the milieu of emptiness. All is empty.

Buddha used to send his disciples to the funeral pyres to meditate there. The newcomers had to be there for three months in the beginning. Where bodies are burned, they would just sit there and watch, day in and day out. People would be brought in, burned, and then the friends would leave. What kind of life is this? What substance has it got?

Just the other day, the man was so haughty, so proud, so egoistic, that if you had said anything wrong he would have jumped on you. And now where is he? Disappeared in the flames. This is what life is. "Sooner or later I am also going to be on the funeral pyre and all will be burned. So why bother, why make so much fuss? It is only a few days' dream. And those few days are not much in the eternity of time, they are just momentary."

Let this body of emptiness grow around you; you will be protected by it.

The second body is *nirmankaya*: the first arising of compassion. When all is empty, when everybody is on the funeral pyre, then compassion arises. It is not to be cultivated, remember; it arises out of the first body. If you cultivate it you still believe in the ego. If you cultivate it you still believe in character, if you cultivate it you still believe in virtue. And if there is no self, what is virtue? If there is no self, what is character? If there is no self, then what is good?

First settle into nobodiness and then the second body arises of its own accord. Nirmankaya means the body of creation. It is strange – the first body is the body of emptiness, and the second body is the body of creation. But this is the insight of all the great buddhas, that if you become a nobody, a great creation arises out of you. The whole starts flowing through you; you become a vehicle, a passage, a medium, a voice, for the whole.

And with the second body arising, the first experience will be of great compassion. Of course in the beginning it will be partial, conditional, caused by the suffering of others. You see an old man dying on the road and compassion arises, you see somebody starving and compassion arises – it has a cause outside. If nobody is dying and nobody is starving, there will be no compassion. In the second body, compassion comes and goes; it arises in certain situations and disappears in certain other situations.

Out of the second, the third crystallizes. The third body is called *sambhogkaya*: the body of bliss. In the third body, compassion is unconditional. It does not arise and does not disappear; it remains, it abides. It is not a question of whether somebody is suffering or not; in the third body, one simply is compassion. In the second body, compassion is a relationship; when there is a need it happens. In the third body, compassion becomes your very state of being: need or no need, it is there. It is like a light burning in the night; it goes on radiating whether somebody is in the room or not. Whether somebody needs light or not, is not the point; the light goes on radiating.

In the third body, the body of bliss, compassion is a natural phenomenon. Just as you go on breathing, even while you are asleep you go on breathing, a buddha is compassionate even while asleep. A buddha is simply compassionate. Compassion is not something that arises like a wave and disappears. Now compassion is oceanic.

And the fourth body is called *swabhavakaya*: the body of the ultimate nature, of spontaneity, of your innermost being as it is. In the fourth body, all distinctions disappear, dualities are transcended. Good/bad, self/no-self, mind/no-mind, samsara/nirvana, God/devil – all dualities are transcended. One simply is, with no distinctions, with no categories, with no divisions. This is the existential body; this is the real thing to be attained.

Each seeker after truth passes through these four bodies.

An excellent means is to have the four provisions.

How to attain these four bodies? There are four provisions. The first is: observe. Observe without evaluation, observe everything, don't miss any opportunity to observe – because it is not a question of what you are observing, the question is that observation is growing. Observe everything – the trees, the birds, the animals, the people, the traffic, your own mind and its traffic, your own reactions, others' reactions. Use every situation to observe, so that observation becomes deep-rooted in you.

And the second is: analyze, but only after you have observed – don't mix them. At first, observation has to be simple observation, with no analysis, no judgment, no evaluation. When you have observed, then analyze, then go into details, then dissect. Then see its parts, how it is made, because each experience is very complex. If you really want to understand it you will have to dissect it into its parts.

And then the third is: choose that which brings more and more bliss, silence, serenity and calmness to you.

And the fourth is: discard all that which brings tension, anxiety, anguish and hell to you.

These are the four provisions. If you follow these four provisions, four bodies will arise in you.

In order to bring any situation to the path quickly as soon as it is met, join it with meditation.

And remember, each situation has to become an opportunity to meditate. What is meditation? Becoming aware of what you are doing, becoming aware of what is happening to you.

Somebody insults you: become aware. What is happening to you when the insult reaches you? Meditate over it; this is changing the whole gestalt. When somebody insults you, you concentrate on the person – "Why is he insulting me? Who does he think he is? How can I take revenge?" If he is very powerful you surrender, you start wagging your tail. If he is not very powerful and you see that he is weak, you pounce on him. But you forget yourself completely in all this; the other becomes the focus. This is missing an opportunity for meditation. When somebody insults you, meditate.

Gurdjieff has said, "When my father was dying, I was only nine. He called me close to his bed and whispered in my ear, 'My son, I am not leaving much to you, not in worldly things, but I have one thing to tell you that was told to me by *my* father on his deathbed. It has helped me tremendously; it has been my treasure. You are not very grown up yet, you may not understand what I am saying, but keep it, remember it. One day you will be grown up and then you may understand. This is a key: it unlocks the doors of great treasures.'"

Of course Gurdjieff could not understand it at that moment, but it was the thing that changed his whole life. And his father said a very simple thing. He said, "Whenever somebody insults you, my son, tell him you will meditate over it for twenty-four hours and then you will come and answer him."

Gurdjieff could not believe that this was such a great key. He could not believe that "This is something so valuable that I have to remember it." And we can forgive a young child of nine years old. But because this was something said by his dying father who had loved him tremendously, and immediately after saying it he breathed his last, it became imprinted on him; he could not forget it. Whenever he remembered his father, he would remember the saying.

Without truly understanding, he started practicing it. If somebody insulted him he would say, "Sir, for twenty-four hours I have to meditate over it – that's what my father told me. And he is here no more, and I cannot disobey a dead old man. He loved me tremendously, and I loved him tremendously, and now there is no way to disobey him. You can disobey your father when he is alive, but when your father is dead how can you disobey him? So please forgive me, I will come after twenty-four hours and answer you."

And he says, "Meditating on it for twenty-four hours has given me the greatest insights into my being. Sometimes I found that the insult was right, that that's how I am. So I would go to the person and say, 'Sir, thank you, you were right. It was not an insult, it was simply a statement of fact. You called me stupid; I am.'

"Or sometimes it happened that meditating for twenty-four hours, I would come to know that it was an absolute lie. But when something is a lie, why be offended by it? So I would not even go to tell him that it was a lie. A lie is a lie, why be bothered by it?"

But watching, meditating, slowly, slowly he became more and more aware of his reactions, rather than the actions of others.

This is what Atisha says:

In order to bring any situation to the path quickly as soon as it is met, join it with meditation.

Whatsoever happens – good, bad, success, failure – immediately become aware of what is happening. Don't miss a single moment. Don't lag behind – be present to it, and you will be surprised, errors will start disappearing from your life. And then whatsoever you do will be right.

People ask me what is right and what is wrong, and my answer is: If something arises out of awareness, it is right. If something arises out of unawareness, it is wrong. Right and wrong is not a question of what you do, but of how you do it. It is not a question of what, but of how – meditatively or nonmeditatively, alert, awake, or doing things as if you are a sleepwalker.

The concise epitome of heart instruction: work with "five forces."

These are the five forces. The first force is intensity, totality. If you really want to have a transformed life, if you really want to become a light unto yourself, if you really want to know the ultimate mystery of existence and the ultimate ecstasy of being alive, then the first force is intensity, totality. Whatsoever you do, do it intensely, to the optimum. Don't be lousy, don't be lazy, don't be partial. Go into it wholeheartedly, let it become a total absorption.

If you dance, dance so totally that the dancer disappears and only the dance remains, and it will be a transformation. If you love, love totally, so totally that there is no lover found. The lover is found only if you are holding something back. That which you are holding back becomes the lover. If you are holding something back, that which you are holding back becomes the dancer, the singer. If you are totally in the dance, in the song, in the love, who is left behind there to say, "I am the lover, I am the dancer"? Nothing is left.

And totality transforms.

It is only at one hundred degrees intensity that one evaporates from the material into the spiritual, from the earth into the sky, from the ordinary into the extraordinary.

The second force is familiarization: do and be what you really want to do and be. Life is lived according to gestalts that you have created around yourself. If you really want to be something else, then familiarize yourself with it. If you want to play the guitar, practice. If you want to dance, practice. If you want anything to happen in your life, imbibe more and more of it and drop all that is against it. And the way to drop it is not to use it, because by using it you create ways for it to come into you again and again and again.

The third force is the force of white seeds. "White seeds" is a metaphor. Atisha means, drop all that is black. Don't go on cultivating the black seeds of anger, jealousy, hatred, possessiveness, domination. Drop all black seeds. Even if they arise, watch, absorb them in the heart, and they will become white seeds. And what are the white seeds? Love, compassion, service, sincerity, sensitivity, awareness – these are the white seeds. If one day you want to have white flowers in your life, you will have to sow white seeds.

And the fourth force is reproach – to completely abjure ego-oriented thoughts. Watch: whatsoever arises out of the ego, whatsoever is an ego trip, immediately disconnect yourself from it. Even to linger with it for a little while is dangerous, because lingering will give it energy. The moment you know it is an ego trip, immediately disconnect yourself.

And everybody knows when they are going on an ego trip. It is not an art to be learned, everybody is born with it. You know it; you can go with it in spite of your knowing – that is another matter – but you know it. Whenever pride arises, whenever the ego raises its head, you know it. Cut that head immediately in a single blow.

And the fifth force is the force of the dedication of all virtue to the welfare of others. Whatsoever good happens to you, immediately share it. This is one of the most fundamental things in Buddhism. Don't hoard it, don't be a miser. If love has arisen, share it, shower it. If you cannot find people, shower it on the trees, on the rocks, but shower it. Don't hoard it – because if you hoard it, it turns into poison; if you hoard it, it goes sour and bitter. Share it.

And the more you share, the more will be coming into you from unknown sources. Slowly, slowly, you will be able to know the ways of inner economics. The outer economics is hoard if you want to have things. And the inner economics is just the opposite: hoard, and you will not have it. Give, and you will have it; give more, and you will have more of it.

The third sutra:

The instructions for transference in the Mahayana are the "five forces."
Behavior is important.

All these five forces can be significant only if you behave, if you act according to them. If you simply contemplate over them they are meaningless, they will remain impotent. Actualize them in your life.

And the last sutra:

The purpose of all dharma is contained in one point.

That point is the ego. The ego is false. If you live according to the false ego, your whole life will remain false. If you live without the ego your whole life will have the flavor of reality, truth and authenticity.

Think, meditate, practice.

And the more you share, the more will be coming into you from unknown sources. Slowly, slowly, you will be able to know the ways of inner economics. The outer economics is hoard if you want to have things. And the inner economics is just the opposite: hoard, and you will not have it. Give, and you will have it; give more, and you will have more of it.

The sutra:

The instructions for transference in the Mahayana are the "five forces."
Behavior is important.

All these five forces can be significant only if you behave, if you act according to them. If you simply contemplate over them they are meaningless, they will remain impotent. Actualize them in your life.

And the last sutra:

The purpose of all dharma is contained in one point.

That point is the ego. The ego is false. If you live according to the false ego, your whole life will remain false. If you live without the ego your whole life will have the flavor of reality, truth and authenticity.

Think, meditate, practice.

Enough for today.

Chapter 6
Empty Yourself

Can you explain to us the difference between emptying oneself and effacing oneself? And what is the role of individuality in dissolution?

The process of emptying oneself and the process of effacing oneself have nothing in common. Not only are they different, they are diametrically opposite.

Emptying oneself brings individuality, more and more individuality. Emptying oneself means emptying oneself of all that is implied in personality.

Personality is a farce, personality is pseudo, personality is that which is given to you by the society. Personality is imposed on you from the outside; it is a mask. Individuality is your very being. Individuality is that which you bring into the world, individuality is God's gift.

Personality is ugly because it is pseudo. And the more personality you have, the less is the possibility for individuality to grow. The personality starts occupying the whole of your space. It is like a cancerous growth. It goes on growing, it possesses you totally. It leaves no space for individuality to have even its own corner. The personality has to be dropped, so that the individuality can be.

Individuality is a non-egoistic phenomenon; it is pure am-ness, it has no "I" in it. Personality is nothing but "I": it has no am-ness in it. Personality is aggressive, violent, dominating, political. Individuality is silent, loving, compassionate; it is religious.

Emptying oneself means emptying of all content – just as you empty a room of all the junk that has gathered there, down the years. When you have emptied the room of all the furniture and all the things, you have not destroyed the room, not at all; you have given it more roominess, more space. When all the furniture is gone, the room asserts itself, the room *is*.

Effacing oneself means destroying the room itself – destroying the very space of your being, destroying the very uniqueness of your existence, destroying the gift of God. Effacing yourself means becoming a slave.

Individuality gives you mastery; it makes you very authentic, grounded, rooted. It gives you substance; you are no longer dream stuff. It gives you solidity, it gives you clarity, transparency, vision. It makes you aware of the beauty of existence, it makes you aware of the beauty of all. Effacing yourself destroys you, it is suicidal. You are not dropping your personality, you are dropping your very uniqueness. You are becoming more and more shadowy, rather than becoming more substantial. You are becoming a slave.

And the ironical thing is that if you efface yourself, the ego will remain. Now it will become a very subtle ego, so subtle that it will be almost impossible to detect it. Now it will claim humbleness, nobodiness, humility. But the claim will persist. It will say, "Look, I have effaced myself. I am no more."

But when you say, "I am no more" you *are* – otherwise who is saying, "I am no more?"

A so-called saint was once asked, "Are you God?"

He said, "No" – but immediately he added, "The sun rises in the morning, but it does not declare 'I am the sun.'"

In a vicarious way he is saying, "I am God. But I am like the sun which rises every morning but does not declare 'I am God.'"

I told the man who had related the incident to me, "Go back to that so-called saint, and tell him that the sun does not say, 'I am not the sun' either." The sun does not say, "I am the sun" or "I am not the sun" – not because the sun is enlightened, but simply because it cannot speak! If it could speak, it would have declared it in a thousand and one ways. In fact it *is* declaring in a thousand and one ways: "I am here!" It is declaring it in the flowers, in the birds; it is declaring all over: "I am here!"

Once Krishnamurti was asked, "Why do you go on talking?"

He said, "This is simply my nature, to talk." He said, "I talk in the same way as the flower releases its fragrance."

The flower cannot talk, it has its own language; the fragrance is its language. The sun cannot talk, but the light that radiates from it is its way of communicating the fact: "I am here, I have arrived."

In Japan there is a saying: "Flowers don't talk." That saying is utterly wrong – they talk. Of course they speak their own language. The Tibetan speaks his language; will you say that he does not talk? The Chinese speaks his own language; will you say he does not talk? Just because you cannot understand, will you say he is not talking? The Chinese has his own language, so does the sun, so do the flowers, so do the animals, the birds, the rocks. In millions of languages the whole world asserts itself.

But the humble person starts saying, "I am not. I am not an ego, I have effaced myself." But who is saying these things? The person who has emptied himself will not say such things. He will say, "I am, and I am for the first time. But now in my I-am-ness "I" is only linguistic, a way of saying it. Existentially, there is only am-ness."

And let this be the criterion for whether you are emptying yourself or effacing yourself. If you are emptying yourself you will become more and more blissful, because you will become more and more spacious. You will become more and more available to God and to God's celebration. You will become open to existence and all its joys and all its blessings.

But if you are effacing yourself you will become more and more sad and heavy, you will become more and more dull and dead – because effacing oneself is nothing but a slow suicide. Beware of it. And you have to be aware, very aware, because they both look alike.

The real danger in spiritual growth is from things which are diametrically opposite but look very alike. The real problem does not arise from things which are apparently opposite; the real problem arises with things which are not so apparently opposite, and yet they are opposite.

The real opposite of hate is not love, the real opposite of love is not hate – it is so apparent, who can be deceived by it? The real opposite of love is pseudo-love: love that pretends to be love, and is not. One has to be watchful there.

The real opposite of compassion is not anger. The real opposite of compassion is cultivated compassion: compassion that is not within you but is only in your character, compassion that you have painted on your circumference.

The real opposite of your smiles are not tears, but smiles which are painted, smiles which don't go any deeper than the lips, which are nothing but exercises of the lips. No heart collaborates with them, no feeling stands behind them. There is nobody behind the smile, the smile is just a learned trick. Tears are not opposite to smiles, they are only complementaries. But the false smile is the real opposite.

Remember it always, the false is the enemy of the true. If your smile is true and your tears are true, they are friends, they will help each other because they both will strengthen the truth of your being. If your tears are false and your smiles are false, then too, they are friends; they will strengthen your falsity, your personality, your mask.

The conflict is between the real and the unreal or pretended. Emptying oneself is of tremendous value, but effacing yourself is dangerous. Effacing yourself is a subtle way of the ego – the ego coming from the back door.

And naturally it will make you more and more serious. That's why your so-called saints look so serious. Their seriousness has a reason in it. The reason is, they are maintaining humbleness which is not really there. And to maintain something which is not really there is arduous, hard. One has to be continuously on guard. Just a little slip here and there, and the reality will assert, and it will destroy all that you have maintained for so long. It will destroy your respectability.

Anything that has to be maintained will keep you serious and sad, deep down afraid of being caught red-handed, of being caught in your falsity. You will escape from people if you are carrying something false in you. You will not allow anybody to be friendly, to be intimate with you, because in intimacy the danger is that the other may be able to see something which strangers cannot see. You will keep people at a distance; you will run and rush away from people. You will have only formal relationships, but you will not really relate, because to really relate means to expose yourself.

Hence your so-called saints escaped into the monasteries. It was out of fear. If they were in the marketplace they would be caught; it would be discovered that they are cheating, that they are deceiving, that they are hypocrites. In the monasteries they can maintain their hypocrisy and nobody will ever be able to detect it. And moreover, there are other hypocrites there; they can all maintain their conspiracy together more easily than each single hypocrite can maintain his alone.

Monasteries came into existence for escapists. But you can live even in the world in a monastic way, keeping people always at a distance, never allowing anybody access to your inner being, never opening up, never allowing anybody to have a peek into you to see who you are, never looking into people's eyes, avoiding people's eyes, looking sideways. And always in a hurry, so that everybody knows you are so occupied, you don't have any time to say hello, to hold somebody's hand, to sit with somebody informally. You are so busy, you are always on the go.

You will not even allow intimacy with those who are close to you – husbands, wives, children – with them also you will have a formal relationship, an institutional relationship.

Hence marriage has become an institution. It is really ugly to see something so tremendously beautiful becoming an institution. And if people look so miserable it is natural. If you live in institutions you will be miserable.

You ask me: "Can you explain to us the difference between emptying oneself and effacing oneself?"

Effacing oneself is the way of the ego, emptying oneself is the way of understanding. In emptying yourself you simply understand the ways of the ego – and in that understanding, the ego disappears of its own accord. You don't drop it, you don't have to drop it. You don't fight with it. It is not found.

When you look within with attention, with the light of awareness, you cannot find any ego there. So the question does not arise of why or how one should efface oneself. There is nothing to efface! That which is, is, and cannot be effaced. And that which is not, is not, and there is no need to efface it.

Emptying oneself simply means *seeing* oneself. And then many things start dropping, because you were unnecessarily carrying them. In the first place, they don't exist. They are ghosts, nightmares; they disperse themselves when the light is brought in. Emptying oneself is a meditative process. Just looking in, deeply, with no prejudice, with no prefabricated ideology, neither for nor against, just looking in, and emptying starts happening.

And when you have emptied all content – thoughts, desires, memories, projections, hopes – when all is gone, for the first time you find yourself, because you are nothing but that pure space, that virgin space within you. Unburdened by anything, that contentless consciousness, that's what you are! Seeing it, realizing it, one is free. One is freedom, one is joy, one is bliss.

But effacing oneself is dangerous. It means you have accepted already that the ego is there and it has to be effaced. You have accepted an illusion, and now you want to destroy it. You have missed the first point. You have accepted that the rope is a snake, and now you are trying to kill the snake. You will be in great trouble. You will never be able to kill the snake, because in the first place there is none. You can go on beating the rope, but what about the snake? The snake will remain there.

The snake exists in your illusion; the snake does not exist outside, otherwise you could have killed it. But how can you kill a snake which is not? You are fighting with a shadow, and you are bound to be defeated.

Let this fundamental be remembered always: if you fight with anything false, you will be defeated. The false cannot be defeated, because it is false. How can you defeat something which is non-existential? There is no way. The only way is, bring light and see.

Ihi passiko, come and see! In that very seeing, the snake is not found. The rope is there, the snake has disappeared. Now there is no need to efface yourself, no need to fight.

There are millions of people who try to become humble, but their whole effort is nonsense, sheer stupidity.

Once a man asked me, "Are you an egoist or a humble person?"

I said. "Neither. *neti neti*, neither this nor that. I cannot be either."

He said, "What are you talking about? One has to be either an egoist or a humble person."

I said, "You don't understand. You know nothing; you have never gone within yourself. If you are humble, you are an egoist standing on his head. Humbleness is an expression of the ego. I am neither. I am simply whatsoever I am, neither humble nor egoistic, because I have seen that there is no ego. How can there be humbleness then?"

Humbleness is diluted ego. But if there is no ego, how can you dilute it? If there is no snake, how can you take the poisonous teeth of the snake away? That's what humbleness is. The poisonous teeth have been removed from the snake; now the snake cannot hurt, now the snake cannot bite, now the snake cannot do any harm – but the snake is there.

Those teeth were false, because the snake itself is false.

Buddha is neither egoistic nor humble. Both are impossible for the man of understanding. The ignorant person can be egoistic, can be humble – both are aspects of ignorance. And the ignorant person can try to efface the ego, because it is so respectable not to have the ego. One becomes a saint by effacing the ego, one attains great prestige and power by effacing the ego. But it is the same game; the game has not changed.

My message to you is, please don't efface yourself. Be yourself, look within yourself, and in that very seeing, the ego disappears. Even to say "disappears" is not right: the ego is not found, it has never been there. Its existence depended on your not looking within yourself. Seen, it is no longer there – it has never been there.

And then you are individuality, uniqueness, a unique expression of the divine. And then there is great rejoicing. You start blooming, the spring has come. You start dancing, you start singing. Great gratitude arises in you that God has made you a unique individual.

There has never been a person like you before, there is nobody else like you right now in the whole world, and there will never be anybody like you. Just see how much respect God has paid to you. You are a masterpiece – unrepeatable, incomparable, utterly unique. Even the hardest heart, the rocklike heart, will start melting in gratitude. Tears will start flowing, tears of bliss and joy, tears which laugh.

But please remember, empty yourself, don't efface yourself.

Chapter 7
Learning the Knack

**My mind has difficulty understanding the existence of beginninglessness.
Would you please talk about it?**

Reality is indefinable. Reality simply is; there is no way to say *what* it is. It is not a "what," it is not even a "that," it is this. It is this-ness: you can experience it, but it cannot be explained.

And reality is beginningless and endless. The mind has a beginning and an end, hence the mind and reality cannot meet. The mind cannot comprehend the eternal. The mind exists in time, in fact the mind *is* time; it exists in the past and the future. And remember, time consists of only two tenses, the past and the future. The present is not part of time, the present is part of eternity.

Hence the mind is never found in the present. It is always wavering, either towards the past or towards the future. It moves into that which is not, or into that which is not yet. Its whole skill consists in dreaming. It is rooted in the non-existential, hence it cannot understand existence itself. It is like darkness. How can darkness comprehend light? How can death comprehend life? If death can comprehend life then death will have to *be* life. If darkness has to comprehend light then darkness will have to *be* light.

And so is the case with the mind. If the mind wants to comprehend reality, it will have to come out of the past and the future. But coming out of the past and the future, it is no longer the mind at all. Hence the insistence of all the great masters of the world that the door to reality is no-mind.

Slip out of the mind, and you will know what it is: the beginningless, the endless. Remain confined to the mind, and you will be puzzled; reality remains inconceivable.

I cannot explain it to you, because in explaining I will have to use the mind. Trying to understand it, you will have to use the mind. I can be silent with you, and if you can also be silent with me then there is understanding. Understanding is not of the mind. Then there is great intelligence, great insight. Suddenly you know, and you know from a totally different center of your being; you know from the heart. Your knowing has the quality of love, not of knowledge. Your knowing has the quality of transcendence. It is no longer scientific knowledge, reducible to concepts. It is poetic vision, it is mystic experience.

If you really want to understand, you will have to lose the mind. You will have to pay the price of losing the mind. But if you insist, "I have to understand through the mind," then only one thing is possible. The mind will convince you, slowly, slowly, that there is nothing which is beginningless, nothing which is endless, nothing which is indefinable, nothing which is unknowable.

The mind will reduce your experience to the measurable, the fathomable, the knowable – and the knowable is ordinary, mundane. The unknowable is sacred. And only with the unknowable does life become a benediction, only with the unknowable are you thrilled with the wonder of life and existence. Suddenly a song is born in your heart – a song that cannot be contained, a song that starts overflowing, a song that starts reaching others. A dance is born in you – a dance that has to be shared, a dance about which you cannot be miserly, a dance that makes you generous. A love is born in you – a love that is so infinite that it can fill the whole infinite existence. That is real understanding. But it happens only when the mind is dropped.

Don't try to do the impossible. Trying to understand reality through the mind is like pulling yourself up by your own shoestrings. Maybe you can hop a little bit, but that hopping is not going to help; you will be back on the ground again and again, and it will be very tiring. Just by pulling your own shoestrings you cannot fly into the sky; that is not going to give you wings.

Slowly, slowly, learn the art of contacting reality without the mind interfering. Sometimes when the sun is setting, just sit there looking at the sun, not thinking about it – watching, not evaluating, not even saying, "How beautiful it is!" The moment you say something, the mind has come in.

The mind consists of language. Don't use language. Can't you just see the sunset and its beauty? Can't you be overwhelmed by its beauty? Can't you be possessed by its grandeur? What is the point of bringing language in? Nobody is asking you to say anything. The sun does not understand your language, the clouds that have become so beautiful and luminous in the setting sun are unable to understand your language. Why bring it in? Put it aside; be in direct contact, be thrilled. If tears come to your eyes, good. If you start dancing, good. Or if you simply remain unmoving, stoned on the beauty of the sun, intoxicated, you will have gained a little experience – a little experience that goes very far, a little glimpse of no-mind.

And there are a thousand and one situations every day. Holding the hand of your woman or your man, there is no need to talk. People are continuously talking – yakkety-yakkety-yakkety. And the reason why they are talking is that they are afraid to be silent, they are afraid to see the truth, they are afraid to see their utter emptiness, they are afraid to expose themselves, they are afraid to look deep into the other. Continuous talking keeps them on the surface, occupied, engaged.

Holding the hand of your woman or man, why not sit silently? Why not close your eyes and feel? Feel the presence of the other, enter into the presence of the other, let the other's presence enter into you; vibrate together, sway together; if suddenly a great energy possesses you, dance together – and you will reach to such orgasmic peaks of joy as you have never known before. Those orgasmic peaks have nothing to do with sex, in fact they have much to do with silence.

And if you can also manage to become meditative in your sex life, if you can be silent while making love, in a kind of dance, you will be surprised. You have a built-in process to take you to the farthest shore.

People make love in such an ugly way that if children sometimes see their parents making love, they think they are wrestling, fighting – that Daddy is going to kill Mum! Groaning, breathing in an ugly way, violent, their movements have no elegance. It is not a dance; certainly it is not a dance.

And unless it becomes a dance it will remain very, very physiological; it won't have any spirituality in it. But it is impossible. Unless your whole life is saturated with those moments that come when the mind ceases, your love life cannot move into silence.

The night is full of stars. Lie down on the earth, disappear into the earth. We come from the earth, one day we will be going back to the earth to rest forever. At night sometimes, lying on the lawn, disappear into the earth. Look at the stars – just look, a pure look. Don't start thinking about the names of the stars, the names of the constellations. Forget all that you know *about* stars, put aside all your knowledge, just see the stars. And suddenly there will be a communion; the stars will start pouring their light into you, and you will feel an expanding of consciousness. No drug can do it.

Drugs are very artificial, arbitrary and harmful methods to know something which is naturally available, which is easily available, beneficially available. Just watching the stars, you will start feeling high, you will start soaring high.

Make as much as you can of all the opportunities that life and existence allow you. Never miss a single opportunity when you can drop the mind, and slowly, slowly you will know the knack of it. It is a knack – it is certainly not a science, because it has no fixed methods.

Somebody may be thrilled by the stars, somebody may not be. Somebody may be thrilled by the flowers, somebody else may not be affected at all. People are so different that there is no way of determining it in a scientific way; it is not a science. It is not even an art, because an art can be taught.

So I insist on the word *knack*. It *is* a knack. You have to learn it by doing a few experiments with yourself. And once you have the knack…and everybody can have it, because every child is born with it. Every child brings wondering eyes into existence. Soon we force dust into his eyes; we cover his pure mirror with dust. Sooner or later, he becomes knowledgeable – and the sooner he does, the more happy we are. Our happiness is really in poisoning the child.

If the child sees that the parents are very happy because he has become knowledgeable, he starts gathering more and more knowledge. He starts forgetting the knack that he had brought with him into this life, that was inborn. By the time he comes out of the university he has completely forgotten one of the most beautiful things that was given to him by God: the capacity to wonder, the capacity to see without thinking, the capacity to contact reality without the mind continuously interfering, distorting.

You will have to regain it.

The sage is the person who regains his childhood; hence he is called "the twice born." Jesus says, "Unless ye are born again, you will not be able to enter into my kingdom of God." And the kingdom of God is *here*, but you have to be reborn – reborn as a no-mind.

And I am not saying that when you are reborn as a no-mind you cannot use the mind. The mind has its limited uses. Use it. When you are working in your office, I am not telling you to be a no-mind. When you are working in your shop or in the factory, I am not saying to be a no-mind. I am saying be perfectly a mind. Use the mind but don't carry it continuously, twenty-four hours, day in and day out, with yourself. Don't go on dragging it. Use it as you use a chair. You don't go on carrying your chair everywhere, wherever you go, just because you may need it.

The mind is a beautiful instrument *if* you know how to be a no-mind too.

The mind is impotent, incapable of knowing the beginningless and the endless. The mind exists between birth and death; it knows nothing beyond birth and beyond death.

You were here before you were born, and you will be here after you are dead. The mind has a very limited existence, very momentary – one day it comes, another day it is gone. You are forever. Have some experience of your forever-ness.

But that is possible only through no-mind. No-mind is another name for meditation

? **Yes!**

This simple word "yes" contains all the religions of the world. It contains trust, it contains love, it contains surrender. It contains all the prayers that have ever been done, are being done, and will ever be done. If you can say yes with the totality of your heart, you have said all that can be said. To say yes to existence is to be religious, to say no is to be irreligious.

That's my definition of the atheist and the theist. The atheist is not one who denies God, and the theist is not one who believes in God – not necessarily so, because we have seen great theists who never believed in any God. We have known Buddha, Mahavira, Adinatha: we have known tremendously enlightened people who never talked about God. But they also talked about yes; they *had* to talk about yes.

God can be dropped as an unnecessary hypothesis, but yes cannot be dropped. Yes is the very spirit of God. And yes can exist without God, but God cannot exist without yes. God is only the body, yes is the soul.

There are people who believe in God and yet I will call them atheists, because their belief has no yes behind it. Their belief is bogus, their belief is formal; their belief is given by others, it is borrowed. Their parents, priests and teachers have taught them that God is; they have made them so much afraid that they cannot even question the existence of God. And they have given them promises of great things if they believe in God. There will be great rewards in heaven if you believe, and great punishments in hell if you don't believe.

Fear and greed have been exploited. The priest has behaved with you almost like the psychologist behaves with the rats upon which he goes on experimenting. The rats in psychological experiments are controlled by punishment and reward. Reward them, and they start learning the thing for which they are rewarded; punish them, and they start unlearning the thing for which they are punished.

The priests have behaved with men as if men are rats. Psychologists are not the first to dehumanize humanity; priests were the pioneers. First the priests behaved with men as if they were rats, now the psychologists are behaving with rats as if they are men. But the process is the same, the technique exactly the same.

There are people who are theists – believers in God, churchgoers, worshippers – and yet in their hearts there is no yes; in their hearts there is doubt. On the surface they behave religiously, deep down they are suspicious. And it is the depth that determines you. It is not what you do that is decisive, it is what you feel at the deepest core of your being that determines you, that creates you. And there are atheists who go on saying there is no God, but they are not in any way different from the believers. Their disbelief has as much doubt in it as the belief of the believers.

In Soviet Russia, in China, and in other red countries, disbelief is the belief; not to believe is to be a conformist, to believe is to be a revolutionary. The state goes on teaching that there is no God. If people are taught continuously, conditioned continuously, they become whatsoever they are conditioned for. It is a kind of mass hypnosis.

Theists, atheists, both are victims. The really religious person has nothing to do with The Bible or the Koran or the Bhagavadgita. The really religious person has a deep communion with existence. He can say yes to a roseflower, he can say yes to the stars, he can say yes to people, he can say yes to his own being, to his own desires. He can say yes to whatsoever life brings to him; he is a yea-sayer.

And in this yea-saying is contained the essential prayer.

The last words of Jesus on earth were: "Thy kingdom come, thy will be done. Amen."

Do you know this word amen, what it means? It simply means "Yes, Lord, yes. Let thy will be done. Don't listen to what I say, I am ignorant. Don't listen to what I desire; my desires are stupid – bound to be so. Go on doing whatsoever you feel right – go on doing it in spite of me." That is the meaning of the word *amen*.

Mohammedans also end their prayer with *amin* – it is the same word.

Your question is tremendously significant. First, it is not a question, hence it is significant. It is a declaration, it is a dedication, it is surrender, it is trust.

You say: "Beloved Osho, YES!"

This is the beginning of real sannyas. If you can say yes with totality, with no strings attached to it, with no conditions, with no desire for any reward, if you can simply enjoy saying yes, if it is your dance, your song, then it is prayer. And all prayers reach God – whether God is mentioned or not, whether you believe in God or not. All prayers reach God. To reach him, a prayer has only to be an authentic prayer.

But I would like to tell you that your yes should not only be a prayer. It should become your very lifestyle, it should become your flavor, your fragrance. Down the ages, religions have been teaching people life-negation, life-condemnation. Down the ages, religions have been telling you that you are sinners, that your bodies are the houses of sin, that you have to destroy your life in order to praise the Lord, that you have to renounce the world to be able to be accepted by the Lord. This is all holy cow dung, utter nonsense.

Life-affirmation, not life-negation, is religion – because God is life, and there is no other God. God is the green of the trees and the red of the trees and the gold of the trees. God is all over the place. Only God is. To deny life means to deny God, to condemn life means to condemn God, to renounce life means you are thinking yourself wiser than God.

God has given you this life, this tremendously valuable gift, and you cannot even appreciate it. You cannot welcome it, you cannot feel any gratitude for it. On the contrary, you are complaining and complaining and complaining. Your heart is full of grudges, not gratitude.

But this is what you have been taught by the priests down the ages. Priests have lived on it; this has been their basic strategy to exploit people.

If life is lived in its totality, the priest is not needed at all. If you are already okay as you are, if life is beautiful as it is, what is the need for a priest? What is the need of a mediator between you and God? You are directly in contact with God: you are living in God, breathing in God, God is pulsating in you. The priest will be utterly useless, and so will be all his mumbo jumbo, his religion and scriptures. He can be significant only if he can create a rift between you and

God. First the rift has to be created, then he can come and can tell you, "Now I am here, I can bridge the rift." But first the rift has to be there, only then can it be bridged.

And of course, you have to pay for it. When the priest does such great work bridging the rift, you have to pay for it. And in fact deep down, he is not interested in bridging it. He will only pretend that he is bridging it; the rift will remain. In fact he will make it more and more unbridgeable; the more unbridgeable it is, the more important he is. His importance consists in denying life, destroying life, making you renounce it.

I teach you a tremendous total yes to life. I teach you not renunciation but rejoicing. Rejoice! Rejoice! Again and again, I say rejoice! – because in your rejoicing you will come closest to God.

When the dancer disappears in his dance, he is divine. When the singer disappears in his song, he is divine. Rejoice so deeply, so totally, that you disappear in your rejoicing: there is rejoicing, but there is nobody who is rejoicing. When it comes to such an optimum, there is a transformation, a revolution. You are no more the old dark ugly self. You are showered with blessings. For the first time you come to know your grandeur, the splendor of your being. Say yes to life, say a total yes to life. That's what sannyas is all about. I don't give you concepts, dogmas, creeds. I only give you a certain life-affirmative lifestyle, a philosophy of life reverence.

> You told us that truth can't be transmitted or transferred, it can be attained only by experience. Many years ago when I was converted to Catholicism and when I took the "holy communion," I had genuine, pure feelings of love for Jesus and felt I had attained the "truth."
>
> ? As I see it today, I simply fell victim to a vicious fallacy induced by the priests through a kind of self-hypnosis, and had adored and worshipped nothing more than a piece of bread. I had to face the fact that I had attained, by experience, the wrong truth.
>
> How to distinguish between these cases of unconscious self-delusion and the "real thing"? How to avoid deception?

Farid, truth cannot be transferred, truth cannot be handed over to you by somebody else, because it is not a commodity. It is not a thing, it is an experience. In fact, the word *experience* is not exactly the right word. It will be truer to say that it is an experiencing; this is the first thing to be understood.

I have to use language which is already there, created by the centuries, with all kinds of fallacies in it – obviously. Language is created for day-to-day use, language is created for the mundane world; as far as it goes, it is good. It is perfectly adequate for the marketplace, but as you start moving into deeper waters it becomes more and more inadequate – not only inadequate, it starts becoming utterly wrong.

For example, think of these two words, experience and experiencing. When you use the word *experience* it gives you a sense of completion, as if something has come to a completion, as if the full stop has arrived. In life there are no full stops. Life knows nothing of full stops; it is an ongoing process, an eternal river. The goal never arrives; it is always arriving, but it never arrives. Hence the word *experience* is not right. It gives a false notion of completion, perfection; it makes you feel as if now you have arrived. *experiencing* is far more true.

In reference to true life all nouns are wrong, only verbs are true. When you say, "This is a tree," you are making a wrong statement existentially. Not linguistically, not grammatically, but existentially you are making a wrong statement, because the tree is not a static thing, it is growing. It is never in a state of is-ness, it is always becoming. In fact to call it a tree is not right: it is tree-ing. A river is rivering.

If you look deeply into life, nouns start disappearing, and there are only verbs. But that will create trouble in the marketplace. You cannot say to people, "I went to the rivering," or, "This morning I saw a beautiful treeing." They will think you have gone mad. Nothing is static in life, nothing is at rest.

A great scientist, Eddington, is reported to have said that the word *rest* has no corresponding reality to it, because nothing is ever at rest, everything is moving. It is all movement.

So let me say that truth is an experience in the sense of experiencing. You can never declare, you can never claim "I have it." You can only be humble about it – "It is happening" – and then you will not be deceived. The deception comes because you start claiming "I have it." Then the ego arises saying, "I have the truth. Only I have the truth, nobody else does. I have arrived." And the ego raises its head.

Truth is an experiencing. You cannot claim it, it is very mercurial. If you want to grab it, it will disappear from your fist. You can have it only with an open hand, not with a fist. When you make a noun out of it, you are trying to grab it in a fist; it will disappear. Let it remain a verb. Don't say, "I have arrived." Simply say, "The pilgrimage has started. I am a pilgrim, I am moving."

If the ego does not arise, nobody can deceive you. That is the second thing to be remembered. It is always the ego that deceives and is deceived. If you don't have any ego, there is no possibility of you ever being deceived. But if you have the ego, then others will deceive you. What to say of others? – you will deceive yourself.

The ego is the fundamental deception; don't help it to grow in you, don't nourish it. And the greatest thing that nourishes it is experiences, particularly spiritual experiences. You have seen Christ, you have seen Buddha; you have seen kundalini rising in your spine, the serpent uncoiling; you have seen great light, you have seen a lotus flowering inside your head, you have seen the heart chakra opening, and all that crap – beautiful sounding words, but only fools are deceived by them.

If fools disappear from the world, all esotericism will disappear. There will be great poetry, but no esotericism in it. There will be immense mystery, but no esotericism in it.

The third thing is that whenever you have some experience – spiritual or otherwise, wise or otherwise – whenever you have some experience, remember, you are not it. It is a content in consciousness – and all contents have to be dropped. Only then does the mind disappear. The mind is nothing but all the contents together; the accumulation of contents is the mind.

Just look, watch. What is your mind? What is meant by the word *mind*? What exactly does it consist of? All your experiences, knowledge, the past, accumulated – that is your mind. You may have a materialist's mind, you may have a spiritualist's mind, it doesn't matter a bit; the mind is the mind. The spiritual mind is as much a mind as the materialist mind. And we have to go beyond the mind.

Don't trust in the content – watch it, and let it pass. And yes, sometimes the content is so tremendously enchanting, so hypnotizing, that one would like to cling to it. When spiritual, so-called spiritual, experiences start happening, it is really very tempting – more tempting than anything in the world. When you see great light inside, it is so tempting to cling to it, to claim, "I have arrived" – or at least to believe deep inside yourself, "I have arrived. While everybody else is groping in darkness, light has happened to me."

This is just a new kind of darkness, because you are again being caught, trapped, by the content. These two things have to be remembered: the content and the consciousness. The consciousness never becomes content, and the content never becomes consciousness. The consciousness is a pure mirror, it only reflects.

Now, what does it matter to the mirror whether a beautiful woman is standing before it, or an ugly woman? Do you think it matters? Do you think the mirror starts thinking of clinging to the reflection of a beautiful woman – Sophia Loren? "Don't let her go, cling." Or do you think the mirror feels very repulsed if some ugly woman is there? It doesn't matter. What does it have to do with the mirror?

The mirror remains unaffected; it simply goes on reflecting whatsoever is the case. If it is darkness it reflects darkness, if it is morning it reflects morning. If somebody is dead it reflects death. If a child starts giggling, laughing, jumping, it reflects that. A roseflower is reflected with the same quality as it reflects a thorn; no distinction is made.

This state is really spiritual.

You ask me: "How to distinguish between these cases of unconscious self-delusion and the real thing?"

The real thing never appears as a thing. The real thing is not a thing, the real thing is the mirrorlike consciousness.

Always remember, always and always: "I am the witness." Don't get identified with any content, otherwise you will be falling into error. If you become identified with any content, howsoever beautiful and spiritual it appears, you have gone wrong, you have gone astray.

And the temptation is certainly great. What to say when inside you see a great melody arising – *anahat*, the soundless sound, the sound of one hand clapping? It is such a beautiful experience, one would like to be drowned in it for ever and ever. Or when suddenly inside, fragrances are released….

And remember, whatsoever can happen outside can happen inside too, because each sense has two doors to it, and each sense has two potential possibilities. One is for the outside, the other is for the inside. Your eyes can see light and colors and rainbows in the clouds, and the stars outside; and your eyes have another aspect, the other side of your eyes.

If you close your eyes and learn how to see within, you will be surprised. A far more beautiful sky opens its doors for you. A far more unbelievably beautiful world welcomes you; it has great splendor. You could never have imagined that things could ever be so beautiful. Stones turn into diamonds. Naturally, one would like to cling. Great treasures are there; one would like to hoard them. And there is nobody to compete with you; you are alone, and the whole kingdom is yours.

And just as your nose has the capacity to smell beautiful flowers, it has an inner capacity too. Once you turn in, you will come to smell fragrances which are not of this world – and it is very natural to be caught by them.

But all these experiences are hindrances, obstacles. The real seeker when he moves inwards has to be more alert than he had ever been on the outside. He has to be really alert not to be caught by anything.

And I am not saying don't enjoy. Enjoy – but remember that you are not it. Enjoy, it is your *right* to enjoy – but remember: "I am the witness of it all." If that witnessing is remembered, you will never be "goofed," you will never be deceived. Otherwise you can be deceived again and again.

To summarize: the spiritual experience is not an experience, but experiencing. Second, experiencing is a content; and you are not the content, you are just a mirror. If this much is remembered, then there is no pitfall for you. Then your path is straight.

I simply cannot understand your generalizations about male and female type. Sometimes you acknowledge male and female principles regardless of gender. But most of the time you talk of woman being the "primitive" one, finding the "wolf" in the man. What of the woman who finds herself naturally the initiator or sees the cat, not the wolf, in her man? Some men are really longing to be passive. Some women may need to assert themselves to grow. How can it be simply a matter of women's lib making women "sophisticated" and over-rational?

My statement that women are more primitive than men is not to condemn them, it is to condemn men. By "primitive" I mean more natural, more in tune with existence. Civilization is a falsification, civilization is going astray from nature. The more man becomes civilized, the more he is hung up in the head. He loses contact with his heart.

The heart is still primitive. And it is good that the universities have not yet found a way to teach the heart and make it civilized. That is the only hope for humanity to survive. The woman is the only hope for humanity to survive. Up to now, man has been dominant, and man has been dominant for a very strange reason. The reason is that deep down man feels inferior. Out of inferiority, just to compensate for it, he started dominating the woman.

Only in one sense is he stronger than the woman, and that is in muscular strength. In every other way the woman is far stronger than the man. The woman lives longer than the man, five to seven years longer. The woman suffers less through diseases, illnesses, than the man.

One hundred and ten boys are born to every hundred girls. But by the time they reach sexual maturity the number is equaled – ten boys have disappeared down the drain.

The woman has more resistance to illnesses and diseases of all kinds. More men go mad, the number is almost double. And more men commit suicide; again the number is double.

In every possible way except the muscular, the woman is far superior. But to have muscular strength is not really something very superior; it is animalistic. In that sense a wolf is far superior, a tiger even more, a lion still more.

Man must have become aware of his inferiority millions of years ago. And this is one of the psychological mechanisms: whenever you become aware of a certain inferiority, you have to compensate for it. The ugly person tries to look beautiful, pretends to be beautiful in every possible way. He will try with clothes, with cosmetics, he will go to beauticians, to plastic surgeons. It is over-compensation; somehow he knows that he is not beautiful and he has to be beautiful. The inferior person tries to be superior. And because of muscular strength, the man could prove to be the master, and he has dominated the woman down the ages.

But the time has come now for a great change. The future belongs to women, not to men, because what man has done, down through these ages, has been so ugly. Wars and wars and wars – that is his whole history. All the great that man has created is…Genghis Khan, Tamerlane, Nadirshah, Alexander, Napoleon, Adolf Hitler, Mao Zedong – people like these.

Yes, there have been a few men like Gautam Buddha, Jesus Christ, Krishna – but have you noted one point? They all look feminine. In fact that was one of Friedrich Nietzsche's criticisms of Buddha and Jesus Christ, that they look feminine, that they are womanish.

Buddha certainly looks feminine. Whenever a man moves into the heart, something in him goes feminine. He becomes more round, more soft, more vulnerable.

Friedrich Nietzsche cannot understand Gautam Buddha…because Nietzsche says the most beautiful thing that ever happened to him, the most beautiful thing he ever saw, was not the stars, not the sunset or the sunrise, not beautiful women, not roses and lotuses – no, nothing like that…. You cannot imagine what was the most beautiful thing that he had come across. He says that soldiers parading with naked swords, and the swords shining in the sunlight – that was the most beautiful experience. The sound of their boots was the most musical thing that he had ever come across – not Mozart, not Wagner, no, but the sound of boots. And the regiment moving with naked swords shining in the sun was the most beautiful thing he had seen.

Of course he cannot understand Buddha. It is Friedrich Nietzsche who has been the father of this century, and this century is one of the ugliest. He is the father of two world wars, and he may be waiting for the third, waiting to give birth to the third. He says war is the most beautiful thing in the world, because it brings that which is greatest in man to the surface.

He himself went mad, which seems very logical; such a man must go mad. And when he became mad he started signing his letters as "Anti-Christ Friedrich Nietzsche." Even in his madness he could not forget one thing, that he was anti-Christ. Everything else was forgotten: he could not recognize his friends, he could not even recognize his own sister who had looked after him his whole life, but he could not forget one thing, that he was anti-Christ.

Yes, there have been a few buddhas. But if you look closely at them you will find they are more feminine than masculine. All the great artists of the world slowly, slowly start growing a quality of feminineness, grace, elegance, exquisiteness. A certain flavor of softness, relaxedness, calmness and quietness surrounds them. They are no longer feverish.

What I am teaching here is really to turn the whole world feminine.

But Jacky Angus must be coming from that ugly movement called Women's Lib. Not only is woman to be liberated, man also has to be liberated. The woman has to be liberated from her past, and the man has to be liberated from his past. We need liberation, we need a liberated human being. And remember, when I use the word *man* the woman is included. But women have become very touchy about it.

Once I was talking in a very sophisticated club of women in Calcutta. In some reference I made the statement "All men are brothers." And some woman who must have been like Jacky Angus stood up, very angry, furious. And she said, "Why do you go on making statements only about men? All men are brothers – and what about women? Why don't you say all women are sisters and sisterhood is strong?"

I said to the woman, "Lady, I am sorry. I will make a compromise: I will say all men are sisters. What else can I do? If I say all women are sisters, some man may get angry at me."

Don't be foolish. When I am talking, try to be a little more sympathetic. You will not find any more sympathetic person than me, I make no distinctions between men and women; both have suffered. In fact suffering always comes like that, it is a double-edged sword. If you make somebody suffer, you have to suffer. If you make somebody a slave, you have to become a slave too; it is mutual.

The day women are liberated will be a great day of liberation for men too. But don't make the whole thing ugly. Otherwise there is every possibility – I fear that the possibility is there, and it is a great possibility that in fighting with men, women may lose something which is valuable. Something which has not yet been crushed and destroyed by men may be destroyed by women themselves in fighting with men. If you fight ferociously you will lose the beauty of femininity; you yourself will become as ugly as men.

It has not to be decided by fighting, it has to be decided by understanding. Spread more and more understanding. Drop these ideas of being men and women! We are all human beings. To be a man or a woman is just a very superficial thing. Don't make much fuss about it, it is not anything very important; don't make it a big deal.

And what I say sometimes may look like generalizations, because each time I cannot put in all the conditions; otherwise my talking to you would become very much burdened with footnotes. And I *hate* books with footnotes! I simply don't read them. The moment I see footnotes I throw the book away – it has been written by some pundit, some scholar, some foolish person.

You say: "I simply cannot understand your generalizations about male and female type…."

I am always talking about types; the gender is not included. Whenever I say "man" I mean the man-type, and whenever I say "woman" I mean the woman-type. But I cannot each time say "man-type," "woman-type." And you are right that there are women who are not women, who are wolves; and there are men who are not wolves, who are cats. But then whatsoever I say about the man-type will be applicable to women who are wolves, and whatsoever I say about women will be applicable to men who are cats.

I am not talking about the biological distinction between man and woman, I am talking about the psychological one. Yes, there are men who are far more feminine than any woman, and there are women who are far more masculine than any man. But this is not a beautiful state; this is ugly, because this is creating a duality in you. If you have the body of a man and the mind of a woman, there will be a conflict, a social struggle in you, a civil war in you. You will be continuously in a tug of war, fighting, tense.

If you are a woman physiologically, and you have the mind of a man, your life will dissipate much energy in unnecessary conflict. It is far better to be in tune. If a man in the body, then a man in the mind; if a woman in the body, then a woman in the mind.

And the Women's Lib movement is creating unnecessary trouble. It is turning women into wolves, it is teaching them how to fight. Man is the enemy; how can you love the enemy? How can you be in an intimate relationship with the enemy?

The man is not the enemy. The woman, to be really a woman, has to be more and more feminine, has to touch the heights of softness and vulnerability. And the man, to be really a man, has to move into his masculinity as deeply as possible. When a real man comes in contact with a real woman, they are polar opposites, extremes. But only extremes can fall in love, and only extremes can enjoy intimacy. Only extremes attract each other.

What is happening now is a kind of uni-sex: men becoming more and more feminine, women becoming more and more masculine. Sooner or later, all distinctions will be lost. It will be a very colorless society, it will be boring.

I would like the woman to become as feminine as possible, only then can she flower. And the man needs to be as masculine as possible, only then can he flower. When they are polar opposites, a great attraction, a great magnetism, arises between them. And when they come close, when they meet in intimacy, they bring two different worlds, two different dimensions, two different richnesses, and the meeting is a tremendous blessing, a benediction.

Enough for today.

Chapter 8
Krishnamurti's Solo Flute

? **When does the boat reach the other shore?**

There is no other shore, this is the only shore there is. And it is not a question of reaching somewhere else, it is a question of awakening here and now. It is never there, it is always here; it is never then, it is always now. This moment contains the totality of reality.

The boat I am talking about is not really a boat. I am talking about becoming aware. Man has fallen asleep – man is already where he needs to be, where he is meant to be. Man *is* in paradise. The garden of Eden has never been left, nobody can expel you from it. But you can fall asleep, and you can start dreaming a thousand and one things. Then those dreams become your reality, and the reality fades far away, becomes unreal.

You need not go anywhere. Meditation is neither a journey in space nor a journey in time, but an instantaneous awakening. If you can be silent now, *this* is the other shore. If you can allow the mind to cease, not to function, this is the other shore.

But the mind is very clever and cunning; it distorts every great teaching. It jumps upon words, catches hold of the words, and starts giving meanings to them which are not real meanings.

Yes, I talked about the other shore. And your mind must have caught the words "the other shore, the boat." "Where is the other shore, and where is the boat, and how can I get to the boat, how can I get into it, and when will I reach the other shore?"

You misunderstood the whole thing. Be awake, and this shore becomes the other shore, and this very moment becomes eternity. This very body the buddha, and this very place the lotus paradise.

And awakening does not need time; not even a split second is needed for it to happen. It is only a question of a tremendous desire arising in you, of such a quality of intensity that you become afire with it. In that fire, the old is gone and the new has arrived. The old was never there in the first place, you only believed in it. And the new has always been the case, you had only forgotten it.

I declare to you that this is the only world there is, and this is the only life there is. Don't start thinking of some other life somewhere after death, beyond the seven skies, in heaven. Those are all just mind dreams, mind trips, new ways to fall asleep again.

Hence my insistence that no sannyasin has to leave the world, because leaving the world is part of a project, part of a dream of reaching to the other world. And because there is none, all your efforts will be in vain. You are not to go to the monasteries or to the Himalayas; you are not to escape from here. You have to become awakened here.

And in fact it is easier to be awakened here than in a Himalayan cave. Have you not observed it? If you are suffering from a nightmare, awakening is easier. If you are having a sweet dream, awakening is more difficult. If in your dream you are on a honeymoon with your beloved, who wants to be awakened? In fact the person who tries to wake you up will look like the enemy. But if you are followed by a tiger and it is a question of life and death, and you are running and running and the tiger is coming closer and closer and closer, and you start feeling his breath on your back, then suddenly you will be awake. It is too much to tolerate, it is unbearable.

In a Himalayan cave you will be dreaming sweet dreams. That's what people are doing in the monasteries – dreaming beautiful dreams of God, of angels, of heaven, of eternal peace and joy. In the world, people are suffering from nightmares – the nightmares of the share market, the nightmares of power politics. It is easier to be awakened here. If you cannot awaken here, you cannot wake up anywhere else.

But remember, let me repeat it again, there is no other reality, there is only one reality. But the one reality can be seen in two ways: with sleepy eyes, dreamy eyes, eyes full of dust, and then what you see is distorted; and the same reality can be seen without sleep, without dreaming eyes, without dust. Then whatsoever you see is the truth – and truth liberates.

? **While you were pointing the finger to the moon you said today, "Men have to become more masculine." What is this masculine?**

Masculinity can have two directions, just as feminineness can have two directions. The masculine mind can be aggressive, violent, destructive – that is only one of the possibilities. Men have tried that, and humanity has suffered much from it. And when men try this negative aspect of masculinity, women naturally start moving into the negative feminineness, just to keep together with men. Otherwise the rift will be too great, unbridgeable. When the feminine is negative it is inactivity, lethargy, indifference. The negative man can only have a bridge with a negative woman.

But there is a positive aspect too. Nothing can be only negative; every negativity has a positive aspect too. Every dark cloud has a silver lining, and every night is followed by a dawn.

Positive masculinity is initiative, creativity, adventure. These are the same qualities, but moving on a different plane. The negative masculine mind becomes destructive, the positive masculine mind becomes creative. Destructiveness and creativeness are not two things, but two aspects of one energy. The same energy can become aggression and the same energy can become initiative.

When aggression is initiative it has a beauty of its own. When violence becomes adventure, when violence becomes exploration, exploration of the new, of the unknown, it is tremendously beneficial.

And so is the case with the feminine. Inactivity is negative, receptivity is positive. They both look alike, they look very similar. You will need very penetrating eyes to see the difference between the inactive and the receptive. The receptive is a welcome, it is an awaiting, it has a prayer in it. Receptivity is a host, receptivity is a womb. Inactivity is simply dullness, death, hopelessness. There is nothing to wait for, nothing to expect, nothing is ever going to happen. It is falling into lethargy, it is falling into a kind of indifference. And indifference and lethargy are poisons.

But the same thing that becomes indifference can become detachment, and then it has a totally different flavor. Indifference looks like detachment, but it is not; indifference is simply no interest. Detachment is not absence of interest – detachment is absolute interest, tremendous interest, but still with the capacity of non-clinging. Enjoy the moment while it is there and when the moment starts disappearing, as everything is bound to disappear, let it go. That is detachment.

Lethargy is a negative state. One is like a lump of mud just lying there – no possibility of growth, no exuberance, no flowering. But the same energy can become a pool, a great pool of energy – not going anywhere, not doing anything, but the energy accumulating and accumulating and accumulating.

And scientists say that at a certain point the quantitative change becomes a qualitative change. At a hundred degrees heat the water evaporates. At ninety-nine degrees it has not evaporated yet; at ninety-nine point nine degrees it has still not evaporated. But just point one degree more, and the water will take a quantum leap.

Positive feminineness is not like lethargy, it is like a tremendous pool of energy. And as the energy gathers and accumulates, it goes through many qualitative changes.

A man, to be really masculine, has to be adventurous, has to be creative, has to be able to take as many initiatives in life as possible. The woman, to be really a woman, has to be a pool of energy behind the man, so the adventure can have as much energy as possible. Energy will be needed so that the adventure can have some inspiration, so that the adventure can have some poetry, so that the adventurous soul can relax in the woman and be replenished with life, rejuvenated.

Man and woman both together, moving positively, are one whole. And the real couple – and there are very few real couples – is one in which each has joined with the other in a positive way. Ninety-nine percent of couples are joined together in a negative way. That's why there is so much misery in the world.

I repeat it again: the man has to be masculine and the woman has to be feminine, but in a positive way. Then to be together is a meditation, then to be together is really a great adventure. Then to be together brings new surprises every day. Then life is a dance between these two polarities, and they help each other, they nourish each other.

Man alone will not be able to go very far. Woman alone will be just a pool of energy with no possibility of any dynamic movement. When both are together they are complementary. No one is higher than the other; complementaries are never higher and lower, complementaries are equal. Neither the man nor the woman is higher, they are complementaries. Together they make a whole, and together they can create a holiness which is not possible for either separately.

That's why Jesus or Buddha look a little less rich than Krishna, and the reason is that they are alone. Krishna is more total. Hence, in India, Krishna is thought to be the perfect *avatar*, the perfect incarnation of God. Buddha is thought to be partial, so is Mahavira a partial manifestation of God, and so is Jesus. Krishna has something of totality in him.

And one thing more. If it was only a case of an outer meeting of man and woman, it would not have been so important. It is also a case of a meeting deep down in the being of each man and woman, because each man is a woman inside too, and each woman is a man inside too. The outer meeting and merging with the other is really a lesson, an experiment, to prepare for the inner meeting.

Each man is born out of a man and a woman. Half of you comes from your father and half of you comes from your mother. You are a meeting of polar opposites.

Modern psychology, particularly the Jungian school of psychology, accepts this, is based on this, that man is bisexual and so is woman. If your conscious mind is that of a man, then your unconscious will be that of a woman, and vice versa.

But to manage the inner meeting is difficult in the beginning, because the inner is invisible. First you have to learn the lesson with the visible. Meet with the outer woman, meet with the outer man, so that you can have a few experiences of what this meeting is all about. Then, slowly, slowly, you can search withinwards and find the same polarity there.

The day your inner man and woman meet, you are enlightened. That day is a day of great celebration, not only for you but for the whole existence. One man has arrived back again. Out of millions and millions, one man has arrived.

It is said that when Buddha became enlightened, flowers showered from the sky. These are not historical facts, they are poetic expressions, but of tremendous significance. The whole existence must have danced, must have sung, must have showered millions of flowers – because it is a rare phenomenon. A groping soul suddenly has become integrated, a fragmentary soul has become crystallized. One man has become God: it has to be celebrated. It is a blessing to the whole existence.

But the first lesson has to be learned outside, remember. Unless you have known the woman on the outer plane, in all her richness, in all her sweetness and bitterness; unless you have known the man on the outside, in all his beauty and in all his ugliness, you will not be able to move into the inner dimension. You will not be able to allow the yin and yang, Shiva and Shakti, to meet inside.

And that meeting is of utter importance, of ultimate importance, because only with that meeting do you become a god – never before it.

Although I have not been to Krishnamurti's latest discourses in Bombay, I have heard that he has talked against sannyas in them. It seems to me that this attitude is a device that helps both his work and yours, that he does not mean what he says. Please comment.

J. Krishnamurti is an enlightened man – you need not defend him. He does mean what he says, he is against sannyas. That's his approach towards life, a very narrow approach of course. He has a very tunnel-type of vision. Of course whatsoever he says is right according to his tunnel vision, but his vision is very narrow.

He can say sannyas is wrong, he can say I am wrong. Still, I cannot say that he is wrong, because I have a wider vision, very inclusive. If I can say Buddha is right, Zarathustra is right, Lao Tzu is right, Tilopa, Atisha, and many, many more are right, I can also say Krishnamurti is right.

Yes, there are people for whom his vision will be of help, but those people will be very few. In fact the people for whom his vision is right may not need his help at all – because to need help from a master is what sannyas is all about, to need help from a master is the fundamental of disciplehood. Whether you call it disciplehood or not does not matter.

Krishnamurti is very much against the words *disciple* and *master*. But that's what he has been doing for fifty years. He is a master who says that he is not a master. And the people who listen to him and follow him are disciples who think they are not disciples.

It does not matter what you think. What matters is what you are. He is a master and he has disciples. He denies that he is a master; that is part of his device. In this egoistic world it is very difficult for people to surrender, to drop their egos. For the egoists who cannot drop their egos he opens a door. He says, "You can keep your ego; you don't need to be a disciple, you don't need to be a sannyasin." The egoists feel very good that they need not bow down to anybody. But listening to him continuously again and again, deep down the bowing starts happening, the surrender starts happening.

He does not claim that he is a master. But whatsoever a master requires, he requires from his listeners. The master says, "Listen without thinking, listen totally, without any interference from your thoughts." And that's what *he* requires from his disciples whom he does not call disciples. It is a very sophisticated game. He can say sannyas is wrong – he *has* to say it.

And whenever he is in India – and soon wherever he will be, in every meeting of his he will find my sannyasins. That irritates him very much, and it must be even more irritating that when he talks against sannyas and against sannyasins, my sannyasins laugh and enjoy it.

He has been asking them, "Why do you come to me? If you have already got a master there is no need to come." To one of my sannyasins he said in a private interview, "If you have got a master, you need not come here."

And my sannyasin said, "But my master says 'Go everywhere. Wherever you find something can be learned, go there!' This is his teaching and we are following him, and we are not here to follow you!"

Naturally he gets very irritated. But you need not defend him. And this is the beauty, that he cannot accept me but I can accept him. It makes no problem for me. I accept all kinds of people and all kinds of philosophies; my vision is wide enough.

In fact why is he so much against masters and disciples? It is a wound that has healed but the scar is still left. He was forced to be a disciple against his will. He was a small child when he was adopted by Annie Besant and the theosophists, only nine years old, completely unaware of what was being done to him. And he was forced to follow a very rigid discipline.

Twenty-four hours a day he was being trained, because one of the theosophist leaders, Leadbeater, had this idea, this vision, that this boy was going to become a world teacher – a *jagatguru*, a master of the whole world – that he was going to become the vehicle of Lord Maitreya, that he had to be prepared so he could receive the new incarnation of Buddha in his body. So he was tortured in many ways.

He was not allowed to eat like other children, he was not allowed to play with other children, as any child would like to. He was guarded. He was not allowed to go to ordinary schools, he was almost completely kept a prisoner. And then getting up early at three o'clock in the morning, and then the ritual bath, and so many, many rituals – Tibetan, Chinese, Indian, Egyptian…he must have become tired.

And the last wound happened when his brother Nityananda died. There were two brothers, Krishnamurti and Nityananda, and both were being prepared, because there was a little suspicion as to who was really going to be the master. Nityananda died from this rigid discipline, this almost insane imposition. His death was a trauma for Krishnamurti; he had loved his brother tremendously. There was no other outlet for his love. He had been taken away from his family; his mother had died and his father was not able to look after them, he was just a small clerk. Both the children were adopted by Annie Besant and they had to travel all around the world learning different esoteric disciplines. It was very hard on them. There is every possibility Nityananda died simply because of too much training.

And then those masters whom Krishnamurti had not chosen out of love…they were like prisoners and the masters were like jailers. He carried a very wrong notion about masters; it was very difficult for him to get free from their trap. Finally he got free from their trap – how long can you hold someone? When he became a young man, and strong enough to get out of the trap, he simply rushed out, and declared, "I am nobody's master, and I am not going to be a world teacher, and this is all nonsense!"

Since then, the scar has remained. Since then he has been talking about things like masters, disciplines, meditations, disciplehood, and he has been against all of them. It is natural. In fact he has never known a master, and he has never known disciplehood – because these are not things that can be imposed on you, these are things which you accept out of joy and love.

You are far more fortunate than him. You have chosen me out of joy, out of love, and you are free to leave me at any moment. He was not free to leave. He did not choose these people. And there is every possibility that many wrong things were done to him when he was a child.

It is almost an established fact that Leadbeater was a homosexual. The point was even raised in court that he was sexually exploiting children. Just think of a nine-year-old child if sexually mishandled – he will have a very deep wound from it; it will be difficult for him to erase the scar.

You can ask the psychologists: if a child is in some way sexually exploited, his whole life becomes disturbed. If a girl was somehow sexually exploited against her will, or when she was not aware of what was happening, she will never be at ease sexually, never. The fear will come again and again.

There is every possibility that something like this happened. Krishnamurti never talks about these things, there is no point in talking about these things, all those old fogies are dead. But somewhere there is a scar. Hence his antagonism to masters, to disciplehood, to sannyas, to all kinds of methods. This shows something about his history; it shows nothing about masters and disciples.

What does he know about Buddha and the disciples that Buddha had? What does he know about Atisha and the masters Dharmakirti, Dharmarakshita and Yogin Maitreya – what does he know about these people?

And one thing more, a calamity happened. Annie Besant and Leadbeater never allowed him to read ancient scriptures because they were afraid he would lose his originality. So he was kept utterly ignorant of all the great traditions of the world.

And if you don't know anything about Atisha and Dharmakirti, you will miss something. Dharmakirti was the master who told Atisha to move to another master, Dharmarakshita, "because what I have known, I have given to you. I can give you the rest too, but that has never been my path. Go to Dharmarakshita, he has followed another route. He will give you something more, something more authentic. I have only heard about it, or only seen it from the mountain-top. I give you emptiness. Now, to learn compassion, go to Dharmarakshita."

What beautiful people they must have been! And Dharmarakshita told him, "I know only the feminine kind of compassion, the passive kind. For the active, you must go to another master, Yogin Maitreya; he will teach you."

These are not people who are possessive, who are jealous, who want to dominate. These are people who give freedom! Krishnamurti is utterly unaware of all the great traditions of the world – he only knows the theosophists.

And that was one of the ugliest things that happened in this century. All kinds of fools gathered under the banner of theosophy, it was a hotchpotch. It was an effort to create a synthesis of all that is good out of all the religions. But no such synthesis is possible. And if you make such a synthesis you will only have a corpse on your hands, not an alive body, breathing, pulsating.

It is as if you love many women – one woman has beautiful eyes, you take the eyes out; another woman has a beautiful nose, you cut off the nose – and so on and so forth. Put all the parts together, assemble them, and you will have a corpse. Making the corpse you have killed twenty beautiful women, and the end result is just utter stupidity.

That's what theosophy did. Something is beautiful in Hinduism, something is beautiful in Taoism, something is beautiful in Mohammedanism, something is beautiful in Judaism, and so on and so forth. Collect all that, put it together, put it in a mixer and mix it, and what you will have will be just a corpse.

Krishnamurti unfortunately had to live with these people. But he has tremendous intelligence. Anybody in his place would have been lost, anybody else in his situation would not have been able to come out of the cage. And the cage was so beautiful, so alluring – thousands of followers were available. But he had the courage, he had the guts and intelligence to renounce all that, to simply move out of the whole trap.

It was difficult for him, very difficult; even to survive was difficult. I respect the man, I respect him tremendously. And I can understand why he is against masters, disciples, sannyas.

You say, "Although I have not been to Krishnamurti's latest discourses in Bombay, I have heard that he had talked against sannyas in them. It seems to me that this attitude is a device that helps both his work and yours, that he does not mean what he says."

He says what he means, he means what he says. His narrow vision is very clear. That is one of the most beautiful things about narrow visions, they are clear. The wider the sky, the less the clarity; the bigger the vision, the less the clarity.

And my vision contains all. His vision is very exclusive, my vision is very inclusive. His vision is only his. My vision contains Buddha, Zarathustra, Moses, Mahavira, Mohammed, and millions more. And remember, I am not trying to make a synthesis here. I am not trying to choose what is beautiful in one and what is beautiful somewhere else. No, I accept every tradition as it is – even though sometimes it goes against me, even though sometimes there are points which I would not like to be there. But then who am I? Why should I bring my choice into it?

I accept every tradition as it is, without interfering with it. This has never been done before, and this may not be done again for centuries, because to have such inclusive vision is very confusing. Being with me, you can never have certainty. The more you are with me, the more and more the ground under your feet will disappear. The more you are here with me, the more and more your mind will be taken away, and with it all certainty.

Yes, you will have transparency, but no certainty.

With Krishnamurti everything is certain, absolutely certain. He is one of the most consistent men who has ever walked on the earth, because he has such a narrow vision. When you have a very narrow vision you are bound to be very consistent.

You cannot find a more inconsistent person than me, because I have to make space for so many contradictory standpoints. There is nothing in common between Bahauddin and Atisha, there is nothing in common between Rinzai and Mohammed, there is nothing in common between Mahavira and Christ. And yet they all have met in me, and they are all one in me. And I have not chosen, I have not interfered, I have simply digested them all.

A tremendously new kind of symphony, I will not call it a synthesis but a symphony, is arising here. In a synthesis something dead is produced. In a symphony, in an orchestra, all instruments are playing, but in a tremendous harmony.

Krishnamurti is a solo flute player. I am an orchestra; the flute is accepted. Of course my orchestra will not be accepted by Krishnamurti, he is a solo flute player. And a beautiful flute player he is, I appreciate him. I can appreciate him, but he cannot appreciate me. What does he know about the orchestra? I know everything about the flute, because it is part of my orchestra, just a small part. But for him the flute is all.

Don't try to defend him, there is no need. He can defend himself, he is quite capable. I can understand his criticism of sannyas. If he had not criticized it, that would have been a surprise. If he really wants to surprise me he should stop criticizing my sannyasins – it would be unbelievable, it would be really a shock to me!

But let that old man continue, and you please continue going to listen to him. Provoke him. Just sit in the front row, and whenever he criticizes sannyas, applaud, laugh. And then he will be really in a rage. He is the only enlightened person in the world who can get angry. And that's perfectly beautiful. I love him, I respect him – and I love him and respect him as he is. But he cannot love and respect me; that too I can understand.

Like Krishna and Buddha and Nanak and Jesus, your message is love. How are your misunderstood sannyasins vehicles for your message of love to the world?

Krishna has talked about love, Buddha too, Jesus, Nanak and Kabir, they all have talked about love. But nobody has talked about love like me. Their love is very ethereal, abstract; their love is not of this world at all. Their love is philosophical. The way they define their love and the way I define my love are totally different. I accept love in its whole spectrum, all the colors of it, the whole rainbow of it. They are choosers; they say, "Only the color blue is love, all other colors are not love." Or somebody says, "Only the color green is love, all others are not love."

They condemn earthly love, they condemn sensuous love, they condemn the body. And that's where the difference is. To me, love is a ladder. One part of the ladder is resting on the earth – not only resting but really rooted in the earth – and the other end is touching heaven.

They talk only of the other end. And because they talk only of the other end, it becomes humanly impossible to reach it, because the lower part is denied, and the higher can be reached only through the lower. You will have to pass over the lower rungs of the ladder, otherwise how are you going to reach the higher part?

There have been people like Charvaka in India, and Epicurus in Greece, who believe only in the lower part of the ladder and deny the higher part.

I accept the totality of it. I accept the mud, I accept the lotus, and I accept all that is in between. Hence I am bound to be misunderstood by everybody. The spiritual people will misunderstand me because they will think I am a materialist – that I don't believe in the soul, that my preaching of love is nothing but a preaching of sex, that in the name of love I am only teaching people sexuality. And the materialists, the Epicureans, the Charvakas, they are also going to misunderstand me, obviously. They will say that my talk of sex and earthly love is only a trap to take you to those non-existential abstractions – ecstasy, samadhi, God.

I am going to be misunderstood by both the materialists and the spiritualists. And the same is going to be the case with my sannyasins. You are going to be misunderstood everywhere – in every culture, in every society, by every religion, by every ideology. To be with me is risky; you will have to be misunderstood. You will have to accept it as a fact of your existence.

And the reason is clear; it is because nobody in the past has accepted the whole spectrum. I accept the whole spectrum because to me, the lower and the higher are not separate, they are one. The lower contains the higher, and the higher contains the lower. The mud is unmanifest lotus, and the lotus is manifest mud. I don't condemn the mud, because in condemning the mud the lotus is condemned. And I don't condemn the lotus, because if you condemn the lotus the mud loses all meaning; then it is simply mud and nothing else.

I accept this earth and I accept this heaven. I accept both the body and the soul, the outer and the inner. My teaching is that of total acceptance.

You will be misunderstood. And it is not only that you will be misunderstood – there is every possibility that you will misunderstand me too, because many of you will think that sex is all. And you can find quotes from my books easily supporting your standpoint. And many of you will misunderstand that sex has to be transcended, that only samadhi is the truth and that sex is just something to be bypassed, transcended and surpassed. Both these things are going to happen. Those who really understand me will see the point, and will see what I am doing here. I am creating a materialist spirituality, or a spiritualist materialism. It has never been done before. And whenever something is done for the first time, it is natural that it will be misunderstood.

A middle-aged American lady whose husband had recently died went to a spiritualist to get in touch with him as she was feeling lonely. Contact having been established, she said, "Hello, honey! How you doin'?"

Honey: "Fine. In fact I'm a hell of a lot better off than I was before."

Lady: "How do you pass the time, honey?"

Honey: "Well, I wake up, make love, have breakfast, make love, have lunch, make love, have supper, make love, sleep, make love, wake up, make love – day in and day out."

Lady: "Where are you, honey? In heaven?"

Honey: "No, I'm a bull in Koregaon Park, Pune."

That possibility is there, you can misunderstand me. And there are also others at the other extreme. Anybody who chooses one part of my teaching is bound to misunderstand me.

You have to take me in toto, in my totality. Of course the totality is very confusing, because it contains the polar opposite. It is easier to choose one part – the materialist or the spiritualist; it is easier, you feel consistent. To choose me in my totality you will have to live a very inconsistent life – one moment this, another moment that. But that is my whole message.

If one really wants to live life in all its richness, one has to learn how to be inconsistent, how to be *consistently* inconsistent, how to be able to move from one extreme to another – sometimes rooted deep in the earth and sometimes flying high in heaven, sometimes making love and sometimes meditating.

And then, slowly, slowly, your heaven and your earth will come closer and closer, and you will become the horizon where they meet.

Chapter 9
Watching the Watcher

Grasp the principle of two witnesses.
Always rely on just a happy frame of mind.
Even though you are distracted, if you can do it, it is still mind training.
Always observe the three general points.
Change your inclination and then maintain it.
Do not discuss defects.
Don't think about anything that concerns others.
Train first against the defilement that is greatest.
Abandon all hopes of results.

The first sutra:

Grasp the principle of two witnesses.

It is one of the most important sutras, one of the very fundamentals of inner alchemy. Let it sink deep in your heart. It can transform you, it can give you a new birth, a new vision, a new universe. It has two meanings; both meanings have to be understood.

The first meaning: there are two kinds of witnesses. One kind is the people that surround you. You are constantly aware that you are being watched, witnessed. It creates self-consciousness in you. Hence the fear when you are on a stage facing a big crowd. Actors feel it, poets feel it, orators feel it – and not only the beginners but even those who have wasted their whole life in acting. When they come on the stage a great trembling arises in them, a great fear, as to whether they will be able to make it or not.

With so many eyes watching you, you are reduced to an object. You are no more a subjectivity, you have become a thing. And you are afraid because they may not appreciate you. They may not feed your ego, they may not like you, they may reject you. Now you are in their hands. You are reduced to a dependent slave. Now you have to work in such a way that you will be appreciated. You have to buttress their egos, so that in response you can hope they will buttress your ego.

When you are with your friends you are not so afraid. You know them, they are predictable, you depend on each other. But when you face the anonymous crowd, more fear arises. Your whole being starts trembling, your whole ego is at stake – you can fail. Who knows? Your success is not guaranteed.

This is the first kind of witness. Others are witnessing you, and you are just a beggar. This is the situation in which millions of people live. They live for others, hence they only appear to live, they don't live in reality. They are always adjusting to others, because they are happy only if others are happy with them. They are compromising constantly, they are selling their souls, for a simple reason – so their ego can be strengthened, so that they can become famous, well known.

Have you observed something of immense value, that whenever a poet, a novelist or a scientist gets a Nobel prize, immediately after that his creativity declines? No Nobel laureate has been able to produce anything valuable compared to the things that he created before he received it. What happens? Now you have attained the goal of the ego, there is no further to go, so there is no more need to adjust to people. Once a book becomes famous the author dies.

That's what happened with Kahlil Gibran's The Prophet. That's what happened with Rabindranath's Gitanjali. And that is almost the rule, not the exception. Once you are famous you stop compromising. For what? You are already famous. And when you stop compromising, people start neglecting you, ignoring you. Your whole creativity was rooted in the desire of the ego; now the ego feels at rest, all creativity disappears.

This is the situation in which ninety-nine point nine percent of people live. You know only one kind of witness – the other. And the other is always anxiety-creating.

Jean-Paul Sartre rightly says, "The other is hell." The other does not allow you to relax. Why do you feel so relaxed in your bathroom, in your bathtub? – because the other is not there. But relaxing in your bathtub, if you suddenly become aware that somebody is looking at you through the keyhole, suddenly all relaxation disappears. You are tense again. You are being watched.

To create fear in people, down the ages, the priests have been telling you that God is constantly watching you – constantly watching you, day in and day out. You may be asleep; he never sleeps, he goes on sitting by the bed and watching. He not only watches you, he watches your dreams and your thoughts too. So you are not only going to be punished for your acts, but for your dreams, for your thoughts, your desires and your feelings.

The priests created great fear in people. Just think of God watching continuously. No moment, not even a single moment, is allowed when you can be yourself. That was a great strategy for reducing people to things.

Why do we hanker for the attention of others? – because as we are, we are hollow. As we are, we are *not*. As we are, we don't have a center of being. We are just noise, a crowd, a house full of servants quarreling with each other because the master is absent or fast asleep. We hanker for other people's attention so that at least we can create a pseudo-center. If the real is missing, at least we can depend on a pseudo-center. It will give you an appearance of togetherness, it will make you a person. You are not an individual – individuality is the fragrance of a really centered being, one who knows who he is.

But if you are not an individual, then at least you can be a person, you can attain personality. And personality has to be begged. Individuality is your innermost growth. It is a growth; you need not beg it from anybody else, and nobody can give it to you. Individuality is your unfoldment. But personality can be begged, people can give it to you – in fact, only other people can give it to you.

If you are alone in the forest you will not have any personality, remember. You will have individuality but no personality at all. If you are alone in the Himalayas, who are you – a saint or a sinner? There is nobody to appreciate you or condemn you, there is nobody to make you famous or notorious, there is nobody except yourself. In your total aloneness, who are you? A sinner or a saint? A very, very famous person, VVIP, or just a nobody?

You are neither. You are neither a very, very important person nor a nobody, because for both the other is a must. The eyes of others are needed to reflect your personality. You are neither this nor that. You are, but you are in your reality; you are not created by others. You are as you are, in your utter nudity, authenticity.

This is one of the reasons why many people thought it wise to escape from the society. It was not really to escape from the society, it was not really against society, it was just an effort to renounce the personality.

Buddha left his palace. He is not a coward and he is not an escapist, so why did he leave the palace? Rabindranath has written a beautiful poem about it. He left the palace; for twelve years he roamed in the forests, practiced and meditated. And the day of ultimate rejoicing came, he became enlightened. Naturally, the first thing that he remembered was that he had to go back to the palace to deliver the good news to the woman he had loved, to the child that he had left behind, to the old father who was still hoping that he would come back.

It is so human, it touches the heart. After twelve years he returned. His father was angry, as fathers will be. His father could not see who he was, could not see what he had become, could not see his individuality which was so loud and so clear. The whole world was becoming aware of it, but his father was blind to it. He was still thinking about him in terms of the personality that was no longer there, that he had renounced the day he left the palace.

In fact Buddha had to leave the palace just to renounce his personality. He wanted to know himself as he was, not what others were thinking about him. But the father was now looking into his face with the eyes of twelve years ago. He again said to Buddha, "I am your father, I love you – although you have hurt me deeply and have wounded me deeply. I am an old man, and these twelve years have been a torture. You are my only son, and I have somehow tried to live so that you could come back. Now you are back, take charge of the empire, be the king! Now let me rest, it is time for me to rest. You have committed a sin against me, and you have been almost murderous towards me, but I forgive you and my doors are still open."

Buddha laughed. He said, "Sir, be a little more aware of whom you are talking with. The man who left the palace is no more; he died long ago. I am somebody else – look at me!"

And the father became even more angry. He said, "Do you want to deceive me? I don't know you? I know you more than you know yourself! I am your father, I have given birth to you, in your blood my blood circulates – and I don't know you?"

Buddha said, "Still I pray, sir…. You have certainly given birth to me. I came through you, that's true, but you were only a vehicle. And just because somebody has come riding on a horse, it does not mean that the horse knows the rider. I have passed through the doors of your body, but that does not mean that you know me. In fact, twelve years ago, even I did not know who I was. Now I know! Look into my eyes. Please forget the past – be here now!"

But the father was incapable. With his old eyes, full of tears of anger and joy, he could not see what had happened to Buddha. "What nonsense is he talking about, that he has died and is reborn, that he is a totally different individuality? That he is no more a personality, that he is an individuality?"

In dictionaries, "personality" and "individuality" are synonyms. They are not synonymous in life. The personality is false, a pretension, a facade. Individuality is your truth.

Why do we want many, many people to give attention to us? Why do we hanker for this? To create personality. And the more personality you create around yourself, the less is the possibility of knowing your individuality.

And when Buddha went to see his wife, she was even more angry. She asked only one question, a very significant one. She said, "I have only one question to ask you. I have waited for all these years, and I have only one question. The question is simple, but *be honest*." She still thinks that Buddha can be dishonest! "Be honest, be true, and just tell me one thing. Whatever you have attained in the forest, was it impossible to attain it here in the palace? Is God only in the forest and not here in the marketplace?"

Her question is of tremendous significance.

Buddha said, "Yes, the truth is as much here as it is there. But it would have been very difficult for me to know it here, because I was lost in a personality – the personality of the prince, the personality of a husband, the personality of a father, the personality of a son. The personality was too much. I never left the palace really, I was only leaving my personality behind so that there would be nobody to remind me who I was, and I could answer the question 'Who am I?' on my own. I wanted to encounter myself. I was not interested in others' answers."

But everybody else is interested in others' answers. How much you love it when somebody says, "You are so beautiful."

Sarvesh was saying to Mukta, "I feel a little lost." Naturally. He is one of the best ventriloquists the world knows; he has lived the life of a showman – always on the stage, lights flooding him from everywhere, thousands of people absolutely alert, watching what he is doing with great appreciation. He has talent, genius, and he has lived flooded with others' attentions.

Now naturally in this commune nobody comes to say to him, "Sarvesh, you are great. Sarvesh you are this, you are that." He must be feeling a little bit lost. That is a problem for people who are public figures, it is very difficult for them to drop their personality.

But he is trying, and I am certain that he will succeed. It is going to happen. On one hand he has hankered for the attention of others, but sooner or later you become tired of it too, because it is just artificial food. Maybe it tastes good, maybe its flavor is beautiful, but it does not nourish, it does not give you vitality.

Personality is a showpiece. It can deceive others, but it cannot deceive you, at least not for long. That's why Sarvesh has come here, tired, exhausted by all the attention. But old habit persists a little longer. Sooner or later he will start enjoying himself, sooner or later he will start enjoying his individuality.

And the day you can enjoy your individuality, you are free – free from dependence on others. If you ask for their attention you have to pay for it in return. It is a bondage. The more you ask people to be attentive towards you, the more you are becoming a thing, a commodity, which can be sold and purchased.

That's what happens to all public figures – to politicians, to showbiz people. This is one kind of witnessing; you want to be witnessed. It gives you respectability, and in order to have respectability you will have to create character and morality. But all that character and all that morality is just hypocrisy. You create it with a motivation, so that others can be attracted towards you.

If you want respectability you will have to be a conformist, you will have to be obedient to the society and its demands. You will have to live according to wrong values, because the society consists of people who are fast asleep – their values cannot be right values.

Yes, but there is one thing: you can become a saint. That's how thousands of your saints are. They have sacrificed everything at the altar of respectability. They have tortured themselves, they have been suicidal, but they have gained one thing. They have become saints, people worship them.

If you want that kind of worship, respectability, sainthood, then you will become more and more false, more and more pseudo, more and more plastic. You will never be a real rose. And that is the greatest calamity in life that can happen to a man, to be a plastic rose and not to be a real rose.

The second kind of witnessing is totally different, just the polar opposite. It is not that you hanker for others' attention; on the contrary, you start paying attention to yourself. You become a witness to your own being. You start watching your thoughts, desires, dreams, motives, greeds and jealousies. You create a new kind of awareness within you. You become a center, a silent center which goes on watching whatsoever is happening.

You are angry, and you watch it. You are not just angry, a new element is introduced into it: you are watching it. And the miracle is that if you can watch anger, the anger disappears without being repressed.

The first kind of saint will have to repress it. He will have to repress his sexuality, he will have to repress his greed. And the more you repress anything, the deeper it goes into your unconscious. It becomes part of your basement and it starts affecting your life from there. It is like a wound that is oozing with pus, but you have covered it. Just by covering it, you don't become healthy, it does not heal. In fact by covering it you are helping it to grow more and more. Your saints stink, stink of all kinds of repressions.

The second kind of witnessing creates a totally different kind of person. It creates the sage. The sage is one who knows who he is, not according to others. The sage is one who lives a life according to his own nature, not according to others' values. He has his own vision and the courage to live it.

The sage is rebellious. The saint is obedient, orthodox, conventional, traditional, conformist. The sage is nonconformist, nontraditional, non-conventional, rebellious. Rebellion is the very taste of his being. He is not dependent on others. He knows what freedom is, and he knows the joys of freedom. The saint will be followed by a big crowd. The sage will have only the chosen people who will be able to understand him.

The sage will be misunderstood by the masses, the saint will be worshipped. The sage will be condemned by the masses, maybe even murdered. Jesus is crucified and the pope is worshipped. Jesus is a sage and the pope is a saint.

The saint has character and the sage has consciousness. And there is a tremendous difference. They are as different as the earth and the sky. Character is imposed for some ulterior motives – to gain respectability in this world and to have more and more heavenly pleasures. Consciousness has no future, no motivation, it is a joy unto itself. It is not a means to some end, it is an end unto itself.

To be with a saint is to be with an imitator. To be with a sage is to be with something true and authentic. To be with a saint is to be with a teacher, at the most. To be with a sage is to be with a master. These are the two witnesses.

Atisha says:

Grasp the principle of two witnesses.

Avoid the first and plunge into the second. There is another meaning to this sutra too. The other meaning is, first witness the objects of the mind. This is a higher meaning than the first. Witness the objects of the mind.

Patanjali calls it *dhyana*, meditation – from the same word come Zen and *ch'an*. Witness the objects, the contents, of the mind. Whatsoever passes before you, watch it, without evaluating, judging or condemning. Don't be for or against, just watch, and dhyana, meditation, is created.

And the second is, witness the witness itself – and samadhi is created, satori is created, the ultimate ecstasy is created. The first leads to the second. Start watching your thoughts but don't stop there. When thoughts have disappeared then don't think that you have arrived. One more thing has to be done, one more step. Now watch the watcher. Now just witness the witnessing. Nothing else is left, only you are. Just suddenly become aware of awareness itself, and then dhyana is transformed into samadhi. By watching the mind, the mind disappears. By watching the witness, the witness expands and becomes universal.

The first is a negative step to get rid of the mind. The second is a positive step to get rooted in the ultimate consciousness – call it God or nirvana or whatever you wish.

The second sutra:

Always rely on just a happy frame of mind.

If you are unhappy, that simply means that you have learned tricks for being unhappy, and nothing else. Unhappiness depends on the frame of your mind. There are people who are unhappy in all kinds of situations. They have a certain quality in their mind which transforms everything into unhappiness. If you tell them about the beauty of the rose they immediately start counting the thorns. If you say to them, "What a beautiful morning, what a sunny day!" they will look at you as if they are surprised by your statement. They will say, "So what! One day between two dark nights! It is only one day between two dark nights, so what is the big deal? Why are you looking so fascinated?"

The same thing can be seen from a positive reference; then suddenly each night is surrounded by two days. And then suddenly it is a miracle that the rose is possible, that such a delicate flower is possible among so many thorns.

Everything is the same. All depends on what kind of frame you are carrying in your head. Millions of people are carrying crosses; naturally, obviously, they are burdened. Their life is a drag. Their frame is such that it immediately becomes focused on everything that is negative.

It magnifies the negative; it is a morbid approach towards life, pathological. But they go on thinking, "What can we do? The world is such."

No, the world is not such! The world is absolutely neutral. It has thorns, it has roses, it has nights, it has days. The world is utterly neutral, balanced, it has all. Now it depends on you as to what you choose. If you have decided to choose only the wrong, you will live in a wrong kind of world, because you will live in your own chosen world.

That's how people create hell and heaven on the same earth. It looks very unbelievable that Buddha lived on this earth with the same kind of people, and lived in paradise. And you also live on the same earth with the same kind of people, and you live in hell.

Now, there are two possibilities. The political mind says, "Change the world." The religious mind says, "Change the frame of your mind."

Religion and politics are diametrically opposite. There is a possibility one day of a meeting of science and religion. Sooner or later, science and religion are bound to meet, because their approach is very similar. Maybe the direction is different – science searches the outer, and religion the inner. But the search, the quality of the search, is the same. The spirit of the search is the same.

But I don't see any possibility that politics and religion can ever meet. Politics always thinks the world is wrong; change the society, the economic structure, this and that, and everything will be okay. And religion says the world has always been the same and will remain the same; you can change only one thing – the context of your mind, the space of your mind.

Always rely on just a happy frame of mind.

Let it become one of the fundamental rules of your life. Even if you come across a negative, find something positive in it. You will always be able to find something. And the day you become skillful at finding the positive in the negative, you will dance with joy.

Try it, try the new vision of life. Think in terms of optimism, don't be a pessimist. The pessimist creates hell around himself and lives in it – you live in the world you create.

Remember, there is not only one world, there are as many worlds as there are minds in the world. I live in my world, you live in your own world. They are not only different, they never overlap. They are utterly different, they exist on different planes.

Atisha makes it a fundamental rule for his disciples to live in a happy frame of mind. Then you start turning each opportunity into a challenge for growth. For example, somebody insults you. Now it is so clear that you have been insulted, how can you practice a happy frame of mind now? Yes, it can be practiced. Insult a buddha and you will know.

Gautam Buddha was insulted once. He was passing by a village, and the villagers were very against him. It was impossible for them to comprehend what he was teaching. Compared to the buddhas, the whole world is always very primitive, very unsophisticated, very stupid. The people gathered and insulted him very much.

Buddha listened very silently and then he said, "If you are finished, can I take leave of you, because I have to reach the other village, and they must be waiting for me. If you are not finished, then when I return tomorrow morning you can come again and finish your job."

One man from the crowd asked, "Have you not heard us? We have been insulting you, abusing you. We have been using all kinds of dirty words, anything that we can find."

Buddha laughed. He said, "You have come a little too late – you should have come ten years ago. Then I was in the same frame of mind as you are; then I would have replied, and replied well. But now this is simply an opportunity for me to be compassionate, to be meditative. I am thankful to you that you allowed me this opportunity. This is just a test – a test of whether or not I have anything of the negative lurking anywhere in my unconscious mind.

"And I am happy to declare to you, friends, that not even a single shadow of the negative has passed through my mind. I have remained utterly blissful, you have not been able to affect me in any way. And I am tremendously happy that you gave me such a great opportunity. Very few people are as kind as you are."

This is how one should use situations, this is how a sannyasin should use negative opportunities for inner growth, for inner understanding, for meditativeness, for love, for compassion. And once you have learned this happy frame of mind, this positive vision of life, you will be surprised that the whole existence starts functioning in a totally different way. It starts mothering you. It starts helping you in every possible way, it becomes a great friend.

And to know this is to know God. To know this, that existence mothers you, is to know God. There is no other God – just this feeling, this tremendous feeling, this penetrating feeling, that the existence loves you, protects you, helps you and showers many, many blessings on you; that the existence is graceful towards you, that you are not alienated, that you are not a stranger, that this is your home.

To feel that "This existence is my home" is to know God.

The third sutra:

Even though you are distracted, if you can do it, it is still mind training.

Yes, sometimes you will be distracted. You are not yet all buddhas – there will be times when you will be distracted, there will be times when you will be dragged down by the negative, sucked in by the old habit. And by the time you know, it has already happened; you are miserable. The shadow has fallen on you, that sunlit peak has disappeared, you have fallen into the dark valley.

Then what to do in those moments? Atisha says:

Even though you are distracted, if you can do it, it is still mind training.

What does he mean by "if you can do it?" This is of great importance. If you can be attentive to your inattention, if you can be aware that you have fallen into the trap of the negative, it is still meditation, it is still mind training, you are still growing.

Yes, many times you will fall, it is natural. And many times you will forget, it is natural. And many times you will be trapped and it will take time for you to remember. But the moment you remember, remember *totally*. Wake up totally and say, "I have fallen."

And see the difference. If you ask the ordinary religious person he will say, "Repent – punish yourself." But Atisha is saying: If you are attentive, that's enough. Be attentive to your inattention, be aware that you have not been aware, that's all. No repentance is needed. Don't feel guilty; it is natural, it is human. To fall many times is not something to feel guilty about. To commit errors, to go astray, is part of our human frailty and limitations. So there is no need to repent.

Repentance is ugly. It is like playing with your wound, fingering your wound. It is unnecessary, and not only unnecessary but harmful – the wound may become septic, and fingering your wound is not going to help it heal either.

If you have fallen, just know that you have fallen, with no guilt, with no repentance. There is no need to go anywhere to confess it, just knowing it is enough. And knowing it, you are helping your awareness to grow. Less and less will you fall, because knowing will become more and more strong in you.

The fourth sutra:

Always observe the three general points.

What are the three general points? The first is regularity of meditativeness. Remember, it is very difficult to create meditation, it is very easy to lose it. Anything higher takes much arduous effort to create, but it can disappear within a moment. To lose contact with it is very easy.

That is one of the qualities of the higher. It is like growing a roseflower – just a little hard wind and the rose has withered and the petals have fallen, or some animal has entered the garden and the rose is eaten. It is very easy to lose it, and it was so long a journey to create it.

And whenever there is a conflict between the higher and the lower, always remember, the lower wins easily. If you clash a roseflower with a rock, the roseflower is going to die, not the rock. The rock may not even become aware that there has been a clash, that it has killed something beautiful.

Your whole past is full of rocks, and when you start growing a rose of awareness in you, there are a thousand and one possibilities of it being destroyed by your old rocks – habits, mechanical habits. You will have to be very watchful and careful. You will have to walk like a woman who is pregnant. Hence the man of awareness walks carefully, lives carefully.

And this has to be a regular phenomenon. It is not that one day you do a little meditation, then for a few days you forget about it, and then one day you do it again. It has to be as regular as sleep, as food, as exercise, as breathing. Only then will the infinite glory of God open its doors to you.

So the first general point is: be regular.

The second general point is: don't waste your time with the nonessential. Don't fool around. Millions of people are wasting their time with the nonessential, and the irony is that they know that it is nonessential. But they say, "What else to do?" They are not aware of anything more significant.

People are playing cards, and if you ask them, "What are you doing?" they say they are killing time. Killing time? Time is life! So you are really killing life. And the time that you are killing cannot be recaptured again; once gone, it is gone forever.

The man who wants to become a buddha has to drop the nonessential more and more, so that more energy is available for the essential. Take a look at your life, how many nonessential things you are doing – and for what? And how long you have done them – and what have you gained? Are you going to repeat the same stupid pattern your whole life? Enough is enough! Take a look, meditate over it. Say only that which is essential, do only that which is essential, read only that which is essential. And so much time is saved and so much energy is saved, and all that energy and time can easily be channeled towards meditation, towards inner growth, towards witnessing.

I have never seen a man who is so poor that he cannot meditate. But people are engaged in foolish things, utterly foolish. They don't look foolish, because everybody else is also doing the same.

But the seeker has to be watchful. Take more note of what you are doing, what you are doing with your life – because to grow roses of awareness much energy will be needed, a reservoir of energy will be needed. All that is great comes only when you have extra energy. If your whole energy is wasted on the mundane, then the sacred will never be contacted.

And the third general point is: don't rationalize your errors and mistakes. The mind tends to rationalize. If you commit some mistake, the mind says, "It had to be so, there were reasons for it. I am not responsible, the very situation made this happen." And the mind is very clever at rationalizing everything.

Avoid rationalizing your own errors and mistakes, because if you rationalize you protect them. Then they will be repeated. Avoid rationalizing your errors. Stop rationalization completely. Reasoning is one thing, rationalization is totally another. Reasoning can be used for some positive purposes, but rationalization can never be used for any positive purpose.

And you will be able to find when you are rationalizing, you can deceive others but you cannot deceive yourself. You know that you have fallen. Rather than wasting time in rationalizing and convincing yourself that nothing has gone wrong, put the whole energy into being aware.

All these general points are to help you so that you can block the leaks of your energy. Otherwise God goes on pouring energy into you, and you have so many leakages that you are never full. Energy comes, but leaks out.

The fifth sutra:

Change your inclination and then maintain it.

Change your inclination from the mind to the heart. That is the first change. Think less, feel more. Intellectualize less, intuit more. Thinking is a very deceptive process, it makes you feel that you are doing great things. But you are simply making castles in the air. Thoughts are nothing but castles in the air.

Feelings are more material, more substantial. They transform you. Thinking about love is not going to help, but feeling love is bound to change you. Thinking is very much loved by the ego, because the ego feeds on fictions. The ego cannot digest any reality, and thinking is a fictitious process. It is a kind of dreaming, a sophisticated dreaming. Dreams are pictorial and thinking is conceptual, but the process is the same. Dreaming is a primitive kind of thinking, and thinking is a civilized kind of dreaming.

Change from the mind to the heart, from thinking to feeling, from logic to love.

And the second change is from the heart to the being – because there is a still deeper layer in you where even feelings cannot reach. Remember these three words: mind, heart, being. The being is your pure nature. Surrounding the being is feeling, and surrounding feeling is thinking. Thinking is far away from being but feeling is a little closer; it reflects some glory of the being. It is just as in the sunset the sun is reflected by the clouds and the clouds start having beautiful colors. They themselves are not the sun, but they are reflecting the light of the sun.

Feelings are close to being, so they reflect something of the being. But one has to go beyond feelings too. Then what is being? It is neither thinking nor feeling, it is pure am-ness. One simply is.

Thinking is very selfish and egoistic. Feeling is more altruistic, less egoistic. Being is no-ego, egolessness – neither selfishness nor altruism but a spontaneity, a moment-to-moment responsiveness. One does not live according to oneself, one lives according to God, according to the whole.

Feeling is half, and no half can ever satisfy you. Thinking and feeling are both halves and you will remain divided. Being is total, and only the total can bring contentment.

And the ultimate, the fourth change, is from being to non-being. That is nirvana, enlightenment; one simply disappears, one simply is not. God is, enlightenment is. Light is, delight is, but there is nobody who is delighted. *Neti neti*: neither this nor that, neither existence nor nonexistence – this is the ultimate state. Atisha is slowly, slowly taking his disciples towards it.

Let me repeat: from thinking to feeling, from feeling to being, from being to non-being, and one has arrived. One has disappeared and one has arrived. One is no more, for the first time. And for the first time one really is.

The sixth sutra:

Do not discuss defects.

The mind tends to discuss the defects of others. It helps the ego to feel good. Everybody is such a sinner; when everybody is such a sinner, comparatively one feels like a saint. When everybody is doing wrong, it feels good that "At least I am not doing *that* much wrong."

Hence people talk about others' defects; not only do they talk about them, they go on magnifying them. That's why there is so much joy in gossiping. When the gossip passes from one hand to another hand, it becomes richer. And when it passes back again, something will be added to it. By the evening, if you come to know the gossip that you started in the morning, you will be surprised. In the morning it was just a molehill, now it is a mountain. People are very creative, really creative and inventive.

Why are people so interested in gossiping about others, in finding fault with others, in looking into others' loopholes and defects? Why are people continuously trying to look through others' keyholes? The reason is, this helps to give them a better feeling about themselves. They become Peeping Toms, just to have a good feeling, "I am far better." There is a motivation. It is not just to help others – it is not, whatsoever they say, notwithstanding what they say. The basic reason is, "If others are very ugly, then I am beautiful." They are following Albert Einstein's theory of relativity.

I have heard: Mulla Nasruddin was staying in a hotel. A telegram had arrived from home and he was in a hurry to catch the train. He rushed. But when he reached downstairs and looked at his luggage the umbrella was missing. He had to go up to the room again and by the time he reached the fourteenth floor the room had already been given to somebody else – a newlywed couple.

Although he was in a hurry and he might miss the train if he lingered there a little longer, the temptation was great. So he looked through the keyhole to see what was happening.

A newlywed couple – they were also in a hurry, they had already waited too long; the marriage ceremony and the church and the guests and all that – somehow they had got rid of all of them and they were lying naked on the bed, talking sweet nothings. And the young man was saying to the woman, "You have such beautiful eyes. I have never seen such beautiful eyes! To whom do these eyes belong?"

And the woman said, "To you! To you, and only to you!"

And so on, the list went on. "These beautiful hands, these beautiful breasts," and this and that – this went on and on. And Mulla had completely forgotten about the train and the taxi waiting downstairs. But then suddenly he remembered his umbrella. When the list was about to be completed, he said, "Wait! When you come to the yellow umbrella, that belongs to me."

People are unconsciously doing many things. If they become conscious these things will drop. Atisha says: Don't ponder over others' defects, it is none of your business. Don't interfere in others' lives, it is none of your business.

But there are great moralists whose whole work is to see who is doing wrong. Their whole life is wasted; they are like police dogs sniffing here and there. Their whole life's work is to know who is doing wrong.

Atisha says: That is an ugly trait and a sheer wastage of time and energy. Not only is it a wastage but it strengthens and gratifies the ego. And an ego more gratified becomes more of a barrier.

And remember, it is not only a question of not discussing others' defects. Don't even be too much concerned about your own defects. Take note, be aware, and let the matter be settled then and there. There are a few other people who brag about their own defects....

It is suspected by psychologists that Saint Augustine's autobiography, his confessions, are not true. He bragged about his defects. He was not *that* bad a person. But man is really unbelievable. If you start bragging about your qualities, then too, you go to extremes. If you start bragging about sins, then too, you go to the extreme. But in both ways you do only one thing.

What Saint Augustine is doing is simple. By bragging about his defects and sins and all kinds of ugly things, he is preparing a context. Out of such a hell he rose and became a great saint. Now his saintliness looks far more significant than it would have looked if he had been simply a good person from the very beginning.

And the same is the case with Mahatma Gandhi in India. In his autobiography he simply exaggerates about his defects and goes on talking about them. It helps him in a very vicarious way. He was so low, he was in such a seventh hell, and from there he started rising and became a great mahatma, a great saint. The journey was very arduous. This is very ego-fulfilling.

Don't discuss others' defects, don't discuss your own defects. Take note, and that is that. Atisha says awareness is enough, nothing else is needed. If you are fully aware of anything, the fire of awareness burns it. There is no need for any other remedy.

Don't think about anything that concerns others.

And that's what you go on thinking. Ninety-nine percent of the things that you think about concern others. Drop them – drop them immediately!

Your life is short, and your life is slipping out of your fingers. Each moment you are less, each day you are less, and each day you are less alive and more dead! Each birthday is a death day; one more year is gone from your hands. Be a little more intelligent.

Do not think about anything that concerns others.
Train first against the defilement that is greatest.

Gurdjieff used to say to his disciples – the first thing, the very, very first thing, "Find out what your greatest characteristic is, your greatest undoing, your central characteristic of unconsciousness." Each one's is different.

Somebody is sex-obsessed. In a country like India, where for centuries sex has been repressed, that has become almost a universal characteristic; everybody is obsessed with sex. Somebody is obsessed with anger, and somebody else is obsessed with greed. You have to watch which is your basic obsession.

So first find the main characteristic upon which your whole ego edifice rests. And then be constantly aware of it, because it can exist only if you are unaware. It is burnt in the fire of awareness automatically.

And remember, remember always, that you are not to cultivate the opposite of it. Otherwise, what happens is a person becomes aware that "My obsession is anger, so what should I do? I should cultivate compassion." "My obsession is sex, so what should I do? I should practice brahmacharya, celibacy."

People move from one thing to the opposite. That is not the way of transformation. It is the same pendulum, moving from left to right, from right to left. And that's how your life has been moving for centuries; it is the same pendulum.

The pendulum has to be stopped in the middle. And that's the miracle of awareness. Just be aware that "This is my chief pitfall, this is the place where I stumble again and again, this is the root of my unconsciousness." Don't try to cultivate the opposite of it, but pour your whole awareness into it. Create a great bonfire of awareness, and it will be burned. And then the pendulum stops in the middle.

And with the stopping of the pendulum, time stops. You suddenly enter into the world of timelessness, deathlessness, eternity.

And the last sutra:

Abandon all hopes of results.

The ego is result-oriented, the mind always hankers for results. The mind is never interested in the act itself, its interest is in the result. "What am I going to gain out of it?" If the mind can manage to gain, without going through any action, then it will choose the shortcut.

That's why educated people become very cunning, because they are able to find shortcuts. If you earn money through a legal way, it may take your whole life. But you can earn money by smuggling, by gambling or by something else – by becoming a political leader, a prime minister, a president – then you have all the shortcuts available to you. The educated person becomes cunning. He does not become wise, he simply becomes clever. He becomes so cunning that he wants to have everything without doing anything for it.

The mind, the ego, are all result-oriented. The being is not result-oriented. And how can the non-being ever be result-oriented? It is not there at all in the first place.

Meditation happens only to those who are not result-oriented.

There is an ancient story:

A man was very much interested in self-knowledge, in self-realization. His whole search had been to find a master who could teach him meditation. He went from one master to another, but nothing was happening.

Years went by, he was tired, exhausted. Then someone told him, "If you really want to find a master you will have to go to the Himalayas. He lives in some unknown parts of the Himalayas; you will have to search for him. One thing is certain, he is there. Nobody knows exactly where, because whenever somebody comes to know of him he moves from that place and goes even deeper into the Himalayan ranges."

The man was getting old, but he gathered courage. For two years he had to work to earn money for the journey, then he made the journey. It is an old story. He had to ride on camels and horses and then go on foot, and then he reached the Himalayas. People said, "Yes, we have heard about the old man, very ancient he is, one cannot say how old – maybe three hundred years old, or even five hundred years old; nobody knows. He lives somewhere, but the location cannot be given to you. Nobody is aware of where exactly you will find him, but he is there. If you search hard you are bound to find him."

The man searched and searched and searched. For two years he was roaming in the Himalayas – tired, exhausted, dead exhausted, living only on wild fruits, leaves and grass. He had lost much weight. But he was intent that he had to find this man; even if it took his life, it would be worth it.

And can you imagine? One day he saw a small hut, a grass hut. He was so tired that he was not even able to walk, so he crawled. He reached the hut. There was no door; he looked in, there was nobody inside. And not only was there nobody inside, but there was every sign that for years there had been nobody inside.

You can think what would have happened to that man. He fell on the ground. Out of sheer tiredness he said, "I give up." He was lying there under the sun in the cool breeze of the Himalayas, and for the first time he started feeling so blissful, he had never tasted such bliss! Suddenly he started feeling full of light. Suddenly all thoughts disappeared, suddenly he was transported – and for no reason at all, because he had not done anything.

And then he became aware that somebody was leaning over him. He opened his eyes. A very ancient man was there. And the old man, smiling, said, "So you have come. Have you something to ask me?"

And the man said, "No."

And the old man laughed, a great belly laugh which was echoed by the valleys. And he said, "So now you know what meditation is?"

And the man said, "Yes."

What had happened? That assertion which came from his deepest core of being – "I give up" – in that very giving up, all goal-oriented mind efforts and endeavors disappeared. "I give up." In that very moment he was no more the same person. And bliss showered on him. He was silent, he was a nobody, and he touched the ultimate stratum of non-being. Then he knew what meditation is.

Meditation is a non-goal-oriented state of mind.

This last sutra is tremendously significant:

Abandon all hopes of results.

And then there is no need to go anywhere, God will come to you. Deep down say, "I give up." And silence descends, benediction showers.

Meditate over these sutras, they are meant only for meditators. Atisha is not a philosopher, he is a *siddha*, a buddha. What he is saying is not some speculation. These are clear-cut instructions given only to those who are ready to travel, to go on the pilgrimage into the unknown.

Chapter 10
Miracles Are Your Birthright

? **What is so attractive about missing?**

It has a tremendous attraction, because it is only through missing that the ego can survive. It is only through searching, seeking, desiring, that the ego exists; it exists in the tension between that which is and that which should be.

The moment the "should" disappears, the ego collapses. Hence all ethical systems, all moralities, are nourishments for the ego. The moral man is the most egoistic man in the world. And the mechanism is very simple. Seeking, searching, you live in the future, which is not; and the ego can exist only with that which is not, because it itself is not.

If you are in the moment, in the present, the ego has no possibility of surviving even for a single moment. The present is and the ego is not, like light is and darkness is not. Bring light in, and darkness disappears. Even to say that it disappears is not right, because it was not there in the first place, so how can it disappear? It was a pure absence. The absence of light, that's what darkness is.

The absence of the present, that's what the ego is. Not to be herenow, that's what the ego is – not to be herenow, to be somewhere else, seeking and searching for a faraway goal, looking at a faraway distant star. The farther away the goal, the bigger the ego.

Hence people who are not worldly have bigger egos than the so-called poor worldly people. Spiritual people have bigger egos, naturally; their goal is very far away, distant, beyond death, above the seven skies. God is their goal, or *moksha* or nirvana – goals which look almost impossible.

The possible goal can give you only a small ego, and that too only for the time being. Once the goal is achieved you will start feeling frustrated. That's what happens every day. You wanted a beautiful house, now you have got it, and suddenly frustration sets in. The ego needs a new goal to survive; now it starts fantasizing about a bigger palace.

You were seeking and searching for a woman; now you have got her, and the moment you have got her you are finished with her. It may take a few days for you to recognize the fact, that is another matter, but you are finished with her. Now your ego needs another woman so that the journey can continue.

The ego is constantly journeying from the present to some non-existential future. If you ask me, this is my definition of *samsara*, the world. The ego journeying from the present to the future is the world. And the ego not journeying at all, simply being herenow, is the end of samsara: you are in nirvana, samadhi, enlightenment. Hence enlightenment cannot be reduced to a goal. If you reduce it to a goal, you have missed the whole point.

All the buddhas of all the ages have been telling you a very simple fact: Be – don't try to become. Within these two words, be and becoming, your whole life is contained. Being is enlightenment, becoming is ignorance. But you have been taught to become this, to become that. And the mind is so cunning, and the ways of the ego are so subtle that it even turns God, nirvana, enlightenment, truth, into goals; it starts asking how to achieve them. They are not to be achieved, they cannot be achieved; the achieving mind is the only barrier. They are already here. You have to drop the achieving mind, you have to forget journeying from this point to that, you simply have to relax and be, and all is attained.

Lao Tzu calls it *wu-wei*, action without action. You have not moved a single inch, and you have arrived; this is wu-wei. You have not gone anywhere, you have not even thought of going anywhere, and you are already there. Suddenly the recognition comes, "I never lost the home, I only fell asleep and started dreaming about achieving."

Those who give you goals are your enemies. Those who tell you what to become and how to become it, are the poisoners. The real master simply says, "There is nothing to become. You are already that, it is already the case. Stop running after shadows. Sit silently and *be*. Sitting silently, doing nothing, the spring comes and the grass grows by itself".

? Because I am only a beginner in the search for reality, could you define for me the four terms: truth, God, spiritual, fact.

If you are only a beginner in the search, please come back, don't go ahead. Don't become more of an expert in the spiritual search, because the experts are the losers. Don't become more knowledgeable, become more innocent. Drop all that you know, forget all that you know. Remain wondering, but don't transform your wondering into questions, because once the wonder is changed into a question, sooner or later the question will bring knowledge. And knowledge is a false coin.

From the state of wonder, there are two paths. One is of questioning – the wrong path – it leads you into more and more knowledge. The other is not of questioning but enjoying. Enjoy the wonder, the wonder that life is, the wonder that existence is, the wonder of the sun and the sunlight and the trees bathed in its golden rays. Experience it. Don't put in a question mark, let it be as it is.

Remain ignorant if you ever want to become enlightened. Remain innocent, childlike, if you ever want a communion with existence and reality. Remain in wonder if you want the mysteries to open up for you. Mysteries never open up for those who go on questioning. Questioners sooner or later end up in a library. Questioners sooner or later end up with scriptures, because scriptures are full of answers.

And answers are dangerous, they kill your wonder. They are dangerous because they give you the feeling that you know, although you know not. They give you this misconception about yourself that now questions have been solved. "I know what The Bible says, I know what the Koran says, I know what the Gita says. I have arrived." You will become a parrot; you will repeat things but you will not know anything. This is not the way to know – knowledge is not the way to know.

Then what is the way to know? Wonder. Let your heart dance with wonder. Be full of wonder: throb with it, breathe it in, breathe it out. Why be in such a hurry for the answer? Can't you allow a mystery to remain a mystery? I know there is a great temptation not to allow it to remain a mystery, to reduce it to knowledge. Why is this temptation there? – because only if you are full of knowledge will you be in control.

Mystery will control you, knowledge will make you the controller. Mystery will possess you. You cannot possess the mysterious; it is so vast and your hands are so small. It is so infinite, you cannot possess it, you will have to be possessed by it – and that is the fear. Knowledge you can possess, it is so trivial; knowledge you can control.

This temptation of the mind to reduce every wonder, every mystery, to a question, is basically fear-oriented. We are afraid, afraid of the tremendousness of life, of this incredible existence. We are afraid. Out of fear we create some small knowledge around ourselves as a protection, as an armor, as a defense.

It is only cowards who reduce the tremendously valuable capacity of wondering to questions. The really brave, the courageous person, leaves it as it is. Rather than changing it into a question, he jumps into the mystery. Rather than trying to control it, he allows the mystery to possess him.

And the joy of being possessed, and the benediction of being possessed, is invaluable. You cannot imagine what it is, you have never dreamt about it – because to be possessed by the mystery is to be possessed by God.

You say: "Because I am only a beginner...."

You are fortunate that you are only a beginner. There are many who have become experts; they will have to come back home, and it is going to be a long, long arduous journey. They have accumulated so much knowledge that dropping it is going to be a difficult task. If you are really a beginner, be happy. You have not gone far away, you are just beginning. Come back.

There is no need to define these beautiful words, because they are not only words. You want me to define truth. Do you know, has anybody ever defined truth? Is it definable at all? What is a definition? A definition means a tautology – you put the same words in a different way. What are your definitions, in fact? Synonyms.

Just look at your definitions and you will find you have been paraphrasing. But how can paraphrasing define anything? The second thing that you think is the definition, in its own turn needs another definition. Definitions are either tautologies or just stupid.

For example, ask what the mind is and the knowers, the knowledgeable, say, "It is not matter." And then ask them, "What is matter?" And they say, "It is not mind." What kind of defining is going on? Mind is not matter; this becomes a definition. Matter is not mind; this becomes a definition. Both remain indefinable; you have not defined anything, you have simply shifted the problem from one place to another.

You can befool only fools.

And the truth means the whole, all that is, the total. All that is – how can you define it? It is unbounded, infinite. Definition means drawing a line around it, locating it, saying, "This is it." But there is no way to define truth, because there is no way to draw a line around it. It is infinite, it is eternal, it has no beginning, no end.

People who have tried to define truth say, "Truth is that which is." But that is tautology. The question remains the same, the mystery remains unsolved. "Truth is that which is" – what have you added? Have you made it a little simpler than before? You can call it "that which is" or you can call it truth, or you can call it God, but you are simply using names, words, labels, for something which is basically indefinable.

Truth cannot be defined, although it can certainly be experienced. But experience is not a definition. A definition is made by the mind, experience comes through participating. If somebody asks, "What is a dance?" how can you define it? But you can dance and you can know the inner feel of it.

God is the ultimate dance. You will have to learn ecstatic dancing to experience God. God is the dance where the dancer disappears. Then the experience arrives, showers on you, and you *know*. But that knowing is not knowledge, that knowing is wisdom.

Truth cannot be defined. Lao Tzu says if you define it you have already made it untrue. He lived a long life; it must have been really long because the story is that for eighty-two years he lived in his mother's womb, so when he was born he was already eighty-two years old. Then if he lived for at least eighty-two more years, he must have lived very long. But he never wrote a single word.

His whole life his disciples were again and again asking, requesting, "Write something. You are getting older and older and older, and one day you will have to leave the body. Leave your last testament." But he would laugh and not say a thing, or he would keep silent as if he had not heard.

Then when he became very old, he started moving towards the Himalayas. He said to his disciples, "Now I am going to the Himalayas, never to return again. My whole life I have been a wanderer, and the Himalayas are the best place to die. I lived beautifully, I lived the most ecstatic life possible. I would also like to die most ecstatically, most aesthetically. I would like to die in the silence of the Himalayas, in those beautiful mountains."

When he was leaving the border of China, the guard at the border prevented him. He said, "I won't allow you to leave the country unless you write something." He must have been a very perceptive man, the guard. The world is in his debt for one of the greatest things that has ever been written – the Tao Te Ching. There is no other book comparable to it.

Finding no way to avoid it, because the guard wouldn't allow him to go and he wanted to leave the country as fast, as quickly, as possible – death was coming closer and he wanted to die in the silence of the Himalayas – compelled to write, he sat in the guard's room for three days and completed the book, Tao Te Ching.

But the first thing that he wrote was, "Tao cannot be said. Once said, it is no more Tao."

You can understand what he means. He is saying that if you read the first statement, there is no need to go any further. "Truth cannot be said. Once said, it is no more true" – this is his declaration. Now, if you understand, the book is finished. What can be said about the truth? Yes, it can be lived, experienced. You can love, live, be – but definition is not possible. If you want definitions you will have to go to a university. Professors define what truth is, and each professor of philosophy defines it in his own way, and there are millions of definitions, and all are false. No definition can ever be true.

What to say about truth – even the small experiences of life cannot be defined. What is love? Or what is the taste of sugar on your tongue? How to define it? What is beauty when you see it in a lotus flower?

One of the greatest modern philosophers, G.E. Moore, has written a book, *Principia Ethica*, in which he tries to define what good is. Of course, that is the first question in the world of ethics: what is good? And for two hundred or two hundred and fifty pages, he tries hard this way and that, and cannot define it. And he was one of the most perceptive people this century has produced.

Defeated, tired, exhausted, in the end he says good is indefinable. It is as indefinable as the color yellow. If somebody asks, "What is yellow?" – there is a marigold flower, and somebody asks, "You call it yellow? What is yellow?" – how are you going to define it? What more can you say? Yellow is yellow, good is good, beauty is beauty. But these are tautologies; you are not defining anything, you are simply repeating words.

What is truth? There is no way to define it.

I am not teaching philosophy to you, I am sharing my truth with you. Don't ask for definitions. If you have the courage, then take a plunge into the experience that is made available here: take a jump into meditation, and you will know. And still, even when you know, you will not be able to define it.

And you ask, "What is God?"

That is another name for truth – the lover's name. "Truth" is the name given by the meditator to totality. "God" is the name given to totality, to truth, by a lover, by a devotee. Both arrows point to the same phenomenon, but the lover can't think in terms of abstract words. "Truth" is very abstract: you cannot hug truth, can you? You cannot kiss truth – or can you? You cannot say hello to truth, you cannot hold hands with truth. "Truth" is impersonal; it is the word given by the meditator who does not want to bring any personality into it.

"God" is the name given out of love, out of a personal relationship with existence. The lover wants to say "Thou," the lover wants to say "Hi," the lover wants to have a communion, a dialogue. It is the same totality, but the lover makes it personal. Then truth becomes God.

And you ask, "What is spiritual?"

To be in relationship with truth or God is to be spiritual. Remember, to be in relationship – not to talk about spirituality, not to follow a certain creed, dogma, church, but to be in direct immediate relationship with existence is spirituality. To be in tune with the whole, to feel the harmony and the joy and the sheer celebration of being here, that is spirituality. It has nothing to do with going to the church or the temple, it has nothing to do with reciting the Koran or The Bible or the Gita. It has nothing to do with any kind of worship ritual, it has something to do with communion – communion with the trees, communion with the stars, communion with the rivers, communion with all that is. It is communion with this multidimensional expression of God, it is having a dialogue with the whole. The quality of mad love is needed, then you are spiritual. Spirituality is not a head trip; it is a heart-to-heart dialogue, and ultimately a being-to-being dialogue.

And fourth, you ask, "What is a fact?"

A fact is the truth seen with unawareness, seen with blindness, seen with closed eyes, seen unintelligently, unmeditatively. Then the truth becomes a fact.

For example, you come across a buddha. If you look at him unconsciously he is just a fact, a historical fact; he is born on a certain day and is going to die on a certain day. He is the body that you can see with your eyes; he is a certain person, a personality. History can take note of him, you can have a picture of him.

But if you look, not with unconsciousness but with great consciousness, with awareness, with great light, silence, then the fact is no longer there – there is truth. Then Buddha is not somebody who is born on a certain date, he is somebody who is never born and is never going to die. Then Buddha is not the body, the body is just an abode. Then Buddha is not the confined being that appears to you, he represents the total, the whole. Then Buddha is a ray of the infinite, a gift of the beyond to the earth. Then suddenly the fact has disappeared; now there is truth.

But history can take no note of truth; history consists of facts. In India we have two different systems. One we call history; history takes note of the facts. Another we call *purana*, mythology; it takes note of the truth. We have not written histories about Buddha, Mahavira or Krishna, no. That would have been dragging something immensely beautiful into the muddy unconsciousness of humanity. We have not written histories about these people, we have written myths. What is a myth? A myth is a parable, a parable that only points to the moon but says nothing about it – a finger pointing to the moon, an indication, an arrow, saying nothing.

Go to a Jaina temple and you will be surprised. You will find twenty-four statues of twenty-four great enlightened masters, the twenty-four *tirthankaras*. And the most striking thing will be this, that they all look absolutely alike. This is impossible – there are not even two persons absolutely alike in the world, not even twins are absolutely alike. So how was it possible – and the time span is big, thousands of years – for twenty-four tirthankaras to be exactly alike?

This is not history. These statues don't depict the real persons, no, not at all. They are not pictorial representations. Then what are they? They represent something of the inner, they represent something of meditativeness, they represent something of inner stillness, something of the being. Those twenty-four statues are just representations, visible representations, of something which is invisible.

Sitting before these statues, if you silently go on watching, you will be surprised. Something starts happening inside you. The statue is a form of objective art; it synchronizes with the inner form of your being. The posture of the statue synchronizes with your posture. If you sit in the same posture – with erect spine, half-opened eyes, just looking at the tip of your nose, doing nothing, as if you are also a marble statue, all white, within and without – then you will know that you are not facing ordinary statues, you are confronting great symbols. This is mythology.

Mythology is bound to be poetic, because only poetry can give a few glimpses of the unknown.

It is said that wherever Buddha moved, trees would start blooming out of season. Now, this is poetry, pure poetry; it did not happen as a fact. But this shows something; there is no other way to say it. It says whenever Buddha is contacted, even trees start blooming out of season – so what to say about man?

It is said that wherever Mohammed would move in the desert's hot sun, and there was fire everywhere, a small cloud, a white cloud, would go on moving above him just to give him shade like an umbrella. This is poetry, beautiful, but it is not a historical fact. A man like Mohammed is protected by existence, a man like Mohammed is in every way cared for by existence. One who has surrendered to existence is bound to be cared for by existence. One who has trusted totally, how can existence be uncaring about him? To say this, there is this metaphor of the cloud just hanging over his head wherever he would go.

Jesus dies on the cross, and then after three days is resurrected. This is poetry, not history. This is not fact, this is truth. It simply says that those who die in God and for God attain to eternal life. Those who are ready to die for God are resurrected on another plane of being; they lose the physical body but they gain the luminous body. They are no more part of the earth but they become part of the sky; they disappear from time but they appear in eternity.

But all the religions have been trying to prove that these are facts. And in trying to prove that these are facts they have simply proved that they are fools. These are not facts, these are symbolic truths.

Whatsoever you see around you is a fact. You see a tree, a green tree, full of sap and flowers – it is a fact. But if you meditate and one day suddenly your eyes open, open to the real, and the tree is no more just a tree – the green of it is nothing but God green in it, and the sap running through it is no more a physical phenomenon but something spiritual – if one day you can see the *being* of the tree, the God of the tree, that the tree is only a manifestation of the divine, you have seen the truth.

Truth needs meditative eyes. If you don't have meditative eyes, then the whole of life is just dull dead facts, unrelated to each other, accidental, meaningless, a jumble, just a chance phenomenon. If you see the truth, everything falls into line, everything falls together in a harmony, everything starts having significance.

Remember always, significance is the shadow of truth. And those who live only in facts live an utterly meaningless life.

You have said that enlightenment is always total, never partial. Still you compare your state of no-mind with an orchestra while that of Krishnamurti is compared with that of a single flute player. Has not the enlightened one access to all knowledge? Why that tunnel vision of Krishnamurti?

Enlightenment is always total. If it is an orchestra it is a total orchestra, if it is only a solo flute then it is an absolutely total solo flute. Existence is always total, so is enlightenment always total. The small flower is as total as the sun. Totality is a totally different phenomenon than quantity; it is concerned with quality.

Krishnamurti's solo flute is as total as my orchestra, my orchestra is not more total. Totality cannot be more or less. You think in terms of quantity, that's why the question has arisen. I am talking about quality. Each act of the enlightened person is total. Whether he is drinking tea or painting a great painting, playing music or just sitting silently doing nothing, each act is total. Krishnamurti is a solo flute player – and a few solo flute players are needed as much as orchestras are needed. They enhance the beauty of existence, they make life richer.

Drop your mind that goes on comparing in terms of quantity. Raise your level of consciousness a little higher and start thinking of quality, and then there is no problem.

Krishnamurti is doing what he can do best. I would not like him to become an orchestra, no. That would impoverish the world. He should go on doing what he is doing; that gives color to life, variety.

I cannot become a solo flute player – not that it is not beautiful, but it is simply not my way.

I enjoy being an orchestra. I would like Atisha to play with me, and Bahauddin and Kabir and Nanak and Lao Tzu and Zarathustra and many, many more. I would like to play with them all and become part of this orchestra.

This is *my* way. There is nothing higher or lower. Once you are enlightened, there is nothing higher or lower; there cannot be. If a lotus flower becomes enlightened it will be a lotus flower. If a rose becomes enlightened it will be a rose. They both have the same quality of being enlightened, but the rose will remain a rose and the lotus will remain a lotus.

You ask me, "You have said that enlightenment is always total, never partial."

Yes, it is never partial. And Krishnamurti is not a partial flute player. He is a total flute player; he is totally in his act, utterly in his act. He says he is fortunate that he has not read the Vedas, The Bible, the Koran, the Upanishads, Tao Te Ching. Why? – because they might have disturbed him, might have left a few traces behind, might have become part of his being. He wants to be simply himself, in utter purity.

My approach is totally different. I would like to have as big a company of enlightened people with me as possible. It is a difficult company, because they are all such different people; to become a host to all of them is troublesome. But I enjoy it. The more troublesome it is, the more I enjoy it. It is a beautiful challenge. You cannot understand how difficult it is to have Buddha, Mahavira, Mohammed and Moses staying together with you. Mahavira stands naked, and Buddha does not like it at all. And because Buddha is not naked, Mahavira is not happy either. To have all these people stay with you is a great challenge.

Krishnamurti lives alone. It has its own challenge, but that is not my choice. I am not saying that my choice has to be his choice, I am not saying that he has to do what I am doing. I am perfectly happy doing my thing, and I am perfectly happy that he is doing his thing.

Many people have asked me questions saying that I have spoken on dead masters, so many, but why don't I sometimes speak on a living master?

Let Krishnamurti die, then I will speak on him. There is a reason for it. I know how difficult it is even to keep so many dead masters together, but you can manage with dead masters – if I tell Mahavira to stand in this corner, he *has* to stand in this corner. But a living master won't listen; he will start meddling, he will start arguing with others. And sometimes I need a little sleep too.

You say, "Has not the enlightened one access to all knowledge?"

Enlightenment has nothing to do with knowledge at all. The enlightened one has no access to knowledge. Yes, he has every access to innocence – and Krishnamurti playing his flute is as innocent as I am with my orchestra. It is not a question of knowledge, it is a question of wisdom. Wisdom is a totally different phenomenon – wisdom is innocence. You can even call it ignorance, that will do, but please don't call it knowledge. It is closer to ignorance than to knowledge.

Socrates is reported to have said in his last days, "I know only one thing, that I know nothing." This is enlightenment, knowing only one thing, "I know nothing." The moment all knowledge disappears, the ego disappears, the personality disappears, then the separation between you and existence disappears. Again you are clean, pure, one with the whole.

And you also ask, "Why that tunnel vision of Krishnamurti?"

That you have to ask Krishnamurti, not me. That is not my business. He loves it, that's how he has grown. For centuries, for many, many lives, he has been moving towards a tunnel vision. And the tunnel vision has its own beauties, because whatsoever you see, you see very clearly because your eyes are focused.

Hence the clarity of Krishnamurti. Nobody has ever been so clear, so crystal clear. Nobody has ever been so logical, so rational; nobody has ever been so analytical. His profundity in going into things and their details is simply unbelievable. But that is part of his tunnel vision. You cannot have everything, remember. If you want clarity you will need tunnel vision; you will have to become more and more focused on less and less.

That's how they define science: "Knowing more and more about less and less." And if science ever succeeds in its ultimate goal, then we will have to say, "Knowing everything about nothing." That can be the only logical conclusion of knowing more and more about less and less. Where will it lead? It will lead to a point where you know all about nothing.

Science is a tunnel vision. Krishnamurti is a scientific individuality, very scientific. Hence his appeal for all those who love analysis, dissection, who love going into minute details. He is just the opposite of Lao Tzu. Lao Tzu says, "Everybody seems to be so clear; only I am confused."

A man of the quality of Lao Tzu, a man of ultimate enlightenment, saying this: "Everybody seems to be so clear about everything, except me. I am so confused, I am so muddle-headed, that I don't know what is what. Everybody walks with such certainty, and I hesitate at each step. Everybody goes so straight, without looking sideways. And I walk like a man in winter crossing a cold, icy cold stream."

Lao Tzu is just the opposite of J. Krishnamurti. He has no tunnel vision. His vision is so wide, so spread out, it cannot be very clear. It is bound to be hazy, misty, but that too has its own beauty. Krishnamurti's statements have logic. Lao Tzu's statements have poetry.

My vision is even wider than Lao Tzu's. I include Lao Tzu and many more. Obviously Lao Tzu could not have included me. Twenty-five centuries have passed; in those twenty-five centuries great enlightened people have happened on the earth. I claim the whole heritage, as nobody has ever claimed before.

Lao Tzu had never heard about Krishna, Lao Tzu had never heard about Patanjali. Patanjali had never heard about Lao Tzu or Chuang Tzu or Lieh Tzu. Buddha had no awareness of Zarathustra or Moses.

Now the world has become a small village, a global village, and the whole history of humanity is ours. I am in a totally different situation. I know everything about Lao Tzu, Chuang Tzu, Lieh Tzu, Confucius, Mencius, Milarepa, Marpa, Tilopa, Naropa, Bodhidharma, Mahakashyap, Sariputra, Mahavira, Adinatha, Moses, Abraham, Jesus, Francis, Kabir, Nanak, Dadu, Meera, Rabiya – all. The whole world is available to me.

I see the whole sky, all the stars, all the constellations; my vision is bound to be the most poetic. But the deeper you go into poetry, the less and less logical it becomes. The deeper you go into poetry, it becomes more and more love-like and less and less like logic. At the very rock bottom of poetry, all clarity disappears. Nothing is clear, but everything is beautiful, everything is mysterious. Nothing is clear but everything is simply fantastic.

Krishnamurti has his way, and I am happy that he is in the world. He is at the other extreme. If he is gone, I will miss him more than anybody else in the world.

But I can understand your question. This is not the only question; you have asked many more about the same thing. It seems it has hurt you deeply that I criticized Krishnamurti. You don't understand me yet. This is my way of paying respects to him. This is my way of declaring that there exists another enlightened person in the world.

If my orchestra does not suit you, then the only alternative possible is the solo flute-playing of J. Krishnamurti. There is no other, no third person who can be of any help to you. Either Krishnamurti or me – there is no other alternative. Right now there is no other alternative.

Krishnamurti is *bound* to criticize me; I can understand it. His standpoint is simple and clear, my standpoint is a little more unclear. Sometimes I will appreciate him tremendously, because I would like him to also become part of my orchestra. And sometimes I will criticize him, because my own liking is not for solo flutes.

I feel you share a lot of esoteric points with people who have no way of validating what you are saying. What is the importance of hearing about the sixth or the sixteenth Jaina Tirthankara, or other esoteric information, to the person in Oshkosh or Brooklyn going to work on the crowded bus or subway every day? What is the relevance of hearing that Jesus was once in India or that a Rosicrucian sect of spirits working from the other side possessed Hitler?

Fools are everywhere – as much in Oshkosh and Brooklyn as they are in Bombay and Pune. No country has any claim on fools. And fools are always searching for something esoteric – only nonsense appeals to them. And sometimes I talk nonsense, because I am not here only to help those who are not fools. I am also throwing my net wider and wider; some fools have to be caught by me too. They are good people!

Now just look, from where have you come? How were you caught? Those stupid theories about the sixth or sixteenth tirthankaras, or the Rosicrucian secret masters, Koothumi, K.H., directing Adolf Hitler and the whole Nazi movement....

There is a deep urge in man to know things which are worthless, to know things which make you feel special – because only *you* know those things and nobody else does. Man wants to be special, and nothing makes you more special than so-called esoteric knowledge. That is why esoteric knowledge remains important. All kinds of rubbish go on in the name of esoteric knowledge – that the earth is hollow, that inside the earth there are great civilizations. And there are people who still believe in it, and in many more such stories.

Man lives such a dull and drab life that he wants some sensation. Those who are a little wiser, they read scientific fiction or detective stories. Those who are not so wise, they read spiritual fiction.

And these things were said by me when I was surrounded by a certain group of fools. They were not interested in anything else. And I have to respond to you; as you grow, my responses will be higher and higher. The day you have understood the whole stupidity of the human mind I will not need to talk to you; just sitting silently will be more than enough.

These things were told by me to a certain group of people who were only interested in those things. It would have been absolutely pointless to talk about anything else with those people. Now that they have almost disappeared, and now that a totally different quality has come here, I can go more into the world of the truth. But still I have to use words, and words distort.

Only silence communicates the truth as it is. Please get ready as soon as possible, so that we can just be together, merging into each other's energies, being lost in each other. And miracles *are* possible. What I cannot say in years can be communicated in a single moment of silence, and what can never be said can transpire when between me and you there is no barrier of thought – when my silence and your silence are just present to each other, mirroring each other just as two mirrors mirror each other.

My real work has not yet started. I am just preparing the ground, preparing the people who will be able to take part in the real work. This is just the preliminary stage. So don't waste time, get ready for great things, great things are waiting for you. But the only readiness from your side will be a tremendous silence – and then there will be no need to talk at all.

It is really a torture for me to talk to you. You cannot imagine how difficult it is for me to force myself to talk to you continuously. It is just like walking on a tightrope. Words have disappeared in me; I have to bring them back again and again. It is arduous, tiring. But it cannot be stopped unless you say, "I give up."

The day you are able to say, "Now I am ready to be silent. I don't hope for anything, I am ready to renounce hoping. I am ready to renounce all ideas of spirituality, God, truth, nirvana, enlightenment, I would just like to enjoy being with you, this moment, here, now" – then miracles will start happening.

Yes, out of season you are going to bloom.

And remember, you are entitled to all those miracles, they are your birthright.

Enough for today.

Chapter 11
Expelled from the World

? I don't understand. You said that longing is in and of itself divine. Yet you have
often said that all desiring, even for God, is mundane and not spiritual.

Longing in its purity is divine, longing when it longs for nothing is divine. The moment an object of the longing arises, it becomes mundane. Longing is a pure fire that purifies, longing is a smokeless fire, a smokeless flame. But the moment it becomes attached to any object whatsoever – worldly, otherworldly; money, meditation, God, nirvana, it doesn't matter – any object, and the longing is no more pure, it is contaminated by the object. Then the object becomes more important than the longing itself. Then the longing is only a means, it is no more the end in itself.

And the whole effort of sannyas is to help you drop all objects of longing. Longing will not disappear – in fact, the more objects are dropped, the more intense, the more total the longing will become, because the energy involved in the objects will be released. And there comes a moment when one is simply thirsty – not thirsty for something, but just simply thirsty. Hungry – not hungry for something, just a pure fire of longing. And that very pure fire consumes you, reduces you to ashes. And out of that, something new is born.

This is the meaning of the parable of the phoenix, this is the significance of the parable of the phoenix. The bird dies out of a fire that arises within his own being, is consumed by it, disappears into it, and then is resurrected.

And this is the meaning of Jesus' resurrection too, his dying on the cross and being reborn. Jesus says again and again, "Unless ye are born again, ye will not be able to enter into my kingdom of God."

But how to be born again unless you die first? An ultimate death has to precede it before the ultimate birth can happen.

I can understand your confusion – because on the one hand I say, "Longing is in and of itself divine…." I repeat it again, it is so. And there is no contradiction when I say that all desiring, even for God, is mundane and not spiritual. Longing *is* divine. Long for, and you have fallen. This is the original fall. You have lost the purity, the virginity of longing; it has become muddy, it has fallen on the earth, its wings are cut.

There is no contradiction in these two statements. Whenever you find a contradiction in my statements make it a point to meditate over them, because essentially there cannot be a contradiction. Apparently there may be, but now you have to start doing some homework too.

Meditate, look at all the possible aspects, all the possible meanings, and you will be surprised. When you are able to see the consistency, the intrinsic consistency, when you are able to go beyond the contradiction, it will be a moment of great insight. It will fill you with light, it will make you delighted, because it is a discovery, and each discovery helps growth.

Often I have the feeling that I am not doing something I ought to be doing, or
? **doing something I should not be doing; that something has to change and fast –**
a schooldays' worry that I am not going to make the grade, that I might be expelled.

This is how we all have been brought up. Our whole education – in the family, in the society, in the school, in the college, in the university – creates tension in us. And the fundamental tension is that you are not doing that which you ought to do.

Then it persists your whole life; it follows you like a nightmare, it goes on haunting you. It will never leave you at rest, it will never allow you to relax. If you relax, it will say, "What are you doing? You are not supposed to relax; you should be doing something." If you are doing something it will say, "What are you doing? You need some rest, it is a must, otherwise you will drive yourself crazy – you are already on the verge."

If you do something good, it will say, "You are a fool. Doing good is not going to pay, people will cheat you." If you do something bad it will say, "What are you doing? You are preparing the way to go to hell, you will have to suffer for it." It will never leave you at rest; whatsoever you do, it will be there condemning you.

This condemner has been implanted in you. This is the greatest calamity that has happened to humanity. And unless we get rid of this condemner inside us we cannot be truly human, we cannot be truly joyous and we cannot participate in the celebration that existence is.

And now nobody can drop it except you. And this is not only your problem, this is the problem of almost every human being. Whatsoever country you are born in, whatsoever religion you belong to, it doesn't matter – Catholic, communist, Hindu, Mohammedan, Jaina, Buddhist, it does not matter to what kind of ideology you belong, the essential is the same. The essential is to create a split in you, so one part always condemns the other part. If you follow the first part then the second part starts condemning you. You are in an inner conflict, a civil war.

This civil war has to be dropped, otherwise you will miss the whole beauty, the benediction of life. You will never be able to laugh to your heart's content, you will never be able to love, you will never be able to be total in anything. And it is only out of totality that one blooms, that the spring comes, and your life starts having color and music and poetry.

It is only out of totality that suddenly you feel the presence of God all around you. But the irony is that the split has been created by your so-called saints, priests and churches. In fact the priest has been the greatest enemy of God on the earth.

We have to get rid of all the priests; they are the root cause of human pathology. They have made everybody ill at ease, they have caused an epidemic of neurosis. And the neurosis has become so prevalent that we take it for granted. We think that this is all life is about, we think this is what life is – a suffering, a long, long, delayed suffering; a painful, agonizing existence; an autobiography of much ado about nothing.

And if we look at our so-called life, it seems so, because there is never a single flower, never a single song in the heart, never a ray of divine delight.

It is not surprising that intelligent people all over the world are asking what the meaning of life is. "Why should we go on living? Why are we so cowardly as to go on living? Why can't we gather a little courage and put a stop to all this nonsense? Why can't we commit suicide?"

Never before in the world were there so many people thinking that life is so utterly meaningless. Why has this happened in this age? It has nothing to do with this age. For centuries, for at least five thousand years, the priests have been doing the harm. Now it has reached to the ultimate peak.

It is not our work, we are victims. We are the victims of history. If man becomes a little more conscious, the first thing to be done is to burn all the history books. Forget the past, it was nightmarish. Start anew from ABC, as if Adam is born again. Start as if we are again in the garden of Eden, innocent, uncontaminated, unpolluted by mean priests.

The priests have been very mean, because they discovered something tremendously significant for themselves: divide a man, split a man, make him basically schizophrenic and you always remain in power. A divided man is a weak man. An undivided man, an individual, has strength – strength to accept any adventure, any challenge.

A man was looking for a good church to attend and found a small one in which the congregation was reading with the minister. They were saying, "We have left undone those things we ought to have done and we have done those things which we ought not to have done."

The man dropped into a seat and sighed with relief as he said to himself, "Thank goodness, I've found my crowd at last."

Go to any church and you will find your crowd, you will find replicas of your being. Maybe the language is a little bit different, the ritual a little bit different, but the fundamentals are the same. The fundamental is: man has to be reduced to a civil war.

The first day when you recognize this, what the priests have done to you, is a day of great insight. And the first day when you drop all this nonsense is the day of the beginning of liberation.

Do what your nature wants to do, do what your intrinsic qualities hanker to do. Don't listen to the scriptures, listen to your own heart; that is the only scripture I prescribe. Yes, listen very attentively, very consciously, and you will never be wrong. And listening to your own heart you will never be divided. Listening to your own heart you will start moving in the right direction, without ever thinking of what is right and what is wrong.

So the whole art for the new humanity will consist in the secret of listening to the heart consciously, alertly, attentively. And follow it through any means, and go wherever it takes you. Yes, sometimes it will take you into dangers – but then remember, those dangers are needed to make you ripe. And sometimes it will take you astray – but remember again, those goings astray are part of growth. Many times you will fall. Rise up again, because this is how one gathers strength – by falling and rising again. This is how one becomes integrated.

But don't follow rules imposed from the outside. No imposed rule can ever be right, because rules are invented by people who want to rule you. Yes, sometimes there have been great enlightened people in the world too – a Buddha, a Jesus, a Krishna, a Mohammed. They have not given rules to the world, they have given their love. But sooner or later the disciples gather together and start making codes of conduct. Once the master is gone, once the light is gone and they are in deep darkness, they start groping for certain rules to follow, because now the light in which they could have seen is no more there. Now they will have to depend on rules.

What Jesus did was his own heart's whispering, and what Christians go on doing is not their own hearts' whispering. They are imitators – and the moment you imitate, you insult your humanity, you insult your God.

Never be an imitator, be always original. Don't become a carbon copy. But that's what is happening all over the world – carbon copies and carbon copies.

Life is really a dance if you are an original – and you are *meant* to be an original. And no two men are alike, so my way of life can never become your way of life.

Imbibe the spirit, imbibe the silence of the master, learn his grace. Drink as much out of his being as possible, but don't imitate him. Imbibing his spirit, drinking his love, receiving his compassion, you will be able to listen to your own heart's whisperings. And they *are* whisperings. The heart speaks in a very still, small voice; it does not shout.

Listen to the master's silence so one day you can listen to your own innermost core. And then this problem will never arise: "I am doing something that I should not do, and I am not doing something that I should do." This problem arises only because you are being dominated by outer rules; you are imitators.

What is right for a Buddha is not right for you. Just look how different Krishna is from Buddha. If Krishna had followed Buddha we would have missed one of the most beautiful men of this earth. Or if Buddha had followed Krishna he would have been just a poor specimen. Just think of Buddha playing on the flute; he would have disturbed many people's sleep, he was not a flute player. Just think of Buddha dancing; it looks so ridiculous, just absurd.

But the same is the case with Krishna. Sitting underneath a tree with no flute, with no crown of peacock feathers, with no beautiful clothes, just sitting like a beggar under a tree with closed eyes, nobody dancing around him, nothing of the dance, nothing of the song, and Krishna looks so poor, so impoverished.

A Buddha is a Buddha, a Krishna is a Krishna, and you are you. And you are not in any way less than anybody else. Respect yourself, respect your own inner voice and follow it.

And remember, I am not guaranteeing you that it will always lead you to the right. Many times it will take you to the wrong, because to come to the right door one has to knock first on many wrong doors. That's how it is. If you suddenly stumble upon the right door, you will not be able to recognize that it is right.

There are many people who come here directly, they have never been to anybody else. It is almost impossible to have any contact with them. They cannot understand what is happening here, they have no background, they have no context for it. They have not learned what is wrong, so how can they understand what is right?

But when people come here, and they have lived with many, many so-called masters and lived with many, many seekers and been part of many schools, when they come here something immediately is lit in their hearts. They have seen so much that now they can recognize what is true.

So remember, in the ultimate reckoning no effort is ever wasted, all efforts contribute to the ultimate climax of your growth. So don't be hesitant, don't be worried too much about going wrong. That is one of the problems; people have been taught never to do anything wrong, and then they become so hesitant, so fearful, so frightened of doing wrong, that they become stuck. They cannot move, something wrong may happen. So they become like rocks, they lose all movement.

I teach you: Commit as many mistakes as possible, remembering only one thing: don't commit the same mistake again. And you will be growing. It is part of your freedom to go astray, it is part of your dignity to go even against God. And it is sometimes beautiful to go even against God. This is how you will start having a spine; otherwise there are millions of people, spineless.

Because I say such things, many people are angered. Just the other day a journalist came here. He had come to cover what is happening here in this ashram, and he wanted to have both stories – the people who are for it, and the people who are against it. So he went around the town. He talked to police officers, he went to see the mayor of Pune. And what the mayor said was really beautiful, I loved it.

He said, "This man is so dangerous that he should be expelled from Pune – not only from Pune but from India, not only from India but from the world!"

I loved it. And I started thinking about it. Where will they expel me from the world? That's a really fantastic idea! If they can manage it, I am willing to go.

Why is there so much anger? The anger has a reason in it, it has a rationale behind it. The rationale is that I am trying to give you a totally new vision of religious life – and if the new vision succeeds, then all the old visions will have to die.

Forget all about what you have been told, "This is right and this is wrong." Life is not so fixed. The thing that is right today may be wrong tomorrow, the thing that is wrong this moment may be right the next moment. Life cannot be pigeonholed; you cannot label it so easily, "This is right and this is wrong." Life is not a chemist's shop where every bottle is labeled and you know what is what. Life is a mystery; one moment something fits and then it is right. Another moment, so much water has gone down the Ganges that it no longer fits and it is wrong.

What is my definition of right? That which is harmonious with existence is right, and that which is disharmonious with existence is wrong. You will have to be very alert each moment, because it has to be decided each moment afresh. You cannot depend on ready-made answers for what is right and what is wrong. Only stupid people depend on ready-made answers, because then they need not be intelligent. There is no need; you already know what is right and what is wrong, you can cram the list, the list is not very big.

The Jews have ten commandments, so simple, you know what is right and what is wrong. But life goes on changing continuously. If Moses comes back, I don't think he will give you the same ten commandments – he cannot. After three thousand years, how can he give you the same commandments? He will have to invent something new.

But my own understanding is this, that whenever commandments are given they create difficulties for people, because by the time they are given they are already out of date. Life moves so fast; it is a dynamism, it is not static. It is not a stagnant pool, it is a Ganges, it goes on flowing. It is never the same for two consecutive moments. So one thing may be right this moment, and may not be right the next.

Then what to do? The only possible thing is to make people so aware that they themselves can decide how to respond to a changing life.

An old Zen story: There were two temples, rivals. Both the masters – they must have been so-called masters, must have really been priests – were so much against each other that they told their followers never to look at the other temple.

Each of the priests had a boy to serve him, to go and fetch things for him, to go on errands. The priest of the first temple told his boy servant, "Never talk to the other boy. Those people are dangerous."

But boys are boys. One day they met on the road, and the boy from the first temple asked the other, "Where are you going?"

The other said, "Wherever the wind takes me." He must have been listening to great Zen things in the temple; he said, "Wherever the wind takes me." A great statement, pure Tao.

But the first boy was very much embarrassed, offended, and he could not find how to answer him. Frustrated, angry, and also feeling guilty because, "My master said not to talk with these people. These people *really* are dangerous. Now, what kind of answer is this? He has humiliated me."

He went to his master and told him what had happened. "I am sorry that I talked to him. You were right, those people are strange. What kind of answer is this? I asked him, 'Where are you going?' – a simple formal question – and I knew he was going to the market, just as I was going to the market. But he said, 'Wherever the winds take me.'"

The master said, "I warned you, but you didn't listen. Now look, tomorrow you stand at the same place again. When he comes ask him, 'Where are you going?' and he will say, 'Wherever the winds take me.' Then you also be a little more philosophical. Say, 'If you don't have any legs, then? Because the soul is bodiless and the wind cannot take the soul anywhere!' What about that?"

Absolutely ready, the whole night he repeated it again and again and again. And next morning very early he went there, stood on the right spot, and at the exact time the boy came. He was very happy, now he was going to show him what real philosophy is. So he asked, "Where are you going?" And he was waiting....

But the boy said, "I am going to fetch vegetables from the market."

Now, what to do with the philosophy that he had learned?

Life is like that. You cannot prepare for it, you cannot be ready for it. That's its beauty, that's its wonder, that it always takes you unawares, it always comes as a surprise. If you have eyes you will see that each moment is a surprise and no ready-made answer is ever applicable.

And all the old religions have supplied you with ready-made answers. Manu has given his commandments, Moses has given his commandments, and so on and so forth.

I don't give you any commandment. In fact the very word commandment is ugly. To command somebody is to reduce him to a slave. I don't give you any orders, you are not to be obedient to me or to anybody else. I simply teach you an intrinsic law of life. Be obedient to your own self, be a light unto yourself and follow the light and this problem will never arise.

Then whatsoever you do is the thing to do, and whatsoever you don't do is the thing that has not to be done.

And remember, don't go on looking back again and again, because life goes on changing. Tomorrow you may start thinking what you did yesterday was wrong. It was not wrong yesterday, it may look wrong tomorrow. There is no need to look back; life goes ahead. But there are many drivers who go on looking in the rear-view mirror. They drive onwards but they look backwards; their life is going to be a catastrophe.

Look ahead. The road that you have passed, you have passed. It is finished, don't carry it any more. Don't be unnecessarily burdened by the past. Go on closing the chapters that you have read; there is no need to go back again and again. And never judge anything of the past through the new perspective that is arriving, because the new is new, incomparably new. The old was right in its own context, and the new is right in its own context, and they are incomparable.

What I am trying to explain to you is: drop guilt! – because to be guilty is to live in hell. Not being guilty, you will have the freshness of dewdrops in the early morning sun, you will have the freshness of lotus petals in the lake, you will have the freshness of the stars in the night. Once guilt disappears you will have a totally different kind of life, luminous and radiant. You will have a dance to your feet and your heart will be singing a thousand and one songs.

To live in such rejoicing is to be a sannyasin, to live in such joy is to live a divine life. To live burdened with guilt is simply to be exploited by the priests.

Get out of your prisons – Hindu, Christian, Mohammedan, Jaina, Buddhist, communist. Get out of all your prisons, get out of all your ideologies, because ideologies supply you ready-made answers. If you ask the communist a question he will have to look in *Das Kapital*. In the same way, if you ask the Hindu he turns the pages of the Gita.

When are you going to use your own consciousness? When? How long are you going to remain tethered to the dead past? The Gita was born five thousand years back; life has changed so much. If you want to read the Gita, read it as beautiful literature – but just like that, no more than that. It is beautiful literature, it is beautiful poetry, but it has no dictums to be followed and no commandments to be followed. Enjoy it as a gift from the past, as the gift of a great poet, Vyasa. But don't make it a discipline for your life; it is utterly irrelevant.

And everything becomes irrelevant, because life never remains confined. It goes on and on; it crosses all borders, all boundaries, it is an infinite process. The Gita comes to a full stop somewhere, the Koran comes to a full stop somewhere, but life never comes to a full stop, remember it. Remind yourself of it.

And the only way to be in contact with life, the only way not to lag behind life, is to have a heart which is not guilty, a heart which is innocent. Forget all about what you have been told – what has to be done and what has not to be done – nobody else can decide it for you.

Avoid those pretenders who decide for you; take the reins in your own hands. *You* have to decide. In fact, in that very decisiveness, your soul is born. When others decide for you, your soul remains asleep and dull. When you start deciding on your own, a sharpness arises. To decide means to take risks, to decide means you may be doing wrong – who knows, that is the risk. Who knows what is going to happen? That is the risk, there is no guarantee.

With the old, there is a guarantee. Millions and millions of people have followed it, how can so many people be wrong? That is the guarantee. If so many people say it is right, it *must* be right.

In fact the logic of life is just the opposite. If so many people are following a certain thing, be certain it is wrong, because so many people are not so enlightened and cannot be so enlightened. The majority consists of fools, utter fools. Beware of the majority. If so many people are following something, that is enough proof that it is wrong.

Truth happens to individuals, not to crowds. Have you ever heard of a crowd becoming enlightened? Truth happens to individuals – a Tilopa, an Atisha, a Nanak, a Kabir, a Farid.

Truth happens to individuals.

Be an individual if you really want truth to happen to you.

Take all the risks that are needed to be an individual, and accept the challenges so that they can sharpen you, can give you brilliance and intelligence.

Truth is not a belief, it is utter intelligence. It is a flaring-up of the hidden sources of your life, it is an enlightening experience of your consciousness. But you will have to provide the right space for it to happen. And the right space is accepting yourself as you are. Don't deny anything, don't become split, don't feel guilty.

Rejoice! And I say to you again, rejoice *as you are*.

? Why does so much controversy surround you?

If it were not so, it would have been really a surprise, it would have been a miracle, it would have been unbelievable. This is the natural course. This is what was happening to Socrates. And what was his mistake? His mistake was that he was trying to tell the truth as it is. His mistake, his only mistake, was that he was not ready to compromise with the stupidities of the crowd. He lived in continuous controversy; he died because of those controversies.

Do you think Jesus lived a noncontroversial life? Then why was he crucified? A reward for a noncontroversial life? He lived continuously in controversy; it is bound to be so. So it was with Buddha, so it was with Bodhidharma, so it has always been, and it seems so it is always going to be.

Truth creates controversy, because it shocks people, it shatters their illusions. And they want to cling to their illusions; those illusions are very consoling, comfortable, convenient and cozy. They don't want to leave their dreams, they are not ready to drop their investments in all kinds of foolish projects – and that's what truth requires of them. They feel angry, they want to take revenge.

It's absolutely natural. I am going to live in controversy – and this is only the beginning. Wait for the day they expel me from the world! I am really enchanted: where will they send me? It will be worth it, worth all the trouble of going there and living out of the world.

This is only the beginning, this is just the spark. Soon the whole forest will be on fire, and this fire is going to spread all over the earth…because I am not fighting against Hindu fanaticism, I am not fighting against Mohammedan fanaticism, I am simply fighting against all kinds of fanaticism.

Socrates was only fighting against the lies that were prevalent in the small city of Athens; it was a very small place. Buddha was against the Hindu beliefs, Jesus was fighting the Judaic heritage. My fight is multidimensional: I am fighting with Jews, I am fighting with Hindus, I am fighting with Buddhists, I am fighting with Jainas, I am fighting with Mohammedans. My fight is not addressed to anybody in particular. Hence I am bound to create so many enemies, more than anybody has ever done.

But certainly I am also going to create just as many friends, more than anybody has ever done, because life keeps a balance. If you have so many enemies you will have as many friends, if you have so many friends you will have as many enemies. Life always keeps a balance, life never loses balance. So the more enemies there are, the more friends there will be.

The whole thing seems to be very intriguing, very interesting. And remember, you cannot satisfy all – that is not possible, and I am not interested in it either.

Two thousand five hundred years ago, Aesop told this story:

It was a bright sunny morning in a mountain village. An old man and his grandson were going to the market in the large town in the valley to sell a donkey. The donkey was beautifully groomed and brushed and they set off happily down the steep path. In a while they passed some people lounging by the side of the path.

"Look at that silly pair!" said one of the onlookers. "There they go, scrambling and stumbling down the path, when they could be riding comfortably on the back of that sure-footed beast."

The old man heard this and thought it was right. So he and the boy mounted the donkey, and thus continued their descent.

Soon they passed another group of people gossiping by the wayside. "Look at the lazy pair, breaking the back of that poor donkey!"

The old man thought they were right, and since he was the heavier, he decided to walk while the boy rode.

In a little while they heard more comments. "Look at that disrespectful child – he rides while the old man walks!"

The old man thought they were right, and it was only proper that he should ride while the boy walked.

Sure enough, they soon heard this: "What a mean old man, riding at his ease while the poor child has to try to keep up on foot!"

By this time the old man and the boy were becoming increasingly bewildered. When they finally heard the criticism that the donkey would be all worn out and no one would want to buy him after the long walk to the market, they sat down, dejected, by the side of the road.

After the donkey had been allowed to rest for a while, they continued the journey, but in a completely different manner. Thus it was, late that afternoon, that the old man and the boy were seen gasping breathlessly into the marketplace. Slung on a pole between them, hung by his tied feet, was the donkey!

As Aesop said: "You can't please everyone. If you try, you lose yourself."

I cannot please everybody, and neither am I interested in pleasing everybody. I am not a politician; the politician tries to please everybody. I am here only to help those who really want to be helped. I am not interested in the mob, in the crowd. I am only interested in those sincere seekers who are ready to risk all – *all* – to attain themselves.

This is going to anger many, this is going to create much controversy, because I am a very noncompromising person. I will say only that which is true to me, whatsoever the consequence. If I am condemned for it or murdered for it, that's perfectly okay. But I am not going to compromise, not an iota.

I have nothing to lose, so why compromise? I have nothing to gain, so why compromise? All that could have happened has happened. Nothing can be taken away from me, because my treasure is of the inner. And nothing can be added to it, because my treasure is of the inner.

So I am going to live the way I want to live. I am going to live in my own spontaneity and authenticity. I am not here to fulfill anybody's expectations. I am not interested in being called a spiritual person or a saint either. I don't need any compliments from anybody, I don't want the crowd to worship me. All those stupid games are finished.

I am in that state where nothing can happen any more; it is beyond happening. So I will go on saying things which offend people. It is not that I want to offend them, but what can I do? If truth offends them, then it offends them. I am going to live life the way it is happening to me. If it is not according to their expectations, either they can change their expectations or they can feel angry, miserable, and go on clinging to their expectations.

I am utterly free from their opinion, it does not matter to me at all.

The controversies will become more and more. And because I am controversial, my people are bound to be controversial too. Because I am controversial, you will also be offensive, you will also have to suffer. You will also have to be ready to be persecuted in many ways.

But remember one thing. To live a life of compromise is worse than death. And to live a life of truth, even if it is for a single moment, is far more valuable than to live eternally in lies. To die for truth is far more valuable than to live in lies.

? What is your idea of heaven?

There is no heaven and there is no hell. They are not geographical, they are part of your psychology. They are psychological. To live a life of spontaneity, truth, love and beauty is to live in heaven. To live a life of hypocrisy, lies and compromises, to live according to others, is to live in hell. To live in freedom is heaven, and to live in bondage is hell.

You can decorate your prison cell beautifully, but that makes no difference, it is still a prison cell. And that's what people have been doing, they go on decorating their prison cell. They give it beautiful names, they go on painting it, putting new pictures on the walls, arranging the furniture in new ways, purchasing more and more things – but they live in prisons.

Your marriage is a prison, your church is a prison, your nationality is a prison. How many prisons you have created! You are not living in one prison, your prisons are like Chinese boxes: a box within a box within a box within a box, it goes on. You are like an onion: peel it, another layer, peel that, another layer. Destroy one prison and you find another inside. This is what hell is.

To reach the very core of the onion, where all layers have been dropped and there is only nothingness in your hands, that is freedom, nirvana, *bodhichitta*. The consciousness of a buddha, the pure consciousness of a buddha, that is heaven.

And my idea of heaven is not something far away, a heaven in the sky where only angels live…. Do you know that angels don't perspire? They don't need any deodorants. And do you know, in heaven there are no pubs, because pubs are not needed. There are rivers of wine, so you can jump into the rivers and drink to your heart's content. And there are beautiful women who never grow old, who are stuck at the age of eighteen. Centuries and centuries have passed, but they are stuck at the age of eighteen. They have golden bodies. Just think of it! It looks more like a nightmare. Golden bodies? With eyes of sapphire?

No, that is not my idea of heaven. In that way, I am an old Jew….

The minister said to his friend, "Rabbi, I dreamed of a Jewish heaven the other night. It was very lifelike, and it seemed to me to just suit the Jewish ideal. It was a crowded tenement district with Jewish people everywhere. There were clothes on lines from every window, women on every stoop, pushcart peddlers on every corner, children playing stick-ball on every street. The noise and confusion were so great that I woke up."

The rabbi said, "By a strange coincidence, Father Williams, I dreamed the other night of an Episcopalian heaven. It was very lifelike, and it seemed to me just the ideal of Episcopalians. It was a neat suburb, with well-spaced English Tudor and manor houses, with beautiful lawns, each with its own flowerbed, with clean wide tree-lined streets, and all was suffused in warm sunshine."

The vicar smiled. "And the people?"

"Oh," murmured the rabbi, "there were no people."

My idea of heaven is not unearthly. Heaven is here – you just have to know how to live it. And hell too is here, and you know perfectly well how to live it. It is only a question of changing your perspective, your approach towards life.

The earth is beautiful. If you start living its beauty, enjoying its joys with no guilt in your heart, you are in paradise. If you condemn everything, every small joy, if you become a condemner, a poisoner, then the same earth turns into a hell – but only for you. It depends on you where you live, it is a question of your own inner transformation. It is not a change of place, it is a change of inner space.

Live joyously, guiltlessly, live totally, live intensely. And then heaven is no more a metaphysical concept, it is your own *experience*.

Enough for today.

Chapter 12
Buddha in the Supermarket

One of the essential laws of nature seems to be relationship, interdependence. I have watched two birds fly, intimate with each other and with the wind, so easy and without strife, in perfect harmony. What is the secret of this that seems so hard for human beings? Please Osho, say something about relationship.

The most fundamental thing to be remembered is that life is dialectical. It exists through duality, it is a rhythm between opposites. You cannot be happy forever, otherwise happiness will lose all meaning. You cannot be in harmony forever, otherwise you will become unaware of the harmony. Harmony has to be followed by discord again and again, and happiness has to be followed by unhappiness. Every pleasure has its own pain, and every pain has its own pleasure.

Unless one understands this duality of existence, one remains in unnecessary misery. Accept the total, with all its agonies and all its ecstasies. Don't hanker for the impossible; don't desire that there should be only ecstasy and no agony.

Ecstasy cannot exist alone, it needs a contrast. Agony becomes the blackboard, then ecstasy becomes very clear and loud, just as in the darkness of night the stars are so bright. The darker the night, the brighter are the stars. In the day they don't disappear, they simply become invisible; you cannot see them because there is no contrast.

Think of a life without death, and it will be unendurable pain, an unendurable existence. It will be impossible to live without death. Death defines life, gives it a kind of intensity; because life is fleeting, each moment becomes precious. If life is eternal, then who cares? One can wait for tomorrow forever – then who will live now and here? Because tomorrow there is death, it forces you to live now and here. You have to plunge into the present moment, you have to go to its ultimate depth, because who knows, the next moment may come, may not come.

Seeing this rhythm, one is at ease, at ease with both. When unhappiness comes one welcomes it, when happiness comes one welcomes it, knowing that they are partners in the same game.

This is something which has to be continuously remembered. If it becomes a fundamental remembrance in you, your life will have a totally new flavor – the flavor of freedom, the flavor of unclingingness, the flavor of non-attachment. Whatsoever comes, you remain still, silent, accepting.

And the person who is capable of being still, silent, accepting of pain, frustration and misery, transforms the very quality of misery itself. To him, misery also becomes a treasure; to him, even pain gives a sharpness. To him, even darkness has its own beauty, depth, infinity. To him, even death is not the end but only a beginning of something unknown.

You say, "One of the essential laws of nature seems to be relationship, interdependence."

They are not synonymous. Relationship is one thing, interdependence totally another. Relationship means you are separate; you are independent and so is the other, and you decide to relate. Relationship is not interdependence, it is a contract between two independent persons. Hence all relationships are false, because basically independence is false. Nobody is independent – and if you are not independent how can you relate? With whom can you relate?

Life is interdependence. Nobody is independent, not for a single moment can you exist alone. You need the whole existence to support you; each moment you are breathing it in and out. It is not relationship, it is utter interdependence. Remember, I am not saying it is dependence, because the idea of dependence again presumes that we are independent. If we are independent then dependence is possible. But both are impossible; it is interdependence.

What do you say? Are waves independent from the ocean or are they dependent on the ocean? Neither is true. They *are* the ocean, neither independent nor dependent. The ocean cannot exist without the waves, the waves cannot exist without the ocean. They are utterly one, it is a unity.

And so is our whole life. We are waves of a cosmic ocean of consciousness. That means love can have three dimensions. One is that of dependence; that's what happens to the majority of people. The husband is dependent on the wife, the wife is dependent on the husband; they exploit each other, they dominate each other, they possess each other, they reduce each other to a commodity. In ninety-nine percent of cases, that's what is happening in the world. That's why love, which can open the gates of paradise, only opens the gates of hell.

The second possibility is love between two independent persons. That too happens once in a while. But that too brings misery, because there is constant conflict. No adjustment is possible; both are so independent and nobody is ready to compromise, to adjust with the other.

Poets, artists, thinkers, scientists, those who live in a kind of independence, at least in their minds, are impossible people to live with; they are eccentric people to live with. They give freedom to the other, but their freedom looks more like indifference than like freedom, looks more as if they don't care, as if it doesn't matter to them. They leave each other to their own spaces. Relationship seems to be only superficial; they are afraid to go deeper into each other, because they are more attached to their freedom than to love, and they don't want to compromise.

And the third possibility is of interdependence. That happens very rarely, but whenever it happens a part of paradise falls on the earth. Two persons, neither independent nor dependent but in a tremendous synchronicity, as if breathing for each other, one soul in two bodies – whenever that happens, love has happened. Only call this love. The other two are not really love, they are just arrangements – social, psychological, biological, but arrangements. The third is something spiritual.

You also say, "I have watched two birds fly, intimate with each other and with the wind, so easy and without strife, in perfect harmony."

Yes, it creates jealousy. But birds are not aware; they have no consciousness, they exist below consciousness. Their harmony looks like harmony to you, not to them. And their joy on the wing is your interpretation, not theirs. Remember it: it is your interpretation. They can't interpret; they have not yet evolved that consciousness which can interpret, which can look back, which can look forward, which can observe and look into things. Their behavior is mechanical.

Man is a higher being, man has the capacity to be conscious. And with consciousness, trouble begins. The higher you move, the more dangerous becomes every step. If you fall, you will be falling from such heights that you will disappear somewhere in the valley. In the valley you can walk unconsciously, there is no fear. But when you are moving towards the top, reaching to the peak, you will have to be more and more conscious.

Man is very close to God, the closest. Hence the responsibility and the danger, the hazard, the adventure. You can fall. And what is the fall?

Because you are capable of being conscious, there are two possibilities. You can become *self*-conscious – that is the fall. If the self overpowers your consciousness, you have fallen. If consciousness does not allow the self to overpower it, if you simply are conscious and there is no self in it – a consciousness without a center, a consciousness without anybody being there to be conscious – then you are rising and rising and rising and the climax is not far away. Maybe a few steps more, and you will have arrived home. Then you will know what harmony is. And you will know the eternal harmony of existence, the silence that has never been broken; from the beginningless beginnings to the endless end, it continues the same. Then you will know the virgin purity of existence, which has never been polluted.

What can poor birds and animals know of it?

But I can understand, sometimes it creates great jealousy. Two birds on the wing in such harmony, in such love and intimacy, not only between themselves but with the wind, with the sun, with the rain, and man starts feeling, "Why can't I be so happy? Why can't I relate with such beauty? Why can't I enjoy the wind and the rain and the sun so relaxedly?"

It is not because you are lower than the birds, it is because you are higher and much more is required of you. It is because you are higher that God's criterion for you is higher too. Yes, a drunkard looks lost, without any anxiety, without any worry, and Buddha also looks without any worry and without any anxiety; Buddha also looks drunk. But do you think they exist on the same plane? The drunkard has fallen from consciousness, and the buddha has risen from the self.

Self-consciousness is human. If you fall from consciousness you will have a certain forgetfulness of anxiety. If you rise from the self you will not only have a forgetfulness of anxiety; anxieties simply evaporate, they exist no more.

You *can* become buddhas. You have the capacity, the potential, to become a buddha. The birds are poor. But man has fallen so low that he even starts feeling jealous of poor birds.

You ask, "What is the secret of this that seems so hard for human beings?"

The secret is consciousness. Consciousness brings freedom. Freedom does not mean only the freedom to do right; if that was the meaning of freedom, what kind of freedom would it be? If you are only free to do right, then you are not free. Freedom implies both the alternatives – to do right, to do wrong. Freedom implies the right to say yes or to say no.

And this is something subtle to be understood. Saying no feels more of a freedom than saying yes. And I am not philosophizing, it is a simple fact you can observe in yourself. Whenever you say no, you feel more free. Whenever you say yes, you don't feel free, because yes means you have obeyed, yes means you have surrendered – where is the freedom? No means you are stubborn, keeping aloof; no means you have asserted yourself, no means you are ready to fight. No defines you more clearly than yes. Yes is vague, it is like a cloud. No is very solid and substantial, like a rock.

That's why psychologists say that between seven and fourteen years of age each child starts learning to say no more and more. By saying no, he is getting out of the psychological womb of the mother. Even when there is no need to say no, he will say no. Even when to say yes is in his favor, he will say no.

There is much at stake; he has to learn to say no more and more. By the time he is fourteen, sexually mature, he will say the ultimate no to the mother; he will fall in love with a woman. That is his ultimate no to the mother, he is turning his back on the mother. He says, "I am finished with you, I have chosen my woman. I have become an individual, independent in my own right. I want to live my life, I want to do my own thing."

And if the parents insist, "Have short hair," he will have long hair. If the parents insist, "Have long hair," he will have short hair. Just watch a little longer. When hippies become parents then they will see, their children will have short hair – because they will have to learn no.

If the parents insist, "Cleanliness is next to God," the children will start living in every kind of dirt. They will be dirty. They won't take a bath, they won't clean themselves, they won't use soap. And they will find rationalizations that soap is dangerous to the skin, that it is unnatural, that no animal ever uses soap. They can find as many rationalizations as possible, but deep down all those rationalizations are just cover-ups. The real thing is, they want to say no. And of course when you want to say no, you have to find reasons.

Hence, no gives you a sense of freedom; not only that, it also gives you a sense of intelligence. To say yes needs no intelligence. When you say yes, nobody asks you why. When you have already said yes, who bothers to ask you why? There is no need of any reasoning or argument, you have already said yes. When you say no, why is bound to be asked. It sharpens your intelligence, it gives you a definition, a style, freedom. Watch the psychology of the no.

It is so hard for human beings to be in harmony, because of consciousness. Consciousness gives freedom, freedom gives you the capacity to say no, and there is more possibility to say no than to say yes. And without yes, there is no harmony. Yes is harmony. But it takes time to grow up, to mature, to come to such a maturity where you can say yes and yet remain free, where you can say yes and yet remain unique, where you can say yes and yet not become a slave.

The freedom that is brought by no is a very childish freedom. It is good for seven-year-olds up to fourteen-year-olds. But if a person gets caught in it and his whole life becomes a no-saying, then he has stopped growing.

The ultimate growth is to say yes with such joy as a child says no. That is a second childhood. And the man who can say yes with tremendous freedom and joy, with no hesitation, with no strings attached, with no conditions – a pure and simple joy, a pure and simple yes – that man has become a sage. That man lives in harmony again. And his harmony is of a totally different dimension than the harmony of trees, animals and birds. They live in harmony because they cannot say no, and the sage lives in harmony because he does not say no. Between the two, the birds and the buddhas, are all human beings – un-grown-up, immature, childish, stuck somewhere, still trying to say no, to have some feeling of freedom.

I am not saying don't learn to say no. I am saying learn to say no when it is time to say no, but don't get stuck with it. Slowly, slowly, see that there is a higher freedom that comes with yes, and a greater harmony. A peace that passeth understanding.

Is relationship there because love is not?

Yes. Love is not a relationship. Love relates, but it is not a relationship. A relationship is something finished. A relationship is a noun; the full stop has come, the honeymoon is over. Now there is no joy, no enthusiasm, now all is finished.

You can carry it on, just to keep your promises. You can carry it on because it is comfortable, convenient, cozy. You can carry it on because there is nothing else to do. You can carry it on because if you disrupt it, it is going to create much trouble for you.

Relationship means something complete, finished, closed. Love is never a relationship; love is relating. It is always a river, flowing, unending. Love knows no full stop; the honeymoon begins but never ends. It is not like a novel that starts at a certain point and ends at a certain point. It is an ongoing phenomenon. Lovers end, love continues. It is a continuum. It is a verb, not a noun. And why do we reduce the beauty of relating to relationship? Why are we in such a hurry? – because to relate is insecure, and relationship is a security, relationship has a certainty. Relating is just a meeting of two strangers, maybe just an overnight stay and in the morning we say good-bye. Who knows what is going to happen tomorrow? And we are so afraid that we want to make it certain, we want to make it predictable. We would like tomorrow to be according to our ideas; we don't allow it freedom to have its own say. So we immediately reduce every verb to a noun.

You are in love with a woman or a man and immediately you start thinking of getting married. Make it a legal contract. Why? How does the law come into love? The law comes into love because love is not there. It is only a fantasy, and you know the fantasy will disappear. Before it disappears settle down, before it disappears do something so it becomes impossible to separate.

In a better world, with more meditative people, with a little more enlightenment spread over the earth, people will love, love immensely, but their love will remain a relating, not a relationship. And I am not saying that their love will be only momentary. There is every possibility their love may go deeper than your love, may have a higher quality of intimacy, may have something more of poetry and more of God in it. And there is every possibility their love may last longer than your so-called relationship ever lasts. But it will not be guaranteed by the law, by the court, by the policeman.

The guarantee will be inner. It will be a commitment from the heart, it will be a silent communion. If you enjoy being with somebody, you would like to enjoy it more and more. If you enjoy the intimacy, you would like to explore the intimacy more and more.

And there are a few flowers of love which bloom only after long intimacies. There are seasonal flowers too; within six weeks they are there in the sun, but within six weeks again they are gone forever. There are flowers which take years to come, and there are flowers which take many years to come. The longer it takes, the deeper it goes.

But it has to be a commitment from one heart to another heart. It has not even to be verbalized, because to verbalize it is to profane it. It has to be a silent commitment; eye to eye, heart to heart, being to being. It has to be understood, not said.

It is so ugly seeing people going to the church or the court to get married. It is so ugly, so inhuman. It simply shows they can't trust themselves, they trust the policeman more than they trust their own inner voice. It shows they can't trust their love, they trust the law.

Forget relationships and learn how to relate. Once you are in a relationship you start taking each other for granted. That's what destroys all love affairs. The woman thinks she knows the man, the man thinks he knows the woman. Nobody knows either. It is impossible to know the other, the other remains a mystery. And to take the other for granted is insulting, disrespectful.

To think that you know your wife is very, very ungrateful. How can you know the woman? How can you know the man? They are processes, they are not things. The woman that you knew yesterday is not there today. So much water has gone down the Ganges; she is somebody else, totally different. Relate again, start again, don't take it for granted.

And the man that you slept with last night, look at his face again in the morning. He is no more the same person, so much has changed. So much, incalculably much, has changed. That is the difference between a thing and a person. The furniture in the room is the same, but the man and the woman, they are no more the same. Explore again, start again. That's what I mean by relating.

Relating means you are always starting, you are continuously trying to become acquainted. Again and again, you are introducing yourself to each other. You are trying to see the many facets of the other's personality. You are trying to penetrate deeper and deeper into his realm of inner feelings, into the deep recesses of his being. You are trying to unravel a mystery which cannot be unraveled.

That is the joy of love: the exploration of consciousness. And if you relate, and don't reduce it to a relationship, then the other will become a mirror to you. Exploring him, unawares you will be exploring yourself too. Getting deeper into the other, knowing his feelings, his thoughts, his deeper stirrings, you will be knowing your own deeper stirrings too. Lovers become mirrors to each other, and then love becomes a meditation. Relationship is ugly, relating is beautiful.

In relationship both persons become blind to each other. Just think, how long has it been since you saw your wife eye to eye? How long has it been since you looked at your husband? Maybe years. Who looks at one's own wife? You have already taken it for granted that you know her. What more is there to look at? You are more interested in strangers than in the people you know – you know the whole topography of their bodies, you know how they respond, you know everything that has happened is going to happen again and again. It is a repetitive circle.

It is not so, it is not really so. Nothing ever repeats; everything is new every day. Just your eyes become old, your assumptions become old, your mirror gathers dust and you become incapable of reflecting the other.

Hence I say relate. By saying relate, I mean remain continuously on a honeymoon. Go on searching and seeking each other, finding new ways of loving each other, finding new ways of being with each other. And each person is such an infinite mystery, inexhaustible, unfathomable, that it is not possible that you can ever say, "I have known her," or, "I have known him." At the most you can say, "I have tried my best, but the mystery remains a mystery."

In fact the more you know, the more mysterious the other becomes. Then love is a constant adventure.

> **I feel like the frog in the fairy tale who gets kissed and starts growing up to be the handsome prince. But I'm still wearing froggy clothes and they are too tight and the princess isn't interested and wouldn't it be nice just to be a frog again? Help!**

You seem to be very old fashioned. The world has changed a lot since these kinds of stories were written. Now just the vice versa exists. Touch a prince and he becomes a frog, kiss a prince and immediately there is a frog.

This fable is no longer applicable. But it will be good to go a little deeper into it. Why were such kinds of stories invented? – why in the first place? What is their psychology? The psychology is to cover up something ugly about human beings. The reality is that the moment you kiss a woman or a man, the moment you fall in love with a man or a woman, immediately the process starts that the man starts becoming a frog, the woman starts becoming a frog.

Now, this is a fact, and you all know it. And these fables were created to cover up this reality. These fables were created to deceive you, that this is not so, that in reality you can kiss a frog and he becomes a prince. To deceive you about the reality of life, these stories were created. Small children read these stories and believe in them, and later on they are very much disillusioned.

These stories are fantasies, wish fulfillments. That's how man would like things to be. Kiss a frog and the frog is transformed into a handsome prince. These are wish fulfillments; it does not happen, what happens is just the contrary. But how to hide it? How not to look at it? Create beautiful fables around it.

Ninety-nine percent of our religion and a hundred percent of our literature consists of deceptions. It goes on talking about things as they are not, never have been, and never will be.

But man is the animal who lives through illusions. He cannot live with reality; reality is too much, it hurts. Have you not seen it in your own life? Fall in love with a woman; she was so beautiful when she was unavailable; when she was beyond your grasp she was like a Cleopatra. And once you are married to her you are fed up with her, bored to death. Now you cannot believe how you managed to see Cleopatra in this woman; she looks utterly ugly in every possible way.

And the same is the case from her side. She was thinking you were a charming prince, like the princes in the fables who come on their beautiful horses. She thought she had found her charming prince. And when she lives with the reality, he snores in the night, he stinks, and he has such dirty habits – he smokes, she cannot even kiss him because he smells so much of smoking. And suddenly she becomes aware that the charming prince was never there in reality; he was a projection, she had projected him.

Every day the person becomes more and more ordinary. The reality is: kiss a prince and he becomes a frog. But then how to live?

If all these realities are made known, then life will become impossible. So we create fantasies, fables, fictions, to create some consolation, to create a little cozy atmosphere. If it is not real, at least you can dream, you can fantasize, you can believe that if it is not real today, tomorrow it is going to be real. Go on kissing the frog, and sooner or later he will become a prince. These are make-believes.

People believe in the immortality of the soul because they are conscious of death – not that they *know* the soul is immortal, but just because they see everybody dying, they know the certainty of death. Now, how to escape from a certainty? Create a fiction.

Remember, I am not saying that the soul is not eternal, I am simply saying that people's belief that the soul is eternal is a fiction. The belief is a fiction.

People believe in a God who cares, because they feel so uncared for. Nobody cares about them, they feel so left alone, nobody seems to be interested in them; whether they live or die will not matter. They have to create a father figure high in heaven who cares for them. Even if nobody cares, God cares. It is a great solace.

In the name of religion, in the name of literature, in the name of poetry, music, we have been creating fictions – we create a few buffers around ourselves, so the shocks of reality don't reach to us.

You must have seen buffers in railway trains. Between two bogies, two compartments, there are buffers, so if somehow some accident happens, the compartments don't run into each other and the shock of the accident can be absorbed by the buffers. Cars have springs so that you don't feel the bumps on rough roads. Those springs go on absorbing the bumps, the shocks; they are shock absorbers.

Man has created many psychological shock-absorbers around himself. And what I would like to say to you is this: that unless you drop all shock absorbers you are never going to be free.

Only truth liberates. And in the beginning, truth shocks very much – but that's how it is, that's how things are, that's how nature functions. You have to open yourself, you have to be vulnerable to all the shocks of life. It will hurt, it will wound, you will cry, you will weep, you will be in a rage against life. But slowly, slowly you will start seeing that truth is truth, and it is pointless to be in a rage against truth. And once the rage has subsided, the truth has a beauty of its own. Truth liberates.

The real work of a master is to destroy the absorbers of the disciples. And it is really very hard work – hard in the sense that the disciples resist in every possible way. They protect their absorbers, and if they feel that there is some danger, they create more absorbers around themselves. If they see that somebody is after them to snatch their absorbers, they become very defensive, very protective and they create more armors around themselves.

The real master cannot give you solace, he can only give you freedom. He can give you bliss, but he cannot give you consolation. And he will have to destroy many things in you which you have cherished for long, nourished for long. He will have to take away all the clothes that protect you, he will have to leave you nude in reality.

It frightens, it scares, but that is the only way you can grow. Growth has to be *with* reality, not against reality. And once you have tasted something of reality as it is, you will never gather any other buffers, shock absorbers, around you again.

You say, "I feel like the frog in the fairy tale who gets kissed and starts growing up to be the handsome prince."

You must be dreaming. Things are not done that way here. You came here, as a charming prince. You have been kissed, and now you are a frog. But there is nothing wrong with being a frog – frogs are beautiful people.

You say, "But I'm still wearing froggy clothes…." Of course – you are still a frog!

"And they are too tight" – you are imagining – "and the princess isn't interested and wouldn't it be nice just to be a frog again?"

What are you talking about? You don't need any help, you already are one! Accept your frogginess and forget all about the princess. In fact I have never seen a frog interested in a princess – foolish idea! Become interested in another frog! And in that way I can help you. I have so many frogs here.

? You have said that Krishnamurti can get angry. How is that possible, as in enlightenment there is no one there to be angry?

In enlightenment there is nobody there to get angry, and there is nobody there *not* to get angry either. So whatsoever happens, happens. Krishnamurti does not get angry the way you get angry. Everything with an enlightened person happens on a totally different plane. His anger comes out of his compassion. Your anger comes out of hate, aggression, cruelty. He becomes angry – sometimes he starts pulling his hair out, he hits his own forehead – but out of compassion.

Just think, for fifty years or more he has been teaching a certain kind of truth to the world, and nobody understands him. The same people gather each year to listen to him – the *same* people.

Once he was talking in Bombay…somebody reported this to me, and the person who reported it to me is an old lady, older than Krishnamurti. She saw Krishnamurti when he was a child, she has seen him and listened to him for fifty years. And because she is a little deaf, very old, she sits in the front on a chair. And for fifty years Krishnamurti has been saying that there are no methods for meditation, that meditation is not needed at all. Just be in the present and live your life, that's enough meditation, no other technique is needed….

For one and a half hours he poured his heart out, and at the end the lady stood up and asked, "How to meditate?" Now, what do you suppose he should do? He hit his head.

This is not *your* anger. This is so unbelievable! He is tired of this lady, but this lady is not tired of him. She comes to every talk to listen to him, and asks the same stupid questions.

When I say Krishnamurti can get angry, I don't mean that he can get angry like you get angry. His anger is out of compassion. This situation is unbelievable! He wants to help this lady and he feels so helpless. He tries this way and that. His message is very simple, singular, one-dimensional. For fifty years he has been saying only a single word. In essence his whole teaching can be printed on one side of a postcard. He has been saying it in as many possible ways as one can invent, but it is the same citadel that he attacks from the north, from the south, from the west, from the east. And still people go on listening to him and go on asking the same old foolish questions.

He certainly gets angry. And when a man like Krishnamurti gets angry, he is pure anger. Many in India have felt very disappointed with Krishnamurti because he gets angry. They have a certain concept that a buddha should not get angry. They go with a prejudice. And when they see that Krishnamurti *can* get angry, they are disillusioned, "So this man is not a buddha, he has not become enlightened yet."

I say to you that he is one of the most enlightened persons who has ever walked on this earth. Still he can get angry, but his anger comes out of compassion; it is condensed compassion. He cares about you, so much so that he becomes angry. This is a totally different quality of anger.

And when he becomes angry he is real anger. Your anger is partial, lukewarm. Your anger is like a dog who is not certain how to behave with a stranger. He may be a friend of the master, so he wags his tail; he may be an enemy, so he barks. He does both together. On one hand he goes on barking, on the other hand he goes on wagging his tail. He is playing the diplomat, so whatsoever the case turns out to be, he can always feel right. If the master comes and he sees that the master is friendly, the barking will stop and his whole energy will go into the tail. If the master is angry with the intruder, then the tail will stop completely, and his whole energy will go into barking.

Your anger is also like that. You are weighing up how far to go, how much will pay; don't go beyond the limit, don't provoke the other person too much.

But when a man like Krishnamurti becomes angry he is pure anger. And pure anger has a beauty because it has totality. He is just anger. He is like a small child, red-faced, just anger all over, ready to destroy the whole world.

That's what happened to Jesus. When he went into the great temple and saw the moneychangers and their tables inside the temple, he was in a rage. He became angry – the same anger that comes out of compassion and love. Single-handed, he drove all the moneychangers out of the temple and overturned their boards. He must have been really very angry, because driving all the moneychangers out of the temple single-handed is not an easy thing.

And reports say – I don't know how far they are right, but reports say that he was not a very strong man. Reports say that he was not even a very tall man; you will be surprised, he was only four feet six inches. And not only that – on top of it he was a hunchback. I don't know how far those reports are true, because I don't want to go to court! But it is there in the books, ancient books, very ancient books.

So how did this hunchback, four feet six inches high, drive out all the moneychangers single-handed? He must have been pure rage!

Indians are angry about that. They cannot trust that Jesus is enlightened – just because of this incident.

People have their prejudices, their ideas. Rather than seeing into reality, rather than looking into an enlightened man, they come ready with so many concepts, and unless he fits them he is not enlightened. And let me tell you, no enlightened person is going to fit with your unenlightened prejudices; it is impossible.

It happened, a lady came to me. She had been a follower of Krishnamurti for many years, then a small thing disturbed the whole thing and the whole applecart was upturned. The thing was so small that I was surprised. There was a camp in Holland where Krishnamurti holds a camp every year, and the woman had gone there from India. Nearabout two thousand people had gathered from all over the world to listen to him. The next morning the lectures were going to start, and the woman had gone shopping. And she was surprised, Krishnamurti was also shopping. An enlightened person shopping? Can you believe it? Buddha in a supermarket? And not only that – he was purchasing a necktie. Enlightened people need neckties? And not only *that* – the whole counter was full of neckties and he was throwing them this way and that, and he was not satisfied with *any*.

The woman watched, looked at the whole scene, and fell from the sky. She thought, "I have come from India for this ordinary man who is purchasing neckties. And even then, of *thousands* of neckties of all colors and all kinds of material, nothing is satisfying to him. Is this detachment? Is this awareness?"

She turned away. She didn't attend the camp, she came back immediately. And the first thing she did was to come running to me, and she said, "You are right."

I said, "What do you mean?"

She said, "You are right that it was useless wasting my time with Krishnamurti. Now I want to become a sannyasin of yours."

I said, "Please excuse me, I cannot accept you. If you cannot accept Krishnamurti, how can I accept you? Get lost!…Because here you will see far more disappointing things. What are you going to do with my Mercedes Benz? So before it happens, why bother? What are you going to do with my air-conditioned room? Before it happens, it is better that you go and find some Muktananda, etcetera. You have not been able to understand Krishnamurti, you will not be able to understand me."

People like Krishnamurti live on a totally different plane. Their anger is not your anger. And who knows that he was not just playing with those ties for this stupid old woman? Masters are known to devise things like that. He got rid of this stupid old woman very easily.

In Italy, a poor country, we have only three things – the pope, the pizza and gossip. Now in coming to India, we have lost the pizza and with you as the pope, please at least let us have the gossip!

I am not averse to gossiping. In fact, I love it. But what to do with this old man, Atisha? Every day I decide to gossip a little, and he says no. And I have to be a little respectful towards him. And the problem is not so much with Atisha, the problem is the sutra that is coming. I will find a legal way to wriggle out of it. But gossiping is difficult – but if you promise me not to tell anybody, I will….

A man was walking down the street looking into shop windows and his gaze stopped on a small overnight shaving-kit bag in a shop. What stopped him was the price – an exorbitant three hundred dollars.

His curiosity got the better of him and he was compelled to go in and ask about it, although he did not need one. "Why is this little bag so expensive?" he asked.

The shopkeeper replied, "It is made out of a very special leather."

"Even if it was made out of alligator skin or mink-lined it wouldn't be so costly," said the inquiring man.

The shopkeeper answered, "The story behind this small bag is special. The leathersmith's uncle is a rabbi and this bag is made entirely out of foreskins."

"I can see that that would be unique," the man came back. "But three hundred dollars is still too high a price!"

The shopkeeper then said, "It is very convenient. When you rub it, it turns into a large suitcase."

Enough for today.

Chapter 13
Don't Make Wicked Jokes

Abandon poisoned food.
Don't be consistent.
Don't make wicked jokes.
Don't wait for an opportunity.
Don't strike at the heart.
Don't transfer the cow's load to the bull.
Don't back the favorite.
Don't have wrong views.
Don't fall for the celestial demon.

The first sutra:

Abandon poisoned food.

According to the mystic traditions of the East, all that you think you are is nothing but food. Your body is food, your mind is food, your soul is food. Beyond the soul there is certainly something which is not food. That something is known as *anatta*, no-self. It is utter emptiness. Buddha calls it *shunya*, the void. It is pure space. It contains nothing but itself; it is contentless consciousness.

While the content persists, the food persists. By "food" is meant that which is ingested from the outside. The body needs physical food; without it, it will start withering away. This is how it survives; it contains nothing but physical food.

Your mind contains memories, thoughts, desires, jealousies, power trips, and a thousand and one things. All that is also food; on a little more subtle plane it is food. Thought is food. Hence when you have nourishing thoughts your chest expands. When you have thoughts which give you energy you feel good. Somebody says something good about you, a compliment, and look what happens to you – you are nourished. And somebody says something wrong about you, and watch – it is as if something has been snatched away from you, you are weaker than you were before.

The mind is food in a subtle form. The mind is nothing but the inner side of the body; hence what you eat affects your mind. If you eat non-vegetarian food you will have a particular kind of mind; if you eat vegetarian food you will certainly have a different kind of mind.

Do you know this immensely important fact about Indian history? India never attacked any country in its whole history of ten thousand years – never, not a single aggressive act. How was it possible? Why? The same humanity exists here as exists everywhere else, but it is just that a different kind of body created a different mind.

You can watch it yourself. Eat something and watch, eat something else and watch. Keep notes, and you will become aware and surprised to find that each thing that you digest is not only physical, it has a psychological part to it. It makes your mind vulnerable to certain ideas, to certain desires.

Hence, down the ages, there has been a search for a kind of food that will not strengthen the mind but will help it to finally dissolve; a kind of food which, instead of strengthening the mind, will strengthen meditation, no-mind. No fixed and certain rules can be given, because people are different and each one has to decide for himself.

And watch what you allow into your mind. People are completely unaware; they go on reading everything and anything, they go on looking at the TV, any silly stupid thing. They go on listening to the radio, they go on chitchatting, chattering with people, and they are all pouring rubbish into each other's heads. Rubbish is all that they have.

Avoid such situations in which you are unnecessarily burdened with rubbish. You already have too much as it is, you need to be unburdened of it. And you go on collecting it as if it is something precious.

Talk less, listen only to the essential, be telegraphic in talking and listening. If you talk less, if you listen less, slowly, slowly you will see that a cleanliness, a feeling of purity, as if you have just taken a bath, will start arising within you. That becomes the necessary soil for meditation to arise. Don't go on reading all kinds of nonsense.

Once I used to live in a house where the neighbor was a madman who was very much interested in newspapers. He would come every day to collect all the newspapers from me. If sometimes he was ill or I was not at home, then he would come later on.

Once it happened, for ten days I was away, and when I came back he came again to collect all the newspapers. I said to him, "But these are old now – ten days old."

He said, "What does it matter? It is the same rubbish! Only the dates change."

It must have been a very sane moment in that madman's life. Yes, there are insane moments in so-called sane people's lives, and vice versa. He was telling the truth, saying, "It is the same old nonsense. What does it matter? I have time, and I have to remain occupied."

I asked him, "What did you do for these ten days?"

He said, "I was reading the old newspapers – reading them again and again and again."

Leave a few gaps in your mind unoccupied. Those moments of unoccupied consciousness are the first glimpses of meditation, the first penetrations of the beyond, the first flashes of no-mind. And then if you can manage to do this, the other thing is to choose physical food which does not help aggression and violence, which is not poisonous.

Now even scientists agree with this, that when you kill an animal, out of fear he releases all kinds of poisons. Death is not easy. When you are killing an animal, out of fear a great trembling arises inside. The animal wants to survive; all kinds of poisons are released.

When you are in fear you also release poisons in the body. Those poisons are helpful; they help you to either fight or take flight. Sometimes it happens that in anger you can do things which you could never have imagined yourself doing. You can move a rock which ordinarily you could not have even shaken, but anger is there and poison is released.

In fear, people can run so fast that even Olympic runners will be left behind. Just think of yourself running if somebody is behind you with a dagger to kill you. You will do the best you can do, your whole body will be geared to function at its optimum.

When you kill an animal there is anger, there is anxiety, there is fear. Death is facing him; all the glands of the animal release many kinds of poisons. Hence the modern idea is that before killing an animal, make him unconscious, give him anaesthesia. In modern butcheries, anaesthesia is being used. But that does not make much difference, only a very superficial difference, because at the deepest core where no anaesthesia can ever reach, death has to be encountered. It may not be conscious, the animal may not be aware of what is happening, but it is happening as if in a dream. He is passing through a nightmare.

And to eat meat is to eat poisoned food.

Avoid anything that is poisoned on the physical plane, avoid anything that is poisoned on the mental plane. And on the mental plane things are more complicated. If you think you are a Hindu, you are poisoned; if you think you are a Mohammedan, you are poisoned. If you think you are a Christian, a Jaina, a Buddhist, you are poisoned. And you have been poisoned slowly, so slowly that you have become attuned to it. You are addicted to it.

You have been spoon-fed since the very first day; from your mother's breast, you have been poisoned. All kinds of conditionings are poisons. To think of oneself as a Hindu is to think of oneself opposed to humanity. To think of oneself as German, as Chinese, is to think of oneself opposed to humanity, is to think in terms of enmity, not friendship.

Think of yourself only as a human being. If you have any intelligence, think of yourself only as a simple human being. And when your intelligence grows a little more you will drop even the adjective "human"; you will think of yourself only as a being. And the being includes all – the trees and the mountains and the rivers and the stars and the birds and the animals.

Become bigger, become huge. Why are you living in tunnels? Why are you creeping into small dark black holes? But you think you are living in great ideological systems. You are *not* living in great ideological systems, because there *are* no great ideological systems. No idea is great enough to contain a human being; being-hood cannot be contained by any concept. All concepts cripple and paralyze.

Don't be a Catholic and don't be a communist, just be a human being. These are all poisons, these are all prejudices. And down the ages you have been hypnotized into these prejudices. They have become part of your blood, your bones, your very marrow. You will have to be very alert to get rid of all this poisoning.

Your body is not poisoned as much as your mind is. The body is a simple phenomenon, it can be easily cleaned. If you have been eating non-vegetarian foods it can be stopped, it is not such a big deal. And if you stop eating meat, within three months your body will be completely free of all the poisons created by non-vegetarian foods. It is simple. Physiology is not very complicated.

But the problem arises with psychology. A Jaina monk never eats any poisoned food, never eats anything non-vegetarian. But his mind is polluted and poisoned by Jainism as nobody else's is.

The real freedom is freedom from any ideology. Can't you simply live without any ideology? Is an ideology needed? Why is an ideology needed so much? It is needed because it helps you to remain stupid, it is needed because it helps you to remain unintelligent. It is needed because it supplies you ready-made answers and you need not find them on your own.

The real man of intelligence will not cling to any ideology – for what? He will not carry a load of ready-made answers. He knows that he has enough intelligence so that whatever situation arises, he will be able to respond to it. Why carry an unnecessary load from the past? What is the point of carrying it?

And in fact the more you carry from the past, the less you will be able to respond to the present, because the present is not a repetition of the past, it is always new, always, always new. It is never the old; it may sometimes appear like the old, but it is not old, there are basic differences.

Life never repeats itself. It is always fresh, always new, always growing, always exploring, always moving into new adventures. Your old ready-made answers are not going to help you. In fact they will hinder you; they will not allow you to see the new situation. The situation will be new, and the answer will be old.

That's why you look so stupid in life. But to remain stupid seems cheaper. To be intelligent needs effort, to be intelligent means you have to grow. And growth is painful. To be intelligent means you have to be continuously alert and aware; you cannot fall asleep, you cannot live like a somnambulist.

And to be intelligent has a few more dangers too. To be intelligent is very difficult because you have to live with the stupid crowds. To live with blind people and have eyes is a dangerous situation; they are bound to destroy your eyes. They cannot tolerate you, you are an offense.

Hence Jesus is crucified, Socrates is poisoned, Al-Hillaj is killed, Sarmad is beheaded. These were the most intelligent people that have ever walked on the earth. And how have we behaved with them? Why did a man of the intelligence of Socrates have to be killed? He became intolerable. His presence became such an offense. To look into his eyes meant to look in the mirror. And we are so ugly that rather than accepting the fact that we are ugly, the easier course is to destroy the mirror and forget all about your ugliness, and start living again in the old dream that you are the most beautiful person in the world.

We destroyed Socrates because he was a mirror. Hence people have decided it is better to remain mediocre, it is better to remain unintelligent.

Just the other day, I was reading a report. A few psychologists in England have discovered that by the time great politicians reach the highest posts, their intelligence is already withering away. Just think of a man of eighty-four becoming a prime minister! Those psychologists have warned the whole world that this is dangerous. People who have gone beyond the age of sixty, seventy, eighty, they become prime ministers and presidents. This is dangerous for the world, because they have so much power and so little intelligence left.

But those psychologists are not aware of another thing that I would like to tell you. In fact people choose them to be prime ministers and presidents because they are no longer intelligent. People don't like intelligent persons. People like people who look like them, who are like them; they feel they are not strangers. Intelligent people will be strangers.

I can't think of any country which could choose Socrates to be the prime minister – impossible. He is so different, his approach to life is so different, his insight into things is so deep. No country could afford, or no country could be so courageous, as to make him the prime minister, because he would bring chaos. He would start changing each and everything, because each and everything needs to be changed.

This rotten society has to be destroyed completely; only then can a new society be created. Renovation is not going to help. We have been renovating the same old ruins for centuries. No more props, no more renovations, no more whitewash! All that is needed is to demolish it, and let us create a new society. Let us bring a new human being, *homo novus*. Let us give birth to something new, a new mind, a new consciousness.

People choose dull dead persons to be in power because you can be safe with them. Now, India is very safe with Morarji Desai; he is not going to do a single thing. He will keep everything intact, he will keep this country's ugly bureaucracy as it is. He will not change anything; his whole effort will be to stop change. Jaiprakash Narayan was thinking of bringing about a total revolution, and what has happened is total failure.

Countries choose mediocre people to be in power, because they will save their tradition, their conventions, their prejudices. They will protect their poisons. Instead of destroying them, they will enhance them and strengthen them.

It is certainly dangerous to have unintelligent people in powerful posts. And it is becoming more and more dangerous, because they have more and more power and less and less intelligence. But why does it happen? There is a subtle logic in it. People don't want to change. Change is arduous, change is difficult.

If you change your poisonous foods you will be surprised; a new intelligence will be released in you. And this new intelligence will make it possible not to go on stuffing yourself with nonsense. This new intelligence will make you capable of dropping the past and its memories, of dropping unnecessary desires and dreams, dropping jealousies, angers, traumas and all kinds of psychological wounds.

Because you cannot drop psychological wounds, you become victims of psycho-fraud. The world is full of psychoanalysts of many kinds, they come in all shapes and sizes. The world is full of all kinds of psychotherapies. But why are so many psychotherapies needed? They are needed because you are not intelligent enough to heal your own wounds. Instead of healing them, instead of opening them to the winds and to the sun, you go on hiding them. You need psychotherapists to help you to open your wounds to the sun so that they can be healed, so that they can be allowed to heal.

But it is very difficult to find a real psychotherapist. Out of a hundred psychotherapists, ninety-nine are psychofrauds, not psychotherapists.

You will be surprised to know that more psychotherapists and psychoanalysts commit suicide than people in any other profession. The number is almost double. Now, what kind of people are these? And how were they going to help others? What were they doing their whole lives helping people?

More psychoanalysts go mad, insane, than people in any other profession of the world. The number is almost double. Why?…and they were helping other people towards sanity, when they themselves were insane. There is every possibility that they became interested in psychotherapy because of their insanity. It was an effort to find a cure for themselves.

And you will be surprised to know that psychotherapists of one kind go for psychotherapy to psychotherapists of another kind. The Freudian goes to the Jungian, the Jungian goes to the Freudian, and so on and so forth. This is a very strange situation.

If intelligence is released in you, you will be able to do all that is needed. You will be able to heal your own wounds, you will be able to see your own traumas, you need not go to a primal therapist.

I am allowing all kinds of therapies in this commune. In fact, in no other place in the world are so many psychotherapies available – sixty in all. Why am I allowing these therapies? Just because of you, because you are not yet ready to release your intelligence.

As the commune goes deeper and deeper into inner realizations, therapies can be dropped. When the commune has really bloomed, there will be no need of any therapy. Then love is therapy, intelligence is therapy. Then living day to day, moment to moment, aware and alert, is therapy. Then all kinds of things that you do during the day, cleaning and cooking and washing, they are all therapy.

Therapies are here only for the time being. The day I become convinced that now the major part of you has gone beyond therapies, therapies will disappear, because then the major part will be able to pull the minor part into intelligence also.

We are trying to create an intelligent kind of life. I am not much of a religious person, I am not a saint, I have nothing to do with spirituality. All those categories are irrelevant about me. You cannot categorize me, you cannot pigeonhole me. But one thing can be said, that my whole effort is to help you release the energy called love-intelligence. If love-intelligence is released, you are healed.

And the third kind of poisoned food is spiritual. That's what the self is. The self needs continuous attention. It feeds on attention, attention is its food. It is not only the politician who hankers for attention, more and more attention from more and more people. Your so-called saints are doing the same.

There is no difference between saints and politicians and actors, no difference at all. Their basic need is the same – attention: "More people should pay attention to me, more people should look up to me." That becomes food for the ego, and it is the subtlest kind of poisoned food.

These three things are implied in the first sutra. Atisha says:

Abandon poisoned food.

Physical, psychological, spiritual. Let your physiological body be pure of all poisons and toxins, and your mind be unburdened from all kinds of rubbish and junk. And let your soul be free from the idea of the self. When the soul is free from the idea of "I" you have arrived at that inner space called no-self, anatta. That is freedom, that is nirvana, that is enlightenment. You have come home. Now there is nowhere to go; now you can settle, rest and relax. Now you can enjoy the millions of joys that are being showered upon you by existence.

When these three poisoned foods are dropped, you become empty. But this emptiness is not a negative kind of emptiness. You are empty in the sense that all poisons, all contents, are gone. But you are full, full of something which cannot be named, full of something which devotees call God.

Atisha cannot use that word; he is not a devotee, he is not a *bhakta*. He cannot use any word for it, he remains completely silent about it. He says: Drop this, drop this, drop this, and then whatsoever remains is you, the real you.

And the second sutra is a very, very significant sutra.

Don't be consistent.

Have you ever heard anything like that, "Don't be consistent"? When you hear it for the first time or read it for the first time, you will think there has been some mistake, maybe a proof mistake or something. Because your so-called saints have been telling you just the opposite. "Don't be inconsistent," they say. "Be consistent."

It is here that Atisha is superb. He says:

Don't be consistent.

Why? What is consistency? Consistency means living according to the past. With what will you be consistent? If you want to be consistent you can have only one reference, and that is the past. To be consistent means to live according to the past, and to live according to the past is not to live at all. To live according to the past is to be dead. Then your life will be just a repetition.

To be consistent means you have already decided that now there is no more to life, that you have already come to a full stop; you don't allow life to have anything new to give to you, you have closed your doors. The sun will rise, but you will not allow its rays to enter into your room. And the flowers will bloom, but you will remain unaware of their fragrance. Moons will come and go, but you will remain stagnant. You have stopped being a river.

A river cannot be a consistent phenomenon. Only a pond can be consistent, because it is nonflowing. The flow by its very nature has to be inconsistent, because it has to face new situations, new challenges. New spaces are constantly coming upon it; it has to respond spontaneously, not according to the past.

The consistent man is a logical man, his life is one-dimensional. He lives in arithmetic, he follows logic. If anything goes against logic he simply avoids seeing it; he pretends that it is not there, because it is so disturbing to his logic.

And the logical man is the poorest man in the world, because life consists not only of logic, but of love too. And love is illogical. Only a very small part of life is logical, the superficial part. The deeper you go, the more and more you move into the illogical, or, to be more accurate, the supralogical.

Logic is good in the marketplace, but not in the temple, not in the mosque, not in the church. Logic is good in the office, in the shop, in the factory. Logic is not good when you are with your friends, when you are with your beloved, with your children. Logic is good when you are dealing in a businesslike way. But life is not all business; there is something far more valuable in life than any business. Allow that too.

A professor of philosophy went to a doctor and asked for advice on how to improve his sex life.

"You seem to be in good physical condition," said the doctor, after an examination. "You run ten miles a day, every day for seven days, then phone me."

A week later, the professor telephoned. "Well," said the physician, "has the running improved your sex life?"

"I don't know," said the professor. "I am seventy miles from home now."

This is the way a logical mind functions. It is one-dimensional. Life is multidimensional. Don't confine it, don't make it linear, don't live like a line. Live the multidimensions of it, the multi-phases of it, and then you cannot be consistent, because life is paradoxical – one moment it is joy, another moment it is sadness. If you are very consistent, then you have to go on smiling; whether your heart is crying or smiling, that doesn't matter, you have to be consistent. You have to be Jimmy Carter and go on smiling.

I have heard that his wife has to close his mouth every night, because at night also he goes on smiling. If you practice such a thing the whole day, naturally, how can you relax so suddenly at night? It becomes a fixed pattern.

Life consists of sadness too. And sadness is also beautiful; it has its own depth, its own delicacy, its own deliciousness, its own taste. A man is poorer if he has not known sadness; he is impoverished, very much impoverished. His laughter will be shallow, his laughter will not have depth, because depth comes only through sadness. A man who knows sadness, if he laughs, his laughter will have depth. His laughter will have something of his sadness too, his laughter will be more colorful.

A man who lives life in its totality is a rainbow; he lives the whole spectrum of it. He cannot be consistent, he has to be inconsistent.

Atisha is giving you something tremendously valuable. Live all the moods of life; they are your own and they all have something to contribute to your growth. Don't become confined to a small space. Howsoever comfortable and cozy it looks, don't become confined to a small space. Be an adventurer. Search and seek all the facets of life, all the aspects of life.

It is said that you cannot write a novel about a good man. And that is true; a good man really has no life. What novel can you write about him? At the most you can write a character certificate saying that he is good – and that is his whole life. He does not have much of a life, because he has no multidimensionality.

Live, and allow all that is possible. Sing, dance, cry, weep, laugh, love, meditate, relate, be alone. Be in the marketplace, and sometimes be in the mountains.

Life is short. Live it as richly as possible, and don't try to be consistent. The consistent man is a very poor man. Of course the society respects the consistent man, because the consistent man is predictable. You know what he is going to do tomorrow, you know how he is going to react. He is manageable, he can be easily manipulated. You know what buttons to push and how he will act. He is a machine; he is not truly a man. You can put him on and off and he will behave according to you; he is in your hands.

The society respects the consistent man; the society calls consistency "character." And the real man has no character. A real man is characterless, or beyond character. A real man cannot afford character, because character can be afforded only at the cost of life. If you renounce life, you can have character. If you don't renounce life, you will have many characters, but you will not have character. If you don't renounce life, how can you have a character? Each moment life is new, and so are you.

Society will not respect you, you will not be a respectable citizen – but who cares? Only mediocre people care about the respect of the society. The real person cares about only one thing: Whether I am living my life or not, whether I am living it according to my own vision or not, it is my life, and I am responsible to myself.

The most important responsibility is not to the nation or to the church or to anybody else. The real responsibility is to yourself. And it is that you have to live your life according to your own light and you have to move wherever life leads, without any compromise.

The man of character compromises. His character is nothing but an effort to guarantee the society, "I am not dangerous," and to declare to the society, "I will follow the rules of the game, I am utterly at your disposal."

The saint has character, hence he is respected. The sage has no character, hence it is very difficult to recognize him. Socrates is a sage, Jesus is a sage, Lao Tzu is a sage but they are very difficult to recognize, almost impossible, because they don't leave any trace behind them. They don't fit into any mold, they are pure freedom. They are like birds flying in the sky, they don't leave any footprints.

It is only for a very few sensitive souls to find a sage as a master, because the mediocre follow the saint. Only very, very intelligent people attune themselves to a sage, because the sage has no character and he cannot fulfill any of your expectations. He is bound to offend you, he is bound to disappoint you, he is bound to shake you and shatter you in many, many ways.

Slowly, slowly, he will make you as free as he himself is.

And now the third sutra, the most dangerous. I have been really worried about it.

Don't make wicked jokes.

What is a wicked joke? First I will have to tell three just to explain. And three, because it is a very esoteric number.

The first:

With a buzz and a beep and a whirr, a strange spaceship descends to Earth. Two bizarre creatures emerge and float to the ground. They are a young Martian couple, both scientists, here on an exploratory visit. They decide that the best way to find out about Earth is to communicate with some of the inhabitants, so off they bounce in search of some likely candidates. They enter an apartment building in the mysterious way Martians have of doing these things, and settle upon a newly-wedded couple by the names of Everett and Gladys Sprinkle (honest!).

Well, Everett and Gladys are as surprised as could be, but quickly adjust, in that special way newlyweds have of adapting to startling surprises. With one thing and another, the talk finally ends up on the subject of reproduction. The Martian male astounds the Sprinkles by offering to demonstrate the way people reproduce on his planet. Before they can protest in their embarrassment, he grabs the Martian woman, places the eight chubby fingers of his single hand on her forehead, and while he sparkles and she twinkles, an opening appears in her side and a tiny baby Martian hops out and starts prancing around Everett and Gladys' living room.

The Martian male then asks them how it is done on Earth. They hem and haw a bit, and finally decide that it would be too difficult to describe. So, in the interest of interplanetary cooperation, they take off their clothes and give a demonstration.

The Martians watch their performance, enthralled. When it is all over, the Martian woman asks, "When will the Earth child come out?" Gladys shakes her head and tells her that it will take nine months. The Martians are amazed at this, scratch their heads a bit, and then the male asks, "But if it isn't coming out right now, how come you were both so excited towards the end?"

The second:
A man went to see his doctor because he was feeling under the weather. The doctor asked the usual questions such as had the man been drinking or eating too much.

"No," said the man.

"Well, perhaps you have had too many late nights?" queried the doctor.

"No," the man replied.

The doctor thought about the problem for a while and then asked, "Much sex?"

"Infrequently," came the reply.

"Is that two words or one?"

And the third:

A woman walked into a supermarket to buy some broccoli. She went up to a man in the vegetable department and said, "Sir, do you have any broccoli?"

The man replied, "No, ma'am, none today. Come back tomorrow."

A few hours later, the woman was back again, asking the man, "Sir, do you have any broccoli?"

"Look, lady, I already told you, we don't have any broccoli today."

The lady left, only to return again that same day. By this time, the man was exasperated and said, "What does t-o-m spell in the word *tomato*?"

She replied, "Tom."

"And what does p-o-t spell in the word *potato*?" he asked.

"Pot," was the reply,

He then said, "And what does f-u-c-k spell in the word *broccoli*?"

She looked puzzled and said, "There's no fuck in *broccoli*."

He sighed a deep sigh and exclaimed, "Lady, that's what I've been trying to tell you all day"

I don't know whether they are wicked jokes or not, but one thing is certain, Atisha would have enjoyed them.

In fact, by "wicked jokes" he means something totally different. He means: Don't say anything against anybody, don't hurt anybody when they are not present, don't hurt anybody behind their back.

The translation is not exact. Atisha's whole meaning is: Don't gossip about people with a deliberate intention to hurt them, because that is not really joking, that is not fun, that is not humorous. Atisha can't be against the sense of humor, it is impossible. No man of his intelligence and awareness can be against the sense of humor. In fact, it is people like Atisha who have given the best religious humor to the world. Atisha comes from Gautam Buddha's tradition – the same lineage as the Zen people. And Zen is the only religion which has accepted humor as prayer. It is not possible, not possible at all, that Atisha had no sense of humor.

Then the sutra cannot be really against jokes. It is against hurting people. What he is saying is going deeper into the psychology of the joke, into the rationale behind the joke. It is what Sigmund Freud did one thousand years later. Sigmund Freud thinks that when you joke about somebody there is every possibility that you are aggressive, that you have anger, that in a vicarious way you are pretending to be humorous but you really want to be offensive.

But that cannot be decided by anybody else from the outside; only you can be the judge. If there is a deliberate effort in your mind to offend somebody, to hurt somebody, if it is violence disguised as humor, avoid it. But if it is not violence but just a pure sense of humor, the sense of fun – the sense of not taking life seriously, not taking it too seriously, then there is no problem.

If I meet Atisha some day, I am going to teach him a few jokes. And my feeling is he will enjoy it.

Jokes can be just pure humor without any violence in them. Sometimes on the surface one may think there is some violence, but the point is not what others think, the point is what your intention is. It is a question of intention. You can smile with an intention to offend, then smiling becomes a sin. Anything can become a sin if deep down the desire is to do violence. And anything can become virtue if deep down there is a desire to create more joy in life, more laughter in life.

My own understanding is that there is nothing more valuable than laughter. Laughter brings you closest to prayer. In fact only laughter is left in you when you are total. In everything else you remain partial, even in lovemaking you remain partial. But when you have a really heartfelt belly laugh, all the parts of your being – the physiological, the psychological, the spiritual – they all vibrate in one single tune, they all vibrate in harmony.

Hence, laughter relaxes. And relaxation is spiritual. Laughter brings you to the earth, brings you down from your stupid ideas of being holier-than-thou. Laughter brings you to reality as it is. The world is a play of God, a cosmic joke. And unless you understand it as a cosmic joke you will never be able to understand the ultimate mystery.

I am all for jokes, I am all for laughter.

Atisha has been wrongly translated. What he actually means is: Don't be violent, even in your words. Even while joking, don't be violent, because violence breeds more violence, anger will bring more anger, and it creates a vicious circle that has no end.

The fourth:

Don't wait for an opportunity.

Because the opportunity is now, the opportunity is here. So those who say, "We are waiting for an opportunity," are being deceptive, and they are not deceiving anybody but themselves.

The opportunity is not going to come tomorrow. It has already arrived, it has always been here. It was here even when you were not here. Existence is an opportunity; to be is the opportunity.

Don't wait for an opportunity.

Don't say, "Tomorrow I will meditate, tomorrow I will love, tomorrow I will have a dancing relationship with existence." Why tomorrow? Tomorrow never comes. Why not now? Why postpone? Postponement is a trick of the mind; it keeps you hoping, and meanwhile the opportunity is slipping by. And in the end you will come to the cul-de-sac – death – and there will be no more opportunity left.

And this has happened many times in the past. You are not new here, you have been born and you have died many, many times. And each time the mind has played the same trick, and you have not yet learned anything.

Atisha says:

Don't wait for an opportunity. Don't strike at the heart.

He says: Criticize people's minds, criticize their ideologies, criticize their systems of thought, criticize everything – but never criticize anybody's love, never criticize anybody's trust. Why? – because love is so valuable, trust is so immensely valuable. To destroy it, to criticize it, to shatter it in any way, is the greatest harm one can do to anybody.

You can criticize the mind – it *should* be criticized – but not the heart. Whenever you see something of the heart, avoid the temptation to criticize it.

Just the opposite is the case with people. They can tolerate your ideology, they can tolerate your mind, but the moment they see your love, your trust, they jump upon you. They cannot tolerate your trust; it is too much. They will say that this is hypnosis, that you have been hypnotized, you have been deceived, you are living in an illusion; that love is madness, love is blind; logic has eyes, and love is blind.

The truth is just the opposite. Logic is blind; criticize it! Love has eyes, only love has eyes, because only love can see God. Criticize beliefs, because beliefs are nothing but doubts hidden behind beautiful words. Criticize beliefs, but don't criticize anybody's trust.

And what is the difference? Trust has the quality of love. Belief is just a rational approach. If somebody says, "I believe in God because these are the proofs for God," then criticize him, because proofs can only prove the belief. But don't criticize somebody who says, "I love God. I don't know why, I simply love God. I am in love. There are no proofs, in fact there is every proof against him, but still I love God."

Remember the famous statement of Tertullian, a great Christian mystic: *Credo quia absurdum....* Somebody asked him, "Why do you believe in God?" He said, "Because God is absurd. Because God cannot be believed in, that's why I believe in God."

Everything else can be believed, only God cannot be believed. But in believing that which cannot be believed, one grows. That is reaching for the impossible.

So whenever you see somebody in love, somebody in trust, avoid the temptation to criticize. It is easy to criticize, it is easy to throw poison at somebody's love affair. But you don't know that you have been destructive, you don't know that you have destroyed something of immense beauty. You have thrown a rock on a roseflower.

Don't transfer the cow's load to the bull.

People are always finding scapegoats. Because they cannot answer the strong person, they take revenge on the weak.

There is a story about Mulla Nasruddin. He was in the court of a great king, he was the jester of the court. He said something very funny, but the king felt offended, and he slapped Mulla Nasruddin. Now, Mulla wanted to slap him back, but that was risky, that was dangerous, so he slapped the man who was standing by his side.

The man was taken aback; he said, "What are you doing? I have not done anything to you."

And Mulla said, "Why are you arguing with me? You can slap the man who is standing by your side. The world is big; by the time it comes back again we will see. Just let it go – pass it on!"

That's what people are doing, *actually* doing. It is not just a story. The husband has been humiliated by the boss and he comes home and is angry at the wife for no reason at all. Or maybe he finds a reason; a reason can always be found, they are so simple to find. There is too much salt in the vegetables or the chappati is burnt, or something – anything! He will find a reason, and he will convince himself that he is angry because of this reason. The reality is that he is angry at his boss. But the boss is a powerful man; to say anything could be dangerous, he might lose his job. So he smiled when the boss was insulting him; he went on wagging his tail. Now he is projecting the boss onto the wife.

If the story is happening in the West, then the wife can also jump on him. But if it is happening in the East, the wife cannot do anything. In the East, husbands have been telling their wives that husbands have to be treated as gods. The wife cannot say anything; she will have to wait for the child to come back from school and then she will do with the child whatsoever she wanted to do with the husband. She will beat the child. The child is late, his clothes are torn again, he has done this and that again, he has been playing with the wrong boys again.

And what can the child do? He will go into his room and beat or destroy his toys. In this way it goes on shifting.

Atisha is saying: Please don't shift things; otherwise your whole life you will be just shifting and shifting. Take the responsibility, take the risk. Respond to the situation, whatsoever the cost.

Don't transfer the cow's load to the bull. Don't back the favorite.

Don't have likes and dislikes. Be just, be fair, don't decide through your prejudices, your likes and dislikes. Just decide the case on its own merit, and your life will have the beauty of truth, your life will have the strength of truth.

Don't have wrong views.

All views are wrong. Life should be lived without views, life should be lived in immediate contact with reality. But if it is not possible, then at least don't have wrong views. What are wrong views? Views which are rooted in prejudice, hate, anger, greed, ambition, violence.

The first thing is, don't have any kind of views. Live life without a philosophy to live by. No philosophy is needed to live life; in fact the best and most glorious life is the life which is lived without any philosophy – simple, innocent, spontaneous.

But if it is not possible right now, then start by at least dropping wrong views. Don't live through prejudice, don't live through anger, don't live through hatred, don't live through greed and ambition, don't live through dreams. Be more real, more realistic. Be a little more alert and watchful, watching each act cautiously, because each act creates a chain of actions. Whatsoever you do will remain in the world even when you are gone, because the chain will continue. If you cannot do something beautiful in the world, at least don't do something ugly.

The highest possibility is to live without any views, to just live, to just be. The second best is to at least drop the negative part and follow the positive. And slowly, slowly you will see that if you can drop the negative, the positive can also be dropped. In fact to drop the negative is more difficult than to drop the positive.

The person who can drop the no can easily drop the yes, because the no is more ego-strengthening than the yes. The person who can drop anger, hatred and greed can easily drop the positive feelings. And to remain transcendental to all dualities is the ultimate goal of Atisha and all the great masters.

And the last sutra:

Don't fall for the celestial demon.

The ego is called the celestial demon. Remember constantly, each moment of your life has to become a constant remembrance, that the ego is very subtle and it has very cunning ways to come back again and again. It follows you to the very last, it hopes to the very last that you will be trapped. Beware of it.

This ego is called in Christian, Mohammedan and Judaic scriptures the devil. It is your own mind, the very center of your own mind.

In the beginning, just try for a few moments to live without any "I". You are digging a hole in the earth in the garden; just dig the hole, just become the digging, and forget that "I am doing it." Let the doer evaporate. You will perspire in the sun, and there will be no doer, and the digging will continue. And you will be surprised how divine life is if the ego can disappear even for a single moment.

Taking a shower, just let the water fall on you, but don't be there as an "I". Relax, forget the "I", and you will be surprised. The shower is not only cooling your body, it cools your innermost core too.

And if you search, you will find so many moments in ordinary life every day when the ego can be put aside. And the joy is so great that once you have tasted it you can do it again and again. And slowly, slowly you become capable of putting it off, unless it is absolutely necessary.

And then that day of blessing also comes when you know it is not necessary at all. You say the final good-bye to it. The day the ego dies, you have reached the point of no-self. That is your real being. Nonbeing is your real being. Not to be is to be for the first time.

Enough for today.

Chapter 14
Other Gurus and Etceteranandas

Can you say something about death and the art of dying?

The first thing to be known about death is that death is a lie. Death exists not; it is one of the most illusory things. Death is the shadow of another lie – the name of that other lie is the ego. Death is the shadow of the ego. Because the ego is, death appears to be there.

The secret of knowing death, of understanding death, is not in death itself. You will have to go deeper into the existence of the ego. You will have to look, watch, observe, be aware of what this ego is. And the day you have found that there is no ego, that there has never been – it appeared only because you were not aware, it appeared only because you were keeping your own existence in darkness – the day it is understood that the ego is a creation of an unconscious mind, the ego disappears and simultaneously death disappears.

The real you is eternal. Life is neither born nor dies. The ocean continues, waves come and go – but what are waves? Just forms, the wind playing with the ocean. Waves have no substantial existence. So are we, waves, playthings.

But if we look deep down into the wave there is an ocean, and the eternal depth of it and the unfathomable mystery of it. Look deep down into your own being and you will find the ocean. And that ocean *is*; the ocean always is. You cannot say, "It was," you cannot say, "It will be." You can only use one tense for it, the present tense: it is.

This is the whole search of religion. The search is to find that which truly is. We have accepted things which really are not, and the greatest and the most central of them is the ego. And of course it casts a big shadow – that shadow is death.

Those who try to understand death directly will never be able to penetrate into the mystery of it. They will be fighting with darkness. Darkness is non-existential, you cannot fight with it. Bring light, and the darkness is no more.

How can we know the ego? Bring a little more awareness to your existence. Each act has to be done less automatically than you have been doing up to now, and you have the key. If you are walking, don't walk like a robot. Don't go on walking as you have always walked, don't do it mechanically. Bring a little awareness to it, slow down, let each step be taken in full consciousness.

Buddha used to say to his disciples that when you raise your left foot, deep down say "Left." When you raise your right foot, deep down say "Right." First say it, so that you can become acquainted with this new process. Then slowly, slowly let the words disappear; just remember "Left, right, left, right."

Try it in small acts. You are not supposed to do big things. Eating, taking a bath, swimming, walking, talking, listening, cooking your food, washing your clothes – de-automatize the processes. Remember the word *de-automatization*; that is the whole secret of becoming aware.

The mind is a robot. The robot has its utility; this is the way the mind functions. You learn something; when you learn it, in the beginning you are aware. For example, if you learn swimming you are very alert, because life is in danger. Or if you learn to drive a car you are very alert. You have to be alert. You have to be careful about many things – the steering wheel, the road, the people passing by, the accelerator, the brake, the clutch. You have to be aware of everything. There are so many things to remember, and you are nervous, and it is dangerous to commit a mistake. It is so dangerous, that's why you have to keep aware. But the moment you have learned driving, this awareness will not be needed. Then the robot part of your mind will take it over.

That's what we call learning. Learning something means it has been transferred from consciousness to the robot. That's what learning is all about. Once you have learned a thing it is no more part of the conscious, it has been delivered to the unconscious. Now the unconscious can do it; now your consciousness is free to learn something else.

This is in itself tremendously significant. Otherwise you will remain learning a single thing your whole life. The mind is a great servant, a great computer. Use it, but remember that it should not overpower you. Remember that you should remain capable of being aware, that it should not possess you in toto, that it should not become all and all, that a door should be left open from where you can come out of the robot.

That opening of the door is called meditation. But remember, the robot is so skillful, it can even take meditation into its control. Once you have learned it, the mind says, "Now you need not be worried about it, I am capable of doing it. I will do it, you leave it to me."

And the mind is skillful; it is a very beautiful machine, it functions well. In fact all our science, together with all our so-called progress in knowledge, has not yet been able to create something so sophisticated as the human mind. The greatest computers in existence are still rudimentary compared to the mind.

The mind is simply a miracle.

But when something is so powerful, there is danger in it. You can be hypnotized so much by it and its power that you can lose your soul. If you have completely forgotten how to be aware, then the ego is created.

Ego is the state of utter unawareness. The mind has taken possession of your whole being; it has spread like a cancer all over you, nothing is left out. The ego is the cancer of the inner, the cancer of the soul.

And the only remedy, the *only* remedy I say, is meditation. Then you start reclaiming a few territories from the mind. And the process is difficult but exhilarating, the process is difficult but enchanting, the process is difficult but challenging, thrilling. It will bring a new joy into your life. When you reclaim territory back from the robot you will be surprised that you are becoming a totally new person, that your being is renewed, that this is a new birth.

And you will be surprised that your eyes see more, your ears hear more, your hands touch more, your body feels more, your heart loves more – everything becomes more. And more not only in the sense of quantity but in the sense of quality too. You not only see more trees, you see trees more deeply. The green of the trees becomes greener – not only that, but it becomes luminous. Not only that, but the tree starts having an individuality of its own. Not only that, but you can have a communion with existence now.

And the more territories that are reclaimed, the more and more your life becomes psychedelic and colorful. You are then a rainbow – the whole spectrum; all the notes of music – the whole octave. Your life becomes richer, multidimensional, has depth, has height, has tremendously beautiful valleys and has tremendously beautiful sunlit peaks. You start expanding. As you reclaim parts from the robot, you start coming alive. For the first time you are turned on.

This is the miracle of meditation; this is something not to be missed. The people who miss it have not lived at all. And to know life in such intensity, in such ecstasy, is to know that there is no death. Not to know life creates death; ignorance of life creates death.

To know life is to know there is no death, there never has been. Nobody has ever died, I declare, and nobody is ever going to die. Death is impossible in the very nature of things – only life is. Yes, life goes on changing forms; one day you are this, another day you are something else. Where is the child you once were? Has the child died? Can you say that the child has died? The child has not died, but then where is the child? The form has changed. The child is still there in its essentiality, but now you have become a young man or a young woman. The child is there with all its beauty; it has been superimposed by new riches.

And then one day you will become old. Then where is your youth? Died? No, again something more has happened. Old age has brought its own crop, old age has brought its own wisdom, old age has brought its own beauties.

The child is innocent, that is his core. The youth is overflowing with energy, that is his core. And the old man has seen all, lived all, known all; wisdom has arisen, that is his core. But his wisdom contains something of his youth; it is also overflowing, it is radiant, it is vibrant, it is pulsating, it is alive. And it also has something of the child; it is innocent.

If the old man is not young also, then he has only aged, he is not old. He has grown in time, in age, but he is not grown-up. He has missed. If the old man is not innocent like the child, if his eyes don't show that crystal clarity of innocence, then he has not yet lived.

If you live totally, cunningness and cleverness disappear, and trust arises. These are the criteria to know whether one has lived or not. The child never dies but only is metamorphosed. The youth never dies, there is only a new mutation again. And do you think the old man dies? Yes, the body disappears because it has served its purpose, but the consciousness continues the journey.

If death was a reality, existence would be utterly absurd, existence would be mad. If Buddha dies, that means such beautiful music, such splendor, such grace, such beauty, such poetry, disappears from existence. Then the existence is very stupid. Then what is the point? Then how is growth possible? Then how is evolution possible?

Buddha is a rare gem, it happens only once in a while. Millions of people try, and then one person becomes a buddha – and then he dies and all is finished, so what is the point?

No, Buddha cannot die. He is absorbed; he is absorbed by the whole. He continues. Now the continuity is bodiless, because he has become so expanded that no body can contain him except the body of the universe itself. He has become so oceanic that it is not possible to have small manifestations. Now he can exist only in essence. He can exist only as a fragrance, not as a flower. He cannot have a form, he can only exist as a formless intelligence of existence.

The world has grown more and more intelligent. Before Buddha it was not so intelligent, something was missing. Before Jesus it was not so intelligent, before Mohammed it was not so intelligent. They have all contributed. If you understand rightly, God is not something that has happened, but is *happening*.

God is happening every day. Buddha has created something, Mahavira has created something, Patanjali has created something, Lao Tzu, Zarathustra, Atisha, Tilopa – they have all contributed.

God is being created. Let your hearts be thrilled that you can become a creator of God! You have been told again and again that God created the world.

I would like to tell you: we are creating God every day.

And you can see the changes. If you look in the Old Testament, the words that the God of the Old Testament utters look so ugly. Something seems to be very primitive. The God of the Old Testament says, "I am a very jealous God." Can you think of God being jealous? "Those who don't follow me should be crushed and thrown into hellfire. Those who don't obey me, great revenge will be taken on them."

Can you think of these words being uttered by Buddha? No, the concept of God is being polished every day. The God of Moses is rudimentary; the God of Jesus is far more sophisticated, far more cultured. As man becomes cultured, his God becomes cultured. As man has more understanding, his God has more understanding, because your God represents you.

The God of Moses is law, the God of Jesus is love. The God of Buddha is compassion, the God of Atisha is utter emptiness and silence.

We are searching for new dimensions of God, we are adding new dimensions to God, God is being created. You are not just a seeker, you are also a creator. And the future will know far better visions of God.

Buddha does not die, he disappears into our concept of God. Jesus melts into the ocean of our God. And the people who are not yet awakened, they also don't die. They have to come back again and again into some form, because the only possibility of being awakened is through forms.

The world is a context for becoming awakened, an opportunity.

Remember Atisha. He says, "Don't wait for the opportunity" – because the world is the opportunity; we are already in it. The world is an opportunity to learn. It looks paradoxical; time is the opportunity to learn the eternal, the body is the opportunity to learn the bodiless, matter is the opportunity to learn consciousness, sex is the opportunity to learn samadhi. The whole existence is an opportunity. Anger is the opportunity to learn compassion, greed is the opportunity to learn sharing, and death is the opportunity to go into the ego and see "whether I am or I am not. If I am, then maybe death is possible." But if you find for yourself that "I am not," that there is pure emptiness inside, that there is nobody – if you can feel that nobodiness inside you, where is death? What is death? Who can die?

Your question is significant. You ask, "Can you say something about death?" Only one thing, that death is not.

And you ask "...and the art of dying?" When there is no death, how are you going to learn the art of dying? You will have to *live* the art of living. If you know how to live, you will know everything about life and about death. But you will have to approach the positive.

Never make the negative the object of your study, because the negative is not there. You can go on and on and you will never arrive anywhere. Try to understand what light is, not darkness. Try to understand what life is, not death. Try to understand what love is, not hate.

If you go into hate you will never understand it, because hate is only the absence of love. So is darkness the absence of light. How can you understand absence? If you want to understand me, you have to understand me, not my absence. If you want to study this chair, this chair has to be studied – not that when Asheesh has taken it away, you start studying the absence. What will you study?

Always be alert, never get hooked into anything negative. Many people go on studying negative things; their energies are simply wasted. There is no art of dying. Or, the art of living is the art of dying. Live!

But your so-called religious people have been teaching you not to live. They are the creators of death. In a very indirect way they have created death, because they have made you so afraid of living. Everything is wrong. Life is wrong, the world is wrong, the body is wrong, love is wrong, relationship is wrong, enjoying anything is wrong. They have made you so guilty about everything, so condemnatory of everything, that you cannot live. And when you cannot live, what is left? The absence, the absence of life – and that is death. And then you are trembling, trembling before something which is not, which is your own creation. And because you start trembling in great fear of death, the priest becomes very powerful. He says, "Don't be worried, I am here to help you. Follow me. I will save you from hell and I will take you to heaven. And those who are within my fold will be saved, and nobody else will be saved."

Christians go on saying the same thing to people: "Unless you are a Christian you cannot be saved. Only Jesus will save you. The day of judgment is coming closer, and on the day of judgment, those who are with Jesus, he will recognize them, he will sort them out. And the others, millions and millions, will be simply thrown into hell for eternity. Remember, there is no escape; for eternity they will be thrown into hell."

And the same is the attitude of other religions. But out of fear people start clinging to something, whatsoever is available in the close vicinity. If you are accidentally born in a Hindu home or a Jaina or a Jewish home, you become a Jew or a Jaina or a Hindu, as the case may be. Whatsoever is available close by, the child starts clinging to it.

My approach is totally different. I don't say be afraid – that is the strategy of the priest, that is his trade secret. I say there is nothing to fear, because God is in you. There is nothing to fear. Live life fearlessly, live each moment as intensely as possible. Intensity has to be remembered. And if you don't live any moment intensely, then what happens? Your mind hankers for repetition.

You love a woman, your mind hankers for repetition. Why? Why do you hanker for the same experience again and again? You eat certain food, you enjoy it, now you hanker for the same food again and again. Why? The reason is that whatsoever you do, you never do it totally. Hence something remains discontented in you. If you do it totally, there will be no hankering for repetition and you will be searching for the new, exploring the unknown. You will not move in a vicious circle, your life will become a growth. Ordinarily people only go on moving in circles. They appear to move, but they only appear to.

Growth means you are not moving in a circle, that something new is happening every day, every *moment* really. And when does that become possible? Whenever you start living intensely.

I would like to teach you how to eat intensely and totally, how to love intensely and totally, how to do small things with such utter ecstasy that nothing is left behind. If you laugh, let the laughter shake your very foundations. If you cry, become tears; let your heart be poured out through tears. If you hug somebody, then become the hug. If you kiss somebody, then be just the lips, then be just the kiss. And you will be surprised how much you have been missing, how much you have missed, how you have lived up to now in a lukewarm way.

I can teach you the art of living; that implies the art of dying, you need not learn it separately. The man who knows how to live, knows how to die. The man who knows how to fall in love, knows when the moment has come to fall out of it. He falls out of it gracefully, with a good-bye, with gratitude – but only the man who knows how to love.

People don't know how to love, and then they don't know how to say good-bye when the time has come to say it. If you love you will know that everything begins and everything ends, and there is a time for beginning and there is a time for ending, and there is no wound in it. One is not wounded, one simply knows the season is over. One is not in despair, one simply understands, and one thanks the other, "You gave me so many beautiful gifts. You gave me new visions of life, you opened a few windows I might never have opened on my own. Now the time has come that we separate and our ways part." Not in anger, not in rage, not with a grudge, not with any complaint, but with tremendous gratitude, with great love, with thankfulness in the heart.

If you know how to love, you will know how to separate. Your separation will also have a beauty and a grace. And the same is the case with life; if you know how to live, you will know how to die. Your death will be tremendously beautiful.

The death of Socrates is tremendously beautiful, the death of Buddha is tremendously beautiful. The day Buddha died, in the morning he gathered all his disciples, all his sannyasins, and told them, "The last day has come now, my boat has arrived and I have to leave. And this has been a beautiful journey, a beautiful togetherness. If you have any questions to ask, you can ask them, because I will not be available to you physically anymore."

A great silence fell on the disciples, a great sadness. And Buddha laughed and said, "Don't be sad, because that's what I have been teaching you again and again – everything that begins, ends. Now let me teach you by my death too. As I have been teaching you through my life, let me teach you through my death too."

Nobody could gather the courage to ask a question. Their whole life they had asked thousands and thousands of questions, and this was not a moment to ask anything; they were not in the mood, they were crying and weeping.

So Buddha said, "Good-bye. If you don't have any questions then I will depart." He sat under the tree with closed eyes and he disappeared from the body. In the Buddhist tradition, this is called "the first meditation" – to disappear from the body. It means to disidentify yourself from the body, to know totally and absolutely, "I am not the body."

A question is bound to arise in your mind: had Buddha not known it before? He had known it before, but a person like Buddha then has to create some device so that just a little bit of him remains connected with the body. Otherwise he would have died long before – forty-two years before he would have died. The day his enlightenment happened, he would have died. Out of compassion he created a desire, the desire to help people. It is a desire, and it keeps you attached to the body.

He created a desire to help people. "Whatsoever I have known, I have to share." If you want to share, you will have to use the mind and the body. That small part remained attached.

Now he cuts even that small root in the body; he becomes disidentified from the body. The first meditation complete, the body is left. Then the second meditation: the mind is dropped. He had dropped the mind long before; as a master it was dropped, but as a servant it was still used. Now it is not even needed as a servant, it is utterly dropped, totally dropped.

And then the third meditation: he dropped his heart. It had been needed up to now, he had been functioning through his heart; otherwise compassion would not have been possible. He had been the heart; now he disconnects from the heart.

When these three meditations are completed, the fourth happens. He is no more a person, no more a form, no more a wave. He disappears into the ocean. He becomes that which he had always been, he becomes that which he had known forty-two years before but had been somehow managing to delay, in order to help people.

His death is a tremendous experiment in meditation. And it is said that many who were present, just seeing him moving, slowly, slowly…. First they saw the body was no more the same; something had happened, the aliveness had disappeared from the body. The body was there, but like a statue. Those who were more perceptive, more meditative, they immediately saw that now the mind had been dropped and there was no mind inside. Those who were even more perceptive could see that the heart was finished. And those who were really on the verge of buddhahood, seeing Buddha disappear, they also disappeared.

Many disciples became enlightened the day Buddha died, many – just seeing him dying. They had watched him living, they had seen his life, but now came the crescendo, the climax. They saw him dying such a beautiful death, such grace, such meditativeness…seeing it, many were awakened.

To be with a buddha, to live with a buddha, to be showered by his love, is a blessing. But the greatest blessing is to be present when a buddha dies. You can simply ride on that energy, you can simply take a quantum leap with that energy – because Buddha is disappearing, and if your love is great and your connection is deep, it is bound to happen.

It is going to happen to many of my sannyasins. The day I disappear, many of you are going to disappear with me.

Vivek again and again says to me, "I don't want to live a single moment when you are gone." And I say to her, "Don't be worried. Even if you want to live, you will not be able to." Just the other day, Deeksha was saying to Vivek, "Once Osho is gone, I am gone." That is true. But this is not only true about Vivek and Deeksha, this is true of many of you. And this is not something that you have to do, it will simply happen of its own accord. It will be a happening. But it is possible only if you allow total trust to happen.

While I am alive, if you allow total trust to happen, then you can move with me in my death too. But if there is a little doubt, you will think, "But I have still not done many things and I have to live my life. I know that it is sad that the master is leaving, and I know it would have been far better if he was alive, but I have many things to do, I have to live my life"…and a thousand and one desires. If there is a little doubt, it will create a thousand and one desires. But if there is no doubt, then the death of the master is the most liberating experience that has ever happened on this earth.

Buddha was very fortunate to have great disciples. Jesus was not so fortunate, his disciples were cowards. While he was dying they all escaped. While he was on the cross they escaped miles away, in fear that they might be caught. After three days, when the stone was removed from in front of the tomb where his body was kept, there was not a single one of the apostles; only Mary Magdalene the prostitute, and another Mary – two women – had gathered courage.

The disciples were afraid that if they went to see what had happened to the master's body or to take the master's body down, they might be caught. Only two women had enough love. When Jesus' body was taken down from the cross, then too, three women took the body down. All those great apostles were not there.

Jesus was not very fortunate. And the reason is clear: he was starting something new. In the East, buddhas have existed for millions of years. The Western concept of time is not right, the Western concept of time is very small, and it is because of Christianity that it is very small. Christian theologians have even calculated when the world was created – the twenty-third of March. I was wondering, why not the twenty-first? God missed by only two days! On the twenty-third of March, four thousand and four years before Christ, the world was created. A very small idea of time.

The world has existed for millions of years. Now science is coming closer and closer to the Eastern concept of time. In the East, buddhas have existed for thousands and thousands of years, so we know how to be with a buddha – how to live with him, how to trust him, and how to be with him when he is dying, and how to die with him.

Much of it has been forgotten, by courtesy of Christianity and Western education. The modern Indian is not Indian at all. It is very difficult to find Indians in India, almost impossible. Only once in a while do I come across an Indian. Sometimes it happens that people who are coming from faraway countries are far more Indian than the so-called Indians. Three hundred years of Western domination and Western education have made the Indian mind completely disoriented.

The Western mind is coming closer and closer towards understanding buddhas more than the Eastern mind itself does. And the reason is that the West is getting fed up with technology and science, is becoming more and more hopeless, and has seen that what science has promised, it has not been able to fulfill. In fact it has seen that all the revolutions have failed. And now there is only one revolution left – the inner, the revolution of the individual, the revolution that is brought by inner transformation.

Indians are still hoping that with a little better technology, a little better government, a little more money, a little more production, things will all be perfectly okay. The Indian mind is hoping, it is very materialistic. The modern Indian is more materialistic than the people of any other country. The materialist countries are fed up with materialism. It has failed; they are disappointed and disillusioned.

So let me tell you, my sannyasins are more Indian. They may be Germans, they may be Norwegians, they may be Dutch, they may be Italians, French, English, Americans, Russians, Czechs, Japanese, Chinese, but they are far more Indian.

Journalists again and again come and ask, "Why don't we see more Indians here?" And I say, "They are all Indians! There are just a few foreigners – just those few whom you think are Indians, just those few foreigners; otherwise they are all Indians."

To be an Indian has nothing to do with geography, it has something to do with an inner approach towards reality. Modern India has forgotten the ways of the Buddha, and has forgotten how to live with buddhas.

I am trying to reveal that treasure to you again. Let it sink deep in your heart. The first principle is the art of living. Be life-affirmative. Life is synonymous with God. You can drop the word *God* – life *is* God. Live with reverence, with great respect and gratitude. You have not earned this life, it has been a sheer gift from the beyond. Feel thankful and prayerful, and take as many bites of it as possible and chew it well and digest it well.

Make your life an aesthetic experience. And not much is needed to make it an aesthetic experience; just an aesthetic consciousness is needed, a sensitive soul. Become more sensitive, more sensuous, and you will become more spiritual.

Priests have almost poisoned your body into a state of death. You are carrying paralyzed bodies and paralyzed minds and paralyzed souls – you are moving on crutches. Throw away all those crutches! Even if you have to fall and crawl on the ground, that is better than clinging to crutches.

And experience life in all possible ways – good-bad, bitter-sweet, dark-light, summer-winter. Experience all the dualities. Don't be afraid of experience, because the more experience you have, the more mature you become. Search for all possible alternatives, move in all directions, be a wanderer, a vagabond of the world of life and existence. And don't miss any opportunity to live.

Don't look back. Only fools think of the past – fools who do not have the intelligence to live in the present. And only fools imagine about the future, because they don't have the courage to live in the present. Forget the past, forget the future, this moment is all. This moment has to become your prayer, your love, your life, your death, your everything. This is it.

And live courageously, don't be cowards. Don't think of consequences; only cowards think of consequences. Don't be too result-oriented; people who are result-oriented miss life. Don't think of goals, because goals are always in the future and far away, and life is herenow, close by.

And don't be too purposive. Let me repeat it: don't be too purposive. Don't always bring in the idea, "What is the purpose of it?" because that is a strategy created by your enemies, by the enemies of humanity, to poison your very source of life. Ask the question, "What is the purpose of it?" and everything becomes meaningless.

It is early morning, the sun is rising and the east is red with the sun, and the birds are singing and the trees are waking up, and it is all joy. It is a rejoicing, a new day has happened again. And you are standing there asking the question, "What is the purpose of it?" You miss, you miss it totally. You are simply disconnected.

A roseflower is dancing in the wind, so delicate and yet so strong, so soft yet fighting with the strong wind, so momentary yet so confident. Look at the roseflower. Have you ever seen any roseflower nervous? So confident, so utterly confident, as if it is going to be here forever. Just a moment's existence, and such trust in eternity. Dancing in the wind, whispering with the wind, sending out its fragrance – and you are standing there asking the question, "What is the purpose of it?"

You fall in love with a woman and ask the question, "What is the purpose of it?" You are holding the hand of your beloved or your friend, and asking the question, "What is the purpose of it?" And you may still be holding hands, but now life has disappeared, your hand is dead.

Raise the question, "What is the purpose?" and everything is destroyed. Let me tell you, there is no purpose in life. Life is its own purpose; it is not a means to some end, it is an end unto itself. The bird on the wing, the rose in the wind, the sun rising in the morning, the stars in the night, a man falling in love with a woman, a child playing on the street…there is no purpose. Life is simply enjoying itself, delighting in itself. Energy is overflowing, dancing, for no purpose at all. It is not a performance, it is not a business. Life is a love affair, it is poetry, it is music. Don't ask ugly questions like, "What is the purpose?" because the moment you ask it, you disconnect yourself from life. Life cannot be bridged by philosophical questions. Philosophy has to be put aside.

Be poets of life, singers, musicians, dancers, lovers, and you will know the real philosophy of life: *philosophia perennis*.

And if you know how to live…and it is a simple art. The trees are living and nobody is there to teach them. In fact they must be laughing; seeing that you have asked such a question, they must be giggling – you may not be able to hear their giggle.

The whole existence is nonphilosophical. If you are philosophical, then a gap arises between you and existence. Existence simply *is*, for no purpose. And the person who really wants to live has to get rid of this idea of purpose. If you start living without any purpose, with intensity, totality, love and trust, when death comes, you will know how to die – because death is not the end of life, but only an episode in life.

If you have known other things, if you have lived other things, you will be able to live death too. The real man of understanding lives his death as much as he lives his life, with the same intensity, with the same thrill.

Socrates was so thrilled when he was going to be given poison. The poison was being prepared outside his room. His disciples had gathered; he was lying on the bed ready, because the time was coming closer. At six o'clock, exactly as the sun sets, he would be given the poison. People were not even breathing, the clock was coming closer and closer to six o'clock, and this beautiful man would be gone forever. And he had not committed any sin. His only sin was that he used to tell the truth to people, that he was a teacher of truth, that he would not compromise, that he would not bow down to the stupid politicians. That was his only crime; he had not done any harm to anybody. And Athens was to remain poorer forever.

In fact, with the death of Socrates, Athens died. Then it never had the same glory again, never. It was such a crime, killing Socrates, that Athens committed suicide. Greek culture never reached such a height again. For a few days it continued, just echoes of Socrates – because

Plato was his disciple, just an echo. And Aristotle was Plato's disciple, an echo of an echo. Slowly, slowly, as the echoes of Socrates disappeared, Greek culture disappeared from the world. It had seen days of glory, but it committed suicide by murdering Socrates.

His disciples were very much disturbed, but Socrates was thrilled, just as a small child when you take him to the exhibition is so thrilled by everything, each and everything is so incredible. He would get up again and again and go to the window and ask the man who was preparing the poison, "Why are you delaying? Now it is six o'clock!"

And the man said, "Are you mad, Socrates, or something? I am delaying just so that a beautiful man like you can stay a little longer. I cannot delay forever, but this much I can do. A little bit more, linger a little bit more! Why are you in such a hurry to die?"

Socrates said, "I have known life, I have lived life, I know the taste of life. Now I am so curious about death! That's why I am in such a hurry. I am pulsating with great joy – the very idea that now I am going to die, and I will be able to see what death is. I want to taste death. I have tasted everything else, only one thing has remained unknown. I have lived life and known all that life can give. This is the last gift of life, and I am really intrigued."

The man who has lived, really lived, will know how to die.

There is no art of death. The art of life is the art of death, because death is not something separate from life. Death is the highest peak of life, the Everest, the virgin-snow-covered sunlit Everest. It is the most beautiful thing in existence.

But you can know the beauty of death only if you know the beauty of life. Life prepares you for death. But people are not living at all; they are hampered in every possible way from living. So they don't know what life is, and consequently they will not know what death is.

Death is a lie. You don't end with it, you only take a turn. You move on another road; you disappear from this road, you appear on another road. If you are not yet awakened, not yet enlightened, then here you die, there you are born. You disappear from one body and you appear immediately in some womb, because millions of foolish people are copulating all over the world – they are just waiting for you! And there are really so many that it is good that you die unconscious and you choose the new womb unconsciously. If it was a conscious choice, you would go crazy. How to choose? Whom to choose?

Unconsciously you die, unconsciously you are born into the closest possible womb that fits with you. One body is gone, and another is immediately formed.

But if you are enlightened…. And what do I mean by "enlightened"? I mean if you have lived your life with awareness, and you have reached the point of awareness where no dark spot of unconsciousness exists in you, then there is no longer any womb for you. Then you enter into the womb of God – existence itself. That is liberation, moksha, nirvana.

? Morarji Desai once said that if he did set up a commission to investigate us, we would not like the results. If the government does set up a commission, is there any hope at all of its being really open, really impartial?

Politics can never be impartial, politics is partiality. Politics can never be unprejudiced, it is rooted in prejudice. So don't hope for much. It will be fun, that's all; we will enjoy the people who come with the commission. Enjoy it then – if he appoints any commission and the people come here, enjoy it. Give them a feeling of your life that is happening here. Who knows, somebody may be turned on!

But don't trust politicians. The game with politicians is a dangerous game. Friendship is dangerous with them, enmity is dangerous with them. But it cannot be avoided. And what is happening here is so huge that politicians cannot remain out of it for long.

Just the other day, in the Indian parliament they discussed us again – a long discussion. A phone call came from Delhi saying, "Send Krishna Prem, Madhura and the other press people, because now this is the only hot thing that people are talking about."

We are not interested in politicians, in politics – not at all. But we cannot avoid them either. Politics is like the weather: whether you like it or not, it is going to affect you anyway.

It is known now why Nasser suddenly died of a heart attack.... He received a telephone call from Golda Meir, who told him, "Let's make love not war."

Now, whether you make love or you make war, with politicians it is going to be difficult going, tough going.

So, there is no need for any hope. In the first place, I don't think he is going to appoint a commission, for many reasons. One reason is, the other day in parliament somebody raised the question, "Why a commission only for Osho?" And a great shiver went through the whole parliament.

It is reported in the newspapers that the man suggested they appoint a commission to investigate Satya Sai Baba, Guru Maharaj-ji, Maharishi Mahesh Yogi, Muktananda, and other Etcetera Etceteranandas. They were very happy to have a commission investigate my place, my commune, but now there is fear. And that looks logical – if you want to investigate one commune, then why not all? That is the first problem they will have to face.

Secondly, he would like to avoid, to escape from appointing the commission – because who knows what will happen if the commission comes? The people who come and go back to him, they may report that all that appears in the newspapers is false, it is not the true picture. So many people have visited the ashram, and so many members of parliament have come, and whosoever has come has reported to him, "You are unnecessarily prejudiced. Something beautiful is happening, a meeting of East and West is happening."

So he is also afraid deep down. Who knows, the commission may report favorably – then what is he going to do? Once the commission reports favorably, it will become a great problem for him. So he has found a very legal way to escape from appointing the commission. He says that I should write a personal letter to him asking that a commission be appointed to investigate me and my work. He knows perfectly well that for five years I have stopped writing personal letters.

And why should I write a personal letter? If the government wants to know what is happening, it is *their* work to find that out. If they have decided without investigating, then they are being undemocratic. If they say to the world, "We will not allow any television companies from Holland, from England, from Japan or from Australia to cover the work and the commune, because it will not represent the true Indian spirit and the true Indian image"; if they have decided it without investigating at all, then it is their duty to appoint a commission. Why should I ask them to appoint a commission? But this is a legal trick. He knows I don't write personal letters. For five years I have not done so, and I am not going to do it now.

And then he is worried also about something he said in parliament the other day. He said that he has not received any personal letter from me and it is always Yoga Laxmi, the managing trustee, who writes. And she writes, "Osho is only a guest in the commune, so how can we investigate a guest?"

But Laxmi is right, I am simply your guest. And I don't do anything, so what are they going to investigate? They can come and sit with me for twenty-four hours in my room; I don't *do* anything, there is nothing to investigate! The question is of the commune, the work that goes on in the commune: *that* has to be investigated.

But he is not interested in the commune. His interest basically is somehow to create a trap in which he can catch me – because he knows if I am caught or if I am imprisoned, then the whole work will be destroyed easily. The other day in parliament he said it – unconsciously it must have come out of him – "Osho is the ashram, Osho is the commune. So we cannot investigate the commune unless he writes." And I am not going to write. I don't think politicians are of any worth, and I don't think they are worthy to investigate a religious commune.

In fact some day we should think of appointing a commission to investigate the politicians....

Three prime ministers of three great countries are sitting at a dinner party when all of a sudden a loud fart is heard coming from the seat where the lady host is dining. She is barely able to hold herself together when immediately from across the table the French prime minister stands up and in a loud firm voice exclaims, "Excuse me, messieurs-dames, but I must unexpectedly leave. I am not feeling well."

Grateful and relieved, the lady manages to regain her composure, when ten minutes later she lets another fart escape. Dismayed and blushing up to her ears, she watches how the English prime minister stands up and declares, "I am sorry, ladies and gentlemen, but I must retire early tonight. I am not feeling well."

The scene happens once more, and this time the Indian prime minister proudly stands up and says loudly, "Well now, ladies and gentlemen, it is my honor and my duty to go home."

Get it?

I don't have any respect for these politicians and political leaders. I have respect for them as human beings, but not as politicians. Politics is the most ugly phenomenon on the earth, and politicians, the ugliest human beings. I have tremendous respect for human beings, but I can't have any respect for the ugly politics that goes on.

There is no need to have any hope. First, they will not appoint any commission, afraid that it may turn against them. And it is not going to be easy either; if they appoint a commission we are first going to give tough tests for the commission too, to find out whether they are really capable of investigating a commune. What do they know about it? What do they know about the therapies that are going on here? First *they* will be examined. A group of fifty therapists will examine them in every possible way. Unless we are satisfied that they are worthy to investigate, we won't allow them inside the gate.

First, they are not going to appoint a commission. He is afraid – whom to appoint? Where are they going to find people who understand primal therapy, bioenergetics, encounter, psychodrama, psychosynthesis and psychoanalysis? And he is afraid that if he appoints somebody who understands these things, he will be in support of us. He can appoint a retired senile judge – but he will not know anything about it, and that will be really hilarious.

I don't think he is going to, but if he does appoint a commission, enjoy it. Let them come, and have real fun with the whole thing. At least let them carry back some joy, some laughter, from here. What they report is irrelevant, because what happens almost always is this: before they come here, the report will already be ready. That's what happens. The report will be prepared by somebody else. But we are not interested in their reports.

I had only said to appoint a commission so that the government can have at least a show of democracy. It is utterly undemocratic to prevent media people reaching Pune. It is so undemocratic what they tell people – now we even have letters in our possession. To one sannyasin, an Indian ambassador in America wrote, "If you want to go to Pune, then forget all about it; we are not going to give you any entry visa. But if you want to go to any other ashram, write, and we are ready to give it to you."

Just see the foolishness of the man – writing it!

Now in Bombay, on the passports of sannyasins they are writing "This visa is not valid for Pune." So it seems Pune is no longer part of India. A tourist is entitled to tour the whole of India, except Pune! But why prevent people from coming to Pune? Just Koregaon Park would have been enough!

In every possible way, they are doing whatsoever they can do to hassle and hinder us. They have tried one thing that they are very clever at doing – to find some flaw in our finances. They have not been able to do it. Sadly, the finance minister had to declare yesterday in parliament, "Their finances are absolutely okay and we could not find any flaw in them." So now they are at a loss as to what to do.

In fact there is nothing that they can find here which is being done against the law. But just their prejudices, their old rotten minds, their traditional minds…. They cannot believe that a phenomenon like me is even possible in India. But it is happening, and it is going to grow. It is growing. And the more they hinder it, the more it will grow. That is an inner logic of things: the more hindrances there are, and the more challenges, the more it is going to grow.

If Jesus had not been crucified, there would have been no Christianity. If one day the politicians decide to crucify me, I will be the happiest person in the world.

Enough for today.

Chapter 15
The Smokeless Flame

You must have told us so many times already, but I still don't get it: what is the seed of desire? Is it only in the existence of mind? And how is the desire of the body for sex related to the mind?

The energy called desire has been condemned for centuries. Almost all the so-called saints have been against it, because desire is life and they were all life-negative. Desire is the very source of all that you see, and they were against all that which is visible. They wanted to sacrifice the visible at the feet of the invisible; they wanted to cut the roots of desire so there would no longer be any possibility of life.

A tremendously great urge to commit total suicide has dominated humanity down the ages.

I have a totally different concept of desire. First, desire itself is God. Desire without any object, desire without being goal-oriented, unmotivated desire, pure desire, is God. The energy called desire is the same energy as God.

Desire has not to be destroyed, it has to be purified. Desire has not to be dropped, it has to be transformed. Your very being is desire; to be against it is to be against yourself and against all. To be against it is to be against the flowers and the birds and the sun and the moon. To be against it is against all creativity. Desire is creativity.

The Eastern scriptures are perfectly right when they say that God created the world because a great desire arose in him – a desire to create, a desire to manifest, a desire to make many from one, a desire to expand. But these are only metaphors; God is not separate from desire. Desire means a longing, a great longing, to expand, to become huge, to be enormous – as huge as the sky.

Just watch people, watch desires, and you will understand what I mean. Even in your ordinary desires, the basic thing is present. In fact what the man who wants to have more and more money really wants is not money but expansion, because money can help you expand. You can have a bigger house, you can have a bigger garden, you can have this, you can have that – your territory will be bigger, your freedom will be bigger. With more money you will have more alternatives to choose from.

The man who is after money may not know why he is after the money. He may himself think and believe that he loves money, but that is only on the surface of his consciousness. Go deeper into his unconscious, help him to meditate, and you will be surprised and he will be surprised to find that the desire for money is not really the desire for money, it is the desire to expand.

And the same is the case with all other desires. Men want more power, more fame, longer life, better health, but what are they desiring in these different things? The same, exactly the same: they want to be more. They don't want to remain confined, they don't want to be limited. It hurts to feel that you are definable, because if you are definable then you are just an object, a thing, a commodity. It hurts that you have limitations, because to have limitations means to be imprisoned.

But all these objects of desire, sooner or later, disappoint. Money becomes possible one day, and yet expansion has not happened; you may have a little more freedom of choice, but that does not satisfy. The desire was for the infinite, and money cannot purchase the infinite. Yes, you have more power, you are more well-known, but that doesn't really matter in the long run. Millions of people have lived on this earth and were very famous, and now nobody even knows their names. Everything has disappeared into dust – dust into dust, not even traces are left. Where is Alexander the Great? What is he? Would you like to be a dead Alexander the Great or an alive beggar? Ask yourself, and your being will say it is better to be alive and be a beggar than to be dead and be an Alexander.

If you watch carefully, money, power, prestige – nothing satisfies. On the contrary, they make you more discontented. Why? – because when you were poor there was a hope that one day the money was going to happen and all would be settled and settled forever, and then you would relax and enjoy. Now that has happened, and there seems to be no sign of any relaxation. In fact, you are more tense than before, you are more anxiety-ridden than before.

Money has brought a few blessings, but in the same measure it has brought many curses too. You can have a bigger house, but now you will have less peace. You can have a bigger bank balance, but you will also have a bigger madness, anxiety, neurosis, psychosis. Money has brought a few things which are good; in the wake of it many other things have arrived which are not good at all. And if you look at the whole thing, the whole effort has been a sheer wastage. And now you cannot have even the hope that the poor man can have.

The rich man becomes hopeless. He knows now the money will go on increasing and nothing is going to happen – just death, only death. He has tasted all kinds of things; now he only feels a tastelessness. A kind of death has already happened, because he cannot conceive of how to fulfill that desire for expansion.

But desire in itself is not wrong. The desire for money, the desire for power, the desire for prestige, are wrong objects for desire – let it be very clear. By having wrong objects of desire, desire itself does not become wrong. You can have a sword and you can kill somebody – that does not make the sword something wrong. You can also save somebody with the same sword. Poison can kill and poison can become medicine too. In the right hands, poison is nectar; in the wrong hands, nectar is poison.

This is the essential wisdom of all the buddhas of all the ages. What the priests say is one thing; what the buddhas have brought to the world is totally different, it is diametrically opposite.

Desire has to be purified and transformed, because it is your energy – you don't have any other energy. How to transform desire? One way, the ordinary way, the mediocre way, is to change the object. Don't go after money, start going after God. You are frustrated with money – become religious, go to the church, to the temple, to the mosque. Let your desire have a new object called God, which is as illusory as the object called money, even more illusory, because what do you know about God? Money at least is something visible, objective; you have known it, you have seen it. What do you know of God? You have only heard the word. God remains a word unless experienced. God remains an empty word unless you pour some content into it through your own existential experience.

People, when they are frustrated with worldly desires, start changing the object: they start making otherworldly objects of desire – heaven, paradise, and all the joys of heaven. But it is the same trick, the mind is again befooling you. This is not the way of the intelligent person, this is the way of the stupid.

What is intelligence? Intelligence means the insight that no object can fulfill your desire. No object, I say, and I say it categorically, no object can ever fulfill your desire. Your desire is divine. Your desire is as big as the sky – even the sky is not a limit to it. No object can fill it. Then what is to be done? The intelligent person stops desiring objects. He makes his desire pure of all objects – worldly, otherworldly. He starts living his desire in its purity, moment to moment. He is full of desire, full of overflowing energy. His ordinary life becomes so intense, so passionate, that whatsoever he touches will be transformed. The baser metal will become gold, and the dead tree will come to bloom again.

It is said of Buddha that wherever he moved, dead trees would start growing leaves; out of season, trees would bloom. These are beautiful poetic expressions of a certain metaphysical truth. Buddha is pure desire, just desire. Not a desire for anything; he has abandoned all objects.

Let me remind you, first he abandoned the world. He was a prince, he was born to be a king. Seeing the futility of money, seeing the futility of all kinds of relationships, seeing the futility of all that the world can give – he was only twenty-nine years old – he escaped. He did well, because after thirty it becomes more difficult, more and more difficult.

Hippies are right. They say, "Don't believe a man who is over thirty." Buddha escaped at the right time – he was exactly twenty-nine – because the more you become experienced in worldly ways, the more cowardly you become. Religion is for the courageous, religion is for the brave, religion is for the young, those who are still able to take the risk, those who are still able to gamble.

Buddha escaped. Seeing the futility, he escaped in search of God, in search of truth. He replaced his desire for the world with the desire for God, truth, nirvana. For six years he worked hard. By the time he was thirty-five he was utterly spent. He had done all that was possible, humanly possible, to do. He fasted for months, meditated, practiced yoga. And in those days there were different kinds of schools. He went from one teacher to another, from one school to another, he practiced all possible methods. And one day it suddenly flashed.

He was crossing the river Niranjana. It is a small river – when I went to see the river I could not believe the story. The story says that he could not cross the river Niranjana, he could not swim it, because he was so weak. The river is so narrow, the river is so small, but he must have been very weak from years of fasting. It is said that he had fasted so long that you could count his bones, his ribs. He had become simply bones, he was a skeleton; his stomach had completely disappeared, his stomach and his back had become one. He must have been really weak; he could not cross the river, and was hanging onto the root of a tree, having no energy to get out of the river.

In that moment, a great insight happened. Insights happen only in such moments. When the frustration is total, when the disappointment is complete, when the disillusionment is utter, when there is nothing left to hope for…in that moment he saw the pointlessness of it all. The worldly objects were meaningless; he had had all of them and they did not satisfy. And those otherworldly desires were just as foolish as the worldly desires. In that moment, in that insight, he became objectless.

Let me tell you, the scriptures report it very wrongly. They say that in that moment he became desireless. But try to understand what I am trying to convey to you. He became objectless, not desireless. You cannot become desireless. Desire is your very life, your breath, your heartbeat; desire is your being. But certainly a transformation happened; he became objectless. This-worldly, otherworldly, all desires in toto disappeared as objects, not desire as energy. There was no object; pure energy was felt, a desiring for nothing, a pure desire moving nowhere, a pure desire herenow.

That very night he attained enlightenment. Having nothing to desire, he rested under a tree and fell asleep. For the first time he really slept. When there is nothing to desire, there is nothing to dream about either, because dreams are reflections of your desires. Dreams are reflections of your frustrations, dreams are reflections of your repressions, dreams reflect your day-life. That night there was no dream, it was a dreamless deep sleep.

Patanjali says dreamless deep sleep is closest to samadhi – just one step more, and you have come home. And that one step happened early in the morning. Rested, Buddha opened his eyes. For the first time in his life there was nowhere to go, nothing to do. For the first time in life he must have been at a loss. Now what? There was nothing to cling to, nothing to hold on to. There must have been an utter emptiness. Time must have stopped. There was no program any more. Every day he used to get up with so many ideas to be cultivated, so many methods to be practiced, so many religious rituals to be done, and all that. Today there was nothing left! Utter emptiness.

But do you think he died? No, he was born. Objects were not there. Now the desire was pure – just a throb, a pulsation, just a passion for nothing in particular. Resting under the tree with open eyes, he must have been seeing the sky in the east becoming red, and then the sunrise. And with the rising sun and with the sky turning red, and with the last star of the night disappearing, he became enlightened.

What does this word enlightenment mean? It simply means desire was freed from all objects. He became pure love, compassion, pure life. And this pure life has tremendous beauty and ecstasy; with this pure life you have attained the infinite. Desire remains small because you confine it to small objects, desire remains small because you desire small things. Seeing it, people start desiring big things – but big things are also small things; howsoever big they are, they have limitations.

Just think of your God. How big is he? Egyptians used to say he is seven feet tall – nothing much. There are many Dutch sannyasins here. Whenever I see a Dutch sannyasin, I remember the Egyptians and the Egyptian gods. Indians say he has three faces. So what? Our politicians have one thousand and one faces, and everyone has many faces. Only three? When you talk to your wife you have one face, when you talk to your girlfriend you have another face, when you talk to your servant still another, when you talk to your boss still another. Just watch the whole day, how many faces you have! And God seems to be very poor – only three faces? How does he manage with only three faces?

All concepts of God are bound to be limited. Concepts as such are bound to be limited. Even if you say he is infinite, what do you mean? What do you mean by infinite? Try to comprehend the meaning of the word *infinite* and you will be in a difficulty. Even your word infinite will be found to be finite. You can say he is unbounded, but just think, what do you mean? The boundary must be somewhere; how could it be that one just goes on and on and on? There must be a boundary – maybe it is very far away, far, far away, maybe you will never reach it, but what do you mean by "unbounded"? You simply mean unmeasured, nothing more.

What do you mean when you say the ocean is unfathomable? Do you think there is no bottom to it? The bottom is there, although we may not have fathomed it. Our ways of measurement are small, our yardsticks are small.

Any word that we can use is bound to remain limited. Hence, those who have known God, they say nothing can be said about him. Buddha did not even say this much, that nothing can be said about him, because he said if you say nothing can be said about him, you have already said something. You have already defined him! "Nothing can be said about him" is a statement, and all statements define.

You can move from small objects to bigger and bigger objects, but still your desire, your life, will not feel fulfilled. It cannot feel fulfilled unless it is really infinite, not in conceptions but in experience, and unless you taste the infinity of existence.

Desire is beautiful, there is nothing wrong in it – only free it from objects. With freedom from objects, desire is divine.

You say, "You must have told us so many times already, but I still don't get it...."

Just by my saying it, you are not going to get it. You will have to move into experience. It is not a philosophical system of thought that I am conveying to you. I am only pointing towards a path; the path has to be followed. You will not get it just by listening to me. Yes, you can get it if you sit silently by my side. You can get it in the intervals, when I am here and you are here and no word interferes, intervenes.

Words don't communicate. On the contrary, for higher things they become barriers. For lower things they are bridges; the higher you move, the less and less they are bridges, the more and more they are walls.

You say, "You must have told us so many times already, but I still don't get it...."

I will go on saying it again and again, but remember, you will not get it just by listening to me. You will have to be something like me. You will have to imbibe me, you will have to digest me. It is not something verbal that is happening here, it is something existential. It is a love affair.

I am not a teacher, I am not teaching you anything, I am simply imparting something to you. What has happened to me, I am inviting you to partake of it. Be my guest, let me be your host. And if you can even be a guest for a single moment, that which has not been understood for so long will be immediately understood. And not only will it be understood, you will be surprised how you went on missing it. It is so simple; to have understood it would have been simple.

But it is a question of an energy communication. And, slowly, slowly, I will turn the commune into an energy communication. Words can take you only so far, then it has to become a meeting of energies. You have to be electrified by me. You have to allow my pure desiring, my pure energy. It is objectless; I don't desire a thing, I am simply desire. If you allow yourself to come in contact with this energy, there will be a transformation, a turning point, a conversion.

You say, "What is the seed of desire?"

There is no seed of desire. Desire is the seed of all. Desire is the ultimate seed. God desired to be man, God desired to expand, God desired to create.

Desire is the seed of everything!

If you ask me, I will say God is desire – that's why he could desire. Only desire can desire.

You ask, "Is it only in the existence of mind?"

No. The mind has only a very tunnel vision. The mind is as if you are hiding behind a door and looking through the keyhole. Yes, sometimes you can see a bird on the wing, but for only a split second, and then it is gone. You see somebody passing by – a beautiful woman, a beautiful man, or a dog – just for a moment, and it is gone. A moment before, it was not there; a moment afterwards, it is no more there. That's how the mind creates time. It is a keyhole.

You see a bird on the wing, and you see it only for just a second. Before that, it was not – do you think it was not? It was, but for you it was in the future, because it was not in front of your keyhole. And after a moment it is no more again – do you think it is no more? It still is, but for you it is past.

Mind is limited, hence it creates divisions – past, present and future. The present is that which for a moment appears on the screen of the mind, and the past is that which is no more on the screen, and the future is that which is not yet. But let me tell you: all is, and always is. Nothing ever goes out of existence, and nothing ever comes into existence. Everything persists, remains.

Time is a false notion created by the mind.

Eternity is truth, timelessness is truth.

Somebody asked Jesus, "Tell us something more about the kingdom of God. What will be special there? Something unique. Yes, we have heard that there will be pleasure, but pleasure we know – maybe it will be thousands and thousands of times greater, but we know what pleasure is. We have heard there will be celestial music – okay, we know something about music. But what will be special?"

And you will be surprised what Jesus said. It is not recorded in the Christian scriptures, but there are a few sayings scattered here and there in other scriptures. This is recorded by the Sufis. Jesus said, "There shall be time no longer." A tremendously significant answer. There shall be time no longer – this will be special. You have known everything, but you have not known timelessness. "There shall be time no longer" means there shall be mind no longer. Mind and time are synonymous.

In the ultimate reckoning, time is mind, mind is time. Both are aspects of the same coin, they both disappear together. Drop one, and the other is gone also.

You ask me, "What is the seed of desire?"

There is no seed of desire. Desire is the ultimate seed of all other seeds.

And you ask, "Is it only in the existence of mind?"

No. The mind has only a little glimpse of desire, just a flickering glimpse of desire. Mind knows nothing of desire; mind only knows about desiring this and desiring that. Desiring money, desiring power, desiring prestige – mind knows about desires for objects. When the objects are no more there, desire is no more part of the mind. Then desire is beyond mind; then desire is simply an overflowing energy.

William Blake says desire is energy and energy is delight. I have heard a rumor that Sargama, one of our sannyasins, is a direct descendant of William Blake. We have beautiful people here. William Blake is one of the most beautiful persons who has ever walked on the earth, one of the most penetrating mystics. Sargama must have something of William Blake's quality in him. But it may be just a rumor, because I have heard another rumor also that William Blake had no son at all. But that may be applicable only to legal sons; one can have illegal sons.

William Blake's insight is true. Desire is energy, energy is delight. Contemplate over it. Just pure desire, just overflowing energy, for no particular object, for no destination.

That's what you have to remember when you come to me for an energy darshan, for a "close-up." Just become pure desire, just an overflowing desire, for nothing in particular. Don't wait for any experience. Experiences will come, but don't wait for them. If you wait, you will miss, because when you are waiting for an experience you are no more in the herenow. You have already missed the point; the mind has come in. The object has obstructed the purity of desire.

When you are in an energy darshan with me, when you are partaking of something of my energy, just be pure desire – going nowhere, moving nowhere, just thrilled for no reason at all, just madly ecstatic for no reason at all. And in those few moments you will have the contact with me, because those few moments are my reality.

But if you are sitting there, waiting to have some great experience of light inside, then maybe you may experience some light, but you have missed. You have thrown the diamonds away and gathered pebbles on the shore. You may be waiting for your kundalini to rise, you may have a certain sensation rising in your spine, but what is it? It is pointless. It may give you a kick, a spiritual kick, but then it is gone.

With me, just be pure desire – swaying with me, moving with me, dancing with me, allowing me to penetrate you to your deepest core, to the deepest core of your desire, to the very seed. And then something immense, something incredible, something you cannot imagine, is possible – an entry of the beyond into you, the meeting of the earth and sky.

You say, "Is it only in the existence of mind?"

No, the mind is a barrier. It allows desire only little outlets – and desire is an ocean. The mind has to be dropped, not desire; the mind has to be dropped so that you can have *total* desire.

And you ask, "And how is the desire in the body for sex related to the mind?"

The mind is not separate from your body, it is the inner part of the body. You are separate from the body and the mind, both. You are an entity, transcendental, you are a witness to the mind and the body, both. But your mind and your body are both one and the same energy. The body is visible mind, the mind is invisible body. The body is the exterior mind, and the mind is the interior body.

Hence sex is not only physical. It is far more cerebral, it is far more psychological than physical. In fact, sex is triggered not by your physiology but by your psychology. The physiology cooperates with it, but deep down sex comes from the inner body to the outer body.

You may be aware, you may not be aware, because you are not at all aware of what goes on happening to you. But watch, the first thing about sex happens in the head, in the mind. And then immediately the body is affected, because the body and the mind are not separate.

There can be a physiological sex too. That's what happens when you go to a prostitute; it is physiological, it is just a relief for the body. The body is overburdened with energy and you don't know what to do with it. You have to throw it out somehow to unburden yourself, so that you can feel a little relaxed, because you have too much energy and you are so uncreative that you don't know what to do with it.

You can't sing a song totally. If you can, you will be surprised; the energy disappears into the song and becomes the song. There is no need to go to a prostitute. But you cannot dance, you cannot play on the guitar, you are so uncreative.

Prostitutes will exist in the world unless man becomes more creative. And now in the West where the Women's Liberation movement is demanding equality in everything, even male prostitutes have come into existence. They were bound to, because why should there be only female prostitutes? Why not male prostitutes too? Equality is equality.

Man is uncreative. Have you observed? Any time when you are creative, sex disappears. If you are painting and totally absorbed in it, you don't have any sexual desire. Sex simply does not cross the threshold of your mind; it is simply not there.

Only in deep creativity are people celibate, in no other way. Your saints, so-called saints, are not celibate – because they are so uncreative, they cannot be. It is impossible; it is just against the very science of energy. They are doing nothing, sitting in the temples and ashrams repeating Ram-Ram, Ram-Ram, or just stupidly playing with their malas – how can they be celibate? How can *brahmacharya* happen to them? It happens only when creativity takes all your energy, and no energy is left as a tension in you.

Poets can be celibate more, painters can be celibate more, dancers can be celibate more, musicians can be celibate more. I am not saying that they are all celibates, I am saying that whenever a poet is a poet, he can be celibate – because a poet is not twenty-four hours a day a poet. It is very rare to find a poet who is twenty-four hours a day a poet. Then he becomes a seer, then he becomes a *rishi*, then he is no more an ordinary poet.

It is from people like these who were for twenty-four hours poets that great poems like the Upanishads, the Koran and the Gita were born. It is not ordinary poetry. Ordinary poets are only once in a while poets, otherwise they are ordinary people – maybe far worse. Ordinary painters are only once in a while painters.

It is said about a great Indian poet, Rabindranath, that whenever he was in the mood to create, he would close his doors and disappear into his room for days together – three or four days. No food, no bath, he would not even come out. Only when his energy had moved into creativity and he was unburdened would he open his door and come out. And people who saw him coming out of his room after four days of fasting and remaining lost in his creativity, all observed that his face was no more the same. He looked as if he had gone to some other world. He looked so delicate, like a roseflower; he looked so beautiful, so feminine, so graceful, so buddhalike. But only for a few hours would that fragrance surround him, and then it would disappear. And even for months together, the mood might not come.

Poets are only once in a while poets. And when you read a whole poem, the whole poem is not a poem either. Only a few lines here and there are really poetry; the other lines are just managed by the poet, they did not descend on him.

A great poet, Coleridge, died. He left forty thousand incomplete poems. Many times in his life he was asked, "Why don't you complete these things? They are so tremendously beautiful, and only one line is missing. Just complete one line and the poem will be complete."

But Coleridge always refused. He said, "I will not complete it unless it comes from the beyond. I am not going to do it. These lines have come from the beyond, I have just noted them down. I am not the writer, I am not the author, I am just a steno; I have simply noted down something that has been dictated from the beyond. And that one line is missing. I cannot add it, because many times I have tried to add it, and I have always failed. It looks so ugly, it looks so different, so mundane, so mediocre. It does not have that luminosity."

When Rabindranath for the first time translated his great book Gitanjali into English, he was a little worried as to whether the translation had come through or not. English was not his mother tongue, in the first place. And secondly, to translate prose is one thing, it is easy; to translate poetry is very difficult, and more so to translate poetry from a language like Bengali which is so poetic. The whole language is poetic, its flavor is of poetry.

He was worried: "Has the translation come true to the spirit of my original?" He showed it to one great Englishman, C.F. Andrews. Andrews went through it, and at just four points he said, "Four words have to be changed, grammatically they are wrong." Naturally, Rabindranath changed them.

Then when he read Gitanjali and his poems for the first time in a poets' gathering in London, he was surprised, he could not believe his ears. One English poet, Yeats, stood up and said, "Everything is perfectly right, but at just four points something is very mundane, something is not poetic. The whole poetry flows beautifully, but at four points the river comes across rocks."

With a trembling in his heart, Rabindranath asked, "What are those four points?" And they were exactly the same as those which C.F. Andrews had suggested. Rabindranath told him, "These are C.F. Andrews' words, he knows English better than me."

Yeats said, "That is right – it is better English, but not better poetry. The grammar is right, but poetry is not grammar. The language is right, but poetry is not only language. Poetry is something that hovers above language and grammar. Please go back to your old words!"

Rabindranath got his Nobel prize with this book, Gitanjali.

All poets are not always poets, all poems are not poems. Hence you may not be able to understand what I am trying to convey to you, but whenever a poet is a poet, he is celibate. Sexuality simply disappears, evaporates. And whenever a poem is born in a poet he is part of God, he is a creator. In that moment it is impossible to give any object to your desire. Sex gives an object to your desire. Sex is not pure, cannot be, because the object is always there.

The moment sex becomes pure, it is samadhi.

The mind and the body both are sexual. The body has come out of sex, and the mind is always hankering for objects, hence it is sexual. But both can be purified through creativity.

My message, my key, my golden key to transform your energies, is creativity. Be more and more creative, and slowly, slowly you will see a transformation happening of its own accord.

Your mind will disappear, your body will have a totally different feel to it, and constantly you will remain aware that you are separate, that you are a pure witness.

And that pure witness is pure desire and nothing else.

I am not against desire. I am all for desire, but I am not for desires with objects. Let objects disappear, and then you will have a desire like a flame without any smoke. It brings great liberation.

? I understand everything that you say, but why does my life still remain unchanged?

To understand something intellectually is one thing, but to understand something intellectually is not going to transform your life. You will remain the same. To understand something intellectually is really to deceive yourself. You have not understood, the mind has only pretended to have understood. This is a trick, because if you really understand it then change is bound to happen. And the mind does not want any change.

The mind is very traditional, conventional, conformist, orthodox. The mind is never revolutionary; it is against all change. And the change I am talking about is a total change.

You say, "I understand everything that you say…."

You only *believe* that you understand. You understand the words, naturally. My words are simple, I don't know many words. In fact, if you count, I must be using not more than four hundred words. But see the turnout! I am not a man of language. You can understand what I am saying as far as words are concerned – but do you comprehend it? That is the question, that is the crux of the matter. Do you comprehend what is being imparted to you?

You must have a very philosophical bent of mind. Meditate over this anecdote:

A patient of his, a great philosopher in his thirties, eagerly responded at the beginning of therapy to each interpretation his analyst made by saying, "I hear you, I hear you."

"I'm sorry," said the doctor. "I didn't know you were a little deaf."

"I'm not. I *hear* you. It means I comprehend," said the philosopher.

"Well, what is it that you comprehend?"

The philosopher paused. "Jesus," he finally replied, "I don't know."

Understanding is not the question, but comprehension. Understanding is of the head; comprehension is something deeper, of the heart. And if it is really total then it is even deeper, of the being.

When you understand something then you have to do something about it. When you comprehend something you need not do anything about it; the very comprehension is enough to change you. If you comprehend something, it has already changed you; there is no need to do anything about your comprehensions.

Please don't try to understand me intellectually. I am not an intellectual, in fact I am anti-intellectual. I am not a philosopher, I am very anti-philosophic. Try to comprehend me.

And how does one try to comprehend? How does one try to understand in the first place?

Understanding means listening with the head, continuously interpreting, evaluating, judging: "This is right, this is wrong. Yes, this is true, I have read about it. This must be right, because Jesus also said it in the same way. This is also in the Gita and in the Vedas."

This goes on, this constant chattering inside that you call understanding. And then out of this hotchpotch you create a hypothesis, and you think this is what I have been telling you. Comprehension cannot come this way; this is the way to prevent comprehension.

Listen silently with no inner chattering, with no inner talk, without evaluating. I am not saying believe what I say, I am not saying accept what I say. I am saying there is no need to be in a hurry to accept or reject. First at least listen – why be in such a hurry? When you see a roseflower, do you accept or reject it? When you see a beautiful sunset, do you accept or reject it? You simply see it, and in that very seeing is a meeting.

Don't let your mind wander. Listen silently, attuned, and then something will stir in the heart. Truth has that quality, it stirs the heart. Truth has the quality of being self-evident, it needs no proofs.

If what I am saying has anything of truth in it, it will be understood by your heart. But the mind has to give way. And then you will not need to change your life according to it, it will be changed of its own accord.

? What? What?? What???

You remind me of a story. A man was troubled for many years with a sore arm. He had been to many doctors and could not find out what was causing the problem. Finally a friend urged him to see a doctor who was famous for his ability to diagnose illnesses. The doctor was very expensive and he had to wait a long time for an appointment. Finally he sat waiting in the office. The doctor walked in, handed him a jar and told him to return it the next day with his first morning's urine. Then he promptly left the room.

The man was infuriated! "He did not even look at me," he thought. "And how can he tell what is wrong with my arm from my urine?"

The next morning, the man, still angry, peed in the jar. Then he had his wife pee in it, then he had his daughter pee in it. Then as he walked out the door he saw his dog peeing on a tree and he got some of that also. He gave the urine to the doctor and sat there laughing to himself.

Just then, the doctor re-entered the room and exclaimed, "Please sir, this is no laughing matter! Your wife has been fooling around on you, your daughter is pregnant, your dog has worms, and if you don't stop jerking off, your arm will never get better!"

Now you ask me, "*What? What?? What???*"
I am not this kind of doctor, you will have to go somewhere else.

? Why can't I feel any wonder in existence?

You are too knowledgeable, you know too much. And all that you know is just holy cow dung – all knowledge always is. Wisdom is a totally different matter. Knowledge is all rot, junk;

you gather it from here and there, it is not your own. It has no authenticity, it has not grown in your being, you have not given birth to it.

But it gives you a very gratified ego to feel "I know." And the more you become settled in the idea of "I know," the less and less will you feel wonder in life. How can a man of knowledge feel wonder? Knowledge destroys wonder. And wonder is the source of wisdom, wonder is the source of all that is beautiful, and wonder is the source for the search, the real search. Wonder takes you on the adventure to know the mysteries of life.

The knowledgeable person already knows – knows nothing, but thinks that he already knows. He has come to a full stop. He has not reached anywhere, he has not known anything. He is a computer, his mind is simply programmed. Maybe he has MAs, PhDs, DLitts, maybe he has been to the biggest education centers of the world and he has accumulated much information, but that information is destroying his sensitivity to feel the mystery of the flowers, the birds, the trees, the sunlight and the moon, because he knows all the answers.

How can he see any beauty in the moon? He already knows everything about the moon. And if you say to him, "My beloved's face looks like the full moon," he will laugh. He will say, "You are simply foolish. How can you compare the moon with your beloved's face? There is no comparison possible!"

He is mathematically right, scientifically right, but poetically wrong. And life is not only science. Just as Jesus said, "Man cannot live by bread alone," I say to you, "Man cannot live by science alone." A few windows are to be left open for poetic experiences, so some sun, some wind and some rain can come from real existence.

You cannot be thrilled by life if you are too full of knowledge.

I used to go for a long walk every evening when I was in the university. A professor used to follow me. For two or three days I tolerated it, and then I said, "Either you stop coming, or I will have to stop coming."

He said, "Why?"

I said, "You are destroying my whole walk."

He said, "How?"

He knew too much about everything, and he would talk. "This tree belongs to that species." Now, who bothers? The tree is beautiful; it is dancing in the wind, the foliage is so young, so fresh. The green of it, the red of it, the gold of it, all is so beautiful – and he is talking about the species. He was a very, very informed man about everything. A bird on the wind, he would immediately label it. He was a great labeler.

I said, "Please, either you stop coming – you are destroying my evening walk – or I will have to stop."

You must be too burdened. You are, I know you. You are burdened with great scriptures, mountains of scriptures; nothing can ever surprise you.

A man comes into a bar, obviously nervous and obviously in a hurry, walks over to the counter, picks up an empty glass and starts eating it. When he is finished he goes over to the wall, walks up the wall, walks along the ceiling, walks down the other wall and disappears out the door.

The barkeeper can't believe his eyes. "What the hell," he says, "is going on here?"

A man who has been sitting on a bar stool and seen the whole thing, says with a shrug of his shoulders, "Don't worry, I know that guy. It's always the same thing with him -- comes and goes without even saying hello."

There are millions of people who are living like this. Miracles are happening all around but they can't see anything, they are blind with their knowledge.

Drop your knowledge. Knowledge is worthless, wonder is precious. Regain the wonder that you had when you were a child – and the kingdom of God belongs only to those who are able to become children again.

I am in a jam. I love three women. This is hell, and this has been going on for three months. Now what to do?

You must be something of a man! One woman is enough. You need legal protection. But if you have tolerated it patiently for three months, wait a little more. Time settles everything. And women are always more perceptive than men – if you cannot do anything, they are bound to do something.

John and Mary began making love in a railway cutting. As their lovemaking progressed, they rolled down onto the railway tracks in the path of the oncoming express.

The driver, seeing the two bodies ahead on the line, halted the train just in time. Now, delaying the train is a serious offense, and at the trial the judge demanded an explanation.

"Now look, John," he said, "I am a man of the world and I can understand you and your girlfriend having a little fun. But why didn't you get out of the way of the train?"

"Well, it's like this, Your Honor," said John. "I was coming, the train was coming and Mary was coming, and I thought that whoever could stop would stop!"

Enough for today.

Chapter 16
The University of Inner Alchemy

? **Yes and no!**

Man is a dilemma, he is both yes and no. It is not abnormal in you, it is the normal state of humankind. Man is half earth, half sky; part matter, part consciousness; part dust, part divine. Man is a tension. Friedrich Nietzsche says "a rope stretched between two infinities."

The past is that of an animal and the future is that of God. And between the two is man – half animal, half angel. The no comes from the past, the yes is a possibility for the future. Doubt comes from darkness, trust is the by-product of light. The higher self in you is always trusting, the lower is cunning and always doubting. And you are both, as you are now.

Man is naturally schizophrenic. Schizophrenia is not a disease; it is not pathology, it is the state of normal human beings. It starts looking like a pathology only when it goes to the extreme, when yes and no are so divided that there is not even an "and" to bridge them. When they become unbridgeable, then it becomes pathological. Otherwise every human being is always in a kind of duality, in a state of either/or. No other animal is in that state. Dogs are simply dogs, and lions are lions, and trees are trees, and rocks are rocks. They don't have any duality, there is no division.

Man is dual, double, divided. It is his misery, but it is also the possibility for his bliss. It is his agony, but out of this agony ecstasy can be born. No animal can be ecstatic except man. Have you seen any animal ecstatic – ecstasy like a Buddha, a Ramakrishna? There is no possibility of coming across an animal which is so ecstatic. Even the rosebush with so many beautiful flowers is not ecstatic in the sense Jesus is. The rosebush is simply a rosebush; there is no exuberance, there is no overflowing, there is no rejoicing. It is a matter of fact – not that something incredible is happening, not that something from the beyond has descended, not that God has been realized, not that light has come and penetrated to the deepest core of your being and you are full of it and you are enlightened.

The bird on the wing is free, but knows nothing about freedom. Only man, even though he may be imprisoned, knows about freedom. Hence the misery; the bondage on one hand, and the vision of freedom on the other. The reality, the ugly reality, and the tremendously luminous possibility.

Man can be miserable as no other animal can ever be miserable. Have you seen any animal crying its heart out, weeping, committing suicide? Have you seen any animal laughing, a belly laughter that shakes the very foundations? No, all these things are possible only for man. Hence the grandeur of man, hence his dignity, and hence his anxiety too.

The anxiety is over whether you are going to make it or not, whether this time it is going to happen or not. The anxiety is a natural consequence of two diametrically opposite possibilities: one can fall into hell, and one can rise into heaven.

Man is just a ladder, and you move on this ladder like a yo-yo. One moment you are in heaven, another moment you are in hell. One moment suddenly the sunlit peak, another moment the darkest valley that you have ever come across. One moment love, sharing; another moment anger, miserliness. One moment such an expanded heart that you can contain the whole world, and another moment you are so mean that you cannot imagine you had this possibility to be so mean. Man goes on moving between these two infinities continuously like a pendulum.

Your question is significant, because it is everybody's question. It is not a question, it is far more existential. It is a problem; no answer can help, some solution has to be searched for.

Now, there are two possibilities for the solution. One is to fall back and be satisfied with your animalness. Be satisfied – that's what millions are trying to do; drink, eat, sleep, and forget all about the greater challenges of life. Eat, drink and be merry, because tomorrow we shall be no more. That's what the materialist says.

The materialist has accepted the lower self; he denies the higher self just in sheer self-defense. He does not deny it because he knows that it is not; no – he knows nothing about it. He denies it because if he does not deny it then that either/or opens up again. Again one is in a problem, again something has to be done, again the at-easeness is lost. Again the journey, the wandering, and the discomfort and the inconvenience and the insecurity of the journey.

It is better to say that the higher does not exist, that there is no God, that there has never been any God, that there is no soul, that there is nothing inner, that man has no interiority, that man is just what he is from the outside, that man is his behavior and there is no soul in him.

From Pavlov to B.F. Skinner, this is what is being taught to the world by the so-called scientific psychologists, the behaviorists, that man is only behavior. There is no one inside, just as there is no one inside a machine. The machine is just a functional unity; it has no organic unity in it, it has no soul. You can dismantle it, you can rearrange it again.

That's what scientists hope, that sooner or later they will be able to dismantle man and reassemble him. At least theoretically, it seems possible for them. It is not possible. You cannot dismantle and reassemble man, because there is something which is nonmechanical in man. And that nonmechanical part is his glory. But it is better to deny it; it makes life easier, it makes life less anxious, it makes life less of a problem. You can go on living the shallow day-to-day life of so-called pleasures – eat, drink and be merry.

Those who decide for that are renouncing the opportunity Atisha is talking about. They are renouncing the opportunity to become gods. They are settling for something very low, they are settling for something very cheap, they are missing something very essential. Yes, you can be at ease with the lower self, you can settle with the doubting self. But then there is no growth. And there will be no ecstasy, because there will never be any buddha born in you. You will never come to know anything of Christ-consciousness. You will remain in darkness – of course at ease, but what is the point of being at ease?

Far more valuable is creative discontent, far more valuable is the insecurity of the unknown, far more valuable is a homeless wandering in search of the real home.

Religion is for those who don't accept the lower as the be all and end all. I am not saying deny the lower, remember, because there are foolish people who go to the other extreme. One stupid type of people denies the higher, says it does not exist, and settles with the lower. The other stupid kind denies the lower, says there is no lower, there is only the higher. One says God is illusion, the world is truth. The other says the world is illusion, God is truth.

In my approach, both are being stupid, because both are doing the same thing. Both want to be at ease; both are denying the polar opposite, both are denying the possibility of any inner tension. And remember, it is the inner tension that gives you aliveness. And the bigger the tension, the more alive you are.

You know, you have experienced it. Everybody has experienced it, more or less – the attraction of the opposite. A man is attracted to a woman, and vice versa – why? The negative pole of electricity is attracted towards the positive pole, and vice versa – why? Why the attraction for the opposite? Because in that very attraction, life arises. In that tension, how can you remain dead? In that very tension you start pulsating.

Those who settle and choose one against the other become stale, become dead. The materialist becomes superficial, and your so-called spiritualist also becomes phony. Your so-called materialist lives with shallow pleasures, and your so-called spiritualist lives in imagination, in fantasy. Both are missing life and its life-giving tensions. Man has to live with both, and in such a way that neither is denied and yet both become complementary to each other. Yes need not be against no; there is no necessity that the no should be against the yes. They can define each other, they can nourish each other.

That's my whole effort here. I bring you a new dispensation, that the earth and the sky have to be accepted together. Body and soul, the world and God, have to be accepted together. Nothing is wrong in the lower, the lower has to become the base for the higher. The lower has to function as the foundation; if you deny it you won't have any foundation.

That's why religious countries, for example India, became poorer and poorer and poorer. They lost their foundations and became very phony. How can you be true if you deny something which is all around you and so real? If you say the world is illusion, maya, how can you be true? You know it is not.

Even the person who says that the world is maya does not try to pass through the wall, he goes through the door. If both are maya, illusion, what is the difference? Can you find any difference between two illusions? Is one a little less an illusion and the other a little more? Even the person who says the world is illusion does not start eating stones. What is the difference between bread and stones then? Both are illusions, both are dreams.

But by denying the world you lose contact with the reality. That's what happened in the East, particularly in India. India became disoriented from reality, it lost its roots in the earth. It became unearthly, a little ghostly. That's my experience of India – India is a ghost, it has lost its body. And nobody else is responsible for it. It could not gather courage to accept the polar opposites. It became poor, it became ugly, it became ill.

India chose this so that it could be at ease with the higher. But the higher can exist only with the lower; this is one thing more of great importance to be remembered. The lower can exist without the higher – it will remain unfulfilled, but it can exist. The higher cannot even exist without the lower.

You cannot have a building – a temple, a church – without the foundations. But you can have the foundations without making the temple. That is possible because the lower comes first and the higher comes later. The lower can come, and the higher may not come.

The East tried the higher without the lower, the temple without the foundations. Now, such a temple can only be in your imagination, it cannot exist in reality. And it creates hypocrisy. The greatest hypocrisy possible in the world has happened in India. The hypocrisy is: we have to live in the lower because the lower is the real, and we have to deny it and talk about the higher. And because the lower is denied, the higher cannot have any substance; it is dream stuff. So people are very much obsessed with money, but they talk of God; obsessed with politics and power, and they talk of God. That remains just talk.

In the West, just the opposite has happened. The lower was accepted, for the same reason – because if there is only one, you can relax. You can drop the creative discontent if there is only one. Hence the attraction for the one; it is an attraction towards suicide.

Think of a world where only men exist and no women. There will be no tension, certainly. There will be great brotherhood, everybody will be gay -- literally gay! But life will lose something, something of immense importance – there will be no tension. It will be like having loose strings on a sitar; you cannot create music. You have to make them tight and tense, only then can you strike music out of them, only then can the hidden become manifest. With loose strings on a sitar how can you create music? They have to be tight, in a certain tension. Only great masters know how much tension is the right tension. And in the right tension the greatest melody is possible.

I teach you the right tension between the lower and the higher, between the body and the soul, between the earth and heaven; a right tension with no antagonism. The lower has not to be denied for the higher, neither has the higher to be denied for the lower. They are together, they are two aspects of the same reality, they interpenetrate.

So I don't say drop your doubt, I don't say drop your no. I say let your no become the tension for your yes, let your no become the background for your yes. Let your no create the context in which the yes will be more meaningful. Only in contrast does meaning arise. You write with white chalk on a blackboard – why? Because only in contrast will the white show; it will be loud and clear. Let no become the blackboard, and yes the white writing on it.

Your trust should not be a blind trust, your trust should be a trust which has eyes. Your trust should not be an impotent trust, a trust which is trust because you are impotent to say no. Your trust should be alive, strong and vital. Your trust will be capable of saying no. Say yes and yet retain the capacity to say no, then you will be surprised – your yes has such sharpness, such brilliance, such intelligence! Then it is not blind, it has eyes to see.

Use no as a foundation for yes, use doubt as manure for the rosebush. Use everything that God has given to you. Nothing, nothing at all, has to be denied; all has to be absorbed, because nothing is unessential or unimportant. Even though sometimes it looks unessential and unimportant, even though sometimes it looks positively harmful and poisonous, it has not to be denied. It has not to be thrown out, because later on, on the way, as you become wiser you will repent if you threw something away, because you will need it in some situation. There are moments when poison is needed as medicine. There are moments of wisdom when just the touch of the wise man and the poison becomes nectar.

I want you to become alchemists. This is an alchemical school, a university for inner alchemy. We are trying to change the baser metal into gold. So remember, I accept your no too, I love your no too. I accept all that you are. I accept all that you are not, even that too. You are accepted whatsoever you are, and you are accepted whatsoever you are not. You are accepted in totality.

From my side there is no question of denying anything, but of transforming it.

What is the ego? Remaining unenlightened, are we always functioning through the ego or are there moments when we are free of it?

Man has no center separate from the center of the whole. There is only one center in existence; the ancients used to call it Tao, *dhamma*, God. Those words have become old now; you can call it truth. There is only one center of existence. There are not many centers, otherwise the universe would not be really a universe, it would become a multiverse. It is a unity, hence it is called the "universe"; it has only one center.

But this is to be meditated upon a little. That one center is my center, your center, everybody's center. That one center does not mean that you are centerless, that one center simply means that you don't have a separate center. Let us say it in different words. You can make many concentric circles on one center, many circles. You can throw a pebble in a silent lake: one center arises from the fall of the pebble and then many concentric circles arise and they go on spreading to the farthest shore – millions of concentric circles, but they all have one center.

Each can claim this center as his own. And in a way it is his center, but it is not only his. The ego arises with the claim, "The center is mine, separate. It is not your center, it is my center; it is me." The idea of a separate center is the root of the ego.

When a child is born he comes without a center of his own. For nine months in the mother's womb he functions with the mother's center as his center; he is not separate. Then he is born. Then it is utilitarian to think of oneself as having a separate center; otherwise life will become very difficult, almost impossible. To survive, and to struggle for survival in the fight of life, everybody needs a certain idea of who they are. And nobody has any idea. In fact nobody can ever have any idea, because at the deepest core you are a mystery. You can't have any idea of it. At the deepest core you are not individual, you are universal.

That's why if you ask the Buddha, "Who are you?" he remains silent, he does not answer it. He cannot, because now he is no more separate. He is the whole. But in ordinary life even Buddha has to use the word *I*. If he feels thirsty he has to say, "I am thirsty. Ananda, bring me a little water, I am thirsty."

To be exactly right, he should say, "Ananda, bring some water. The universal center is a little thirsty." But that will look a little odd. And to say it again and again – sometimes the universal center is hungry, and sometimes the universal center is feeling a little cold, and sometimes the universal center is tired – it will be unnecessary, absolutely unnecessary. So he continues to use the old meaningful word *I*. It is very meaningful; even though a fiction, it is still meaningful. But many fictions are meaningful.

For example, you have a name. That is a fiction. You came without a name, you did not bring a name with you, the name was given to you. Then by constant repetition you start becoming identified with it. You know your name is Rama or Rahim or Krishna. It goes so deep that if all you three thousand sannyasins fall asleep here and somebody comes and calls,

"Rama, where are you?" nobody will hear except Rama. Rama will say, "Who has come to disturb my sleep?" Even in sleep he knows his name; it has reached to the unconscious, it has seeped through and through. But it is a fiction.

But when I say it is a fiction I don't mean it is unnecessary. It is necessary fiction, it is useful; otherwise how are you going to address people? If you want to write a letter to somebody, to whom are you going to write?

A small child once wrote a letter to God. His mother was ill and his father had died and they had no money, so he asked God for fifty rupees.

When the letter reached the post office they were at a loss – what to do with it? Where to send it? It was simply addressed to God. So they opened it. They felt very sorry for the little boy and they decided to collect some money and send it to him. They collected some money; he had asked for fifty rupees but they could collect only forty.

The next letter came, again addressed to God, and the boy had written, "Dear Sir, please next time when you send the money, send it directly to me, don't send it through the post office. They have taken their commission – ten rupees!"

It will be difficult if nobody has a name. Although nobody has a name in reality, still, it is a beautiful fiction, helpful. And nobody knows it more than I do, because I don't think anybody in the whole history of humanity has given as many names as I have given. You can count on me!

Names are needed for others to call you, "I" is needed for you to call yourself, but it is just a fiction. If you go deep into yourself you will find the name has disappeared, the idea of "I" has disappeared; there is left only a pure am-ness, is-ness, existence, being.

And that being is not separate, it is not yours and mine; that being is the being of all. Rocks, rivers, mountains, trees, all are included. It is all-inclusive, it excludes nothing. The whole past, the whole future, this immense universe, everything is included in it. The deeper you go into yourself, the more and more you will find that persons don't exist, that individuals don't exist. Then what exists is a pure universalness. On the circumference we have names, egos, identities. When we jump from the circumference towards the center, all those identities disappear.

The ego is just a useful fiction.

Use it, but don't be deceived by it.

You also ask, "Remaining unenlightened, are we always functioning through the ego or are there moments when we are free of it?"

Because it is a fiction, there are moments when you are free of it. Because it is a fiction, it can remain there only if you go on maintaining it. A fiction needs great maintenance. Truth needs no maintenance, that is the beauty of truth. But a fiction? You have constantly to paint it, to give it a prop here and there, and it is constantly collapsing. By the time you have managed to prop up one side, the other side starts collapsing.

And that's what people go on doing their whole life, trying to make the fiction seem as if it is the truth. Have more money, then you can have a bigger ego, a little more solid than the ego of the poor man. The poor man's ego is thin; he can't afford a thicker ego. Become the prime minister or president of a country, and your ego is puffed up to extremes. Then you don't walk on the earth.

Our whole life, the search for money, power, prestige, this and that, is nothing but a search for new props, a search for new supports, to somehow keep the fiction going. And all the time you know death is coming. Whatsoever you make, death is going to destroy it. But still one goes on hoping against hope – maybe everybody else dies, but not you.

And in a way it is true. You have always seen other people dying, you have never seen yourself dying, so it seems true also, logical also. This person dies, that person dies, and you never die. You are always there to feel sorry for them, you always go with them to the cemetery to say good-bye, and then you are back home again.

Don't be deceived by it, because all those people were doing the same thing. And nobody is an exception. Death comes and destroys the whole fiction of your name, your fame. Death comes and simply effaces all; not even footprints are left. Whatsoever we go on making out of our life is nothing but writing on water – not even on sand, but on water. You have not even written it, and it is gone. You cannot even read it; before you could have read it, it is gone.

But we go on trying to make these castles in the air. Because it is a fiction, it needs constant maintenance, constant effort, day and night. And nobody can be so careful for twenty-four hours. So sometimes, in spite of you, there are moments when you have a glimpse of reality without the ego functioning as a barrier. Without the screen of the ego, there are moments – in spite of you, remember. Everybody once in a while has those moments.

For example, every night when you fall deeply into sleep, and the sleep is so deep that you cannot even dream, then the ego is no more found; all the fictions are gone. Deep dreamless sleep is a kind of small death. In dreams there is a possibility that you may still manage to remember it. People go on managing to maintain their ego even in their dreams.

That's why psychoanalysis tries to go deep into your dreams, because there is less possibility of you maintaining your identity; more loopholes can be found there. In the daytime you are very alert and on guard, continuously there with a shield to protect your ego. In dreams sometimes you forget. But the people who have been studying dreams say that even in dreams the protection remains; it becomes a little more subtle.

For example, you see in a dream that you have killed your uncle. If you go deep into it you will be surprised: you wanted to kill your father, but you killed your uncle. You deceived yourself, the ego played a game. You are such a good guy, how can you kill your own father? And the uncle looks like your father, although nobody really wants to kill their uncle. Uncles are always nice people – who wants to kill one's uncle? And who does not want to kill one's own father?

There is bound to be great antagonism between the father and the son. The father has to discipline the son, he has to curb and cut his freedom and order him and force him to obey. And nobody wants to obey and be disciplined and given shoulds and should-nots. The father is so powerful that the son feels jealous. And the greatest jealousy is that the son wants the mother to be completely his own, and this father always comes in between, he is always there. And not only does the son feel jealous of the father, the father also feels jealous of the son because he is always there between his wife and him.

Mulla Nasruddin's son got married. He came home with his wife and with his friends and relatives; the whole house was full. He went out for something and when he came back he was very much taken aback – his father was hugging his wife and kissing her. This was too much! This is not allowed. He was very angry and said, "What are you doing?"

The father said, "And what have you been doing your whole life? You have been kissing and hugging my wife – and I never said anything to you."

He may not have said anything, but he must have felt like it. There is an antagonism between the father and the son, between the daughter and the mother – a natural antagonism, a natural jealousy. The daughter wants to possess the father but the mother is there; she looks like the enemy.

Uncles are very beautiful people, but in a dream you will not kill your own father. Your moral conscience, part of your ego, will prevent you from doing such a thing. You will find a substitute; this is a strategy.

If you minutely observe your dreams you will find many strategies the ego is still trying to play. The ego cannot accept the fact: "I am killing my own father? I am such an obedient son, respectful towards my father, loving him so much – and I am trying to kill my father?" The ego won't accept the idea; the ego shifts the idea a little bit to the side. The uncle looks almost like the father; kill the uncle, that seems easier. The uncle is only a substitute. This is what goes on even in dreams.

But in dreamless sleep the ego completely disappears, because when there is no thinking, no dreaming, how can you carry a fiction? But dreamless sleep is very small. In eight hours of healthy sleep it is not more than two hours. But only those two hours are revitalizing. If you have two hours of deep dreamless sleep, in the morning you are new, fresh, alive. Life again has a thrill to it, the day seems to be a gift. Everything seems to be new, because you are new. And everything seems to be beautiful, because you are in a beautiful space.

What happened in these two hours when you fell into deep sleep – what Patanjali calls *sushupti*, dreamless sleep? The ego disappeared. And the disappearance of the ego has revitalized you, rejuvenated you. With the disappearance of the ego, even though in deep unconsciousness, you had a taste of God.

Patanjali says there is not much difference between sushupti, dreamless sleep, and samadhi, the ultimate state of buddhahood – not much difference, although there is a difference. The difference is that of consciousness. In dreamless sleep you are unconscious, in samadhi you are conscious, but the state is the same. You move into God, you move into the universal center. You disappear from the circumference and you go to the center. And just that contact with the center so rejuvenates you.

People who cannot sleep are really miserable people, very miserable people. They have lost a natural source of being in contact with God. They have lost a natural passage into the universal; a door has closed.

This century is the first century which is suffering from sleeplessness. We have closed all the other doors; now we are closing the last door, the door of sleep. That seems to be the last disconnection from the universal energy – the greatest danger. And now there are foolish people in the world who are writing books, and with very logical acumen, saying that sleep is not needed at all, it is a wastage of time. They are right, it is a wastage of time. For people who think in terms of money and work, people who are workaholics, for them it is a wastage of time.

Just as there is now Alcoholics Anonymous, soon we will need Workaholics Anonymous. I propose Morarji Desai's name for the president of Workaholics Anonymous.

People who are obsessed with work, they have to be constantly on the go. They cannot rest, they cannot relax. Even when they are dying, they will be doing something or other.

These people are now suggesting that sleep is unnecessary. They are suggesting that sleep is really an unnecessary hangover from the past. They say that in the past, when there was no electricity and no fire, out of necessity people had to sleep. Now there is no need. It is just an old habit imbibed in millions of years; it has to be dropped. Their idea is that in the future sleep will disappear.

And the same is happening behind the iron curtain in Russia too. They are creating new devices so that people can be taught things while they are asleep – a new kind of education, so time is not wasted. It is the last torture that we are going to invent for children. We invented the school; we are not satisfied with that. Small children, imprisoned in schools....

In India, schools and prisons used to be painted the same way, the same color. And they were the same type of building – ugly, with no aesthetic sense, with no trees and birds and animals around them, so that children would not be distracted. Otherwise, who will listen to the foolish mathematics teacher when a cuckoo suddenly starts calling from the window? Or a deer comes into the class, and the teacher is teaching you geography or history.... Children will be distracted, so they have to be taken away from nature, away from society. They have to be forced to sit on hard benches for five hours, six hours, seven hours.

This goes on for years together. Almost one third of life is spent in schools. You have made slaves of them. In their remaining life they will remain workaholics; they will not be able to have a real holiday.

Now these people are thinking, why waste the night time? So children can be put into night education. They will be asleep in bed but their ears will be connected to a central school, and in a very, very subtle subliminal way, messages will be put into their heads. They will be programmed.

And it has been found that they can learn more easily in this way than they learn while they are awake. Naturally, because when you are awake, howsoever you are protected, a thousand and one things distract your mind. And children are so full of energy that everything attracts them; they are continuously distracted. That is just energy, nothing else; there is no sin in it. They are not dead, that's why they are distracted.

A dog starts barking, somebody starts fighting outside, somebody plays a trick on the teacher or somebody tells a joke – and there are a thousand and one things which go on distracting them. But when a child is asleep – and deeply asleep, when dreams are not there – there is no distraction at all. Now that dreamless sleep can be used as part of pedagogy.

It seems we are in every way ready to disconnect ourselves from the universal source of being. Now, these children will be the ugliest possible, because even when there was a possibility of being lost completely beyond the ego, that has also been taken away. The last possibility of ego disappearance is then no longer available. When they could have been in contact with God, they will be taught some rubbish history. The dates when Genghis Khan was born – who bothers, who cares? In fact if Genghis Khan had never been born, that would have been far better. That's what I wrote in my paper, and my teacher was very angry. I had to stand for twenty-four hours outside the class, because I had written, "It is unfortunate that he was born. It would have been very fortunate if he had not been born at all."

But kings and emperors, they go on and on being born just to torture small children; they have to remember the dates and the names for no reason at all. A better kind of education will drop all this crap. Ninety percent of it is crap, and the remaining ten percent can be very much improved. And then life can have more joy, more rest, more relaxation.

Because the ego is a fiction, it disappears sometimes. The greatest time is dreamless sleep. So make it a point that sleep is very valuable; don't miss it for any reason. Slowly, slowly, make sleep a regular thing. Because the body is a mechanism, if you follow a regular pattern of sleep the body will find it easier and the mind will find it easier to disappear.

Go to bed at exactly the same time. Don't take it literally – if one day you are late you will not be sent to hell or anything! I have to be cautious, because there are a few people here who are health freaks. Their only disease is that they are continuously thinking of health. If they stop thinking of health they will be perfectly well. But if you can make your sleep a regular thing, going to bed at almost the same time and getting up at almost the same time…the body is a mechanism, the mind is too, and it simply slips into dreamless sleep at a certain moment.

The second greatest source of egoless experiences is sex, love. That too has been destroyed by the priests; they have condemned it, so it is no longer such a great experience. Such a condemnation for so long, it has conditioned the minds of people. Even while they are making love, they know deep down that they are doing something wrong. Some guilt is lurking somewhere. And this is so even for the most modern, the most contemporary, even the younger generation.

On the surface you may have revolted against the society, on the surface you may be a conformist no more. But things have gone very deep; it is not a question of revolting on the surface. You can grow long hair, that won't help much. You can become a hippie and stop taking baths, that won't help much. You can become a dropout in every possible way that you can imagine and think of, but that won't help really, because things have gone too deep and all these are superficial measures.

For thousands of years we have been told that sex is the greatest sin. It has become part of our blood, bone and marrow. So even if you know consciously that there is nothing wrong in it, the unconscious keeps you a little detached, afraid, guilt-ridden, and you cannot move into it totally.

If you can move into lovemaking totally, the ego disappears, because at the highest peak, at the highest climax of lovemaking, you are pure energy. The mind cannot function. With such joy, with such an outburst of energy, the mind simply stops. It is such an upsurge of energy that the mind is at a loss, it does not know what to do now. It is perfectly capable of remaining in function in normal situations, but when anything very new and very vital happens it stops.

And sex is the most vital thing.

If you can go deeply into lovemaking, the ego disappears. That is the beauty of lovemaking, that it is another source of a glimpse of God – just like deep sleep but far more valuable, because in deep sleep you will be unconscious. In lovemaking you will be conscious – conscious yet without the mind.

Hence the great science of Tantra became possible. Patanjali and yoga worked on the lines of deep sleep; they chose that path to transform deep sleep into a conscious state so you know who you are, so you know what you are at the center.

Tantra chose lovemaking as a window towards God. The path of yoga is very long, because to transform unconscious sleep into consciousness is very arduous; it may take many lives. And who knows, you may or may not be able to persist for so long, persevere for so long, be patient for so long. So the fate that has fallen on yoga is this, that the so-called yogis go on only doing body postures. They never go deeper than that; that takes their whole life. Of course they get better health, a longer life – but that is not the point! You can have better health by jogging, running, swimming; you can have a longer life through medical care. That is not the point.

The point was to become conscious in deep sleep. And your so-called yogis go on teaching you how to stand on your head and how to distort and contort your body. Yoga has become a kind of circus – meaningless. It has lost its real dimension.

In the new commune, I have the vision of reviving yoga again in its true flavor, in its true dimension. And the goal is to become conscious while you are deeply asleep. That is the essential thing in yoga, and if any yogi is teaching anything else it is all useless.

But Tantra has chosen a far shorter way, the shortest, and far more pleasant too! Lovemaking can open the window. All that is needed is to uproot the conditionings that the priests have put into you. The priests put those conditionings into you so that they could become mediators and agents between you and God, so that your direct contact was cut. Naturally you would need somebody else to connect you, and the priest would become powerful. And the priest has been powerful down the ages.

Whosoever can put you in contact with power, real power, will become powerful. God is real power, the source of all power. The priest remained down the ages so powerful – more powerful than kings. Now the scientist has taken the place of the priest, because now he knows how to unlock the doors of the power hidden in nature. The priest knew how to connect you with God, the scientist knows how to connect you with nature. But the priest has to disconnect you first, so no individual private line remains between you and God. He has spoiled your inner sources, poisoned them. He became very powerful but the whole humanity became lustless, loveless, full of guilt.

My people have to drop that guilt completely. While making love, think of prayer, meditation, God. While making love, burn incense, chant, sing, dance. Your bedroom should be a temple, a sacred place. And lovemaking should not be a hurried thing. Go deeper into it; savor it as slowly and as gracefully as possible. And you will be surprised. You have the key.

God has not sent you into the world without keys. But those keys have to be used, you have to put them into the lock and turn them.

Love is another phenomenon, one of the most potential, where the ego disappears and you are conscious, fully conscious, pulsating, vibrating. You are no more an individual, you are lost into the energy of the whole.

Then, slowly, slowly, let this become your very way of life. What happens at the peak of love has to become your discipline – not just an experience but a discipline. Then whatsoever you are doing and wherever you are walking…early in the morning with the sun rising, have the same feeling, the same merger with existence. Lying down on the ground, the sky full of stars, have the same merger again. Lying down on the earth, feel one with the earth.

Slowly, slowly, lovemaking should give you the clue for how to be in love with existence itself. And then the ego is known as a fiction, is used as a fiction. And if you use it as a fiction, there is no danger.

There are a few other moments when the ego slips of its own accord. In moments of great danger: you are driving, and suddenly you see an accident is going to happen. You have lost control of the car and there seems to be no possibility of saving yourself. You are going to crash into the tree or into the oncoming truck, or you are going to fall in the river, it is absolutely certain. In those moments suddenly the ego will disappear.

That's why there is a great attraction to move into dangerous situations. People climb Everest. It is a deep meditation, although they may or may not understand this. Mountaineering is of great importance. Climbing mountains is dangerous – the more dangerous it is, the more beautiful. You will have glimpses, great glimpses of egolessness. Whenever danger is very close, the mind stops. Mind can think only when you are not in danger; it has nothing to say in danger. Danger makes you spontaneous, and in that spontaneity you suddenly know that you are not the ego.

Or – these will be for different people, because people are different – if you have an aesthetic heart, then beauty will open the doors. Just seeing a beautiful woman or a man passing by, just for a single moment a flash of beauty, and suddenly the ego disappears. You are overwhelmed.

Or seeing a lotus in the pond, or seeing the sunset or a bird on the wing – anything that triggers your inner sensitivity, anything that possesses you for the moment so deeply that you forget yourself, that you are and yet you are not, that you abandon yourself – then too, the ego slips. It is a fiction; you have to carry it. If you forget it for a moment, it slips.

And it is good that there are a few moments when it slips and you have a glimpse of the true and the real. It is because of these glimpses that religion has not died. It is not because of the priests – they have done everything to kill it. It is not because of the so-called religious, those who go to the church and the mosque and the temple. They are not religious at all, they are pretenders.

Religion has not died because of these few moments which happen more or less to almost everybody. Take more note of them, imbibe the spirit of those moments more, allow those moments more, create spaces for those moments to happen more. This is the true way to seek God. Not to be in the ego is to be in God.

? **Why do you emphasize the importance of herenow so much?**

Because there is nothing else. Here is the only space, now is the only time. Beyond the herenow, there is nothing. Two thousand years ago, a great Jewish master, Hillel, wrote a little poem in Aramaic. The poem is this:

"If I'm not for myself,
Then who can be for me?
And if I'm only for myself,
Then what am I?
And if not now,
When?"

It is a beautiful statement: if not now, then when? Tomorrow? But the tomorrow never comes.

Hence I emphasize the herenow. Don't let this moment slip by unused, unlived, unpenetrated; squeeze all that you can out of it. Live it passionately and with intensity, so you need not repent later on that you missed your life.

It was after the Second World War; the war had ended. Joe Dink was still in Japan waiting to be discharged. His wife, Irma Dink, was wild with anxiety and jealousy because she read about the goings on between the American soldiers and the Japanese girls.

Finally she could stand it no longer, and she wrote her husband, "Joe, hurry up and come back. What do those girls have, anyway, that the American girls don't?"

"Not a thing," wrote back Joe. "But what they've got, they've got here."

And that is the most important thing. The question is of here and now.

? What is a miracle?

It depends. To me, everything is a miracle. I never come across anything that is not a miracle; only miracles exist. Everything is such a surprise, it is so unbelievable! But if your eyes are closed, if your eyes are full of dust, if your mind is too knowledgeable, if you think you know all, then nothing is a miracle.

To know "I don't know anything" makes everything a miracle. It depends on your inner state, it depends on you. And to live a life without miracles is not to live at all. You can have a million miracles every day, you are entitled to have them. But because you don't know how to connect yourself with the miraculous, you are being cheated by stupid people.

Somebody produces a Swiss-made watch and you think this is a miracle. Then you become victims of ordinary magicians. Don't be befooled.

The seed sprouting into leaves is a miracle – not somebody producing a Swiss-made watch out of nothing. That is just a trick, a very ordinary trick; street magicians are doing it all over the world. They are just simple people, not cunning people, otherwise you would have worshipped them.

While exploring the wilds of South America, a man was captured by savages. They were dancing excitedly around before killing him when the explorer had a bright idea. He would baffle them with magic. Taking a cigarette-lighter from his pocket, he shouted, "I make fire!"

With a flick of the thumb, the lighter burst into flame. The savages fell back and gazed in wonder.

"Magic!" cried the explorer.

"It certainly is," said the chief. "It's the only time I ever saw a lighter work on the first try."

It depends on you, what you call a miracle. As far as I am concerned, there is nothing else except miracles. And drop these stupid kinds of miracles.

Mulla Nasruddin and his wife are sitting one Sunday listening to the radio, when this faith healer comes on and he says, "If you have a part of your body you want healed, place one hand on the radio and the other hand on the afflicted part."

The wife placed one hand on the radio and the other on her heart. The Mulla placed one hand on the radio and the other on his appendage.

So the wife said, "Mulla, he's trying to cure the sick, not raise the dead."

Enough for today.

Chapter 17
Wake Up the Slave

> *Don't seek sorrow for spurious comforts.*
> *All absorptions are effected in one.*
> *One method will correct all wrong.*
> *At the beginning and at the end*
> *There are two things to do.*
> *Be patient, whichever of the two occurs.*
> *Observe two precepts even at the risk of life.*
> *Learn the three difficulties.*
> *Take up the three parts of the principal cause.*
> *Meditate on the three things not to be destroyed.*
> *Make the three inseparable from virtue.*

An ancient story.... Jesus, son of Mary, once came upon an old man who lived on a mountain in the open air without any shelter from heat or cold. Jesus asked him why he had not built himself a house.

"Ah, spirit of God!" said the old man. "Prophets before thee predicted that I would live for only seven hundred years. It is not worth my trouble to settle down."

Life is a wandering, it is not a home. It is a search for the home, but it itself is not the home. It is an inquiry, an adventure. It is not necessarily that you will succeed – success is very rare, because the search is very complex and there are a thousand and one difficulties on the way.

But let this be your first understanding about today's sutras. They are of immense value. When you meditate and when you go deeper into them you will be surprised: these sutras are just like oceans contained in dewdrops.

Mohammed says, "I am like a rider who shelters under a tree, then goes on his way." Yes, this life is an overnight's stay, a caravanserai. Don't settle in it. Use the opportunity to reach higher and higher and higher, because there is no end to heights, to depths. But remember always, don't take life for granted: it is only an opportunity, with immense potential and possibilities. But if you start thinking that you have already arrived because you are alive, you will miss the whole point.

Jesus says again and again, "The world is to be treated as a bridge, not as a stopping place." Use it as a bridge; it can bridge you to God. And when life becomes a bridge to God it is divine. But if you don't use it as a bridge towards God it remains mundane, spurious, illusory, imaginary, fictitious.

The first sutra:

> *Don't seek sorrow for spurious comforts.*

Everybody seeks, searches for bliss, and almost everybody succeeds in finding just the opposite. I say "almost" because a few people have to be left out of the account – a Buddha, a Zarathustra, a Lao Tzu, an Atisha. But they are so few and far between; they are exceptions, they only prove the rule. So I say almost everybody who searches for bliss finds misery and suffering. People try to enter into heaven, but by the time they have arrived suddenly they recognize the fact that it is hell.

There must be a great misunderstanding somewhere. The misunderstanding is that those who seek pleasure will find sorrow – because pleasure is only a camouflage; it is sorrow hiding itself behind a curtain. It is a mask – tears hiding behind smiles, thorns waiting for you behind flowers. Those who see it, and everybody can see it because it is so obvious...everybody comes to experience it again and again. But man is the animal who never learns.

Aristotle has defined man as a rational being. That is sheer nonsense! Man is the most irrational being you can find anywhere. Man can be rational, but is not. It is not the definition of man as he is, it is the definition of man as he should be. A Buddha, yes; a Mohammed, yes – they are rational beings, rational in the sense that they live intelligently, they live wisely, they use each single opportunity to grow, to mature, to be. But as far as millions of human beings are concerned, ninety-nine point nine percent of people, they are not rational beings at all, they are utterly irrational.

Their first irrationality is that they pass through the same experience again and again, yet they learn nothing, they remain the same. How many times have you been angry, and what have you learned out of it? How many times have you been jealous, and what experience have you gained out of it? You go on moving through experiences without in any way being affected by them. You remain un-grownup; your way of life is very irrational, unintelligent.

The intelligent person will be able to see easily that, seeking pleasure, all that is found is sorrow. And what are those pleasures in fact? Very spurious ones. Somebody wants to make a big house, and how much trouble he takes and how much suffering he goes through and how many anxieties and how many nervous breakdowns!

They say that if you are really a successful person you are bound to have a heart attack somewhere between forty-two and forty-eight. If you don't have a heart attack before you are fifty your life is wasted, you are a failure; you have not tried to succeed, you have not been ambitious enough. Ambitious people are bound to have heart attacks; the more ambitious will have nervous breakdowns.

If you don't need the psychiatrist, that simply means you have not used your mind in the ways of ambition. And the whole society is geared towards ambition, the whole educational system produces only ambitious minds. That means potential patients for the psychotherapist. It seems as if there is a conspiracy – that the whole educational system only creates people for doctors, for priests, for psychotherapists.

The whole system seems to be sick, sick unto death. It does not create the healthy, alive, radiant human being; it does not create the joyous, the celebrating, the festive being. It does not teach you how to make your life a festival. Whatsoever it teaches takes you deeper and deeper into hell. And you know it – because I am not talking about some speculative systems of thought, I am talking simply about your psychology, your state of being

Atisha is right. He says:

Don't seek sorrow for spurious comforts.

How much suffering you have created – for what? Somebody wanted a little bigger house, a little bigger bank balance, a little more fame, a little more name, more power. Somebody wanted to become the president or the prime minister. All are spurious, because death will take them away. That is the definition of the spurious.

Only that which cannot be taken away by death is real. Everything else is unreal; it is made of the same stuff dreams are made of. If you are running after things which will be taken away by death, then your life is "a tale told by an idiot, full of sound and fury, signifying nothing." You will never attain to any significance.

And without significance how can there be a song? And without significance how can you ever say that "I have lived"? The tree has not bloomed, the tree has not been fruitful. What to say about fruits and flowers – even leaves have not come.

Millions are born as seeds and die as seeds. From the cradle to the grave, their story is just of drifting. Accidental it is, and the ultimate result is great sorrow. The idea of hell only symbolizes the great sorrow that you create by a wrong kind of living.

Atisha says:

Don't seek sorrow for spurious comforts.

Then what has to be done? Think of something higher – something that is beyond death, something that cannot be destroyed, something that is indestructible, something that transcends time – and sorrow will not be created.

If you search the ultimate, each moment of your life will become more and more peaceful, calm, quiet, cool, fragrant. If you search for the ultimate, if you search for the truth, or God or nirvana or whatsoever you want to call it; if you are in search for the deepest in life and the highest in life and you are not after spurious things, then your very search will bring a new quality to your being. You will feel rooted, integrated; you will feel together. And you will feel a new joy arising in your heart, not coming from the outside.

The real joy never comes from the outside, it is the spurious that comes from the outside – death can take away only that which has come from the outside.

Death happens only on the without, it never happens within. Death happens on the outside, never on the inside; the inside is eternal. Your interiority is beyond death – it has always been here, will always be here, but you are unaware of it. You go on running after shadows, and the real waits for you to look in, to turn in, to tune in.

So the first thing: seek that which is deathless, and sooner or later you will knock on the doors of heaven.

The second thing is: why in the first place do you run after spurious pleasures? This woman, that man…why do you run after spurious pleasures? What is the rationale behind it?

The rationale is that you are already in sorrow. You want somehow to forget all about it; you want to drown yourself in alcohol, in sex, in money, in power politics – you want somewhere to drown yourself.

Politicians can easily say that prohibition is needed, because they have a far more dangerous intoxicant available to them. Morarji Desai can insist for prohibition, because he is drinking out of his power politics; he is drowning himself in a very subtle kind of intoxicant. In fact, no alcohol is more dangerous than politics.

If anything has to be prohibited from the world, it is not alcohol, it is politics. And how many people drink alcohol in India? Not more than seven percent. And how many more people are political? I don't think you can find any person who is not political – very difficult.

You may not be actually in politics, but politics is far more subtle. The husband is trying to dominate over the wife – this is politics. The wife is trying to manipulate the husband in her own way – this is politics. The child is in a tantrum and wants a toy immediately – this is politics. Politics means an effort to dominate the other. And it is very intoxicating; it is the worst kind of alcohol available in the world.

A few people drown in power politics, a few seek shelter in sexuality, a few go to the pub, but many more simply go on searching spurious comforts, go from one comfort to another. When they have achieved one and found that it gives nothing, no nourishment, immediately they start seeking something else. Their life becomes a constant occupation so they need not look at the inner sorrow that is gathering like a cloud, a dark cloud.

So the second meaning of the sutra is: rather than seeking spurious comforts, the best way is to go into your sorrow. Meditate, go deep into it. Don't escape from your misery, because by escaping you will never learn what it is and you will never learn how to transcend it. The beauty is: if you really know the cause of your misery, in that very knowing misery is transcended – because the cause is always and always ignorance and nothing else.

Jesus says: Truth liberates. This is one of the most important statements ever made, very fundamental for every seeker to understand. Truth liberates – not the truth that you gather from scriptures but the truth that you come across through your own experiencing.

You are sad. Go into your sadness rather than escaping into some activity, into some occupation, rather than going to see a friend or to a movie or turning on the radio or the TV. Rather than escaping from it, turning your back towards it, drop all activity. Close your eyes, go into it, see what it is, why it is – and see without condemning it, because if you condemn you will not be able to see the totality of it. See without judging. If you judge, you will not be able to see the whole of it. Without judgment, without condemnation, without evaluation, just watch it, what it is. Look as if it is a flower, sad; a cloud, dark; but look at it with no judgment so that you can see all the facets of it.

And you will be surprised: the deeper you go into it, the more it starts dispersing. If a person can go into his sorrow deeply he will find all sorrow has evaporated. In that evaporation of sorrow is joy, is bliss.

Bliss has not to be found outside, against sorrow. Bliss has to be found deep, hidden behind the sorrow itself. You have to dig into your sorrowful states and you will find a wellspring of joy.

The second sutra:

All absorptions are effected in one.

So Atisha says: There is no need to have many goals, one goal is enough. Inquire into the truth of your life. Only one search is enough to deliver you from all your miseries, sufferings, hells. Inquire into the truth of your being, see all the facets of it – the anger, the greed, the lust. Go into each. And by going into each, you will find always and always the same source of joy, the same spring of joy. Slowly, slowly you will become a festival. Nothing has been added from the outside, but you have discovered yourself. You have come into the kingdom of God.

The third sutra:

One method will correct all wrong.

One goal – truth – and one method. What is that method? I call it meditation, Atisha used to call it awareness, Buddha used to call it mindfulness. These are different words for the same quality – the quality of being attentive, alert, awake.

Atisha is very mathematical; no great mathematician can be so mathematical as he is. He is moving step by step. First he says: Don't seek spurious comforts; that is going astray. Don't escape from your sorrowful state; go into it. Let this become your one goal: the search for the truth of your being. He is not talking about any truth that lives somewhere in the sky, he is not talking about any philosophical truth. He is talking about the truth that you are; he is talking about you. He is utterly psychological, he is not talking about metaphysics.

Then the method…and he goes so quick, not a single word wasted, not a single word superfluous. He is so telegraphic; that is the meaning of the word *sutra*. *Sutra* means very telegraphic. There was a great need in those days when Atisha was writing these sutras – there was a great need to be very, very short, condensed, telegraphic, because books were not available; people had to remember them. And it is better to make very, very condensed sutras so people can remember. Now these are only seven points we are discussing, and can be easily remembered.

One method will correct all wrong.

That method is awareness. There are many illnesses but there is only one health. The quality of health is one, always the same. Whether I am healthy or you are healthy, the feel of health is the same. Diseases are millions, wrongs are many, but the right key that unlocks all the doors, the master key, is only one. And rather than cutting the branches, rather than pruning the leaves, why not cut the very root? There are many people who go on pruning the leaves or cutting the branches; these people are known as moralists.

The moral person is a little-bit-stupid person, stupid in the sense that he thinks that by cutting the leaves he is going to destroy the tree. He is not going to destroy the tree this way. You cut one leaf and the tree will respond with three leaves instead, the foliage will become thicker. You cut one branch and the tree will pour its sap and juices into another branch, and the other branch will become thicker and bigger. This is what happens in your life.

Somebody is against sex; he represses sex, he cuts that branch. Now the whole energy becomes anger. You will find stories in Indian scriptures, stories like the story of Durvasa – a great so-called *mahatma* who repressed his sex totally, and then became all anger, just red-hot anger. It is bound to happen. You cannot destroy any energy – never. It is not possible in the very nature of things. Energies can only be transformed, never destroyed. If you close one outlet, the energy will start flowing from another. If you close the front door, then from the back door...and from the back door it is more dangerous, because it makes your life the life of a hypocrite, it makes your life double. You start living in a dual way: you say one thing, you do another; you show one thing, you are another. You become more and more split.

My emphasis is also exactly the same as Atisha's. You come to me with a thousand and one problems, but my answer is always the same. If you come with anger I say be aware of it, if you come with greed I say be aware of it, if you come with lust I say be aware of it – because awareness cuts the very root. What is the root? Unawareness is the root.

One can be angry only if he is unaware. Try to be angry and aware together and you will find it impossible. Either you will be aware, then anger will not be found, or you will be angry and awareness will have disappeared. Up to now, nobody has been able to manage both together, and I don't think you can prove the exception. Try it. It is possible you may think both are happening, but if you minutely watch you will see: when awareness is there anger is not, when anger is there awareness is not. Unawareness is the root of all illnesses; then awareness is the only medicine.

Buddha says, "I am a physician." And once somebody asked, "You again and again say you are a physician, but I don't see any medicines around you. What medicines do you give?"

He said, "My medicine is only one: it is awareness. I prescribe awareness." And it has not to be brought from the chemist; you have to change your inner chemistry to bring it. You have to change your inner chemistry. Right now your inner chemistry functions in such a way that it produces unawareness, unconsciousness. It can be changed, it can be de-automatized. How to do it you will find in the sutras that are to follow.

But remember, one method is enough to correct all wrong. That method is awareness. And how will you know that you have attained it? Awareness is something inner, it is so deep that nobody can see it. Still, if you become aware, everybody who has a little intelligence, who has eyes to see, will become aware of it – because as awareness happens at the inner core, compassion starts radiating, love starts radiating.

Buddha says: Light the candle of awareness in your heart, and your whole being will radiate compassion. Compassion is the proof. Unless compassion happens, remember, you must be deceiving yourself; you must be doing something else than being aware.

For example, you can try concentration. Concentration is not awareness, and the person of concentration will never show compassion. Compassion is not a consequence of concentration. Concentration means the focusing of the mind, the narrowing of the mind on only one point. The concentrated mind becomes a very powerful mind – but remember it is mind, and very powerful, hence more dangerous than ever. Concentration is the method of science.

Awareness is totally different; it is not focusing, it is unfocused alertness. For example, right now you are listening to me. You can hear in a concentrated way, you can be focused on me; then you will miss the birds and their songs, then you will miss this noise on the road. Then you are not aware, then your mind has become very narrow. Awareness is not the narrowing of the mind but the disappearance of the mind. The narrowing of the mind makes the mind more of a mind – hence the Hindu mind is more of a mind, the Mohammedan mind is more of a mind, the communist mind is more of a mind, because these are all narrowing. Somebody is focused on *Das Kapital* or the *Communist Manifesto*, somebody is focused on the Koran or on *The Dhammapada*, somebody on the Gita, somebody on The Bible – focused people. They create narrow minds in the world. They create conflict, they don't bring compassion.

For thousands of years religions have existed, but compassion is still a dream. We have not been able to create a world that knows what love is, friendship is, brotherhood is. Yes, we talk, and we talk too much about all these beautiful things. In fact the talk has become nauseating, it is sickening. It should stop. No more talk of brotherhood and love and this and that – we have talked for thousands of years for no purpose.

The reason is that the concentrated mind becomes narrow, becomes more of a mind. And love is not the function of the mind, love is the function of no-mind – or call it heart, which means the same. No-mind and heart are synonymous.

Awareness means to listen to me unfocused – alert of course, not fallen asleep, but alert to these birds, their chirping, alert to the wind that passes through the trees, alert to everything that is happening. Concentration excludes much, includes little. Awareness excludes nothing, includes all.

Awareness is a state of no-mind. You are, yet you are not focused. You are just a mirror reflecting all, echoing all; see the beauty of it and the silence and the stillness. Suddenly you are and you are not, and the miracle starts happening. In this silence you will feel a compassion, compassion for all suffering beings. It has not to be practiced either; it comes on its own.

Atisha says: Awareness inside, compassion on the outside. Compassion is the outer side of awareness, the exterior of awareness. Awareness is your interiority, subjectivity. Compassion is relating with others, sharing with others.

The fourth sutra:

At the beginning and at the end there are two things to do.

By the beginning is meant the morning, and by the end, the evening. In the morning remember one thing, says Atisha, that a new day, a new opportunity, has again been given to you. Feel grateful. Existence is so generous. You have wasted so many days, and again one day has been given to you. Existence is so hopeful about you! You have been wasting and wasting and doing nothing; you have wasted so much valuable opportunity and time and energy, but existence still hopes. One day more is given to you.

Atisha says: In the morning remember it is a new day, a new beginning. Have a decision deep in your heart that "Today I am not going to waste this opportunity. Enough is enough! Today I am going to be aware, today I am going to be alert, today I am going to devote as much energy as possible to the single cause, the cause of meditation. I will meditate in all my acts. will do all the activities, the usual day-to-day activities, but with a new quality: I will bring the quality of awareness to them."

Welcome the new day. Feel grateful, happy that existence still trusts in you; there is still a possibility, the transformation can still happen. Start the day with a great decisiveness.

And in the evening again feel gratitude that the day was given to you, and feel gratitude for all that happened – good and bad both, happiness and unhappiness both, because they are all teachers.

Everything is an opportunity. Taken rightly, every moment is a stepping-stone. Failure as much helps you to become alert as success; sometimes in fact failure helps you to become more aware than success. Success helps you to fall asleep. In happiness people forget; in happiness nobody remembers God. In unhappiness suddenly the remembrance comes.

Fortunate is the man who can remember even when he is happy; fortunate is the man who can remember when everything is going good and smooth. When the sea is rough, everybody remembers God; there is nothing special in it, it is just out of fear.

It happened: In the sea there was a ship, a ship which was carrying many Mohammedans to Mecca. They were on a pilgrimage. They were all surprised by one thing: because they were all pilgrims going to the holy of holies, each was praying all the five prayers prescribed for a Mohammedan every day – except a Sufi mystic. But the mystic was so radiant with joy that nobody dared to ask him why.

Then one day the sea was very rough and the captain declared, "There seems to be no possibility that we can be saved, so please do your last prayer. The ship is going to sink." And everybody fell in prayer except the Sufi mystic.

Now this was too much. Many people gathered around the mystic. They were really angry and they said, "You are a man of God. We have watched you, you have never prayed. But we didn't say anything; we felt that this would be disrespectful – you are thought to be a holy man. But now it is unbearable. The ship is sinking, and you are a man of God – if you pray, your prayer will be listened to. Why are you not praying?"

The mystic said, "To pray out of fear is to miss the whole point, that's why I am not praying."

And then they asked, "Then why did you not pray when there was no question of fear?"

He said, "I am in prayer, so I cannot pray. Only those who are not in prayer can pray. But what is the point of their prayer? Empty rituals! I am in prayer, in fact I *am* prayer. Each moment is a prayer."

Prayer is the Sufi word for the same quality for which Atisha will use the word *awareness*.

So in the evening thank again, thank the whole existence. For Atisha there is no God, remember. Even if I use the word *God* it is not Atisha's word; for Atisha the whole existence is divine, there is no personal God.

That has always been the attitude of the meditator. If you are a man of prayer, existence appears as God, as personal. If you are a man of meditation, existence is impersonal, just a wholeness, a divineness. For the man of prayer there is God; for the man of awareness there is godliness but no God.

H.G. Wells is reported to have said that Gautam Buddha was the most godless man, yet the most godly. This is true – most godless because he never believed in any God, yet the most godly because he himself was divine. He himself was as godly as one can ever be or hope ever to be.

So in the evening feel grateful for whatsoever happened during the day. And two things more: remember when you failed in the day in being aware and being compassionate – just remember. Atisha does not say repent, just remember. And let me remind you: when in The Bible Jesus says again and again "Repent!" it is a mistranslation from the Aramaic. In English it has taken on a totally different meaning, a diametrically opposite meaning. It has become repentance – "Feel guilty!"

In Aramaic, repent simply means return, look back; that's all. Take a count back: the day is gone, look back. Just watch again, take note when you failed in awareness – that will help you tomorrow, it will enhance your awareness. And take note when you failed in compassion – that will help you tomorrow to be more compassionate. And also take note when you succeeded in being aware and compassionate. Don't feel any pride for it either – no guilt, no pride. It is not a question of guilt and pride; it is simply taking an account of the day that is gone before you go to sleep, just looking back, with no evaluation – neither condemning oneself as a sinner, nor being very, very proud that "Today I have been so aware, so compassionate; I have done so many good deeds." Nothing of the sort – just noticing back, what happened from the morning to the evening. This is also a method of becoming more aware.

Be patient, whichever of the two occurs.

Remember, whether you succeed in awareness or you fail, be patient. Don't be impatient, because impatience is not going to help. Just watch patiently and wait in tremendous trust that if this much can happen, more is possible. Another leaf will be born tomorrow, another flower will bloom tomorrow.

Also remember that this body is not the only body. Many more you had before, and many more you are going to have in the future. There is no hurry. Be patient, because hurry can only disturb things. Hurry is not going to help, but hinder.

Observe two precepts even at the risk of life.

These two precepts of awareness and compassion are so valuable that even if you sometimes have to sacrifice your life for them, it is worth it. Life is nothing but an opportunity to attain to awareness and compassion. If you don't attain awareness and compassion, what is the point of going on living? It is meaningless.

Just meditate over it. If one is so much ready, so intent, so deeply committed to be aware and compassionate that he is ready to sacrifice his life, will he remain unaware long? Impossible!

This very moment, if this intensity is there, awareness will happen out of this intensity. This intensity will flare up like a light inside, and out of that light, the radiance of compassion.

Life in itself is not meaningful. It is meaningful only if you can sing a song of the eternal, if you can release some fragrance of the divine, of the godly, if you can become a lotus flower – deathless, timeless. If you can become pure love, if you can beautify this existence, if you can become a blessing to this existence, only then does life have significance; otherwise it is pointless. It is like an empty canvas: you can go on carrying it your whole life and you can die under its weight, but what is the point? Paint something on it!

Meaning has to be created in life; meaning is not given already. You are given freedom, you are given creativity, you are given life. All that is needed to create meaning is given. All the essential ingredients of meaning are given, but meaning is not given, meaning has to be created by you. You have to become a creator in your own right.

And when you became a creator in your own right, you participate with God, you become a part of God.

Learn the three difficulties.

There are three difficulties in becoming aware. These are very essential for each seeker to understand. In fact everybody becomes aware, but only when the act is finished. You have been angry – you slapped your wife or you threw a pillow at your husband. Later on when the heat is cooled, the moment has passed, you become aware. But now it is pointless, now nothing can be done. What has been done cannot be undone; it is too late.

Three things, Atisha says, are to be remembered. One is becoming aware while the act is happening. That is the first difficulty for the person who wants to become aware – becoming aware in the act itself.

Anger is there like smoke inside you. Becoming aware in the very thick of it, that is the first difficulty, but it is not impossible. Just a little effort and you will be able to catch hold of it. In the beginning you will see, you become aware when the anger has gone and everything has cooled – you become aware after fifteen minutes. Try – you will become aware after five minutes. Try a little more – you will become aware immediately after one minute. Try a little more, and you will become aware just when the anger is evaporating. Try a little more, and you will become aware exactly in the middle of it. And that is the first step: be aware in the act.

Then the second step, which is even more difficult because now you are going into deeper waters. The second step, or the second difficulty, Atisha calls it, is remembering before the act: when the act has not yet happened but is still a thought in you; it has not been actualized but it has become a thought in your mind. It is there, potentially there like a seed; it can become the act any moment.

Now you will need a little more subtle awareness. The act is gross – you hit the woman. You can become aware while you are hitting, but the idea of hitting is far more subtle. Thousands of ideas go on passing in the mind – who takes note of them? They go on and on; the traffic continues. Most of those ideas never become acts.

This is the difference between sin and crime. Crime is when something becomes an act. No law court can punish you for a thought. You can think of murdering somebody but no law can punish you. You can enjoy, you can dream, but you are not under law unless you act, unless you do something and the thought is transformed into actuality; then it becomes a crime.

But religion goes deeper. It says when you think it, it is already a sin. Whether you actualize it or not does not matter – you have committed it in your inner world and you are affected by it, you are contaminated by it, you are blemished by it.

The second difficulty, Atisha says, is to catch hold when the thought is arising in you. It can be done, but it can be done only when you have crossed the first barrier, because thought is not so solid. But still it is solid enough to be seen; you have to just practice a little bit. Sitting silently, just watch your thoughts. Just see all the nuances of a thought – how it arises, how it takes form, how it remains, abides, and how then it leaves you. It becomes a guest and then when the time comes it leaves you. And many thoughts come and go; you are a host where many thoughts come and go. Just watch.

Don't try from the very beginning with the difficult thoughts, try with simple thoughts. That will make it easier, because the process is the same. Just sit in the garden, close your eyes and see whatsoever thought is passing – and they are always passing. The dog barks in the neighborhood, and immediately a process of thought starts in you. You suddenly remember a dog you had in your childhood and how much you had loved that dog, and then the dog died, and how you suffered.

Then comes the idea of death, and the dog is forgotten and you remember the death of your mother. And with the idea of the mother suddenly you remember your father. And things go on and on. Just the whole thing was triggered by a foolish dog who is not even aware that you are sitting in your garden, who is simply barking because he knows nothing else to keep himself occupied. His barking is nothing but politicking – his politics, power politics.

That's why dogs are very much against uniforms. The policeman, the postman, the sannyasin – and the dogs are very angry. They don't tolerate uniforms. How dare you walk in uniform, trying to dominate them? They are angry against policemen and people like that.

He was not aware of you, he has not barked for you especially, but a chain was triggered. Watch these simple chains, and then slowly, slowly try them with more emotionally involved things. You are angry, you are greedy, you are jealous – just catch hold of yourself in the middle of the thought. That is the second difficulty.

And the third difficulty is to catch hold of this process, which results ultimately in an act, before it becomes a thought. That is the most difficult; right now you cannot even conceive of it. Before anything becomes a thought, it is a feeling. These are the three things: feeling comes first, then comes thought, then comes the act. You may not be aware at all that each thought is produced by a certain feeling. If the feeling is not there, the thought will not come. Feeling becomes actualized in thought, thought becomes actualized in the act.

Now you have to do the almost impossible thing – to catch hold of a certain feeling. Have you not watched sometimes? You don't really know why you are feeling a little disturbed; there is no real thought that can be caught as the cause, but you are disturbed, you feel disturbed. Something is getting ready underground, some feeling is gathering force. Sometimes you feel sad. There is no reason to feel sad, and there is no thought to provoke it; still the sadness is there, a generalized feeling. That means a feeling is trying to come above ground, the seed of the feeling is sending its leaves out of the ground.

If you are able to become aware of the thought, then sooner or later you will become aware of the subtle nuances of the feeling. These are the three difficulties.

Atisha says:

Learn the three difficulties.

And if you can do these three things, suddenly you will fall into the deepest core of your being.

Action is the farthest from the being, then comes thought, then comes feeling. And behind feeling, just hidden behind feeling, is your being. That being is universal. That being is the goal of all meditators, the goal of all those who pray – call it God, *atman*, self, no-self, whatsoever you wish to call it, but this is the goal. And these three barriers have to be crossed. These three barriers are like three concentric circles around the center of being.

Take up the three parts of the principal cause.

Now a very important sutra. The last three sutras are just golden. Keep them in your heart: they will nourish you, they will strengthen you, they will transform you. Particularly for my sannyasins, they are of immense value.

Take up the three parts of the principal cause.

What are those three parts of the principal cause? In the tradition of Buddha there are three famous shelters: *buddham sharanam gachchhami*: I go to the feet of the buddha, I surrender myself to the buddha. *sangham sharanam gachchhami*: I go to the feet of the commune, I surrender myself to the buddhafield. *dhammam sharanam gachchhami*: I surrender myself to the ultimate law which is personified by the buddha and is searched for by the commune, which has become actual in the buddha and is an inquiry in the commune. These three are the most important things for a seeker: the master, the commune, and the dhamma, Tao, logos, the ultimate law.

Unless you are in contact with one who has already realized, it is almost impossible for you to grow. The hindrances are millions, the pitfalls many, the false doors many, the temptations are many; there is every possibility of going astray. Unless you are in the company of someone who knows the way, who has traveled the way, who has arrived, it is almost impossible for you to reach. Unless your hands are in the hands of someone whom you can trust and to whom you can surrender, you are bound to go astray. The mind creates so many temptations – so alluring they are, so magnetic is their power – that unless you are in the power-field of someone whose magnetism is far more powerful than any other kind of temptation, it is impossible to reach. That is the meaning of disciplehood.

Buddham sharanam gachchhami: I surrender to the master.

The master is such a magnetic force that your surrender to the master becomes your protection; hence it is called the shelter. Then you are secure, then you are guarded, then you are protected. Then your hand is in those hands which know where to take you, what direction to give to you.

The second thing is the commune. Each buddha creates a commune, because without a commune a buddha cannot function. A commune means his energy field, a commune means the people who have become joined with him, a commune means an alternate society to the ordinary mundane society which goes after spurious comforts – it is there available to everybody.

A small oasis in the desert of the world is what is meant by a commune created by a buddha – a small oasis in which life is lived with a totally different gestalt, with a totally different vision, with a totally different goal; where life is lived with purpose, meaning, where life is lived with method – even though to the outsiders it may look like madness, but that madness has a method in it – where life is lived prayerfully, alert, aware, awake; where life is not just accidental, where life starts becoming more and more a growth in a certain direction, towards a certain destination; where life is no more like driftwood.

And the third is the dhamma. Dhamma means truth. Buddha represents the dhamma in two ways: one, through his communication, verbal, and second, through his presence, through his silence, through his communion: nonverbal. The verbal communication is only an introduction for the nonverbal. The nonverbal is an energy communication. The verbal is only preparatory; it simply prepares you so you can allow the master to communicate with you energywise, because energywise it is really moving into the unknown. Energywise it needs great trust, because you will be completely unaware where you are going – aware that you are going somewhere, aware that you are being led somewhere, aware that something is happening of tremendous import; but what exactly it is you don't yet have the language for, you don't have any experience to recognize. You will be moving into the uncharted.

The buddha represents dhamma, truth, in two ways. Verbally he communicates with the students; nonverbally, through silence, through energy, he communicates with the disciples. And then there comes the ultimate unity where neither communication nor communion is needed, but oneness has been achieved – where the master and the disciple become one, when the disciple is just a shadow, when there is no separation. These are the three stages of growth: student, disciple, devotee.

Meditate on the three things not to be destroyed.

The buddha, the sangha, the dhamma, meditate over these three things not to be destroyed. The world will be very much against all these three things; the world will be bent upon destroying them. Those who love truth, those who are real seekers, inquirers, they will do everything to protect these three things.

First, the buddha. Why does the world creates so many difficulties for the buddha whenever he appears, in whatsoever form? He may be Krishna, Christ, Atisha, Tilopa, Saraha; he may appear in any form. By buddhahood I mean awareness, awakening. Wherever awakening happens, the whole world becomes antagonistic. Why? – because the whole world is asleep.

There is an Arabic saying: Don't wake up a slave, because he may be dreaming that he is free. Don't wake up a slave; he may be dreaming that he is free, that he is no more a slave.

But the buddha will say: Wake up the slave! Even though he is dreaming beautiful dreams of freedom, wake him up and make him aware that he is a slave, because only through that awareness can he really become free.

The world is fast asleep and people are enjoying their dreams. They are decorating their dreams, they are making their dreams more and more colorful, they are making them psychedelic. Then comes a man who starts shouting from the housetops, "Wake up!" The sleepers feel offended; they don't want to wake up, because they know that once the dream is gone they will be left with their misery and suffering and nothing else. They are not yet aware that behind their misery there is a source of joy that can be found. Whenever something like awakening has happened to them they have always found themselves utterly miserable. So they want to remain drowned in something, whatsoever it is; they want to remain occupied.

The teaching of the buddhas is: Find time and a place to remain unoccupied. That's what meditation is all about. Find at least one hour every day to sit silently doing nothing, utterly unoccupied, just watching whatsoever passes by inside. In the beginning you will be very sad, looking at things inside you; you will feel only darkness and nothing else, and ugly things and all kinds of black holes appearing. You will feel agony, no ecstasy at all. But if you persist, persevere, the day comes when all these agonies disappear, and behind the agonies is the ecstasy.

So the first thing: whenever the buddha appears the world is against him. The world is fast asleep, dreaming, and the buddha tries to wake people up. There are a thousand and one other reasons why the world wants to destroy a buddha, and why Atisha is saying:

Meditate on the three things not to be destroyed.

Had Jesus' disciples known something like this they would have tried in every way to protect Jesus, but they were not aware at all. Jesus could live only three years as a buddha. He could have lived to a very old age, he could have helped millions of people on the path, but the disciples were not aware that a great treasure was in their possession and it had to be protected and guarded.

There are many reasons. One reason why people are against is because whenever a buddha appears in the world he is unique, he cannot be compared to any other buddha of the past; that is the problem. People become accustomed, slowly, slowly, to the past buddhas, but whenever a new buddha arrives he is so new, so unique, so different, that they cannot believe he is a buddha because they have a certain conception.

Those who have known Mahavira, how can they recognize me as a buddha? – because I am not standing naked. Those who have seen Jesus, how they can recognize Atisha as the buddha? – because Atisha is not curing the ill and helping the dead to be raised again, is not helping the blind to see. Atisha is a totally different kind of buddha; he is not serving the poor, his work is on a totally different plane.

The Christian cannot recognize Buddha as a buddha. What to say of the Christian – Mahavira and Buddha were contemporaries, but Jainas don't recognize Gautam Buddha as the awakened one, and Buddhists don't recognize Mahavira as the awakened one. They were contemporaries, in the same province, sometimes lived in the same town and once stayed in the same *serai*. But each buddha has a unique quality, incomparable; hence no previous buddha can be used as a criterion. That creates difficulty.

Buddhas are unrecognizable, because your life has no experience through which you can recognize a buddha. The sexual person can recognize the sexual, the money minded can recognize the money minded, but how can you recognize a buddha? You don't have any experience of awareness. In the buddha you will only see reflected your own mind. It is natural.

The buddha is uncompromising; that creates trouble. He cannot compromise. Truth cannot be compromised with any lies, comfortable lies. The buddha seems to be very unsocial and sometimes antisocial. The buddha never fulfills any expectations of the multitudes – he cannot; he is not here to follow you. There is only one way: you can follow him if you want to be with him, otherwise get lost! He cannot fulfill your expectations. Your expectations are foolish, your expectations are *your* expectations – out of unawareness and blindness. What value can they have?

The buddha is always rebellious, antitraditional, nonconformist. That creates trouble. The buddha does not belong to the past; in fact, the future belongs to the buddha. He is always before his time, he is a new birth of God.

All these things are enough for the society of the blind, mad, power-hungry, ambitious egoists, all kinds of neurotics, psychotics – it is enough for them to be together and to destroy any possibility of there being a buddha.

And they are also against the sangha – even more so. They can tolerate a Buddha if he is alone; they know, what can he do? They have tolerated Krishnamurti more easily than they can tolerate me. What can Krishnamurti do? He can come and talk and people listen, and people have been listening for fifty years and nothing has happened – so he can talk a few years more; there is nothing to be worried about him.

I was also alone, traveling all over the country from one corner to the other corner almost three weeks every month on the train, on the plane, continuously traveling, and there was not much problem. The day I started sannyas the society became alert. Why? – because to create a buddhafield, to create a sangha, means now you are creating an alternate society; you are no more a single individual, you are gathering power, you can do something. Now you can create a revolution.

So people want to destroy all communes. Do you know, communes don't have long lives; very rarely do communes survive – very rarely. Millions of times communes have been created, and the society destroys them sooner or later, and more sooner than later. But a few communes have survived. For example, Buddha's commune still continues – not with the same purity, much garbage has entered into it. It is no more the same crystal-clear water that you can see at Gangotri where the Ganges is born. Now the Buddha's commune is like the Ganges near Varanasi – dirty, dead bodies floating in it, all kinds of garbage being poured into it. But still it is alive. Many have completely disappeared.

For example, no commune of Lao Tzu survives, no commune of Zarathustra survives. Yes, a few followers are there, but they are not communes. No commune of Saraha, Tilopa, Atisha, survives. They all had created communes. But the society is really big, huge, powerful; when the master is alive maybe the commune can survive, but once the master is gone the society starts destroying the commune from all possible directions.

Atisha says:

Meditate on the three things not to be destroyed.

And the third is dhamma, the truth. The world is against the truth, the world lives in lies. Lies are very comfortable, very secure, cozy, and you can create lies according to yourself, according to your needs. Truth is never according to you; you have to be according to the truth, and that is difficult. Many chunks of your being will have to be cut so that you can fit with truth. Your ego will have to be dropped so that you can enter into the temple of truth.

Lies are perfectly beautiful, cheap, everywhere available. You can go shopping and you can purchase bags full of lies, as many as you want. And the best thing about them is that they fit with you, they never require that you should fit with them. They are very friendly; they don't require anything from you, they don't demand, they don't ask for any commitment. They are ready to serve you.

Truth cannot serve you, you will have to serve truth.

Atisha is giving you a great insight. Particularly for my sannyasins it has to be remembered, meditated upon. The buddha is here, the commune has started happening, the truth is being shared. Now it is up to you to help it survive, to protect it, so that it can live long and serve humanity long.

And the last sutra:

Make the three inseparable from virtue.

Let this be your virtue, your religion: serving the buddha, serving the commune, serving the truth. Let this be your only virtue, your only religion.

Enough for today.

Chapter 18
Dropping Out of the Olympics

? **How to slow down?**

Life is not going anywhere; there is no goal to it, no destination. Life is non-purposive, it simply is. Unless this understanding penetrates your heart, you cannot slow down.

Slowing down is not a question of any how; it is not a question of technique, method. We reduce everything into a how. There is a great how-to-ism all over the world, and every person, particularly the modern contemporary mind, has become a how-to-er: how to do this, how to do that, how to grow rich, how to be successful, how to influence people and win friends, how to meditate, even how to love. The day is not far off when some stupid guy is going to ask how to breathe.

It is not a question of how at all. Don't reduce life into technology. Life reduced into technology loses all flavor of joy.

I have come across a book; the name of the book is hilarious. The name is *You Must Relax*. Now the "must" is the problem, but it is there. It is because of the must that nobody is able to relax. Now another must on top of all other musts – You Must Relax – is going to create more tension in your life. Try to relax, and you will find out that you feel more tense than ever. Try harder and you will feel more tense and more tense.

Relaxation is not a consequence, is not a result of some activity; it is the glow of understanding.

This is the first thing I would like to relate to you: life is purposeless. It is very hard to accept it. And why is it so hard to accept that life is purposeless? It is hard because without purpose the ego cannot exist. It is hard to conceive that life has no goal because without any goal being there, there is no point in having a mind, in having an ego.

The ego can exist only in a goal-oriented vision; the mind can exist only in the future. The purpose brings future in; the goal creates the space for thoughts to move, desires to arise. And then naturally there is hurry, because life is short. Today we are here and tomorrow we are gone – maybe the next moment.

Life is very short. If there is a goal to be achieved, there is bound to be hurry. And there is bound to be worry, a constant worry "whether I am going to make it or not" – a trembling heart, a shaking of the foundations. You will remain almost always in an inner earthquake, you will be always on the verge of a nervous breakdown. Have a goal, and sooner or later you will end up on the psychoanalyst's couch.

My vision is that of a goalless life. That is the vision of all the buddhas. Everything simply is, for no reason at all. Everything simply is utterly absurd. If this is understood, then where is the hurry, and for what? Then you start living moment to moment. Then this moment is given to you, a gracious gift from God or the whole or whatsoever you want to call it – Tao, dhamma, logos.

This moment is available to you: sing a song, live it in its totality. And don't try to sacrifice it for any other moment that is going to come in the future. Live it for its own sake.

They say art is for art's sake. It may be so, it may not be so – I am not an artist. But I can say to you: Life is for life's sake. Each moment is utterly for its own sake. To sacrifice it for anything else is to be unintelligent. And once the habit of sacrificing settles, then this moment you will sacrifice for the next, and the next for the next, and so on, so forth – this year for the next year, and this life for the next life! Then it is a simple logical process: once you have taken the first step, then the whole journey starts – the journey that leads you into the wasteland, the journey that makes your life a desert, the journey that is self-destructive, suicidal.

Live in the moment for the sheer joy of living it. Then each moment has the quality of an orgasm. Yes, it is orgasmic. This is how my sannyasins have to live, with no should, with no ought, with no must, with no commandment. You are not here to be with me to become martyrs, you are here to be with me to enjoy life to its fullness. And the only way to live, love, enjoy, is to forget the future. It exists not.

And if you can forget the future, if you can see that it is not there, there is no point in constantly getting ready for it. The moment future is dropped, past becomes irrelevant on its own accord. We carry the past so that we can use it in the future. Otherwise who will carry the past? It is unnecessary. If there is no future, what is the point of carrying the knowledge that the past has given to you? It is a burden which will destroy the joy of the journey.

And let me remind you, it is a pure journey. Life is a pilgrimage to nowhere, from nowhere to nowhere. And between these two nowheres is the now-here. Nowhere consists of two words: now, here. Between these two nowheres is the now-here.

It is not a question of following a certain technique to slow down, because if your basic approach towards life remains the same – goal-oriented – you may try to slow down, and you may even succeed in slowing down, but now you have started another tension in your life. You have to be constantly on guard so that you remain slow; you have to hold yourself continuously so that you remain slow.

You cannot have a free flow of your energies. You will be constantly afraid, because if you forget the technique, immediately the old habit will take possession of you. And the habit is there, because in fact the habit is rooted in the philosophy of your life. You have been taught to become achievers: Achieve something!

From the very first moment a child is born, we start feeding him poisons: ambition, achievement, success, richness, name, fame. We start poisoning his sources of being; we give great attention…twenty-five years are wasted in giving a poisonous education to children. It is one-third of life; it seems to be a wastage. And it is the most important one-third, because by the time a person is twenty-five he has already started declining in many ways. The highest peak of his sexuality is no longer there, it was nearabout when he was seventeen and a half; nearabout eighteen he had the highest sexual peak. By the time he is twenty-five he is already getting old.

Twenty-five years wasted in creating an achiever's mind…. And then there is competition, conflict. On each level of life, everywhere there is politics. Even in private intimate relationship there is politics: the husband trying to control the wife, the wife trying to control the husband, the children trying to control the parents, the parents trying to control the children. There is no intimacy left, because for the achieving mind intimacy is not possible. He only knows how to use the other; he cannot be respectful to the other. He is exploitative. His relationship with life is what Martin Buber calls the "I-it" relationship: everything is reduced into a commodity.

You love a woman: immediately you start reducing her into a commodity, reducing her into being a wife, and she is trying to reduce you from a man into a husband. To be a man is something beautiful, to be a woman is something divine, but to be a wife or to be a husband is simply ugly. Love is no more there, it is law. Intimacy is gone; now it is bargain, business. Now the poetry is dead. And both are in politics now: who dominates whom?

From the most intimate relationship to the most impersonal relationship, it is the same story. The story is that of I-it. That's why we have created an ugly world. And naturally, when there is so much competition and so many competitors, how can you slow down? If you slow down you will be a failure, if you slow down you will never be able to succeed, if you slow down you are lost! If you slow down you will be anonymous, you will not be able to leave your signature in the world. Who will you be if you slow down? Everybody else is not slowing down.

It is almost as if you are in an Olympic race and you ask me, "How to slow down?" If you slow down, you are a drop-out! Then you are no more in the Olympic race. And this whole life has been turned into an Olympic race. Everybody is racing, and everybody has to race to the optimum, because it is a question of life and death. Millions of enemies…we are living in a world where everybody is your enemy, because with whomsoever you are in competition, they are your enemies. They are destroying your possibilities of success, you are destroying their possibilities of success.

In this ambitious world, friendship cannot bloom, love is almost impossible, compassion cannot exist. We have created such an ugly mess, and the root is that we think that there is something to achieve.

There is no difference between a capitalist country or a communist country, it is the same philosophy. Communism is a by-product of capitalism, just as Christianity is a by-product of Judaism. There is not much difference; only words change. The game remains the same – translated into another language, certainly, but the game is the same.

Power politics is as great in a communist country – in fact there is more than there is in a capitalist country – because we never change the foundation, we only go on whitewashing the walls. You can whitewash them, you can change the color; that is not going to make any real difference. And that's what we go on doing in our individual lives too.

One politician came to me and he wanted to learn how to meditate. I asked why. He said "Why? Meditation gives peace, silence, and I want to be silent, I want to be peaceful."

I asked him, "Do you really want to be silent and peaceful?"

He said, "Yes, that's why I have come from so long a distance."

"Then," I said, "the first thing you will have to understand is that the political mind can never be silent and can never be peaceful. You will have to choose. If you want really to enter into the world of meditation, you will have to get out of the world of politics. You cannot ride on two horses, and two horses which are going in diametrically opposite directions."

He said, "That is too much! In fact I had come to you because of my political work. There is so much tension in the mind, I cannot sleep in the night, I cannot rest, I toss and turn, and the whole day and the night too, the same political anxiety continues. I had come to you so that you can teach me a technique of meditation that can help me to relax and compete more efficiently in the world. I am not ready to pay that much for meditation. I want meditation to serve me in my political competition. Twenty years I have been in politics, and yet I have not become the chief minister of my state."

Now, this man cannot meditate. Meditation is not something that can grow in any soil. It needs a basic understanding; the change has to be very fundamental. It needs a new soil to grow in; it needs a new gestalt.

A meditator naturally slows down with no effort. He does not practice it. A practiced thing is never true; it is artificial, arbitrary. Avoid practiced things – at the most they can be actings, they are not true. And only truth liberates.

A meditator is naturally slow – not because he is trying to be slow but just because there is nowhere to go. There is nothing to achieve, there is nothing to become, the becoming has ceased. When becoming ceases, being is. And being is slow, non-aggressive, unhurried.

Then you can savor the taste of each moment with total presence, you can be present to the present; otherwise you are in such a hurry that it is impossible to have any look at that which is. Your eyes are focused on a faraway distant goal, a faraway distant star; you are looking there.

I have heard an ancient story, it happened in Greece. A great astrologer, the most famous of those days, fell into a well. Because in the night he was studying the stars, walking on the road he forgot that there was a well by the side and fell into it.

The sound of his falling and his crying.... An old woman who lived in a hut by the side came out, helped him to get out of the well. He was very happy. He said, "You have saved my life! Do you know who I am? I am the royal astrologer. My fee is very great – even kings have to wait for months to consult me – but for you I will predict your future. You come tomorrow morning to my house, and I will not take any fee."

The old woman laughed and she said, "Forget all about it! You cannot see even two feet ahead – how can you see my future?"

This is the situation of millions of people on this earth. They cannot see that which is, they are obsessed with that which should be. The greatest obsession that humanity suffers is of "that which should be." It is a kind of madness.

The really healthy person has no concern with that which should be. His whole concern is the immediate, that which is. And you will be surprised: if you enter into the immediate, you will find the ultimate in it. If you move into that which is close by, you will find all the distant stars in it. If you move in the present moment, the whole eternity is in your hands. If you know your being, there is no question of becoming. All that you could have ever imagined to become you already are.

You are gods who have forgotten who they are. You are emperors who have fallen asleep and are dreaming that they have become beggars. Now beggars are trying to become emperors – in dreams they are making great efforts to become emperors, and all that is needed is to wake up! And when I say wake up, where can you wake up? In the future? In the past? The past is no more, the future not yet – where you can wake up? You can wake up only now, and you can wake up only here. This is the only moment there is, and this is the only reality there is, and this is the only reality that has always been and will always be.

Change your basic philosophy of that of an achiever. Relax into your being. Don't have any ideals, don't try to make something out of yourself, don't try to improve upon God. You are perfect as you are. With all your imperfections you are perfect. If you are imperfect, you are perfectly imperfect – but perfection is there.

Once this is understood, where is the hurry? Where is the worry? You have already slowed down. And then it is a morning walk with no destination, going nowhere. You can enjoy each tree and each sunray and each bird and each person that passes by.

? Is there any real difference between different races, nationalities, etcetera, etcetera?

There are no real differences, there cannot be. All differences are superficial. The Jew is not different from the Hindu, the Mohammedan is not different from the Christian, the Chinese is not different from the American, the Negro is not different from the English.

Man is one, differences are superficial. Yes, they are there, obviously. A Negro is a Negro: he has black skin, he looks different from the white man. But the difference is not a difference that makes a difference. The difference is so small: just a little more black pigment in his skin, four *annas* worth more – just that is the difference, four annas. And remember, he is four annas *more* than the white man, not less – richer by four annas.

But the difference of the color of the skin or the difference of the length of your nose is not an important difference. Just because you have a long nose, a Jewish nose, you don't become the chosen people of God. Or just because you are born in India you don't become religious either.

These are all stupid ideas. But these stupid ideas have persisted in the world; and not only persisted, have proved great calamities to humanity. They were very ego-gratifying. The Hindu thinks he is the most religious in the world, his country the most sacred – what nonsense they go on talking!

Countries are separate only on the political maps; otherwise it is just one earth. Just thirty years ago, Karachi and Lahore used to be holy land – just thirty years ago. But now they are in Pakistan and very unholy. Now Indians cannot think of a place which is more unholy than Lahore or Karachi. Now they are the unholiest of the unholy, and they used to be part of the holy land. Just a little change of politics, a line drawn on the map – not on the earth; the earth is still undivided.

I have heard a story: When India and Pakistan were going to be divided, there was a madhouse just on the border, and nobody was particularly interested in having that madhouse, neither India nor Pakistan. But it had to go somewhere – and because politicians were utterly uninterested, it was decided to ask the madmen themselves where they want to go.

A great gathering – one thousand madmen were gathered and they were asked, "Where do you want to go?"

And they said, "We don't want to go anywhere, we simply want to remain here."

Again and again, in many ways it was explained to them, "You will not be going anywhere, you will remain here. But still we want to ask where do you want to go – to India or to Pakistan?"

The madmen could not believe their ears. They said, "Now you are creating great suspicion in us, whether we are mad or you are mad! If we are not going to go anywhere, then why should we decide where we should go?"

There was no communication possible. And you see, the mad people were far more right. They are always far more right than your so-called politicians.

Then the leaders decided, just divide it in the middle. And a wall was raised in the middle of the madhouse. I have heard that still the madmen sometimes climb up on the wall and they laugh. The whole thing seems to be so ridiculous. They are exactly in the same place, but some have become Pakistanis and some have become Indians – and just a wall in between. And they still talk about it: "What happened? – because we are the same, you are the same, we don't see any difference! But now we are enemies – we really should not talk."

Differences are not there. Or, if they are there, very small differences like….

Do you know how many Indians it takes to screw in a light bulb? Four. One to hold the bulb, and three to screw him round.

Or, do you know many Californians it takes to change a light bulb? Four. One to change the bulb, and three to share in the experience.

? **Today I saw clearly that I really am causing my *own* suffering and that I don't have to, and something heavy lifted from my chest when I saw that I was not just going around in circles!**
Thank you, thank you, Osho.
But oh, I am so afraid of becoming light and permeable. It is all so embarrassing!

The first experience of freedom is always embarrassing. The first ray of light to the blind is bound to be embarrassing. One who has always lived in chains, a sudden message from the king that he is freed…it is always embarrassing. He had become accustomed to live a certain kind of life, he had evolved a certain style of life. There was security in the prison; he had settled. Now everything unsettles. It is not only the question that the chains are being taken away; now he will have to face the great wide world again. He will have to learn all that he has forgotten, he will have to relearn. It is going to be difficult, and he will look a little amateur compared to others. Even walking on the street without the chains to which he has become accustomed will be a little odd; he will not feel at ease.

When the French revolutionaries freed the prisoners from the great French prison of Bastille, they were surprised: the prisoners were not ready to go out. That was the biggest prison of France, where only people who had been sentenced for their whole life were kept. There were people who had been in the prison for thirty years, forty years, even fifty years.

Now, just think of a person who had come to the prison when he was only twenty, and had lived in the prison for fifty years. He has completely forgotten about the world, how it looks.

Fifty years living in a dark cell with heavy chains…. Those chains had no lock because there was no need ever to unlock them. They were chained for his whole life; they were permanent, heavy. For fifty years he has slept with those chains on hands and feet; he has become utterly accustomed to that life. And the food comes at the right time, he has not to worry about it. It is not much of a food, but still, something is better than nothing. He has no responsibility, he need not care about anything, everything is being done for him.

Maybe, slowly, slowly, he had started thinking that he is not a prisoner but a king whose every need is fulfilled. Others take every care. Maybe, slowly, slowly, he had convinced himself that the people who stand on guard are not there to prevent him from going out, but they are his bodyguards. And this is natural. When you live fifty years in a prison you have to create such rationalizations, such hallucinations, such beautiful theories. We all have done things like this.

Then one day suddenly the revolutionaries came and forced the prisoners to get out. The prisoners fought back – they were not ready. This is something to be understood. Even when they were freed against their will, fifty percent of them came back in the night to sleep at least in their cells. Where else should they sleep?

One more important thing – a very important thing – happened. They demanded their chains, because they could not sleep without them. Fifty years sleeping with that heavy load of chains, it may have started sounding like music. Turning in the night, and the chains and the sound…now without chains they must be feeling so light that sleep was impossible.

This is the situation of all human beings. We are brought up in such a way that we only believe that we are free, but we are not. While nations exist, no man is really free. While politicians go on dominating humanity, the world will remain in slavery. They go on persuading you that you are free. You are not. There are a thousand and one walls around you – maybe very transparent so that you can look through the walls, and that gives you a feeling that you are free, but you are not. While there are religions in your head – Christianity, Hinduism, Mohammedanism, Jainism, Buddhism – you are not free. A mind cannot be free.

Freedom means freedom from the mind.

Only a no-mind knows the taste of freedom.

But to be a no-mind is so risky; you will have to lose all that you have become accustomed to, all that you have become so attached to. All your possessions are contained in your mind: your philosophies, your religions, your concepts, your theories, all are contained in your mind. If you drop the mind – and that's what meditation is all about, dropping the mind – you will feel as if you have been robbed, as if you have suddenly been forced to be naked, as if suddenly inside you have become empty. You will miss that old fullness, although it was only junk. But people's idea is that it is always better to have something than nothing, whatsoever that something is.

Even to be miserable is better than to be nothing, even to be in pain is better than to be nothing. People are so much afraid of being nothing. And nothing is freedom; nothing means no thing, no body, no mind.

And when the first glimpse arrives – just a whiff of no-mind, a small breeze from the beyond – it is embarrassing. Enchanting and embarrassing, both – calling you forth to come out of your grave, and yet scary.

But now, when the call has been heard, it has to be respected. When you have seen a little glimpse that you are the creator of your own misery, it will be very difficult for you now to go on creating it. It is easy to live in misery when you know others are creating it – what can you do? You are helpless. That's why we go on throwing responsibilities on others.

There are people who think they are in misery because of past karma, past life karma. The whole idea is so foolish: put your hand in the fire now and you will be burned next life. Life is immediate. That's what life is – immediacy. Life never postpones. You do something beautiful, and in that very doing you are rewarded; not that you will have to wait many lives for the reward. You do something ugly, and in that very act is the punishment; the punishment is not separate from the act.

This is one of my fundamental things – you have to understand I am against the whole idea of karma. It is a strategy of the mind to throw responsibility on the past. And once the responsibility is thrown on something – whatsoever it is, x, y, z, it doesn't matter what it is – you can relax in your misery and you can remain miserable. What can you do? You start feeling like a victim. Now the past cannot be changed; what has been done has been done, you cannot undo it now, you have to accept it.

It is because of this foolish idea of karma that the East has suffered so much. People are poor, and they say what they can do? They are hungry, starving, dying, and they go on thinking what can they do? They have done something wrong in the past, they have to suffer for it. A great invention of the priests to keep people in misery and yet contented, in great suffering yet creating no trouble for the status quo.

The greatest idea against revolution that has ever been invented is the idea of karma. That's why in the ten-thousand-year history of India there has never been a revolution. Unless the Indian mind changes totally, there is not going to be any revolution. Revolution seems to be absolutely un-Indian. The Indian consciousness is so much burdened with the idea of karma, with the past, that you cannot create any revolt in this country.

This is strange. One of the most ancient lands of the world, and yet a revolution has never happened. People like Buddha, Atisha, Kabir, have walked on this earth, and yet not a single revolution. Yes, revolutionaries have happened – Buddha is a revolutionary – but the country remained unaffected.

In fact, Buddhism disappeared from this country for the simple reason that it was too revolutionary. It didn't fit with the conformist mind of the country, it didn't fit with the idea of accepting that whatsoever is, is; nothing can be done, no hope.

People go on throwing the responsibility on the past, or on fate, *kismet*, or on God. And if these things have become out of date, then the social structure or the economic system of the society, capitalism or communism or fascism – but they need something as an excuse so that they can remain free, free from the arousal of the vision that "I am responsible for my suffering and nobody else."

Even if people drop God, society, karma, etcetera, then they start finding new ways. Freudians will say you are suffering because of the unconscious. Freud says there is no hope for man, man will always remain miserable. All that we can manage is to keep him normally miserable; that is all that can be done. The best that can be done according to Freud is that people can be kept within limits of misery, that's all. Miserable they are going to be, there is no hope of a blissful humanity. Why? – because of the unconscious.

The unconscious instincts are in conflict with society. And Freud says if you allow the unconscious instincts full play, then the society, the culture, the civilization disappears and you will be back in the world of the jungle, and you will suffer. Or, if you allow the society to have control over you, to inhibit your unconscious instincts, then there is a consistent conflict between your unconscious and the social code. And because of that conflict you remain miserable.

There seems to be no way out.

The really religious person is one who stops finding excuses for his misery. It needs guts to accept that "I am responsible," that "This is my choice, I have chosen my life this way," that "My freedom is there, has always been there, to choose whatsoever I want. I can choose misery, I can choose bliss."

Man's soul consists of freedom.

I teach you freedom.

But freedom means taking the responsibility, total responsibility for your life, on your own shoulders, not throwing it onto somebody else.

Ashoka, something beautiful has happened to you, something tremendously significant. Embrace it. Don't feel embarrassed – embrace it. Love it, cherish it, nourish it, welcome it. Some truth has knocked on your door.

You say: "Today I saw clearly that I really am causing my own suffering and that I don't have to, and something heavy lifted from my chest when I saw that I was not just going around in circles. Thank you, thank you, Osho. But oh, I am so afraid of becoming light and permeable!"

I can understand it. It is difficult to drop chains, prisons, bondages, slaveries. We have invested so much in them, and for so long. I can understand.

You say: "It is all so embarrassing!"

It is. But still, now there is no going back. Even if you want to go back, there is no going back. That glimpse will haunt you, that glimpse will follow you like a shadow, that glimpse will remind you again and again: "Ashoka, you are responsible, and you are doing it again. Watch. You are again choosing misery, while the other alternative is available."

One Sufi mystic who had remained happy his whole life – no one had ever seen him unhappy – who was always laughing, who was laughter, whose whole being was a perfume of celebration…. In his old age, when he was dying, on his deathbed and still enjoying death, laughing hilariously, a disciple asked, "You puzzle us. Now you are dying, why are you laughing? What is there funny about it? We are feeling so sad. We wanted to ask you many times in your life why you are never sad. But now, confronting death at least, one should be sad. You are still laughing – how are you managing it?"

The old man said, "It is simple. I had asked my master – I had gone to my master as a young man; I was only seventeen and already miserable, and my master was old, seventy, and he was sitting under a tree, laughing for no reason at all. There was nobody else there, nothing had happened, nobody had cracked a joke or anything, and he was simply laughing, holding his belly. I asked him, 'What is the matter with you? Are you mad or something?'

"He said, 'One day I was also as sad as you are. Then it dawned on me that it is my choice, it is my life.'

"Since that day, every morning when I get up, the first thing I decide is…before I open my eyes I say to myself, 'Abdullah'" – that was his name – "'what do you want? Misery? Blissfulness? What you are going to choose today?' And it happens that I always choose blissfulness."

It is a choice. Try it. When you become aware the first moment in the morning that sleep has left, ask yourself, "Abdullah, another day! What is your idea? Do you choose misery or blissfulness?"

And who would choose misery? And *why*? It is so unnatural – unless one feels blissful in misery, but then too you are choosing bliss, not misery.

It has been good. Now let this insight gather more roots in you, help it. Slowly, slowly you will become more and more attuned to this new feel of life and existence – it is an attunement. And once you have learned how to be in harmony with this inner blissfulness, you will become aware of higher and higher peaks of bliss. There are climaxes and climaxes, peaks beyond peaks. One peak leads to another peak, one small harmony soon opens a door for a bigger harmony, and so on, so forth, ad infinitum.

? **I enjoyed very much your coining the word *etceteranandas*. I wonder how you did it!**

It's simple. You can go and see many saints in India, and you will find that they have no individuality, no uniqueness, no originality, no flavor of their own. They are gramophone records – His Master's Voice – just quoting scriptures like parrots. They are imitators, pseudo, plastic; nothing has happened to them.

I am not saying that they are not saints – they are saints, but nothing has happened to them. Their saintliness is just a cultivated gesture, it is not a happening. They have character – certainly they have character, I am not denying that – but their character is like a garment; it is just a cover up. Deep down they are just the opposite of it. They are saints on the surface in the conscious mind, and they are sinners in the unconscious. And ultimately it is the deeper unconscious that is more decisive than the superficial conscious.

You cannot be a saint if you don't repress the sinner. And when you repress the sinner, the sinner goes deeper into your being. So these saints are in constant conflict, a kind of civil war, fighting with themselves. You can see they don't have any zest for life: they don't have any energy for it, they don't have any cheerfulness. How can they be cheerful? Their whole life is a miserable conflict with themselves. They cannot be at ease, they cannot relax, because they are afraid – if they relax, the sinner is there and if they relax the sinner will raise its head. They have to constantly repress it.

Remember, if you repress something you have to repress it constantly – day in, day out, year in, year out. And the problem is not solved by repressing. In fact it becomes more and more acute, chronic, because whatsoever is repressed becomes more and more powerful. It gathers energy, it becomes a tumor inside you.

You will see more and more fear in your so-called saints' eyes. Character they have: they are good people, they don't do anything bad, they follow the dictates of the society, they fulfill the expectations of the worshippers.

I call them Etceteranandas because no buddha ever follows the dictates of the society, no buddha has any character. Let me repeat it: no buddha has any character. He need not have any character, he has consciousness. He has the real thing – why should he have a plastic flower? When you can grow real roses, why bother about plastic roses? Character is a plastic flower, consciousness is a real rose. No buddha has any character, he has consciousness. He does not live out of readymade programs, he lives moment to moment out of his consciousness; he responds, he does not react.

Etceteranandas are predictable. You know what they are, and you can be perfectly secure that they are going to remain the same tomorrow too. They are dead people; you can depend on them. No buddha is predictable. You cannot say what he is going to be tomorrow or the next moment, because as life changes, his responses change. And life is constantly changing.

Old Heraclitus is right – he is a buddha – he is right when he says you cannot step twice in the same river. No buddha is ever the same again; not even for two consecutive moments is he the same. He moves with life, he is a river, he is not stagnant. He has uniqueness, originality. He speaks, not authoritatively, but on his own authority. Remember the difference. The person who speaks authoritatively derives his authority from somewhere else – from the Vedas, from The Bible, from the Koran, from the tradition, from the state, from the church. The man who speaks on his own authority derives his authority from nowhere. It is his own experience – and experience is self-evident, self-validating.

You ask me how do I manage such coinage of words. I cannot help it. Look at any so-called saint and you will find written on his forehead, Etceterananda.

When Noah had built the ark and the time came to have all the pairs of animals go aboard, Noah named each one as it went by up the gangplank. As a strange looking animal passed by, Noah said, "The name of this animal is hippopotamus."

Noah's wife looked at him and said, "Noah, why in the world did you call that animal, that strange-looking creature, a hippopotamus?"

Noah responded, "Well, it is the only one of the animals that has gone through that really looked like a hippopotamus."

There are people who look like a hippopotamus. I call them respectfully Etceteranandas. It is just out of respect that I have coined the word.

? **How can we know the difference between surrender and dependency,
not just with you but with all that comes up in our lives?**

The difference is so absolutely clear that once you have experienced surrender you will never miss understanding what is surrender and what is dependency.

Surrender is out of love, dependency is out of fear. Dependency is a relationship in which you are hankering for something, desiring something; there is a motive. You are ready to become dependent – that's what you are willing to pay for something. Surrender has no desire in it. It is sheer joy, it is trust, it is unmotivated.

It is like falling in love. In fact it is exactly falling in love – a love that knows no bounds, a love that is totally different from what you ordinarily call love. Your love is again a kind of dependency. You become dependent on the person you love, because in fact you don't love, you are simply finding somebody to cling to; otherwise you feel very lonely. You want to avoid your loneliness, you want somebody to fill your inner black hole, your emptiness.

But real love is not an escape from loneliness, real love is an overflowing aloneness. One is so happy in being alone that one would like to share – happiness always wants to share. It is too much, it cannot be contained; like the flower cannot contain its fragrance, it has to be released.

Surrender is the highest form of love, the purest form of love. You will not feel dependent, because there will be no clinging in it. You will not feel dependent, because it is not out of loneliness that you have surrendered. If you have surrendered out of loneliness then it is not surrender at all, then it is something else.

Another thing: surrender always happens, it is not a doing. You cannot do it – how can you *do* surrender? If you do it, it is not surrender. You are the doer – and if the doer is there then it can be taken back any moment.

Surrender happens; the doer is not found. You simply find yourself melting into somebody, into something. You may find yourself melting into a sunset, and it is surrender. You may find yourself melting into the starry night, and it is surrender. You may find yourself melting into a woman or man, and it is surrender. You may find yourself melting into music, and it is surrender. Surrender has many dimensions, but the taste is the same: you simply find yourself melting. You simply find yourself no more; a kind of egolessness is felt.

You are...in fact you are very much, and yet you are not. Presence and absence both together – surrender is paradoxical. Presence, because the ego is not there, so you are just awareness; and absence because the ego is not there, so you cannot say "I am."

Dependency is ugly, surrender is beautiful. Dependency will make you feel reduced, surrender will make you feel enhanced, expanded. Dependency will create reaction in you to revolt. Surrender will bring more and more trust.

But the distinction is delicate. Once known it is not difficult, but if you have not experienced it yet then surrender will look like dependency, because dependency is what you know.

I cannot explain it to you, I can only indicate a few directions. In the morning when the sun is rising, just sit silently on the riverbank. Watch it. Doing nothing, just sitting silently, watch it. And some time in some blissful moment it will happen: there will be no observer, and nothing observed. The observer becomes the observed. It is not that you are separate from the rising sun – you *are* it.

Sitting by the tree, just close your eyes, feel the tree. Hug the tree, just be one with it, as if you are with your beloved. And sometimes...and it is not predictable; I cannot say that it will happen each time. Only once in a while it will happen – because it has to happen in spite of you, that's why only once in a while.

Or, loving your woman, melt into her warmth. For a moment forget sexuality, for a moment forget all that goes on in your head, in your fantasy. For a moment just melt into the real woman. Don't carry any pornography in your head, don't make sexuality something cerebral. Let your sexuality be a deep sensuousness, sensitivity, a gut feeling. Melt into the woman, as if you are again a child in the mother's womb. Unless you have known this with your beloved, you have not known your beloved. A child again in the mother's womb, absolutely together, all distances gone – and in that moment you will know what surrender is.

But the male ego creates trouble everywhere. Even being with your woman, you are trying to control the situation. Even in our language, ugly expressions have entered: we call it lovemaking. How can you *make* love? Nobody can make love. But it has come into language not without any reason. People are trying to *make* love; even in love they are doers. So the greatest opportunity of knowing surrender is missed.

And now you have manuals: How To Make Love, How To Attain Total Orgasm. And people are reading these manuals and following the instructions. I know of some foolish people who make love to their woman, and by the bedside is the manual and they go on looking into it: how to make total orgasm.

Some moments in life when you are not a doer, not a knower, when you simply *are*, you will have the taste. It can come through beauty, it can come through poetry, it can come through music, it can come through so many doors. God has many doors to his temple.

But my feeling is that you know only dependency, hence the question has arisen. One who has known surrender cannot ask the question. Be in relaxation a few moments. It can be any kind of situations – swimming in the river, relax with the river, or sunning on the beach, relax with the sun – anything. Life is full of opportunities. Remember Atisha. He says life is full of opportunities, life *is* the opportunity. Don't wait for the opportunity, the opportunity is already here.

But you will have to learn a totally different kind of consciousness – not that of a doer, but that kind of consciousness which is simply existing…that simple consciousness, innocent.

And that happens so many times to you here while listening to me. In the pauses, when sometimes I stop…it is there.

Drink it.

? I want to get married. Please give me your blessings.

Have you gone crazy or something? Love is enough; marriage is not going to add anything to it. In fact, why are you in such a hurry to finish some beautiful experience? Wait. When you see that now love is finished, you can get married.

A minister received this thank you letter from a bridegroom he had married: "Dear Reverend, I want to thank you for the beautiful way you brought my happiness to a conclusion."

You are very young, only twenty-two. One should marry only when one is wise enough. Marriage is not for young people. For young people is to fool around. Marriage is for those who have experienced life in many ways, who have seen all the colors, the whole spectrum of it, and are now ready to settle.

My own suggestion is that nobody should marry before forty-two. When you have already had your first heart attack, then marry. Before that it is too early, and foolish. But maybe because you are only twenty-two and foolish the question has arisen.

Five-year-old Steven: "Are you a virgin?"
Four-year-old Susan: "No, not yet."

It takes time. You are too young; wait a little. When you are tired – when you are tired of adventures, when you are tired of your freedom, when you are tired of your openness to life and its millions of opportunities – then you can go to a court and get married. But why now?

Student in the Highlands looking for summer work: "Got any odd jobs?"
Farmer: "Well, you could try milking the bull."

That will be far better. You are in search for some odd jobs…otherwise why?

Love, and love as deeply as possible. And if love itself becomes the marriage, that is another thing, altogether different. If love itself becomes such an intimacy that it is unbreakable, that is another thing, that is not a legal sanction.

Legal sanctions are needed only because you are afraid. You know that your love is not enough; you need the legal support for it. You know perfectly well that you can escape or the woman can escape, hence you need the policeman to keep you together. But this is ugly, to need a policeman to keep you together. That's what marriage is!

I can bless your love, but I cannot bless your marriage. If love itself is your marriage, then all of my blessings are there for you; otherwise wait. There is no hurry. It is better to wait than to repent later on.

Enough for today.

Chapter 19
The Three Rung Ladder of Love

? **Many times I have thought of questions felt to be meaningful. Each time the question resolved itself or seemed absurd after letting it gestate for a while. The paradox is that the words dissolve but the question mark remains.**

The question mark is bound to remain forever, because the question mark has nothing to do with the question at all. It has something to do with the mystery of life itself. Life never becomes known, it always remains a mystery, a question mark – and a question mark which cannot be dissolved. It is in the very nature of existence, it is the very center of existence; there is no way to find any answer or explanation for it.

That's why philosophy fails and poetry succeeds. That's why mathematics fails and music succeeds. That's why logic always lags behind and love reaches, arrives.

The question mark is immensely significant. All questions are absurd. And all questions are sooner or later resolved, are bound to be resolved, because all questions have answers. If you can formulate a question you can find an answer for it, but the question mark is not your formulation. It is there; it is on each leaf of the trees, on each sound of the birds. On each cloud, on each star, on each atom, the question mark is there.

Life is not a problem but a mystery. A problem is that which can be solved – at least theoretically is soluble. A mystery is that which can be lived but can never be solved.

An ancient Hassid story:

An old Hassid master asked one of his disciples, "What do we mean when we use the word *God*?"

The disciple wouldn't answer, the disciple wouldn't look in the eyes of the master. With bent head, ashamed of himself, he remained silent.

The question was asked again and again. Thrice the master asked. The more the master asked, the more silent the disciple became. And the silence was very embarrassing. The disciple has to respect the question of the master – and it was as if he has not even heard; no response from the disciple. The master was irritated and he asked, "Why don't you answer me? What do we mean by the word *God* when we use it?"

And the disciple said, "Because I don't know, how can I answer? I don't know God!"

And the master laughed, a laughter which can happen only to those who have arrived. He said, "And do you think I know?"

Who knows? Who has ever known? But still God is, and still God has to be addressed.

Whoever told you that God is an object of knowledge? God is not an object of knowledge, God is not an object at all. God is the silence that pervades you when words dissolve. God is the question mark that remains, When questions are gone, evaporated. God is the mystery – unresolvable.

I am not here to give answers, I am here to provoke in you the question mark, the ultimate question mark. It is not a question, remember; the ultimate question mark is not a question.

There is no question at all. Simply you are encountering something ineffable, indefinable, infinite, eternal, with no beginning and no end, with no possibility to comprehend it, with no possibility to encompass it. On the contrary, God is the one who encompasses you, God is the one who comprehends you. God is the one for whom you are not a question nor a question mark.

Slowly, slowly, learn the ways of living in mystery. Mind continuously hankers to demystify everything; there is a deep urge in the mind to demystify. Why? – because it can control only when something is demystified. Mystery starts controlling it, hence mind escapes from mysteries. Mind wants explanations, because once something is explained it can be manipulated; once something is no more a secret, then the mind is the master. In the presence of a secret the mind feels simply impotent. The greater the secret, the more the impotence of the mind.

But that is where prayer arises, meditation arises, and all that is beautiful. That is where truth is felt. Mind is not the door to truth, it is a door to power.

Francis Bacon is right when he says, "Knowledge is power." Mind is a power seeker; mind is always after power, more and more power. Hence mind slowly, slowly became too much attached to science; mind *became* science. Science is the search for power. And then automatically science becomes reduced to technology. What is technology? How to manipulate nature. That "how" is technology; know-how is technology. Science prepares the blueprint, science gives the idea how to demystify existence, and then technology implements it.

Religion is not of the mind, religion is of the heart. Mind raises questions, the heart knows only the ultimate question mark.

It is beautiful, it is tremendously important that you became aware of this phenomenon, that questions arise; in the beginning they look meaningful, but soon they are resolved. If one can wait, all questions resolve; there is no need to go anywhere to ask. The mind that is capable of creating a certain question is capable of finding the answer too – in fact if you dissect the question deeply you will find the answer hidden there. The answer is always in the question. The question is only a form of the answer, the question is only the beginning of the answer. The question is the seed and the answer will be the sprout – and the seed contains the sprout.

If you wait a little, if you are a little patient, if you allow the question to move within you, you are capable of solving it. Either it will be solved or you will come to know that it is absurd. There are absurd questions which cannot be solved – and they are not mysteries either, remember, they are simply absurd questions.

For example, linguistically it may look perfectly right, grammatically it may look perfectly right, and existentially it may be absurd. For example, you can ask, "What is the smell of the color red?" Linguistically, grammatically, there is no flaw in it. "What is the smell of the color red?" – the question can be raised, but if you look deep into it, it is not a question, it is simply absurd. Colors have nothing to do with smells; there is no relationship at all. Colors are colors, smells are smells; neither smells have colors, nor colors have smells.

It is just like asking how to see music with the eyes. The question looks perfectly right: How to see music? But music is not an object to be seen, it is not an object for the eyes; it can only be heard, not seen. Beauty can be seen but cannot be heard.

We can make a thousand and one absurd questions. People have asked down the ages… the so-called wise too. In the Middle Ages, the whole Christian world was so concerned, and there was such great argument and controversy on such absurd questions as: How many angels can stand on the point of a needle? Great theologians wrote great treatises on these questions.

In fact, the so-called learned people are always deep down very stupid people. Their learnedness is nothing but a cover up for this inner stupidity. They raise great fuss for nothing, great ado for nothing. They are clever, that is true – clever to create such absurd questions. At least they are able to give to those absurd questions an appearance of rationality.

How many hells are there? In the times of Buddha the question became so important in India…. Hindus believe in three hells, Jainas started believing in seven hells, and then there was really a man of insight, Sanjaya Vilethiputta, who must have been able to laugh at absurdities. He said, "Who says seven? I have exactly counted: there are seven hundred!"

He must have been a wise man, he was simply joking about this absurd controversy. How many hells? How many heavens? How many angels? When did God create the world? Why did God create the world? All are absurd questions: you cannot solve them, because they are not questions in the first place. Neither are they mysteries, because a mystery cannot be formulated in words. It is only a question mark, a question mark in the silent heart – just a great surprise, a wonder, awe. And then each and every thing creates awe.

Allow this question mark to settle in you. The meaningful questions will be solved, the meaningless will be known as absurd; then finally remains only the question mark.

I am happy. You say: "The paradox is that the words dissolve but the question mark remains."

Rejoice! Celebrate! This is a great moment, this is the door to the divine.

? Is there really something like an inferiority complex?

Psychobabble! The psychologists have taken the place of the theologist. The theologian is out of date, the psychologist is in. And psychology has created great psychobabble, great words, strange words, and when you can use great and strange words which are really nothing but gibberish, you can impress people.

Do you know from where the word *gibberish* comes? It comes from the name of a Sufi mystic, Jabbar. He used to talk nonsense, because he came to understand that whatsoever you say is nonsense. Then why even pretend that it is sense?

Jabbar started *really* talking nonsense. He would use sounds, words…nobody could follow what he was saying. Everybody was free to have his own interpretation. The followers of Jabbar were many – because when the master cannot be understood, it is very easy for the disciples to follow him, because then they can interpret.

For example, if you had asked Jabbar, "Do you believe in God?" he would have said, "Hoo hoo!" Now, it is up to you to find out what "Hoo hoo!" means. The very clever one will think it is the last part of Allah-hoo, that the master has given only a hint, and so on, so forth.

Or he will do something absurd. You ask, "What is God?" and he may stand on his head immediately. Now it is up to you to figure it out – and everybody is clever in figuring out things. Somebody will think he had given the indication that everything is topsy-turvy, so whatsoever you have been thinking up to now has to be put upside down. Some disciples even started reading the scriptures backwards!

But one thing was good about it: Jabbar must have enjoyed the whole show! He must have really enjoyed how many interpretations people can find. The English word gibberish comes from Jabbar.

Now the greatest gibberish that is "in" is psychological. Freud really created a new language: psychoanalysis is nothing but a new language. For small things, for things which everybody understands, he will find such difficult words: "Oedipus complex" – for a small thing, that every boy loves his mother. Now if you say every boy loves his mother, nobody can think that you are very learned, but if you say, "This boy suffers from an Oedipus complex," it sounds….

One Jewish lady was talking to the neighbor, and she said, "The psychoanalyst who is treating my son has said that my son suffers from an Oedipus complex."

And the neighbor lady said, "Oedipus schmoedipus! Doesn't matter as long as he is a good boy and loves his mother!"

Now, this word inferiority complex…. There is nothing like inferiority complex, all that is there is the phenomenon of the ego. And because of the phenomenon of the ego, two things are possible. If you are egoistic you are bound to compare yourself with others. The ego cannot exist without comparison, hence if you really want to drop the ego, drop comparing. You will be surprised: where has the ego gone? Compare, and it is there; and it is there only in comparison. It is not an actuality, it is a fiction created out of comparison.

For example, you are passing through a garden and you come across a very big tree. Compare: the tree is so big, suddenly you are so small. If you don't compare, you enjoy the tree, there is no problem at all. The tree is big – so what! So let it be big, you are not a tree. And there are other trees also which are not so big, but they are not suffering from any inferiority complex. I have never come across a tree which suffers from inferiority complex or from superiority complex. Even the highest tree, a Lebanon cedar, even that tree does not suffer from superiority complex, because comparison does not exist.

Man creates comparison because ego is possible only if nourished by comparison continuously. But then you will have two outcomes: sometimes you will feel superior, and sometimes you will feel inferior. And the possibility of feeling inferior is greater than the possibility of feeling superior, because there are millions of people: somebody is more beautiful than you, somebody is taller than you, somebody is stronger than you, somebody seems to be more intelligent than you, somebody is more learned than you, somebody is more successful, somebody is more famous, somebody is this, somebody is that. If you just go on comparing, millions of people…you will gather a great inferiority complex. But it doesn't exist, it is your creation.

Those who are more mad, they suffer from a superiority complex. They are so mad that when they compare they cannot see that there are millions of people who are different in many ways and superior in many ways. They are so obsessed with the ego that they remain closed to anything that is superior; they always look at the inferior. It is said that people like to meet people who are in some way inferior to them; it gives them great nourishment. People like people who support their ego.

The more mad person will suffer from a superiority complex, because he will always choose those things which make him feel superior. But he knows that he is playing a trick. How can he deceive himself? He knows that he has chosen only those points which make him feel superior; he knows what he has not chosen – that is there on the margin, he is perfectly aware of it. So his superiority complex is always shaking: it is made on sand, the house can collapse any moment. He suffers from anxiety because he has made a house on the sand.

Jesus says: Don't make your house on the sand; find a rock.

The more sane person will suffer from an inferiority complex, because he will look all around, will be available to all that is happening all around, and will start collecting ideas that he is inferior. But both are shadows of the ego, two sides of the ego. The superior person deep down carries the inferiority complex, and the person who suffers from inferiority complex deep down carries a superiority complex; he wants to be superior.

Except politicians, I don't think anybody is inferior. I make an exception for politicians. In fact, if somebody does not suffer from an inferiority complex he will not go into politics at all. Politics is the arena for those who suffer from an inferiority complex, because they want to prove to themselves and to the world that they are not inferior: Look, I have become the prime minister, or the president! Now who can say I am inferior? I have proved that I am not inferior. Politics attracts the people who are very egoistic and suffer from inferiority complex.

Artists are just on the other polarity: they suffer from superiority complex. They know they are creators, they know that they have come with a special quality to create something in the world. Politicians suffer from an inferiority complex, and try to reach to higher and higher power posts to prove to themselves and to others that it is not so. Artists suffer from superiority complex; that's why artists constantly quarrel amongst themselves. No artist ever agrees that another artist has contributed anything to the world. They are continuously criticizing each other; they cannot be friends, they are all superior people!

The mystic is the one who has come to see the whole stupidity of it, the whole game of the ego. And these are the three worlds available: the world of the politician – the world of power politics – the world of the artist, or the world of the mystic.

The mystic is one who has seen that all comparison is false, meaningless: he has dropped comparing. The moment you drop comparing, you are simply yourself – neither superior nor inferior. How can you be superior or inferior if you are just yourself?

Just think: the Third World War has happened and everybody else has disappeared from the world, and only Anand Bashir, who has asked this question, is left. The whole world is suddenly gone, only Bashir is left, sitting in Koregaon Park, Pune. Will you be superior or inferior? You will be simply yourself, because there will be nobody to compare with.

A mystic is the one who simply knows that he is himself. He lives his life according to his own light, he creates his own space, he has his own being. He is utterly contented with himself, because without comparison you cannot be discontented either. And he is not an egoist, he cannot be – ego needs comparison, ego feeds on comparison. He is simply doing his thing.

The rose is a rose and the lotus is a lotus, and some tree is very high and some other tree is very small – but everything is as it is.

Just try to see for a single moment without comparing, and then where is superiority and where is inferiority? And where is the ego, the source of it all?

? I am addicted to telling lies. Why do I do it?

It may be just to feel superior! People start telling lies because that gives them a specialty: they can pretend that they know things which nobody else knows. Truth is universal, the lie is private. It is your own creation, nobody else knows about it; you become very special, the knower. If you say the truth you will not be special.

I have heard that in a village there was a wise man. Once it happened that from the palace of the king some very precious diamonds were stolen and the king's people were searching for the stolen treasure. The king had loved those stones so much that at any cost they had to be brought back, but no clue was available.

Then somebody suggested, "We have an old wise man in the town; maybe he can be of some support, some help, some insight he can give. Whenever we are in trouble – we are poor people, we cannot go to very learned scholars, we cannot go to the experts – we always go to our old wise man. It has never been a disappointment; he always finds some beautiful advice for us."

So the authorities went to the wise man. The wise man closed his eyes, meditated a little, and then he said, "Yes, I know who has done it. But before I can tell you, a few promises from you. First, nobody should ever know that I have told you who has stolen the diamonds."

The promise was of course given. Then the wise man said, "You come with me. We will have to go very far away from people, deep in the forest, so nobody can hear something or even guess. And just the chief of you has to come with me." He took the chief, and the chief was very excited: he was just on the verge of discovering the treasure and he was hoping to be rewarded by the king immensely. It was a long walk into the forest. Again and again he said, "Now there is nobody," but the old man said, "Just a little more."

Finally the chief was tired and he said, "Why do you go on making me walk more and more? I am tired, utterly tired. If you know, please say. If you don't know, say it!"

The wise man said, "I know it. Come close to me. I will whisper in your ears, so nobody hears."

The chief said, "You seem to be almost mad. There is nobody here, we have left people miles away."

But the wise man said, "Just in case." And he whispered in the ears of the chief, "It is absolutely certain some thief has done it."

Now, if you say such universal truths you will not be very special. People love gossiping, people love telling lies, inventing lies. By inventing lies they have some special knowledge that nobody else in the world has; it is their own invention, so nobody knows about it. They can decorate it in such a way, they can rationalize, they can create many, many strategies to protect it. And it always brings joy to people when they can befool others; then they know they are wiser than others.

This is an ego trip. The ego is the greatest lie in the world, and the ego always feels good whenever it can feel special. And it is not a question whether you are telling a lie or not; the whole question is whether the other is believing it or not. If the other is believing, at least for the moment it looks like the truth. And when you create many believers in you, it gives you power.

Truth needs no believers. Let me remind you: truth needs no believers. The sun rises in the morning – you don't believe in it, do you? Nobody asks anybody, "Do you believe in the sun, sir? Do you believe in the moon?" If somebody comes and asks, "Do you believe in the sun, do you believe in the moon, do you believe in the trees?" you will think him mad. What is he asking these things for? They are, so there is no question of believing in them.

People believe in lies; truth needs no believers. And when you invent lies you become a great leader. That's how on the earth three hundred religions exist. Truth is one – and three hundred religions! People have shown great inventiveness. When lies are such that nobody can detect them and there is no way to prove for or against, you are protected. So many people go on talking spiritual lies; that is safer.

If you really want to enjoy telling lies, tell spiritual lies – that the earth is hollow, that inside the earth there is the real civilization, that UFO's come from the hollow earth. Tell lies, supernatural, spiritual – that God has not three faces but four. Nobody can prove or disprove how many faces God has; all that will be decisive is with what confidence you can lie. Your confidence will be catching people, it will become contagious. You can look, down the ages it has been happening.

Adolf Hitler has written in his autobiography, *Mein Kampf*, that a lie repeated again and again becomes a truth. And he knows – in fact nobody else knows it so well as he knows; it is his own experience. His whole life he lived on lies, lies so blatant that on the surface of it nobody would have thought that anybody would believe in them.

For example, "The whole world is deteriorating, the whole world is going down to hell because of the Jews." How do the Jews come in? When for the first time he started talking about the Jews, even his friends laughed, even his friends told him, "This is stupid." He said "You simply wait. Go on repeating it, and not only non-Jews are going to believe it, even Jews will believe it. You just go on repeating it."

Beliefs are created by constant repetition. And he made the whole German race believe – one of the most intelligent races on the earth, and it became victim to this stupid man. But he had a few qualities. For example, he was capable of repeating something continuously for years with confidence, from the housetops, with absolute certainty, with no hesitation. It was contagious.

People don't believe in what you say, people believe in the way you say it. And once you have learned the art of telling lies it becomes an addiction, because people start believing in you, you start becoming powerful. And then, if you can manage a few more things, your power will be immense.

For example, if you can manage a certain character, that gives you credibility. If your character is such that people can believe in you more easily, that will help you. The people who live on lies always create a character around themselves; if not a character, then at least an appearance of it.

Hitler was a mahatma. He was not a drinker, he would not touch any intoxicant. How can you not believe in such a person? He would eat only vegetarian food, he would not touch nonvegetarian food. How can you not believe in such a person? He would not drink even tea or coffee, he would not smoke. How can you not believe in such a person? He was a greater mahatma than Morarji Desai, because he would not even drink his own urine. How can you not believe in such a person? You have to believe! He has all the credibility.

He would get up early in the morning, as has been taught down the ages; he would go early to bed. He remained a bachelor almost to the end – I say almost, because only three hours before he died, committed suicide, he got married. I think that is the only thing that he ever did which can be called wise – just three hours before! He must have thought, "Now what can marriage do to me? I am going to die anyway."

Just three hours before…in the middle of the night, when he decided to commit suicide, he called the priest. The priest was awakened, was brought to his underground cell. Just three, four friends were present, the marriage ceremony was done quick and fast, and the only thing that they did after the marriage ceremony was commit suicide – that was their honeymoon. He had remained a bachelor his whole life.

These things give credibility. If you really want to be a liar, if you really want to go on lying, then you have to create proofs that you are a man of character, how can you lie? People will believe you. That's why your saints, who live on so-called spiritual lies, depend on character.

A man who lives on truth need not depend on anything else; truth is enough. But truth does not create belief in people – in fact, truth offends people. People love lies and are always offended by the truth. That is the cause, not only of your addiction – millions are addicted to lies, for the simple reason that people are never offended by lies. In fact they want to hear more and more. They say, "What is new?

Truth is never new. If you are thinking about truth, then there is nothing new under the sun. When you say, "What is new? What is the news?" you are inquiring, "Give me a few more lies, a few more gossips, a few more rumors." And you are ready to believe. In fact the greater the lie is, the greater is the possibility of its belief, because if there is only a small lie it can be detected by people; they have that much intelligence. But if the lie is very big, bigger than their intelligence, they will never be able to detect it. That's why great lies live for centuries.

Now, hell is a lie; there is no hell. And heaven is a lie; there is no heaven. But they have lived for centuries and centuries, and I don't think they are going to disappear. They will live. God as a person is a lie. There is godliness, but there is no God. Whenever I use the word *God* I simply mean godliness, remember it. Translate it always as godliness. There is a quality of godliness in existence, but there is no God. But people want a God, not godliness; they are not interested in godliness.

That's why people like Buddha could not influence much. Buddha and his whole religion disappeared from this country. One of the most fundamental reasons was this: that he emphasized godliness and not God. If godliness is there, then it is a difficult task. You have to grow into godliness; it is not something readymade there that you can possess. It is not something that you can pray to, it is not something that you can desire anything from. It is not already there, it has to be created in the innermost core of your being. It is like love – it has to bloom in you, you have to release the fragrance of it. You have to become godly, only then there is God; otherwise there is no God.

But this is too much. Nobody wants to pay so great a price. Why not believe in a simple lie, that there is a God – a very, very old ancient man with a white beard, sitting on a golden throne, ready to fulfill any of your demands if you truly ask? And that is the trick. If your prayer is fulfilled, the priest can say, "You really asked"; if it is not fulfilled, "There was no trust in your prayer."

In fact there is never trust in your prayer, because when there is trust there is no need to pray. All prayers arise out of doubt. But sometimes – it is just a coincidence – some prayers happen to be fulfilled. It is just a happening, it is just a chance; there is nobody to fulfill them. But when they are fulfilled, the priest can exploit the situation. He can say, "Look – you prayed deeply, trustfully, your prayer is fulfilled."

But this happens only once in a while. Ninety-nine times in a hundred your prayer is not fulfilled. But you know yourself that there was not trust; doubt was there. Even when you were praying, there was doubt whether there is a God, whether he will hear, whether he will listen, whether he will oblige – all kinds of doubts. In spite of all these doubts you say, "Why not try? What you are going to lose? Give it a try. Maybe, perhaps…." You know it. So when it is not fulfilled, the priest can always say to you, "Your trust was not total."

God is a lie as a person. God is a quality, not a personality. You cannot pray to God. You can be in prayer, but when the prayer is really there it is only a quality of love, nothing else. No words to express it, nobody to address it, it is simply a song, a wordless song in the heart, just a stirring of the deepest in you.

People love lies. Truth is arduous. And people also love lies because they make them feel good. You must lie about somebody else: you meet a and you lie about b and you make a feel good; then you meet b and you lie about a and you make b feel good. When you lie about others to people you give them the idea that they are better than others. You can play this game, and if you play it cleverly, cunningly, you can exploit very much.

Mulla Nasruddin and his friend Rahimtullah are standing on a street corner insulting one another. The one calls the other stupid, a cheat, a thief. The other says, "You are a coward, a miser, a hypocrite." Finally they begin insulting each other's families.

Mulla Nasruddin looks Rahimtullah straight in the eye and says, "Your sister is a stinking old whore; for twenty-five paisa she will let a one-eyed leper crawl over her."

Rahimtullah stands there, speechless. A bystander is amazed. He goes over to him and says, "For God's sake, man, how can you just stand there and let the Mulla insult your sister like that?"

Rahimtullah says, "I don't have a sister, I never had a sister, and now that my parents are both dead I never will have a sister."

So the bystander turns to Mulla Nasruddin and says, "Mulla, there is no point your insulting him like that, he does not have a sister."

"Sure," says the Mulla. "Of course not. I know it and he knows it, and now even you know it. But I ask you, how many of the people who had their windows open and were listening to our every word – how many of them also know it?"

People are living in enormous ignorance; they have not lit the candle of light that is there in their hearts. Their interiority is full of darkness. They don't know even themselves – what else can they know? Hence you can lie easily and they will believe it, and you can exploit their belief. The politicians have been doing it, the priests have been doing it, and it has been done down the ages. Exploit people. This is one of the most cunning businesses ever invented by man.

In the name of religion, only lies and lies are being propagated. Hence whenever a man of truth arrives, there is great confusion. Jesus creates confusion because he starts telling the truth as it is, and people have been accustomed to lies. They think their lies are the truth, and now here comes this man and he starts saying something else, something totally different. Either they have to believe in this man...then they have to drop their whole tradition, which is a long, long investment, and only a very few courageous ones can do it. The easier way is to destroy this man, to make this man silent, so they can go on dreaming and believing in their lies.

You ask me, "I am addicted to telling lies. Why do I do it?"

You must have known the ancient art of the politicians and the priests; maybe you unconsciously have stumbled upon it. And now those lies are paying off for you.

I know one man, a very good man in a way. He has never worked, he has never done anything, but he is very good at a few things; at playing cards, at playing chess, at gossiping and things like that he is perfect. Very cultured, very educated – he is a PhD; we had studied together. He has lived his whole life on lies and cheating people.

When I was a professor in the university, sometimes he would come and stay with me for a few days. Once I asked him, "When are you going to stop all this business of telling lies?"

He said, "Never!"

I said, "But sooner or later you will be caught."

He said, "Never...because there are so many millions and millions of people in this world, and I cheat a person only one time; then I forget about him, then I find another victim." And he said, "I have only a small life, maybe seventy, at the most eighty years, and the world is big and victims are so many – I can go on cheating."

He was very clever in making friends, he was very clever at creating a feeling in you that he is a man who can be trusted. Once the trust has arisen, he would immediately deceive you. But that much is certain: he never deceived a person twice. There is no need either, there are so many people.

You must have found some nourishment in telling lies to people. Maybe they pay you more attention, maybe they make you feel that you know more than they know. There are people who go on reading each other's hands. Nobody knows anything. There are people – tarot card readers, experts in I Ching reading.... These are all basically games. You can invent your own game. And if you start playing these games you will become more and more efficient. And these things pay – although what you are gaining is mundane, spurious, and what you are losing is very essential. You are losing your very soul, you are committing suicide, but it feels as if it is paying.

Stop enjoying it, unlearn the whole art! Of course you will feel many difficulties arising, because you must have become dependent on the art of telling lies. Take the risk, let it be hard. For a few days, it will be hard. Stop immediately! Listen to Atisha's advice: three difficulties.

First: if you become aware when you are lying to somebody, immediately, in the middle of it, ask to be forgiven. Say immediately, "This was a lie, and I was again getting into my old trick. Forgive me, please." It will be hard, but there is no other way. When a habit has become very deep-rooted, it has to be hammered.

Second: become aware when you are just preparing to tell a lie. Just as it is on the lips, just on the tongue…stop it then and there, abort it then and there.

And third: become aware when a lie starts arising in your feelings, in the heart.

If you can do these three awarenesses, lying will disappear. And the moment lying disappears, truth arrives. And truth is the only thing worth seeking and searching, because truth liberates

You speak about love and compassion. I know of and feel different forms of love and compassion. Can you explain the different forms of love, and what you mean by compassion?

Love is a ladder, a ladder of three rungs. The lowest rung is sex, the middle is love, and the highest is prayer. Because of these three rungs there are a thousand and one combinations possible.

Real compassion appears only at the third rung when sex energy becomes prayer – the compassion of a buddha, the compassion Atisha is talking about. When passion has been transformed so totally, so utterly that it is no more passion at all, then compassion appears. Real compassion appears only when your sex energy has become prayer.

But compassion can appear on the second rung too, and compassion can appear on the first rung also. Hence there are so many different compassions. For example, if compassion appears on the first rung, when you are living at the lowest level of love-energy, sex, then compassion will be just an ego trip. Then compassion will be very egotistic: you will enjoy the idea of being compassionate. You will really enjoy the other's suffering, because it is the other's suffering that is giving you the opportunity to be compassionate.

Somebody has fallen in the river and is drowning. The sexual person can jump in and save him, but his joy is that he was so good, that he did something beautiful, something great. He will talk about it with pride, he will brag about it. Compassion on the lowest rung, that of sex, will appear only as an ego trip.

That's what millions of missionaries all over the world are doing – serving the poor, serving the ill, serving the uneducated aboriginals, primitives. But the whole joy is that, "I am doing something great." The "I" is strengthened. That is an ugly form of compassion. It is called duty. Duty is a four-letter dirty word.

The second kind of compassion appears when love has arrived. Then compassion is sympathy: you feel, you really feel for the other. You fall into a harmony with the other, the other's suffering stirs you. It is not something to brag about. On the second rung, you will never talk about your compassion, never; it is not something to be talked about. In fact you will never feel that you have done anything special, you will simply feel you have done whatsoever was to be done. You will see that it was human to do it. There is nothing special in it, nothing extraordinary; you have not attained some spiritual merit in doing it. There is nothing like merit in it: it was natural, spontaneous. Then compassion is becoming more soft, more beautiful.

At the third rung, where sex energy becomes prayer, compassion appears as empathy – not even sympathy, but empathy. Sympathy means feeling the other's suffering, but you are still at a distance; empathy means becoming one with the other's suffering – not only feeling it but suffering it, actually going into it. If somebody is crying, sympathy means you feel for the one who is crying, empathy means you start crying. You are not only in a feeling space, you become attuned, you become really one: at-one-ment happens.

A man came to Buddha and asked, "I am very rich and I have no children, and my wife has also died. Now I have all the money in the world. I would like to do some meritorious work. I would like to do something for the poor and the downtrodden. Just tell me, what should I do?"

And it is said Buddha became very sad and a tear rolled down from his eye.

The man was very much puzzled. He said, "Tears in your eyes? And you look so sad – why?"

Buddha said, "You cannot help anybody, because you have not even helped yourself yet. And you cannot do anything compassionate, because your energies are still at the lowest. Your base metal has not yet become gold. In fact," Buddha said, "I am feeling so sorry for you. You want to be of some help to people, but you are not. You don't exist yet, because awareness has not happened, and without awareness how can you be? You don't have a real center from where compassion can flow."

Compassion can have these three categories, and love also has three categories. First, sex. Sex simply means: "Give me – give me more and more!" It is exploitation, it is what Martin Buber calls the I-it relationship: "You are a thing and I want to use you." The man uses the woman, the woman uses the man, the parents use the children and the children use parents, friends use friends. They say, "A friend is a friend only; a friend in need is a friend indeed." Use, reduce the other into a commodity.

To live in the I-it world is to miss the whole wonder of existence. Then you are surrounded by things – not by persons, not by people, not by life, but just material things. The poorest man in the world is one who lives in the I-it relationship. Sex is exploitation.

Love is totally different. Love is not exploitation. Love is not an I-it relationship, it is an I-thou relationship. The other is respected as a person in his own right; the other is not a thing to be used, to be possessed, to be manipulated. The other is an independent person, a freedom. The other has to be communicated with, not exploited. Love is a communication of energies.

Sex is only "Give me, give me, give me more!" Hence the sexual relationship is continuously that of war, conflict, because the other also says "Give me!" Both want more and more, and nobody is ready to give. Hence the conflict, the tug-of-war. And of course whosoever proves more strong will exploit the other. Because man has been muscularly stronger than woman, he has exploited, he has reduced women to utter nonentities; he has destroyed the soul of women. And it was easier for him if the soul was completely destroyed.

For centuries women were not allowed to read; in many religions women were not allowed to go to the temple, women were not allowed to become priests. Women were not allowed any public life, any social life. They were imprisoned in the houses; they were cheap labor, the whole day working, working, working. And they were reduced to sex objects. There has not been much difference between prostitutes and wives in the past. The wife was reduced into a permanent prostitute, that's all. The relationship was not a relationship, it was an ownership.

Love respects the other. It is a give-and-take relationship. Love enjoys giving, and love enjoys taking. It is a sharing, it is a communication. Both are equal in love; in a sexual relationship both are not equal. Love has a totally different beauty to it.

The world is slowly, slowly moving towards love relationships; hence there is great turmoil. All the old institutions are disappearing – they have to disappear, because they were based on the I-it relationship. New ways of communication, new ways of sharing are bound to be discovered. They will have a different flavor, the flavor of love, of sharing. Nonpossessive they will be; there will be no owner.

Then the highest state of love is prayer. In prayer there is communion. In sex there is the I-it relationship, in love the I-thou relationship. Martin Buber stops there; his Judaic tradition won't allow him to go further. But one step more has to be taken: that is "neither I nor thou" – a relationship where I and thou disappear, a relationship where two persons no more function as two but function as one. A tremendous unity, a harmony, a deep accord, two bodies but one soul. That is the highest quality of love: I call it prayer.

Love has these three stages, and compassion accordingly has three stages, and both can exist in different combinations.

Hence there are so many kinds of love and so many kinds of compassion. But the basic, the most fundamental, is to understand this three-rung ladder of love. That will help you, that will give you an insight into where you are, what kind of love you are living in and what kind of compassion is happening to you. Watch. Beware not to remain caught in it. There are higher realms, heights to be climbed, peaks to be attained.

? I don't understand you. Please don't confuse me. I have come here to attain some clarity.

You have come to the wrong place. Confusion is my technique to bring clarity. You are feeling confused because you must have come with certain prejudices and I am shattering them. Hence the confusion, hence you are feeling chaos. You had come here to be made more certain about your prejudices. I am not here to help your prejudices, I am not here to help your traditions, your conditionings. My work consists in demolishing you completely, because only when you are utterly demolished the new is born. When the old ceases to exist, the new appears – and that new has clarity.

Clarity is not certainty, certainty is not clarity. Clarity comes not out of mind and its projections and ideas and philosophies, clarity comes out of the mirrorlike quality of no-mind. Clarity simply means that you have no idea of what is, that you have no philosophy to cling to, that you have no ideology – Christian, Hindu, Mohammedan, communist – that you are simply without any ideology, without any philosophy, without any scripture: empty, utterly empty.

That virginity is clarity. Then all dust is gone and the mirror reflects that which is.

You say: "Osho, I don't understand you."

It is not a question of understanding at all. I am not trying in any way to make myself understood by you. It is not a question of understanding, knowing; it is a question of feeling, seeing, being. But that's what happens to many people: they come with a certain idea, with a certain language that they understand. I use different methods that they have never even heard about. They come with their expectations, their ideologies, their language. I speak a totally different language, and I have no ideology to teach you. I have nothing to teach you; I am not a teacher at all. I have nothing to convey to you, I have no message. You will have to learn my language; otherwise there is going to be more and more misunderstanding and more and more confusion.

Did you hear about the PE lecturer who went to the doctor and said, "When I was twenty it was like steel – so solid I could not bend it at all. When I was thirty I could bend it, but only a wee bit, mind you. Now I'm sixty-four, I can tie a knot in it."

After listening to this, the doctor asked what it was that he wanted to know. And the lecturer replied, "Am I getting stronger, doctor?"

Meditate over it. Different languages....

An inexperienced young man visits a house of prostitution. He is surprised at the politeness of the girl. In the morning he gets dressed and is about to depart.

"How about some money?" says the girl.

"Oh, no," he replies, "you have been kind enough already."

The traveling saleswoman goes to bed with the farmer's son. Trying to get something going, she says to him, "Would you trade sides with me? Roll over me and I will roll over you, and we will be more comfortable."

"Oh, that's all right, ma'am. I'll just walk to your side of the bed."

He does so. This happens several more times. Finally she says, "I don't think you know what I really want."

"Yes I do," he replies. "You want the whole darn bed, but you ain't gonna get it!"

The draft board examiners eyed the swishy young man with suspicion. They had orders to watch out for potential draft evaders feigning homosexuality. After subjecting the chap to an extensive physical and psychological examination, one of the examiners declared, "Well, fellah, it looks like you are going to make a good little soldier."

"Fabulous!" replied the young man. "When do I meet him?"

Enough for today.

Chapter 20
Diogenes and the Dog

? **What is this attachment to misery? And why is it so difficult to be happy?**

Misery has many things to give to you which happiness cannot give. In fact, happiness takes away many things from you. Happiness takes all that you have ever had, all that you have ever been; happiness destroys you. Misery nourishes your ego, and happiness is basically a state of egolessness. That is the problem, the very crux of the problem. That's why people find it very difficult to be happy. That's why millions of people in the world have to live in misery…have decided to live in misery. It gives you a very, very crystallized ego. Miserable, you are. Happy, you are not. In misery, crystallization; in happiness you become diffused.

If this is understood then things become very clear. Misery makes you special. Happiness is a universal phenomenon, there is nothing special about it. Trees are happy and animals are happy and birds are happy. The whole existence is happy, except man. Being miserable, man becomes very special, extraordinary.

Misery makes you capable of attracting people's attention. Whenever you are miserable you are attended to, sympathized with, loved. Everybody starts taking care of you. Who wants to hurt a miserable person? Who is jealous of a miserable person? Who wants to be antagonistic to a miserable person? That would be too mean.

The miserable person is cared for, loved, attended to. There is great investment in misery. If the wife is not miserable the husband simply tends to forget her. If she is miserable the husband cannot afford to neglect her. If the husband is miserable the whole family, the wife, the children, are around him, worried about him; it gives great comfort. One feels one is not alone, one has a family, friends.

When you are ill, depressed, in misery, friends come to visit you, to solace you, to console you. When you are happy, the same friends become jealous of you. When you are *really* happy, you will find the whole world has turned against you.

Nobody likes a happy person, because the happy person hurts the egos of the others. The others start feeling, "So you have become happy and we are still crawling in darkness, misery and hell. How dare you be happy when we all are in such misery!"

And of course the world consists of miserable people, and nobody is courageous enough to let the whole world go against him; it is too dangerous, too risky. It is better to cling to misery, it keeps you a part of the crowd. Happy, and you are an individual; miserable, you are part of a crowd – Hindu, Mohammedan, Christian, Indian, Arabian, Japanese. Happy? Do you know what happiness is? Is it Hindu, Christian, Mohammedan? Happiness is simply happiness. One is transported into another world. One is no more part of the world the human mind has created, one is no more part of the past, of the ugly history. One is no more part of time at all. When you are really happy, blissful, time disappears, space disappears.

Albert Einstein has said that in the past scientists used to think that there were two realities – space and time. But he said that these two realities are not two – they are two faces of the same single reality. Hence he coined the word *spaciotime*, a single word. Time is nothing else but the fourth dimension of space. Einstein was not a mystic, otherwise he would have introduced the third reality also – the transcendental, neither space nor time. That too is there, I call it the witness. And once these three are there, you have the whole trinity. You have the whole concept of *trimurti*, three faces of God. Then you have all the four dimensions. The reality is four-dimensional: three dimensions of space, and the fourth dimension of time.

But there is something else, which cannot be called the fifth dimension, because it is not the fifth really, it is the whole, the transcendental. When you are blissful you start moving into the transcendental. It is not social, it is not traditional, it has nothing to do with human mind at all.

Your question is significant: "What is this attachment to misery?"

There are reasons. Just look into your misery, watch, and you will be able to find what the reasons are. And then look into those moments when once in a while you allow yourself the joy of being in joy, and then see what differences are there. These will be the few things: when you are miserable you are a conformist. Society loves it, people respect you, you have great respectability, you can even become a saint; hence your saints are all miserable. The misery is written large on their faces, in their eyes. Because they are miserable they are against all joy. They condemn all joy as hedonism; they condemn every possibility of joy as sin. They are miserable, and they would like to see the whole world miserable. In fact only in a miserable world can they be thought to be saints. In a happy world they would have to be hospitalized, mentally treated. They are pathological.

I have seen many saints, and I have been looking into the lives of your past saints. Ninety-nine out of a hundred of them are simply abnormal – neurotic or even psychotic. But they were respected – and they were respected for their misery, remember. The more misery they lived through, the more they were respected. There have been saints who would beat their body with a whip every day in the morning, and people would gather to see this great austerity, asceticism, penance. And the greatest was one who would have wounds all over his body – and these people were thought to be saints!

There have been saints who have destroyed their eyes, because it is because of the eyes that one becomes aware of beauty, and lust arises. And they were respected because they had destroyed their eyes. God had given them eyes to see the beauty of existence; they became blind by their own decision.

There have been saints who cut their genital organs. And they were respected very much, tremendously, for the simple reason that they had been self-destructive, violent with themselves. These people were psychologically ill.

There have been saints who have been worshipped because they were capable of fasting for long periods, were experts in fasting. It is a certain expertise, you need a little training. Not much intelligence is needed; the training is very ordinary and any stupid person can go through it and learn it. You just have to be able to enjoy suffering – and only the ill person enjoys suffering. If you can remain for ten, twelve days on a fast, only the first four, five days are difficult. Then the body metabolism becomes attuned to not eating. In fact, it starts eating itself.

The body has a dual mechanism in it; for emergency purposes the body has a dual mechanism. You eat, you get energy from the outside, because every day you need a certain quantity of energy to live by. If you don't do that, then the body has some stored energy for emergency times; that's what fat is. Fat is emergency food, stored food. If a person is normal, healthy, he can live for three months without food; that much fat the body contains.

In the ancient days when the body was developing and man was coming down from the trees and was becoming a hunter, it was not possible every day to find food. Some days you would find it, some days you would not find. Man started gathering some storage inside; the body has learned this.

The more afraid you are of tomorrow, the more fat you will gather. That's why women gather more fat. Down the ages they have been more afraid – they have been made more afraid by men. They gather more fat. And women are more capable of going on a fast than men. Women need more fat also because they will have to go through pregnancy, and eating becomes difficult in pregnancy. They will have to eat their own stored food. In fact to be on a fast is nothing but eating yourself, it is cannibalism. Reduced to the truth, a man who fasts is a cannibal; he eats himself. That's why when you fast, every day one or two pounds of weight start to disappear. Where is it going? You are eating it; it is your need, everyday need. That much energy is used by your machine, by your body.

Great saints were doing long fasts, just torturing themselves. But it is not much of an intelligent thing. Just for a few days, the first week, it is difficult; the second week it is very easy; the third week it becomes difficult to eat. The fourth week you have completely forgotten. The body enjoys eating itself and feels less heavy, obviously, with no problems to digest. And the whole energy that is continuously being used in digestion becomes available to the head. You can think more, you can concentrate more, you can forget the body and its needs.

But these things simply created miserable people and a miserable society. Look into your misery and you will find certain fundamental things are there. One: it gives you respect. People feel more friendly towards you, more sympathetic. You will have more friends if you are miserable. This is a very strange world, something is fundamentally wrong with it. It should not be so, the happy person should have more friends. But become happy and people become jealous of you, they are no more friendly. They feel cheated; you have something that is not available to them. Why are you happy? So we have learned down the ages a subtle mechanism: to repress happiness and to express misery. It has become our second nature.

My sannyasins have to drop this whole mechanism. You have to learn how to be happy, and you have to learn to respect happy people and you have to learn to pay more attention to happy people, remember. This is a great service to humanity. Don't sympathize too much with people who are miserable. If somebody is miserable, help, but don't sympathize. Don't give him the idea that misery is something worthwhile. Let him know perfectly well that you are helping him, but "This is not out of respect, this is simply because you are miserable." And you are not doing anything but trying to bring the man out of his misery, because misery is ugly. Let the person feel that the misery is ugly, that to be miserable is not something virtuous, that "You are not doing a great service to humanity."

Be happy, respect happiness, and help people to understand that happiness is the goal of life – *Sat-Chit-Anand*. The Eastern mystics have said God has three qualities. He is sat: he is truth, being. He is *chit*: consciousness, awareness. And, ultimately, the highest peak is *anand*: bliss. Wherever bliss is, God is. Whenever you see a blissful person, respect him, he is holy.

And wherever you feel a gathering which is blissful, festive, think of it as a sacred place.

We have to learn a totally new language, only then this old rotten humanity can be changed. We have to learn the language of health, wholeness, happiness. It is going to be difficult because our investments are great.

That is why it is so difficult to be happy and so easy to be miserable. One thing more: misery needs no talents, anybody can afford it. Happiness needs talents, genius, creativity. Only creative people are happy.

Let this sink deep in your heart: only creative people are happy. Happiness is a by-product of creativity. Create something, and you will be happy. Create a garden, let the garden bloom, and something will bloom in you. Create a painting, and something starts growing in you with the growing painting. As the painting comes to the finish, as you are giving the last touches to the painting, you will see you are no more the same person. You are giving the last touches to something that is very new in you.

Write a poem, sing a song, dance a dance, and see: you start becoming happy. That's why in my commune creativity is going to be our prayer to God. This commune is not going to be of those sad, long faces who are not doing anything, just sitting under trees or in their huts, vegetating. This commune is going to be a commune of artists, painters, poets, sculptors, dancers, musicians – and so many things are there to be done!

God has only given you an opportunity to be creative: life is an opportunity to be creative. If you are creative you will be happy. Have you seen the joy in the eyes of a mother when the child starts growing in her womb? Have you seen the change that happens to the woman when she becomes pregnant? What is happening? Something is flowering in her, she is being creative, she is going to give birth to a new life. She is utterly happy, tremendously joyous, a song is in her heart.

When the child is born and the woman sees the child for the first time, see the depth of her eyes, the joy of her being. She has gone through much pain for this joy, but she has not gone into this pain for the pain's sake. She has suffered, but her suffering is tremendously valuable; it is not ascetic, it is creative. She has suffered to create more joy.

When you want to climb to the highest peak of the mountains, it is arduous. And when you have reached the peak and you lie down, whispering with the clouds, looking at the sky, the joy that fills your heart – that joy always comes whenever you reach any peak of creativity.

It needs intelligence to be happy, and people are taught to remain unintelligent. The society does not want intelligence to flower. The society does not need intelligence; in fact it is very much afraid of intelligence. The society needs stupid people. Why? – because stupid people are manageable. Intelligent people are not necessarily obedient – they may obey, they may not obey. But the stupid person cannot disobey; he is always ready to be commanded. The stupid person needs somebody to command him, because he has no intelligence to live on his own. He wants somebody to direct him; he seeks and searches his own tyrants.

Politicians don't want intelligence to happen in the world, priests don't want intelligence to happen in the world, generals don't want intelligence to happen in the world. Nobody really wants it. People want everybody to remain stupid, then everybody is obedient, conformist, never goes outside the fold, remains always part of the mob, is controllable, manipulatable, manageable.

The intelligent person is rebellious. Intelligence is rebellion. The intelligent person decides on his own whether to say no or yes. The intelligent person cannot be traditional, he cannot go on worshipping the past; there is nothing to worship in the past. The intelligent person wants to create a future, wants to live in the present. His living in the present is his way of creating the future.

The intelligent person does not cling to the dead past, does not carry corpses. Howsoever beautiful they have been, howsoever precious, he does not carry the corpses. He is finished with the past; it is gone, and it is gone forever.

But the foolish person is traditional. He is ready to follow the priest, ready to follow any stupid politician, ready to follow any order – anybody with authority and he is ready to fall at his feet. Without intelligence there can be no happiness. Man can only be happy if he is intelligent, utterly intelligent.

Meditation is a device to release your intelligence. The more meditative you become, the more intelligent you become. But remember, by intelligence I don't mean intellectuality. Intellectuality is part of stupidity.

Intelligence is a totally different phenomenon, it has nothing to do with the head. Intelligence is something that comes from your very center. It wells up in you, and with it many things start growing in you. You become happy, you become creative, you become rebellious, you become adventurous, you start loving insecurity, you start moving into the unknown. You start living dangerously, because that is the only way to live.

To be a sannyasin means to decide that "I will live my life intelligently," that "I will not be just an imitator," that "I will live within my own being, I will not be directed and commanded from without," that "I will risk all to be myself, but I will not be part of a mob psychology," that "I will walk alone," that "I will find my own path," that "I will *make* my own path in the world of truth." Just by walking into the unknown you create the path. The path is not already there; just by walking, you create it.

For stupid people there are superhighways where crowds move. And for centuries and centuries they have been moving – and going nowhere, going in circles. Then you have the comfort that you are with many people, you are not alone.

Intelligence gives you the courage to be alone, and intelligence gives you the vision to be creative. A great urge, a great hunger arises to be creative. And only then, as a consequence, you can be happy, you can be blissful.

Why can I remember the useless things for years, but not the essential ones? I forget the essential almost immediately.

You are fortunate – fortunate in the sense that at least you hear the essential. People don't hear at all, so there is no question of forgetting. People only hear the nonessential. Mind feeds on the nonessential, the useless, trivia.

The essential is a beautiful word, it comes from essence. The essential feeds your essence, hence it is called essential. The nonessential only decorates your surface; the nonessential remains on the circumference, it never reaches to the center of your being. Only the essential reaches to the center.

But your circumference is thick, it does not allow the essential to reach to the center; it hinders. It is a strategy of the mind, because if your being becomes more powerful, the mind loses its grip on you. There is a great conflict between the circumference and the center: who is going to dominate whom? The circumference is dominating. The circumference only allows that which nourishes it, and does not allow that which nourishes the essence – and everything has to pass through the circumference.

Scientists say that only two percent is allowed to reach to the core; ninety-eight percent is prevented from reaching. That's why you have poor souls – rich minds and poor souls, knowledgeable minds but foolish souls. You don't have wisdom. Unless you start doing something deliberately about it, this is going to remain so.

Mind loves the nonessential; it is always hungry for gossip. Something utterly useless, and it listens so attentively.

I have heard about a priest. He was giving a discourse to his congregation, and almost everybody was fast asleep – that's what people do in churches, temples. In fact, people who suffer from sleeplessness, they go to the churches, to the temples. If everything fails, tranquilizers don't work any more, just go to a religious discourse – it never fails, it immediately succeeds.

So almost everybody was asleep. And that was not the problem, because the priest knew, it was his whole life's experience. But a few people were there who were snoring too, and that was a great disturbance. So out from nowhere, unconnected with the discourse, he started telling a story.

He said, "Once it happened I was passing through a desert. There was nobody, just I was there with my donkey, and suddenly the donkey started speaking to me!"

Everybody was fully awake. Everybody! Not a single person was asleep. And then he dropped the story then and there, started his discourse again. One man stood up and said, "But what happened? What did the donkey say?"

The priest said, "You are so much interested in what the donkey said, you all became fully awake. But you are not interested in what I am saying."

Muza Dai Boo, an Arab merchant, was in the marketplace one day when he felt terrible cramps. He just couldn't control himself, and let out a long loud fart.

People stared at him from all sides. Mortally embarrassed, he ran back to his house, packed his few belongings and journeyed far away. For years he traveled from town to town, but always avoided his home town.

At last, an old and weary man, he decided to return. He had grown a long beard and his face had aged enough so that he was sure he would not be recognized. His heart longed for the old familiar streets.

Once in town, he went directly to the marketplace. There, to his surprise, he saw the street had been paved. He turned to the man nearest him and said, "My friend, how smooth this street is! When, by the grace of Allah, was it so neatly paved?"

"Oh, that," said the man. "That was done three years, four months and two days after Muza Dai Boo farted in the marketplace."

People never forget the stupid things of life. Muza Dai Boo they have forgotten, nobody recognizes him – but *that* has become something historical.

It is so with everybody's mind, it is nothing special to you.

You say: "Why can I remember only the useless things and for years, but not the essential ones?"

The essential ones are against your mind. The mind is continuously afraid of allowing any truth to enter you. It finds a thousand and one ways to avoid the truth, because the truth is going to shatter it. It allows only that which is supportive. And because mind itself is rubbish, it collects rubbish, and very joyously.

What Buddha has said will be forgotten. Buddha used to repeat each statement three times. Once somebody asked, "Why do you repeat three times?"

He said, "Because I know, the first time you don't hear at all. The second time you hear, but you hear something else that I have not said. The third time I hope that you hear that which is said, exactly that which is said."

It is very difficult to read Buddhist scriptures, because each statement repeated three times becomes very tiring. So now they have invented a device: they write the statement and they make three stars, so you know three times…no need to *read* three times.

If somebody came to Buddha to surrender, he had to surrender three times. He had to say, "*Buddham sharanam gachchhami, sangham sharanam gachchhami, dhammam sharanam gachchhami*" – three times. Why? Buddha is reported to have said, "The first time you may have said it but may not have meant it. The second time you may have meant it, but may not have meant that which I mean by it. The third time I hope that you are exactly doing what is expected."

It is not a formal thing to say, "*Buddham sharanam gachchhami*, I go to the feet of the Buddha." If it is formal it is meaningless. If you are simply repeating it because others are repeating it, it is useless. And people are imitators.

Once it happened, I was staying in a house and I told the friend with whom I was staying that people are imitators.

He said, "All?"

I said, "All."

He said, "Then give me a demonstration."

I said, "You wait."

I told him, "When the next person comes to see me, the moment he enters, you touch my feet, put a hundred-rupee note at my feet."

And it happened: when the next people came to see me – three people came to see me together – he immediately touched my feet and left a hundred-rupee note there, and all three touched my feet and left hundred-rupee notes immediately!

I said, "What do you say now? And these are the people who have been coming to see me for years, and not even a single *paisa* – and suddenly hundred-rupee notes!"

I asked them, "Why did you do this?"

They said, "Why? – because we thought maybe this is what we have to do. If it is being done, then it must be done.

People are imitators. In temples and mosques, in churches, you will find them bowing down. Somebody is bowing down to a cross – why? Can you really answer why you go on bowing down to the cross? – because your parents have been doing it. And ask the parents, Why? – because their parents have been doing it, and so on and so forth. People simply imitate. Imitation is easy, it remains on the surface. It is not a commitment, commitment goes to the heart.

You will have to be very conscious, you will have to learn two things. One: the moment you see something nonessential is there, don't pay any attention to it, bypass it. There is no need even to look at it, there is no need to read it.

If you start reading only the essential, our cities will become far more beautiful because boards and advertisements on the walls will disappear. They are there because you go on reading them. And the same thing: "Livva little hot, sippa Gold Spot." Whenever you pass, again you read it: "Livva little hot…." It is unconscious! And if you read it too many times – "Livva little hot, sippa Gold Spot" – one day you will sippa Gold Spot! How long can you avoid it?

The whole advertising depends on your foolishness. Just constant repetition. That's why the latest thing is not to have fixed lights for advertisements; they go on, off. "Livva little hot…" you have read once, the light goes off. It comes again: "Livva little hot…" again you have to read it! If it remains constant you will read it only once and you will go home. But if it changes while you are passing, it changes four or five times, then four or five times you have to read it.

The whole science of advertising depends on your foolishness. Just go on repeating, and people start purchasing. Anything can be sold. In the old days the economists used to say that this is a fundamental law; it is no more. What they used to think a fundamental law was: wherever there is demand, there is supply. Now it is just vice versa: wherever there is supply, there is demand. First supply anything – just create a hypnotic atmosphere about it, and anything repeated too many times becomes a hypnosis.

Beware of the nonessential. Nobody can force you, if you are aware, to cling to the nonessential. And if you don't cling to the nonessential, if you don't gather the nonessential, passages will be available from the circumference to the center, and the essential can go in.

That's why it happens to many sannyasins…. Just now Haridas has said that he used to go outside the ashram; now it is becoming more and more difficult to go outside. Why is it becoming more and more difficult to go outside? Nobody is prevented from going outside, but it becomes difficult on its own, because you see so much nonsense – and you have to see it, because it is there; you have to listen to it.

Once you have started living in the essential, slowly, slowly many things that you used to do before – going to the movies, reading the novels, seeing the TV, listening to the radio, gossiping with people – start disappearing. And the energy that is involved in them becomes available for the essential.

Buddha has said that the sannyasin should not look more than four feet ahead while he is walking on the road – just four feet ahead. Why? So that you need not see all that is going on around. It is beautiful, it is significant.

Listen to that which will help your soul to grow. Read that which will provoke aspirations for God. See that which will give you a new vision, new eyes, clarity. Life is short, energy is limited.

Don't be foolish, don't go on wasting it on the nonessential. But you have to be *conscious*, only then the nonessential can be dropped. And the first thing is to drop the nonessential; only then the second thing is possible – to get attuned with the essential.

Seeing the false as the false is the beginning of seeing the true as the true.

? Is it ever possible to paint a totally satisfying painting?

While painting, each moment can be totally satisfying. But once the painting is complete it can never be totally satisfying, because if it is totally satisfying the painter will have to commit suicide. There will be no need to live any more.

That's why I say life is longing, pure longing – longing to attain higher and higher peaks, longing to go deeper and deeper into existence. But each moment can be utterly satisfying; that difference has to be remembered. When you are painting, each brush, each color that you throw on the canvas, each moment of it, is totally satisfying. There is nothing more to it. You are utterly lost, possessed, if you are a creator.

If you are only a technician then it is not so. The technician is not lost while he is painting, he is separate from his painting. He is just using his knowledge. He knows how to paint, that's all. There is nothing in his heart to paint – no vision, no poetry, no song. He has nothing to create, but just the technology. He is a technician, not an artist. He can paint – but while painting it is not meditation for him, it is not a love affair for him. He is doing it; he is a doer, separate. But the creator is not separate while he is creating, he is one with it. He is utterly lost, he has forgotten himself.

That's why when painters are painting they forget about food, forget about thirst, forget about sleep. They forget about the body so much that they can go on painting for eighteen hours without feeling at all tired. Each moment is absolutely satisfying.

But once the painting is complete, a great sadness descends on the real painter. These differences have to be remembered. When the painting is complete, the technician feels very happy: a good job done, finished. He is feeling tired; it was a long tiring process, no contentment on the way. He was just waiting for the result, he was result-oriented. He wanted to finish it somehow, and now it is finished. He takes a deep sigh of relief. He is happy, not while he is painting but only when the painting is complete.

Just the opposite happens to the creator. He is happy while he is painting; once the painting is complete, a great sadness descends on him. "So it is over? That peak, that climax, that orgasmic experience is over? That thrill, that adventure, that going into the unknown is over?"…just as lovers feel sad after a deep orgasm: a subtle sadness, beautiful in itself, of tremendous value – far more valuable than the happiness of the technician, because out of this sadness another painting will arise, out of this sadness another longing to soar high, another aspiration to reach beyond, another search, another inquiry, another pregnancy. The painter will be pregnant soon, will feel full, so full that he will have to share it again.

It is said that when Gibbon, the great historian, finished his great work about world history…. Thirty-three years it took to finish it, and he was so tremendously happy for those thirty-three years that it is said that he didn't age. He remained exactly the same, as if time never passed, as if time has stopped.

But the day it was finished he started crying. His wife could not believe it. She said, "You are crying? You should be happy, you should dance! The work is complete."

Gibbon said, "The work is complete. Now what is left for me? My life is complete." And within five years he aged so much, and by the seventh year he was gone.

It is said that Vincent van Gogh, the great Dutch painter, committed suicide when he felt that he had done the perfect painting. It is possible. If the painter feels the perfect has happened, then there is no point in living. The creator lives to create. The singer lives to sing, the dancer lives to dance, the lover lives to love, the tree lives to bloom – if it has bloomed and the perfect flowers have come, then what is the point of prolonging a futile, meaningless existence?

Your question is significant. You ask: "Is it possible to paint a totally satisfying painting?"

Yes and no. Yes, while you are painting it will be totally satisfying. And no, once it is over you will feel great sadness. But that sadness is also creative, because it is only out of that sadness you will again start moving towards the sunlit peaks.

And in this life nothing really is ever perfect or can ever be perfect.

You will be surprised that I believe in an imperfect God. You will be shocked, because at least all the religions are agreed on one thing, that God is perfect. I don't agree, because if God is perfect then Friedrich Nietzsche is right that God is dead. God is perfectly imperfect – that much I can say. Hence there is growth, evolution; hence there is movement. It is always, always coming closer and closer to perfection, but it is never perfect and it will never be perfect.

Nothing ever is perfect. In fact imperfection has a beauty of its own, because imperfection has a life. Whenever something is perfect – just think, contemplate – whenever something is really perfect, life will disappear from it.

Life can exist only if something is still imperfect and has to be perfected. Life is the effort to perfect the imperfect. Life is the ambition to make the ugly beautiful. Something of imperfection is a must for life to exist, for life to go on growing and flowing.

Nothing ever is perfect. Or if something any time happens to be perfect, in the East we have a right vision of it. We say whenever a person becomes perfect, that is his last life. The scriptures give different reasons for it; my reason is totally different. I say yes, when Buddha is perfect he will not come back, because perfection means life is no more possible. He will disappear into the cosmos.

Rabindranath, a great Indian poet and mystic, prayed his last prayer to God: "Send me back. Remember, I am not perfect. Send me back. Your world was too beautiful and you gave me such a precious life. And I don't want to disappear yet: I have yet to sing many songs, I have yet to paint many paintings, there is yet much in my heart which needs to bloom. Send me back, I am not perfect! Send me back."

That was his last prayer; he died praying this way. It is one of the most beautiful prayers and one of the most beautiful ways to die. How can one thank God more than this? "Your world was beautiful, I loved your world; I was not worthy of it but you made me. I am not worthy to be sent back, but still, your compassion is great. At least one time more, send me back."

Life remains growing. Nothing ever is perfect – or whenever something is perfect it disappears, it goes into annihilation. The Buddhist word is nirvana. Nirvana means annihilation, nirvana means cessation. Literally, nirvana means "blowing out the candle." Just as you blow out a candle and suddenly the light is gone, gone forever, has disappeared into nothingness – that is nirvana. All the buddhas say whosoever becomes perfect moves into nirvana, goes into annihilation.

Don't hanker for a perfect painting otherwise the painter will die. And you have yet to sing many songs.

And the painting cannot be perfect, the song and the dance cannot be perfect, for a few more reasons. One: when you visualize it in the deepest core of your heart, it is a totally different thing. When you start painting it, you are translating it from the subtle to the gross. In that very transforming, in that very translation, much is lost.

Hence no painter ever feels satisfied when he finishes his painting. It is not the same as that which he wanted to paint – similar, but not the same. He has some vision to compare, it has fallen very short. Hence he starts another painting.

Rabindranath again has to be remembered. He wrote six thousand songs – seems to be the greatest poet the world has ever known – and each song is a beauty. But when he was dying he was crying, he was saying to God, "The song that I wanted to sing, I have not sung yet."

An old friend was by the side of the bed, and the old friend said, "What are you saying? Have you gone mad? You have sung six thousand songs. In Europe, Shelley is thought to be one of the greatest poets. He has sung only two thousand songs. You have defeated him three times. You should be happy and contented!"

Rabindranath opened his tear-filled eyes and he said, "I am not. Yes, six thousand songs I have sung, but you don't know the inner story. The inner story is, I wanted to sing only one song! But because it never was possible.... I tried once, failed; I tried again, I failed. Six thousand times I have failed. Those are all efforts, and I am not satisfied with any of them. That which I wanted to sing is still unsung."

In fact nobody can sing it.

Buddha used to declare in every town, wherever he would go, "Please don't ask these eleven questions." In those eleven questions, all important questions were included: God, soul, death, life, truth, everything important was included. Why? "Because," he would say, "they cannot be answered. Not that I don't know, but to bring them to words is impossible."

There was an ancient mysterious wall which stood at the edge of a village and whenever anyone climbed the wall to look onto the other side, instead of coming back he smiled and jumped to the other side, never to return. The inhabitants of the village became curious as to what could draw these beings to the other side of the wall. After all, their village had all the necessities of living a comfortable life.

They made an arrangement where they tied a person's feet, so when he looked over and wished to jump, they could pull him back.

The next time someone tried to climb the wall to see what was on the other side, they chained his feet so he could not go over. He looked on the other side and was delighted at what he saw, and smiled. Those standing below grew curious to question him and pulled him back. To their great disappointment he had lost the power of speech.

Those who have seen cannot say. That which has been seen cannot be painted, cannot be reduced to words. But still each one has to give a try. The world goes on becoming more and more beautiful because of these efforts. The world is beautiful because of the six thousand songs that Rabindranath tried, although he failed to sing the song that he wanted. Those six thousand failures have made the world far more beautiful than it ever was. It will not be the same world again, those six thousand songs will go on resonating.

So go on painting, go on creating. Yet I tell you again and again, you will never be satisfied. I bless you that you should never be satisfied, but let each moment of your creativity be a great contentment. But when something is finished, move ahead. You have infinite capacities to create; you are unlimited, you don't have any limits to your potential. You are not aware what you can do, and you will never be aware unless you do it!

Hence the greatest creators are aware how poor has been their creation, because they become aware, more and more aware, how much more is possible. The ordinary person who has never created anything is not aware what he can do. There is no other way to know what you can do unless you do it. And while doing it you can see that what you wanted to do, what was very clear in your inner world, has become very dim and ordinary when it has been brought to the outer.

You will try again. Each effort will become better and better and better, more and more perfect, but never perfect.

? I am very much afraid of sex, because I am afraid of death. I have been told since my childhood by my society and religion that it is sex that brings death. What is the truth about it?

Can't you see a simple fact, that even your great saints die? Buddha and Christ and Zarathustra and Lao Tzu where are they? If it is through sex that death comes, then your celibates must be alive, they will never die. Then all the Catholic monks will live forever and will make the world so ugly. Then all the nuns will live forever – the world will become a monastery, monks and nuns, monks and nuns.

Everybody dies, death has nothing to do with sex. Death has something to do with birth, and birth has already happened, so death cannot be avoided now. One part has already happened and the second part cannot be divided and separated from it.

In fact, the people who are very sexual live longest. That's what scientific researchers have found: the sexual people live longest. Not only that, the great creators – painters, poets, musicians, singers, actors – they are all very sexual. Nothing has yet been said about the mystics, but I say to you, the mystics are the most sexual people in the world. Of course their sex is without any object; they are simply sexual. It is pure energy, pure longing, pure desire. They desire nothing, their sex has no object, it is unaddressed; it is simply a tremendous pool of energy. But they are sexual.

Sex is life, and wherever you see life you will find sex somewhere, in some way. The day sex disappears you will start dying, because it is sex energy that keeps you alive. Drop the foolish ideas that you have been taught. This has been done to many people in different ways. A thousand and one inhibitions and taboos have been created, and the best way to make you afraid of sex is to associate it with death. This is the simple, simple logic priests have discovered. And priests have been the most cunning people in the world. They must have discovered in the very beginning that if you join sex with death, then you can make people afraid of sex. Once they are afraid of sex, they are afraid of intelligence, creativity, they are afraid of being, they are afraid of freedom, they are ready to become slaves.

Death has nothing to do with sex. Sex or no sex, death is going to happen. In fact, if you can move deep into sex and transform its energy into love, and can move deep into love and transform its energy into prayer, you will come to know that there is no death. That is the only way to know something of immortality.

Two men were talking and it came out that one of them was a Mormon. "How many wives do you have?"

"Only one."

"How many wives does your father have?"

"Only one," he replied. "But my grandfather had sixty-five wives."

Mormons have many wives.

"How did he ever arrange his sex life?"

"That was easy. My grandfather lived in one house, and a mile down the road his sixty-five wives lived in another house. He had a runner, and each night, for example, he would tell his runner to run down the mile and tell wife number ten to get ready for the night. The next night he would have his runner run down the mile and have wife number thirty-five get ready – and so on, etcetera."

"Your grandfather must have been a remarkable man. But forgive my curiosity, I want to know how long he lived."

"Hell, the old man lived till he was ninety-eight years of age. And the funny part was that the runner died at the age of fifty, which proves a great moral: It is not the sex that kills you, but rather the running after it."

? You are always talking about no-mind, dropping the mind, becoming mindless. My understanding of this is that you are referring not to the whole mind (that is, not "mindless" in the ordinary sense of the word) but only to that analytical quality of mind which causes separation and prevents or hinders experiencing anything totally at any one time.

But perhaps I have misinterpreted your words to fit my own ideas?

This is what the analytical mind is. Yes, that is exactly what I mean: dropping the analytical mind. But when you drop the analytical mind nothing is left, because mind is pure analysis and nothing else. Once the analytical mind is dropped, logic is dropped, reason is dropped, because those are methods for analysis. Once the analytical mind is dropped, what is left of thought? Thought is basically analytical; it is the process of categorization, labeling, analyzing. Then what is left? Mind is gone – only heart is left, intuition is left.

But if you love words you can say "the synthetical mind" is left. But that makes no difference at all; that will simply show that you are very much clinging to your analytical mind. Now you will call it "synthetical mind."

Sigmund Freud created analysis, psychoanalysis, and then Assagioli created synthesis, psychosynthesis. And both are not basically different, both are aspects of the same coin. Sigmund Freud tries to analyze, and Assagioli tries to synthesize – but whether you analyze or synthesize, you use the same mind.

There is a state called no-mind: I am talking about that. It knows nothing of analysis, nothing of synthesis. It simply knows not; it is innocent of knowledge. It is pure being, presence, a mirror that reflects that which is.

Analyze a little more. And then you will find, if analysis is dropped, then nothing is left behind.

There was once a man who got into a nearly fatal automobile accident. He spent a week in the hospital in a coma before regaining consciousness. When he came to, the doctor was at his bedside and he asked the doctor what had happened.

The doctor replied, "Well, I have a little bad news and a little good news. I will tell you the bad news first. You have been in a very serious automobile accident which crushed both of your legs. While you were in a coma we had to amputate both legs in order to save your life."

"Oh, my God!" cried the man. "You mean both my legs have been cut off? I will never be able to walk again? I will have to spend the rest of my life in a wheelchair? Oh, this is the worst thing that could happen," said the man in deep anguish. Gathering himself together a bit, he queried, "Well, what is the good news?"

Replied the doctor, "The man down the hallway has offered to buy your shoes for eleven dollars."

Once the analytical mind is gone, what is left? Just the shoes – you can sell them. But even for eleven dollars, it is not such good news.

? Who is a lazy man?

It depends. To a workaholic, the answer will be totally different. To a workaholic almost everybody is lazy. But to the laziest, almost everybody is a workaholic.

It happened: There was an emperor in Japan who was himself very lazy and loved lazy people. Lazy people are good people, they have never been mischievous – they cannot be, because mischief needs activity. You have to be very active, only then you can be mischievous. Just think, if Alexander the Great had been a little lazy, Adolf Hitler a little lazy, the world would have been so beautiful. All the mischief comes from the active people. Lazy people have never done any harm, that much can be absolutely said.

The king loved lazy people. He said to his prime minister, "Nobody has done anything for these beautiful people called lazy. I want to do something. It is not their fault that they are lazy,

God has made them that way. And in a way they are very good because they don't harm anybody. They need state protection. So you declare that whosoever is lazy can come and be part of the palace. He has to be served as a government guest and he can live his lazy life without any worry and without any torture from the so-called active people."

The prime minister said, "It will be very difficult, because many who are not lazy will also come, and there will be great difficulty how to decide who is who."

And that's exactly what happened. Thousands of people started coming. The king was puzzled, he had never thought that so many people are lazy. Then a device was made: they were all placed in straw huts and in the middle of the night fire was put to the straw huts. Almost everybody ran out, except four – they simply went inside their blankets, they refused to move out. They said, "If God wants to kill us, it's okay. If he wants to save us, he will find some way."

So those four were accepted as royal guests. They were!

It is difficult – how to decide? Alexander thought that Diogenes was lazy, and Diogenes thought that Alexander was mad. Alexander tried to conquer the whole world – this is sheer madness – and Diogenes was so lazy that he remained naked, because it was such a botheration to put the clothes on and off. And then sometimes you have to wash them, and you have to look for Bahadur, and the soap, and this and that – it is a long sequence of things.

Diogenes had only one begging bowl. That too one day he threw in the river, because it was such a botheration to clean it. And the day he threw it, he saw a dog that gave him the inspiration. He was going towards the river, thirsty, with his begging bowl, and the dog was also thirsty and he was also going to the river.

The dog ran fast, jumped into the river, drank to his heart's content. And Diogenes thought, "So the dog is far more intelligent. Without any begging bowl, and he is doing well. Why do I go on carrying this weight?" He threw the begging bowl, he thanked the dog; they became friends. They became so friendly that they started sharing the place – where the dog used to live Diogenes also started living. It was just a big pipe, the dog used to live there; that became the house of Diogenes too.

When Alexander went to see Diogenes – naturally, polar opposites are always attracted – he was lying down on the sand by the side of the river in the early morning sun, warm, naked, he was enjoying, singing a song. The dog was sitting by his side, also enjoying the morning. Alexander came with all his paraphernalia, the generals and the prime ministers, and they declared, as was part of the court mannerism, that "Alexander the Great is here!"

Diogenes looked at the dog and laughed. Alexander could not understand why he looked at the dog; he asked why. Diogenes said, "I looked at the dog because only he will understand. These fools that you have brought with you, they will not understand at all. This dog is very wise. In the first place he never speaks – so wise, never utters a word, just keeps everything secret. And he is the only one who can understand that one who declares that he is great, can't be. Greatness need not be declared; it is there, or it is not there."

Shocked, Alexander could not believe that this would be the way he would be received, but still he was impressed by the man – he was so joyous. He said, "I feel a little jealous of you.

Next time, if God asks me, 'Alexander, what do you want to become?' I will ask to become Diogenes."

Diogenes again looked at the dog. And it is said that the dog smiled. Alexander could not believe what was happening, what was transpiring. He said, "What is the meaning of it?"

Diogenes said, "It is so foolish to wait for the next life. We live moment to moment, me and my friend, and you are hoping for the next life. If you are so jealous of Diogenes, who is preventing you? Is God preventing you? Throw off the clothes – and tell these foolish people to go! And the bank is so big, we can share. That is our house. First only the dog used to live here, then I became a part of it; you can also become a part of it. We have nothing else, so there is no quarrel, no competition, nothing."

It must have been one of the greatest moments in history. Just to think of it.... Alexander said, "I am happy that I came. I have seen a man worth seeing. Can I do something for you?"

Diogenes said, "You just move a little to the left, because you are hindering the sun. Nothing else is needed, because we don't need anything."

You ask me: "Who is a lazy man?"

It is very relative. My own suggestion is: act only when it is essential. And even while doing things, don't become a doer, become a non-doer. Let God do things through you, then action and inaction are one.

That's what Lao Tzu says: Wu-wei – action through inaction. Then action and laziness are no more opposite but complementaries. A real man will have both the capacities: he can act; he can be lazy, he can rest.

What ordinarily happens is that people become addicted, either to work or to laziness – and that is wrong. Don't become addicted. Do, but don't become a doer. And then even while doing things you will remain at rest, perfectly at rest.

Alexander on the circumference and Diogenes at the center: that is my definition of a total man.

Mulla Nasruddin once told me, "My uncle has the laziest rooster in the world."

"How can you tell?" I asked him.

"At sunrise, he just waits until some other rooster crows, then he nods his head."

Enough for today.

Chapter 21
Vagabonds of the Soul

Train impartially in every area; it is important to have trained deeply
and pervasively in everything.
Always meditate on specific objects.
You should have no concern for other factors.
Therefore, apply yourself to important matters.
Don't do things backwards.
Don't vacillate.
Train as though cut off.

Once a Jaina monk came to see me. He asked, "Is hell real? Is there really a hell?" Instead of answering him, I asked him, "And where do you think you are living?" Man lives in hell, because man is upside down. You need not go to some stupid yoga teacher to learn the headstand posture, because you are already doing it. Everything is in the wrong order. For centuries you have been messed up; a chaos has been created in you instead of a cosmos. You are just a kind of madness. Whatever you think is normal is not normal at all. It appears normal, because you have lived with these people from your very childhood and you have started thinking that these are the only people, so they must be normal.

It is as if one was born in a madhouse and from the very beginning was acquainted only with mad people; he will think them normal. In fact, if he ever comes across somebody who is sane, he will be very puzzled, he will not be able to believe his own eyes. He will think this man has gone crazy.

Man is a chaos. Let this idea sink deep into your heart, because only then the desire to create a cosmos out of this chaos arises. The moment you realize that you are standing on your head, a great moment has arrived. Now you cannot go on standing on your head any more: you have to do something, it is inevitable. You have to act – and that very act becomes religion.

Religion is against society, because society lives on this so-called normal madness of people. Society wants people to be abnormal; only then can they be exploited, only then can they be reduced into machines, only then can they be reduced to slaves – and happily, and without any revolt.

For thousands of years, man has lived in an imprisoned state. Those prisons have been given beautiful names: you call them churches, religions, ideologies. Somebody lives in a Catholic prison and somebody lives in a communist prison, and both go on bragging about their prison, that their prison is far better. But any person who lives through some ideology is a prisoner, because every ideology narrows down your consciousness, becomes chains on your being. Anybody who belongs to any crowd out of fear, out of conditioning, out of a kind of hypnosis, is not truly a man, is not yet born. The opportunity has been given to him, but he is wasting it.

You have been taught values which are not really values; you have been taught things which are basically poisonous. For example, you have been told not to love yourself, and you have been told so many times that it looks like a simple fact, truth. But a man who is incapable of loving himself will be incapable of loving anybody else. The man who cannot love himself cannot love at all.

You have been told to be altruistic and never selfish. And it looks so beautiful – but it only *looks* beautiful; it is destroying your very roots. Only a really selfish person can be altruistic, because one who is not rooted in his self, is not selfish, will not bother about anybody else. If he cannot care for himself, how can he care for anybody else? He is suicidal; naturally he will become murderous.

Your whole society up to now has been a society of murderers. A few people commit suicide; they become saints. A few more go on committing murder; they become great politicians, great leaders – Genghis Khan, Nadir Shah, Tamerlane, Alexander, Napoleon, Adolf Hitler, Stalin, Mao. But both are neurotic, both are unhealthy.

You have to be taught new values. Atisha's sutras will help you immensely. He is really a revolutionary, a really religious man – a man who *knows*, not through scriptures but by his own experience; a man who has looked deep into the misery of man, a man who is really so full of compassion that he wants to help, to be of some help to the suffering humanity. And the suffering humanity is not helped by creating more hospitals or by making more people educated. The suffering humanity can be helped only by giving it a new soul.

People like Mother Teresa of Calcutta are simply serving the status quo. That's why they are respected by the status quo. They are given gold medals, prizes, awards, and the society thinks Mother Teresa is the symbol of real saintlihoodness. It is not so; she is simply in the service of a rotten society. Of course the rotten society respects her. She is not a revolutionary, she is not a religious person.

And this is something to be understood: society respects only those saints who are not really sages but are agents – agents who help the society to continue as it is, agents of the establishment.

Atisha is not for the establishment. He wants to create a new man, a new humanity, as always buddhas have dreamed about. Their dreams remain yet unfulfilled.

Here I am, again dreaming a great dream of giving birth to a new man. You are my hope, in the same way Atisha had hoped with his own disciples. These sutras were not written as a book, these sutras were given to his disciples to meditate on.

The first sutra:

Train impartially in every area; it is important to have trained deeply and pervasively in everything.

The first thing is impartiality: one should be unprejudiced, and nobody is unprejudiced. And that is a basic requirement to grow into a greater vision. To come out of the prisons, the first thing is to drop prejudices – prejudices called Hinduism, prejudices called Mohammedanism, prejudices called Christianity. One has to drop all prejudices. How can you ever know truth if you have already decided what it is? If you are already functioning from a conclusion, you will never arrive to truth – never! It is impossible.

Don't start by a priori assumptions, don't start by any belief. Then only are you a true seeker. But everybody starts by belief – somebody believes in The Bible, somebody else in the Koran; somebody believes in the Gita, and somebody in Dhammapada. And they *start* by belief.

Belief means you don't know, still you have taken something for granted. Now your whole effort will be to prove it right, it will become your ego trip. Each belief becomes an ego trip, you have to prove it right. If it is wrong, then you are wrong; if it is right, then you are right. And every person is nothing but a bag full of beliefs.

Remember, *all* beliefs are stupid. I am not saying that those beliefs are basically untrue – they may not be, they may be – but to believe is stupid. To know is intelligent. It may be that when you come to know, it may be the same thing that you were told by others to believe; but still to believe in it is wrong, and to know it, right – because once you believe in something that you have not known, you have already started gathering around yourself a darkness which will not help you to know, to see. You are already becoming knowledgeable. And knowing happens to those who are not knowledgeable, but innocent. Knowing happens to those eyes which are absolutely without the dust of knowledge.

The first thing Atisha says: Be impartial, start without any conclusion, start without any a priori belief. Start existentially, not intellectually; these are two different dimensions, not only different but diametrically opposite.

Somebody can start his journey into love by studying about love, by going to the library, by looking in the Encyclopedia Britannica to learn what love is. This is an intellectual inquiry. He may gather much information, he may write a treatise, and some foolish university may give him a PhD but he knows nothing of love. Whatsoever he is writing is only intellectual, it is not experiential. And if it is not experiential, it is not true.

Truth is an experience, not a belief. Truth never comes by studying about it: truth has to be encountered, truth has to be faced. The person who studies about love is like the person who studies about the Himalayas by looking at the map of the mountains. The map is not the mountain! And if you start believing in the map, you will go on missing the mountain. If you become too much obsessed with the map, the mountain may be there just in front of you, but still you will not be able to see it.

And that's how it is. The mountain *is* in front of you, but your eyes are full of maps – maps of the same mountain, maps about the same mountain, made by different explorers. Somebody has climbed the mountain from the north side, somebody from the east. They have made different maps: Koran, Bible, Gita – different maps of the same truth. But you are too full of the maps, too burdened by their weight; you cannot move even an inch. You cannot see the mountain just standing in front of you, its virgin snow peaks shining like gold in the morning sun. You don't have the eyes to see it.

The prejudiced eye is blind, the heart full of conclusions is dead. Too many a priori assumptions and your intelligence starts losing its sharpness, its beauty, its intensity. It becomes dull. Dull intelligence is what is called intellect. Your so-called intelligentsia is not really intelligent, it is just intellectual. Intellect is a corpse. You can decorate it, you can decorate it with great pearls, diamonds, emeralds, but still a corpse is a corpse.

To be alive is a totally different matter. Intelligence is aliveness; it is spontaneity, it is openness, it is vulnerability, it is impartiality, it is the courage to function without conclusions. And why do I say it is a courage? It *is* a courage because when you function out of a conclusion the conclusion protects you, the conclusion gives you security, safety. You know it well, you know how to come to it, you are very efficient with it. To function without a conclusion is to function in innocence. There is no security, you may go wrong, you may go astray.

One who is ready to go on the exploration called truth has to be ready also to commit many errors, mistakes, has to be able to risk. One may go astray, but that is how one arrives. Going many, many times astray, one learns how not to go astray. Committing many mistakes one learns what is a mistake, and how not to commit it. Knowing what is error, one comes closer and closer to what is truth. It is an individual exploration; you cannot depend on others' conclusions.

Hence Atisha says:

Train impartially in every area; it is important to have trained deeply and pervasively in everything.

The second thing he says: Let your life be as multidimensional as possible, don't live one-dimensionally. Monks, nuns and the so-called priests have all lived, down the ages, one-dimensionally. They live a very narrow life; they move as trains move, on fixed rails. They go on doing the same ritual, the same prayer, day in, day out, year in, year out, life in, life out; they go on repeating. Their whole life moves in circles. And they are not rich, they cannot be – richness comes by living life in all its dimensions.

A religious person should explore in every possible way, should try to experience life in all its tastes, sweet and bitter, good and bad. The really religious person will be very experimental. He will experiment with music, he will experiment with dance, he will experiment with poetry, with painting, with sculpture, with architecture. He will go on experimenting with everything, everything that becomes available; he will be a child exploring everything. And that makes your inner life rich.

Do you know, all great discoveries are made by people who are not one-dimensional. One-dimensional people can never make discoveries; it is impossible, because a discovery happens only like crossbreeding. A mathematician starts writing poetry: now you can be certain something is on the way. His whole training is that of a mathematician, his approach is that of mathematics, and he starts writing poetry. Now, no poet can write poetry like this; this is going to be something new, because something of the mathematics is bound to filter in. And mathematics and poetry having a meeting is a crossbreeding.

Scientists say children that are born out of crossbreeding are stronger, more beautiful, more intelligent. But man is so stupid that he never learns. Now everybody knows that it is good to bring an English bull for an Indian cow; that is perfectly beautiful and that is being done. But as far as man is concerned we remain stupid. It would be beautiful if people marry different races, different backgrounds, different cultures. A Siberian marrying someone in Africa – then something is really going to happen, some miracle.

My own suggestion is – because within a few years we are going to find out other planets where evolution has almost reached to the point that it has reached on the earth, or a few planets where it has even reached higher – my own suggestion is for interplanetary marriages. Then miracles will start happening. A Martian marrying a Puneite: then something is going to happen, something really new which has never happened before!

Atisha says: Experiment, experience as many dimensions as are available to you.

Become a gardener, become a shoemaker, become a carpenter – that's what is going to happen in my commune. All dimensions have to be made available, and people have to experiment and enjoy and explore. It is not that when you do some scientific work, something happens only in the outside world. When you are doing some scientific work, something happens inside your consciousness: your consciousness starts taking a form, a scientific form. If this person starts painting, then the painting will have something of the science in it. And if the painter starts becoming a physicist, certainly his vision is going to give birth to new things.

All great discoveries up to now have been made by people who were trained for something else, but were courageous enough to enter into arenas where they were amateurs. Less courageous people remain clinging with the thing that they know best. Then they go on doing it their whole life. And the more they do it, the more efficient they become; the more efficient they become, the less capable of trying anything new.

A country remains alive only if people are multidimensional. America is now the most alive country in the world for the simple reason that people are trying every kind of thing. From mathematics to meditation, everything is being tried. America is just on the verge of a great step; if a new step is going to happen anywhere, it is going to happen in America. It can't happen in India. It can't happen because Morarji Desai and people like that won't allow it to happen in India – rigid, stale minds, having no vision of the future, having no vision of what is going to happen tomorrow, having no idea of what is really happening today.

In America, people go on changing their jobs – three years is the average limit when people change their jobs. Three years also is the average limit when people change their towns. Three years is also the average limit when people change their spouses. The number three is very esoteric.

When a man has lived with many women, has done many kinds of work – has been a cobbler, has been a carpenter, has been an engineer, has been a painter and a musician – naturally he is very rich. Each woman that he has lived with has imparted some color to him, and each work that he has done has opened a new door into his being. Slowly, slowly many doors of his being are opening; his consciousness expands, he becomes huge, enormous.

You *are* your experience. Hence, experience more. Before settling, experience as much as possible. The real person never settles; the real person always remains homeless, a wanderer, a vagabond, a vagabond of the soul. He remains continually in search, he remains an inquirer, a learner – he never becomes *learned*. Don't be in a hurry to become learned, remain a learner. To become learned is ugly, to remain a learner has tremendous beauty and grace in it, because it is life itself.

Train impartially in every area; it is important to have trained deeply
and pervasively in everything.

Whatsoever you are learning, learn it in its totality. Don't let it be just a hit-and-run affair, go into it as if it is your whole life. Stake everything! Be total, whatsoever you do, because it is only out of totality that one learns. It is only when you are totally into something that mysteries are revealed to you. If you are totally in love, then love reveals its mysteries; if you are totally in poetry, then the world of poetry opens its heart.

If you are totally in love with anything, that is the only possible way to have a rapport with that certain dimension. So be total, and go to the very depth of it. Don't just go on swimming in many rivers; become a diver, go to the rock bottom of everything – because the deeper you go into anything, the more and more deep you will become. Depth calls the depth, height provokes the height. Whatsoever we are doing outside simultaneously goes on happening inside. This is a fundamental law of life.

Atisha says: Discipline in many, many things, be total, go into depth, to the very roots of everything – because the secrets are in the roots, they are not in the flowers. Flowers are only expressions of joy, but the secrets are not there. Secrets are hidden in the roots, secrets are always hidden in darkness. You will have to go into dark depths, then only you will know the secrets. And the more you experience life in its multidimensionality, the richer will be your soul. It depends on you, how rich you make your soul, or how poor you live.

Millions of people are living a life of poverty – and I don't necessarily mean the outer poverty. I know rich people, and so poor that sometimes even beggars are richer than they are. I know rich people who can afford everything but have never experimented with anything, who are simply vegetating comfortably, who are simply dying, slowly, slowly…existing comfortably, but not living – no intensity, no flair, no flame, no fire, just a cold life. Comfortably they will live and comfortably they will die – but in fact they will never have lived.

And one who has never lived, how can he die?

Death is the ultimate mystery. That gift is given only to those who have lived really intensely, who have burned their torch of life from both the ends together. Only then it happens sometimes that in a single moment of intensity the whole life is revealed. In a single moment of total intensity, the whole eternity opens its doors to you, you are welcomed by God.

God is not found by praying on your knees; God is not found in the temples and churches. God is found in intense living – a life of depth, depth and totality, and a death also of depth and totality. Live totally and die totally, and God is yours and truth is yours.

The second sutra:

Always meditate on specific objects.

First thing: by meditation Atisha never means concentration, remember. Concentration and meditation are polar opposites. Concentration narrows down your mind; it is focusing on one point. It includes only something and excludes everything else. Meditation is all-inclusive, it excludes nothing. It is not a narrowing down of the mind, it is an expansion of consciousness. Concentration is of the mind, meditation is of consciousness. Concentration is mind, meditation is no-mind. Concentration is a tension: you will be tired of it sooner or later. You cannot concentrate for a long time, it is effort. But one can be meditative twenty-four hours, because it is relaxation.

So remember, Atisha says:

Always meditate – he means always relax – *on specific objects*.

What does he mean by "specific objects"? Sadness, anger, greed, lust – the negatives; love, beauty, joy, freedom – the positives.

Begin with the negative, because you are living in the negative. When sad, meditate on it. Don't be in a hurry to get rid of it, don't be in a hurry to get occupied somewhere else so that you can forget it. That will be missing an opportunity, because sadness has its own depth, sadness has its own beauty, sadness has its own taste. Live it, relax into it, *be* it – and without any effort to escape, without any effort to get occupied somewhere else. Let it be there – enjoy! It is a flowering of your being. Sadness too is a flowering of your being.

And you will be surprised: if you can meditate on sadness, sadness will reveal its secrets to you – and they are of tremendous value. And sadness, once it has revealed its secrets to you, will disappear. Its work is done, its message delivered. And when sadness disappears, joy arises.

Joy arises only when sadness disappears out of meditation; there is no other way. Joy wells up when you have broken the ice of sadness that surrounds it. In fact, sadness is like the shell that surrounds the seed; it is protective, it is not the enemy. Once the seed has dropped its protection, is surrendered into the soil, the shell has died, only then the sprout is born.

It happens inside exactly like that. Meditate on anything negative, and slowly, slowly you will be simply taken by surprise – that sadness turns into joy, that anger turns into compassion, that greed turns into sharing, and so on, so forth. This is the science of inner alchemy: how to change the negative into the positive, how to change the base metal into gold.

But remember, never start with the positive because you don't know anything of the positive. And that's what is being taught by many people in the world – the "positive thinkers" they are called. They don't know anything about the inner alchemy. You don't begin with gold. If you already have gold, then what is the point of beginning at all? You don't need alchemy. You have to begin with base metal, the base metal has to be changed into gold. And the base metal is what you have, is what you are. Hell is what you are; it has to be transformed into heaven. Poison is available; it has to be transformed into nectar. Start with the negative.

All the buddhas have insisted: Go via *negativa*, because the negative brings the positive, and the negative brings the positive so easily. You don't drag it, you don't impose it upon yourself. If you start with the positive, as the so-called positive thinkers are teaching, you will become phony. What will you do? How will you start with joy? You may start smiling, but that smile will be painted: it will be just on the lips, not even skin-deep.

Start with the negative and you don't need to think about the positive at all. If you meditate on the negative, if you go deeply into it, to the deepest root of it, suddenly an explosion happens: the negative disappears and the positive has arrived. In fact it has always been there, hidden behind the negative. The negative was a shelter. The negative was needed because you were not yet worthy enough; the negative was needed so that you could become worthy enough to receive the positive.

The world is the negative pole of God. You need not renounce it, you have simply to be meditative in it. And one day you will see the world has disappeared and there is God and only God.

Bayazid of Bistam, a Sufi mystic, used to say in his later years, "First I used to ask people, 'Where is God?' And then one day it happened, I started asking people where God is not. One day there was no God and I was asking where he is; the next day there was only God, and I was asking 'Is there a place where he is not?'" The same world, but your eyes are different now; you are not the same.

Always meditate on specific objects.

Start with the negative and you will find the positive. Dig a well. First you find only earth, rocks, garbage. Slowly, slowly you come to the water. First it is very dirty, then it becomes purer and purer and purer. Exactly the same way one has to dig a well within one's own being. The beginning has to be negative, and the end is of itself positive. Your work has to be with the negative; the positive is the reward.

The third sutra:

You should have no concern for other factors.

Atisha says: While you are meditating on any specific subject – for example, sadness – then be it and forget everything else, as if nothing else exists. Just be totally sad. Savor it, taste it, let it sink in you, soak in it; just be a sponge.

That's what meditation is all about: just be a sponge. And when this mood is there, soak in it to your total capacity, to the optimum. Meditating on sadness, be it. Meditating simply means dropping the distinction between the observer and the observed; let the observer become the observed. Drop that old dichotomy of object and subject; disappear into the object of your meditation. Don't stand aloof, don't be a spectator. Secrets are not revealed to the spectators; secrets are revealed only to those who take a jump, who dive deep into something, people who don't hold themselves back.

And if you are totally sad, you are just on the verge of a discovery: sadness will evaporate. At a certain intensity, at a certain point, it simply evaporates as dewdrops evaporate in the morning sun. Once the heat has reached a certain intensity, the dewdrops disappear. Exactly like that the sadness will disappear, and suddenly, out of nowhere, joy has arrived, the guest has arrived. Now be a host to it. Now meditate on it, again be one with it. Now *be* joy. Don't stand aloof again. Don't start thinking, "Such a beautiful experience is happening, I am having the experience of joy." Don't start creating a distance between you and the joy. Be the joy. Dance it, sing it. Manifest it, be it!

Therefore, apply yourself to important matters.

Life is short, energy limited, very limited. And with this limited energy we have to find the unlimited; with this short life we have to find the eternal. A great task, a great challenge! So please, don't be concerned with unimportant matters.

What is important and what is unimportant? In Atisha's definition, or in the definition of all the buddhas, that which can be taken by death is unimportant and that which cannot be taken by death is important. Remember this definition, let this be a touchstone. You can judge anything immediately on this touchstone.

Have you seen the touchstone on which gold is judged? Let this be a touchstone for what is important: Is death going to take it away from you? Then it is not important. Money then is not important – useful, but not important, has no import. Power, prestige, respectability – death will come and efface them all, so why make so much fuss about them for the few days you are here? This is a caravanserai, an overnight stay, and by the morning we go.

Remember, only that which you can take with you when you leave the body is important. That means, except meditation, nothing is important. Except awareness, nothing is important, because only awareness cannot be taken away by death. Everything else will be snatched away, because everything else comes from without. Only awareness wells up within; that cannot be taken away. And the shadows of awareness – compassion, love – they cannot be taken away; they are intrinsic parts of awareness.

You will be taking with you only whatsoever awareness you have attained; that is your only real wealth. All else is "ill-th," not well-th.

Don't do things backwards.

This is a very significant sutra. I said to you in the beginning, people are upside down, in a permanent headstand posture. People are living backwards. Life moves forward, people live backwards in many, many ways.

The first meaning is: the heart has to be the master and the head the servant. But people are upside down: the head has become the master and the heart has become the servant. Logic rules, love is not even heeded. Personality has become more important than individuality. Personality is that which is conferred on you by others, individuality is that which is given to you by God. Personality is just a mask, persona; individuality is your uniqueness.

The society wants you to have beautiful personalities; the society wants you to have personalities which are comfortable for the society, convenient for the society. But the person is not the real thing, the individual is the real thing. The individual is not necessarily always comfortable to the society – in fact he is very inconvenient.

Jesus must have been very inconvenient; otherwise people don't kill, don't murder, don't crucify. If Jesus were really a personality, there would have been no trouble. He would have been a well-respected rabbi; the masses would have worshipped him, Jews would have remembered him as a great saint. But he was an individual. Individuals don't fit easily with others, individuals fit only with other individuals – and then too, the harmony is not imposed, enforced, the harmony is natural. But individuals don't fit with personalities. Light cannot be adjusted with darkness, that is the trouble.

Jesus may have been too much of a troublemaker, because he only worked for three years, and in only three years he created so much offense that people had to kill him. And Jews are not dangerous people, Jews are business-minded people. In fact for these two thousand years Jews have been crying and weeping deep down, because they killed Jesus and missed the opportunity of the greatest business possible. Christianity is the greatest firm on the earth! Jews must have been very jealous.

This time when it was going to happen they didn't miss. Sigmund Freud was a Jew; he started another business, psychoanalysis. This time they did not miss – all the important psychoanalysts are Jews. Now psychoanalysis is big business.

Jesus must have offended terribly; they could not tolerate him even for a single day. So too Socrates, Buddha and Mahavira – all individuals have suffered because of the phony society. The truth becomes intolerable. But though they may have suffered from the outside, from the inside they lived a blissful life, they lived an orgasmic life. Each moment of their life was an orgasm, a deep love affair with existence.

Unless you start living right-side-up, you will go on missing being an individual, you will never become authentic. The head is good, but only as a servant, not as a master. The heart has to be the master; feelings should dominate thoughts. And once this has happened then another step can be taken: being should dominate feelings.

These are the three layers: thoughts, the outermost; and being, the innermost; and feeling, in between, the bridge. Move from thoughts to feelings and from feelings to being, and start *living* from being. That does not mean that you don't have any feelings – you will have feelings, but those feelings will follow being; they will have the flavor of being, the heartbeat of being. It does not mean that you will not be able to think – you will be able to think far more intelligently, but now your thinking will have the juiciness of your feelings and the light of your being; your thoughts will be luminous.

Right now it is just the other way: thoughts are dominating feelings. And because of this domination, everything has gone topsy-turvy; because of this domination you cannot reach to the being, because thought is impotent to reach to the being. The inner is capable of reaching the outer, not vice versa. The center can touch the circumference, but not vice versa.

Future has become more important to you than the present. Present should be the central and everything should go round it. "That" has become more important than "this," "then" has become more important than "now." Change these values. Unless you change these values you are not sannyasins. Let "now" be more important, let "here" be more important, let "this" be more important.

Upanishads say, "Thou art that." I say to you: "Thou art this" – because "that" means far away, as if God is far away. "Thou art that" – no. "Thou art *this*": this very moment, this air that surrounds you, these chirping birds, this railway train passing by, these trees, this sun, these people, I and you, this silence where neither I am, nor you are. Thou art this. Let "this" become more important than "that" and your life will have a totally different quality to it.

Because life goes ahead and your mind is past-oriented, mind and life never meet. Mind goes backwards, lives backwards. Mind is a rear-view mirror. Use it when the occasion arises. Yes, the rear-view mirror in the car has some important function to fulfill. But if you become obsessed with the rear-view mirror, and you only look into the rear-view mirror and drive the car looking always into the rear-view mirror, then there is going to be danger. Then there are going to be accidents and accidents and nothing else.

And that's what has been happening to humanity. Look: three thousand years of history and you will find only accidents and accidents and accidents. In three thousand years we have fought five thousand wars. What more accidents do you want? And in these three thousand years, what have we done to the earth, to nature? We have destroyed the ecology. Now if something is not done immediately, the earth may become uninhabitable.

The earth has been poisoned by us, we are killing it. And we have to *live* on it, and we are turning it into a corpse! It has started stinking in many places. We have given nature and earth a cancer: nature has given us life, and we are giving death to nature in return. And the basic reason, the basic cause, is that we have been listening to the mind which moves backwards.

Mind means past. Mind has no idea of the present, cannot have any idea of the present. Mind only means that which has been lived, known, experienced – the accumulated past. It cannot have any contact with the present; it will have that contact only when the present is no more present and has become past. And life moves ahead. We live in the present and we move in the future, and mind never lives in the present and always clings to the past. This is the dichotomy, the greatest calamity. This is the knot that has to be cut.

Atisha says: *Don't do things backwards*.

Another meaning of this sutra is: remember life can be really lived only if you live it naturally. If you impose artificial commandments over it, you will destroy it.

For example, I told you: unless you love yourself you cannot love anybody else. Hence I say to you, be selfish, because only out of selfishness is altruism born. But you have been told again and again that you are worthless. You have been told that you have no value – that as you are, you are only worth condemnation; that as you are, you are bound to hell. You have to be worthy, you have to change, you have to become a saint, this and that. One thing is certain: that as you are, you are not of any worth. How can you love yourself?

And when a person cannot love himself and hates himself, he hates everybody else, he hates the whole world. By hating himself he becomes life-negative, and the person who is life-negative is life-destructive.

Your monks and nuns have all been life-negative; they have not affirmed life, they have not nourished life, they have not beautified life, they have not been a blessing to the world. They have been a curse! Your monasteries should disappear; we don't need monasteries. We certainly need sannyasins, but they should live *in* the world, part of the world, transforming the world. But the basic transformation that has to happen is that they should be lovers of themselves.

The person who does not love himself becomes a masochist, he starts torturing himself. And these masochists have been worshipped as saints down the ages. And a person who is a masochist cannot be anything else than a sadist too, because he who tortures himself would like everybody to be tortured. Torturing becomes his sacrifice to God.

So there have been masochists, there have been sadists. And because in life you cannot find any quality purely, so you will not find masochists and sadists separate. It is almost always the case that the same person is both: sado-masochist – everybody is like that. You have been conditioned by your religions in such a way that you are against yourself and against others. On the one hand you torture yourself with beautiful rationalizations, and on the other hand you torture others, again with beautiful rationalizations.

Life has become a torture chamber, a concentration camp; it is no more a celebration. It should be a celebration. If nature is allowed to take its own course, it is *bound* to be a celebration.

So the last thing to be remembered:

Don't do things backwards.

Go with nature, don't try to go upstream. Go with the stream of life. Go with the river, don't push the river. Don't try to conquer nature – you cannot; you can only destroy it, and destroy yourself in the effort. The very idea of conquering nature is violent, ugly. Victory is not going to be against nature, victory is possible only with nature.

Don't vacillate.

Your mind will vacillate. Mind is vacillation, mind is either/or, mind is always in that space of "to be or not to be." If you really want to grow, mature, if you really want to know what this life is all about, don't vacillate. Commit, involve! Involve yourself with life, get committed to life, don't remain a spectator. Don't go on thinking whether to do or not – "Should I do this or that?" You can go on vacillating your whole life, and the more you vacillate, the more trained you become in vacillation.

Life is for those who know how to commit – how to say yes to something, how to say no to something decisively, categorically. Once you have categorically said yes or no to something, then you can take a jump, then you can dive deep into the ocean.

People are just sitting on the fence. Millions of people are fence-sitters – this way or that, just waiting for the opportunity to come. And the opportunity will never come, because it has already come, it is there!

My own suggestion is that even if sometimes it happens that you commit to the wrong thing, even then it is good to commit, because the day you will know it is wrong you can get out of it. At least you would have learned one thing: that it is wrong, and never to get into anything like that again. It is a great experience; it brings you closer to truth.

Why do people vacillate so much? – because from the very childhood you have been told not to commit any mistakes. That is one of the greatest teachings of all the societies all over the world – and very dangerous, very harmful. Teach children to commit as many mistakes as possible, with only one condition: don't commit the same mistake again, that's all. And they will grow, and they will experience more and more, and they will not vacillate. Otherwise a trembling…and time is passing by, out of your hands, and you are vacillating.

I see many people standing on the shore vacillating, whether to take the jump or not. Here it happens every day.

Just a few days ago, one young man came to me. For three years he has been vacillating whether to take sannyas or not. I said, "Decide either yes or no, and be finished with it! And I am not saying decide yes, I am only saying decide. No is as good as yes. But wasting three years? If you had taken sannyas three years ago," I told him, "by this time you would have known whether it is worth it or not; at least one thing would have been decided. Vacillating three years, nothing has been decided. You are in the same space, and three years have gone by."

Atisha says: *Don't vacillate. Train as though cut off.*

This is the secret of meditation, the last sutra today.

Train as though cut off.

Mind is vacillation. The discipline of a meditator is to become so watchful of the mind, so alert to the mind and its stupidities – its hesitations, its tremblings, its vacillations – to become so watchful that you are cut off.

That is the whole purpose of watching: watching cuts you off.

Watch anything in the mind, and you are cut off. Watching is a sword.

If a thought is moving in your mind, just watch it – and suddenly you will see the thought is there, you are here, and there is no bridge left. Don't watch, and you become identified with the thought, you become it; watch, and you are not it. Mind possesses you because you have forgotten how to watch. Learn it.

Just looking at a roseflower, watch it; or at the stars, or the people passing on the road, sit by the side and watch. And then slowly, slowly close your eyes and see the inner traffic moving – thousands of thoughts, desires, dreams, passing by. It is always rush hour there.

Just watch as somebody watches a river flowing by, sitting on the bank.

Just watch – and watching, you will become aware that you are not it.

Mind is being identified with it. No-mind is being disidentified with it. Don't be a mind, because in fact you are not a mind. Then who are you? You are consciousness. You are that watchfulness, you are witnessing, you are that pure observation, that mirrorlike quality that reflects everything but never becomes identified with anything.

Remember, I am not saying that you are conscious. I am saying you are consciousness: that is your true identity. The day one knows, "I am consciousness," one has come to know the ultimate, because the moment you know, "I am consciousness," you also know all is consciousness, on different planes. The rock is conscious in its own way, and the tree is conscious in its own way, and the animals and the people. Everybody is conscious in his own way, and consciousness is a multifaceted diamond.

The day you know, "I am consciousness," you have known the universal truth, you have come to the goal.

Socrates says, "Man, know thyself." That is the teaching of all the buddhas: Know thyself. How are you going to know yourself? If mind remains too much and goes on clamoring around you, goes on making great noise, you will never hear the still small voice within. You have to become disidentified with the mind.

George Gurdjieff used to say, "My whole teaching can be condensed into one word, and that is disidentification." He is right. Not only his teaching can be condensed into one word, all the teaching of all the masters can be condensed into one word: disidentification. Don't be identified with the mind.

That is the meaning of Atisha. He says:

Train as though cut off.

Discipline yourself into deep awareness, so that you are cut off from the mind. If you can have only a single moment of this cut-offness, the first satori has happened. In the second satori you become capable of cutting off from the mind whenever you want. In the first satori it happens accidentally: meditating, watching, one day it happens almost like an accident. You were groping in the dark and you have stumbled upon the door. The first satori is a stumbling on the door.

The second satori is becoming perfectly aware where the door is, and whenever you want to, you can go to the door – whenever you want to go. Even in the marketplace, surrounded by all the clamor of the market, you can go to the door. Suddenly you can become cut off.

And the third satori is when you are absolutely cut off, so that even if you want to join with the mind, you cannot. You can use it like a machine, separate from you, but even in your deep sleep you are not identified with it.

These are the three satoris, three samadhis. First, accidental stumbling; second, becoming more deliberate, conscious in reaching to the door; and third, becoming attuned so deeply with the door that you never lose track of it, that it is always there, always open. This is the state called satori in Japan, samadhi in India. In English it is translated as ecstasy. That word is beautiful; literally it means "standing out." Ecstasy means standing out, standing out of the mind.

Atisha's last sutra: *Train as though cut off*, is exactly the same as the meaning of the word *ecstasy* – so cut off from the mind that you are standing out, that mind is there but you are not it. Some people have also started translating samadhi not as ecstasy but as instasy. That too is beautiful, because it is not standing out; it is standing out of the mind if you think of the mind, but if you think of consciousness then it is standing in.

As far as mind is concerned ecstasy is the right word, but as far as consciousness is concerned instasy is far better. But both are aspects of the same thing: standing out of the mind is standing in consciousness, knowing that "I am not mind" is knowing "I am consciousness, *aham brahmasmi*." That is the meaning of the Upanishad saying, I am God, I am consciousness.

Enough for today.

Chapter 22
The Greatest Joke There Is

? **What is innocence, what is beauty?**

To live in the moment is innocence, to live without the past is innocence, to live without conclusions is innocence, to function out of the state of not knowing is innocence. And the moment you function out of such tremendous silence which is not burdened by any past, out of such tremendous stillness which knows nothing, the experience that happens is beauty.

Whenever you feel beauty – in the rising sun, in the stars, in the flowers, or in the face of a woman or a man – wherever and whenever you feel beauty, watch. And one thing will always be found: you had functioned without mind, you had functioned without any conclusion, you had simply functioned spontaneously. The moment gripped you, and the moment gripped you so deeply that you were cut off from the past.

And when you are cut off from the past you are cut off from the future automatically, because past and future are two aspects of the same coin; they are not separate, and they are not separable either. You can toss a coin: sometimes it is heads, sometimes it is tails, but the other part is always there, hiding behind.

Past and future are two aspects of the same coin. The name of the coin is mind. When the whole coin is dropped, that dropping is innocence. Then you don't know who you are, then you don't know what is; there is no knowledge.

But you *are*, existence is, and the meeting of these two is-nesses – the small is-ness of you, meeting with the infinite is-ness of existence – that meeting, that merger, is the experience of beauty.

Innocence is the door; through innocence you enter into beauty. The more innocent you become, the more existence becomes beautiful. The more knowledgeable you are, the more and more existence is ugly, because you start functioning from conclusions, you start functioning from knowledge.

The moment you know, you destroy all poetry. The moment you know, and *think* that you know, you have created a barrier between yourself and that which is. Then everything is distorted. Then you don't hear with your ears, you translate. Then you don't see with your eyes, you interpret. Then you don't experience with your heart, you *think* that you experience. Then all possibility of meeting with existence in immediacy, in intimacy, is lost. You have fallen apart.

This is the original sin. And this is the whole story, the biblical story of Adam and Eve eating the fruit of the tree of knowledge. Once they have eaten the fruit of knowledge they are driven out of paradise. Not that somebody drove them out, not that God ordered them to get out of paradise, they themselves fell. Knowing they were no more innocent, knowing they were separate from existence, knowing they were egos…knowing created such a barrier, an iron barrier.

You ask me, "What is innocence?"

Vomit knowledge! The fruit of the tree of knowledge has to be vomited. That's what meditation is all about. Throw it out of your system: it is poison, pure poison. Live without knowledge, knowing that "I don't know." Function out of this state of not knowing and you will know what beauty is.

Socrates knows what beauty is, because he functions out of this state of not knowing. There is a knowledge that does not know, and there is an ignorance that knows. Become ignorant like Socrates and then a totally different quality enters your being: you become a child again, it is a rebirth. Your eyes are full of wonder again, each and everything that surrounds surprises. The bird on the wing, and you are thrilled! The sheer joy of seeing the bird on the wing – and it is as if you are on the wing.

The dewdrop slipping from a lotus leaf and the morning sun shining on it and creating a small rainbow around it, and the moment is so overwhelming…the dewdrop slipping off the leaf, just on the verge of meeting with the infinite, disappearing into the lake – and it is as if you start slipping, as if your drop starts slipping into the ocean of God.

In the moment of innocence, not knowing, the difference between the observer and the observed evaporates. You are no more separate from that which you are seeing, you are no more separate from that which you are hearing.

Listening to me, right now, you can function in two ways. One is the way of knowledge: chattering inside yourself, judging, evaluating, constantly thinking whether what I am saying is right or wrong, whether it fits with your theories or not, whether it is logical or illogical, scientific or unscientific, Christian or Hindu, whether you can go with it or not, whether you can swallow it or not, a thousand and one thoughts clamoring inside your mind, the inner talk, the inner traffic – this is one way of listening. But then you are listening from so far away that I will not be able to reach you.

I go on trying but I will not be able to reach you. You are really on some other planet: you are not here, you are not now. You are a Hindu, you are a Christian, you are a Mohammedan, you are a communist, but you are not here now. The Bible is there between me and you, or the Koran or the Gita. And I grope for you but I come across the barrier of the Koran, I grope for you but there is a queue of priests between me and you. This is the way of knowledge, this is the way of remaining deaf, of remaining blind, of remaining heart-less.

There is another way of listening too: just listening, nothing between me and you. Then there is immediacy, contact, meeting, communion. Then you don't interpret, because you are not worried whether it is right or wrong. Nothing is right, nothing is wrong. In that moment of innocence one does not evaluate. There is nothing to evaluate with, no criterion, no a priori knowledge, no already-arrived conclusion, nothing to compare with. You can only listen, just as one listens to the running sound of water in the hills, or a solo flute player in the forest, or somebody playing on the guitar. You listen.

But the person who has come to listen as a critic will not listen. The person who has come simply to listen, not as a critic but to enjoy the moment, will be able to listen to the music. What is there to understand in music? There is nothing to understand. There is something to *taste*, certainly; there is something to drink and be drunk with, certainly, but what is there to understand?

But the critic, he is not there to taste, he is not there to drink – he is there to understand. He is not listening to the music because he is so full of mathematics. He is continuously criticizing, thinking. He is not innocent; he knows too much, hence he will miss the beauty of it. He may arrive at some stupid conclusions, but he will miss the whole moment. And the moment is momentous!

If you can listen, *just* listen, if you can see, *just* see, then this very moment you will know what innocence is.

And I am not here only to explain to you what innocence is, I am here to give a taste of it. Have a cup of tea! I offer it to you, each moment it is being offered. Sip it – feel the warmth of the moment and the music of it and the silence and the love that overflows. Be encompassed with it. Disappear for a moment with your mind – watching, judging, criticizing, believing, disbelieving, for, against. For a moment be just an openness, and you will know what innocence is. And in that you will know what beauty is.

Beauty is an experience that happens in innocence, the flower that blooms in innocence. Jesus says, "Unless you are like small children you will not enter into my kingdom of God."

Sometimes I believe you and sometimes I disbelieve you. How long am I to live in this duality? How am I to drop this duality and unite? Please explain.

Who has told you to believe in me? If you believe you will disbelieve too. Nobody can believe without disbelieving. Let it be settled once for all: nobody can believe without disbelieving. Every belief is a cover-up for disbelief.

Belief is only the circumference of the center called doubt; because the doubt is there you create belief. The doubt hurts, it is like a wound, it is painful. Because the doubt is a wound it hurts; it makes you feel your inner emptiness, your inner ignorance. You want to cover it up. But hiding your wound behind a roseflower – do you think it is going to help? Do you think the roseflower will be able to help the wound disappear? Just the contrary! Sooner or later the roseflower will start stinking of the wound. The wound will not disappear because of the roseflower; in fact the roseflower will disappear because of the wound.

And you may be able to deceive somebody else who is looking from the outside – your neighbors may think that there is no wound, but a roseflower – but how can you deceive yourself? That is impossible. Nobody can deceive himself; deep down somewhere you will know, you are bound to know, that the wound exists and you are hiding it behind a roseflower. And you know the roseflower is arbitrary: it has not grown in you, you have plucked it from the outside, while the wound has grown inside you; you have not plucked it from the outside.

The child brings the doubt in him – an inner doubt, that is natural. It is because of the doubt he inquires, it is because of the doubt he questions. Go with a child for a morning walk in the woods, and he brings so many questions that you feel bored, that you want to tell him to shut up. But he goes on asking.

From where are these questions coming? They are natural to the child. Doubt is an inner potential; it is the only way the child will be able to inquire and search and seek. Nothing is wrong about it. Your priests have been telling you a lie, that there is something wrong about doubt. There is nothing wrong about it. It is natural, and it has to be accepted and respected. When you respect your doubt, it is no longer a wound; when you reject it, it becomes a wound.

Let it be very clear: doubt itself is not a wound. It is a tremendous help, because it will make you an adventurer, explorer. It will take you to the farthest star in search of truth, it will make you a pilgrim. It is not unhealthy to have doubt. Doubt is beautiful, doubt is innocent, doubt is natural. But the priests have condemned it down the ages. Because of their condemnation, the doubt which could have become a flowering of trust has become just a stinking wound. Condemn anything and it becomes a wound, reject anything and it becomes a wound.

My teaching is: the first thing to be done, is not to try to believe. Why? If doubt is there, doubt is there! There is no need to hide it. In fact, allow it, help it, let it become a great quest. Let it become a thousand and one questions – and ultimately you will see it is not the questions that are relevant, it is the question mark! Doubt is not a search for belief; doubt simply is groping for the mystery, making every effort to understand the un-understandable, to comprehend the incomprehensible – a groping effort.

And if you go on searching, seeking, without stuffing yourself with borrowed beliefs, two things will happen. One: you will never have any disbelief. Remember, doubt and disbelief are not synonymous. Disbelief happens only when you have already believed, when you have already deceived yourself and others. Disbelief comes only when belief has entered in; it is a shadow of belief.

All believers are disbelievers – they may be Hindus, they may be Christians, they may be Jainas. I know all of them: all believers are disbelievers, because belief brings disbelief, it is the shadow of belief. Can you believe without disbelieving? It is impossible; it cannot be done in the nature of things. If you want to disbelieve, the first requirement is to believe. Can you believe without any disbelief entering from the back door? Or can you disbelieve without having any belief in the first place? Believe in God, and immediately the disbelief comes in. Believe in afterlife and disbelief arises. Disbelief is secondary, belief is primary.

What you want to do is what millions of people in the world want to do: they don't want the disbelief, they want only the belief. I cannot help, nobody can help. If you only are interested in belief, you will have to suffer the disbelief also. You will remain divided, you will remain split, you will remain schizophrenic. You cannot have the feel of organic unity; you yourself have barred it from happening.

What's my suggestion? First, drop believing. Let beliefs be dropped, they are all rubbish! Trust in doubt, that's my suggestion; don't try to hide it. Trust in doubt. That is the first thing to bring in your being: trust in your doubt. And see the beauty of it, how beautifully trust has come in.

I am not saying believe, I am saying *trust*. The doubt is a natural gift; it must be from God – from where else can it be? You bring doubt with you: trust in it, trust in your questioning. And don't be in a hurry to stuff and hide it with borrowed beliefs from the outside – from the parents, from the priests, from the politicians, from the society, the church. Your doubt is something beautiful because it is yours; it is something beautiful because it is authentic. Out of this authentic doubt some day will grow the flower of authentic trust. It will be an inner growth, it will not be an imposition from the outside.

That is the difference between belief and trust: trust grows inside you, in your interiority, in your subjectivity. Just as doubt is inner, so is trust. And only the inner can transform the inner.

Belief is from the outside; it can't help because it can't reach to the innermost core of your being, and it is there that the doubt is.

From where to start? Trust your doubt. That's my way of bringing trust in. Don't believe in God, don't believe in the soul, don't believe in the afterlife. Trust in your doubt, and immediately a conversion has started. Trust is such a powerful force that even if you trust in your doubt you have brought light in. And doubt is like darkness. That small trust in doubt will start changing your inner world, the inner scene.

And question! Why be afraid? Why be so cowardly? Question – question all the buddhas, question me, because if there is truth, truth is not afraid of your questioning. If buddhas are true, they are true; you need not believe in them. Go on doubting them…and still one day you will see trust has arisen.

When you doubt, and you go on in doubting to the very end, to the very logical end, sooner or later you will stumble upon a truth. Doubt is groping in darkness, but the door exists. If Buddha could get to the door, if Jesus could get to it, if Atisha could get to it, if I can get to it, why can't you? Everybody is capable of getting to the door – but you are afraid of groping, so you sit in your dark corner believing in somebody who has found the door. You have not seen that somebody, you have heard about him from others who have heard it from others, and so on, so forth.

How do you believe in Jesus? Why? You have not seen Jesus! And even if you had seen him you would have missed. The day he was crucified, thousands had gathered to see him, and do you know what they were doing? They were spitting on his face! You may have been in that crowd, because that crowd was not different at all. Man has not changed.

Darwin says man has evolved out of the monkey. Maybe, but since then evolution seems to have stopped. It must have been an accident, some monkey must have fallen from the tree and could not get back. Maybe he was fractured or became afraid of falling again, so he started living on the earth. When you live in the trees you can live with all your four hands or four legs, but when you live on the earth you have to stand on two legs.

Because the monkey was able to look all over the place from the trees…he had always lived that way, looking all over the place; there was no danger, he could see far away. Once he was on the ground, living on all fours was dangerous. He could not see all around, he could see only just two, three feet in front of himself, and he was afraid – that was not his way of living. He had lived always in a kind of security in the trees, looking all over the place. Wherever the enemy was, he was aware; he could protect himself. Out of sheer fear he had to stand on two legs on the ground. Just think of that hilarious situation: a monkey trying to stand on two legs! All the monkeys must have laughed uproariously, "Look at that fool, what he is trying to do!"

Since then evolution seems to have stopped. Nothing has happened since then. Man has lived almost the same way, his mind has not changed. Yes, things have changed: we live in better houses with better plumbing…I am not talking about India!

Some sannyasin has just asked me, "Osho, You say life is beautiful. I could have believed you – but two things, women and Indian plumbing, they don't allow me to believe in it."

Women can be changed – but Indian plumbing? No!

We have better roads and better vehicles to carry you from one place to another, great technology – man has landed on the moon – but man has not changed. That's why I say many of you must have been in the crowd that was spitting on Jesus, and many of you must have been in the crowd that was witnessing Mansoor's murder, who were throwing stones at the murdered mystic. You have not changed.

How can you believe in Jesus? You were spitting on his face when he was alive, and now you believe in him, after two thousand years? It is just a desperate effort to hide your doubt. Why do you believe in Jesus?

If one thing can be dropped from the Jesus story, the whole of Christianity will disappear. If one thing, only one thing, the phenomenon of resurrection – that after being crucified and remaining dead three days, Jesus came back again – if this part can be dropped, the whole of Christianity will disappear. You believe in Jesus because you are afraid of death, and he seems to be the only man who has come back again, who has defeated death.

Christianity became the greatest religion in the world. Buddhism could not become that great, for the simple reason that the fear of death helps people to believe in Christ more than in Buddha. In fact to believe in Buddha needs guts, because Buddha says, "I teach you total death." This small death – he is not satisfied with it. He says: This small death won't do, you will be coming back again. I teach you the total death, the ultimate death. Annihilation I teach, so that you will never come back again, so that you will disappear, you will be diffused in existence, you won't *be* any more, any longer; not even a trace will be left behind.

In India Buddhism disappeared, completely disappeared. Such a great, so-called religious country, and Buddhism completely disappeared. Why? People believe in religions which teach that you will live after death, that the soul is immortal. Buddha was saying that the only thing worth realizing is that you are not. Buddhism could not survive in India, because it didn't give you a cover-up for your fear.

Buddha did not say to people, "Believe in me." Hence his teaching disappeared from this country, because people want to believe. People don't want truth, they want belief. Belief is cheap. Truth is dangerous, arduous, difficult; one has to pay for it. One has to seek and search, and there is no guarantee that you will find it, there is no guarantee that there is any truth anywhere. It may not be at all; the goal may not exist.

People want belief, and Buddha said…his last message to the world was "*appa dipo bhav*; be a light unto yourself." He had said this because his disciples were crying. Ten thousand sannyasins surrounding him…of course they were sad, and tears were falling; their master was leaving. And Buddha said to them, "Don't cry. Why are you crying?"

One of the disciples, Ananda, said, "Because you are leaving us, because you were our only hope, because we had hoped and hoped long that it is through you we will attain to truth."

It was to answer Ananda that Buddha said, "Don't be worried about that. I cannot give you truth; nobody else can give it to you, it is not transferable. But you can attain it on your own. Be a light unto yourself."

The same is my attitude. You need not believe in me. I don't want believers here, I want seekers, and the seeker is a totally different phenomenon. The believer is not a seeker. The believer does not want to seek, that's why he believes. The believer wants to avoid seeking, that's why he believes. The believer wants to be delivered, saved, he needs a savior. He is always in search of a messiah – somebody who can eat for him, chew for him, digest for him. But if I eat, your hunger is not going to be satisfied. Nobody can save you except yourself.

I need seekers here, inquirers, not believers. Believers are the most mediocre people in the world, the least intelligent people in the world. So forget about belief, you are creating trouble for yourself. You start believing in me, then disbelief arises – it is bound to arise, because I am not here to fit with your expectations.

Mohan Bharti comes from a Jaina family. It took great courage for him to become a sannyasin of mine. But the traditional mind is there; you cannot so easily get rid of it. So very deep down in the unconscious there are lurking expectations of how I should be. Then disbelief is bound to arise.

I live in my own way, I don't consider you. I don't consider anybody at all – because if you start considering others you can't live your life authentically. Consider and you will become phony. I know if I can live in a grass hut, thousands and thousands of Indians will come to worship me. If I can live naked, millions will think of me as a saint, a great saint. If I can eat only once a day, and that too by begging, the whole country will be happy with me. But I can't do these things, they are not natural to me.

It may have been natural for Mahavira to be naked; hence he was naked. And remember, people were not happy, because the people who were surrounding Mahavira had believed in Krishna and Rama, and they were not naked. So they were expecting Mahavira to behave like Krishna; they were expecting a flute, and he had none. They must have searched – in fact there was nowhere to search, he was standing naked! He was not fulfilling their expectations. Where is the crown of peacock feathers? They had known Krishna; he was a totally different individual, a totally different expression of existence. Very colorful he was, a rainbow, with peacock feathers as a crown, with beautiful flowers as garlands, the dress, the garments made of the best silk possible.

And he had ornaments on his body, diamonds, gold, ornaments like women. In those days, men used to have ornaments. That seems to be more natural, because in nature the male animal is more ornamental than the female. The male peacock has those beautiful feathers, the female peacock has no beautiful feathers at all. It is enough for her to be the female; that is enough. The male has to substitute something because he is not female: he has to look beautiful, he has to be ornamental. The male peacock dances, remember, not the female. That dance is a substitute. He wants to look as beautiful as possible – he is afraid he may not be chosen!

It is the male cuckoo that gives the call; that beautiful sound, that song, comes from the male cuckoo. The female simply sits, waits; just to be female is enough. Look in nature and you will be surprised: female animals are not ornamental at all. In the ancient days it was so with men too. The female is beautiful as she is, nature has made her beautiful.

So in those days of Krishna, five thousand years back, the male used to have beautiful garments, flowers, ornaments, and Hindus were accustomed to that idea. And then came Mahavira, standing naked, with no ornaments, no garments, nothing to beautify his body, just utterly naked. Not only that, he used to pull out his own hair. He must have looked a little crazy.

Only crazy people pull out their hair; when madness possesses you, you pull out your hair. He was pulling it for a certain different reason – because hair gives a certain beauty.

And the people who don't have hair, the bald people like me, have to create beautiful theories! They say that bald people are the most sexual. The whole theory is that people go bald in three ways. A few people start from the front: they are the most sexual. A few people start from the back: they are not sexual, they only think they are sexual. And a few people start in the middle: it is better not to say anything about them! Hair gives beauty. Bald people must feel something has to be substituted, and they have created the rumor all over the world that bald people are very sexual.

Krishna and Rama were very aesthetic people, and Mahavira was totally different, very austere. But that was natural to him; he was beautiful in his nakedness, as beautiful as Krishna was with all his garments and ornaments. In fact, ancient scriptures say that Mahavira may have been the most beautiful man in the world. That may have been one of the reasons why he went naked. If you have a well-proportioned body, if your body is really beautiful, who cares about clothes?

Ugly people are very much worried about clothes, because that's how somehow they manage. Now, a woman who has an ugly body will not be ready to go naked on the beach. She will be very much against beaches; she will be very much against going naked, nude people and nudist camps. The only thing she is really against is that she knows that if she goes naked it will be a really horrible scene!

Whenever a country becomes beautiful, people start becoming nude. Whenever it has happened that a race has become beautiful, people start going nude. There is no need to hide. We hide only the ugly part. But clothes are helpful to people who don't have beautiful bodies. You may not have a beautiful chest, manly chest, but you can wear stuffed coats and they can give a feel – at least to the outsiders.

A man was searching on a nude beach…he was searching for his wife. A policeman was looking at him. He became suspicious and asked him, "What are you searching for? And for hours you have been searching…searching for some hidden treasure?"

He said, "No, just a sunken chest."

You can have stuffed clothes which can give a shape to your body.

Mahavira must have been beautiful – that's my feeling too – must have been a rare, beautiful man. But it was not expected, hence people were against him. No village, no town, was hospitable to him. He was driven away from villages and towns, stones were thrown at him, wild dogs were released behind him so that they could chase him out of the town – just because he was nude! He was not doing any harm to anybody; the most harmless person you can think of, he would not even do harm to the ants. In the night he used to sleep only on one side. He would not change from one side to the other, because who knows, an ant may have crawled behind him in the night and if he turns over the ant may be killed. He would not walk in the night, because some insect may be killed. He would not walk on grass, on lawns; he would not walk in the rainy season, because so many insects are born in the rainy season.

Such a harmless man, but yet people misbehaved with him. And the only reason? – he was not fulfilling their expectations.

No buddha has ever fulfilled anybody's expectations. In fact that's why he becomes a buddha: he never compromises. If you have any expectations about me you will again and again be in trouble, because I don't consider your expectations.

George Gurdjieff used to say to his disciples one of the most fundamental things: "Don't consider others, otherwise you will never grow." And that's what is happening in the whole world, everybody is considering others: "What will my mother think? What will my father think? What will the society think? What will my wife, my husband…?" What to say of the parents – even parents are afraid of children! They think, "What will our children think?"

One man came to me and he said, "Since I have become a sannyasin, my children think that I have gone crazy, they laugh at me. Nothing hurts me more than this, that my own children… they look at me from the window, they don't come inside the room! They whisper to each other – I don't know what, but they talk about me. They think something has gone wrong."

People are considering each other – and then there are millions of people to consider. If you go on considering each and everybody, you will never be an individual, you will be just a hodgepodge. So many compromises made, you would have committed suicide long ago.

It is said people die at the age of thirty and are buried at the age of seventy. Death happens very early – I think thirty is also not right, death happens even earlier. Somewhere near twenty-one, when the law and the state recognize you as a citizen, that is the moment when a person dies. In fact, that's why they recognize you as a citizen: now you are no more dangerous, now you are no more wild, now you are no more raw. Now everything has been put right in you, fixed right in you; now you have been adjusted to the society. That's what it means when the nation gives you the right to vote: the nation can trust now that your intelligence has been destroyed – you can vote. There is no fear about you; you are a citizen, you are a civilized man. You are no more a man then, you are a citizen.

My own observation is, people die nearabout twenty-one. Then whatsoever is, is a post-humous existence. On the graves we should start writing three dates: birth, death, and posthumous death.

First you believe in me – that's where you go wrong, don't believe in me – and then you disbelieve. Then you get caught up in the conflict, and the problem arises, What to do? How to get out of this duality? You create the duality and then you want to get out of it. I will not tell you how to get out of it, I will tell you how not to get into it. Why in the first place should you get into it?

They define a witty person as one who knows how to get out of difficulties, and the wise one as one who knows how never to get into them. Be wise. Why not cut the very root? Don't believe in me, be a fellow traveler with me. That's what my sannyasins are: they are not believers, they are fellow travelers. They are walking with me into the unknown; they are walking with their own feet, on their own. I don't carry you on my shoulders, I don't want you to be cripples your whole life; I don't give you any crutches, you have to walk on your own.

Yes, I know the way, I have walked on it, I know all the pitfalls on the way. I will go on shouting loudly at you, "Beware, there is a pitfall!" But still it is up to you to decide whether to fall into it or not. If you fall into it I don't condemn you, I respect your freedom. If you don't fall into it I don't reward you, I take it for granted this is how an intelligent person behaves. So there is no reward with me and no punishment with me, there is no hell and no heaven, there is no sin, no virtue. This is my joy – to share. If it is your joy to share it with me, good; we can go along as far as you decide to come along with me. The moment you want to have a separate way, it's perfectly good, we will depart with a good-bye.

There is no need to believe in me, there is no need to cling onto me. And then there is no question of disbelief, and the duality never arises, and you need not find a way to get out of it. Please don't get into it.

? What is exactly your attitude about death?

A mystic who was being led to the gallows saw a big crowd running on before him. "Don't be in such a hurry," he said to them. "I can assure you, nothing will happen without me."

That's my attitude towards death: it is the greatest joke there is. Death has never happened, cannot happen in the very nature of things, because life is eternal. Life cannot end; it is not a thing, it is a process. It is not something that begins and ends; it has no beginning and no end. You have always been here in different forms, and you will be here in different forms, or, ultimately, formless. That's how a buddha lives in existence: he becomes formlessness. He disappears from the gross forms totally.

Death is not there, it is a lie – but it appears very real. It only appears very real, it is not. It appears so because you believe too much in your separate existence. It is in believing that you are separate from existence that you give reality to death. Drop this idea of being separate from existence, and death disappears.

If I am one with existence, how can I die? Existence was there before me and will be there after me. I am just a ripple in the ocean, and the ripple comes and goes, the ocean remains, abides. Yes, you will not be there – as you are you will not be there. This form will disappear, but the one who is abiding in this form will go on abiding, either in other forms or ultimately in formlessness.

Start feeling one with existence, because that's how it is. That's why my insistence again and again to let the distinction between the observer and the observed disappear, as many times during the day as possible. Find a few moments – whenever you can find, wherever you can find – and just let this distinction and difference between the observer and the observed disappear. Become the tree you are seeing and become the cloud you are looking at, and slowly, slowly you will start laughing at death.

This mystic who was being led to the gallows must have seen the utter lie of death, he could joke about his own death. He was being led to the gallows, he saw a big crowd running on before him; they were going to see the crucifixion....

People are very much interested in such things. If they hear that somebody is being murdered publicly, thousands of people will gather to see it. Why this attraction? Deep down you are all murderers, and this is a vicarious way to enjoy it. That's why films about murder and violence, detective novels, are so much in vogue, popular. Unless a film has murder in it and suicide in it and obscene sex in it, it never becomes a box office hit. It never succeeds, it fails. Why? – because nobody is interested in anything else. These are deep desires in your being. Seeing them on the screen, there is a vicarious enjoyment as if you are doing it; you become identified with the characters in the film or in the novel.

Now this mystic was being led to the gallows. He saw a big crowd running on before him. "Don't be in such a hurry," he said to them. "I can assure you nothing will happen without me. You can walk easily, slowly, there is no hurry. I am the person they are going to kill, and nothing is going to happen without me."

This is my attitude about death. Laugh! Let laughter be your attitude about death. It is a cosmic lie created by man himself, created by the ego, by selfconsciousness.

That's why in nature no other animal, bird, tree is afraid of death. Only man, and he makes so much fuss out of it…his whole life trembling. Death is coming closer, and because of death he cannot allow himself to live totally. How can you live if you are so afraid? Life is possible only without fear. Life is possible only with love, not with fear. And death creates fear.

And who is the culprit? God has not created death, it is man's own invention. Create the ego, and you have created the other side of it – death.

? I cannot believe that I am. What is wrong with me?

It is impossible. It is impossible to say that "I am not" – because even to say that you have to be. One of the great philosophers of the West, the modern father of philosophy in the West, was Descartes. His whole life was an inquiry for something indubitable, which cannot be doubted. He wanted a foundation, and a foundation which cannot be doubted; only then the right edifice can be built upon it. He searched, very sincerely he searched.

God can be doubted, the other life can be doubted, even the existence of the other can be doubted. I am here, you can see me; but who knows, you may be dreaming, because in dream also you see the other, and in dream the other seems as real as in the so-called real life. You never doubt in your dream. In fact, in the real life you may doubt sometimes, but in the dream it is indubitable.

Chuang Tzu is reported to have said, "My greatest problem is one which I am unable to solve. The problem is that one night I dreamed that I am a butterfly. Since that night I am confused."

A friend asked, "What is your confusion? Everybody dreams, there is nothing special about it. Why be so worried about it, that you are a butterfly in a dream? So what?"

He said, "Since that day I am puzzled, I cannot decide who I am. If Chuang Tzu can become a butterfly in the dream, who knows – when the butterfly goes to sleep, she may dream that she is Chuang Tzu. Then am I really Chuang Tzu or just a butterfly dreaming? If this is possible, that Chuang Tzu can become a butterfly, then that too is possible. A butterfly resting in the afternoon sun underneath the shadow of a tree may be dreaming that she has become a Chuang Tzu. Now who am I? – a butterfly dreaming, or Chuang Tzu dreaming?"

It is difficult. Even to decide the other is, is difficult, very difficult.

Descartes searched long. Then he stumbled upon only one fact, and that fact is "I am." That cannot be doubted, that's impossible, because even to say, "I am not," you are required.

Wife: "I think I hear burglars. Are you awake?"
Husband: "No!"

Now, if you are not awake, how can you say "No"? That "No" presupposes that you are awake.

You ask me: "I cannot believe that I am."

It is not a question of belief; you *are*. Who is this who cannot believe? Who is this who is full of doubt? Can doubt exist without a doubter? Can dream exist without a dreamer? If the dream is there, one thing is absolutely certain: the dreamer is there. If the doubt is there, then one thing is absolutely certain: the doubter is there.

This is the foundation of all religions: "I am." It need not be believed – there is no question of belief, it is a simple fact. Close your eyes and try to deny it. You cannot deny it, because in the very denial you will be proving it.

But this age is the age of doubt. And remember, any age that is the age of doubt is a great age. When great doubts arise in the human heart, great things are bound to happen. When great doubts arise, great challenges arise.

Now this is the greatest challenge for you – to go deeper into this doubter who doubts even the existence of his own being. Go into this doubt, go into this doubter. Let this become your meditation, and reaching deeper into it you will see that this is the only indubitable fact in existence, the only truth which cannot be doubted.

And once you have felt it, trust arises.

? Are all minds Jewish?

There is some truth in it, it is so. To be a Jew has nothing to do with any race. Jewishness is really a quality – the quality that calculates, the quality that thinks always in terms of business. That's why the other day I said to you that it is really unbelievable how the Italians could snatch the greatest business from the Jews. It is really unbelievable, it is a miracle, because the Vatican is the greatest business on the earth. All the Rockefellers and all the Morgans and all the Fords put together still fall short.

Jewishness is a quality; it can be found in a Hindu, it can be found in a Jaina, it can be found in a Christian, in a Buddhist. It is the quality of calculation. It can become great intelligence, it can also become great cunningness – both alternatives are there.

Jews have given the greatest minds to the world; the people who have dominated this century were all Jews. Karl Marx, Sigmund Freud, Albert Einstein, the three great minds who have dominated, who have left their immense impact on modern humanity, were all Jews. Jews snatch more Nobel prizes than anybody else. That is one part: the mind can become very intelligent. But the other part is, it can become very cunning, mean, calculative.

On his way home from the market, where he bought a beautiful horse at a very good price, Moses is surprised by a storm – and the Siberian storms are really frightening!

"My God, if you grant me safety," he prays, "I promise to sell my horse and give the money to the poor."

As soon as he uttered these words, the snow stopped and the sky cleared up. So Moses arrived home safely.

The following week, with a heavy heart, he went to the market to sell his horse. But he took a goose with him.

"How much for the horse?" Old Isaac asked him.

"The horse is sold with the goose," answered Moses. "Two rubles for the horse, and a hundred rubles for the goose! "

That calculativeness, that cunningness – now he is even deceiving God!

One small boy – must have been Jewish – was going to the synagogue. His mother had given him two small coins, one for himself and one to be offered to God in the synagogue. On the way he was playing with the coins, and one coin slipped from his hand, went into a hole. The boy stood there, looked at the sky and said, "So take your coin! Here goes your coin, God! You are omnipotent, so you can find it anywhere. It will be a little difficult for me."

Just a small boy – but he finds a way out of the problem. This quality is Jewishness.

Ibrahim Silberstein, a rich merchant, invites all his friends to a party to celebrate his twenty-five years of marriage.

On his invitation card is written: "The presents of the guests who cannot visit us on this occasion will be returned."

One of his clients, Zacharia, after receiving the invitation, borrows a magnificent silver chandelier from the jewelry shop and tells his wife, Esther, "I have got a great idea, dear! We will send this chandelier as a present to the Silbersteins, but we won't visit them, so it won't cost us anything as they will return it to us!"

Zacharia sends the chandelier and patiently waits for the return of the present. One week goes by, then two, then three: no sign of the chandelier. Very nervous, Zacharia finally decides to go and see the Silbersteins. Silberstein warmly greets his generous friend: "Ah, finally, there you are! I knew you were coming. Just this morning I was saying to my dear wife, Rebecca, 'If my old friend Zacharia does not come today, ah well, too bad, tomorrow we will have to send the chandelier back to him!'"

This quality, wherever it is found, is Jewishness.

If you try to watch your own mind you will find a Jew hidden there. Whenever you calculate and whenever you start living mathematically, whenever your life becomes just a business, just a logic; whenever you lose love, whenever you lose the quality to share, to risk, to gamble; whenever you lose the quality of giving wholeheartedly for the sheer joy of giving, beware of the Jew within.

But the Jew is very difficult to destroy, because it pays you. It helps you to succeed in the world, it helps you to become famous in the world, it offers you the whole world. If you are really calculative, the whole world is yours. The temptation is great. If you are tempted by the world and all that it can offer, you cannot get rid of the inner Jew.

And unless you get rid of the inner Jew you will never be religious, you will never have innocence – and without innocence there is no beauty, no benediction.

Enough for today.

Chapter 23
Behind the Master's Hands

Where is the witness when the observer and the observed become one?

The observer and the observed are two aspects of the witness. When they disappear into each other, when they melt into each other, when they are one, the witness for the first time arises in its totality.

But this question arises in many people; the reason is that they think the witness is the observer. In their minds, the observer and the witness are synonymous. It is fallacious; the observer is not the witness, but only a part of it. And whenever the part thinks of itself as the whole, error arises.

The observer means the subjective, and the observed means the objective. The observer means that which is outside the observed, and the observer also means that which is inside.

The inside and the outside can't be separate; they are together, they can only be together. When this togetherness, or rather oneness, is experienced, the witness arises. You cannot practice the witness. If you practice the witness you will be practicing only the observer, and the observer is not the witness.

Then what has to be done? Melting has to be done, merging has to be done. Seeing a roseflower, forget completely that there is an object seen and a subject as a seer. Let the beauty of the moment, the benediction of the moment, overwhelm you both, so the rose and you are no more separate, but you become one rhythm, one song, one ecstasy.

Loving, experiencing music, looking at the sunset, let it happen again and again. The more it happens the better, because it is not an art but a knack. You have to get the knack of it; once you have got it, you can trigger it anywhere, any moment.

When the witness arises, there is nobody who is witnessing and there is nothing to be witnessed. It is a pure mirror, mirroring nothing. Even to say it is a mirror is not right; it will be better to say it is a mirroring. It is more a dynamic process of melting and merging; it is not a static phenomenon, it is a flow. The rose reaching you, you reaching into the rose: it is a sharing of being.

Forget that idea that the witness is the observer; it is not. The observer can be practiced, the witness happens. The observer is a kind of concentration, and the observer keeps you separate. The observer will enhance, strengthen your ego. The more you become an observer, the more you will feel like an island – separate, aloof, distant.

Down the ages, the monks all over the world have been practicing the observer. They may have called it the witness, but it is not the witness. The witness is something totally different, qualitatively different. The observer can be practiced, cultivated; you can become a better observer through practicing it.

The scientist observes, the mystic witnesses. The whole process of science is that of observation; very keen, acute, sharp observation, so nothing is missed. But the scientist does not come to know God. Although his observation is very, very expert, yet he remains unaware of God. He never comes across God; on the contrary, he denies that God is, because the more he observes – and his whole process is that of observation – the more he becomes separate from existence. The bridges are broken and walls arise; he becomes imprisoned in his own ego.

The mystic witnesses. But remember, witnessing is a happening, a by-product – a by-product of being total in any moment, in any situation, in any experience. Totality is the key: out of totality arises the benediction of witnessing. Forget all about observing. It will give you more accurate information about the observed object, but you will remain absolutely oblivious of your own consciousness.

Science is objective, art is subjective, religion is neither – *neti neti*, neither this nor that. Then what is religion? Religion is the meeting of the object and the subject, religion is the meeting of the lover and the beloved. Religion is the disappearance of the separation, of the duality. And in that separation energy is released; energy that was confined by the dual, that was kept separate, simply dances in utter unity.

That unity is witnessing. It happens only once in a while to you, and even then you don't take much note of it, because it comes like a flash and it is gone. And because you don't understand it, you don't preserve the experience. In fact you neglect it, you ignore it; it seems to be dangerous.

It happens when you are in a deep orgasmic state, when the woman and man meet and merge and disappear into each other. It happens only for a single moment at the highest peak. When their energies are no more two, when the energies have penetrated into each other so deeply that you cannot call them two at all...that orgasmic peak is the moment where witnessing arises. This is the whole secret of Tantra. Tantra discovered that in orgasmic ecstasy witnessing arises on its own accord. It is a gift from God, a natural gift to enter into samadhi.

But it happens in all creative experiences, because all creative experiences are orgasmic; in a subtle sense, there is something of the sexual and the sensuous in them. When a painter looks at the trees, then the green and the red and the gold of the trees is not the same as when you look at the trees. His experience is orgasmic, he is utterly lost in it. He is not there as an observer, he falls in deep rapport. He becomes one with the green and the red and the gold of the trees.

The painter knows that looking at the beautiful existence is an orgasmic experience. Hence, while the painter is painting, he becomes absolutely nonsexual; he becomes celibate. He is already experiencing orgasmic joy, he need not go into sex at all. Celibacy comes naturally to him.

Thousands of poets and painters and musicians have remained celibate, and with no effort. Monks remain celibate with great effort. Why? The monk is uncreative; in his life there is no orgasmic experience, his mind hankers for the sexual experience. The poet, the musician, the artist, the dancer who is capable of being lost into whatsoever he is doing, is having orgasmic experiences on a higher plane; sex is not a necessity. If once in a while such a person moves into sex, it is not out of need, it is just playfulness, it is simple playfulness. And when sex has the quality of playfulness it is sacred. When it is out of need it is a little bit ugly, because out of need you exploit the other, and out of need it can never take you to the highest orgasmic peak. You remain always discontented somewhere or other, because out of need means there is a motive, there is goal-orientation. There is manipulation, exploitation, an effort to use the other as a means. When you are simply playful, it is totally different.

D.H. Lawrence is right when he says that he experienced God in sexual orgasm. But his sexuality is totally different from the sexuality of the monks. They will not be able to understand Lawrence.

Lawrence was one of the most misunderstood men of this century – one of the most beautiful, one of the most creative, one of the most precious, but the most misunderstood. And the reason is that his experience has a totally different quality. When he is talking about sexual orgasm, he is not talking about your sexual orgasm, he is talking about *his* sexual orgasm. Only very rare people will be able to understand him. He is a natural *tantrika* – unaware of the science of Tantra, but he stumbled upon it. Somehow a window has opened in his life; his sensuality is spiritual.

It is not a question of what you do, it is a question of how you do it. And ultimately it is a question whether you do it or you allow it to happen. If you allow it to happen, then whenever there is a creative meeting you will suddenly become a witness. The observer and the observed become one in it – in fact it happens only when they become one.

? Please say something about the relationship of consciousness and energy.

Modern physics has discovered one of the greatest things ever discovered, and that is: matter is energy. That is the greatest contribution of Albert Einstein to humanity: e is equal to MC2, matter is energy. Matter only appears…otherwise there is no such thing as matter, nothing is solid. Even the solid rock is a pulsating energy, even the solid rock is as much energy as the roaring ocean. The waves that are arising in the solid rock cannot be seen because they are very subtle, but the rock is waving, pulsating, breathing; it is alive.

Friedrich Nietzsche has declared that God is dead. God is not dead – on the contrary, what has happened is that matter is dead. Matter has been found not to exist at all. This insight into matter brings modern physics very close to mysticism, very close. For the first time the scientist and the mystic are coming very close, almost holding hands.

Eddington, one of the greatest scientists of this age, has said, "We used to think that matter is a thing; now it is no more so. Matter is more like a thought than like a thing."

Existence is energy. Science has discovered that the observed is energy, the object is energy. Down the ages, at least for five thousand years, it has been known that the other polarity – the subject, the observer, consciousness – is energy.

Your body is energy, your mind is energy, your soul is energy. Then what is the difference between these three? The difference is only of a different rhythm, different wavelengths, that's all. The body is gross – energy functioning in a gross way, in a visible way.

Mind is a little more subtle, but still not too subtle, because you can close your eyes and you can see the thoughts moving; they can be seen. They are not as visible as your body; your body is visible to everybody else, it is publicly visible. Your thoughts are privately visible. Nobody else can see your thoughts; only you can see them – or people who have worked very deeply into seeing thoughts. But ordinarily they are not visible to others.

And the third, the ultimate layer inside you, is that of consciousness. It is not even visible to you. It cannot be reduced into an object, it remains subject.

If all these three energies function in harmony, you are healthy and whole. If these energies don't function in harmony and accord you are ill, unhealthy; you are no more whole. And to be whole is to be holy.

The effort that we are making here is how to help you so that your body, your mind, your consciousness, can all dance in one rhythm, in a togetherness, in a deep harmony – not in conflict at all, but in cooperation. The moment your body, mind and consciousness function together, you have become the trinity, and in that experience is God.

Your question is significant. You ask, "Please say something about the relationship of consciousness and energy."

There is no relationship of consciousness and energy. Consciousness is energy, purest energy; mind is not so pure, body is still less pure. Body is much too mixed, and mind is also not totally pure. Consciousness is total pure energy. But you can know this consciousness only if you make a cosmos out of the three, and not a chaos. People are living in chaos: their bodies say one thing, their bodies want to go in one direction; their minds are completely oblivious of the body – because for centuries you have been taught that you are not the body, for centuries you have been told that the body is your enemy, that you have to fight with it, that you have to destroy it, that the body is sin.

Because of all these ideas – silly and stupid they are, harmful and poisonous they are, but they have been taught for so long that they have become part of your collective mind, they are there – you don't experience your body in a rhythmic dance with yourself.

Hence my insistence on dancing and music, because it is only in dance that you will feel that your body, your mind and you are functioning together. And the joy is infinite when all these function together; the richness is great.

Consciousness is the highest form of energy. And when all these three energies function together, the fourth arrives. The fourth is always present when these three function together. When these three function in an organic unity, the fourth is always there; the fourth is nothing but that organic unity.

In the East, we have called that fourth simply "the fourth" – *turiya*; we have not given it any name. The three have names, the fourth is nameless. To know the fourth is to know God. Let us say it in this way: God is when you are an organic orgasmic unity. God is not when you are a chaos, a disunity, a conflict. When you are a house divided against yourself there is no God.

When you are tremendously happy with yourself, happy as you are, blissful as you are, grateful as you are, and all your energies are dancing together, when you are an orchestra of all your energies, God is. That feeling of total unity is what God is. God is not a person somewhere, God is the experience of the three falling in such unity that the fourth arises. And the fourth is more than the sum total of the parts.

If you dissect a painting, you will find the canvas and the colors, but the painting is not simply the sum total of the canvas and the colors; it is something more. That "something more" is expressed through the painting, color, canvas, the artist, but that "something more" is the beauty. Dissect the roseflower, and you will find all the chemicals and things it is constituted of, but the beauty will disappear. It was not just the sum total of the parts, it was more.

The whole is more than the sum total of the parts; it expresses through the parts, but it is more. To understand that it is more is to understand God. God is that more, that plus. It is not a question of theology, it cannot be decided by logical argumentation. You have to *feel* beauty, you have to *feel* music, you have to feel *dance*. And ultimately you have to feel the dance in your body, mind, soul.

You have to learn how to play on these three energies so that they all become an orchestra. Then God is – not that you see God, there is nothing to be seen; God is the ultimate seer, it is witnessing. Learn to melt your body, mind, soul; find out ways when you can function as a unity.

It happens many times that runners.... You will not think of running as a meditation, but runners sometimes have felt a tremendous experience of meditation. They were surprised, because they were not looking for it – who thinks that a runner is going to experience God? – but it has happened, and now running is becoming more and more a new kind of meditation. It can happen in running. If you have ever been a runner, if you have enjoyed running in the early morning when the air is fresh and young and the whole world is coming back out of sleep, awakening, and you were running and your body was functioning beautifully, and the fresh air, and the new world again born out of the darkness of the night, and everything singing all around, and you were feeling so alive.... A moment comes when the runner disappears, there is only running. The body, mind and soul start functioning together; suddenly an inner orgasm is released.

Runners have sometimes come accidentally on the experience of the fourth, turiya, although they will miss it because they will think it was just because of running that they enjoyed the moment; that it was a beautiful day, that the body was healthy and the world was beautiful, and it was just a certain mood. They will not take note of it. But if they take note of it, my own observation is that a runner can more easily come close to meditation than anybody else. Jogging can be of immense help, swimming can be of immense help. All these things have to be transformed into meditations.

Drop old ideas of meditations, that just sitting underneath a tree with a yoga posture is meditation. That is only one of the ways, and may be suitable for a few people but is not suitable for all. For a small child it is not meditation, it is torture. For a young man who is alive, vibrant, it is repression, it is not meditation. Maybe for an old man who has lived, whose energies are declining, it may be meditation.

People differ, there are many types of people. To someone who has a low kind of energy, sitting underneath a tree in a yoga posture may be the best meditation, because the yoga posture is the least energy-expensive – the least. When the spine is erect, making a ninety-degree angle with the earth, your body expends the least energy possible. If you are leaning towards the left or towards the front, then your body starts spending more energy, because the gravitation starts pulling you downwards and you have to keep yourself, you have to hold yourself so that you don't fall. This is expenditure. An erect spine was found to need the least spending of energy.

Then sitting with your hands together in the lap is also very, very useful for low-energy people, because when both the hands are touching each other, your body electricity starts moving in a circle. It does not go out of your body; it becomes an inner circle, the energy moves inside you.

You must know that energy is always released through the fingers, energy is never released from round-shaped things. For example, your head cannot release energy, it contains it. Energy is released through the fingers, the toes of the feet and the hands. In a certain yoga posture the feet are together, so one foot releases energy and it enters into the other foot; one hand releases energy and it enters into the other hand. You go on taking your own energy, you become an inner circle of energy. It is very resting, it is very relaxing.

The yoga posture is the most relaxed posture possible. It is more relaxing than even sleep, because when you are asleep your whole body is being pulled by gravitation. When you are horizontal it is relaxing in a totally different way. It is relaxing because it brings you back to the ancient days when man was an animal, horizontal. It is relaxing because it is regressive; it helps you to become an animal again.

That's why in a lying posture you cannot think clearly, it becomes difficult to think. Try it. You can dream easily but you cannot think easily; for thinking you have to sit. The more erect you sit, the better is the possibility to think. Thinking is a late arrival; when man became vertical, thinking arrived. When man used to be horizontal, dreaming was there but thinking was not there. So when you lie down you start dreaming, thinking disappears. It is a kind of relaxation, because thinking stops; you regress.

The yoga posture is a good meditation for those who have low energy, for those who are ill, for those who are old, for those who have lived the whole life and now are coming closer and closer to death.

Thousands of Buddhist monks have died in the sitting lotus posture, because the best way to receive death is in the lotus posture – because in the lotus posture you will be fully alert, and because energies will be disappearing, they will be becoming less and less every moment. Death is coming. In a lotus posture you can keep alertness to the very end. And to be alert while you are dying is one of the greatest experiences, the ultimate in orgasm.

And if you are awake while you are dying you will have a totally different kind of birth: you will be born awake. One who dies awake is born awake. One who dies unconscious is born unconscious. One who dies with awareness can choose the right womb for himself; he has a choice, he has earned it. The man who dies unconsciously has no right to choose the womb; the womb happens unconsciously, accidentally.

The man who dies perfectly alert in this life will be coming only once more, because next time there will be no need to come. Just a little work is left: the other life will do that work. For one who is dying with awareness, only one thing is left now: he has had no time to radiate his awareness into compassion. Next time he can radiate his awareness into compassion. And unless awareness becomes compassion, something remains incomplete, something remains imperfect.

Running can be a meditation – jogging, dancing, swimming, anything can be a meditation. My definition of meditation is: whenever your body, mind, soul are functioning together in rhythm it is meditation, because it will bring the fourth in. And if you are alert that you are doing it as a meditation – not to take part in the Olympics, but doing it as a meditation – then it is tremendously beautiful.

In the new commune we are going to introduce all kinds of meditations. Those who enjoy swimming, they will have opportunities to go for a swimming meditation. Those who enjoy running, they will have their group to run for miles. Each according to his need – only then this world can be full of meditation; otherwise not.

If we give only a fixed pattern of meditation, then it will be applicable only to a few people. That has been one of the problems in the past: fixed patterns of meditation, not fluid – fixed, so they fit certain types and all others are left in the darkness.

My effort is to make meditation available to each and everybody; whosoever wants to meditate, meditation should be made available according to his type. If he needs rest, then rest should be his meditation. Then "sitting silently doing nothing, and the spring comes and the grass grows by itself" – that will be his meditation. We have to find as many dimensions to meditation as there are people in the world. And the pattern has not to be very rigid, because no two individuals are alike. The pattern has to be very liquid so that it can fit with the individual. In the past, the practice was that the individual had to fit with the pattern.

I bring a revolution. The individual has not to fit with the pattern, the pattern has to fit with the individual. My respect for the individual is absolute. I am not much concerned with means; means can be changed, arranged in different ways.

That's why you find so many meditations going on here. We don't have enough opportunities here, otherwise you would be surprised how many doors God's temple has. And you would be surprised also that there is a special door only for you and for nobody else. That's God's love for you, his respect for you. You will be received through a special door, not through the public gate; you will be received as a special guest.

But the basic fundamental is, whatsoever the meditation, it has to fill this requirement: that the body, mind, consciousness, all three should function in unity. Then suddenly one day the fourth has arrived: the witnessing. Or if you want to, call it God; call it God or nirvana or Tao or whatsoever you will.

In a deep embrace with you,
In orgasmic play with existence,
Little more of you,
Little less of me.

Darshan, that's what is already happening to you. Every day you are disappearing – and it is so obvious. Every day something of you is evaporating: more and more, I am becoming your being. Soon Darshan will not be found there at all.

And that is the moment of great blessings – when the disciple disappears, when the disciple is only a vehicle of the master. And the master is nobody except the whole. The master is one who is not, the master is one who has already disappeared into God. The master is already a hollow bamboo and God is using him as a flute.

When the disappearance also has happened to the disciple, the first experience is that of meeting and merger with the master – because the disciple does not know what God is, he knows only the master. The master is his or her God. Once the disciple disappears into the master and allows the master to enter into the innermost core of his being, the second experience is that the master has never been there.

Hidden behind the master's hands were God's hands, hidden behind the master's words were God's messages. The master was only a singer, singing the songs of the infinite and the eternal.

It is happening to you. I am utterly happy with you, all my blessings are for you.

You say: "In a deep embrace with you, in orgasmic play with existence, little more of you, little less of me."

This is happening, this will go on happening. Your prayer is going to be fulfilled in *this* life. I can guarantee only for a very few people; it is very difficult to guarantee, but for Darshan I can guarantee: in this very life it is going to be fulfilled.

? What is this longing in me that no relationship can satisfy, that no tears relieve, that is not changed by many and beautiful dreams and adventures?

It is so, not only with you but with everybody who has a little intelligence. It is not detected by the stupid people, but the intelligent person is bound to stumble upon the fact sooner or later – and the more intelligent you are, the sooner it will be – that no relationship can satisfy.

Why? – because every relationship is only an arrow towards the ultimate relationship; it is a milestone, it is not a goal. Every love affair is just an indication of a bigger love affair ahead – just a little taste, but that little taste is not going to quench your thirst or satisfy your hunger. On the contrary, that little taste will make you more thirsty, will make you more hungry.

That's what happens in every relationship. Rather than giving you contentment, it gives you a tremendous discontentment. Each relationship fails in this world – and it is good that it fails; it would have been a curse if it was not so. It is a blessing that it fails.

Because each relationship fails, that's why you start searching for the ultimate relationship with God, with existence, with the cosmos. You see the futility again and again, that it is not going to be satisfied by any man, by any woman; that each experience ends in tremendous frustration, begins in great hope and leaves you in great hopelessness. It is always so, it comes with great romance and ends in a bitter taste. When it happens again and again, one has to learn something – that each relationship is only an experimentation to prepare you for the ultimate relationship, for the ultimate love affair.

That's what religion is all about.

You say: "What is this longing in me that no relationship can satisfy?"

That is the longing for God. You may know it, you may not know it. You may not be able yet to articulate it, exactly what it is, because in the beginning it is very vague, cloudy, surrounded by great mist. But it is the longing for God, it is the longing to merge with the whole, so there is no separation any longer.

You cannot merge with a man or a woman forever, the separation is bound to happen. The merger can only be momentary, and after that moment is gone you will be left in great darkness. After that flash, that lightning, is gone, the darkness is going to be even more than it was before. That's why millions of people decide not to go into any love relationship – because at least one is accustomed to one's darkness, one has not known anything else. There is a kind of satisfaction: one knows that this is what life is, that there is no more to it, so there is no discontent.

Once you have tasted love, once you have seen a few moments of joy, of that tremendous throbbing when two persons are no longer two…. But you fall again and again from that peak; and each time you fall the darkness is far darker than before, because now you know that light is. Now you know that there are peaks, now you know that life has much more to offer to you, that this mundane existence of going to the office every day and coming home and eating and sleeping – that this mundane existence is not all, that this mundane existence is only the porch of the palace.

If you have never been invited in and you have lived always in the porch, then you think this is what life is, this is your home. Once a window opens and you can see inside the palace – the beauty of it, the grandeur of it, the splendor of it – or once you are invited in for a moment and then thrown out again, now the porch can never satisfy you. Now this porch is going to be a heavy burden on your heart. Now you are going to suffer, your agony is going to be great.

This is my observation, that the people who are very uncreative are more satisfied than the people who are creative. The creative person is very much unsatisfied, because he knows much more is possible and it is not happening. Why is it not happening?

The creative person is constantly searching; he cannot rest, because he has seen a few glimpses. Once in a while a window has opened and he has seen beyond. How can he rest? How can he feel comfortable and cozy in that stupid porch? He knows about the palace, he has seen the king too, and he knows, "That palace belongs to me; it is my birthright." All that is needed is how to enter into the palace, how to become a permanent resident in it. Yes, momentarily he has been inside, and he has been thrown out again and again.

The more sensitive a person is, the more you will find him in discontent. The more intelligent, the more discontent will be found there. It has always been so.

You come from the West to the East; you see the beggar on the road, the laborer carrying mud on his head, and you feel a little bit surprised: their faces don't show discontentment. They have nothing to be contented with, but somehow they are satisfied. And the so-called Indian religious people think it is because of religion that they are satisfied. And the so-called Indian saints go on bragging about it: "Look! the West has everything, science and technology has provided the West with every possible comfort, and yet nobody is contented. And in our country people are so religious that they have nothing, yet they are contented." The saints of this country go on bragging about it, but their whole bragging is based on a fallacy. The people of this country – the poor people, the uneducated people, the starving people – are not contented because they are religious, they are contented because they have no sensitiveness. They are contented because they are not creative, they are contented because they have never seen any glimpse.

The West is becoming discontented because the comfort, the convenience, all that science has provided for them, has given them so much time to explore, to meditate, to pray, to play music, to dance, that a few glimpses have started happening. They are becoming aware that there is much more to life than appears on the surface; one has to dive deep.

The East is simply poor – and poverty makes people insensitive, remember. A poor person has to be insensitive, otherwise he will not be able to survive at all. If he is very sensitive, the poverty will be too much. He has to grow a thick skin around himself as a protection, otherwise how will he survive? He has to become very blind, only then can he live in a poor country. Otherwise the beggar is there, the ill people are there on the street, dying: if he is not insensitive, how is he going to work at all? Those beggars will haunt him. He has to close his doors.

You can see it happening on the Indian streets. The Western visitor for the first time becomes very puzzled: a man is dying on the street and no Indian takes any note of it, people go on passing. This happens every day.

If they start taking note of it, they will not be able to live at all; they have not any time for such luxuries. This is a luxury! They cannot take the person to the hospital, they have no time. If they start being so compassionate they will start dying themselves, because who is going to earn for their family? They have to become utterly blind and deaf. They go on moving like zombies, seeing nothing. Whatsoever is happening by the side is nothing to do with them, it is none of their business; everybody is suffering his own karma.

The beggar dying on the street is suffering from his own karma – maybe he was a murderer in the past life. You need not worry about him, in fact you should be happy that he is suffering from his karma; now his karma is finished. Next birth he will be born a king, or something like that – beautiful rationalizations to keep yourself blind, insensitive.

It is very difficult for the poor person to have some aesthetic sense, he cannot afford it. If he has aesthetic sense then he will feel his poverty too much, it will become unbearable. He cannot have a sense for cleanliness, he cannot have a sense for beauty. He cannot afford these things – what is the point of having the sensitivity for them? It will be a torture, constant torture. He will not be able to sleep in his ugly house with all kinds of dirt, with all kind of rotten things – they are his only possessions! He seems to be very satisfied – he *has* to be; he cannot afford dissatisfaction.

It has nothing to do with religion, remember. All poor people are satisfied, without any exception. You can go to Africa and you will find the poor people satisfied; they are even poorer than Indians and their satisfaction is far deeper. You can go to Indian aboriginal tribes, which are the poorest in the world, but you will see on their faces a kind of satisfaction, as if nothing is wrong, all is right. They have to believe that all is right, they have to constantly autohypnotize themselves that all is right; otherwise how will they be able to sleep and how will they be able to eat?

Once a country becomes rich, it becomes sensitive. Once a country becomes rich, affluent, it becomes aware of many, many dimensions of life that have always been there but one had no time to look at. The rich country starts thinking of music, painting, poetry, and ultimately meditation – because meditation is the last luxury. There is no greater luxury than meditation. Meditation is the last luxury, because it is the ultimate love affair.

It is good that you are not satisfied with your relationships. Indians are very satisfied, because in fact there is no relationship at all. It is marriage, it has nothing to do with relationship. Parents decide it, and astrologers and palmists. It has nothing to do with the persons who are going to get married; they are not even asked, they are simply put into a certain situation where they start living together. It is not a relationship. They may produce children, but it is not love; there is nothing of romance in it. But one thing is good about it: it is very stable. When there is no relationship there is no possibility of divorce. Divorce is possible only if there is love. Try to understand me. Love means great hope, love means "I have arrived." Love means "I have found the woman or the man." Love means the feeling that "We are made for each other." Love means now there is no need to search any more.

If you start with such great hope, by the time the honeymoon is over the relationship will be over. These great hopes cannot be fulfilled by human beings. You are hoping that the woman is a goddess; she is not. She is hoping the man is a god; he is not. Now, how long can they go on deceiving each other? Sooner or later they will start seeing the actual. They will see the fact, and the fiction will start evaporating.

No relationship can satisfy, because every relationship begins with great hope, and that is not possible to be fulfilled. Yes, that hope can be fulfilled, but it can be fulfilled only when you have fallen in love with the whole. No part can fulfill it. When you have fallen in love with the total, when the merger happens with the total, only then will there be contentment. There will be nobody who is contented, there will be simply contentment. And then there is no end to it.

I am all for love, because love fails. You will be surprised – I have my own logic. I am all for love, because love fails. I am not for marriage, because marriage succeeds; it gives you a permanent settlement. And that is the danger: you become satisfied with a toy, you become satisfied with something plastic, artificial, manmade.

That's why in the East, particularly in India.... It is a very ancient country, and ancient countries become cunning just as old people become cunning. Out of cunningness this country decided for child marriage, because once somebody is adolescent hope starts arising – longing, romance, poetry; now it will be difficult. The best way that India found was child marriage, marriage of children. They don't know what marriage is, they don't know what relationship is, they don't know what love is – they are not even hungry for it – sex has not yet become a mature thing in them. Let them get married.

Just think – a three-year-old girl being married to a five-year-old boy. Now they will grow together, just as brothers and sisters grow together. Have you ever felt any desire to divorce your sister? I don't think anybody ever divorces one's own sister, there is no need. You take it for granted. Everybody thinks his mother is good, beautiful; his sister is beautiful, his brother is beautiful. You take these things for granted.

There was only one relationship which was available for you to choose out of your own freedom: your spouse, your woman, your man. In India we destroyed even that freedom. Husbands and wives were as much given as brothers and sisters. And when you have grown together for years a certain kind of friendship, a certain kind of association, arises. You become accustomed to each other.

This is not relationship, this is not love. But India had decided for stability – and an ancient country knows perfectly well love can never be stable. Choose love and you choose trouble.

In the West love has become more and more important, and with it all kinds of troubles have arisen. The family is falling apart, disappearing really. People are changing their wives and husbands so many times that everything seems to be just in a chaos.

I have heard about one Hollywood actress, that she married for the thirty-first time. After three days she became aware that this man had once also been her husband before. Now even to remember for so many times…. People change, their faces change. Now, this cannot happen in India. Even after lives your wife will remember you; even after lives you cannot escape, there is no escape.

But I am all for love, and I am against marriage, particularly the arranged kind, because the arranged marriage gives you satisfaction. And love? – love can never satisfy you. It gives you more and more thirst for a better and better love, it makes you more and more long for it, it gives you tremendous discontentment. And that discontent is the beginning of the search for God. When love fails many times, you start looking for a new kind of lover, a new kind of love, a new quality of love. That love affair is prayer, meditation, sannyas.

It is good that no longing for ordinary love affairs is ever going to be satisfied. The longing will be intensified more; no relationship is going to fulfill you. They will make you more frustrated, and no tears will relieve it, they cannot. They may help for the moment, but again you will be full of pain and agony. Nothing is changed by many and beautiful dreams and adventures, nothing is changed. Yet I say go through them. Nothing is changed, but you are changed by going through all those dreams and beautiful adventures. Nothing is changed in the world.

Just think, this question has arisen in you. This is a change. How many people are there who ask this type of question? This question is not an ordinary question; it is not out of curiosity. I can feel the pain, the agony; I can feel your tears, I can see your frustrations in it, I can see all that misery and suffering you must have gone through. It is almost tangible.

Nothing changes in the world. But, falling again and again, something changes in you – and that is revolution. Even to ask such a question means you are on the verge of a revolution. Then a new adventure is needed. Old adventures failed, and a new one – not in the sense that you have to search for a new man or a new woman – a new one in the sense that you have to search in a new dimension is needed. That dimension is the dimension of the divine.

I say to you: I am fulfilled and contented. Atisha is fulfilled and contented, not by any relationship of the world, not by any love affair of the world, but having a love affair with the whole existence is utterly fulfilling.

And when one is fulfilled, one starts overflowing. He cannot contain his own contentment. He is blessed, and so much is he blessed that he starts blessing others. He is so much blessed that he becomes a blessing to the world.

? What is a contemporary mind?

Contemporary mind is a contradiction in terms. Mind is never contemporary, it is always old. Mind is past – past and past and nothing else; mind means memory. There can be no contemporary mind; to be contemporary is to be without mind.

If you are herenow, then you are contemporary with me. But then, don't you see, your mind disappears; no thought moves, no desire arises: you become disconnected with the past and disconnected with the future.

Mind is never original, cannot be. No-mind is original, fresh, young; mind is always old, rotten, stale.

But those words are used – they are used in a totally different sense. I can understand your question – in that sense, those words are meaningful. The mind of the nineteenth century was a different mind; the questions they were asking, you are not asking. The questions that were very important in the eighteenth century are now stupid questions. "How many angels can dance on the point of a needle?" was one of the greatest theological questions in the middle ages. Now can you find such a stupid person who will think that this is an important question? And this was discussed by the greatest theologians; not small people, great professors were writing treatises on it, conferences were arranged. How many angels? Now who cares? It is simply irrelevant.

In Buddha's time, a great question was: "Who created the world?" It has persisted for centuries, but now fewer and fewer people are worried about who created the world. Yes, there are some old-fashioned people, but very rarely such questions are asked of me. But Buddha was encountered every day. Not a single day must have passed when somebody did not ask the question, "Who created the world?" Buddha had to say again and again that the world has always been there, nobody has created it; but people were not satisfied. Now nobody cares. Very rarely somebody asks me the question, "Who created the world?" In that sense, the mind goes on changing as time goes on changing. In that sense, the contemporary mind is a reality.

Husband to wife: "I said we are not going out tonight, and that is semi-final."

Now this is a contemporary mind. No husband in the past would have said that. It was always final; the last word was his.

Two high-class English ladies met each other by accident while out shopping in London. One noticed the other was pregnant and asked, "Why, darling, what a surprise! You obviously got married since I last saw you! "
The second said, "Yes. He's a wonderful man; he's an officer in the Ghurka rifles."
The questioner was horrified. "A Ghurka! Darling, are not they all black?"
"Oh no," she said. "Only the privates."
The questioner exclaimed, "Darling, how contemporary!"

In that sense, there is a contemporary mind....

Have you heard about the latest family game? It is called incest.
Little sister to brother in bed: "Hey, you are better at this than Daddy."
"Yes, Mummy says so too!"

Otherwise, there is no contemporary mind. Fashions come and go; if you think of fashions then there are changes. But basically all mind is old. Mind as such is old, and there can be no modern mind; the most modern mind is still of the past.

The really alive person is a herenow person. He does not live out of the past, he does not live for the future; he lives only in the moment, for the moment. The moment is all. He is spontaneous; that spontaneity is the fragrance of no-mind. Mind is repetitive, mind always moves in circles. Mind is a mechanism: you feed it with knowledge, it repeats the same knowledge, it goes on chewing the same knowledge again and again.

No-mind is clarity, purity, innocence. No-mind is the real way to live, the real way to know, the real way to be.

❓ Why are politicians so mean?

They are mean because they are stupid. Stupidity has always the shadow of meanness. The more intelligent you are, the less mean you are. The utterly intelligent person cannot have any meanness; it is impossible. He can have only love and compassion.

The stupid person has to be mean because that is the only way he thinks he can win. The intelligent person has no desire to win, the intelligent person is already victorious in his intelligence. The intelligent person is already superior in his intelligence, he has not to compete for it. The stupid person has to continuously compete. And because he is stupid, he cannot rely on his intelligence, he has to rely on something else: he becomes mean, cunning, deceptive, a hypocrite.

To me, stupidity is the only sin, and everything else is just a by-product of it. And intelligence is the only virtue; everything else that we have known as virtue follows it like a shadow.

Two politicians are returning home from the bar, late at night, drunk as usual. As they are making their way down the sidewalk one of them spots a heap of dung in front of them just as they are walking into it.

"Stop!" he yells.

"What is it?" asks the other.

"Look!" says the first. "Shit!"

Getting nearer to take a good look at it, the second drunkard examines the dung carefully and says, "No, it isn't, it's mud."

"I tell you, it's shit," repeats the first.

"No, it isn't," says the other.

"It's shit!"

"No!"

So finally the first angrily sticks his finger in the dung and puts it to his mouth. After having tasted it, he says, "I tell you, it is shit."

So the second politician does the same, and slowly savoring it, says, "Maybe you are right. Hmm."

The first politician takes another try to prove his point. "It's shit!" he declares.

"Hmm, yes, maybe it is," answers the second, after his second try.

Finally, after having had enough of the dung to be sure that it is, they both happily hug each other in friendship, and exclaim, "Wow, I'm certainly glad we didn't step on it!"

Enough for today

Chapter 24
Bring In the New Man

> What is this urge to do something, to create? To free your message, your word, unto the world? I feel like I am in a hurry and that all the people in the commune have the same feeling. It is as if there is no time left, as if any day, this very moment, can be the last moment.
>
> Am I dying? I am exploding each and every moment. What is that? What is this urge? Please say something for this thirst.

Man is dying, mankind is dying. And in fact there is not much time left. And this is felt not only here around the commune, it is felt everywhere by sensitive, intelligent, creative people. Only the mediocre are unaware of it; only the politicians go on rushing into the danger, the calamity, that awaits, totally unaware where they are going and where they are leading the world.

But people of sensitivity, awareness, meditativeness, people of the heart, are everywhere feeling that the danger is very close, that mankind can commit suicide any moment, that the future was never so uncertain as it is today, that the tomorrow may really never come.

These are moments of great turmoil, but they can become of great creativity too. When one is encountering death, one can bring one's total potential into manifestation. When there is no time left you cannot postpone. Hence the hurry.

When death is very imminent, life flares up to the optimum. And that is what is happening to all creative people around the world, and more so around this commune, because my whole approach is such that only the very creative ones will be attracted to it.

I teach sensitivity. Down the ages, religions have been teaching just the opposite – how to become insensitive – because the more insensitive you are the more you can remain aloof, distant, detached. Because it was thought that to attain to God one has to renounce the world, it was a natural consequence, a logical consequence, that one should learn how to be more and more insensitive to beauty, to music, to love, to people, to life itself. In the past, religion has been teaching people how to be unintelligent, because sensitivity and intelligence go together, insensitivity and stupidity go together.

Your so-called saints are not intelligent people at all, but you have worshipped them. And you have worshipped them for the wrong reason – because they were insensitive, because they had dulled their consciousness, because they had grown thick skin around themselves. The spring will come but they will remain unaffected, the clouds will gather and they will remain unaffected. The peacock will dance but they will remain unaffected, the night sky will be full of stars but they will be completely unaware of it. That was the whole discipline in the past: how to become like a rock, so that the world cannot overpower you. It was a kind of paranoia, it was based in fear.

I teach you just the opposite: be sensitive, be alert, be loving, be sensuous – because God is not against the roseflower, God is in it. If you can sensuously feel the velvetyness of the rose you have touched God himself. God is not against the stars and the sun and the moon, he is in them. If you can allow them to enter into your being, if you allow them to stir your heart, if you can allow them to drive you crazy in a dance of joy and celebration, you will be coming closer and closer to home. I teach sensitivity, I teach love.

The people who have gathered around me have a totally different quality to them. This is not an ordinary ashram, it is a commune of creators – artists, painters, singers, musicians. All kinds of talented people have come to me; only they can understand what I am saying. People understand according to their own inner capabilities. I may say one thing, you may understand something else. Communication is not easy, language is not adequate, and you will understand only that for which you have come.

I have gathered around me a special kind of people. Hence this urge will be felt by almost everybody, that something has to be done. First, it will be a very, very vague kind of feeling, just a silent voice within your being, heard yet not heard, understood yet not understood…a whisper, not very clear, a little muddy, not very transparent. In the beginning this is bound to be so. You will hear it like a song: it will be more poetry than prose, it will come to you like dreams, visions. Slowly, slowly the unconscious will be able to communicate to the conscious.

And that's what meditation is all about: learning the way to bridge the unconscious with the conscious, so that your own being can give you indications where to move, where to go, so that you don't need a leader, so that you become a guide to yourself, so that you can become a light unto yourself.

You are not dying, but this will be felt like that because you are part of humanity and humanity *is* dying. All that is human is disappearing, and all that is inhuman is becoming more and more dominating and powerful.

Man is being reduced to a machine, and mechanical values are becoming dominant. The artist is not respected, but the technician is. Poetry is not loved, but plumbing is. The dancer is no more in the center of life, but the businessman, the bureaucrat, the politician are. All that is beautiful is becoming irrelevant to man, because that which is beautiful cannot be used as a means to anything. That which is beautiful is an end unto itself. You cannot use poetry in war; you will need the scientist, not the poet. And you cannot use musicians in the marketplace; there you will need economists.

This whole life is geared around wrong things. Money is more important than meditation. This is a very topsy-turvy situation: man is standing on his head. Man is dying, and the death is very slow. And remember, when death is very fast you can avoid it, because you become intensely aware of it. When it comes very, very slow, a slow poisoning….

For example, a person goes on smoking every day. All the experts go on saying that this is dangerous to you, that this will kill you, but he smokes every day and it doesn't kill him! So you may write it on every packet of cigarettes – nobody bothers about your warnings that "This is harmful to health," that "This is harmful to life." Who cares? – because experience says something else! You smoke every day, dozens of cigarettes, and you don't die and you have not died yet.

You believe in your experience. The poison is very, very slow: if a person goes on smoking one dozen cigarettes every day, then it will take twenty years to poison the whole system. Now, twenty years is a long time, and man has a very, very short vision, he is shortsighted.

The world is being poisoned very slowly. The rivers are being polluted, the oceans are being polluted, the lakes are dying. Nature is being destroyed. We are exploiting the earth so much that sooner or later we will not be able to live on it. We are not behaving well with nature.

Our whole approach is wrong, it is destructive. We only take from the earth, and we never give anything back. We only exploit nature. The ecology is broken, the circulation is broken; we are not living in a perfect circle, and nature is a perfect circle: if you take from one hand and you give from another, you don't destroy it. But we are doing it: we only go on taking, and all the resources are being spent. But this poisoning is happening slowly, slowly. You don't see it happening because it takes a long time. And then there are politicians who go on gathering more and more atomic weapons – more atom bombs, more hydrogen bombs, super-hydrogen bombs – as if man has decided to commit suicide.

This is what is being felt by you. You have the heart of a poet or the heart of a painter, the heart of a lover. You have immense potential for creativity. You are sensitive, hence you are feeling it. But the feeling is as if "I am dying." No, not you – something far more important is happening, something far more dangerous too.

Individuals have always died, it is not a problem. It is, in fact, part of recycling. Your body goes back to the sources to be renewed, your being moves back into the eternal to be rested, and then you come back again, fresh, young. Life tires, life exhausts, death is a rest. For the individual, death is a blessing – but not for humanity itself; then it is a curse. Individuals go on dying and they go on coming back. But humanity is needed for them to come back. This earth is a beautiful planet and it is in the wrong hands. Hence you are feeling that something is to be done very urgently. Yes, it is urgent, because death is coming closer.

This century's end is going to see either the total destruction of humanity, and with it the total destruction of life on this earth, or a new man being born – a new man who will not hate life, as in the past it has been done; a new man who will love life; a new man who will not be negative in any way, but will be affirmative; a new man who will not desire life after death, but will live moment to moment in sheer joy – who will think of this life as a gift and not as a punishment; who will not be antagonistic to the body, who will respect the body as the temple of the soul; who will love, and who will not be afraid of love; who will move in all kinds of relationships and yet be able to remain himself.

To be in relationship and become dependent is the sign of weakness. And to escape to the Himalayas or to some Catholic monastery because of the fear of becoming dependent is again the sign of weakness; it is cowardly.

To live in relationship and yet remain independent, that is what courage is. The new man will be courageous. In the past, only two kinds of cowards have existed on the earth, the worldly kind and the otherworldly kind – but both are cowards. The really brave man will live in the world and yet not be of it. Either this is going to happen, or a total destruction. Now there is no third alternative. Man cannot survive as he is. Either he has to change himself, transmute himself, or he has to die and vacate the earth.

This is what is felt, this is why you are in such a hurry. That's why I am in such a hurry. My sannyasins can be the new man, my sannyasins can herald the new age. Hence my sannyasins are going to be opposed by all past-oriented people: by Hindus, by Christians, by Mohammedans, by Jainas, by Buddhists – by almost everybody. They are going to be opposed, and that is natural because we are trying to bring a new future in. To bring that new future we will have to destroy the past, because unless the past ceases to exist, the future cannot come into existence.

The past has to die. We have to drop our clinging with the past. What does it mean when you say that "I am a Hindu"? It means you cling to a certain past tradition. What do you mean when you say that "I am a Mohammedan"? You cling to something past.

But when you say, "I am a sannyasin, a neo-sannyasin," you don't cling to any past. Your eyes are focused on the future. Your roots are in the present and your branches are moving towards the future. Then the past is irrelevant. I want you to remember it again and again that the past has to be made irrelevant. You have to cut yourself off from the past.

You say, "What is this urge to do something?"

Yes, something has to be done. You have to give birth to yourself, and you have to prepare the way for the new man.

"What is this urge to do something, to create? to free your message, your word, unto the world?"

Yes, it has to be shouted from the housetops, it has to be hammered – because people are deaf, people are blind, they will not hear what is being said to them.

Just the other day, Neeraj sent me a beautiful parable from Pierre Delattre's Tales of a Dalai Lama. In this beautiful book comes this parable:

All the monks had seen the spirit come out of the wall long enough to utter just one word. But each monk had heard a different word. The event is immortalized in this poem:

The one who wanted to die heard *live*.
The one who wanted to live heard *die*.
The one who wanted to take heard *give*.
The one who wanted to give heard *keep*.
The one who was always alert heard *sleep*.
The one who was always asleep heard *wake*.
The one who wanted to leave heard *stay*.
The one who wanted to stay, *depart*.
The one who never spoke heard *preach*.
The one who always preached heard *pray*.
Each one learned how he had been in someone else's way.

What I am saying has to be conveyed to as many people as possible, and as fast as possible. Use all modern media to reach as many people as possible. Still, be aware that it is very difficult to communicate. It is almost an impossibility to communicate; still it has to be done. Even if fragments of what I am saying are understood, it will be enough to create the field, the energy field, in which the new man can be conceived.

Even if people misunderstand it...it is better to understand the truth, but even if the truth is misunderstood it is better than a lie. Something of the truth will remain in the misunderstanding too. And truth is a potential power, a great power. Even if a fragment, just a seed of truth, falls into your heart, sooner or later you will become the garden of Eden. It cannot be avoided. Just a drop, and the whole ocean will find its way towards you.

It has to be done. You have to create my message in as many forms as possible. Compose music, play on the guitar or on the flute, because it is easier to stir the heart of the people, to wake it up through music than through words. Dance, but dance in a new way so your dance becomes a teaching of meditation. Dance in such a way that the one who looks at you starts feeling that it is not only a dance but something more, something plus; so that he starts feeling the vibe of meditation that is happening inside you.

Paint: paint pictures which can become objects of meditation, paint pictures of the inner sky of buddhas. The modern painting is pathological. If you look at Picasso's paintings you cannot look long, you will start feeling uneasy. You cannot have Picasso paintings in your bedroom, because then you will have nightmares. If you meditate on a Picasso painting long enough you will go mad, because those paintings are out of Picasso's madness.

Go to Ajanta, Ellora, Khajuraho, Konarak, and you will see a totally different world of creativity. Looking at the statue of a buddha, something in you starts falling in tune. Sitting silently with a buddha statue, you start becoming silent. The very posture, the very shape, the face, the closed eyes, the silence that surrounds a marble statue will help you to get connected with your own inner sources of silence.

Gurdjieff used to say that there are two kinds of art. One he used to call objective art, and the other he used to call subjective art. Subjective art is absolutely private, personal. Picasso's art is subjective art; he is simply painting something without any vision for the person who will see it, without any idea of the person who will look at it. He is simply pouring out his own inner illness; it is helpful for himself, it is therapeutic.

I am not saying that Picasso should stop painting, because if he stops painting he is bound to go mad. It is painting that is keeping him sane; his painting is like vomiting. When you have eaten something wrong, when you have a food poisoning, vomiting is the most healthy way to throw the toxins, the poisons, outside the system; it will help. Picasso's paintings are like vomiting. He is suffering from many illnesses, all the illness that humanity is suffering from. He simply represents humanity, he is very representative.

He represents the whole madness that is happening in millions of people. He is a sensitive soul; he has become so attuned with the pathology of mankind that it has become his own pathology. Hence the appeal of his paintings, otherwise they are ugly. Hence his great name – because he deserves it, he represents the age. This is Picasso's age: what you cannot say about yourself, he has said it. What you cannot pour out of yourself, he has poured it on the canvas. But it is a subjective phenomenon. It is therapeutic to him, but it is dangerous to everybody else.

The ancient art was not only art; it was, deep down, mysticism. Deep down, it was out of meditation. It was objective, in Gurdjieff's terminology. It was made so that if somebody meditates over it, he starts falling into those depths where God lives.

Khajuraho or Konarak – if you meditate there, you will know what the Tantra masters were doing. They were creating in stone something that is felt in the ultimate orgasmic joy. It was the most difficult thing to do, to bring ecstasy into the stone. And if the stone can show the ecstasy, then everybody can move into that ecstasy easily.

But people who go to Khajuraho are foolish people. They look either at Khajuraho sculpture as obscene – then they miss the whole point, then they are seeing something which is within their own unconscious; or they are too moralistic – then they don't meditate on any statues, they are in a hurry to get out of the temple somehow, they just throw glances.

Khajuraho sculpture is not just to see, it is for meditation. Sit silently and meditate for hours. If one goes to Khajuraho, one should live at least for three months there, so he can meditate on each possible inner posture of orgasmic joy. And then, slowly, slowly, the at-onement, slowly, slowly, the harmony; then suddenly you are transported into another world – the world of those mystics who created this temple. This is objective art.

So too is the Taj Mahal. On a fullmoon night, if you sit silently by the side of it, not being bothered about the history of the Taj Mahal and who created it and why – those are all nonsense, irrelevant facts, they don't matter: Shah Jahan and his beloved, and his memory of his beloved, he created it…. Don't be bothered by the guides; tip them before they start torturing you, and get rid of them!

Shah Jahan has nothing to do with the Taj Mahal, in fact. Yes, he created it, he created it as a memorial for his wife, but he is not the essential source of it. The essential source is in the Sufi way of life, it is in Sufism. Basically it was created by Sufi masters; Shah Jahan was just instrumental. The Sufi masters have created something of immense value. If you silently sit in the full moon night just looking at the Taj Mahal, sometimes with open eyes and sometimes with closed eyes, slowly, slowly you will feel something that you have never felt before. Sufis called it *zikr*, remembrance of God.

The beauty of the Taj Mahal will remind you of those realms from where all beauty, all benediction comes. You will become attuned with the Sufi way of remembering God: beauty is God.

Don't try to repress this urge. Create in any way that suits you. My message has to be delivered in all possible mediums.

In the new commune we are going to have many guilds. The sculptors will have their own guild and they will sculpt, and the poets will have their own guild, and the painters and the carpenters and the dancers and the musicians and the novelists and the filmmakers. All possible media have to be used to approach as many people as possible, to approach as many different kinds of people as possible – because one who can understand poetry may not understand prose, and one who can understand music may not understand painting, and one who can understand sculpture may not understand poetry.

And the message is so important because the whole future of humanity depends on it. Nowhere else is the experiment being done on such a great scale. There is no other community on the whole earth which is working in such a way as this commune. This is the greatest therapeutic center in the world now.

We need a great therapeutic center so that the modern mind can be helped to vomit, cathart all that has gone wrong in it. Then we will need creators. And once somebody has catharted and thrown out all that is wrong, a great urge will arise in him to create.

Once pathology disappears, everybody becomes a creator. Let it be understood as deeply as possible: only ill people are destructive. The people who are healthy are creative. Creativity is a kind of fragrance of real health. When a person is really healthy and whole, creativity comes naturally to him, the urge to create arises.

This urge is being felt by many just like you. Do something for it – and whatsoever you do is good. Follow your own urge, don't distort it. In the beginning it will remain vague, but if you follow it, soon it will become clear, more and more clear. And if you start doing something about it, things will become very clear very soon.

There are many things which become clear only when you do something about them. For example, the poet is never really aware of the poetry unless he has written it. It remains a very vague cloudy phenomenon. Once he writes it down it starts taking shape, form; it becomes crystallized into words. No painter is ever able to say anything about what he wants to paint, unless he has painted it.

It is said that the best way to learn is to teach. And I agree with it, because what you want to learn you will not be really clearly aware of unless you start teaching it.

In the future, education will have that dimension. My own vision is that each student should be given an opportunity to teach too. The students who are reading and studying for their master's degree should be allowed to go to lower classes to teach; those who are working for their bachelor's degree, they should be allowed to teach the lower classes.

Every student should be a teacher also, and vice versa. Every teacher once in a while should sit with the students and start learning again. Each teacher once in a while should be a student, and each student once in a while should be a teacher too. This difference between the teacher and the taught has to be dissolved; the teacher and the taught are part of one process.

And the same is true about other phenomena. The therapist and the patient – the therapist should not remain always a therapist, once in a while he should lie down on the couch and let the patient be the therapist and he becomes the patient. And immense will be the benefit out of it. The patient will learn many things that he was not able to learn while he was functioning as a patient: by becoming the therapist, by trying to solve the problem of the therapist – because now the therapist is the patient – he will be able to see many things more clearly. And the therapist as a patient will be able to see more clearly the problem, the anxiety, the anguish of the patient, because he will be standing in the shoes of the patient; now he will know where it pinches.

The therapist and the patient should not be divided, they should become part of one team. It is a therapy team, and sometimes the therapist plays the role of the patient and sometimes the patient plays the role of the therapist – the roles are interchangeable and so on and so forth. A couple making love…the man should not always remain the man, and the woman should not always remain the woman. Sometimes the man should be the wife, passive, and the woman should be the husband, active; they should change roles. The husband and wife should not remain frozen, they should be more melting: once in a while the wife should play the active role, take initiative making love, and the husband should be just passive, receptive. Love will have a greater richness that way than it has today. In fact all frozen roles have to be by and by dissolved. Life has to become more liquid.

So do whatsoever you can do, and by doing it, you will know what was the urge. Be articulate, try to convey the message, and don't be afraid.

A great fear arises when you are trying to deliver something immensely valuable; great fear arises, one starts feeling nervous. There is no need to feel nervous, because it is nothing to do with you. The urge is coming from the innermost sources of your being, it is divine. You are in the hands of God; be instrumental, you need not be worried.

You need not be proud if something good happens, you need not be ashamed if something goes wrong. Surrender both right and wrong unto the feet of God, and be free of your self-consciousness – because if you are not free of your self-consciousness you will never really be a creator in my sense of the word.

The real creator has no self. The real creation comes out of no-self, the real creation comes out of inner emptiness. When one is utterly empty, one is full of God. Not to be is the way for God to enter you. If you are too much, he is not there. If you are not, only he is there. And creativity is part of the creator.

No man ever creates; it is always God who creates. Hence the poet while he is creating is divine, and the painter while he is painting is divine. The only thing: if he is self-conscious then God is not there, then whatsoever he will do will be subjective art.

But if he is not there, if he is drowned in painting, completely lost, has forgotten himself and there is no self-consciousness, there is no ego, then God is there. When you find a painter painting, utterly lost, linger around. God is very close by – far more close than you will find him in the temples, in the mosques, in the churches.

When a singer is singing, sit by the side. Feel, God is very close by. When somebody is playing on the flute, hide behind a tree and listen, and you will be able to see something, something that is not of this world, something that is of the beyond. Creativity is always from the beyond.

? What is life?

Life is not something that can be defined. And life is not one thing, either; there are as many lives as there are people. Life is not a singular phenomenon. My life has a taste of its own, your life has its own individuality. The life of a tree certainly is not your life, and the life of a river is not the life of the tree.

Life is a multiplicity, life has millions of forms. How can it be defined? No definition will do justice to it. Yes, it can be lived, it can be tasted, but it cannot be defined. And your definition will simply show your experience. It will not say anything about life, it will only say something about how you have understood your life. It will not be relevant to anybody else's life. Remember this, then life is felt as a tremendous mystery.

Sol Greenberg was the only Jewish man in a small Texas town. He had given freely of his wealth and was particularly kind to the black population. And then Greenberg died.

Since he had no relatives, Greenberg bequeathed all his worldly goods to the townspeople. In order to show their respect and appreciation they decided to bury Greenberg in grand style.

They dressed him up in a cowboy outfit, complete with ten gallon hat and gold spurs. They had a solid gold Cadillac built, placed Greenberg behind the wheel and then dug a hole large enough to accommodate the car and its deceased occupant.

As they were lowering the Caddy into the ground, two blacks stood nearby and one commented to the other, "Ah tell ya, man, them Jewish folks sure knows how to live!"

The definition depends on you. The definition is always going to be your definition, how you conceive life, it will not be *the* definition of life. For the money mad, life will have the sound of money, of solid gold. For the power mad, the power maniac, life will have a different taste. For the poet, of course, life will have something of poetry in it.

It differs individual to individual, it depends. But one thing is central, essential, and that I would like to tell you. One thing is very essential: anybody who is really alive will be herenow. Whatsoever the form and whatsoever the expression of his individual life, one thing will be essentially there: the quality of being herenow.

Past is no more, future is not yet, so those who live in the past don't live, they only think they live. And those who live in the future can't live, because how can you make anything out of the future which has not come yet?

But that's how people are living. Millions live in the past, and the remaining millions live in the future, and it is very rare to find a person who lives herenow. But that is the real person, that is the person who is really alive. Life needs only one thing: to be rooted in the present. There is nowhere else for it to be rooted. Past is memory, future is imagination; both are unreal.

The real is this moment – thisness.

You ask me, "What is life?"

This is it!

You will have to learn how to unburden yourself from past and future, then you will be able to live like a roseflower or like a bird or like an animal, like a tree. Then you will have the same greenness, then you will have the same life juice flowing in you.

As I see it, millions of people on the road are not alive but walking zombies, they are dead people. In their eyes you will not find life flowing, life juices flowing. Their life is utterly meaningless – it is meaningless because it is not life.

In the old days, a minister had a Negro named Ezra in his household. Ezra was smart and ambitious, but he couldn't read or write.

One Sunday the minister saw Ezra in church, scribbling away industriously through the sermon. Afterwards the minister asked him, "Ezra, what were you doing in church?"

"Takin' notes, suh. Ah's eagah to l'arn."

"Let me see," said the minister, and he glanced over Ezra's notes, which looked more like Chinese than English.

"Why, Ezra," he chided, "this is all nonsense!"

"Ah thought so," said Ezra, "all the time you was preaching it."

Life is not there readymade, available. You get the life that you create, you get out of life that which you put into it. First you have to pour meaning into it. You have to give color and music and poetry, you have to be creative. Only then will you be alive.

The second essential thing: that only those few people who are creative know what life is. The uncreative never know, because life is in creativity, life *is* creativity. Can't you see how life goes on creating? It is a continuum of creativity, constant creativity, every moment creativity.

In fact God is not a creator. It is better to call him "creativity," because verbs are truer than nouns. Nouns look like things, verbs are processes – alive, flowing, dynamic. God is more creativity than a creator. Whenever you are creating, you will have the taste of life, and it will depend on your intensity, on your totality. Life is not a philosophical problem, it is a religious mystery. Then anything can become the door – even cleaning the floor. If you can do it creatively, lovingly, totally, you will have some taste of life.

Here in the ashram you will see people cleaning the floors, cleaning the bathrooms, structuring rooms, making furniture. But you will see a totally different quality: whatsoever their work is, they are doing it out of immense love. And you will see joy. That joy is not coming out of the work, that joy is coming out of their totality in the world, out of their surrender to the work. No work in itself can give you joy unless you pour joy into it.

So don't ask what life is, ask how to enter into life. The door is now, here – and you have to be creative, only then will you be able to enter the door; otherwise you will go on standing in the doorway without entering the palace.

So the second essential is: be creative. If these two things are fulfilled, you will know what life is.

? Is there such a thing as right or wrong?

There is no such thing as right or wrong, because something may be right this moment and it may not be right the next moment. Something may be wrong today and may not be wrong tomorrow.

Right and wrong are not fixed entities, they are not labels that you can put on things, "This is right" and "This is wrong." But this has been done up to now. Right and wrong have been decided by people. And because people have decided right and wrong, they have misguided the whole humanity.

Manu decides in one way: what he thinks is right becomes right for millions and millions of Hindus for thousands of years. It is so stupid, it is unbelievable! How can people go on following Manu for five thousand years? Everything else has changed. If Manu comes back he will not be able to recognize the world at all; everything has changed. But the Hindu mind goes on following the categories that Manu has fixed.

Still, after five thousand years, there are millions of people in India who are not treated like people. What to say, that they are not treated like people – they are not even treated like cattle. Even cows are far more important than alive people. Cows are worshipped, cows are holy, and the untouchables, the *sudras*, the rejected people – rejected by Manu, five thousand years ago – are burned.

And even a man like Vinoba Bhave is ready to go on fasting if cow slaughter is not completely stopped in the country, totally stopped. But he is completely silent, he does not say a single word, that the untouchables are being killed, burned alive, their women raped, their children murdered, butchered. Villages of untouchables, whole villages are being effaced from the earth, and Vinoba Bhave is not thinking of going on a fast. Who bothers about these untouchables? They are not part of humanity, they are not human beings. Cows have to be saved, because Manu worships the cow.

It may have been right at that moment; I am not against Manu, I am against the foolish followers of Manu. It may have been right at that time, because the cow was very, very important, it was the center of the whole economy; particularly the Indian economy was based on the cow. It was an agricultural society, and the cow was the source of many things: of the bulls, the bullocks, the manure, the milk – it was immensely important, it was perfectly right to save it. But now the world is living in a totally different way. Manu had a very small world; now we have the whole earth to think of, it is not only a question of a small sect. But once right has been fixed, people go on following blindly; it has been like that up to now.

For example, in the ten commandments Moses says, "Do not worship any other god than the true God. Don't make idols of the true God and don't worship any other gods." It was a totally different world; three thousand years have passed. In fact, in those ten commandments there is not a single commandment which says anything about atheists. It says, "Don't worship any other god." It does not say, "Don't disbelieve in God," because there was no disbeliever. Atheism was not at all in the air.

Now the most fundamental thing will be to teach people how not to be atheists, because atheism is very prevalent. Almost half of the earth has gone communist, it is atheist, and the remaining half is only formally theist. Now the most fundamental commandment should be, "Don't be atheists, don't be disbelievers, don't be doubters." Now trust should be the most fundamental teaching to be given to people.

As time changes, rights change, wrongs change. And you can see it in your own life – every day things are different, and you go on clinging to your fixed ideas. The man who lives with fixed ideas lives a dead life. He is never spontaneous and he is never in a right relationship with the situation that exists. He is never response-able; he functions out of his old conclusions which are no longer relevant, he does not look at the situation itself.

So, according to me there is no such thing as right and no such thing as wrong. Then what do I teach? I teach awareness – not labeling, not categorizing. I teach awareness. I teach you to be fully aware in every situation, and act out of your awareness. Or, in different words I can say: Any action that happens through awareness is right; any action that happens through unawareness is wrong.

But see the emphasis. The emphasis is not on the action itself, the emphasis is on the source – awareness or unawareness. If you act fully aware, then whatsoever you do is right. If you move mechanically and do things unconsciously as if you are a sleepwalker, a somnambulist, then whatsoever you do is wrong.

Awareness is right, unawareness is wrong.

But if you go to the priests, they will teach you what is right and what is wrong. They will not give you insight, they will give you dead categories. They will not give you light, so that you can see in every situation what to do and what not to do; they want you to depend on them.

They don't give you insight into things, so you have to remain dependent forever. They give you crutches, but they don't make you stand on your own feet.

Avoid the priests. Whenever you go to any kind of experts, their whole effort in fact is how to make you dependent on them.

The star of a Broadway hit was visiting friends when talk got around, as usual, to psychiatry. "I must say," said the hostess, "I think my analyst is the best in the world! You can't imagine what he has done for me. You ought to try him."

"But I don't need analysis," said the star. "I could not be more normal – there is nothing wrong with me."

"But he is absolutely great," insisted her friend. "He will find something wrong."

There are people who live on finding something wrong with you. Their whole trade secret is to find something wrong with you. They cannot accept you as you are; they will give you ideals, ideas, ideologies, and they will make you feel guilty and they will make you feel worthless, dirt. In your own eyes, they will make you feel so condemned that you will forget all about freedom.

In fact you will become afraid of freedom, because you will see how bad you are, how wrong you are – and if you are free, you are going to do something wrong, so follow somebody. The priest depends on it, the politician depends on it. They give you right and wrong, fixed ideas, and then you will remain guilty forever.

I say to you: There is nothing right and nothing wrong. I don't want you to depend on me, and I don't give you any fixed ideas. I simply give you indications, hints, which have to be worked out by you. And the hint that I give to you is awareness. Become more aware, and it is a miracle....

If you are angry, the priest will say anger is wrong, don't be angry. What will you do? You can repress anger, you can sit upon it, you can swallow it, literally, but it will go into you, into your system. Swallow anger and you will have ulcers in the stomach, swallow anger and sooner or later you will have cancer. Swallow anger and you will have a thousand and one problems arising out of it, because anger is poison. But what will you do? If anger is wrong, you have to swallow it.

I don't say anger is wrong, I say anger is energy – pure energy, beautiful energy. When anger arises, be aware of it, and see the miracle happen. When anger arises, be aware of it, and if you are aware you will be surprised; you are in for a surprise – maybe the greatest surprise of your life – that as you become aware, anger disappears. Anger is transformed. Anger becomes pure energy; anger becomes compassion, anger becomes forgiveness, anger becomes love. And you need not repress, so you are not burdened by some poison. And you are not being angry, so you are not hurting anybody. Both are saved: the other, the object of your anger, is saved, and you are saved. In the past, either the object was to suffer, or you were to suffer.

What I am saying is that there is no need for anybody to suffer. Just be aware, let awareness be there. Anger will arise and will be consumed by awareness. One cannot be angry with awareness and one cannot be greedy with awareness and one cannot be jealous with awareness. Awareness is the golden key.

Chapter 25
We Are Ancient Pilgrims

*You should find freedom by means of both examination and investigation.
Don't brag. Don't be consumed by jealousy. Don't act capriciously.
Don't expect thanks.
This quintessential elixir of advice by which the advancement of the five
decays is changed into the bodhi path is transmitted through Dharmakirti.
By awakening the karmic energy of previous training, and by virtue of my
intense interest, I ignored misery and bad reputation and sought instruc-
tion to control ego-clinging. Now, even when I die, I'll have no regret.*

Man's greatest longing is for freedom. Man *is* a longing for freedom. Freedom is the very essential core of human consciousness: love is its circumference and freedom is its center. These two fulfilled, life has no regret. And they both are fulfilled together, never separately.

People have tried to fulfill love without freedom. Then love brings more and more misery, more and more bondage. Then love is not what one has expected it to be, it turns out just the opposite. It shatters all hopes, it destroys all expectations and life becomes a wasteland – a groping in darkness and never finding the door.

Love without freedom naturally tends to be possessive. And the moment possessiveness enters in, you start creating bondage for others and bondage for yourself – because you cannot possess somebody without being possessed by him. You cannot make somebody a slave without becoming a slave yourself. Whatsoever you do to others is done to you.

This is the basic principle to be understood, that love without freedom never brings fulfillment.

And there have been people who have tried the other extreme, freedom without love. These are the monks, the escapists, the people who renounced the world. Afraid of love, afraid of love because it brings bondage, they renounce all the situations where love can flow, grow, can happen, is possible. They escape into loneliness. Their loneliness never becomes aloneness, it remains loneliness. And loneliness is a negative state; it is utterly empty, it is sad.

One can be a solitary, but that does not bring solitude. Solitariness is just physical aloneness, solitude is spiritual aloneness. If you are just lonely…and you will be if you have renounced the world. If you have escaped from the world out of fear you will be lonely, the world will haunt you, and all kinds of desires will surround you. You will suffer millions of nightmares, because whatsoever you have renounced cannot be dropped so easily.

Renunciation is repression and nothing else. And the more you repress a thing, the more you need to repress it. And the more you go on repressing it, the more powerful it becomes. It will erupt in your dreams, it will erupt in your hallucinations. People living in the monasteries start hallucinating, people going to the Himalayan caves sooner or later are no more in contact with reality. They start creating a reality of their own – a private reality, a fictitious reality.

The Christian will talk to Christ. In his lonely cave he creates Christ, just so that he can have somebody there, just so that he is not lonely. And many methods of hallucinating have been developed by these monks. If you fast, hallucination becomes easier. The body becomes weaker, you start losing control over reality. The more weak the body is, the more is the possibility of hallucination. People in fever, illness, start hallucinating. The exact same rule: torture the body, weaken the body, starve the body and hallucinations will be easier.

You can have Jesus Christ or Krishna or Gautam Buddha – great company you can have, but it is all imagination. The Hindu will never see Christ, and the Christian will never see Krishna. You will see only whatsoever you believe in, you will see only whatsoever you create by your belief; it is a projection.

It will be difficult to project it in the marketplace, because there will be so many people who will deny your projection. They will take you to the psychiatrist, they will think you have gone nuts. If you start talking to Christ in the marketplace you will end up in some hospital.

But in the Himalayan cave there is nobody else, you are free to create whatsoever you want to your heart's content. Loneliness is such a misery that one starts believing in one's own hallucinations, to have company. But this is madness.

On the one hand is the person, the worldly person, who has tried to find love without freedom and has failed. His life is nothing but a long, long slavery to many, many people, to many, many things. He is chained, body, mind, soul; he is not free to have even a slight movement. That is one failure; the majority of humanity is caught in that extreme.

A few escape from the world: seeing the misery, they start searching for the other extreme – freedom, *moksha*, nirvana. But they become neurotic, psychotic, they start living in their own dreams. Loneliness is so much that one has to create something to be with.

Both these extreme efforts have failed. Hence humanity stands on a crossroads. Where to go? The past has utterly failed. All the efforts that we have done in the past proved wrong, led to cul-de-sacs. Now where to go, what to do?

Atisha has an important message to deliver to you. That is the message of all the buddhas, of all the enlightened people of the world. They say: Love and freedom are not separate things, you cannot choose. Either you will have to have both, or you will have to drop both. But you cannot choose, you cannot have one.

Love is the circumference, freedom is the center.

One has to grow in such delicate balance, to where love and freedom can bloom together. And they can, because in a few rare individuals it has happened. And if it has happened to only a single individual in the whole history, it can happen to every human being. It is your potential, your birthright.

Meditation is the balance.

Meditation is the bird with two wings: freedom and love.

My effort here in this buddhafield is to give you both the wings together: be loving and be free, be loving and be nonpossessive. Be free but don't become cold; remain warm, warm with love.

Your freedom and your love have to grow hand in hand, in deep embrace, in a kind of dance, helping each other. And then the total man is born, who lives in the world and is not of the world at all. Then the man is born in whom extremes meet and merge and become complementaries; then the man is rich. Just to love without freedom is to be impoverished, or just to be free without love is to live in loneliness, sadness, darkness. Freedom is needed for love to grow, love is needed so that freedom can be nourished.

My sannyasin has to remember constantly not to choose between these two. Both have to be absorbed together, digested together. Love has to become your circumference, your action, and freedom has to become your being, your center, your soul.

The first sutra:

You should find freedom by means of both examination and investigation.

Freedom can be of three types, and those three types have to be understood well. The first is freedom from, the second is freedom for, and the third is just freedom – neither from nor for. The first, freedom from, is a reaction. It is past-oriented; you are fighting against the past, you want to get rid of it, you are obsessed with it.

Psychoanalysis tries to give you this freedom, freedom from – from the past traumas, childhood wounds. Primal therapy is based basically on the past. You have to go backwards to free yourself from the past, you have to reach to the first primal scream, then you will be free. So freedom means – for primal therapy, for psychoanalysis and for other therapies – that the past has to be dropped. You have to fight with it, you have to somehow manage to disentangle yourself from the past; then you will be free.

As far as this freedom is concerned, Karl Marx and Sigmund Freud are not opposed to each other; they both agree. Karl Marx says one has to become free from the past, all past social structures, economic structures. His approach is political, Freud's approach is psychological, but both are rooted in the idea of freedom from.

All political reforms are reactions – and when you react you are never free. This has to be understood. It only gives you an appearance of freedom, but it is never true freedom. Out of reaction, total freedom is not possible. Out of reaction, true freedom is not possible. And only total freedom is true freedom.

You can go against the past, but just in being against it you are caught by it from the back door. That's why it has happened again and again that with whomsoever you are fighting, you become like him. Choose your enemies very carefully, because you will be determined by them! Fighting with them, you will have to learn their strategies, obviously. You will have to learn their tactics, you will have to learn their ways. Slowly, slowly, enemies become very alike – more alike than friends.

It happened in Soviet Russia…. When the revolution came and the communists changed the whole social structure, the czar was killed, and a strange phenomenon came into existence. The people who had killed the czar turned out to be greater czars than the czars themselves. Josef Stalin proved to be far more terrible than Ivan the Terrible. Ivan is nothing compared to Josef Stalin.

And it is a natural phenomenon. I am not blaming Josef Stalin at all, I can understand what really happened. If you fight with the czar you have to learn his ways, and by the time you are the winner you have learned the ways so skillfully, so efficiently, they have become your ways. You start practicing the same on your enemies. That's why every revolution has failed. Persons change but the structures remain the same, because the idea of freedom from is basically wrong.

The second idea is freedom for; it is future-oriented. The first is political, the second is more poetic, visionary, utopian. Many people have tried that too, but that too is not possible, because future-oriented you can't live in the present – and you have to live in the present. You don't live in the past, you don't live in the future, you have to live in the present.

Visionaries only imagine. Beautiful utopias they have imagined, but those utopias never become reality, cannot become reality.

If you react to the past, you are determined by the past. If you forget the past and look at the future, you are still driven by the past, you just are not aware of it. Looking at the future you dream beautiful dreams, but they can't change reality. The reality remains the same; dreams are very ineffective, impotent.

The first, freedom from, is a reaction. The second, freedom for, is revolution. The third, just freedom, is rebellion. It is present-oriented. The first is political, the second is poetic, the third is mystic, religious.

What do I mean when I say "just freedom"? Neither for nor against, no past, no future, just being herenow, just living moment to moment with no ideology, with no utopia.

The real sannyasin, the real mystic, is not against the past, is not for the future. He is so utterly absorbed by the present that he has no time, no energy, for the past and the future. This is how the rebel is born.

The rebel is the most beautiful phenomenon in the world. Buddha is a rebel, so is Jesus; Atisha is a rebel, so is Kabir. These are rebels. You will misunderstand them if you think of them as if they were revolutionaries; they were not. Neither were they reactionaries. Their orientation is totally different, their orientation is now, here. They don't live for any ideal, and they don't live against any ideal. They don't have any ideas; no ideology exists in the consciousness.

The sheer purity of this moment…they live it, they enjoy it, they sing it, they dance it. And when the next moment comes, they live the next moment with the same joy, with the same cheerfulness. They move moment to moment, they don't plan ahead.

That's why in the East, where mystics have been a great force, nothing like communism has happened. The idea is Western, the idea cannot be conceived to have happened in the Eastern consciousness. And nothing like future utopias – More's Utopia or other utopias, there are so many utopian socialists – nothing like that has happened either.

But something totally different has happened: a Buddha, an Atisha – individuals living moment to moment in such sheer joy that their joy is contagious. Whosoever comes in contact with them is overwhelmed, starts looking at reality with new eyes. They give you a new insight into the herenow. This is "just freedom." Meditate over it.

There is no need for any psychology either, and that's why psychology has not happened in the East. There is no need to go into past traumas, and in fact even if you go into past traumas you are never free of them. Maybe you become more accepting, more understanding, but you are never free of them.

Whatsoever the founder of primal therapy, Arthur Janov, says about the post-primal man, he has not been able to create a single post-primal man. He himself is not a post-primal man. Totally free from the past, totally free from past wounds – it is not possible. The way it is done by psychoanalysis and kindred therapies, it is not possible. The past is not there. From what are you trying to get free?

In fact, under the impact of a charismatic psychotherapist you start creating a past according to him. This happens: if you go to the Freudian you create a Freudian past, and if you go to the Jungian you create a Jungian past. Now this is a well-known fact, that the patients start creating, fantasizing, the past that is expected by the therapist. The Jungian patient starts going into past lives very easily and starts bringing great mysteries, esoteric, occult. It never happened to any patient with Freud. The Freudian patient brings what Freud expects: libido, sexual fantasies, strange sexual fantasies, incest and all kinds of sexual wounds. They never surface in Jungian psychotherapy. The primal patient starts bringing screams which may not have any reality.

But people are very obliging: if you give them an idea, they oblige you by fulfilling it. In fact the patient starts feeling very, very compassionate toward the therapist – he is working so hard, poor fellow – so sooner or later he starts obliging. Now there are hundreds of psychotherapies in the West, and each psychotherapist becomes convinced that he is right. His patients befool him. And the same patients go to another psychotherapist and they befool the other too. The patients are playing a great game, and that is happening unconsciously.

Mind is so vast, you can always choose a few fragments which will be satisfying to a particular philosophy, to a particular psychology, to a particular therapy. Man is a vast continent, man is not a small phenomenon. It can contain many Freuds, many Jungs, many Adlers. And you can always choose – there is so much in you that you can always find ways of choosing certain fragments which fit with the therapy you are going through.

The East has not created anything like communism, and it has not created anything like psychoanalysis, for a certain reason. The reason is that the mystic is not trying to be free from the past, the mystic is not trying to be free for something in the future. The mystic's effort for freedom, what he calls *moksha*, total freedom, has nothing to do with that which is no more, and has nothing to do with that which is not yet. His whole concern is this moment, this small crystal-clear moment.

And to be in this moment is to be in meditation.

To be utterly in this moment is to be in meditation.

And when meditation happens you will see two wings growing in you: one will be of love – Atisha calls it compassion – another will be of freedom. And they will both start growing together. This brings fulfillment. Then there is no grudge, no regret. Atisha is right; he says:

Now, even when I die, I'll have no regret.

Life has been a fulfillment. I have known its mysteries. I have loved, I have lived in freedom, I have known all that was needed to be contented. I am utterly fulfilled. Life has been fruitful. Life has not been a wastage, it has been a constant enrichment, and I have bloomed and the lotus has opened.

To die with your inner lotus fully in bloom, to die in love, in freedom, is the proof that one has known life, is the proof that one has really lived. All others only go through empty gestures; they are not living.

You should find freedom by means of both examination and investigation.

How to find this freedom? How to find this essential core of your being? It happens in meditation. Atisha calls meditation "awareness." And awareness has to be developed; it is only a seed in you, it can become a tree. And two things he suggests will be helpful: one is examination and the other is investigation.

Examination means, never allow anything to pass your mind without observing it minutely. Socrates is reported to have said that a life is worthless if you have not lived it through examination. An unexamined life is a worthless life.

Examination is the first step: becoming alert to what passes through your mind. And there is constant traffic – so many thoughts, so many desires, so many dreams are passing by. You have to be watchful; you have to examine each and everything that passes through the mind. Not a single thought should pass unawares, because that means you were asleep. Become more and more observant.

And the second step is investigation. First observe, examine, and then start looking into the roots. Why does a certain thing happen again and again? You become angry again and again: examination will simply show you that anger comes and goes. Investigation will show you the roots of anger, from where it comes – because it may be, it is almost always so, that anger is only a symptom of something else which is hidden. It may be your ego that feels hurt and you become angry, but the ego keeps itself hiding underground. It is like roots of the trees: you see the foliage but you don't see the roots.

By examination you will see the tree, by investigation you will see the roots. And it is only by seeing the roots that a transformation is possible. Bring the roots to the light and the tree starts dying. If you can find the root of your anger, you will be surprised that the anger starts disappearing. If you can find the root of your sadness you will be again surprised.

First examine what is constantly there in your mind, what is being repeated again and again. You don't have many thoughts. If you examine minutely you will see that you have only a few thoughts repeated again and again – maybe in new forms, new colors, new garments, new masks, but you have only a very few thoughts.

And if you go into it minutely you will be surprised: you have one basic thought.

Gurdjieff used to say to his disciples, "First find out your main characteristic." And each person has a main characteristic – it may be greed, it may be anger, it may be sex, jealousy, it may be something else. Find out which is the main characteristic, which is the center around which all your thoughts and moods move. If you can find the center, you have found the root.

And the miracle is that once the root is found you need not cut it, it is cut in the very finding of it. This is the inner secret of transformation.

Watch: again and again you become sad. Suddenly out of nowhere…everything was going good, and something clicks and you become sad. And again it is gone, and by the evening it is back, and so on, so forth. Why does this happen?

First examine, then investigate. By examination and investigation the quality called awareness will be born in you. Once awareness is there you have the sword which can cut all the roots of all the diseases. And once awareness is born, slowly, slowly you are getting out of the past and out of the future and you are entering the present. You are becoming more present to the present. You are attaining to a kind of presence which was never there; you are becoming luminous. And in this presence, when you can feel the moment passing by, all your senses will become so pure, so sensitive, so sensuous, so alert and alive, that the whole life will take a new intensity. You will attain to a great zestfulness. The world will be the same, and yet not the same: the trees will look greener, the roses rosier, the people more alive, more beautiful – the same world, and the pebbles on the shore start looking like diamonds and emeralds.

When awareness is very, very deep-rooted, when you are present to the present, you attain to a psychedelic vision of life. That's why mystics talk of so much beauty, and you don't find it. Mystics talk of immense celebration going on, and you don't see any celebration anywhere. Mystics talk of great music, but you don't hear any music.

And the mystics are right – a great music is passing by, but you are deaf. Great beauty is all around, but you are blind. The whole existence is celebrating this very moment, as much as it was celebrating when Atisha was alive. Existence is celebration.

But your heart is dead. Only your physical heart is beating, your spiritual heart is completely nonfunctioning. And without it you will not be able to see the celebration of life. How can you feel grateful to God if you don't see the celebration? How can you feel thankful to God if you don't see the gift? For what to be thankful? You can only be full of complaints, regrets, grudges. You can only be angry at existence. Why have you been created, why this suffering? You see only suffering, because your eyes can only see suffering. Otherwise existence is a blessing, a benediction.

The second sutra:

Don't brag.

Atisha is really beautiful, very telegraphic. His sutras look as if he is taking quantum jumps, they seem to be unrelated. They are not; there is an inner relationship – because when this psychedelic vision happens to you, you will start bragging. When this awareness happens to you, the last but one assault of the ego is bound to happen too. It is inevitable. You will start feeling holier-than-thou. You will start moving like a saint, you will start feeling, exhibiting, that you are not an ordinary mortal, that you are extraordinary, that you are not of this world, that you are transcendental.

And although all these things are right, Atisha says: Please don't brag. He is not saying that you are lying. All these things are true; when awareness happens, miracles start happening. Each moment becomes such a miracle, and you start soaring high, you start attaining to new peaks in everything. Whatsoever you do becomes such a delight, and wherever you move, life appears to be so divine. And you can see too, that wherever you move you bring a certain sacredness to the place. Not that these are lies; these are happening. But if you start bragging, all these things will disappear, because the ego has entered in such a subtle way, and you could not examine it and you could not investigate it.

Ego will ride on your spiritual experiences now. One has now to be very careful. The non-meditator can be careless – he can afford to be careless, because he has nothing to lose. But the meditator cannot be careless, he has much to lose. Treasures are there now and they can be lost within a second.

When you start moving to the higher realms you can fall very easily – and the fall is going to be great. If you fall walking on M.G. Road there is not much danger, but if you fall from Everest it is very dangerous, you may not survive at all.

So those who start moving in the world of meditation have to learn to be very careful. The path is narrow, and just by the side of the path is the great abyss. A single wrong step and you will fall – and you will fall badly. It may take years or even lives for you to attain to the same height again. And if you fall once from a certain space, the tendency is that again you will fall from the same space; that becomes your habit.

My observation is this: that meditators learn habits of always falling from a certain stage, so whenever that state is again there, they fall. Great effort is needed to reach it again, but now it becomes a point where the mind suddenly takes the wrong step, habitually, mechanically. So it is better to be aware when for the first time you are moving high, so no habit of falling is created in you.

Don't brag.

Spiritual experiences should not be talked about. If a great need arises in you to talk about it you can go to your master, you can share with your master. There is no danger in it, because sharing with the master is always helpful. In the first place, whatsoever you bring to the master he will make you feel that it is nothing: "Don't be stupid, this is just bullshit. Forget all about it." Even if you bring nirvana to him, he will say, "This is nothing – throw it out! Leave it where you leave your shoes" – even nirvana!

That is one of the secrets of the master in his work on the disciple. He will never pat your back, he will never say, "Great! You are so great, you have attained!"

Secondly, he will always make you be aware that experiences, howsoever beautiful, are still experiences. The real is not that which is experienced, but the one who experiences. His emphasis will always be towards the witness, towards the inner subjectivity, not towards the object.

Somebody sees great light – and it is really a great rejoicing when you see inner light. You don't walk on the earth; you are so delighted you lose all weight, gravitation no longer functions on you. You feel as if, if you want, you can fly.

But if you go to the master he will say, "So what? This happens to everybody. This is nothing special, others are doing far better. This is only an experience, and experience means something outside. Remember the experiencer, remember the one who is experiencing the light. You are not it: you are the witness of it. Yes, light is there, but you are not it. You are the one who has seen the light. Remember the seer."

we are ancient pilgrims   373

Masters are great artists in pulling legs. You may go standing upright and they will pull your leg and you will fall flat on the ground. And the next time when some great spiritual experience happens, you will be afraid even to go to the master and tell about it. This is very essential.

And the third thing: there are things which, if you talk about them, if you start exhibiting them, the energy that is needed to nourish them starts moving into exhibiting them.

The seed needs to be hidden in the soil. It should not be brought out again and again; if you bring it out you will kill it. And these spiritual experiences are like great seeds. The disciple has to learn the art of keeping secrets. This is one of the very essential parts of being with a master: the capacity to keep secrets.

I have heard: a man was in search of a master who has attained to the ultimate secret. He went to many but was frustrated finally, disappointed. Then he heard that far away, deep in the desert, there is an old man who has attained to the ultimate secret, but to persuade him is very difficult; he does not accept disciples easily.

This man was challenged. He sold all that he had and traveled to the desert. It took three years for him to reach there. Utterly tired, weary of the whole search…many times he had decided to turn back, but it was against his ego, the ego of the seeker – "What will people say? Back home they will laugh and they will say, 'We had told you so before!'"

So he persisted, persevered, and finally reached. Yes, the old man had something; it was so apparent, it was so transparent. He had seen many masters, but all bogus, hocus-pocus; this man had something. He looked into the eyes of the old man and he saw such depth as he had never seen.

The old man was sitting under a tree, and the whole vibe around the tree was so immense that the man was overwhelmed. He started feeling drunk. He fell at the feet of the old man and said, "I have come to find the ultimate secret. Can you tell it to me?"

And the master said, "Then for three years you will have to be silent, not a single word has to be uttered. Serve me for three years in absolute silence. If you can manage that, then I can tell you the secret, because the secret has to be kept secret. If you can manage silence for three years, that will be an indication that you are capable of keeping something within yourself."

The man agreed. Those three years were really long, almost like three lives…desert, nobody else, just this old man, and silence – the silence of the desert, the silence of the old man, and three years. It appeared as if many, many years had passed. When the three years were over, the man asked, "Now, sir, three years are over. Tell me the secret."

The master said, "Now you have to make a promise that you will never tell this secret to anybody – never, *never*. An absolute promise is needed."

The man said, "I promise! I promise to you, I promise to God, with my whole heart, that never will I reveal this secret to anybody."

The old man started laughing. He said, "That's good. So what do you think, if you can keep it a secret for your whole life, cannot I? This is the promise that I have given to my own master: I cannot reveal it! But I will tell you one thing," he said. "The same thing happened with my master. Three years I had remained silent, and it was as long as it has been long to you. And then the day came, and I was so happy that for three years I had kept silent. Exactly the same thing happened! I asked him about the secret and he said, 'Promise that you will never reveal the secret to anybody.' I promised, and he laughed the way I have laughed, and he said, 'So what do you think, if you can keep it a secret, cannot I?'

"So in fact there is no secret. The whole art is of *keeping* it; it is not a question of the secret. My own understanding is that the same has been happening again and again. This must have happened with my master and his master, and so on, so forth. There seems to be no secret, but we have learned a lot by keeping it!"

See the point: if you can keep a secret…whether the secret is worth keeping or not, that is not the point. Whether there is a secret or not, that is not the point. The master may have whispered in your ear that "Two plus two is four: now keep it a secret." That will do – it is not a question of what it is, the question is can you keep something inside you?

Just the other night I was telling Radha, "Now you have to keep this a secret." I have not told any secret to her, but she has promised. "Yes," she said, "I will keep it." I told her, "You are a gossip, one of the greatest gossipers in the commune, so you have to keep it a secret." And she has promised. I don't know what secret she has promised for, but now she has to keep it! The art is in keeping it.

Don't brag.

Don't exhibit. A natural tendency of the mind is to exhibit. And when you have something special – for example, you can read somebody's thoughts – it is very natural to go and show it to people.

Once a Mohammedan young man was with me for many years – a very stubborn fellow – and whatsoever I gave him to do, he would put his whole energy into it. Then one day it happened that he started reading people's thoughts. It was very difficult for me to keep him silent about it. And this is trespass, to read anybody's thoughts; it is entering into his privacy.

Because I told him to keep it to himself, never to practice it, he kept it. Out of keeping it a secret and not exhibiting and not practicing it, another quality arose out of it: he became able to put a thought in your mind very easily without your knowing. Whatsoever he would like to put in your mind, you would immediately act accordingly. He became a kind of Delgado, and without any electrodes. He discovered it suddenly….

I had sent him for a journey; he was sitting on a bus, and just the *idea*, just the idea, suddenly came in his mind: if he can read people's thoughts, cannot he put a thought in somebody's mind? out of nowhere?

Because I had not told him anything about it, he tried. He just tried with the person who was sitting in the seat ahead of him: "Fall down from your seat" – and the man fell down! He himself was shocked, but then he thought it may be just a coincidence, the man was just going to fall down. So he tried on another, and again it happened. He became so afraid, and the idea started torturing him: "Why not take the whole bus down the hill?" He had to stop the driver and get down from the bus in the middle of the journey.

He came back to me and he said, "This is very dangerous. I tried on two persons; it worked, and then the idea came to me, 'Why not try with the whole bus?'"

If you enter into the world of meditation, these are small things which start happening. Avoid them, never use them, never exhibit, and don't talk about them – because if you talk, people will say, "Now show some proof." If you talk about them they will ask for the proof. Then you will start practicing them and soon you will lose the energy.

The energy is needed for inner nourishment. When something is growing in you the whole energy has to be turned into manure. Don't use it outside in any way. The best way to begin is: *Don't brag*.

The third sutra:

Don't be consumed by jealousy.

Now, you will be at a loss to find the relationship, but it is there. Atisha is saying that you may not brag but others may brag; then jealousy will arise. Others may start showing their spiritual powers, and by showing their spiritual powers they may be worshipped by people, respected by people, thought to be great saints. You are holding a secret in your heart, and you know you can do greater miracles than they can do. They are being worshipped by people, and nobody knows anything about you, you are just a nobody. Jealousy may arise, and if jealousy arises, that is the negative part of bragging. Then, sooner or later, you will start bragging.

One more point to be understood.... It happens that when for the first time a meditator attains to some psychic energy, some psychic power, the tendency, a natural tendency, is to exhibit it. And if he exhibits, sooner or later he will lose the power. Then a great problem arises: he cannot do it now, but now he has respectability. He is worshipped and people expect him to do miracles. Now what is he going to do? He will have to turn to magic, he will have to start learning tricks, to maintain his prestige.

That's what happened to Satya Sai Baba and people like that. The first things that they had done were real, the first few experiments that they had done were not phony. But then the energy disappears. And by that time you have become famous, and people start gathering, foolish people, stupid people, and they expect you, and your whole ego depends on your exhibition.

Now the only possible alternative is to learn magic tricks so that you can go on maintaining your prestige. If you brag, sooner or later you will become a victim of magical tricks. You will have to learn, and deceive people.

Don't be jealous, because if you are jealous it will be impossible for you to keep the secret long.

And the fourth:

Don't act capriciously.

Don't irritate people unnecessarily by pretending to be holier than others, by pretending to be saintly, by pretending to be special. Don't irritate people, don't act in such ways. Why? – because difficulties are going to arise on their own, so don't, please, add to them.

Your very presence is going to create troubles for you, so at least avoid as much as possible irritating people. If you pretend to be holier, then you will create competitors. If you pretend that you are special, then there will be others who will deny. Argumentations will arise, unnecessary controversies, enmities.

Atisha is saying this for a very special reason. The special reason is that the very presence of a person who has some spiritual quality is enough to create trouble for him, because blind people don't like people with eyes. Those who have lived always in darkness don't like people who bring light to them, they hate them – because the presence of a man of light is insulting, it makes them feel inferior.

And this happens of its own accord, so please don't in any way do anything to enhance it more. Even if you keep everything secret, a few people are going to know about it. Its presence is such that a few people are bound to find you. Even if you escape to the Himalayas, a few people are bound to search and seek you out, because there *are* seekers. There are people who are very sensitive, there are people who have been looking for lives for something to happen in their life. You will become known. There is no need to brag, there is no need to be jealous. Try to hide yourself as much as you can; still you will become known.

You cannot hide a light underneath a bush; it will show. You cannot hide a light, it will radiate. And once seekers start gathering around you, and disciples come and devotees come, the society at large is going to be very irritated with you, the society is going to be angry with you. The society will try to destroy you and your whole work and your whole commune.

Why? – because you are undermining the society, you are cutting its very roots. It lives in ambition, and you are teaching a non-ambitious life. It lives in Machiavellian ways, and you are teaching the ways of the Buddha. It lives through jealousy, violence, possessiveness, and you are teaching love. You are undermining its very foundation, you are destroying its very roots. It cannot forgive you, it will take revenge. So it is better to be very cautious.

Don't expect thanks.

It is natural, when you attain closer and closer to God, it is very natural to feel that people will be thankful to you. You are bringing a gift to them, the greatest gift there is, the gift of God. It is very natural to feel that people will be thankful to you. Don't expect it; expect just the contrary, that people will never be able to forgive you. The greater the gift you bring to them, the greater will be their anger. They will crucify you, they will poison you – expect things like that.

Even Jesus was not expecting that so much torture was going to be done to him, that so much suffering was going to be created for him. From the cross he shouted to God, "Have you forsaken me? Why? Why is this happening to me? What wrong have I done?" Deep down somewhere he was not expecting that crucifixion was going to happen.

Atisha is very clear in his advice to his disciples:

Don't expect thanks.

On the contrary, expect that people will be angry, irritated, revengeful, they will become antagonistic to you. Hope for the best and expect the worst. If they don't kill you, be thankful to them.

A disciple of Buddha was going to spread his master's word. Buddha asked him, "Where will you be going, in what direction, to what province?" And he said that he was going to a remote corner of Bihar – it was called Sukha – "because no other disciple of yours has ever gone to that part."

Buddha said, "Before you decide, answer three questions. First, do you know the people of that province are very violent, easily irritable, murderous? It is dangerous to go to them, that's why no other disciple has even thought of going to them. If they insult you, and they are going to insult you, how are you going to respond? What will happen in your heart?"

And the disciple said, "You know perfectly well what will happen in my heart, because you know my heart, because you are my heart. Why such unnecessary questions? But because you ask, I have to answer. If they insult me, deep down in my heart I will feel thankful to them that they only insult me; they could have beaten me."

Buddha said, "Now the second question. They will beat you, you are going to be beaten. Then what will happen to you? Then what will you think?"

The disciple said, "You know perfectly well. I will be thankful to them, because I will think they are only beating me when they could have killed me."

Buddha said, "Now the third question. They can kill you. And if they kill you, what will happen to you? What will you think in your heart?"

The disciple said, "You know perfectly well, you are unnecessarily asking me. But because you ask, I have to answer. If they kill me, while I am being killed I will be thankful, because they have given me a beautiful opportunity, the greatest challenge."

Can you be thankful even to those who are killing you? The greatest challenge!

"I will be thankful to them because they are killing me and taking my life away from me – a life in which I may have committed some wrong. Now there is no possibility; I will never commit any wrong. A life in which I may have fallen from my awareness…now they are taking that life away from me, I cannot fall from my awareness any more. I will be thankful to them, utterly thankful, because when somebody is being killed, if he can remain alert, that is his last life, he will not be coming back to the earth. I will think they are my friends, they are delivering me from bondage. I will always remember them with tremendous gratitude in my heart."

Buddha said, "Now you can go wherever you want, because wherever you go you will be able to radiate my energy. You will be able to share my love and my compassion and you will be able to make people alert, aware. You are ready."

Atisha says: *Don't expect thanks*. On the contrary, be thankful if something wrong is being done to you. That is natural; you should know well, you should expect it. If it doesn't happen, that is a miracle. If Jesus is not crucified, if Socrates is not poisoned, if Mahavira is not beaten again and again, if many efforts and attempts are not made on Buddha's life, that will be a miracle. These things have to be expected. That's how the greater part of humanity lives – in darkness, in such darkness; from their darkness you cannot expect more.

*This quintessential elixir of advice by which the advancement of the five
decays is changed into the bodhi path is transmitted through Dharmakirti.*

The original master is Gautama the Buddha, but Atisha's master is Dharmakirti. The disciple
never forgets the master, even when he himself becomes enlightened. Then too his gratitude
remains; in fact it grows, it becomes total, absolute. Atisha remembers his master Dharmakirti.
It was Dharmakirti who told him to go to Dharmarakshita to learn something more, and it was
Dharmakirti who told him, "After Dharmarakshita you go to Yogin Maitreya to learn something
more." But he was following the guidance of his master, Dharmakirti.

Dharmakirti is one of the very famous Buddhist masters. Many of his disciples became
enlightened. Atisha is only one of his disciples, but the most famous. He says:

This quintessential elixir of advice...

"This nectar that I have poured into the previous sutras has nothing to do with me. I am not
the author of these sutras. These truths were transmitted to me from my master, and they were
transmitted to my master from his master. Originally they come from Gautama the Buddha.
"These sutras are not mine," he is saying. "They don't have my signature on them, I am just a
vehicle, a medium, transmitting whatsoever has been given to me. I am instrumental."

See the egolessness of the person, and remember it. And what is the quintessential elixir
of this whole advice? That is how to transform the five decays into the *bodhi* path. What are
the five decays?

Meditate on two states. One is the state of sleep in which the greater part of humanity is.
People are living like somnambulists; mechanical is their life, unconscious is their behavior.
They are not aware who they are, they are not aware what they are doing, they are not aware
where they are going. Their life is accidental, a driftwood.

In this state also, *bodhichitta* – Buddha-consciousness, or Christ-consciousness, or
Krishna-consciousness, whatsoever name you choose, you can choose – exists. Even in
those people who are perfectly asleep, not even a glimpse of awareness, *bodhichitta* exists,
the Buddha-consciousness exists, but it is covered in rubbish. And the rubbish comes from
five senses – the eyes, the ears and the other senses.

The senses go on pouring into you all kinds of impressions from the outside. Whatsoever
you see immediately reaches inside, whatsoever you read reaches inside, whatsoever you
hear reaches inside. And your *bodhichitta* is like a diamond covered with layers and layers of
impressions. This is one state.

Whatsoever these five senses bring to you is going to be taken away by death, because
whatsoever comes from without, death will disconnect you from it. It can never become part of
you, it remains apart. It remains a foreign element in you, it never becomes your nature.

The second state is of the awakened one, the buddha, the enlightened one, who is
absolutely alert. A transformation happens in him. He also has five senses, but now his five
senses function in a totally different way. His five senses start pouring his compassion to the
outside world.

To the person who is asleep, the five senses bring only impressions from the outside. To the person who is awake, these same five senses start pouring his love, his energy, his compassion, into the world.

When *bodhichitta* is discovered, when inner consciousness is known, you are no more a beggar. You don't take anything from without. On the contrary, you become an emperor, you start pouring your being into the outside world; you beautify it, you become a blessing to it. This is the transformation.

If you are alert, you will give something to the world, you will be a giver. Remember, the more you give, the more you have – because the more you pour into the world, from the unknown sources of existence more and more goes on flowing into you. You are connected with the oceanic. The *bodhichitta* is the door of the oceanic. That ocean is God. From that ocean springs go on flowing into you. You just share.

Jesus says, "Those who save will lose, and those who lose will save."

Share, and you will have more. Give, and you will get from the beyond. The transformed person is continuously giving. He has so much to give, he is overflowing.

This quintessential elixir of advice by which the advancement of the five decays is changed into the bodhi path is transmitted through Dharmakirti.

"My master, Dharmakirti," Atisha says, "has given me this secret of transforming the energies, their direction. Now the five senses are no more accumulating unnecessary rubbish which is going to decay and stink. But now they have become passages of an overflowing divine energy."

By awakening the karmic energy of previous training, and by virtue of my intense interest, I ignored misery and bad reputation and sought instruction to control ego-clinging.

He is saying: "I could find Dharmakirti only because of my past searches. For lives I have been searching."

And the same I say to you: You are not new people, you are ancient seekers. Otherwise, there are people living in the neighborhood who have not even seen me, and who will never see and who will never hear, and who will never know what is happening here. Just living a few feet away, and they will not know that something of immense value is happening here!

And you have come from far, faraway corners of the world. You must have been seeking for many lives. You have gathered a certain energy that knows where the buddhafield is, and you are attracted towards that buddhafield. You know where the magnet is.

By awakening the karmic energy of previous training...

He said, "It must have been because in my past lives I have been disciplining myself in many ways, that I must have gathered a certain karmic energy, that I could find the master, that I was fortunate enough to find the master."

...and by virtue of my intense interest...

...my passionate desire to know the truth. Only two things are needed: energy to seek, and passionate interest to put that energy into a certain direction.

I ignored misery and bad reputation...

When you come to a master, and the master is really a master, the society will be against you, the society will create misery for you. You will have to suffer many kinds of things – bad reputation.

I ignored misery and bad reputation...

"It must have been because of my past karmic energy, it must have been because for many lives I have been seeking and searching."
Everybody is an ancient pilgrim.

I ignored misery and bad reputation...

It is very difficult to ignore misery and bad reputation. Now for my sannyasins I am creating a thousand and one kinds of difficulties. The world will be against you: wherever you will go, you will have a bad reputation, mm? Just to be associated with me will be enough for people to condemn you, ridicule you, think of you as if you are mad or something.

Only those who are real seekers will be able to ignore all this misery and bad reputation. Those who are just curious, they will not be able to do it. Only the fortunate ones, only the courageous ones, only the true seekers, will be able to ignore everything, will be able to sacrifice everything, will be able to stake everything.

Once you have come in contact with a living master, then all else is meaningless; then everything can be staked, it can be easily sacrificed.

...and sought instruction to control ego-clinging.

"I dropped the people, I ignored what they say. Instead, I poured my whole energy into one thing: how to drop this idea of ego, how to drop ego-clinging."

All these sutras are nothing but the whole science of destroying ego. Once the ego is no more there, once you are no more separate from existence, once you don't think yourself separate from existence, immediately you are enlightened. Here the ego disappears; there God appears – immediately, instantly.

Now, even when I die, I'll have no regret.

I hope my sannyasins will also be able to say that one day.

Now, even when I die, I'll have no regret.

It is possible only if *bodhichitta* is attained. It is possible only if you have come to know your innermost essential core – that it is not personal, that it is universal; that it is not mortal, that it is immortal; that it has nothing to do with time and space, that it is eternity itself.

Amritasya putrah: we are sons of immortality.

Once you have known it, life is not a regret.

Life is a blessing, a benediction.

Meditate on Atisha, listen to his advice; it is of immense value. It is not a philosophy, it is a manual to discipline yourself, it is a manual of inner transformation. It is the book that can help you grow into wisdom. I call it *The Book of Wisdom*.

Enough for today.

Chapter 26
The Illogical Electron

? Freedom can be willed, love not. Please comment.

Freedom can be willed because it is your own decision to remain in a prison. It is your own responsibility. You have willed your slavery, you have decided to remain a slave, hence you are a slave. Change the decision, and the slavery disappears.

You have invested in your unfreedom. Any moment you see the point, you can drop it; instantly it can be dropped. Nobody has forced unfreedom on you, it is your choice. You can choose to be free, you can choose to be unfree; you are so free that you can choose either. This is part of your inner freedom – not to choose it is part of your freedom. Hence it can be willed.

But love cannot be willed. Love is a by-product of freedom; it is the overflowing joy of freedom, it is the fragrance of freedom. First the freedom has to be there, then love follows. If you try to will love, you will create only something artificial, arbitrary. A willed love will not be true love, it will be phony.

And that's what people are doing. Love cannot be willed, and they go on willing it. What can be willed, freedom, they go on ignoring. They go on thinking that somebody else is responsible for their slavery and their life of slavery. This is a very topsy-turvy conception of your own life. You are upside-down.

Change the vision: will freedom, and love will come of its own accord. When love comes on its own accord only then it is beautiful, because only then it is natural, spontaneous.

Willed love will be a kind of acting. You will be pretending – what else can you do? You will be moving through empty gestures – what else is possible? You cannot be ordered to love somebody, you cannot order yourself to love somebody. If it is not there, it is not there; if it is there, it is there. It is something beyond your will. In fact it is just the opposite of will: it is surrender.

When one is totally dissolved into freedom and when one is really free, the ego disappears. The ego is your bondage, the ego is your prison. In total freedom there is no ego found. Surrender happens, you start feeling one with existence – and that oneness brings love.

? **Many see the work that goes on around you as a model for the holistic approach to life. Please talk about this.**

The old man is dying. And it is good news that the old man is on his deathbed, because the new can be born only when the old is gone, utterly gone. The old has to cease. The old has existed long, and the old man has been a curse, because he was rooted in very stupid conceptions of life.

The old man was based on superstitions. The most basic flaw in the concept of the old man was perfectionism: he wanted to be perfect, and the very idea of perfectionism drives people crazy. The perfectionist is bound to be a neurotic, he cannot enjoy life till he is perfect.

And perfection as such never happens, it is not in the nature of things. Totality is possible, perfection is not possible.

That is the fundamental of the holistic approach. And there is a tremendous difference between perfection and totality. Perfection is a goal somewhere in the future, totality is an experience herenow. Totality is not a goal, it is a style of life. If you can get into any act with your whole heart, you are total. Totality brings wholeness and totality brings health and totality brings sanity.

The perfectionist completely forgets about totality. He has some idea how he should be, and obviously time will be needed to reach that idea. It can't happen now – tomorrow, day after tomorrow, this life, maybe next life…so life has to be postponed.

That's what the old man has been doing hitherto, postponing, postponing. The man in the past has not really lived; his life was nothing but a sequence of postponements.

I teach you to live herenow with no idea of the future at all. The future will be born out of your lived present. If the present has been lived totally, the future will have even more totality to it. Out of totality more totality is born.

But if you have an idea what you want to be in the future, today you will live very partially because your main concern becomes the future. Your eyes become focused on the future, you lose contact with the real and the present – and the tomorrow will be born out of the real with which you are not in contact. The tomorrow will come out of today, and today was unlived.

The English word devil is very beautiful. If you read it backwards it becomes lived. That which is lived becomes divine, and that which is not lived becomes devil. Only the lived is transformed into godliness; the unlived turns poisonous. Today you postpone, and whatsoever remains unlived in you will hang around you like a weight. If you had lived it you would have been free of it. It would not have haunted you, it would not have tortured you.

But man up to now has been taught not to live but to hope – hope that tomorrow things will be such that you will be able to live, hope that tomorrow you will be worthy to live, hope that tomorrow you will be Jesus Christ or Gautama the Buddha.

You are never going to be Jesus the Christ or Gautama the Buddha, you are simply going to be yourself. You are not a carbon copy of anybody else. It would have been ugly to be another Christ or another Buddha; that would have been a great insult to your humanity. Man has dignity because man has originality.

The old concept was to live according to a certain pattern – the Buddhist pattern, the Christian pattern, the Hindu pattern. The old was not in favor of the individual, it was in favor of a certain pattern. That pattern creates slavery.

I teach the individual, I teach the unique individual. Respect yourself, love yourself, because there has never been a person like you and there never will be again. God never repeats. You are utterly unique, incomparably unique. You need not be like somebody else, you need not be an imitator, you have to be authentically yourself, your own being. You have to do your own thing.

The moment you start accepting and respecting yourself you start becoming whole. Then there is nothing to divide you, then there is nothing to create the split. Hitherto, man has been schizophrenic. And I am not saying that a few people have been schizophrenic: the whole humanity has been schizophrenic. Leave a few exceptions – a Krishna, a Lao Tzu here and there – you can count them on your fingers. They don't constitute humanity, they are exceptions, and the exceptions only prove the rule. But the greater part of humanity has lived a schizophrenic life, a divided life, fragmentary.

And how did man become so split? First thing: you are not acceptable as you are, so reject yourself. Rather than respecting yourself, reject yourself; rather than respecting yourself, respect some idea, some imaginary idea, of how you should be. Don't live the real, try to live the "should" – and then you are split, you have become two. You are that which you are, but that you reject, repress. And you want to be that which you are not, and that which you are not you love and you respect and you worship. You have become two.

Not only that you have been split in two, you have been made many – because you were taught that the body is your enemy, that you have to get rid of the body. You were taught that many things in you have to be cut off, that you are not as you should be, that great changes have to be done.

Naturally you started rejecting your sex, you started rejecting your desires, you started rejecting your anger. And all these rejected parts are energies to be transformed. They are not your enemies, they are friends in disguise.

Anger transformed becomes compassion, sex transformed becomes prayer, greed transformed becomes sharing. But in the past it was told again and again, repeated down the ages, that you had to reject this, reject that. If you listen to the old teachings you will be surprised – you are rejected almost ninety-nine percent. Only one percent, some imaginary soul of which you are not aware at all, is accepted in you. And all that you are aware of is rejected.

These fragments do not allow you to become one piece, and unless you become one piece there is no peace possible. Unless you are a togetherness, integrated, crystallized, you will not know what God is – because God speaks only to those who are real, God speaks only to those who are not a crowd, not noisy.

When there are many in you, you are a crowd, and the crowd is noisy. When you become one, there is silence. Only by becoming one will you attain to silence, and in that silence you can hear the voice of God, in that silence you can start feeling the presence of the divine. And when you are one, you will be able to have a communion with the whole. By being a whole yourself, you become capable of having a communion with the whole.

Man has lived very partially – in fragments, in guilt, in fear. A new man is needed, urgently needed. Enough is enough: say good-bye to the old man. The old has created only wars, violence; it has created sadists, masochists, it has created a very ugly human being. It has made people pathological, it has not allowed a natural, healthy, sane humanity to be born.

Just the other day, somebody asked, "Who is a masochist and who is a sadist?"

A masochist is a person who loves to have a cold shower every morning, but takes instead a warm one. And the sadist is a person who, if asked by a masochist, "Please, please, hit my head hard," says "No!"

People are torturing themselves and torturing others in every possible way. In the name of religion, in the name of morality, in the name of nationality, people are torturing each other, killing each other. Beautiful names have been found for very pathological, insane things. Insanities are called "nationalities," insanities are called "moralities" – beautiful labels on very ugly things.

But it is time that we get rid of it all. And if we don't get rid of it all soon enough, then the cup will be full. Man is going to die if the new does not arrive; the old cannot survive. There is no possibility for the old to survive, it has come to its tether's end. It has lived more than expected.

I teach you a new man, a new humanity, which will not think of the future and which will not live with shoulds and oughts, which will not deny any natural instinct, which will accept its body, which will accept all that is given by God with deep gratitude.

Your body is your temple, it is sacred. Your body is not your enemy. It is not irreligious to love your body, to take care of your body – it is religious. It is irreligious to torture your body and to destroy it. The religious person will love his body because it is the temple where God lives.

You and your body are not really two, but the manifestation of one. Your soul is your invisible body, and your body is your visible soul. I teach this unity, and with this unity, man becomes whole. I teach you joy, not sadness. I teach you playfulness, not seriousness. I teach you love and laughter, because to me there is nothing more sacred than love and laughter, and there is nothing more prayerful than playfulness.

I don't teach you renunciation, as it has been taught down the ages. I teach you: Rejoice, rejoice, and rejoice again! Rejoicing should be the essential core of my sannyasins.

Yes, my approach to life is holistic, because to me, to be whole is to be holy.

? Do I rightly understand you that if you and your beloved can transmute your sexual energy into spirituality, that this relationship will not be satisfying either? Your seeming contradictions on love confuse me.

Nellie, confusion is my way of working on you. I confuse you so that clarity becomes possible. People are very much certain, they already think they know. And because of their certainty they are closed. If you already know, then there is no need to seek and search. For what? If you already know, then you can keep your doors and windows closed.

People are much too certain, and that is a great problem. They have to be made uncertain again, they have to be shaken in their certainties; their dogmas and creeds have to be taken away. Hence confusion arises. What is confusion? – when you start losing grip on your old certainty. You were feeling that you know, and suddenly you start feeling that you don't know. You were thinking you have the answer, and suddenly you become aware that the question is there and the answer was just imposed.

It happens to every new disciple here – and Nellie is a new sannyasin; just the other day she has become a sannyasin. For a few days you will become more and more confused. It is a good sign, it means you are listening to me.

There are a few people who go on listening to me and are never confused. That simply means they have not heard; their ears are full of wax, they are deaf. There are people who not only don't become confused, but listening to me they become even more certain. That means they have heard something else that was not said.

Two moving-men were struggling with a big crate in a doorway. They pushed and tugged until they were exhausted but it would not move.

Finally, the man on the outside said, "We had better give up, we will never get it in."

The fellow on the inside said "What do you mean, get it in? I thought you were trying to get it out!"

If you become confused by listening to me, that means you have heard me. The more intelligent you are, the more confused you will become. And I use contradiction as a technique, I go on contradicting myself.

Why do I contradict myself? I am not teaching a philosophy here. The philosopher has to be very consistent – flawless, logical, rational, always ready to argue and prove his statements. I am not a philosopher. I am not here giving you a consistent dogma to which you can cling. My whole effort is to give you a no-mind.

Be perfectly clear about it. My effort is not to strengthen a certain mind, my effort is just the opposite of it: to give you a state of no-mind – a state which has no knowledge, a state which functions from not knowing, a state of innocence.

I use contradiction as a device. I say one thing, out of your old habit you cling to it; the next day I have to contradict it. When I contradict it you have to drop it. But you may start clinging to the new thing that I have said; I will have to contradict it again.

This will go on, you will go on clinging to this, to that. One day suddenly you will become aware what is happening. I don't allow you any certainty, nothing to cling to. And if I contradict, what is the point of clinging at all? Then why not wait? I will contradict, and then you will have to leave it, and it is painful. Once you cling to a thing and then you have to leave it, it is painful, it creates anxiety.

So those who have listened to me for a long time, listen simply. They simply listen, they don't cling. They know perfectly well, now that they are aware of the game, that tomorrow I will contradict. So why carry it for twenty-four hours? The pain of carrying the weight, and then the pain of dropping it…slowly, slowly it dawns in your awareness that there is no need to cling; this man contradicts. This man is consistently inconsistent.

Once you have understood that, you listen to me as one listens to music. You listen to me as one listens to the wind passing through the pine trees, you listen to me as one listens to the birds singing in the morning. You don't say to the cuckoo, "Yesterday your song was different," and you don't go to the roseflower and say, "Last season the flowers were bigger" – or smaller – "Why are you contradicting yourself?"

You don't say to the poet, "In one of your poems you said this, and in another poem you have said something else." You don't expect a poet to be consistent, so you don't ask. Poetry is not a theory, it is not a syllogism, it is a song.

I am not a philosopher. Always remember that I am a poet, not a philosopher. Remember always that I am not a missionary, but a musician playing on the harp of your heart. Songs will go on changing…you need not cling to anything, then there will be no confusion at all.

The people who are always hankering for consistency can never enter into the mystery of life. Consistency is something manmade, it is arbitrary. Existence is not consistent. And now even physicists agree with the poets and the mystics.

You must be aware that modern physics believes in the theory of uncertainty; modern physics believes in the illogical behavior of atoms, of the unpredictability of the behavior of electrons. It was such a shock to the modern physicists, because they had always believed that matter behaves consistently. The whole foundation of science has been shaken; these twenty years, it has been such a shock. People have not yet become aware of it, because the theories are so complicated and so subtle that they will never become part of common knowledge. And they are so against common sense – they look more like fairy tales, stories written for children.

The electrons jump from one spot to another, and between the two they don't exist. Now, can it be believed? An electron jumping from spot a to spot b, and between the two he is not? And I am using "he" knowingly, deliberately, because you cannot use "it" any more. A great mystery...they call it a quantum leap. A special word has been coined – quantum, because in the middle it is not found.

It is as if from New York you come to Pune, but in the space between the two you are not. You simply disappear from New York and you appear in Pune. Now there is a possibility some day.... Right now it is science fiction, but the possibility is there that one day it may happen that there will be no need to take long journeys, wasting time. Time has limitations.

For example, if you want to go to the nearest star it will take four years – the nearest star! And that too only if you go with the speed of light. And it is immense, the speed of light: one hundred and eighty-six thousand miles per second. If you go at this speed, which seems almost impossible, then it will take four years to reach the closest star.

And then there are stars which are a hundred years, two hundred, one thousand, two thousand, one million, two million years away. There are stars so far away that we have not been able to detect them yet.

How can journeys be made to faraway stars? The only possibility is if one day we manage to do what the electron is already managing to do...a machine in which you enter here and you disappear, and another machine on the star, one million years away, and you appear there. Between the two, no traveling time is lost: you simply dematerialize here and you materialize somewhere else. It is a possibility. If the electron can do it, why not man? Man is nothing but millions and millions of electrons, so the possibility is there.

Even to think of it seems to be mind-blowing. But modern physics says electrons are behaving in a very mysterious way – illogical, unpredictable, confusing.

I am not a philosopher who is trying to make a system of thought. I am a mystic who is trying to convey the mysteries that have become available to me. I will confuse you.

It is like a friend of mine who is a jigsaw puzzle fiend. One day his kids were playing with his puzzles and they put his Marilyn Monroe puzzle back in the same box with his Revolutionary War puzzle.

I asked him how he made out with things all mixed up.

"Oh," he said, "I did all right. But I never realized that George Washington had such sexy legs."

Life is a very mixed puzzle. Whatsoever you make out of it is going to be arbitrary, you cannot figure it out in reality. My suggestion to my sannyasins is to forget all about figuring out what it is. Rather, live it; rather, enjoy it! Don't analyze it, celebrate it.

So, you will have to put up with me, you will have to tolerate my contradictions. They appear as contradictions only to you. From my side I am simply talking mysteries, and mysteries are bound to be illogical. But your question is relevant and significant.

You ask: "Do I rightly understand you that even if you and your beloved can transmute your sexual energy into spirituality, that this relationship will not be satisfying either?"

Yes, it will not be satisfying either. In fact, it will create in you the greatest discontent that you have ever felt, because it will make you aware how much is possible. It will make you aware of the tremendous moment of that orgasmic unity, of that spiritual transmutation. But it will remain only momentary. With the outer, nothing can become permanent. And once the moment is gone, the higher was the peak, the lower will be the valley, and you will fall deep down in darkness.

But it will make you aware of one thing, that if male and female energy can have a meeting which is nontemporal, then there will be eternal contentment.

How to manage it? Out of this question the whole science of Tantra was born. How to do it? It can be done. It cannot be done with the beloved outside – it cannot be done *without* the beloved outside, remember that too, because the first glimpse comes from the beloved outside. It is only a glimpse, but with it comes a new vision that, deep down inside yourself, there are both the energies present – male and female.

Man is bisexual – every man, every woman. Half of you is male and half of you is female. If you are a woman, then the female part is on top and the male part is hidden behind, and vice versa. Once you have become aware of this, then a new work starts: your inner woman and inner man can have a meeting and that meeting can remain absolute. There is no need to come back from the peak. But the first vision comes from the outer.

Hence Tantra uses the outer woman, the outer man, as part of inner work. Once you have become aware that you have a woman inside you or a man inside you, then the work takes on a totally new quality, it starts moving in a new dimension. Now the meeting has to happen inside; you have to allow your inner woman and man to meet.

In India we have had that concept for at least five thousand years. You may not have seen the statues of Shiva as *ardhanarishwar*: half man, half woman. That is the picture of everybody's being, inner being. You must have seen *shivalinga*: it symbolizes the male. But *shivalinga* is placed in the female sexual organ, it is not alone; they are together. That again represents the inner duality, the inner polarity, but the polarity can meet and merge.

With the outer, the merger will be only for the moment. Then great frustration and great misery...and the higher the moment, the deeper will be the darkness that follows it. But the meeting can happen inwardly.

First learn that the peak is possible, and then feel grateful to the woman who has given you the peak, feel grateful to the man. Tantra worships the woman as the goddess and the man as the god. Any woman who helps you to attain to this vision is a goddess, any man that helps you to attain to this vision is a god. Love becomes sacred because it gives you the first glimpses of the divine. Then the inner work starts. You have worked without, now you have to work within.

Tantra has two phases, two stages: the outer, the extrovert Tantra, and the inner, the introvert Tantra. The beginning has to be always from the without; it is because we are there, so we have to start from the place we are and then move inwards. When the inner man and woman have met and melted, and when you are no more divided inside, you have become one – integrated, crystallized, *one* – you have attained. This is enlightenment.

But right now everything is upside down. You have completely forgotten the inner; the outer has become your whole life. This is as if somebody is standing on his head and has forgotten completely how to stand on his feet again. Now, standing on your head your life will be really difficult. If you want to go somewhere, if you want to do something, everything will become very, very difficult, almost impossible.

And that is what is happening. People are upside down, because the without has become more important than the within. The without has become all-important, and the within is completely ignored, forgotten.

The real treasure is within. From the without, you can get only hints of the inner treasure; from the without, only arrows pointing to the innermost core of your being; from without, only milestones. But don't cling to a milestone, and don't think that this is the goal and you have arrived.

Remember that the ordinary man is living a very abnormal life, because his values are upside down. Money is more important than meditation, logic is more important than love, mind is more important than heart. Power over others is more important than power over one's own being. Mundane things are more important than finding some treasures which death cannot destroy.

Larry went to an Italian restaurant, and just as the waiter was about to serve, he tripped and dumped a whole bowl of minestrone right in Larry's lap.

Was Larry angry? Was he even slightly ruffled?

He simply looked up with great dignity and disdain and said, "Waiter, I believe there is a soup in my fly."

Things are completely upside down. The fly is not in the soup, the soup is in the fly. And that's why there is so much misery. Everybody seems to be simply running after shadows, knowing perfectly well that there is nothing to happen, that nothing is ever going to happen, but what else to do? Standing by the side of the road when everybody is rushing looks silly. It is better to go on rushing with the crowd.

Let this sink deep in your heart: that unless the within becomes more important than the without, you are living a very abnormal life. The normal person is one whose within is the source of everything that he is doing. The without is only a means, the within is the end.

The love affair that you have with a woman or a man is a means to the end. The end is having a love affair with your inner woman or inner man. The outer has to be used as a learning situation; it is a great opportunity.

I am not against the outer love affair, I am all for it, because without it you will never become aware of the inner. But remember, don't get stuck in the outer.

Why is there such an expression as "the dirty old man"? I am getting on and I suspect people are beginning to think about me in exactly those words.

It is because of a long, long repressive society that the dirty old man exists. It is because of your saints, your priests, your puritans, that the old dirty man exists.

If people are allowed to live their sexual life joyously, by the time they are nearing forty-two – remember, I am saying forty-two, not eighty-four – just when they are nearing forty-two, sex will start losing its grip on them. Just as sex arises and becomes very powerful by the time one is fourteen, in exactly the same way by the time one is forty-two it starts disappearing. It is a natural course. And when sex disappears, the old man has a love, has compassion, of a totally different kind. There is no lust in his love, no desire, he wants to get nothing out of it. His love has a purity, an innocence; his love is a joy.

Sex gives you pleasure. And sex gives you pleasure only when you have gone into sex; then pleasure is the end result. If sex has become irrelevant – not repressed, but because you experienced it so deeply that it is no more of any value.... You have known it, and knowledge always brings freedom. You have known it totally, and because you have known it, the mystery is finished, there is nothing more to explore. In that knowing, the whole energy, the sexual energy, is transmuted into love, compassion. One gives out of joy. Then the old man is the most beautiful man in the world, the cleanest man in the world.

There is no expression in any language as the clean old man. I have never heard it. But this expression, the dirty old man, exists in almost all languages. The reason is that the body becomes old, the body becomes tired, the body wants to get rid of all sexuality – but the mind, because of repressed desires, still hankers. When the body is not capable, and the mind continuously haunts you for something which the body is incapable of doing, really the old man is in a mess. His eyes are sexual, lusty; his body dead and dull. And his mind goes on goading him. He starts having a dirty look, a dirty face; he starts having something ugly in him.

It reminds me of the story of the man who overheard his wife and her sister discussing his frequent out-of-town business trips. The sister kept suggesting that the wife should worry about her husband being unchaperoned at those posh resort convention hotels with so many attractive, unattached career women around.

"Me worry?" said the wife. "Why, he'd never cheat on me. He's too loyal, too decent...too old."

The body sooner or later becomes old; it is bound to become old. But if you have not lived your desires they will clamor around you, they are bound to create something ugly in you. Either the old man becomes the most beautiful man in the world, because he attains to an innocence the same as the innocence of a child, or even far deeper than the innocence of a child – he becomes a sage. But if desires are still there, running like an undercurrent, then he is caught in a turmoil.

A very old man was arrested while attempting to sexually molest a young woman. Seeing such an old man, eighty-four, in court, the magistrate reduced the charge from rape to assault with a dead weapon.

If you are becoming old, remember that old age is the climax of life. Remember that old age can be the most beautiful experience – because the child has hopes for the future, he lives in the future, he has great desires to do this, to do that. Every child thinks that he is going to be somebody special – Alexander the Great, Josef Stalin, Mao Zedong – he lives in desires and in the future. The young man is too much possessed by the instincts, all instincts, exploding in him. Sex is there. Modern research says that every man thinks once at least about sex every three seconds. Women are a little better, they think of sex every six seconds. It is a great difference, almost double; that may be the cause of many rifts between husbands and wives.

Once every three seconds sex somehow flashes in the mind. The young man is possessed by such great natural forces that he cannot be free. Ambition is there, and time is running fast, and he has to do something and he has to be something. All those hopes and desires and fantasies of childhood have to be fulfilled; he is in a great rush, in a hurry.

The old man knows that those childish desires were *really* childish. The old man knows that all those days of youth and turmoil are gone. The old man is in the same state as when the storm has gone and silence prevails. That silence can be of tremendous beauty, depth, richness. If the old man is really mature, which is very rarely the case, then he will be beautiful. But people only grow in age, they don't grow up. Hence the problem.

Grow up, become more mature, become more alert and aware. And old age is the last opportunity given to you: before death comes, prepare. And how does one prepare for death? By becoming more meditative.

If some lurking desires are still there, and the body is getting old and the body is not capable of fulfilling those desires, don't be worried. Meditate over those desires, watch, be aware. Just by being aware and watchful and alert, those desires and the energy contained in them can be transmuted. But before death comes, be free of all desires.

When I say be free of all desires I simply mean be free of all objects of desires. Then there is a pure longing. That pure longing is divine, that pure longing is God. Then there is pure creativity with no object, with no address, with no direction, with no destination – just pure energy, a pool of energy, going nowhere. That's what buddhahood is. Atisha calls it *bodhichitta*, Buddha-consciousness.

? Why is India so poor?

The so-called saints are responsible. Down the ages, India has lived with a wrong philosophy – a philosophy that teaches other-worldliness, a philosophy that teaches that the world is illusion and only the other world is true. You have not seen the other world, the true world; you have to believe. And the world that you have seen, and see every day and experience every day, is illusory, is maya.

This foolish philosophy is the root cause of India's poverty. If the world is illusory then why care about science, why care about technology? What is the point? If the world is illusory, poverty is also an illusion, the beggar on the street is also an illusion, the starving person is also an illusion.

The West has lived with the idea that only this world is real. Hence it has become rich, at least outwardly rich. The West has denied the other world: God is dead. And the West started becoming rich only when it started dropping the idea of the other world; then its whole energy was focused on this world. It became rich materially, but it became poor spiritually.

The other world is also real, and real on a higher plane. The East became poor materially. The other world is real, but the other world can only be based on the reality of this world. This world functions as a foundation. So maybe, once in a while, a person in India was able to become inwardly rich. But the millions, the masses, remain outwardly poor. And because there is no foundation, they have remained inwardly poor too.

These attitudes have been two halves of one whole. The new man I talk about, and the new humanity, will not be Eastern or Western. It will not believe in this world only or in that world only, it will believe in the totality of man. It will believe in the body of man, it will believe in the soul of man; it will believe in the material, it will believe in the spiritual. In fact the new humanity will think of spirituality and materiality as two aspects of one phenomenon. Then the world will be rich in both ways, within and without.

India has to get rid of its otherworldly obsession. It has to learn to love this world too, it has to learn that this world is also real. The very moment that happens will be a great change in India's life. But the saints, the so-called saints, still go on teaching that this world is unreal. And the poor people are consoled by it, so they go on clinging to the philosophy. If the world is unreal, this consoles: there is nothing to be worried about, it is only a question of a few years, then you will enter into the real world. So why bother?

The Eastern mind remains unscientific because of this basically wrong philosophy; science can be created only if the world is accepted as real. And if science is there, then technology is there, and technology is the only way to create riches. The so-called saints are responsible, and the so-called leaders, the politicians, are responsible, because the politicians go on teaching anti-scientific attitudes to the country. Gandhi's philosophy is anti-scientific. You will be surprised to know that he was against railway trains, the post office, the telegraph, modern medicine. He was against the basic technologies which can help the country. And he still remains the father figure, he still dominates the Indian mind, particularly the Indian politician's mind.

India has to get rid of Gandhi, otherwise it cannot become rich. But Gandhi also consoles, because he praises the poor man. He calls the poor man *daridra narayan*: he says that God is in the poor man, the poor man is divine. His teaching is that the rich man is something wrong and the poor man is something right. Poverty has some spirituality in it, according to him.

If you praise poverty as spirituality, naturally the poor person's ego is gratified. Hence the poor people in India go on worshipping Gandhi; every town has his statue. The poor man has nothing else to feel gratified about. This idea gives him great contentment, that he has something spiritual in him, his poverty is spiritual.

There is nothing spiritual in poverty. Poverty is ugly, unspiritual, irreligious. The poor man is the cause of all that is wrong in the world, because out of poverty all kinds of sins and crimes arise. The poor man has not to be gratified, he has to be made aware, "Do something and get out of your poverty." If you go on praising the poor man he will become more and more poor to become more and more spiritual. The poorer he is, the more divine.

A farm laborer got a wire from home; it announced that his wife had just given birth to quintuplets. He decided it was time to look for a better-paying job.

"Tell me," said the employment agent at the firm where he applied, "Do you have any sales ability? Can you type, run a computer or drive a truck?"

Sadly he answered, "No."

The interviewer asked, "Then what can you do?"

He reached into his pocket, brought out the telegram and said, "Here, read this."

India's whole creativity consists in bringing more and more children into the world. There is no reason to be surprised by India's poverty. Every day thousands are born. Medicine has helped people to live long, medicine has helped people to die later and later. The death rate has tremendously changed: just thirty years ago, out of ten children born in India nine were going to die before the age of one. Now nine live, only one dies. The death rate has been changed but the birthrate remains the same.

Now there are only two possibilities: either drop the birthrate or raise the death rate. There are only two possibilities: either kill people in some way or other.... And that's what happens again and again – natural calamities kill people, great diseases spread and kill people, wars come and kill people. But they are all lagging behind; they are not able to cope with modern medicine. Unless the birthrate declines there is no possibility for India to see good days. But the Indians are accustomed to having many children. It is very manly, it is thought to be a great blessing from God: the more children you have, the more blessed you are.

These foolish ideas have to be changed, but it is very difficult to change them. Because I am against all these ideas, the Indian masses are against me. They want to be supported... their saints go on saying to them that a child is a gift of God, their saints go on blessing them. Now each child brings a new curse; it is no longer a blessing.

The politicians are afraid that if they force birth control on the country then the people won't vote for them, so they cannot enforce birth control. So they deliver sermons on *brahmacharya*, celibacy; they themselves are not celibate, and they go on teaching people celibacy. And people love these ideas, these are the ideas they have loved for centuries so they feel very good: this is their culture, their culture is being praised. This is the right way to control population – celibacy.

And how many people are going to do it? That is not the point at all. A cultural idea, praised for centuries, feels very ego-satisfying.

Celibacy is not going to work. Birth control will have to be brought in. If people willingly accept it, good. If they don't accept it willingly, then it has to be forced on them. People cannot be left to destroy the whole country. But if you talk about enforcing birth control they say then you are not a democrat.

You stop people by force in many things: thieves are not allowed to steal – is it non-democratic? Thieves should be allowed, given freedom – democracy means freedom! Murders are not allowed. Now giving birth to so many children is far more of a crime than stealing; in fact it is a far bigger crime than murder.

Things have changed, situations have changed. Now to bring an unnecessary child into the world is far more a crime than killing a person. It is not a question of democracy, it is a question of survival. Democracy is good, but democracy can exist only if the country can survive. The country is dying, starving. Unless birth control is enforced totally, this country cannot be rich.

My attitude is very clear, my approach is absolutely clear, but the country's old mind is not ready to listen. People come to me and they say, "What you are doing for India's poverty? Why don't you run hospitals, and why don't you distribute free food from the ashram?"

This has been done for at least ten thousand years. Ashrams have been distributing free food for ten thousand years: it has not helped. How it is going to help if one more ashram goes on distributing free food? There are so many hospitals – it has not helped; how it is going to help if we run a few more hospitals?

That is not my approach. I want to cut the very root of the problem, I am not interested in pruning the leaves. But people are duped and dulled by the saints, by the leaders, by the moralists.

Karl Marx seems to be right, at least in a certain sense, that religion has been used as an opium to dupe people and dull their intelligence. Real religion is not opium, but real religion is rare. It exists only when there is a living master – otherwise priests go on pretending that they have the keys of religion. They don't have any keys; all that they do is serve the politicians.

There is a conspiracy between organized religion and the state – between church and state. Together they dominate people, together they reduce people into slavery. If the people are poor it is easier to force them into slavery; if people are poor it is easier to give them beliefs, superstitions. If people are poor they are always afraid of hell and always greedy for heaven. The priest can dominate them and the politician can also dominate them because they are so poor.

In poverty, people lose intelligence. Intelligence needs a certain nourishment. It is a well known scientific fact that if certain vitamins are missing in your food you will not be intelligent. And I am really worried, because those are the vitamins which are missing in Indian food. Indian food is very deficient – hence you see the intelligence is on a very low level. Even the so-called intelligentsia of India doesn't seem to be very intelligent. Intelligence is needed to transform this country, its poverty.

And that's what my work is here: to create more intelligence through meditation; to create more intelligent people by destroying their superstitions, beliefs; to create more alert people, so they can be more responsive to the real situation that exists in the country and in the world.

Only in this way can we cut the very root of the problem.

? Why am I here?

This is a very philosophical question.

There is a story about two big beefy American football players in philosophy class, sitting at their final examination. The exam question was just one word: "Why?"

All the students began writing madly, filling exam book after book. The two football players looked at each other and shrugged. The first wrote two words on his exam paper: "Why not?" and left the room. The second fellow wrote one word: "Because" and left with his friend.

Not knowing what to do, the professor gave the first fellow the grade of A, and the second fellow the grade of A minus.

This is really a philosophical question: "Why am I here?"
I don't know. Why not? Or – because.

Three newly deceased candidates for heaven sit in the waiting room of Saint Peter's office. Finally Saint Peter returns from lunch and asks the receptionist to send in the first candidate.

"How did you die, and why do you think you are eligible for heaven?" Saint Peter asked.

"Well," said the man, "for some time I suspected my wife was cheating on me. This morning a neighbor called and confirmed the awful truth. He told me a guy had entered our apartment a half hour ago and had not come out. Furiously I rushed home, burst into the apartment, and found my wife lying naked on the bed. I started to search the apartment in a jealous rage. I looked through the whole flat – under the bed, in the closets, behind curtains, everywhere.

I found no one. Finally, out of sheer frustration and blind rage, I picked up the refrigerator, carried it out onto the back porch and threw it down into the back yard, three stories below. The exertion and excitement must have been too much for me, I must have died right then and there of a heart attack."

"Well," said Saint Peter, "that's a very unusual way to die, but entirely moral. Admitted. Send in the next candidate."

The second candidate told an even more surprising story. "Saint Peter," he said, "if you will excuse the expression, I swear to God I was minding my own business taking a nap in the hammock out in the back yard. I heard a noise and looked up just in time to see a full-size refrigerator falling on me from the third floor."

"Hmmm," said Saint Peter. "Most tragic and most circumstantial. But, again, entirely proper and moral. Admit this man and send in the next candidate."

"Saint Peter," said the third candidate, "I know you are not going to believe a word I say, I just know it. I got called to this lady's apartment to fix her refrigerator. I was working on it when all of a sudden she screamed, 'Here comes my husband! For God's sake, hide!' So help me, Saint Peter, the last thing I remember was climbing into the refrigerator and closing the door."

I don't know why you are here. Why not? Because!

Enough for today.

Chapter 27
The Soul Is a Question

❓ **Why is it so difficult to relate?**

Because you are not yet. There is an inner emptiness and the fear that if you relate with somebody, sooner or later you will be exposed as empty. Hence it seems safer to keep a distance with people; at least you can pretend you are.

You are not. You are not yet born, you are only an opportunity. You are not yet a fulfillment – and only two fulfilled persons can relate. To relate is one of the greatest things of life: to relate means to love, to relate means to share. But before you can share, you must *have*. And before you can love you must be full of love, overflowing with love.

Two seeds cannot relate, they are closed. Two flowers can relate; they are open, they can send their fragrances to each other, they can dance in the same sun and in the same wind, they can have a dialogue, they can whisper. But that is not possible for two seeds. Seeds are utterly closed, windowless – how to relate?

And that is the situation. Man is born as a seed; he can become a flower, he may not. It all depends on you, what you do with yourself; it all depends on you whether you grow or you don't. It is your choice – and each moment the choice has to be faced; each moment you are on the crossroads.

Millions of people decide not to grow. They remain seeds; they remain potentialities, they never become actualities. They don't know what self-realization is, they don't know what self-actualization is, they don't know anything of being. Utterly empty they live, utterly empty they die. How can they relate?

It will be exposing yourself – your nudity, your ugliness, your emptiness – safer, it seems, to keep a distance. Even lovers keep distance; they come only so far, and they remain alert to when to turn back. They have boundaries; they never cross the boundaries, they remain confined to their boundaries.

Yes, there is a kind of relationship, but it is not that of relating, it is that of possession: the husband possesses the wife, the wife possesses the husband, the parents possess the children, and so on and so forth. But to possess is not to relate. In fact to possess is to destroy all possibilities of relating. If you relate, you respect; you cannot possess. If you relate, there is great reverence. If you relate, you come very close, very, very close, in deep intimacy, overlapping. Still the other's freedom is not interfered with, still the other remains an independent individual. The relationship is that of I-thou, not that of I-it – overlapping, interpenetrating, yet in a sense independent.

Khalil Gibran says: "Be like two pillars that support the same roof, but don't start possessing the other, leave the other independent. Support the same roof – that roof is love."

Two lovers support something invisible and something immensely valuable: some poetry of being, some music heard in the deepest recesses of their existence. They support both, they support some harmony, but still they remain independent. They can expose themselves to the other, because there is no fear. They know they *are*. They know their inner beauty, they know their inner perfume; there is no fear.

But ordinarily the fear exists, because you don't have any perfume. If you expose yourself you will simply stink. You will stink of jealousies, hatreds, angers, lust. You will not have the perfume of love, prayer, compassion.

Millions of people have decided to remain seeds. Why? When they can become flowers and they can also have a dance in the wind and the sun and the moon, why have they decided to remain seeds? There is something in their decision: the seed is more secure than the flower. The flower is fragile; the seed is not fragile, the seed looks stronger. The flower can be destroyed very easily; just a strong wind and the petals will blow away. The seed cannot be destroyed so easily by the wind, the seed is very protected, secure. The flower is exposed – such a delicate thing, and exposed to so many hazards: a strong wind may come, it may rain cats and dogs, the sun may be too hot, some foolish man may pluck the flower. Anything can happen to the flower, everything can happen to the flower, the flower is constantly in danger. But the seed is safe; hence millions of people decide to remain seeds. But to remain a seed is to remain dead, to remain a seed is not to live at all. It is secure, certainly, but it has no life. Death is secure, life is insecurity. One who really wants to live has to live in danger, in constant danger. One who wants to reach to the peaks has to take the risk of getting lost. One who wants to climb the highest peaks has to take the risk of falling from somewhere, slipping down.

The greater is the longing to grow, the more and more danger has to be accepted. The real man accepts danger as his very style of life, as his very climate of growth.

You ask me: "Why is it so difficult to relate?"

It is difficult because you are not yet. First be. Everything else is possible only afterwards: first be.

Jesus says it in his own way: "First seek ye the kingdom of God, then all else shall be added unto you." This is just an old expression for the same thing that I am saying: First be, then all else shall be added unto you.

But being is the basic requirement. If you are, courage comes as a consequence. If you are, great desire for adventure, to explore, arises – and when you are ready to explore, you can relate. Relating is exploring – exploring the other's consciousness, exploring the other's territory. But when you explore the other's territory, you have to allow and welcome the other to explore *you*; it cannot be one-way traffic. And you can allow the other to explore you only when you have something, some treasure within you. Then there is no fear. In fact you invite the guest, you embrace the guest, you call him in, you want him in. You want him to see what you have discovered in yourself, you want to share it.

First be, then you can relate – and remember, to relate is beautiful. Relationship is a totally different phenomenon; relationship is something dead, fixed, a full point has arrived. You get married to a woman; a full point has arrived. Now things will only decline. You have reached the limit, nothing is growing any more. The river has stopped and it is becoming a reservoir. Relationship is already a thing, complete; relating is a process. Avoid relationships, and go deeper and deeper into relating.

My emphasis is on verbs, not on nouns; avoid nouns as much as possible. In language you cannot avoid, that I know; but in life, avoid – because life is a verb. Life is not a noun, it is really "living" not "life." It is not love, it is loving. It is not relationship, it is relating. It is not a song, it is singing. It is not a dance, it is dancing.

See the difference, savor the difference. A dance is something complete; the last touches have been made, now there is nothing else to do. Something complete is something dead. Life knows no full point; commas are okay, but no full points. Resting places are okay, but no destination.

Instead of thinking how to relate, fulfill the first requirement: meditate, be, and then relating will arise out of it on its own accord. One who becomes silent, blissful, one who starts having overflowing energies, becomes a flower, has to relate. It is not something that he has to learn how to do, it starts happening. He relates with people, he relates with animals, he relates with trees, he relates even with rocks.

In fact, twenty-four hours a day he relates. If he is walking on the earth, he is relating with the earth…his feet touching the earth, he is relating. If he is swimming in the river he is relating with the river, and if he is looking at the stars he is relating with the stars.

It is not a question of a relationship with somebody in particular. The basic fact is, if you *are*, your whole life becomes a relating. It is a constant song, a constant dance, it is a continuum, a riverlike flow.

Meditate, find out your own center first. Before you can relate with somebody else, relate · with yourself: that is the basic requirement to be fulfilled. Without it, nothing is possible. With it, nothing is impossible.

As you drove away today I felt I am afraid of forgetting…. Is there anything I need to remember?

Yes, there is a great need to remember yourself. Your question is really significant. I call a question significant when it is existential, when it is not intellectual, when it is not bookish, when it does not come out of your knowledge but comes out of your existential experience. It has a totally different quality to it.

Yes, there is something to be remembered. But that something is not outside you, that's why you cannot figure it out. You simply felt a fear, as if you are forgetting something, a very vague kind of fear – something felt, but not yet clearly felt. Something is there, lurking in the unconscious, in the darkness of your soul: you felt afraid of forgetting.

And really then it becomes a great question: What am I afraid of forgetting? Is there anything I need to remember?

A Zen master was dying. At the last moment, when all his disciples had gathered, he opened his eyes and said, "What is the answer?"

The disciples were dumbfounded, they could not figure it out: "What is the answer?"

So the master started laughing, and he said, "So okay, what is the question?"

He was posing a very, very existential thing: What is the answer? Even before the question is asked, he is asking what is the answer? The question is not asked, because it cannot be asked. But the question is there, it is there in everybody's soul. One may be alert about it, one may not be alert about it, one may be completely oblivious of it; but the question is there in everybody's soul.

The soul is a question, it is a quest. Hence the master is asking, "What is the answer?"

The disciples could not figure it out, because this is not the way; people ask first about the question, then they ask about the answer.

And something exactly like that has happened to you. Afraid of forgetting – forgetting what, that is not clear. Just a feeling, a cloud passed by…and the feeling must have been intense.

Is there anything I need to remember?" you ask.

It is you yourself. Self-remembering is needed. Buddha used to call it right-mindfulness, *sammasati*; Mahavira used to call it *vivek*, awareness; George Gurdjieff used to call it self-remembering, Kabir used to call it *surati*. But they all mean the same thing.

You don't know who you are. You are – that much is certain. In fact only that is certain, and nothing else. The existence of others is not certain.

The English philosopher, Berkeley, had gone for a morning walk with Dr. Johnson. Dr. Johnson was very critical of Berkeley's ideas, because Berkeley used to say that the whole world is an idea; it is not a reality, but just an idea, an idea in the mind of God. We are ideas in the mind of God – just ideas, pure ideas, not real entities.

Again and again he was hammering Dr. Johnson's head with the same philosophy – that morning it was too much. He was saying, "All these trees and this sun and this sky, all these are ideas." Enough is enough! Dr. Johnson was a realist, a down-to-earth man. He took a rock from the road and hit hard on the feet of Berkeley. Berkeley screamed in deep pain, blood started oozing out of his feet, and he said, "What are you doing? Have you suddenly gone mad?"

And Dr. Johnson said, "But it is just an idea, this rock. Why are you screaming? Why do you look so angry?"

It is not reported what Berkeley said, but there is a parallel story in Indian history, which takes a beautiful turn.

A Buddhist came to the court of a king. He was a great mystic, and belonged to a certain school of Buddhists who preceded Berkeley by at least two thousand years. His was the same idea: it is called *vigyanvad* – the whole existence is nothing but ideas.

The king must have been a man like Dr. Johnson – very earthbound, very realistic, pragmatic. The philosopher was very argumentative; he defeated the king's court, all the learned men that the king had gathered around himself. The king was feeling humiliated, so he said, "Now the last argument, the real argument."

They had a mad elephant which was brought into the courtyard of the palace. The poor mystic, the philosopher, was left alone in the courtyard, and he was trembling…and then the mad elephant was left. The mad elephant rushed towards the philosopher – and you can imagine, what happened to Berkeley was nothing compared to it: he jumped and shouted and cried and begged for his life.

The king was standing on the balcony with the whole court, and they were laughing. So now it was proved that the elephant is not just an idea, it is not just a dream.

The philosopher was crying with folded hands and asking, "Save me, please!" At the last moment he was saved – just at the last moment. Even after he was saved he was trembling for hours, the elephant was so ferocious.

The king said to him, "So now what do you think? Is the elephant real or not?"

He said, "No, sir. It is just an idea."

The king said, "Then why were you screaming and why were you begging for your life?"

The philosopher said, "That was an idea too. My crying, my effort to be saved, your kindness to save me – all are ideas; they don't really exist, just figments of the mind." This is going to the very logical conclusion of it! He said, "Don't be so happy – because I *myself* am an idea and nothing else."

The king said, "Then we will put you back, and we will bring the mad elephant!"

And the philosopher said, "I will beg for my life again! But that doesn't matter; that doesn't change my argument and my position. The philosophy remains intact."

In fact there is no way to prove that others exist, because you have never touched anybody and you have never seen anybody. When you see somebody, you don't see him really; all that happens is that a picture is seen inside your brain. It may correspond to some reality, it may not correspond. There is no way to know, because we cannot know reality directly.

Always it is through the senses that we know reality. Senses may be deceiving – and you know perfectly well that under the impact of alcohol they deceive, under the impact of psychedelics they deceive very much. One can act in a stupid way, in a suicidal way, under the impact of some psychedelic.

One woman in New York took LSD and thought that she could fly. And when you are under the impact of LSD you simply believe it, it is so. It is not a question of a dream or a desire or a fantasy; it is so real, it is more real than the world outside, than the objective world. She simply flew out of the window from the ninth floor, dashed on the ground, died. This type of accident has been happening all over the world.

The existence of others, the existence of the outside world, is not absolutely certain. Berkeley still remains unrefuted, there is no way to refute him. The only thing that is absolutely certain is your own existence. The dream may be false, but the dreamer cannot be. Even for the false dream to exist there is a need of a real dreamer; to be deceived, at least somebody is needed to be deceived.

The world may be illusion, but who is an illusion? At least some consciousness is needed, absolutely needed, categorically needed; without some consciousness the illusion cannot exist. The rope may not be the snake, the snake may be the illusion. But the person who has the illusion is not an illusion himself.

This has to be remembered, that "I am real." This has to be remembered, that "I am the only certain reality – everything else may be, or may not be."

We never look inwards for this absolute reality; and we go on living a life without basing it on this rock of certainty. Hence our lives are just castles in the air, or at the most, sandcastles; signatures made on water – you have not even completed it, and the signature is gone. Our lives are like that – one moment we are here, another moment we are gone, and that moment could have been used for self-remembering.

Only people who use their life for self-remembering are using this great opportunity.

A man runs into an old friend who has become a drunkard. "But why do you drink so much?" he asks him.

"To forget," the drunkard replies.

"To forget what?" asks his friend.

"Oh," says the drunkard, scratching his head, "I forgot."

A man goes to the psychoanalyst. "Doctor," he says, "you have to help me. I have a terrible problem: I forget everything, absolutely everything."

"So tell me about this problem," replies the therapist, preparing his notepad.

"What problem?" asks the man, puzzled.

We are in this forgetfulness, we *are* this forgetfulness.

I loved your question. You say: "As you drove away today I felt I am afraid of forgetting. Is there anything I need to remember?"

You need to remember yourself. You need to become a flame of inner awareness – an awareness so deep that even in dreams it will be present; an awareness so crystallized that even in deep sleep, dreamless sleep, it will be there burning like a light.

Even in deep sleep the man of awareness knows that he is fast asleep; that is part of his awareness. You don't know, even while you are awake, that you are. The man of awareness knows, even while asleep, that he is.

Buddha's chief disciple, Ananda, asked him once, "*Bhante*, a few things puzzle me very much, and one of the most puzzling things is this, that in the night I have watched you many times – it is so beautiful to watch you while you are asleep – but you always sleep in the same posture and you maintain the same posture from the beginning to the end. When you go to sleep you are in this posture; in the night, many times I wake up and look at you, and you are in the same posture: the hand is resting in the same place, and the feet and the head. And in the morning also when I see you, you are in the same posture. How is this possible?"

Buddha said, "Because I remain awake. The body sleeps, but my own sleep is gone for ever. The body rests, but I am alert."

This alertness is needed. This alertness will make available to you all the mysteries of existence. First become acquainted with the mystery that you are, then you have the master key: it can open all the locks of existence.

I have fallen in love and suffered much. After listening to you I felt unwilling to let go of the dream that the deep rich experience my love affair brings will not ultimately lead to satisfaction. How can I go beyond this attachment that is so rich, yet so painful?

Love is both. It is rich and it is painful, it is agony and it is ecstasy – because love is the meeting of the earth and the sky, of the known and the unknown, of the visible and the invisible.

Love is the boundary that divides matter and consciousness, the boundary of the lower and the higher. Love has roots in the earth; that is its pain, its agony. And love has its branches in the sky; that is its ecstasy.

Love is not a single phenomenon, it is dual. It is a rope stretched between two polarities. You will have to understand these two polarities: one is sex, another is prayer. Love is the rope stretched between sex and prayer; part of it is sex, part of it is prayer.

The sexual part is bound to bring many miseries, the part that belongs to prayer will bring many joys. Hence it is difficult to renounce love, because in renouncing one is afraid the joys that come will also be renounced. One is not able either to be totally in it, because all those pains again and again remind you to renounce it. This is the misery of the lover: the lover lives in a tension, pulled apart.

I can understand your problem. This is the basic problem of all lovers, because love brings both, many thorns and many flowers, and they both come together. Love is a rosebush. One does not want those thorns, one would like the rosebush to be all flowers and no thorns; but they come together, they are aspects of one energy.

But I am not saying to you to renounce love, I am not saying to you to become detached. What I am saying to you is: make it more and more prayerful. My whole approach is that of transformation, not of renunciation. You must have misunderstood me. I am not against sex, but I am all for making sex a prayer. The lowest can be possessed by the highest, then the pain of it disappears.

What pain is there in sexuality? Because it reminds you of your animality – that is the pain. It reminds you of the past, it reminds you of your biological bondage, it reminds you that you are not free, you are under the slavery of the instincts given by nature; that you are not independent from nature, that your strings are pulled by nature, that you are just a puppet in the hands of unknown unconscious forces.

Sex is felt like a humiliation. In sex you start feeling you are losing your dignity, hence the pain. And then the fulfillment is so momentary; sooner or later any intelligent person will become aware that the satisfaction is momentary and followed by long nights of pain.

The ecstasy is just like a breeze, it comes and goes and leaves you in a desertlike state, utterly frustrated, disappointed. You had hoped much; many things were promised by the instinctual part of you, and nothing has been delivered.

In fact sex is a strategy of nature to perpetuate itself. It is a mechanism that keeps you reproducing, otherwise people will disappear. Just think of a humanity where sex is no longer an instinct and you are free, at your own will, to go into sex or not. Then the whole thing will look so absurd, the whole thing will look ridiculous. Just think – if there is no instinctive force pulling you, I don't think anybody will be ready to go into sex. Nobody goes by consent; reluctantly, resisting, one goes into it.

If you read about and study the sexual patterns of different species of animals and insects you will be very much puzzled: how could this be done if it was left to the species themselves? For example, there are spiders which, while the male makes love to her, the female starts eating him. By the time the love is finished, the male is finished! Now think of these spiders if they are free to choose: the moment they see the female they will escape as far as they can. Why should they commit suicide, knowing it perfectly well? They have seen other males disappearing the same way – every day it is happening – but when the instinct possesses them they are just a slave to it. Trembling, afraid, still they make love, knowing perfectly well this is the end. When the male is having the orgasm, the female starts eating him.

The female bedbug has no opening, so it is very difficult to make love to her. The male bug first has to make a hole in her. You can easily see whether the female bedbug is a virgin or not, because each time love is made, a scar is left – it is really screwing! – but willingly she allows it. It is painful, and there is danger to her life, because if the male makes the hole in some wrong place she will be dead – and there are stupid males too! But still the risk has to be taken; there is some such unconscious force that it has to be accepted.

If sex were left to your decision I don't think people would go into it. There are reasons why people make love hiding from the public, from people – because it looks so ridiculous. Just making love in public, you know that others will see the ridiculousness of it; you yourself know it is ridiculous. One feels one is falling below humanity; the great pain is there, that you are dragged backwards.

But it brings a few moments of utter purity and joy and innocence too. It brings a few moments of timelessness, when suddenly there is no time left. It brings a few moments of egolessness too, when in deep orgasmic spasm the ego is forgotten. It gives you a few glimpses of God, hence it cannot be renounced either.

People have tried to renounce it. Down the ages monks have been renouncing it, for the simple reason that it is so humiliating, so against the dignity of human beings. To be under the impact of some unconscious instinct is dehumanizing, demoralizing. The monks have renounced it, they have left the world, but with it all the joy in their life has also disappeared. They become very serious and sad, they turn suicidal. Now they don't see any meaning in life, all life becomes meaningless. Then they simply wait for death to come and deliver them.

It is a delicate problem; how to solve it? Monks have not been able to solve it. On the contrary, they created many perversions in the world. All the perversions that are condemned by your so-called saints are created by those same people. The first idea of homosexuality arose in the monasteries, because men were kept together, away and aloof from women, and women were kept together, aloof and away from men.

There are Catholic monasteries where no woman has entered for one thousand years. Not even a small baby of six months old is allowed. Just the very idea seems to be very horrible; these monks seem to be really dangerous – even a six-month-old girl is not allowed in the monastery. What does it show? What fear! What paranoia!

Naturally the monks huddle together, then their instincts start creating new ways, start inventing perversions; they turn homosexual. Homosexuality is really very religious, it is a by-product of religion. Religion has given many things to the world; homosexuality is one of them.

All kinds of perversions.... Now you don't hear of any woman making love to the devil; the devil seems to have lost all interest in women suddenly! There is no devil. But if you keep women away from all possibilities of falling in love, of being in love, then the mind will start creating its own projections, and of course those projections will be very, very colorful. And those projections are bound to happen, you cannot avoid them.

So monks and nuns have not been able to solve the problem, they have even messed up the whole thing more. And the worldly person, the sensuous, the indulgent person, has not been able to solve it either. He suffers miserably; his whole life is a suffering. He goes on hoping, from one hope to another hope, and goes on failing in every hope, and slowly, slowly a great hopelessness settles in his being.

My approach is neither worldly nor otherworldly.

My approach is not of rejecting something but using it.

My understanding is that whatsoever is given to you is precious. You may know its value, you may not know its value, but it is precious; if it was not so, existence would not have given it to you. So you have to find ways to transform it. You have to make your love more prayerful, you have to make your sex more loving. Slowly, slowly, sex has to be transformed into a sacred activity, it has to be raised. Rather than sex pulling you down into the mire of animality, you can pull sex upwards.

The same energy that pulls you down can pull you upwards, and the same energy can give you wings. It has tremendous power; certainly it is the most powerful thing in the world, because all life arises out of it. If it can give birth to a child, to a new life, if it can bring a new life into existence, you can imagine its potential: it can bring a new life to you too. Just as it can bring a new child into the world, it can give a new birth to you.

And that's what Jesus means when he says to Nicodemus, "Unless you are born again, you will not be able to enter into my kingdom of God" – unless you are born again, unless you are capable of giving birth to yourself – a new vision, a new quality to your energies, a new tuning to your instrument. Your instrument contains great music, but you have to learn how to play on it.

Sex has to become a great meditative art. That's the contribution of Tantra to the world. Tantra's contribution is the greatest, because it give you keys to transform the lowest into the highest. It gives you keys to transform mud into lotuses. It is one of the greatest sciences that have happened – but because of the moralists and the puritans and the so-called religious people, Tantra has not been allowed to help people. Its scriptures have been burned, thousands of Tantra masters have been killed, burned alive. The whole tradition has been almost destroyed, people have been forced to go underground.

Just the other day I received a letter from my sannyasins from America saying that Gurdjieff's people are so persecuted by the government that they have decided to go underground. They have written, "We are afraid that sooner or later this is going to happen to us. Should we start preparing, so that if this happens to us we can also start working in a hidden way?"

It is possible, because it has been always so. Gurdjieff's work also consists in transforming the sexual energy into an inner integration – the organized church is always against any effort of this kind.

My work is hindered in every way, my people are harassed in every way. Just a few days ago, the Indian parliament discussed for one hour what should be done with me – as if this country has no other problem to discuss. So much fear! And I am not doing any harm to anybody; I don't even go outside the gate. And at least this much freedom is everybody's birthright – if someone wants to come to me and wants to be transformed, it is nobody's business to interfere. I don't go to anybody. If people come to me and they want to be transformed...then what kind of democracy is this?

But the stupid politicians and the priests have always been in a conspiracy. They don't want people to be transformed, because transformed people are no longer under their domination. Transformed people become independent, free; transformed people become so aware and so intelligent that they can see through all the games of the politicians and the priests. Then they are nobody's followers; then they start living a totally new kind of life – not the life of the crowd, but the life of the individual. They become lions, they are no more sheep.

And the politicians and the priests are interested that every human being should remain a sheep. Only then can they be the shepherds, leaders, great leaders. Mediocre and stupid people pretending to be great leaders – but that is possible only if the whole humanity remains very low in intelligence, is kept repressed.

Up to now, only two experiments have been done. One was of indulgence, which has failed – which is being tried again by the West and is going to fail, utterly fail. And the other was that of renunciation – which has been tried by the East, and also in the West by Christianity. That too has failed, utterly failed.

A new experiment is needed, urgently needed. Man is in a great turmoil, in a great confusion. Where to go? What to do with oneself?

I am not saying renounce sex, I am saying transform it. It need not remain just biological: bring some spirituality to it. While making love, meditate too. While making love, be prayerful. Love should not be just a physical act; pour your soul into it.

Then slowly, slowly the pain starts disappearing and the energy contained in the pain is released and becomes more and more a benediction. Then agony is transformed into ecstasy.

You say, "I have fallen in love and suffered much."

You are blessed. The really poor people are those who have never fallen in love and never suffered. They have not lived at all. To fall in love and to suffer in love is good. It is passing through fire; it purifies, it gives you insight, it makes you more alert. This is the challenge to be accepted. Those who don't accept this challenge remain spineless.

You say, "I have fallen in love and suffered much. After listening to you I felt unwilling to let go of the dream that the deep rich experience my love affair brings will not ultimately lead to satisfaction."

I am not telling you to drop your love, I am simply telling you a fact – that it will not bring you to ultimate contentment. It is not in my hands to change the nature of things. I am simply stating a fact. If it was in my hands I would have liked you to have ultimate contentment in love. But it doesn't happen. What can we do? Two plus two are four.

It is a fundamental law of life that love brings you to deeper and deeper dissatisfactions. Ultimately love brings you to such a discontent that you start longing for the ultimate beloved, God, you start searching for the ultimate love affair.

Sannyas is an ultimate love affair: the search for God, the search for truth. It is possible only when you have failed many times, loved and suffered, and each suffering has brought you more and more consciousness, more and more understanding. One day the recognition arrives that love can give you a few glimpses – and those glimpses are good, and those glimpses are glimpses of God – but it can only give you glimpses; more than that is not possible. But that too is too much; but without those glimpses you will never seek and search God.

Those who have not loved and suffered never become seekers of God – they cannot; they have not earned that worth, they have not become worthy. It is the sole right of the lover one day to start searching for the ultimate beloved.

Love, and love more deeply. Suffer, and suffer more deeply. Love totally and suffer totally, because this is how the impure gold passes through fire and becomes pure gold.

I am not saying to you, escape from your love affairs: go deeper into them. I help my sannyasins to go into love, because I know love ultimately fails. And unless they know by their own experience that love ultimately fails, their search for God will remain phony.

What is jealousy and why does it hurt so much?

Jealousy is comparison. And we have been taught to compare, we have been conditioned to compare, always compare. Somebody else has a better house, somebody else has a more beautiful body, somebody else has more money, somebody else has a more charismatic personality. Compare, go on comparing yourself with everybody else you pass by, and great jealousy will be the outcome; it is the by-product of the conditioning for comparison.

Otherwise, if you drop comparing, jealousy disappears. Then you simply know you are you, and you are nobody else, and there is no need. It is good that you don't compare yourself with trees, otherwise you will start feeling very jealous: why are you not green? And why has God been so hard on you – and no flowers? It is better that you don't compare with birds, with rivers, with mountains; otherwise you will suffer. You only compare with human beings, because you have been conditioned to compare only with human beings; you don't compare with peacocks and with parrots. Otherwise, your jealousy would be more and more: you would be so burdened by jealousy that you would not be able to live at all.

Comparison is a very foolish attitude, because each person is unique and incomparable. Once this understanding settles in you, jealousy disappears. Each is unique and incomparable. You are just yourself: nobody has ever been like you, and nobody will ever be like you. And you need not be like anybody else, either.

God creates only originals; he does not believe in carbon copies.

A bunch of chickens were in the yard when a football flew over the fence and landed in their midst. A rooster waddled over, studied it, then said, "I'm not complaining, girls, but look at the work they are turning out next door."

Next door great things are happening: the grass is greener, the roses are rosier. Everybody seems to be so happy – except yourself. You are continuously comparing. And the same is the case with the others, they are comparing too. Maybe they think the grass in your lawn is greener – it always looks greener from the distance – that you have a more beautiful wife.... You are tired, you cannot believe why you allowed yourself to be trapped by this woman, you don't know how to get rid of her – and the neighbor may be jealous of you, that you have such a beautiful wife! And you may be jealous of him....

Everybody is jealous of everybody else. And out of jealousy we create such hell, and out of jealousy we become very mean.

An elderly farmer was moodily regarding the ravages of the flood. "Hiram!" yelled a neighbor, "your pigs were all washed down the creek."

"How about Thompson's pigs?" asked the farmer.

"They're gone too."

"And Larsen's?"

"Yes."

"Humphf!" ejaculated the farmer, cheering up. "It ain't as bad as I thought."

If everybody is in misery, it feels good; if everybody is losing, it feels good. If everybody is happy and succeeding, it tastes very bitter.

But why does the idea of the other enter in your head in the first place? Again let me remind you: because you have not allowed your own juices to flow; you have not allowed your own blissfulness to grow, you have not allowed your own being to bloom. Hence you feel empty inside, and you look at each and everybody's outside because only the outside can be seen.

You know your inside, and you know the others' outside: that creates jealousy. They know your outside, and they know their inside: that creates jealousy. Nobody else knows your inside. There you know you are nothing, worthless. And the others on the outside look so smiling. Their smiles may be phony, but how can you know that they are phony? Maybe their hearts are also smiling. You know your smile is phony, because your heart is not smiling at all, it may be crying and weeping.

You know your interiority, and only you know it, nobody else. And you know everybody's exterior, and their exterior people have made beautiful. Exteriors are showpieces and they are very deceptive.

There is an ancient Sufi story:

A man was very much burdened by his suffering. He used to pray every day to God, "Why me? Everybody seems to be so happy, why am only I in such suffering?" One day, out of great desperation, he prayed to God, "You can give me anybody else's suffering and I am ready to accept it. But take mine, I cannot bear it any more."

That night he had a beautiful dream – beautiful and very revealing. He had a dream that night that God appeared in the sky and he said to everybody, "Bring all your sufferings into the temple." Everybody was tired of his suffering – in fact everybody has prayed some time or other, "I am ready to accept anybody else's suffering, but take mine away; this is too much, it is unbearable."

So everybody gathered his own sufferings into bags, and they reached the temple, and they were looking very happy; the day has come, their prayer has been heard. And this man also rushed to the temple.

And then God said, "Put your bags by the walls." All the bags were put by the walls, and then God declared: "Now you can choose. Anybody can take any bag."

And the most surprising thing was this: that this man who had been praying always, rushed towards *his* bag before anybody else could choose it! But he was in for a surprise, because everybody rushed to his own bag, and everybody was happy to choose it again. What was the matter? For the first time, everybody had seen others' miseries, others' sufferings – their bags were as big, or even bigger!

And the second problem was, one had become accustomed to one's own sufferings. Now to choose somebody else's – who knows what kind of sufferings will be inside the bag? Why bother? At least you are familiar with your own sufferings, and you have become accustomed to them, and they are tolerable. For so many years you have tolerated them – why choose the unknown?

And everybody went home happy. Nothing had changed, they were bringing the same suffering back, but everybody was happy and smiling and joyous that he could get his own bag back.

In the morning he prayed to God and he said, "Thank you for the dream; I will never ask again. Whatsoever you have given me is good for me, must be good for me; that's why you have given it to me."

Because of jealousy you are in constant suffering; you become mean to others. And because of jealousy you start becoming phony, because you start pretending. You start pretending things that you don't have, you start pretending things which you *can't* have, which are not natural to you. You become more and more artificial. Imitating others, competing with others, what else can you do? If somebody has something and you don't have it, and you don't have a natural possibility of having it, the only way is to have some cheap substitute for it.

I hear that Jim and Nancy Smith had a great time in Europe this summer. It's so great when a couple finally gets a chance to really live it up. They went everywhere and did everything. Paris, Rome…you name it, they saw it and they did it.

But it was so embarrassing coming back home and going through customs. You know how custom officers pry into all your personal belongings. They opened up a bag and took out three wigs, silk underwear, perfume, hair coloring…really embarrassing. And that was just Jim's bag!

Just look inside your bag and you will find so many artificial, phony, pseudo things – for what? Why can't you be natural and spontaneous? – because of jealousy.

The jealous man lives in hell. Drop comparing and jealousy disappears, meanness disappears, phoniness disappears. But you can drop it only if you start growing your inner treasures; there is no other way.

Grow up, become a more and more authentic individual. Love yourself and respect yourself the way God has made you, and then immediately the doors of heaven open for you. They were always open, you had simply not looked at them.

The last question:

? **Don't you know how to count? One day after the fourth question you said, "Now the seventh question."**

It is really difficult for me. You should be happy that I don't say after the seventh, "The first question."

Little Johnny is in the classroom, learning how to add. "How much is two plus two, Johnny?" asks the teacher.

Johnny hesitates, looks at his hand, and starts counting with his fingers: "One, two, three, four!" he exclaims.

"No, no. Johnny," says the teacher. "You can't use your hands. You have to count in your head. So, how much is four plus four, Johnny?" she asks again.

Johnny hides his hands behind his back and whispering to himself, counts, "One, two, three, four...eight!" he shouts triumphantly.

"No, no, no, Johnny!" replies the teacher angrily. "Now put your hands in your pockets and tell me how much is five plus five?"

Johnny puts his hands in his pockets, concentrates, takes a few minutes and then cries out, "Eleven, ma'am!"

It is really difficult for me to count. I cannot count on my fingers. To keep my fingers at the back will be very difficult, and I don't have pockets!

Enough for today.

Chapter 28
Be a Joke unto Yourself

? **Please explain the difference between a sannyasin and one who is not,
yet lives with a deep commitment to truth.**

Do you know what truth is? Otherwise, how can there be a commitment? Commitment
is possible only if you know. The sannyasin is one who knows that he knows not, the
sannyasin is one whose commitment is not to truth but to the inquiry into truth. And the inquiry
is possible only with someone who knows, who has arrived. The sannyasin is one who is
committed to the person, or to the no-person, around whom he feels the vibe of truth, the vibe
of authenticity.

Your commitment to truth is just an idea. Your truth is just a word, a mind trip. If you want to
make it a real pilgrimage you will have to be a disciple – and to be a disciple is to be a sannyasin.

To be a disciple means to be ready to learn, ready to go into the unknown with someone
who has been in it. Alone, very rarely one has attained to truth. Not that it has not happened –
alone, also, it has happened, but very rarely, just an exception; otherwise one has to learn in
communion with a master.

Then too, it does not happen easily. It is an arduous journey. Dropping the clinging to the
known is not easy. That is our whole investment, that is our whole identity. Dropping the clinging
to the known is dropping the ego, is committing a kind of spiritual suicide; alone, you will not
be able to do it. Unless you see somebody who has committed that suicide and still *is* – in fact
for the first time is…. You will have to look into those eyes which have seen truth, and a glimpse
of the truth will be caught through those eyes. You will have to hold hands with someone who
has known, receive the warmth and the love…and the unknown will start flowing into you.

That's what it means to be with a master, to be a disciple. If you are really committed to truth
you are bound to become a sannyasin. If your commitment to truth is an inquiry then you will
have to learn the ways of learning. And the first thing to learn is to surrender, to trust, to love.

The sannyasin is one who has fallen in love with a person, or a no-person, where he feels
a gut feeling: "Yes, it has happened here." To be with someone who has known is contagious
– and truth is not taught, it is caught.

Your truth is nothing but an idea in your mind – maybe a philosophical inquiry, but a
philosophical inquiry is not going to help. It has to become existential, you have to give proofs
in your life that you are really committed. Otherwise you can go on playing the game of words,
beautiful games of theories, systems of thought – and there are thousands. You can also make
a private system of thought of your own, and you will think this is truth.

Truth is not of your making, truth has nothing to do with your mind. Truth happens, and
it happens only when you have become a no-mind. But how are you going to become a
no-mind? On your own you will remain the mind. You may think about the no-mind, you may
philosophize about the no-mind, you may read the scriptures about no-mind, but you will
remain a mind. On your own, seeking and searching, your ego will feel very good – but that is
the barrier. It is like pulling yourself up by your own bootstraps.

If somewhere you find help is available, don't miss it – because the opportunity is rare, the buddhafield is rare. Only once in a while, somewhere, a buddha arises, a *bodhichitta* happens. Then don't miss the opportunity. If your commitment is really towards truth, you cannot avoid becoming a sannyasin. It is inevitable, because no-mind is learned only by sitting by the side of a no-mind.

If you sit by my side, slowly, slowly your mind will start dispersing like the morning mist. Slowly, slowly a silence will start penetrating you – not of your doing, but coming on its own. A stillness will pervade you.

And the moment you are utterly still, not even a thought moving inside you, that is the moment of illumination. For the first time you have a glimpse of truth – not the idea of truth, but truth itself.

My feelings tell me that until I know you, I can't trust. And yet you say until I trust you, I cannot know you. What to do?

There are two kinds of knowing. One is from a distance: you remain aloof, you remain an observer, a spectator. That's what scientific knowing is; you need not get involved in it, in fact you should not get involved. You should be very objective, you should not allow your subjectivity to interfere with your observation. You should simply be there like a mechanical watcher. You should not be a human being, you should be just a computer.

And this is certain, that sooner or later science is going to be taken over by computers, robots, because they will be more scientific. There will be no subjectivity in them, they will simply see the fact. The fact will not be interfered with in any way, it will remain utterly objective.

That is the way of science – knowing from a distance, keeping aloof, detached. That's how the scientist will know a rose flower, that's how the scientist will know the sunset, that's how the scientist will know the beauty of a woman or a man.

But the problem is, something essential is bound to be missed, something very fundamental, something which is the core of the whole thing. The scientist can know the roseflower – he can know of what it is constituted, he can know all the chemicals, etcetera, but he will never know the beauty of it. He will remain blind to the beauty; his very approach, his methodology, prohibits him.

If you are detached you cannot know beauty. Beauty is known only when you fall *en rapport*, when the observer becomes the observed, when there is no wall between, when every wall has been transformed into a bridge. When there is a kind of melting, when you become the flower and the flower becomes you, then there is a totally different kind of knowing – the way a poet knows. He will know beauty, he will not know the chemicals. He will not know the objective flower, he will know something far deeper. He will know the spirituality of the flower, the spirit of the flower.

And the mystic, his knowing is the highest form of poetic knowing, the ultimate form of poetic knowing. The poet is there only for moments. Sometimes he is a poet, he meets, he mingles, merges into the flower; sometimes he becomes a detached observer. Hence poetry is a kind of mixture of both the knowledges.

Scientific knowledge is purely objective, mystic knowing is purely subjective, poetic knowing is between the two, a mixture of both – a little bit of science, a little bit of religion. But basic knowing can be divided in two, the scientific and the mystic.

Now it depends on you, in what way you want to know me.

You say: "My feelings tell me that until I know you I can't trust you."

These are not feelings – there you are misunderstanding yourself. These are thoughts, these cannot be feelings; that's a sheer misunderstanding. This is the way thoughts speak. Thoughts always say, "Be careful, cautious, move logically" – and of course this is very logical: how can you trust me if you don't know me? It is a logical statement. It is not a statement from your gut level; it cannot be, because gut feelings are very illogical. Gut feelings will say to you the same as I am saying: trust and you will know.

So the first thing to be said is: these are not your feelings, these are your thoughts. You watch again, you go into these so-called feelings again, and you will find they are not coming from the heart, they are coming from the head. The head says, "First know, then trust."

And this is a great strategy, if you believe in the head and its dictation – "First know, then you can trust." Then you will never trust, because knowing cannot happen without trust, mystic knowing cannot happen without trust. Scientific knowing is possible, but scientific knowing is not applicable here.

You can know me scientifically. My doctor comes to examine my body; he knows me in a way. You don't know me in that way, you know me in a totally different way. My doctor is afraid to come to listen to me, because he does not want to lose a patient. If he listens to me, then I will be the doctor and he will be the patient! He comes and he is in a hurry to escape.

Once it happened that he was holding my hand – I had some trouble with my thumb – and something happened to him which was not scientific. Outside the room, he told Vivek, "He is God, he *is* God!" – but since then I have not seen him, he has simply disappeared. Something nonscientific, something which was not of the head. … He felt me for a moment but became frightened.

Watch. If your head is saying these things, these are not feelings. Feelings cannot say these things, because this is not the language of feelings. Feelings say: "Fall in love, and then you will know." Thoughts say: "Doubt, inquire, make certain. When everything is absolutely proved and you are convinced, rationally convinced, then you can trust." And the logic appears very, very clean, there seems to be no trick in it. There is! The trick is that through scientific knowing you cannot know the mystery that is confronting you, you cannot know the poetry that is showering on you, you cannot see the beauty and the grace that is available to you.

You will see my body, you will listen to my words, but you will miss my silences. And they are my real messages. You will be able to see me as I appear on the surface, but you will not be able to penetrate into me as I am at the center.

Knowing the circumference is possible scientifically, but by knowing the circumference of a person love does not arise. And the relationship between the disciple and the master is the crescendo of love, the highest peak of love. Love cannot go higher than that; that is the ultimate in love.

These are your thoughts, not feelings. And if you listen to thoughts you cannot have any communion with me. You will listen to my words, you will listen to my arguments, you will become more knowledgeable, you will go perfectly satisfied that you have something with you. And all that is nonsense. Those words that you have accumulated, the knowledge that you have gathered, are of no use at all.

It is not a question of gathering information here, it is a question of imbibing the spirit; the only way is to trust. It is only through trust that knowing happens.

Science uses doubt as its method, religion uses trust as its method. That is their fundamental difference. Doubt is irrelevant in the world of love, just as trust is irrelevant in the world of things. In the world of I-it, only doubt is significant: you cannot trust things, the scientist cannot just sit there in trust waiting for something to happen. Nothing will happen. He has to doubt, inquire, investigate, dissect. He has to use his mind, his logic, then only some conclusions can be arrived at.

And those conclusions will always remain approximate, they will always remain conditional, because in the future more facts may be known and the whole thing would have to be changed again. They cannot be categorical.

So trust is not the point, it never arises in the world of science; doubt remains the base. If sometimes you come to a conclusion, the conclusion does not become your trust, does not become your faith. It remains an hypothesis.

An hypothesis means that up to now whatsoever has been known supports this theory. It is only up to now; we can't say anything about tomorrow. Tomorrow more facts may be known, and certainly when more facts will be known the hypothesis will have to be adjusted, and the theory would have to be changed.

Science goes on changing every day; it is temporal, it lives in the world of time, because mind is time. Mind cannot live without time; mind is momentary, temporal.

The world of religion functions in a totally different dimension, on a different level. It begins in trust, in love, then a totally different kind of knowing happens.

When you love a woman, you know her. You know her not as the gynecologist knows her, you know her in a totally different way. You don't know her physiology, you don't know her material existence, but you know her spiritual presence. Love, only love, is capable of knowing the spiritual presence. You fall in love not with the physical body, you fall in love with the spiritual presence of a person. But that is available only in trust.

In science, trust is utterly useless. In religion, doubt is utterly useless.

So it is up to you. If you have come here to study what is happening here scientifically, then you are welcome. You can go according to your own thoughts – don't call them feelings, please. You can go on according to your head – don't call it your heart, it is not. You are welcome: be here, study, observe, come to certain conclusions – but they will remain hypotheses.

But if you have come to be transformed, not to be informed only, then you will have to understand that there is a different door. And that door is trust. Trust is an absurd phenomenon, logically absurd. That's why logic always says love is blind, although love has its own eyes, far more deep-going...still, to logic it is blind.

Logic ridicules love, and love smiles knowingly at the whole foolishness of logic.

If you have come here with a logical approach...study, observe, come to some conclusions, but they are not going to transform you; that much you must be aware of. If you have come

be a joke unto yourself

to be transformed, then fall in love. Then forget the head, then let there be a contact heart-to-heart, spirit-to-spirit. Then there is no need to be too much concerned with what you see, your whole concern should be with what you feel. Then you should not be too much concerned in collecting information, but being in celebration with me.

Then don't take much note of what I say, take note of what I am. Listen to my silences, the pauses, the gaps, the intervals – I am more there. Then you will become aware of a totally different world existing here, the buddhafield. It is an energy field; you have to be open and vulnerable to it, only then it can permeate you, pervade you, overwhelm you.

You said the other day that no one is interested any more in questions like "Who created the universe?" But a recent edition of *Time* magazine devoted considerable space to an article entitled "In the beginning: God and science." The basic theme of the article was that science and religion have been brought close together by the "big bang" theory of creation in which the universe is supposed to have come into being through a vast fireball explosion, fifteen or twenty million years ago.
****
Time says that this sounds very much like the story which the Old Testament has been telling all along, namely that the universe began in a single flashing act of creation.
What is wrong with the hypothesis that the universe was created, that it had a beginning? And why do you assert that it did not? Is it not a step in the right direction when science and religion agree?

The first thing to remember is, for three hundred years religion has been losing its territory continuously. First, religion tried to destroy science. It was unable to do it – because you cannot destroy truth, and science was truer, as far as the objective world is concerned, than religion. In fact religion has no authority to say anything about the objective world.

When you are ill you go to the physician, you don't go to the poet. The poet has no authority; he may be a great poet but that is irrelevant when you are ill. He may be a great poet, but when something goes wrong in your bathroom you don't call him, you call a plumber. The plumber may not be a poet at all, but the plumber is relevant there. You don't call Albert Einstein – he may be a great physicist, but what does he know about plumbing?

Religion was proving to be utterly wrong. It was wrong about the objective world. Once science started investigating the objective, organized religion was very much afraid. If there had been a Jesus he would not have been afraid, he would simply have said, "About the objective, listen to science." If a Buddha was there he would have said, "Listen to science."

But there was no buddha in the West where science was growing. And people like Galileo and Copernicus and Kepler were tortured in every possible way because organized religion, the church, became very much afraid: what they were saying was going against their scriptures.

The scientists were saying that the sun does not go around the earth – and The Bible says it does. The scientists were saying the earth goes around the sun...now, if The Bible can be wrong in one thing, then why not in others? That was the problem, that was the fear.

The person who said that the earth goes around the sun was called to the court by the Vatican. Galileo had to appear, in his old age – he was more than seventy, ill, on his deathbed, but he was forced to come to the court to declare there that whatsoever he had said is wrong.

He must have been a man of great humor. He said, "Yes, if it offends you, I declare that whatsoever I have said is wrong – that the earth does not go around the sun, but the sun goes around the earth."

Everybody looked happy, and then Galileo said, "But sir, nothing will change by my statement. The earth will still go round and round the sun – my statement makes no difference! If you are offended by my statement I can take it back, I can refute it. If you want me to write another treatise, I can write that too. But nothing will change by that. Who cares about my statement? Neither the sun nor the earth."

Organized religion tried to kill science – they could not, because truth cannot be killed. Slowly, slowly science has possessed the whole territory of the objective world. Then the natural tendency of mind...science started claiming that which could not be claimed by it. Science created the same fallacy as organized religion, which was saying, "About the objective world also, we are right." They were not. They *are* right about the subjective world; about the interiormost being of existence they are right. But they are not right about the circumference of it, that is not their dimension. But they were claiming that they are right about both.

The same started happening with physicists, chemists and other scientists. In the beginning of this century, science became very arrogant – the same type of arrogance, just the authority shifted from the priests to the scientists. The scientists started saying, "There is no God and there is no soul and there is no consciousness, and all that is rubbish."

This type of arrogance has always remained with man. We have not yet learned anything. This is again the same game being played. When science became very arrogant, naturally religion became defensive. It was losing, it became defensive. So anything that is discovered by science religion tries to appropriate. It tries somehow to make it fit with itself, because the only possibility for it to survive now is if it proves itself to be scientific.

In the beginning it was just the opposite. If a scientist was to survive, the only way was to prove that whatsoever he has found is according to the scriptures, that it proves the scriptures, that it is not against.

Now the whole thing is just vice versa. Now if religion wants to exist in the world, it has continuously to look up to science. Whatsoever science discovers, religion immediately jumps upon and tries to prove, "This is what we have been saying all along."

This "big bang" theory has nothing to do with the religious attitude and the religious theory of creation. In the "big bang" theory there is no God, it is all an accident; it is not creation, remember, because there is no creator in it.

But religion is very defensive, continuously searching for anything to cling to. The "big bang" theory says that in a sudden explosion, in a great flash of light, the world was created. Jump on it; you can always find some way, some logical way. You can say, "Yes, this is right, this is what we have been saying all along. God in the beginning said, 'Let there be light' – and now the theory says there was a great explosion, the world was suddenly created."

But the basic thing is missing – don't be deceived. Religion has been saying that God said, "Let there be light." The base is not the light, the base is God saying, "Let there be light." That God is missing in the "big bang' theory: there is no God, it was a sudden accident, not creation.

And one more thing: this "big bang" theory is not totally accepted, there are many other theories. These are all guesses; they are not proved yet, nothing is proved. In fact I don't think that it can ever be proved how the world came into existence. It is impossible, because nobody was there to witness it, you cannot find an eyewitness, so all that they can do will be just guesswork.

And it happened fifteen or twenty billion years ago. You cannot even be certain whether Krishna ever existed or not, just five thousand years ago. You cannot be certain even about Jesus, whether he was really an historical person or is just a myth – and he was only two thousand years ago. Do you think you can be certain about something that happened twenty billion years ago? All guesses.

And still I say the world was never created, there was no beginning.

Why do I say that there was no beginning? It is so simple. Even if you believe in the "big bang" theory, there must have been something that exploded. Do you think nothing exploded? If there was something, x, y, z, – any name, I am not much interested in such nonsense things, x, y, z, whatsoever it was that exploded – if something was there before the explosion then the explosion is not the beginning. It may be A beginning but it is not the beginning.

And when I say there has never been any beginning, I mean *the* beginning. Something was always there – whether it exploded or whether it grew slowly, in one day or in six days or in one single moment, doesn't matter. There must have been something before it, because only something can come out of something. Even if you say there was nothing, and it came out of nothing, then your nothing is full of something, it is not really nothing.

Hence I say there has never been any beginning and there will never be any end. Maybe a beginning, maybe many beginnings and maybe many ends, but never the first and never the last. We are always in the middle. Existence is not a creation but a creativity. It is not that it begins one day and ends one day. It goes on and on; it is an ongoing process.

That's why I say that all these guesses are useless and there is no need for them and they serve no purpose. This was Buddha's approach too. Whenever somebody would ask a question like, "Who created the world?" – whether the world was ever created or is uncreated – Buddha would answer by other questions. He would ask, "If who created the world is decided, is it going to help your enlightenment? Is it going to help you become more silent, more meditative, more aware?"

Certainly the person would answer, "It is not going to help. Who created the world doesn't matter. It will not help my enlightenment and it will not make me more meditative."

Then Buddha said, "Then why bother about all this? Think of things which can help you to become more meditative, think of things which can help you become free of all the ego-clinging, think of things which can ultimately lead you into the state of samadhi."

My approach is also the same: these are all irrelevant questions. And because of these irrelevant questions there has been so much controversy down the ages and thousands of people have wasted their lives discussing who created the world, when exactly, what was the date – and so on, and so forth.

I think these people were neurotics. I don't think them healthy, normal, sane people. Who cares? For what? It does not matter at all, it is immaterial.

? What is the secret of a joke?

The sudden unexpected turn, that is the secret of a joke – the revelation. You are expecting something and it doesn't happen; what happens is so totally absurd and yet has a logic of its own...it is ridiculous and yet not illogical. That's what suddenly becomes a laughter in you. You see the ridiculousness of it, and also the logic of it. It is unexpected – if it is expected, then it doesn't bring laughter to you. If you know the joke then it doesn't bring laughter to you, because now you know, everything is expected.

Two insects were living in a cemetery. One said to the other: "Want to make love in dead Ernest tonight?"

Now, poor dead Ernest...!

An Englishman on his first trip to America went to one of those stand-up comic nightclubs for the first time. After he had had a couple of drinks, the lights dimmed and Henny Youngman stepped into the spotlight and greeted the crowd with his famous trademark gag: "Take my wife...please."

The crowd belly-laughed. The Englishman was impressed. "By Jove," he said to himself, "I must remember that and try it on the chaps back home."

Now, when somebody says, "Take my wife," you are expecting he will say, "for example." "Take my wife, for example." But he is saying "Take my wife," and then the silence, the little pause..."please." That is unexpected.

Some weeks later, back in London, he stepped to the microphone at a meeting of his club and, with great confidence, snapped out: "Consider my wife. Please."

Now the whole thing is lost. Just a single word makes it a beauty.

The secret of the joke is that it brings you to a point where you are expecting, expecting, expecting that *this* is going to happen; then it never happens. And what happens is so sudden...and because you were expecting something you were coming to a tension, and then suddenly something else happens, and the tension has come to such a climax that it explodes. You are all laughter. It is a tremendous release, it is great meditation. If you can laugh totally, it will give you a moment of no-time, no-mind. Mind lives logically with expectations, laughter is something that comes from the beyond. Mind is always guessing what is going to happen, groping. And something happens which is absolutely contrary to its expectations: it simply stops for a moment.

And that is the moment when the mind stops, when laughter comes from your belly, a belly laugh. Your whole body goes into a spasm, it is orgasmic.

A good laugh is tremendously meditative.

An English gentleman went to his surgeon saying, "Old chap, I have this damned desire to be an Irishman. Can you perform some operation to make me one?"

"Well," replied the surgeon, "it is a fairly risky business, you know. We have to remove ninety percent of your brain."

"Do it," replied the Englishman.

When he awoke from the operation he found his bed surrounded by long-faced doctors. His surgeon stepped forward, saying, "Terribly sorry, old chap, but during the operation the old scalpel slipped and we accidentally removed one hundred percent of your brain!"

"Ah, na fuckin' worries mate!"

? What is your message in short?

Parinirvana – better known in the commune as Paribanana – Buddha's message in short is: Be a light unto yourself. And mine? Be a joke unto yourself!

? Why am I always thinking of money?

What else is there to think about? Money is power. Everybody else is thinking of money, don't be worried. Even those who are thinking of the other world...they have different coins but they are also thinking of money. Money represents power, with money you can purchase power.

Your saints are also thinking of money – they call it virtue. By virtue you can purchase a better house in heaven, a better car, a better woman. A few people are not that greedy, they are thinking only of the money that is current in this world. A few people are more greedy, they think of the other world. And if you are thinking of virtue to attain to paradise, what is it except money?

A man stops thinking about money only when he starts living in the present. Money is the future; money is security for the future, a guarantee for the future. If you have a good bank balance your future is safe. If you have a good character, even life after death is safe.

The whole world is thinking in terms of money. Those who think in terms of power politics are thinking in terms of money, because money is nothing but a symbol for power. That's why you can go on accumulating more and more money, but the desire never leaves you to have still more – because the thirst for power is unlimited, it knows no end.

And people are thirsty for power because deep down they are empty. Somehow they want to stuff that emptiness with something – it may be money, power, prestige, respectability, character, virtue. Anything will do; they want to stuff their inner emptiness.

There are only two types of people in the world: those who try to stuff their inner emptiness, and those very rare precious beings who try to see the inner emptiness. Those who try to stuff it remain empty, frustrated. They go on collecting garbage, their whole life is futile and fruitless. Only the other kind, the very precious people who try to look into their inner emptiness without any desire to stuff it, become meditators.

Meditation is looking into your emptiness, welcoming it, enjoying it, being one with it, with no desire to fill it – there is no need, because it is already full. It looks empty because you don't have the right way of seeing it. You see it through the mind; that is the wrong way. If you put the mind aside and look into your emptiness, it has tremendous beauty, it is divine, it is overflowing with joy. Nothing else is needed.

Only then a person stops thinking about money, stops thinking about power, stops thinking about paradise – because he is already in paradise, because he is already rich, because he is already powerful.

But ordinarily it is not just to do with you; everybody thinks in some way or other about money.

Two mothers were talking. One said to the other, "I haven't seen you in a long time. How is your son and what is he doing?"

She replied, "My son is a famous actor in Hollywood and he's making a fortune. He just built a new home that cost three hundred thousand dollars. What is your son doing?"

Said the other mother, "My son is doing even better. He is gay and lives in Hollywood; he just moved in with an actor who has a three-hundred-thousand-dollar home."

A young woman has decided to put aside some money for a rainy day and informs her husband that each time they make love she will expect him to put five dollars in the piggy bank.

That night, as he begins to make advances, she reminds him of her requirement. He finds that he has only four dollars in his wallet and so the wife agrees to only four-fifths of a love affair. However, as her passion mounts, she offers to lend him a dollar until the next day.

Rachel is pregnant and Sammy, her husband, a very temperamental man, suffers from the pains of celibacy.

Rachel, who manages the household, takes pity on him and gives him a hundred liras to visit the red-light district.

When Sarah, the neighbor, sees Sammy running out of the house, she calls him, "Where are you running to like that? You look so very happy!"

Sammy shows her the money and tells her that he is going to spend it on a beautiful young girl.

"Give me the money!" proposes pretty Sarah. "You won't regret it, you will see!"

Rachel soon comes to know about it. Very indignant, she explodes, "The bitch! When she was pregnant last year, I did the same for Isaac, her husband, for nothing!"

People are continuously thinking of money and money and money. It is nothing special to you, you are a normally abnormal person, as neurotic as everybody else.

But please come out of this neurosis. Live the moment, drop the future, and money loses its glamour. Live the moment with such totality and abandon, as if there is no other moment to come to you again, as if this is the last moment. Then all desire for money and power simply leaves you.

If suddenly you come to know that today you are going to die, what will happen? Will you still be interested in money? Suddenly all desire for money will leave you. If this is the last day, you can't waste it thinking about tomorrow, having more money in the world; there is going to be no tomorrow.

Because we live in the tomorrows, money has become very important. And because we don't live, we only imitate others, money has become very important. Somebody makes a house, and now you are feeling very inferior. You were not at all dissatisfied with your own house just a few days before, but now this man has made a bigger house: now comparison arises, and it hurts, it hurts your ego. You would like to have more money. Somebody has done something else, and your ego is disturbed.

Drop comparing and life is really beautiful. Drop comparing and you can enjoy life to the full. And the person who enjoys his life has no desire to possess, because he knows the real things of life which are worth enjoying cannot be purchased.

Love cannot be purchased. Yes, sex can be purchased. So one who knows what love is will not be interested in money. But one who does not know what love is, is bound to remain interested in money, because money can purchase sex, and sex is all that he knows.

You cannot purchase the starry night. One who knows how to enjoy the night full of stars won't bother much about money. You cannot purchase a sunset. Yes, you can purchase a Picasso – but one who knows how to enjoy a sunset will not be interested at all in purchasing a painting. Life is such a painting, such a moving, alive painting.

But people who don't know how to see a sunset are ready to purchase a Picasso for millions of dollars. They will not even know how to hang it, whether it is upside down or right side up, but they want to show to others that they have a Picasso painting.

I have heard that once a rich man came to Picasso; he wanted two paintings, immediately, and he was ready to pay as much as was demanded. Picasso demanded a fabulous price – thinking that he would not be able to pay it – because only one painting was ready. But the rich man was ready to pay. So Picasso went in, cut the canvas in two, and the rich man thought they were two paintings.

I have heard another story: in an exhibition, a Picasso exhibition, people are appreciating his paintings. All the critics have gathered around a certain painting which looks the most absurd, hence the most appealing – because when something is absurd it is a challenge to your intellect, and every critic is trying to prove that he understands what it is.

And then came Picasso, and he said, "Wait. Some fool has hung it upside down. Let me put it right first." And they were expressing great appreciation for the painting!

If you know how to enjoy a roseflower, a green tree in your courtyard, the mountains, the river, the stars, the moon, if you know how to enjoy people, you will not be so much obsessed with money. The obsession is arising because we have forgotten the language of celebration. Hence money has become the only thing to brag about – your life is so empty.

I will not tell you to renounce money. That has been told to you down the ages; it has not changed you. I am going to tell you something else: celebrate life, and the obsession with money disappears automatically. And when it goes on its own accord, it leaves no scratches, it leaves no wounds behind, it leaves no trace behind.

? What is wisdom?

Stephen Crane writes: I met a seer, he held in his hands the book of wisdom. "Sir," I addressed him, "let me read." "Child…he began."

"Sir," I said, "think not that I am a child, for already I know much of that which you hold."

"Ah, much!" he smiled. Then he opened the book and held it before me. Strange, that I should have gone so suddenly blind.

Wisdom is not knowledge. The knowledgeable person cannot see it, he is blind. Only the innocent person can see it, only a child, one who knows nothing, one who functions from the state of not knowing, can know what wisdom is. Wisdom has nothing to do with knowledge, not at all; it has something to do with innocence. Something of the purity of the heart is a must, something of the emptiness of being is needed for wisdom to grow.

"Only those who are like small children will be able to enter into my kingdom of God." Yes, Jesus is right.

Knowledge comes from without, wisdom wells up within. Knowledge is borrowed, wisdom is original. Wisdom is your insight into existence – not Buddha's insight, not Atisha's insight, not my insight, but your insight, absolutely your insight into existence.

When you are able to see with no dust of knowledge on the mirror of your soul, when your soul is without any dust of knowledge, when it is just a mirror, it reflects that which is. That is wisdom. That reflecting of that which is, is wisdom.

Knowledge gratifies the ego, wisdom happens only when the ego is gone, forgotten. Knowledge can be taught; universities exist to teach you. Wisdom cannot be taught, it is like an infection: you have to be with the wise, you have to move with the wise, and only then will something start moving inside you.

The movement in the disciple is not caused by the master, it is not under the law of cause and effect. It is what Carl Gustav Jung calls "synchronicity." The master is so full of silence, so overflowing with innocence, that his presence triggers a process in you, simply triggers a process in you. Nothing is transferred; your inner being starts remembering that "I also have the same treasure as my master, I had simply forgotten about it. I had moved into the without, keeping the within at the back. The treasure was not lost but only forgotten; I had fallen asleep."

And the asleep person at the most can dream that he is awake. But that too is a dream. That dream is knowledge. The person who is asleep and thinks that he knows…that is knowledge. But the person who really awakes is wise. Knowledge is a false, plastic substitute for wisdom.

Wisdom is true knowledge – rather knowing than knowledge, because it has no full point to it. It goes on growing, it goes on flowing. The man of wisdom goes on learning; there never comes a stop.

Don't be knowledgeable, be wise.

❓ Who are you and what are you doing?

I am not, and I am not doing anything at all. But something is happening, something tremendous is happening – that is another matter, it has nothing to do with my doing it.

"I am not." When I say this, I mean that there is no personality, no person, but just a presence. And the presence without the person looks almost like an absence. It is. The person is absent.

I am only a hollow bamboo, and if you hear some music then it must be from God, it is not from me; it has nothing to do with me. I am not there, I have utterly disappeared. That's what enlightenment is all about. That's what Atisha calls *bodhichitta*.

But things are happening, they always happen. Whenever a person disappears and becomes a presence, immensely valuable things happen around him. A great synchronicity starts functioning. Those who are courageous enough to come close to such a presence start changing, with no effort, just sheer grace, start becoming totally different beings by just being in the buddhafield, in the energy field of a master.

I am not doing anything, and I am not. But still you see me coming, going, talking to you, doing this and that. For that, I will tell you a story.

A Hollywood director once sent out word that he was looking for an actor to play the role of Shakespeare's Hamlet. The actor was to be over six feet tall, young and vigorous and have an excellent command of the language.

On the day of the casting call, many fine tall young men showed up, but among them was a little old Jewish man with a heavy Yiddish accent. The director picked him out immediately and asked, "What do you want?"

The man answered "I vant to be an *hector*. I vant to play Hemlet!"

"Are you kidding or just crazy?" the director asked. "You are only five feet tall and you have an accent so thick I could cut it with a knife. What can you possibly do?"

The little man said, "I vant to hect. Giff me a chance."

Finally the director gave in. "Get up on stage and try it."

The little man stepped out onto the stage. Somehow he looked much taller and full of energy. He began to speak with a booming voice and the perfect king's English: "To be or not to be...."

When he was finished, there was a hush. Everyone was amazed. The director said, "That's unbelievable."

The other actors said, "That's wonderful."

The little Jew just shrugged his shoulders and said, "Dat's *hecting*!"

Enough for today.

For more information:

www.OSHO.com

A comprehensive multi-language website including a magazine, OSHO Books, OSHO TALKS in audio and video formats, the OSHO Library text archive in English and Hindi and extensive information about OSHO Meditations. You will also find the program schedule of the OSHO Multiversity and information about the OSHO International Meditation Resort.

To contact OSHO International Foundation visit: www.osho.com/oshointernational

About the Author

Osho's teachings defy categorization, covering everything from the individual quest for meaning to the most urgent social and political issues facing society today. His books are not written but are transcribed from audio and video recordings of extemporaneous talks given to international audiences over a period of 35 years. Osho has been described by the Sunday Times in London as one of the "1000 Makers of the 20th Century" and by American author Tom Robbins as "the most dangerous man since Jesus Christ."

About his own work Osho has said that he is helping to create the conditions for the birth of a new kind of human being. He has often characterized this new human being as "Zorba the Buddha" – capable both of enjoying the earthy pleasures of a Zorba the Greek and the silent serenity of a Gautam Buddha. Running like a thread through all aspects of Osho's work is a vision that encompasses both the timeless wisdom of the East and the highest potential of Western science and technology.

Osho is also known for his revolutionary contribution to the science of inner transformation, with an approach to meditation that acknowledges the accelerated pace of contemporary life. His unique "Active Meditations" are designed to first release the accumulated stresses of body and mind, so that it is easier to experience the thought-free and relaxed state of meditation.

Two autobiographical works by the author are available:

Autobiography of a Spiritually Incorrect Mystic by Osho,
St. Martin's Griffin (2001) ISBN: 978-0312280710

Glimpses of a Golden Childhood by Osho
The Rebel Publishing House ISBN: 8172610726

The OSHO International Meditation Resort

The OSHO International Meditation Resort is a great place for holidays and a place where people can have a direct personal experience of a new way of living with more alertness, relaxation, and fun. Located about 100 miles southeast of Mumbai in Pune, India, the resort offers a variety of programs to thousands of people who visit each year from more than 100 countries around the world.

Originally developed as a summer retreat for Maharajas and wealthy British colonialists, Pune is now a thriving modern city that is home to a number of universities and high-tech industries. The Meditation Resort spreads over 28 acres in a tree-lined suburb known as Koregaon Park. The resort campus provides accommodation for a limited number of guests, in a new 'Guesthouse' and there is a plentiful variety of nearby hotels and private apartments available for stays of a few days up to several months.

Meditation Resort programs are all based in the Osho vision of a qualitatively new kind of human being who is able both to participate creatively in everyday life and to relax into silence and meditation. Most programs take place in modern, air-conditioned facilities and include a variety of individual sessions, courses and workshops covering everything from creative arts to holistic health treatments, personal transformation and therapy, esoteric sciences, the "Zen" approach to sports and recreation, relationship issues, and significant life transitions for men and women. Individual sessions and group workshops are offered throughout the year, alongside a full daily schedule of meditations.

Outdoor cafes and restaurants within the resort grounds serve both traditional Indian fare and a choice of international dishes, all made with organically grown vegetables from the resort's own farm. The campus has its own private supply of safe, filtered water. www.osho.com/resort.